ISBN 978-0-266-08460-0
PIBN 10947576

English
Français
Deutsche
Italiano
Español
Português

www.forgottenbooks.com

Mythology Photography **Fiction**
Fishing Christianity **Art** Cooking
Essays Buddhism Freemasonry
Medicine **Biology** Music **Ancient
Egypt** Evolution Carpentry Physics
Dance Geology **Mathematics** Fitness
Shakespeare **Folklore** Yoga Marketing
Confidence Immortality Biographies
Poetry **Psychology** Witchcraft
Electronics Chemistry History **Law**
Accounting **Philosophy** Anthropology
Alchemy Drama Quantum Mechanics
Atheism Sexual Health **Ancient History**
Entrepreneurship Languages Sport
Paleontology Needlework Islam
Metaphysics Investment Archaeology
Parenting Statistics Criminology
Motivational

SCHEDULE OF PREMIUMS

Offered by the

Worcester County Horticultural Society

Horticultural Building
30 Elm Street
Worcester, Mass.

For the year

1933

THE ATTENTION OF EXHIBITORS IS PARTICULARLY
CALLED TO THE RULES AND REGULATIONS
GENERAL AND SPECIAL

The Davis Press, Worcester

OFFICERS AND COMMITTEES
of the
WORCESTER COUNTY HORTICULTURAL SOCIETY
For the Year 1933

PRESIDENT
MYRON F. CONVERSE, Worcester, Mass.

VICE-PRESIDENTS
HERBERT A. COOK, Shrewsbury, Mass.   MRS. HOMER GAGE, Worcester, Mass.
S. LOTHROP DAVENPORT, No. Grafton, Mass.

SECRETARY
HERBERT R. KINNEY, of Worcester
Horticultural Hall, 30 Elm Street

TREASURER
BURT W. GREENWOOD, of Worcester

LIBRARIAN
Miss LUCY M. COULSON, of Worcester

TRUSTEES:

Joseph A. Allen	Auburn	James Warr	Worcester
William Anderson	South Lancaster	J. Frank Cooper	Worcester
Elizabeth R. Bishop	Sutton	Mrs. Bertha G. Denny	Worcester
Edward W. Breed	Clinton	Mrs. Alice M. Forbes	Worcester
David L. Fiske	Grafton	Harold J. Greenwood	Worcester
Richard A. Flagg	Boylston	Harry Harrison	Worcester
Allen J. Jenkins	Shrewsbury	Allyne W. Hixon	Worcester
William McAllister	Whitinsville	Mrs. Frances A. Kinnicutt	Worcester
William E. Morey	Shrewsbury	H. Ward Moore	Worcester
Charles Potter	West Boylston	Miss Frances C. Morse,	Worcester
Mrs. Mary D. White	Holden	Harry I. Randall	Worcester
Chandler Bullock	Worcester	Joseph F. Sherer	Worcester
Willis E. Cary	Worcester	Mrs. Amy W. Smith	Worcester
Fred H. Chamberlain	Worcester	George F. E. Story	Worcester
Fred L. Chamberlain	Worcester	Matthew P. Whittall	Worcester

STANDING COMMITTEE ON FINANCE
Myron F. Converse, *Chairman*, 1934   Leonard C. Midgley, 1933
Herbert W. Estabrook, 1935

NOMINATING COMMITTEE
Allen W. Hixon, 1933   Willis E. Cary, 1934   Ernest Hansen 1935

ON LIBRARY AND PUBLICATIONS
Edward W. Breed, *Chairman*   Mrs. Amy W. Smith   William Anderson
Herbert R. Kinney, *Secretary*   Lucy M. Coulson, *Librarian*

ON NOMENCLATURE
S. Lothrop Davenport   Mrs. Amy W. Smith   Charles Potter   Herbert R. Kinney
J. Frank Cooper   Allen J. Jenkins   William Anderson   Leonard C. Midgley

ON ARRANGEMENTS AND EXHIBITIONS
Allen J. Jenkins, *Chairman*
Joseph A. Allen   H. Ward Moore   Elizabeth R. Bishop
Miss Frances C. Morse   Edward W. Breed   James Warr
Mrs. Percy G. Forbes   Lucy M. Coulson   S. Lothrop Davenport
Leonard C. Midgley   Allyne W. Hixon   Albert W. Schneider
President, Myron F. Converse   Charles Potter   William E. Morey
Secretary, Herbert R. Kinney

AUDITORS
Harry C. Midgley   H. Ward Moore   Arthur H. Bellows

JUDGES
PLANTS AND FLOWERS: Allyne W. Hixon, Worcester
FRUIT: S. Lothrop Davenport, North Grafton
VEGETABLES: H. Ward Moore, Worcester

MEDAL COMMITTEE
Myron F. Converse, *Chairman*   Edward W. Breed   Allen W. Hixon

ON WINTER MEETINGS
Myron F. Converse, *Chairman*
Herbert R. Kinney, *Secretary*
Leonard C. Midgley   Burt W. Greenwood
S. Lothrop Davenport   H. Ward Moore

**Office, Library, and Exhibition Hall
30 Elm Street**

GENERAL RULES AND REGULATIONS

1. Strict conformity to the Regulations and Rules will be expected and required, as well for the benefit of exhibitors as for the convenience of the Officers of the Society.

2. Every Flower or Plant entered in a class of named varieties should be correctly named.

3. All articles offered for premiums must remain within the Hall throughout the hours of Exhibition, unless special permission for their removal shall be granted by the Committee on Exhibition, etc.

4. No person shall make more than one entry of the same variety or be awarded more than one premium under the same number.

5. The Judges may correct, before the close of any exhibition, awards made by them, if satisfied that such were erroneous.

6. The cards of exhibitors competing for premiums shall be reversed, until after premiums are awarded.

7. Competitors are expected to conform strictly to the conditions under which articles are invited. Evasion or violation of them may be reported to the TRUSTEES for future disqualification of the offender.

8. Articles offered for premiums must be in the Hall by 2 o'clock of the days of Exhibition except when otherwise specified. Between 2 and 3 o'clock the Hall will be in exclusive charge of the Committee on Arrangements and Exhibitions. Open to the public from 3 to 9 o'clock.

9. Competition for premiums is open to all residents of Worcester County, and it is strictly required that all specimens offered for premiums shall have been grown by the competitors, on their own premises, for at least two (2) months previous to the date of exhibition, except where no restriction is stated in schedule.

10. After the articles are arranged they will be under the exclusive charge of the Judges and Committee of Arrangements, and not even the owners will have liberty to remove them until the exhibition is closed, when they will be delivered as the contributors may direct.

11. Where a certain number or quantity of Plants, Flowers, Fruits or Vegetables is designated in the schedule, there must be neither more nor less than that number or quantity of specimens shown; and in no case can other varieties than those named in the schedule be substituted.

12. The Judges may exclude from competition all inferior specimens and may correct any errors that they think were without deliberate purpose.

13. The Committee on Arrangements has power to change the time of exhibition for any article, if an earlier or later season renders such change desirable.

14. All articles offered for premiums should be correctly named. Indefinite appellations such as "Pippin," "Sweeting," "Greening," etc., will not be considered as names. Any person exhibiting the same variety of Fruit or Vegetable, under different names, or exhibiting as grown by himself Flowers, Fruit or Vegetables grown by another, thereby violating the objects and rules of the Society, shall be debarred from competing for the Society's premiums until reinstated.

15. Competitors will be required to furnish information as to their mode of cultivation, and to present specimens for trial and examinations, if requested.

16. In all exhibitions of Cut Flowers for competition, the number of blooms, clusters, sprays or spikes shown is not restricted except that it is expected the exhibitor shall use only a sufficient number to make a well-balanced display. All shall be of one color and of one variety in the same vase, except Displays, Vases, Baskets, Standards, or otherwise specified in the schedule. The use of foliage must be restricted to that of the varieties shown, except with orchids, carnations, gloxinias and sweet peas. The Judge will consider the quality of the flowers rather than the quantity.

17. The Judges are authorized by the Trustees to invite the assistance of competent and discreet persons in the discharge of their duties.

18. No Judge shall require anything of competitors respecting their exhibits which is not distinctly specified in the schedule.

19. In Table Decorations, collections and displays of Flowers, Fruits, Vegetables, Vases, and Baskets, where the number of exhibits exceeds the number of premiums offered, the Judge *may* award prizes to any worthy exhibits not receiving a premium.

The maximum prize for Vases, Standards, and Baskets shall be two dollars.

20. All premiums that are not claimed within one year after the close of the official year shall be forfeited to the Society.

21. "Downing's Fruits of America," revised edition, will guide the Judge of Fruits in his decisions upon matters at issue.

22. While the Society will take reasonable precautions for the safety of the property of exhibitors, it will be responsible in no case for any loss or damage that may occur.

Scale of Points

CUT FLOWERS AND WILD FLOWERS.—

Arrangement	30 points
Quality of blooms	40 "
Number of varieties	15 "
Properly named	15

LILIES.—

Size and color of bloom	35 points
Number of perfect flowers and buds on stem	35
Arrangement	15
Properly named	15

DISPLAYS.—

Arrangement	40 points
Quality	45 "
Variety	15 "

COLLECTIONS.—

Quality	45 points
Arrangement	25 "
Variety	30 "

Special Funds

OF THE

WORCESTER COUNTY HORTICULTURAL SOCIETY

The following is a list of the Special Funds of the Worcester County Horticultural Society the income of which is devoted to the purpose stated. The date prefixed to each indicates the year in which the fund was established.

1888.   Francis Henshaw Dewey Fund. $1,000.00.
Income to be used for the purchase of books.

1898.   William Eames Fund. $500.00.
Income to be used in prizes for the promotion of apple culture.

1906.   Frederick A. Blake Fund. $1,000.00.
Income only to be used in providing Medals to be awarded to the originators of new varieties of Fruits or Flowers, preference always being given to residents of Worcester County.

In case that the Worcester County Horticultural Society does not find occasion to award medals for New Fruits or Flowers, the said income may be used in special premiums for Orchids or other choice Greenhouse Plants and Flowers.

1907.   Obadiah Brown Hadwen Fund. $1,000.00.
Income to be used for meritorious exhibits of Flowers, Fruits and Vegetables.

1922.   Edwin Draper Fund. $300.00.
Income to be used in prizes for Horticultural exhibitions held under the direction of said Society.

1924.   Miss Frances Clary Morse Fund. $500.00.
Income to be used in prizes for Flowers.

FLOWERS, PLANTS, FRUITS, AND VEGETABLES

A. D. 1933

☞THE COMMITTEE ON ARRANGEMENTS AND EXHIBITIONS would direct the earnest attention of the Judge to *Rule 12*.

12. The Judges may exclude from competition all inferior specimens and may correct any errors that they think were without deliberate purpose.

Special Rules

1. EXHIBITORS WILL ADD VALUE TO THEIR EXHIBITS BY HAVING ALL SPECIMENS CORRECTLY AND LEGIBLY NAMED AND THE NUMBER OF VARIETIES WRITTEN ON THE ENTRY CARDS, NOTICE OF WHICH WILL BE TAKEN BY THE JUDGES IN AWARDING THE PREMIUMS.

2. WHILE IT IS EXPECTED THAT EXHIBITORS WILL TAKE PAINS TO CORRECTLY NAME THEIR EXHIBITS, THE JUDGES WILL NOT EXCLUDE AN EXHIBIT FOR MISTAKE IN NOMENCLATURE.

3. IN ALL EXHIBITIONS OF LILIES THE POLLEN MAY BE REMOVED.

By vote of the trustees, all entries must be made to the Secretary and all cards made out by him or his assistants.

Spring Exhibition

Thursday, March 23, 3 to 9 p. m.
Friday, March 24, 9 a. m. to 9 p. m.
Saturday, March 25, 9 a. m. to 9 p. m.
Sunday, March 26, 12 m. to 9 p. m.

All articles for this exhibition must be in the hall and ready for inspection by the judges by 1 o'clock Thursday

CLASS I	GARDEN DISPLAYS	400.00
CLASS II	PLANT DISPLAYS	150.00
CLASS III	ROCK GARDENS Not to exceed 100 square feet	100.00
CLASS IV	CUT FLOWERS	75.00
CLASS V	FRUIT	75.00
CLASS VI	VEGETABLES	75.00

*   *   *

Frederick A. Blake Fund

CLASS VII	CARNATIONS	25.00

*   *   *

WORCESTER GARDEN CLUB EXHIBIT

Thursday, April 27

All articles for this exhibition must be in the hall and ready for inspection by the judges by 2 o'clock

This exhibition will be open to the public from 3 to 9 p. m.

CUT FLOWERS.—
No. 1. Twenty vases   5.00 4.00 3.00
TABLE DECORATIONS.—
No. 2. For best table decoration, laid
       for four covers, no restric-
       tions. Notify the Secretary
       two days in advance   7.00 6.00 5.00 4.00 3.00
SCALE OF POINTS BY WHICH THE ABOVE CLASS IS TO BE JUDGED
       Arrangement of Flowers and quality   50 points
       Proportion and harmony of flowers
          with accessories   30
          Accessories   20
CARNATIONS.—
No. 3. Vase or Basket, fifty flowers,
       other green permissible   8.00 6.00 4.00
PLANT DISPLAYS.—
No. 4. Plants in Bloom with Foliage
       Plants. Sixty dollars may be
       used in prizes.
APPLE, TWELVE SPECIMENS.—
No. 5. For any variety, eight dollars
       may be used for prizes.
PARSNIP, TWELVE SPECIMENS.—
No. 6. Hollow Crown   2.00 1.50 1.00   .50
No. 7. Any other variety   2.00 1.50 1.00   .50
RHUBARB, TWELVE STALKS.—
No. 8. Any variety   2.00 1.50 1.00   .50
LETTUCE.—
No. 9. Six heads   2.00 1.50 1.00   .50
RADISH.—
No. 10. Two bunches. Six in each bunch   1.50 1.00   .50
POTATO, TWELVE SPECIMENS.—
No. 11. Any named variety   2.00 1.50 1.00   .50

May Exhibition

Thursday, May 11

*All articles for this exhibition must be
in the hall and ready for inspection by
the judges by 2 o'clock*

This exhibition will be open to the public from 3 to 9 p. m.

CUT FLOWERS.—

No. 12.	Twenty vases		3.00	2.50	1.00
No. 13.	Medium basket	3.00 2.50	2.00	1.50	1.00

SPRING BULBS, OPEN CULTURE.—

No. 14. Display   4.00 3.00 2.50 2.00

PANSY.—

No. 15. Twenty vases, one flower
        with foliage in a vase   3.00 2.50 2.00 1.50 1.00   .50

ZONALE GERANIUMS, IN BLOOM.—

No. 16. Six plants   3.00 2.00 1.00   .50

TABLE DECORATIONS.—

No. 17. For best table decoration,
        laid for four covers, no re-
        strictions. Notify the Secre-
        tary two days in advance   7.00 6.00 5.00 4.00 3.00

SCALE OF POINTS BY WHICH THE ABOVE CLASS IS TO BE JUDGED

    Arrangement of Fowers and quality   50 points

    Proportion and harmony of flowers
       with accessories   30

    Accessories   20

PLANT DISPLAYS.—

No. 18. For exhibits—no restrictions as
        to where grown, or by whom
        $60.00 may be used for prizes.
        Notify the Secretary two days
        in advance.

CALENDULA.—

No. 19. Arranged in Bowl or Basket   3.00 2.00 1.00

DANDELION.—
No. 20.   One-half peck   1.50 1.00   .50

LETTUCE.—
No. 21.   Six heads   2.00 1.50 1.00   .50

SPINACH.—
No. 22.   One-half peck   1.50 1.00   .50

RADISH, TWO BUNCHES, SIX IN EACH BUNCH.—
No. 23.   Globe   1.50 1.00   .50

RHUBARB, TWELVE STALKS.—
No. 24.   Linnæus   2.50 2.00 1.50 1.00   .50

ASPARAGUS, TWO BUNCHES, TWELVE SPECIMENS EACH.—
No. 25.   Any variety   3.00 2.50 2.00 1.50 1.00   .50

ONION.—
No. 26.   Two bunches, six in each bunch   1.50 1.00   .50

Thursday, June 8

All articles for this exhibition must be in the hall and ready for inspection by the judges by 2 o'clock

This exhibition will be open to the public from 3 to 9 p. m.

CUT FLOWERS.—
No. 27. Display   4.00 3.00 2.50 2.00 1.50 1.00
No. 28. Standard   3.00 2.50 2.00 1.50 1.00

WILD FLOWERS, TWENTY VASES.—
No. 29. No duplicates   4.00 3.00 2.00 1.50 1.00 .50

AZALEA.—
No. 30. Display in vases   3.00 2.00 1.00

IRIS, GERMAN.—
No. 31. Display   8.00 6.00 4.00 2.00
No. 32. Vase or Basket   3.00 2.50 2.00 1.50 1.00

RHODODENDRON.—
No. 33. Displays in vases   3.00 2.00

PEONIES.—
No. 34. Vase or Basket   3.00 2.50 2.00 1.00

BEGONIA.—
No. 35. Four plants in bloom   3.00 2.00 1.00

ROSES.—
No. 36. Vase of Roses. Five dollars
        may be used in prizes.

ZONALE GERANIUMS.—
No. 37. Twenty vases, one truss in each   3.00 2.00 1.00

STRAWBERRIES, TWENTY-FOUR BERRIES.—
No. 38. Five dollars may be used in prizes.

ASPARAGUS, TWO BUNCHES, TWELVE SPECIMENS EACH.—
No. 39. Any variety   2.50 2.00 1.50 1.00 .50

CUCUMBER.—
No. 40. Three specimens   2.00 1.50 1.00 .50

SPINACH.—
No. 41.   One-half peck   2.50 2.00 1.50 1.00

RHUBARB, TWELVE STALKS.—
No. 42.   Monarch   1.50 1.00 .50·
No. 43.   Victoria   2.50 2.00 1.50 1.00

BEET.—
No. 44. * Twelve specimens   2.00 1.50 1.00 .50

LETTUCE.—
No. 45.   Six heads   2.00 1.50 1.00 .50

ONION.—
No. 46.   Two bunches, six each   2.00 1.50 1.00 .50

Thursday, June 15

All articles for this exhibition must be in the hall and ready for inspection by the judges by 2 o'clock

This exhibition will be open to the public from 3 to 9 p. m.

CUT FLOWERS.—

No. 47.   From hardy plants and shrubs outdoor culture, *to be named*   5.00 4.00 3.00 2.00

ROSES.—

No. 48.   Vase H. P. roses, not to exceed ten blooms   3.00 2.00 1.00

No. 49.   Vase H. T. roses, not exceeding ten blooms   3.00 2.00 1.00

PEONIES.—

No. 50.   Best Display of Peonies. Notify the Secretary two days in advance   5.00 4.00 3.00 2.00

No. 51.   Twenty vases, one flower in each   4.00 3.00 2.00 1.00 .50

FOXGLOVE.—

No. 52.   Vase of twelve spikes   3.00 2.00 1.00 .50

AQUILEGIA.—

No. 53.   Collection   3.00 2.50 2.00 1.00 .50

LUPINUS.—

No. 54.   Vase   3.00 2.00 1.50 1.00

CHERRY, ONE QUART.—

No. 55.   For any named variety five dollars may be used for prizes.

STRAWBERRY, TWENTY-FOUR BERRIES.—

No. 56.   Corsican   1.50 1.00 .50

No. 57.   Senator Dunlap   1.50 1.00 .50

No. 58.   Howard No. 17   3.00 2.50 2.00 1.50 1.00 .50

No. 59.   Any other variety   2.00 1.50 1.00 .50

No. 60.   New varieties   2.00 1.50 1.00 .50

PEA, ONE-HALF PECK.—

No. 61.   Any variety   2.00 1.50 1.00 .50

Rose Exhibition

Thursday, June 22, open from 3 to 9 p. m.

*All articles for this exhibition must be
in the hall and ready for inspection by
the judges by 2 o'clock*

ROSES.—

No. 62.　Twelve blooms of distinct named
varieties of H. P. roses, outdoor
culture　　　　　　　　4.00　3.00　2.00　1.00

No. 63.　Six blooms of distinct named
varieties of H. P. roses, out-
door culture　　　　　　3.00　2.00　1.00　　.50

No. 64.　Collection of cut roses. Twelve
dollars to be used in prizes.

No. 65.　Vase of roses, 12 blooms　3.00　2.50　2.00　1.50　1.00

No. 66.　Vase H. P. roses, not to exceed
ten blooms　　　　　　　3.00　2.00　1.00

No. 67.　Vase H. T. roses, not exceeding
ten blooms　　　　　　　3.00　2.00　1.00

No. 68.　Display of cut climbing roses.
Fifteen dollars may be used in
prizes.

No. 69.　Basket of roses　　　　3.00　2.50　2.00　1.50

* 　 * 　 *

Special Prizes
Miss Frances C. Morse Fund

A.　Table decoration of roses. Flowers
grown by exhibitors　　4.00　3.00　2.00　1.00

* 　 * 　 *

PEONIES.—

No. 70.　Best Display of Peonies.
Notify the Secretary two days in
advance　　　　　　　5.00　4.00　3.00　2.00

AQUILEGIA.—

No. 71.　Bowl　　　　　　　2.50　2.00　1.50　1.00

Special Prizes
Obadiah Brown Hadwen Fund

HARDY FLOWERS, TO BE NAMED.—
B. Display of outdoor varieties   5.00 4.00 3.00 2.00 1.00

*   *   *

STRAWBERRY, TWENTY-FOUR BERRIES.—
No. 72.	Howard No. 17	3.00	2.50	2.00	1.50	1.00	.50
No. 73.	Sample				1.50	1.00	.50
No. 74.	Uncle Joe			2.00	1.50	1.00	.50
No. 75.	Any other variety			2.00	1.50	1.00	.50
No. 76.	Collections, not more than six varieties		5.00	4.00	3.00	2.00	1.00

CHERRY, ONE QUART.—
No. 77. Black Tartarian   2.00 1.50 1.00 .50
No. 78. Gov. Wood   2.00 1.50 1.00 .50
No. 79. Best display, ten dollars may be used for prizes.
No. 80. For varieties not scheduled, five dollars may be used for prizes.

PEA, ONE-HALF PECK.—
No. 81. Thomas Laxton   2.00 1.50 1.00 .50
No. 82. Gradus   2.00 1.50 1.00 .50
No. 83. Any other variety   2.00 1.50 1.00 .50

CABBAGE, THREE SPECIMENS.—
No. 84. Any named variety   2.50 2.00 1.50 1.00

LETTUCE.—
No. 85. Six heads   2.00 1.50 1.00 .50

Thursday, June 29

All articles for this exhibition must be in the hall and ready for inspection by the judges by 2 o'clock

This exhibition will be open to the public from 3 to 9 p. m.

CUT FLOWERS.—
No. 86.   Twenty vases   3.00 2.50 2.00 1.50 1.00   .50

DIANTHUS BARBATUS, (SWEET WILLIAM).—
No. 87.   Twelve vases, three clusters
          in a vase   3.00 2.50 2.00 1.50 1.00   .50

CAMPANULA, (CANTERBURY BELLS).—
No. 88.   Display   4.00 3.00 2.00 1.00

DELPHINIUM.—
No. 89.   One vase, not more than twelve
          spikes   4.00 3.50 3.00 2.50 2.00 1.50 1.00

ROSES.—
No. 90.   Collection of Cut Roses. Ten
          dollars may be used in prizes.

*   *   *

Special Prizes
Offered by Mr. Herbert R. Kinney

C.   Display of Cut Flowers on round
          tables   3.00 2.50 2.00 1.50 1.00
This number is intended for the growers who do not compete in the call for twenty vases or displays during the year.

*   *   *

STRAWBERRY, TWENTY-FOUR BERRIES.—
No. 91.   Downing's Bride   2.00 1.50 1.00   .50
No. 92.   Ten dollars may be used for
          prizes. Preference given to
          worthy varieties of recent
          introduction.
No. 93.   Best display   5.00 4.00 3.00 2.00 1.00

CURRANT, TWENTY-FOUR BUNCHES.—
No. 94.   For any variety, five dollars may be used for prizes.

CHERRY, ONE QUART.—

No. 95.	Coe's Transparent		1.50	1.00	.50
No. 96.	Elton	2.00	1.50	1.00	.50
No. 97.	Black Eagle		1.50	1.00	.50
No. 98.	Montmorency	2.00	1.50	1.00	.50

BEET, OPEN CULTURE.—

No. 99.	Twelve specimens	2.50	2.00	1.50	1.00	.50

CARROT.—

No. 100.	Two bunches, six in each	2.00	1.50	1.00	.50

BEAN, SNAP, ONE-HALF PECK.—

No. 101.	Any named variety	2.50	2.00	1.50	1.00	.50

PEA, ONE-HALF PECK.—

No. 102.	Sutton's Excelsior	2.00	1.50	1.00	.50
No. 103.	Any other variety	2.00	1.50	1.00	.50

CUCUMBER, THREE SPECIMENS.—

No. 104.	Any variety	1.50	1.00	.50

Thursday, July 6

All articles for this exhibition must be in the hall and ready for inspection by the judges by 2 o'clock

This exhibition will be open to the public from 3 to 9 p. m.

CUT FLOWERS.—
No. 105.   Twenty vases   4.00 3.00 2.50 2.00 1.50 1.00
No. 106.   Ten vases.   2.50 2.00 1.50 1.00 .50
This number is intended for the growers who do not compete in call for 20 vases and displays during the year.

BASKET.—
No. 107.   3.00 2.50 2.00 1.50 1.00

JAPANESE IRIS.—
No. 108.   Display, twenty dollars may be used for prizes.

LILIUM CANDIDUM.—
No. 109.   Vase   ·4.00 3.00 2.00 1.00

DELPHINIUM.—
No. 110.   Display, fifteen dollars may be used for prizes.

WILD FLOWERS.—
No. 111.   Twenty vases   2.50 2.00 1.50 1.00 .50

ROSES.—
No. 112.   Display of cut climbing roses. Ten dollars may be used in prizes.

RASPBERRY, BLACK CAP, ONE QUART.—
No. 113.   Named variety   1.50 1.00 .50

RASPBERRY, ONE PINT.—
No. 114.   Latham   2.00 1.50 1.00 .50
No. 115.   Varieties not scheduled, five dollars may be used for prizes.

GOOSEBERRY, ONE QUART.—
No. 116.   Any named variety   2.00 1.50 1.00 .50

CURRANT, TWENTY-FOUR BUNCHES.—

No. 117.	Red Cross		1.50 1.00	.50
No. 118.	Perfection	2.00	1.50 1.00	.50
No. 119.	White Grape		1.50 1.00	.50
No. 120.	Versaillaise	2.00	1.50 1.00	.50
No. 121.	Any other variety	2.00	1.50 1.00	.50

BEAN, SNAP, ONE-HALF PECK.—   0

No. 122.	Wax	2. 0 .00	1.50 1.00
No. 123.	Green Pod	2.50 2.00	1.50 1.0

PEA, ONE-HALF PECK.—

No. 124.	Alderman	2.00	1.50 1.00	.50
No. 125.	Telephone	2.50	2.00 1.50	1.00
No. 126.	Display		3.00 2.00	1.00

DISPLAY OF VEGETABLES.—

No. 127.   Not to exceed 24 square feet, $20.00 may be used for prizes. Notify the Secretary two days in advance.

TOMATO, TWELVE SPECIMENS.—

No. 128.	Any named variety	2.00	1.50 1.00	.50

Sweet Pea Exhibition

Thursday, July 13

All articles for this exhibition must be in the hall and ready for inspection by the judges by 2 o'clock

This exhibition will be open to the public from 3 to 9 p. m.

SWEET PEAS, ANNUAL.—
No. 129. Ten vases, not more than 25
   flower stems in a vase   4.00 3.00 2.00
No. 130. Table Decoration—Sweet Peas,
   laid for four covers, Gypsophila
   may be used. Notify the Secre-
   two days in advance 5.00 4.00 3.00 2.00 1.00
SCALE OF POINTS BY WHICH THE ABOVE CLASS IS TO BE JUDGED
   Arrangement of flowers and quality 50 points
   Proportion and harmony of flowers
    with accessories   30
   Accessories   20

SWEET PEAS.—
No. 131. Basket, any green may be used. 4.00 3.00 2.00 1.00

* * *

Obadiah Brown Hadwen Fund

D. Collection of Sweet Peas, fifteen dollars may be used in prizes.

* * *

CUT FLOWERS.—
No. 132. Display, not exceeding 30
   square feet 4.00 3.00 2.50 2.00 1.50 1.00

LILIUM REGALE.—
No. 133. Fifteen dollars may be used in prizes.

CENTAUREA.—
No. 134. Display, Gypsophila may be
   used   4:00 3.00 2.50 2.00

PETUNIA.—
No. 135.   Twenty vases, one flower in
    each   3.00 2.50 2.00 1.00   .50

APPLE, TWELVE SPECIMENS.—
No. 136.   Any variety   2.00 1.50 1.00   .50

BLACKBERRY, ONE QUART.—
No. 137.   Any variety   1.50 1.00   .50

CURRANTS, TWENTY-FOUR BUNCHES.—
No. 138.   Wilder   2.00 1.50 1.00   .50

CUCUMBER.—
No. 139.   Three specimens   1.50 1.00   .50

CABBAGE, THREE SPECIMENS.—
No. 140.   Any variety   2.00 1.50 1.00   .50

LETTUCE.—
No. 141.   Twelve heads   2.00 1.50 1.00   .50

SQUASH, THREE SPECIMENS.—
No. 142.   Summer   2.00 1.50 1.00   .50

POTATO, TWELVE SPECIMENS.—
No. 143.   Any variety   2.00 1.50 1.00   .50

Thursday, July 20

All articles for this exhibition must be in the hall and ready for inspection by the judges by 2 o'clock

This exhibition will be open to the public from 3 to 9 p. m.

CUT FLOWERS.—
No. 144. Display   4.00 3.00 2.50 2.00 1.50 1.00

GERMAN STOCKS.—
No. 145. Twenty vases, not to exceed
     three spikes in a vase   3.00 2.00 1.00 .50

TABLE DECORATIONS.—
No. 146. For best table decoration
     laid for four covers. Flowers
     to be grown by the exhibitor.
     Notify the Secretary two days
     in advance   5.00 4.00 3.00 2.00 1.00

SCALE OF POINTS BY WHICH THE ABOVE CLASS IS TO BE JUDGED
     Arrangement of flowers and quality   50 points
     Proportion and harmony of flowers
        with accessories   30
     Accessories   20

SWEET PEAS, ANNUAL.—
No. 147. Five vases, 25 flower stems
       in vase   3.00 2.50 2.00 1.50 1.00

BEGONIA, TUBEROUS ROOTED.—
No. 148. Twelve vases   3.00 2.00 1.00

APPLE, TWELVE SPECIMENS.—
No. 149. Yellow Transparent   2.00 1.50 1.00 .50

BLACKBERRY, ONE QUART.—
No. 150. For varieties not scheduled, five dollars may be used for prizes.

PEAR, TWELVE SPECIMENS.—
No. 151. Any named variety, five dollars may be used for prizes.

CORN, TWELVE EARS.—
No. 152.   Sweet, any named variety   2.00 1.50 1.00   .50

TOMATO, TWELVE SPECIMENS.—
No. 153.   Any named variety   2.00 1.50 1.00   .50

BEAN, SHELL, ONE-HALF PECK.—
No. 154.   Any named variety   2.00 1.50 1.00   .50

POTATO, TWELVE SPECIMENS.—
No. 155.   Irish Cobbler   2.00 1. 0 1.00   .50
No. 156.   Any other variety   2.00 1.50 1.00   .50

Thursday, July 27

All articles for this exhibition must be in the hall and ready for inspection by the judges by 2 o'clock

This exhibition will be open to the public from 3 to 9 p. m.

CUT FLOWERS.—
No. 157. Standard   4.00 3.00 2.50 2.00 1.50 1.00
No. 158. Ten vases   2.50 2.00 1.50 1.00 .50
This number is intended for the growers who do not compete in the call for 20 vases and displays during the year.

GLADIOLUS.—
No. 159. Twenty vases, one spike in
          each   4.00 3.00 2.00 1.00

PHLOX, PERENNIAL (SHOULD BE NAMED).—
No. 160. Twelve vases, three clusters
          in each   3.00 2.00 1.00 .50

ANNUALS.—
No. 161. Display   3.00 2.50 2.00 1.50 1.00

APPLE, TWELVE SPECIMENS.—
No. 162. Astrachan   2.00 1.50 1.00 .50
No. 163. Oldenburg   2.00 1.50 1.00 .50
No. 164. Yellow Transparent   2.00 1.50 1.00 .50

BLACKBERRY, ONE QUART.—
No. 165. Any varieties, five dollars may be used for prizes.

PEAR, TWELVE SPECIMENS.—
No. 166. Any variety   1.50 1.00 .50

PEACH, TWELVE SPECIMENS.—
No. 167. Any variety, five dollars may be used for prizes.

PLUM, TWELVE SPECIMENS.—
No. 168. Red June   1.50 1.00 .50

BEAN, SHELL, ONE-HALF PECK.—
No. 169. Dwarf Horticultural   2.00 1.50 1.00 .50
No. 170. Any other variety   2.00 1.50 1.00 .50

CORN, TWELVE EARS.—

No. 171.   Any named variety   2.00 1.50 1.00   .50

SQUASH, THREE SPECIMENS.—

No. 172.   Summer   2.00 1.50 1.00   .50

POTATO, TWELVE SPECIMENS.—

No. 173.   Rose   2.00 1.50 1.00   .50
No. 174.   Varieties not scheduled   2.00 1.50 1.00   .30

VEGETABLES.—

No. 175.   Display, Round Table, $15.00 may be used for prizes.
          Notify the Secretary two days in advance.

Thursday, August 3

All articles for this exhibition must be in the hall and ready for inspection by the judges by 2 o'clock

This exhibition will be open to the public from 3 to 9 p. m.

CUT FLOWERS.—
No. 176. Basket 　　　　　 4.00 3.00 2.50 2.00 1.50 1.00

GLADIOLUS.—
No. 177. Display 　　　　 8.00 6.00 5.00 4.00 3.00

ASTERS.—
No. 178. Twenty vases, one bloom in
　　　　 each 　　　　　 3.00 2.50 2.00 1.00 .50

CHINA PINKS.—
No. 179. Twenty vases, five clusters
　　　　 each 　　　　　　 3.00 2.00 1.00 .50

PHLOX, PERENNIAL (SHOULD BE NAMED).—
No. 180. Twenty vases, one cluster in
　　　　 each 　　　　　 3.00 2.00 1.50 1.00 .50

ZINNIA.—
No. 181. Twenty vases, one flower in
　　　　 each 　　　 3.00 2.50 2.00 1.50 1.00 .50

WILD FLOWERS.—
No. 182. Twenty vases, no duplicates
　　　　　　　　 2.50 2.00 1.50 1.00 .50

* 　 * 　 *

Special Prizes
Offered by Mr. Herbert R. Kinney

E. Table Decorations. For the best
　　 table decorations 　　 3.00 2.50 2.00 1.50 1.00

This call is intended for exhibitors who do not exhibit in other table decorations during the year. Notify the Secretary two days in advance.

APPLE, TWELVE SPECIMENS.—
No. 183.   Oldenburg   .00 1. 0 1.00   .50
No. 184.   Williams   2.00 1.50 1.00   .50

PEACH, TWELVE SPECIMENS.—
No. 185.   Any variety   2.00 1.50 1.00   .50

CABBAGE, THREE SPECIMENS.—
No. 186.   Copenhagen   2.00 1.50 1.00   .50
No. 187.   Any other named variety   2.00 1.50 1.00   .50

CORN, TWELVE EARS.—
No. 188.   Yellow, Sweet   2.50 2.00 1.50 1.00   .50

SQUASH, THREE SPECIMENS.—
No. 189.   Any named variety (excepting
              summer varieties)   2.00 1.50 1.00   .50

TOMATO, OPEN CULTURE, TWELVE SPECIMENS.—
No. 190.   Any named variety   2.00 1.50 1.00   .50

Gladiolus Exhibition

Thursday, August 10

All articles for this exhibition must be in the hall and ready for inspection by the judges by 2 o'clock

This exhibition will be open to the public from 3 to 9 p. m.

GLADIOLUS.—
No. 191. Display. Notify the Secretary two days in advance. Forty dollars may be used in prizes.

No. 192. Standard of Gladioli   3.00 2.50 2.00 1.00 .50

No. 193. Twenty vases, one spike in
each   4.00 3.00 2.00 1.00 .50

ASTER, LARGE FLOWERED, LONG STEM.—
No. 194. Vase of 20 blooms   3.00 2.50 2.00 1.00 .50

SALPIGLOSSIS.—
No. 195. Basket   3.00 2.00 1.00 .50

PHLOX DRUMMONDI.—
No. 196. Display   2.00 1.50 1.00 .50

ANNUALS.—
No. 197. Display, fifteen dollars may be used in prizes.

APPLE, TWELVE SPECIMENS.—
No. 198. Williams   2.00 1.50 1.00 .50
No. 199. For varieties not scheduled, five dollars may be used for prizes.

APPLE, CRAB, TWENTY-FOUR SPECIMENS.—
No. 200. Varieties not scheduled   1.50 1.00 .50

PEAR, TWELVE SPECIMENS.—
No. 201. Clapp's Favorite   3.00 2.50 2.00 1.50 1.00 .50
No. 202. For varieties not scheduled, five dollars may be used for prizes.

PEACH, TWELVE SPECIMENS.—
No. 203. Carman   1.50 1.00 .50
No. 204. Any other variety   1.50 1.00 .50

PLUM, TWELVE SPECIMENS.—
No. 205. Washington   1.50 1.00   .50
No. 206. Japanese varieties, five dollars
           may be used for prizes.

BEAN, SHELL, ONE-HALF PECK.—
No. 207. Dwarf, any variety   2.00 1.50 1.00   .50
· No. 208. Pole, any variety   2.00 1.50 1.00   .50

BEAN, STRING, ONE-HALF PECK.—
No. 209. Kentucky Wonder   2.00 1.50 1.00   .50

CORN, SWEET, TWELVE EARS.—
No. 210. Any named variety   2.50 2.00 1.50 1.00

TOMATO, TWELVE SPECIMENS.—
No. 211. Any named variety   2.50 2.00 1.50 1.00   .50

MUSHROOM, NATIVE.—
No. 212. Collection of edible varieties, prizes will be awarded.

CUCUMBER, FOR PICKLES.—
No. 213. One-half peck   2.00 1.50 1.00   .50

Thursday, August 17

All articles for this exhibition must be in the hall and ready for inspection by the judges by 2 o'clock

This exhibition will be open to the public from 3 to 9 p. m.

ZINNIA, LARGE FLOWERED.—
No. 214. Display, notify the Secretary
        two days in advance   4.00 3.00 2.50 2.00 1.50 1.00
DAHLIA.—
No. 215. Display. Notify the Secretary
        two days in advance   5.00 4.00 3.00 2.00 1.00

* * *

Obadiah Brown Hadwen Fund

DISPLAY OF GARDEN FLOWERS.—
F. Not to exceed 24 square feet.
        Notify the Secretary two days
        in advance   4.00 3.50 3.00 2.50 2.00 1.00

* * *

ASTER, SINGLE OR ANEMONE.—
No. 216. Vase   2.00 1.50 1.00 .50
PLUMS, TWELVE SPECIMENS.—
No. 217. Bradshaw   3.00 2.00 1.50 1.00 .50
No. 218. Imperial Gage   ‛2.00 1.50 1.00 .50
No. 219. Guiei   1.50 1.00 .50
No. 220. For varieties not scheduled, three
        dollars may be used for prizes.
PEACH, TWELVE SPECIMENS.—
No. 221. Five dollars may be used in prizes.
BEAN, POLE, ONE-HALF PECK.—
No. 222. Shell   2.50 2.00 1.50 1.00
No. 223. String, any variety   2.50 2.00 1.50 1.00
CORN, TWELVE EARS.—
No. 224. Sweet, not less than twelve rows 2.50 2.00 1.50 1.00
VEGETABLES.—
No. 225. Display of vegetables from
        Home Gardens to cover 12
        square feet   6.00 5.00 4.00 3.00 2.00 1.00

Thursday, August 24

All articles for this exhibition must be in the hall and ready for insection by the judges by 2 o'clock

This exhibition will be open to the public from 3 to 9 p. m.

CUT FLOWERS.—
No. 226. Display   5.00 4.00 3.50 3.00 2.50 2.00 1.50 1.00
No. 227. Basket   3.00 2.50 2.00 1.50 1.00

ASTER, LARGE FLOWERED.—
No. 228. Twenty vases, three blooms
        in each   3.00 2.50 2.00 1.00 .50

LILIES.—
No. 229. Display   5.00 4.00 3.00 2.00
        Notify the Secretary two days
        in advance.

ZINNIA, LILLIPUT VARIETY.—
No. 230. Twenty vases, three blooms
        in a vase   3.00 2.00 1.00 .50

BEGONIA, TUBEROUS ROOTED.—
No. 231. Display. Ten dollars may be used for prizes.

VERBENA.—
No. 232. Basket or Bowl   2.50 2.00 1.50 1.00 .50

APPLES, TWELVE SPECIMENS.—
No. 233. Porter   1.50 1.00 .50
No. 234. Gravenstein   2.50 2.00 1.50 1.00 .50
No. 235. For varieties not scheduled, five
        dollars may be used for prizes.

PLUM.—
No. 236. Display, no restriction as to
        arrangements   4.00 3.00 2.00 1.00

PEACH, TWELVE SPECIMENS.—
No. 237. Any variety   1.50 1.00 .50

SQUASH, THREE SPECIMENS.—
No. 238. Any named variety   2.50 2.00 1.50 1.00

PEPPER, TWELVE SPECIMENS.—

No. 239. Harris's Early   2.50 2.00 1.50 1.00
No. 240. Bell Type   2.50 2.00 1.50 1.00

VEGETABLES.—

No. 241. Display, not to exceed 24 square feet, $20.00 may be
          used for prizes. Notify the Secretary two days in advance.

Dahlia Exhibition

Thursday, August 31

All articles for this exhibition must be in the hall and ready for inspection by the judges by 2 o'clock

This exhibition will be open to the public from 3 to 9 p. m.

CUT FLOWERS.—

No. 242. Display	5.00	4.00	3.00	2.50	2.00	1.50	1.00
No. 243. Standard		3.00	2.50	2.00	1.50	1.00	.50

This number is intended for the growers who do not compete in call for 20 vases and displays during the year.

DAHLIA.—

No. 244. Display, thirty-five dollars may be used in prizes. Notify the Secretary two days in advance.

LARGE FLOWERED.—

No. 245. Twenty vases, one flower in
each   4.00 3.00 2.00 1.50 1.00

ASTER.—

No. 246. Vase of large flowered   3.00 2.50 2.00 1.00 .50

No. 247. Display, not exceeding
25 square feet   5.00 4.00 3.00 2.00 1.00

SCABIOSA.—

No. 248. Vase   2.50 2.00 1.50 1.00 .50

APPLE, TWELVE SPECIMENS.—

No. 249. Gravenstein	3.00	2.50	2.00	1.50	1.00	.50
No. 250. Maiden's Blush				1.50	1.00	.50
No. 251. Wealthy		2.50	2.00	1.50	1.00	.50

APPLE, CRAB, TWENTY-FOUR SPECIMENS.—

No. 252. Hyslop   2.50 2.00 1.50 1.00 .50

PEAR, TWELVE SPECIMENS.—

No. 253. Bartlett   4.00 3.00 2.50 2.00 1.50 1.00 .50

No. 254. Varieties not scheduled, five dollars may be used for prizes.

PEACH, TWELVE SPECIMENS.—

No. 255.	Champion		1.50	1.00	.50
No. 256.	Oldmixon		2.00	1.00	.50
No. 257.	Elberta	2.50 2.00	1.50	1.00	.50
No. 258.	Seedlings		1.50	1.00	.50
No. 259.	Crawford (early)		2.00 1.50	1.00	.50

No. 260. Varieties not scheduled, five dollars may be used for prizes.

No. 261. New varieties. Five dollars may be used in prizes.

PLUM, TWELVE SPECIMENS.—

No. 262.	Golden Varieties		1.50	1.00	.50
No. 263.	Lombard	2.00	1.50	1.00	.50
No. 264.	Quackenboss		1.50	1.00	.50
No. 265.	Burbank	2.00	1.50	1.00	.50
No. 266.	Moore's Arctic		1.50	1.00	.50

No. 267. For Japanese varieties not scheduled, five dollars may be used for prizes.

No. 268. Other varieties not scheduled, five dollars may be used for prizes.

GRAPE, THREE CLUSTERS.—

No. 269.	Green Mountain	2.00	1.50	1.00	.50
No. 270.	Moore's		1.50	1.00	.50

PEPPER, TWELVE SPECIMENS.—

No. 271.	Squash	2.00	1.50	1.00	.50
No. 272.	Any other variety	2.00	1.50	1.00	.50

TOMATO, TWELVE SPECIMENS.—

No. 273.	Beauty	2.50 2.00	1.50	1.00	.50
No. 274.	Any other variety	2.50 2.00	1.50	1.00	.50

BEAN, ONE-HALF PECK.—

No. 275.	Dwarf Lima	2.00	1.50	1.00	.50
No. 276.	Pole Lima	2.00	1.50	1.00	.50

CABBAGE, THREE SPECIMENS.—

No. 277.	Any named variety	2.00	1.50	1.00	.50

CELERY, BLANCHED (NAMED) SIX SPECIMENS.—

No. 278.	Any variety	2.00	1.50	1.00	.50

CARROT, TWELVE SPECIMENS.—
No. 279.   Any variety   2.50 2.00 1.50 1.00   .50

EGG PLANT.—
No. 280.   Three specimens   2.00 1.50 1.00

MUSHROOM, NATIVE.—
No. 281.   Collection of edible varieties, prizes will be awarded.

Grape Exhibition

Thursday, September 7

*All articles for this exhibition must be
in the hall and ready for inspection by
the judges by 2 o'clock*

This exhibition will be open to the public from 3 to 9 p. m.

CUT FLOWERS.—
No. 282. Twenty vases   5.00 4.00 3.50 3.00 2.50 2.00 1.00
No. 283. Basket   3.00 2.50 2.00 1.50 1.00

DAHLIA.—
No. 284. Fifty vases, one flower in each. Twenty-five dollars
      may be used for prizes.
No. 285. Twelve vases, one flower in each. This number is
      intended for the growers who do not compete in other
      classes for Dahlias during the year.
                            2.50 2.00 1.50 1.00 .50
No. 286. Single varieties, twenty vases   3.00 2.50 2.00 1.00
No. 287. Basket of large flowered   3.00 2.50 2.00 1.00
POMPOM.—
No. 288. Twenty vases, three sprays in
      each   3.00 2.50 2.00 1.00

COSMOS.—
No. 289. Vase or basket   3.00 2.50 2.00 1.50 1.00

MARIGOLD.—
No. 290. Display   3.00 2.00 1.00 .50
      Notify the Secretary two days in advance.

APPLE, TWELVE SPECIMENS.—
No. 291. American Beauty or Sterling   1.50 1.00 .50
No. 292. Twenty-ounce   1.50 1.00 .50

PEAR, TWELVE SPECIMENS.—
No. 293. Louise Bonne de Jersey   1.50 1.00 .50
No. 294. Urbaniste   1.50 1.00 .50
No. 295. Varieties not scheduled, five dollars may be used for
      prizes.

PEACH, TWELVE SPECIMENS.—
No. 296. Crawford (late)   2.00 1.50 1.00 .50
No. 297. Display, no restriction as to
      arrangement   8.00 6.00 4.00 3.00

PLUM, TWELVE SPECIMENS.—
No. 298. Any variety   2.00 1.50 1.00 .50

GRAPE, THREE CLUSTERS.—
No. 299. Brighton   1.50 1.00 .50
No. 300. Campbell   1.50 1.00 .50
No. 301. Lindley   1.50 1.00 .50
No. 302. Ontario   1.50 1.00 .50
No. 303. Worden   2.50 2.00 1.50 1.00 .50
No. 304. Concord   2.50 2.00 1.50 1.00 .50
No. 305. Delaware   2.00 1.50 1.00 .50
No. 306. Niagara   2.50 2.00 1.50 1.00 .50
No. 307. Pocklington   1.50 1.00 .50
No. 308. Moore's Diamond   1.50 1.00 .50
No. 309. For other varieties, ten dollars may be used for prizes.
No. 310. Display of Grapes. Ten dollars may be used for prizes.
No. 311. New varieties, five dollars may be used for prizes.

QUINCE, TWELVE SPECIMENS.—
No. 312. Any variety   2.00 1.50 1.00 .50

CELERY, BLANCHED, SIX SPECIMENS.—
No. 313. Golden   2.50 2.00 1.50 1.00
No. 314. Other varieties   2.50 2.00 1.50 1.00

MELON, THREE SPECIMENS.—
No. 315. Green Flesh   2.00 1.50 1.00 .50
No. 316. Yellow Flesh   2.00 1.50 1.00 .50
No. 317. Water   2.00 1.50 1.00 .50

TOMATO.—
No. 318. Display   4.00 3.00 2.50 2.00 1.00

VEGETABLES.—
No. 319. Display to cover 24 square
      feet. Notify the Secretary
      two days in advance   7.00 6.00 5.00 4.00 3.00

Thursday, September 14

All articles for this exhibition must be in the hall and ready for inspection by the judges by 2 o'clock

This exhibition will be open to the public from 3 to 9 p. m.

No. 320. BASKET   4.00 3.00 2.50 2.00 1.50 1.00

DISPLAY OF FLOWER ARRANGEMENT.—

No. 321. Twelve receptacles, no restrictions as to kind of tables used, not to cover more than 24 square feet. Flowers to be grown by exhibitor. Notify the Secretary two days in advance. Twenty-five dollars may be used in prizes.

SCALE OF POINTS BY WHICH THE ABOVE CLASS IS TO BE JUDGED

Arrangement of flowers	40 points
Proportion and harmony of flowers with receptacles	35
Quality of flowers	25

CELOSIA.—

No. 322. Display   3.00 2.50 2.00 1.50 1.00

Notify the Secretary two days in advance.

*   *   *

Edwin Draper Fund

BEGONIA, TUBEROUS ROOTED.—

G. Fifteen dollars may be used in prizes.

*   *   *

APPLE, TWELVE SPECIMENS.—

No. 323. Hubbardston   2.00 1.50 1.00 .50

No. 324. For other varieties not scheduled, five dollars may be used for prizes.

PEAR, TWELVE SPECIMENS.—

No. 325. Seckel   3.00 2.50 2.00 1.50 1.00 .50

No. 326. Any variety, not scheduled   1.50 1.00 .50

No. 327. Display, no restriction as to arrangement   6.00 5.00 4.00 3.00 2.00

Notify the Secretary two days in advance.

QUINCE, TWELVE SPECIMENS.—

No. 328.   Orange   2.00 1.50 1.00   .50

DISPLAY OF FRUIT.—

No. 329.   Not to exceed 20 square feet, $30.00 may be used for prizes.

*   *   *

Special Prizes
Offered by Miss Frances C. Morse

H.   For most artistic table arrangement of
       Native Fruit.   4.00 3.00 2.00 1.00

*   *   *

POTATO, SIX VARIETIES (NAMED).—

No. 330.   Twelve specimens of each
             5.00 4.00 3.00 2.00 1.50 1.00

SQUASH, THREE SPECIMENS.—

No. 331.   Warren   2.00 1.50 1.00   .50
No. 332.   Golden Hubbard   2.50 2.00 1.50 1.00   .50
No. 333.   For varieties not scheduled, five dollars may be used for prizes.

CABBAGE, THREE SPECIMENS.—

No. 334.   Red   2.00 1.50 1.00   50
No. 335.   Savoy   1.50 1.00   .50
No. 336.   Any other variety   2.50 2.00 1.50 1.00   .50

CAULIFLOWER.—

No. 337.   Three specimens   2.50 2.00 1.50 1.00   .50

TURNIP.—

No. 338.   Twelve specimens   1.50 1.00   .50

BROCCOLI.—

No. 339.   Three specimens   2.00 1.50 1.00   .50

*   *   *

Special Prizes
Offered by Mr. Herbert R. Kinney

VEGETABLES.—

I.   Display of vegetables from Home
       Gardens to cover 16 square feet
            5.00 4.00 3.00 2.50 2.00 1.00

Thursday, September 21

All articles for this exhibition must be in the hall and ready for inspection by the judges by 2 o'clock

This exhibition will be open to the public from 3 to 9 p. m.

CUT FLOWERS.—
No. 340. Display, not exceeding 30 square
      feet   5.00 4.00 3.50 3.00 2.50 2.00 1.50 1.00

COSMOS.—
No. 341. Display. Notify the Secretary
      two days in advance   3.50 3.00 2.00 1.50 1.00 .50

DRIED FLOWERS, STATICE, STRAWFLOWERS, LUNARIA (HONESTY).—
No. 342. Display. Notify the Secretary
      two days in advance   4.00 3.50 2.00 1.00

TABLE DECORATIONS.—
No. 343. For best table decoration laid for four covers, no restrictions. Notify the Secretary two days in advance
      6.00 5.00 4.50 4.00 3.00 2.00 1.50 1.00

SCALE OF POINTS BY WHICH THE ABOVE CLASS IS TO BE JUDGED

Arrangement and quality	50 points
Proportion and harmony of flowers with accessories	30
Accessories	20

MARIGOLD.—
No. 344. Display. Notify the Secretary two days in advance   3.00 2.00 1.00 .50

APPLE, ONE STANDARD BOX.—
No. 345. McIntosh   4.00 3.00 2.00 1.00 .50
No. 346. Any other variety   4.00 3.00 2.00 1.00 .50

APPLE, TWEVLE SPECIMENS.—
No. 347. Sutton Beauty   2.00 1.50 1.00 .50
No. 348. Tompkins King   2.00 1.50 1.00 .50
No. 349. McIntosh   4.00 3.00 2.50 2.00 1.50 1.00 .50

PEAR, TWELVE SPECIMENS.—
No. 350. Bosc   4.00 3.00 2.50 2.00 1.50 1.00 .50
No. 351. Sheldon   4.00 3.00 2.00 1.50 1.00 .50

GRAPE, OPEN CULTURE.—
No. 352. Collection of not less than five
          varieties, three clusters each
                    3.00 2.50 2.00 1.50 1.00 .50

PUMPKIN, THREE SPECIMENS.—
No. 353. Sweet   2.00 1.50 1.00 .50

SQUASH, THREE SPECIMENS.—
No. 354. Bay State ·   2.00 1.50 1.00 .50
No. 355. Blue Hubbard   3.00 2.50 2.00 1.50 1.00
No. 356. Any other variety, not scheduled 2.50 2.00 1.50 1.00

CAULIFLOWER, THREE SPECIMENS.—
No. 357.   2.00 1.50 1.00 .50

VEGETABLES.—
No. 358. Collection not to exceed 25
          varieties   10.00 8.00 7.00 6.00 5.00
          Notify the Secretary two days in advance.

Fruit and Vegetable Exhibition
Thursday, October 5
All articles for this exhibition must be in the hall and ready for inspection by the judges by 1 o'clock

This exhibition will be open to the public from 3 to 9 p. m.

FERNS.—
No. 359. Display, potted plants, named varieties. Twenty dollars may be used in prizes.

SPECIMEN FERN.—
No. 360. One plant   3.00 2.00 1.00

CUT FLOWERS.—
No. 361. Display—$50.00 may be awarded in prizes.

BASKET.—
No. 362. Fifteen dollars may be used in prizes.

HARDY CHRYSANTHEMUM.—
No. 363. Out-door culture. Fifteen dollars may be used in prizes.

APPLE, ONE STANDARD BOX.—
No. 364. Baldwin   4.00 3.00 2.00 1.00 .50
No. 365. Any other variety except McIntosh   4.00 3.00 2.00 1.00 .50

APPLE, TWELVE SPECIMENS.—

366.	Baldwin	4.00	3.50	3.00	2.50	2.00	1.50	1.00	.50
367.	Bellflower						1.50	1.00	.50
368.	Winter Banana						1.50	1.00	.50
369.	Peck's						1.50	1.00	.50
370.	R. I. Greening				3.00	2.00	1.50	1.00	.50
371.	Northern Spy				3.00	2.00	1.50	1.00	.50
372.	Palmer						1.50	1.00	.50
373.	Roxbury Russet				3.00	2.00	1.50	1.00	.50
374.	Cortland					2.00	1.50	1.00	.50
375.	Opalescent						1.50	1.00	.50
376.	Delicious				2.50	2.00	1.50	1.00	.50
377.	Collection, not to exceed 10 varieties	5.00	4.00	3.00	2.50	2.00			

No. 378.   New varieties, five dollars may be used in prizes.
No. 379.   Sweet varieties not scheduled, five dollars may be used for prizes.
No. 380.   For varieties other than sweet not scheduled, fifteen dollars may be used for prizes.
No. 381.   For varieties that have been scheduled, fifteen dollars may be used.

PEAR, TWELVE SPECIMENS.—

No. 382.	Angouleme					1.50	1.00	.50
No. 383.	Clairgeau				2.00	1.50	1.00	.50
No. 384.	Lawrence			3.00	2.00	1.50	1.00	.50
No. 385.	Winter Nelis					1.50	1.00	.50
No. 386.	Anjou		4.00	3.00	2.50	2.00	1.50	1.00	.50
No. 387.	Comice						1.00	.50

No. 388.   For varieties not scheduled, ten dollars may be used for prizes.

GRAPE, OPEN CULTURE.—
No. 389.   For any variety, six clusters, ten dollars may be used for prizes.

PEACH, TWELVE SPECIMENS.—
No. 390.   Any variety, named, ten dollars may be used for prizes.

QUINCE, TWELVE SPECIMENS.—
No. 391.   Champion   2.00 1.50 1.00 .50

CAULIFLOWER.—
No. 392.   Three specimens   2.50 2.00 1.50 1.00

CABBAGE, THREE SPECIMENS.—
No. 393.   Any named variety   2.50 2.00 1.50 1.00 .50

CELERY, BLANCHED, SIX SPECIMENS.—
No. 394.   Golden   2.50 2.00 150 1.00 .50
No. 395.   Any other varieties, not
           scheduled   2.00 1.50 1.00 .50

ENDIVE.—
No. 396.   Six specimens   1.50 1.00 .50

LEEKS.—
No. 397. Twelve specimens   1.50 1.00 .50

ONION, TWELVE SPECIMENS.—
No. 398. For varieties, five dollars may be used for prizes.

PARSLEY.—
No. 399. One-half peck 2.50 2.00 1.50 1.00 .50

SALSIFY.—
No. 400. Twelve specimens   1.50 1.00 .50

TURNIP, TWELVE SPECIMENS.—
No. 401. Purple Top Globe 2.00 1.50 1.00 .50
No. 402. Any variety, not scheduled 2.00 1.50 1.00 .50

Chrysanthemum Exhibition

Thursday, Nov. 9, 3 to 9 p. m.

Friday, Nov. 10, 9 a. m. to 9 p. m.

Saturday, Nov. 11, 9 a. m. to 9 p. m.

Sunday, Nov. 12, 12 m. to 9 p. m.

*All articles for this exhibition must be
in the hall and ready for inspection by
the judges by 1 o'clock Thursday*

CHRYSANTHEMUMS.—

No. 403.	Twelve blooms, not less than six varieties, to be named	12.00	10.00	8.00
No. 404.	Collection of twenty-five large blooms, long stems	20.00	15.00	10.00
No. 405.	Pompoms, display in vases	6.00 5.00	4.00	3.00
No. 406.	Single varieties, display in vases	6.00 5.00	4.00	3.00
No. 407.	Six specimen plants	10.00	8.00	6.00
Nol 408.	One specimen plant	3.00	2.00	1.00
No. 409.	Display of Anemones	6.00 5.00	4.00	3.00

COMMERCIAL GROWERS.—

No. 410.	Chrysanthemums, vase of white	4.00	3.00	2.00
No. 411.	Chrysanthemums, vase of yellow	4.00	3.00	2.00
No. 412.	Chrysanthemums, vase of pink	4.00	3.00	2.00

Note. Six flowers in each, one variety in each vase. Stems not less than two feet.

NON-COMMERCIAL GROWERS.—

No. 413.	Chrysanthemums, vase of white	4.00	3.00	2.00
No. 414.	Chrysanthemums, vase of yellow	4.00	3.00	2.00
No. 415.	Chrysanthemums, vase of pink	4.00	3.00	2.00

Note. Six flowers in each, one variety in each vase. Stems not less than two feet.

CHRYSANTHEMUMS, POMPOMS.—

No. 416.	Basket	5.00 4.00	3.00	2.00

Frederick A. Blake Fund

J. CHRYSANTHEMUMS. Best bloom   4.00 3.00 2.00

* * *

Obadiah Brown Hadwen Fund

K. CHRYSANTHEMUMS. Basket. Fifteen dollars to be
awarded in prizes.

* * *

Special Prizes
Offered by Mrs. Mabel Knowles Gage

L. TABLE DECORATIONS—CHRYSANTHEMUMS.—
Notify the Secretary two days in advance. Fifty dollars
to be used in prizes.

* * *

SPECIAL DISPLAY OF PLANTS.—
No. 417. Three hundred and fifty dollars may be used for prizes.
Persons competing for these premiums, must notify the Sec-
retary previous to 6 p. m. Monday, November 6.
No. 418. For exhibits—no restrictions as to where grown, or by
whom—$75.00 may be used for prizes.

FERN GLOBES.—
No. 419.   3.00 2.00 1.50 1.00

GLASS FERNERY.—
No. 420. Other than Fern Globe   4.00 3.00 2.00 1.00

WILD FRUITS AND BERRIES.—
No. 421. Display   5.00 4.00 3.00 2.50 1.50 1.00

PHYSALIS FRANCHETTII (CHINESE LANTERNS).—
No. 422. Basket   4.00 3.00 2.00 1.00

FRUIT DISPLAY.—
No. 423. No restriction as to arrangement. $40.00 may be used
in prizes. Notify the Secretary two days in advance.

APPLE, FIVE STANDARD BOXES.—
No. 424. Any variety   15.00 10.00 5.00 4.00

APPLES, FORTY-NINE SPECIMENS.—

No. 425.	Baldwin	6.00	5.00	4.00	3.00	2.00	1.00
No. 426.	McIntosh	6.00	5.00	4.00	3.00	2.00	1.00
No. 427.	Delicious		5.00	4.00	3.00	2.00	1.00
No. 428.	Any other named variety		5.00	4.00	3.00	2.00	1.00
No. 429.	Fancy Basket of Apples		3.00	2.50	2.00	1.50	1.00
No. 430.	Fancy Basket of Pears		3.00	3.50	2.00	1.50	1.00

SPECIAL EXHIBITION OF APPLES
WILLIAM EAMES FUND

A.	BALDWIN, BEST TWELVE.—			
	Three premiums	1.50	1.00	.50
B.	TOMPKINS KING.			
	Three premiums	1.50	1.00	.50
C.	PALMER.			
	Three premiums	1.50	1.00	.50
D.	RHODE ISLAND GREENING.			
	Three premiums	1.50	1.00	.50
E.	ROXBURY RUSSET.			
	Three premiums	1.50	1.00	.50
F.	SUTTON BEAUTY.			
	Three premiums	1.50	1.00	.50
G.	McINTOSH.			
	Three premiums	1.50	1.00	.50
H.	ANY OTHER VARIETY.			
	Three premiums	1.50	1.00	.50

*   *   *

BRUSSELS SPROUTS.—

No. 431.	One-half peck	1.50	1.00	.50

CELERY, BLANCHED, SIX SPECIMENS.—

No. 432.	Giant Pascal	2.00	1.50	1.00	.50
No. 433.	Any other variety	2.50	2.00	1.50	.00	.50

ONION, TWELVE SPECIMENS.—

No. 434.	White Globe		1.50	1.00	.50
No. 435.	Yellow Globe Danvers	2.50	2.00	1.50	1.00	.50
No. 436.	Red Globe	2.00	1.50	1.00	.50
No. 437.	Cracker		1.50	1.00	.50
No. 438.	Any other variety	2.00	1.50	1.00	.50

CABBAGE, THREE SPECIMENS.—
No. 439.   2.00 1.50 1.00   .50

PARSNIP, TWELVE SPECIMENS.—
No. 440.   Hollow Crown   2.00 1.50 1.00   .50
No. 441.   Any other variety   2.00 1.50 1.00   .50

SQUASH, THREE SPECIMENS.—
No. 442.   Green Hubbard   2.50 2.00 1.50 1.00   .50

SQUASH.—
No. 443.   Collection   5.00 4.50 4.00 3.00

GOURDS.—
No. 444.   Display   3.00 2.50 2.00 1.00

TURNIP, TWELVE SPECIMENS.—
No. 445.   Purple Top Globe   2.00 1.50 1.00   .50
No. 446.   English varieties, not scheduled 2.00 1.50 1.00   .50

TURNIP, SIX SPECIMENS.—
No. 447.   White Swede   2.00 1.50 1.00   .50
No. 448.   Yellow Swede   2.00 1.50 1.00   .50

POTATO, TWELVE SPECIMENS.—
No. 449.   Green Mountain   2.50 2.00 1.50 1.00
No. 450.   Any other variety   2.50 2.00 1.50 1.00

CORN.—
No. 451.   Field Corn, 12 ears, 8 row flint,
             corn shown flat   3.00 2.00 1.00

GRAINS.—
No. 452.   Best exhibit, five dollars may be used for prizes.

FIELD BEANS.—
No. 453.   Best exhibit, eight dollars may be used for prizes.

————————

Annual Meeting, Wednesday, December 6, 1933.
Premiums will be paid on or after November 20, 1933.

THE LIBRARY OF THE
WORCESTER COUNTY HORTICULTURAL SOCIETY

The Library Committee wish to call your attention to the Library and Reading Room, where the librarian is always ready to extend every facility possible to those in search of horticultural information.

COMMITTEE ON
LIBRARY AND PUBLICATIONS

EDWARD W. BREED, Chairman   MRS. AMY W. SMITH
WILLIAM ANDERSON   HERBERT R. KINNEY
                LUCY M. COULSON, Librarian

SOME OF THE RECENT ACCESSIONS TO THE LIBRARY

Everybody's Garden, by Walter Prichard Eaton
Hortus, by L. H. Bailey and Ethel Zoe Bailey
Pleasures and Problems of a Rock Garden, by Louise Beebe Wilder
Lily Year Book 1932, The Royal Horticultural Society
Practical Carnation Culture, by T. A. Weston
Cactus Culture, by Ellen D. Schulz.
Birds of Massachusetts, Vol. III
How to Grow Roses, by Robert Pyle, J. Horace McFarland and
    G. A. Stevens
Productive Beekeeping, by Frank C. Pellett
Alphabetical Check Iris List, by Mrs. Ethel A. S. Peckham
Rock Garden, by Archie Thornton
Aristocrats of the Trees, by Ernest H. Wilson, M.A., V.M.H.
Rock Garden and Alpine Plants, by Henry Correvon
Our Wild Orchids, by Frank Morris and Edward A. Eames
Principles and Practice in Pruning, by M. G. Kains
Backyard Gardens, by Edward I. Farrington
Commercial Carnation Culture, by J. Harrison Dick
American Rose Annual, 1930
Manual of American Grape Growing, by U. P. Hedrick
The Romance of Our Trees, by Ernest H. Wilson, M.A., V.M.H.
Plant Culture, by George W. Oliver
Hardy Plants for Cottage Gardens, by Helen R. Albee

Wild Flowers of New York, by Homer D. House
Pages from a Garden Notebook, by Mrs. Francis King
Conifers and Their Characteristics, by Coltman & Rogers
Field Book of American Trees and Shrubs, by F. Schuyler
Gladiolus, by Matthew Crawford
Wild Flowers and Ferns, by Herbert Durand
Making the Grounds Attractive with Shrubbery, by Grace Tabor
The Amateur's Book of the Dahlias, by Mrs. Charles H. Stout
Gardening for Women, by Hon. Frances Wolseley
Insect Pests of Farm, Garden and Orchard, by E. Dwight Sanderson and Leonard Marion Peairs
Winter Sunshine, by John Burroughs
Wake-Robin, by John Burroughs
Locusts and Wild Honey, by John Burroughs
Plant Breeding, Grafting and Budding, Fruit Improvement, Small Fruits, Gardening, Useful Plants, Flowers, Trees, Biography Index, by Luther Burbank
Commercial Floriculture, by Fritz Bahr
Cyclopedia of Hardy Fruits, by U. P. Hedrick
A Garden of Herbs, by E. S. Rodhe
Textbook of Pomology, by J. H. Gourley
The Rose in America, by J. Horace McFarland
Trees as Good Citizens, by Charles L. Pack
The Fern Lover's Companion, by George Henry Tilton
Color Standards and Color Nomenclature, by Robert Ridgway
Massachusetts Beautiful, by Wallace Nutting
The Book of Hardy Flowers, by H. H. Thomas
Bulbs and Tuberous Rooted Plants, by C. L. Allen
Practical Plant Propagation, by Alfred C. Hottes
The Chrysanthemum, by Arthur Herrington
Commercial Rose Culture, by Eber Holmes
Lists of Plant Types, by Stephen F. Hamblin
Outside the House Beautiful, by Henrietta C. Peabody
Cultivated Evergreens, by L. H. Bailey
American Fruits, by Samuel Fraser
Wall and Water Gardens, by Gertrude Jekyll
Adventures in My Garden, by Louise Beebe Wilder
The Rock Garden, by E. H. Jenkins
The Little Garden for Little Money, by Kate L. Brewster

The Food Supply of New England, Arthur W. Gilbert
The Practical Book of Outdoor Flowers, by Richardson Wright.
Roses for All Climates, by George G. Thomas
American Landscape Architecture, by P. H. Elwood, Jr., A.S.L.A.
Manual of Tree and Shrub Insects, by E. P. Felt
America's Greatest Garden, by Ernest H. Wilson, M.A., V.M.H.
The Principles of Flower Arrangement, by A. White
Flowers for Cutting and Decoration, by Richardson Wright
The Flower Beautiful, by Clarence Moores Weed
Hardy Perennials, by A. J. Macself
The Iris, by John C. Wister
Bulb Gardening, by A. J. Macself
Annuals and Biennials, by Gertrude Jekyll
More Aristocrats of the Garden, by Ernest H. Wilson, M.A., V.M.H.
Garden Cinderellas, by Helen Fox
Lilies, by W. E. Marshall
Lilies and Their Culture in North America, by William N. Craig
A Little Book of Modern Dahlia Culture, by W. H. Waite
Gardening with Peat Moss, by F. F. Rockwell
The Lilac, by Susan Delano McKelvey
Spraying, Dusting and Fumigating of Plants, by A. Freeman
  Mason
Vegetable Forcing, by Ralph L. Watts
Rock Gardening, by Sir James L. Cotter
American Orchid Culture, by Prof. E. A. White
House Plants, by Parker T. Barnes
Lawn Making, by Leonard Barron
Home Flower Growing, by Emil C. Volz
Flower Growing, by Leonard Barron
Flowering Trees and Shrubs, by R. C. Notcutt
Saunders Orchid Guide
Lawns, by F. F. Rockwell
The New Flora and Silva (English)
Garden Lilies, by Isabella Preston
American Rock Gardens, by Stephen F. Hamblin
Productive Soil, by W. W. Weir, M.S.
Tree Crops, by J. Russell Smith
Bush Fruit Production, by Ralph A. Van Meter
The Gladiolus and Its Culture, by A. C. Beal

Spring Flowering Bulbs, by Clark L. Thayer
The Pear and Its Culture, by H. B. Tukey
Muskmelon Culture, by W. J. Wright
Greenhouses, by W. J. Wright
China, Mother of Gardens, by Ernest H. Wilson, M.A., V.M.H.
Lilac Culture, by John C. Wister
Chrysanthemums, by Alex Laurie
Azalias and Camellias, by H. Harold Hume
The Cactus Book, by A. D. Houghton
Garden Pools, by L. W. Ramsey and Charles H. Lawrence
The Book of Water Gardening, by Peter Bisset
Little Book of Climbing Plants, by Alfred C. Hottes
The Book of Shrubs, by Alfred C. Hottes
Japanese Flower Arrangement, by Mary Averill
A History of Garden Art, by Walter P. Wright
Fertilizers for Greenhouses and Garden Crops, by Alex Laurie and
    J. B. Edmond
If I Were to Make a Garden, by Ernest H. Wilson, M.A., V.M.H.

Worcester County Horticultural Society

SCHEDULE OF PRIZES

Offered to

Children of Worcester County

Exhibitions to be held Saturday, August 12
and Saturday, September 2, 1933
Horticultural Building, 30 Elm Street

Worcester, Massachusetts

Saturday, August 12

All articles must be in the hall by 2 o'clock

The exhibits must be the results of individual effort of the child from the time of planting to the arranging of the exhibit.

Open to Children under 14 years of age

DISPLAY OF FLOWERS.—

No. 1. Not to exceed fifteen vases		2.50	2.00	1.50	1.00	.50

ZINNIA.—

No. 2. Not to exceed 10 vases	·		.75	.50	.25	.25

ASTERS.—

No. 3. Not to exceed 10 vases		.75	.50	.25	.25

PETUNIA.—

No. 4. Not to exceed 10 vases		.75	.50	.25	.25

CALENDULA.—

No. 5. Not to exceed 10 vases		.75	.50	.25	.25

WILD FLOWERS.—

No. 6. Not to exceed fifteen vases		2.00	1.50	1.00	.50
No. 7. Vase of Flowers		1.00	.75	.50	.25

DISPLAY OF VEGETABLES.—

No. 8. Not to exceed 12 varieties							
	2.50	2.00	1.75	1.50	1.25	1.00	.50

BEETS.—

No. 9. Six specimens		.75	.50	.25	.25

SUMMER SQUASH.—

No. 10. Two specimens		.75	.50	.25	.25

STRING BEANS.—

No. 11. Two quarts		.75	.50	.25	.25

POTATO.—

No. 12 Twelve specimens		1.00	.75	.50	.25

SWEET CORN.—

No. 13. Six ears		1.00	.75	.50	.25

TOMATO.—

No. 14. Six specimens		.75	.50	.25	.25

CARROTS.—

No. 15. Six specimens		.75	.50	.25	.25

CUCUMBER.—

No. 16. Two specimens		.75	.50	.25	.25

Open to Children between the ages of 14 and 21

DISPLAY OF FLOWERS.—
No. 17.   Not to exceed 15 vases   2.50 2.00 1.75 1.00

ASTERS.—
No. 18.   Not to exceed 10 vases   1.00 .75 .50 .25

PETUNIA.—
No. 19.   Not to exceed 10 vases   1.00 .75 .50 .25

GLADIOLUS.—
No. 20.   Basket   1.00 .75 .50 .25

ZINNIA.—
No. 21.   Not to exceed 10 vases   1.00 .75 .50 .25

WILD FLOWERS.—
No. 22.   Not to exceed 15 vases   2.00 1.50 1.00 .50
No. 23.   Vase of Flowers   1.00 .75 .50 .25

DISPLAY OF VEGETABLES.—
No. 24.   Not over 15 varieties
                      2.50 2.00 1.75 1.50 1.25 1.00 .50

POTATO.—
No. 25.   Twelve specimens   1.50 1.00 .75 .50 .25

BEETS.—
No. 26.   Six specimens   1.00 .75 .50 .25

CARROTS.—
No. 27.   Six specimens   1.00 .75 .50 .25

SHELL BEANS.—
No. 28.   Two quarts   1.00 .75 .50 .25

STRING BEANS.—
No. 29.   Two quarts   1.00 .75 .50 .25

SWEET CORN.—
No. 30.   Six ears   1.00 .75 .50 .25

TOMATO.—
No. 31.   Six specimens   1.25 1.00 .75 .50 .25

CUCUMBER.—
No. 32   Two specimens   1.00 .75 .50 .25

SUMMER SQUASH.—
No. 33.   Two specimens   1.00 .75 .50 .25

Saturday, September 2

All articles must be in the hall by 2 o'clock

The exhibits must be the results of individual effort of the child from the time of planting to the arranging of the exhibit.

DISPLAY OF FLOWERS.—

| No. 34. | Not to exceed 15 vases | 2.50 | 2.00 | 1.50 | 1.00 | | |

COSMOS.—

| No. 35. | Vase | | .75 | .50 | .25 | .25 | |

CALENDULA.—

| No. 36. | Not to exceed 10 vases | | .75 | .50 | .25 | .25 | |

PETUNIA.—

| No. 37. | Not to exceed 10 vases | | .75 | .50 | .25 | .25 | |

ASTERS.—

| No. 38. | Not to exceed 10 vases | | .75 | .50 | .25 | .25 | |

ZINNIA.—

| No. 39. | Not to exceed 10 vases | | .75 | .50 | .25 | .25 | |

MARIGOLDS.—

| No. 40. | Not to exceed 10 vases | | .75 | .50 | .25 | .25 | |

GLADIOLUS.—

| No. 41. | Basket | | .75 | .50 | .25 | .25 | |

WILD FLOWERS.—

| No. 42. | Not to exceed 15 vases | | 2.00 | 1.50 | 1.00 | .50 | |
| No. 43. | Vase of Flowers | | 1.00 | .75 | .50 | .25 | |

DISPLAY OF VEGETABLES.—

| No. 44. | Not to exceed 12 varieties | | | | | | |
| | 2.50 | 2.00 | 1.75 | 1.50 | 1.25 | 1.00 | .50 |

SHELL BEANS.—

| No. 45. | Two quarts in pods | | .75 | .50 | .25 | .25 | |

BEETS.—

| No. 46. | Six specimens | 1.00 | .75 | .50 | .25 | .25 | |

CARROTS.—

| No. 47. | Six specimens | 1.00 | .75 | .50 | .25 | .25 | |

SWEET CORN.—

| No. 48. | Six ears | 1.00 | .75 | .50 | .25 | .25 | |

TOMATO.—

| No. 49. | Six specimens | 1.00 | .75 | .50 | .25 | .25 | |

WINTER SQUASH.—
No. 50. Two specimens   1.00   .75   .25   .25
POTATO.—
No. 51. Twelve specimens   1.00   .75   .50   .25   .25

Open to Children between the ages of 14 and 21

DISPLAY OF FLOWERS.—
No. 52. Not to exceed 15 vases   2.50 2.00 1.75 1.50
PETUNIA.—
No. 53. Not to exceed 10 vases   1.00   .75   .50   .25
DAHLIAS.—
No. 54. Not to exceed 10 vases   1.00   .75   .50   .25
ZINNIA.—
No. 55. Not to exceed 10 vases   1.00   .75   .50   .25
MARIGOLD.—
No. 56. Not to exceed 10 vases   1.00   .75   .50   .25
COSMOS.—
No. 57. One large vase   1.00   .75   .50   .25
GLADIOLUS.—
No. 58. Basket   1.00   .75   .50   .25
WILD FLOWERS.—
No. 59. Not to exceed 15 vases   2.00 1.50 1.00   .50
No. 60. Vase of Flowers   1.00   .75   .50   .25
DAHLIA.—
No. 61. Vase   1.00   .75   .50   .25
DISPLAY OF VEGETABLES.—
No. 62. Not to exceed 15 varieties
                2.50 2.00 1.75 1.50 1.25 1.00   .50
POTATO.—
No. 63. Twelve specimens   1.50 1.00   .75   .50   .25
CARROTS.—
No. 64. Six specimens   1.25 1.00   .75   .50   .25
BEETS.—
No. 65. Six specimens   1.25 1.00   .75   .50   .25
SWEET CORN.—
No. 66. Six ears   1.25 1.00   .75   .50   .25

TOMATO.—

No. 67. Six specimens   1.25 1.00 .75 .50 .25

CABBAGE.—

No. 68. Two specimens   .75 .50 .25

WINTER SQUASH.—

No. 69. Two specimens   1.00 .75 .50 .25

CELERY.—

No. 70. Three specimens   .75 .50 .25

SHELL BEANS.—

No. 71. Two quarts in the pod   1.00 .75 .50 .25

ONION.—

No. 72. Six specimens   1.00 .75 .50 .25

Prizes will be given for other meritorious exhibits.

Competition is open to all children of Worcester County under two classes. Those under 14 years and those between 14 and 21.

Only one child in a family can compete for the same prize.

The exhibits must be the results of individual effort of the child from the time of planting to the arranging of the exhibit.

All exhibits must be in the Hall ready for inspection by the Judges by 2 p. m. Exhibition will close at 4.30 p. m.

Prizes will be paid at the close of the exhibition.

Vases, plates and everything necessary for the exhibition of the flowers and vegetables will be furnished by the Horticultural Society.

* * *

SPECIAL PRIZES OFFERED
BY SECRETARY HERBERT R. KINNEY

To the ones receiving the two largest amounts under 14 years of age. $3.00. $2.00.

To the ones receiving the two largest amounts over 14 years of age. $3.00. $2.00.

* * *

For further information apply to

HERBERT R. KINNEY,
Secretary.

TRANSACTIONS

OF THE

WORCESTER COUNTY HORTICULTURAL SOCIETY

Reports of the Officers and Lectures

For the year ending December 6, 1933

ALLEN J. JENKINS
Chairman, Committee on Arrangements and Exhibitions

OFFICERS AND COMMITTEES

of the

Worcester County Horticultural Society

For the Year 1933

PRESIDENT

MYRON F. CONVERSE, Worcester, Mass.

VICE-PRESIDENTS

HERBERT A. COOK   MRS. HOMER GAGE
Shrewsbury, Mass.   Worcester, Mass.
S. LOTHROP DAVENPORT, No. Grafton, Mass.

SECRETARY

HERBERT R. KINNEY, of Worcester
Horticultural Hall, 30 Elm Street

TREASURER

BURT W. GREENWOOD, of Worcester

LIBRARIAN

MISS LUCY M. COULSON, of Worcester

TRUSTEES

Joseph A. Allen	Auburn	James Warr	Worcester
William Anderson	So. Lancaster	J. Frank Cooper	Worcester
Elizabeth R. Bishop	Sutton	Mrs. Bertha G. Denny	Worcester
Edward W. Breed	Clinton	Mrs. Alice M. Forbes	Worcester
David L. Fiske	Grafton	Harold J. Greenwood	Worcester
Richard A. Flagg	Boylston	Harry Harrison	Worcester
Allen J. Jenkins	Shrewsbury	Allyne W. Hixon	Worcester
William McAllister	Whitinsville	Mrs.FrancesA.Kinnicutt	Worcester
William E. Morey	Shrewsbury	H. Ward Moore	Worcester
Charles Potter	West Boylston	Miss Frances C. Morse	Worcester
Mrs. Mary D. White	Holden	Harry I. Randall	Worcester
Chandler Bullock	Worcester	Joseph F. Sherer	Worcester
Willis E. Cary	Worcester	Mrs. Amy W. Smith	Worcester
Fred H. Chamberlain	Worcester	George F. E. Story	Worcester
Fred L. Chamberlain	Worcester	Matthew P. Whittall	Worcester

STANDING COMMITTEE ON FINANCE

Myron F. Converse, *Chairman*, 1934   Leonard C. Midgley, 1933
Herbert W. Estabrook, 1935

Office, Library, and Exhibition Hall
30 Elm Street

PRESIDENT'S ADDRESS

To the Members of the
Worcester County Horticultural Society:

The Horticultural fraternity of this locality meets today in annual convention and for the purpose of recounting the events of the twelve months which have passed since our last deliberation.

Into that period there have been packed events which ever will affect the future of mankind. At no other time within my recollection has there been a culmination of circumstances that so greatly affected the spiritual and economic welfare of the people of this great land. The solution of these puzzling questions is still in the making, and in the meantime the very soul of man is being tried.

It is fortunate for the people of this community that during these trying days the work of this Society has continued unabated; thus the loveliness of nature has been reflected through an abundance of flowers in field and garden, and the possibilities of the practice of horticulture have been demonstrated through instructions in cultivation as well as through the realized beauty displayed in the neighborhood gardens and exhibitions.

These results have been obtained through the diligence of people engaged in these undertakings; some through promptings of their particular vocations, while others have persevered because of a leaning toward such a diversion from their usual occupations.

The season's exhibits opened as usual with the Spring Show in March. This was followed by seasonable weekly exhibits in accordance with the schedule prepared by the Committee on Arrangements and Exhibitions. Mr. Allen J. Jenkins has served ably as its chairman for several years.

The Chrysanthemum Show in November was the concluding exhibit of a most successful program.

During the winter months the Society, in accordance with a time-honored custom, conducted a series of lectures which were designed to aid our members in the growing of flowers and in the floral adornment of their homes and grounds.

On March 16th the Annual Reunion was held and was addressed by Mr. Charles B. Rugg who pleasantly related incidents connected with his recent trip to Alaska.

The year's activities in connection with the Library, have afforded opportunity for service, which the Librarian, Miss Coulson, has readily accepted.

The reports which are to follow will deal more specifically with the work of the various departments.

The duties of my office afford me the happy privilege of reporting to you the accomplishments of the year and conveying to our fellow-workers a word of appreciation for their kindly efforts.

Respectfully submitted,

MYRON F. CONVERSE, *President.*

Worcester, Massachusetts
December 6, 1933.

PAST PRESIDENTS

Worcester County Horticultural Society

DAVID L. FISKE
1922-1923

EDWARD W. BREED
1911-1915

LEONARD C. MIDGLEY
1920-1921

SECRETARY'S REPORT

Mr. President and Members of the
Worcester County Horticultural Society:

Our first lecture of the year was "The Call of the North," by Mr. Arthur H. Merritt. There were many fine views of Alaska and the Klondike. Gold was first discovered at Henderson's Creek in 1898. This trip was during midsummer when the country was at its best.

S. Waldo Bailey's illustrated lecture on "Beautiful Berkshires" showed and described many of the arresting scenes of this famous beauty spot.

January 25 and 26 the American Carnation Society held their Annual Meeting and Exhibition in our building. They staged probably the largest carnation exhibition ever held in central Massachusetts.

Our society offered a gold medal for a "Group Arrangement." This was won by Messrs. J. J. Montague and Son, South Woburn, Mass.

President Myron F. Converse offered a silver plate for the best fifty blooms in the exhibition. This was won by Mr. George P. Barr, South Natick, Mass., on the carnation "Laddie."

Mr. Lorenzo F. Kinney, Jr., of Kingston, R. I., opened his lecture on "Rhododendrons and Azaleas" with: "Nature is as beautiful as ever despite the depression now confronting us." He showed many pictures taken in natural colors and described many varieties, some of which do well in New England.

As we have not seen many pictures of China we were pleased to secure Miss Grace M. Boynton, who went to China in 1919, and during a part of her stay there lived within the walls of an imperial garden. She spoke at length about the conditions there and described the pictures shown.

Mr. Carl Stanton's lecture, "Sunshine and Shadow in the Garden," was very beautiful and instructive. He spoke of the garden as a picture and said there were good ones and others not so good. Those he showed seemed to be all good ones and they were interestingly described.

The first "Ladies Day" since leaving Front Street was held February 23. Prof. Robert Illingworth gave two groups of readings, Mrs. Ethel Sleeper Ruggles two groups of songs, and Mr. John Cadieux several solos. Refreshments were served in the west room.

The lecture, "What Plants Know," by Mr. Herbert W. Faulkner, was illustrated by charts that showed many phenomena of plant life. The lecture covered many phases of growth from blossom to seed.

There had been considerable said and written about the "International Peace Garden." Mr. Allen J. Jenkins was invited to tell us something about it. He said that in 1928 Mr. H. J. Islington of Ontario proposed such a scheme. Last year 3000 acres, half in the United States and half in Canada—in the province of Manitoba and in North Dakota—were set aside for a beginning.

Following this talk, Mr. Herbert W. Gleason of Boston, Mass., gave an illustrated lecture, "The Charm of the Little Garden." He showed pictures of many beautiful small gardens and described them in his usual interesting manner.

The Annual Reunion. Reception in the Library at 6:30. Dinner at 7. Invocation by Rev. Vincent E. Tomlinson. Dinner served by Mr. Lunt.

President Converse called on Rev. Vincent E. Tomlinson, who spoke highly of the Society's long service in encouraging horticulture.

President Converse introduced Mr. Charles B. Rugg, guest speaker. Mr. Rugg spoke of his recent trip to Alaska. He described many interesting things he saw there during his six weeks' trip.

Total entries at our regular exhibitions were 2214. This was 72 less than last year: flowers 887, 38 more; fruit 726, 84 less; and vegetables 725, 25 less. These differences could be accounted for by the dry weather in early summer affecting the early fruits and vegetables and no early frosts to spoil the late flowers.

Entries at our Children's Exhibitions were 469, which was 73 less than last year: flowers 240, 17 less; and vegetables 229, a loss of 56.

While the entries showed some decline, this was more than made up by many more of the larger exhibits. Our best Children's Exhibition was on September 2.

The Spring Show was well planned and filled the whole building with an exhibition that pleased our many guests.

Among the outstanding features of the year's exhibitions were table decorations, which would seem to have been much better, even with the larger number of exhibitors. Many of them were exceptionally well combined and arranged.

The tendency is toward a too large and too high flower arrangement for the size of the table. Baskets have been a feature of many of our exhibitions; many of them have been of medium size and not so heavy with flowers or color as formerly. Standards have not been so much of an attraction as it was hoped; many of them have been heavy and of coarse materials.

There were one hundred and fifty entries of cut flowers, consisting of ten and twenty vases and displays, which made the background of many of our exhibitions. Many of these exhibits were not so heavy as formerly. It would seem that there is a tendency to build them too high for the width of the tables and the distance they were viewed from. There is too prominent a showing of boxes.

There have been some excellent exhibits of tuberous rooted begonias.

Mr. Albert W. Schneider's exhibit of gloxinia was probably the best ever seen in Worcester.

The Chrysanthemum Exhibition was a large one, using all of our rooms.

The Auditorium was arranged about the same as usual with the exception of the center being raised with palms and very tall chrysanthemums so that the stage was not in full view from the entrance.

Mr. Potter's exhibit of trailing chrysanthemums "hanging gracefully" in front of the stage was a novelty. There were not so many large blooms as in the past.

loss

than

Chil-

iild-

ions

iuch

y of

nge-

e of

ium

ind-

ed;

con-

iade

hese

that

the

too

ted

ibly

l of

rith

tall

the

ring

not

DISPLAY OF CINERARIAS BY CHARLES POTTER, 1933

Mr. Charles Potter was awarded the Society's Silver Medal for his display of his new geranium, Winfred Robinson.

There was the best showing of vegetables of the season.

The exhibits of wild fruits and berries and the ten entries of gourds attracted much attention.

Prizes offered by Mrs. Homer Gage for table decorations, which were shown in the lecture room and called for chrysanthemums, brought out an entry of twelve tables, most of them very attractive.

It was suggested that it might be well to have the call read chrysanthemums predominating.

New Members

Walter S. Young

Deceased Members

Mr. George S. Graham	Mr. George J. Dudley
Miss Frances C. Morse	Mr. Charles A. Ballou
Mrs. Ellen T. Rockwood	Mr. Edward A. Hackett
Mr. Waldo Lincoln	Mr. Marston Lincoln
Mr. Frank C. Parker	Mrs. Annie E. Knapp
Miss Sarah H. Powers	Mrs. Sara G. Knight
Mr. Francis H. Dewey	Miss Juliet Porter
Mrs. Mary E. Ross	Mr. William I. Allen
Mrs. Emma M. Davis	

Respectfully submitted,

Herbert R. Kinney, *Secretary.*

December 5, 1933.

ANNUAL MEETING OF THE SOCIETY

Wednesday, December 7, 1932

President Myron F. Converse called the meeting to order at 10 o'clock. Thirty-seven were present.

Secretary read the records of the last annual meeting of the Society.

President Converse declared them approved.

President Converse delivered his Annual Address.

Reports were read by the following:

Treasurer, Burt W. Greenwood; Secretary, Herbert R. Kinney; Librarian, Miss Lucy M. Coulson; Finance Committee, President Myron F. Converse; Judge on Vegetables, H. Ward Moore; Judge on Flowers, James Campbell.

On Mr. H. Ward Moore's motion, these reports were accepted and referred to the committee on Publication.

On Mr. Harry Harrison's motion, the recommendation of the Finance Committee to appropriate $8500 for premiums and salaries was approved.

Chairman Richard A. Flagg reported for the Nominating Committee. The report was accepted.

On Mr. Allen Adshead's motion the Secretary was instructed to cast a yea ballot for the candidates as nominated. So voted. President Converse declared them elected.

Mr. H. Ward Moore spoke about changing the date of the Annual Meeting from the first Wednesday to the first Thursday in December. He said that Thursday was our regular day.

Mr. Edward W. Breed would favor the change. It was voted to consider the change next year.

On Mr. Allen J. Jenkin's motion, the meeting adjourned.

HERBERT R. KINNEY, *Secretary.*

ANNUAL MEETING OF THE TRUSTEES

Wednesday, December 14, 1932

President Myron F. Converse called the meeting to order at 2 P.M. Nineteen members were present.

Secretary read the records of the last Annual Meeting of the Trustees.

President Converse declared them approved. President Converse read the following letter:

December 13, 1932

To the Secretary,
Worcester Co. Horticultural Society,
Worcester, Massachusetts.

Dear Sir:

It is the opinion of several of the exhibitors that at the two large exhibitions in March and November there should be an associate judge of plants and flowers, and that the person serving in that capacity be one from outside our Society—one well versed not only in the particular kinds of plants and flowers at these respective exhibitions, but also in the decorative arrangement as well.

Very truly yours,

E. W. Breed.

After some discussion, Mr. Jenkins made a motion to refer this proposition to the Committee on Arrangements and Exhibitions. So voted.

President Converse said that the Trustees would find a list of the present committees in the premium list, which each member has.

He spoke of the harmonious working of these committees during the past year.

He had thought to suggest the placing of Mr. Edward W. Breed on the Medal Committee in place of Mr. Herbert A. Cook. He awaited any other suggestion.

There being none, he asked for a vote on the same committees as last year, with the proposed change on the Medal Committee.

There being no objection, President Converse declared them elected.

President Converse said that at the Annual Meeting of the Society December 7, 1932, the sum of $8500.00 was appropriated for premiums and salaries; this to be apportioned by the Trustees.

The Secretary read the last year's appropriations and said that there had been no serious trouble with our budget.

President Converse called on Mr. H. Ward Moore as the only one of our judges present. He said that in his department it had been quite satisfactory. The small leeway they had was quite an advantage.

Mr. Harry Harrison made a motion that the appropriations be the same as for last year. It was so voted.

Appropriated by the Society for premiums and salaries........			$8,5000.00
Premiums:			
Flowers.	$2,300.00		
Fruits	1,100.00		
Vegetables................	900.00		
Children's Exhibitions.......	300.00		
Spring Exhibition...........	800.00		
Chrysanthemum Exhibition...	200.00		
		$5,600.00	
Salaries:			
Treasurer..................	$300.00		
Secretary..................	800.00		
Librarian..	1,100.00		
Judges...	300.00		
		$2,500.00	
			8,100.00
Not apportioned...........			$400.00

Adjourned.

HERBERT R. KINNEY, *Secretary.*

TREASURER'S REPORT

For the Year Ending December 6, 1933

Statement of Income and Expenditures

INCOME		
Rent:		
Hall............	$1,463.00	
Stores........	34,999.92	$36,462.92
Permanent Funds:		
Membership....	$138.97	
Blake.......	16.00	
Dewey....	63.40	
Draper.....	15.00	
Eames..	22.00	
Hadwen...	58.00	
Morse.....	20.00	333.37
Membership Fees............		10.00
Interest Earned:		
Permanent Funds	$199.54	
Investments	284 21	
Other Interest...	8.06	491.81
Winter Meetings: Tickets.....		141.00
Insurance Premium Refund...		4.93
Other Income:		
Mabel K. Gage..	$50.00	
H. R. Kinney...	37.50	87.50
Temporary Loans........ ...		3,000.00
Total..................		$40,531.53

EXPENDITURES	
Library....................	
Winter Meetings	...
Periodicals.................	
Publications.	....
Premiums:	
1933...	$5,391.75
Special.	87.50
Children........	259.85
Blake Fund.	16.00
Draper Fund.	15.00
Eames Fund..	22.00
Hadwen Fund	58.00
Morse Fund.....	20.00
Expense Accounts:	
Exhibitions......	$289.89
Office..........	401.25
Operating.......	277.27
Miscellaneous..	662.15
Furniture and Fixtures.......	
Maintenance, Furniture and Fixtures..................	
Maintenance, Real Estate .	
Salaries....................	
Interest.	
Interest Added to Investments.	
Interest Added to Permanent Funds....................	
Insurance.	
Light, Heat, Water and Power.	
Janitor Service....	
Mortgage Note Reduction (Front St.)..............	
United States Check Tax.....	
Loans Repaid..............	
Worcester Depositors' Corporation Class "A" Certificate..	
Total.................	

Cash Balance, December 8, 1932 $1,543.96

Cash Balance, December 5, 1933

$42,075.49

Statement of Gains and Losses

s		LOSSES	
Appropriations:		Appropriations..............	$8,500.00
		Depreciation	1,508.09
$40.15		Special and Permanent Fund	
308.25	$348.40	Premiums.....	218.50
———		Expense Accounts.... ...	1,630.56
......	10.00	Insurance.	706.57
Funds	333.37	Interest...	10,639.54
......	87.50	Janitor Service.	2,666.32
......	36,462.92	Light, Heat, Water, etc..	1,324.55
		Maintenance, Furniture and	
		Fixtures..................	183.76
		Maintenance, Real Estate ...	732.21
		Periodicals.................	91.50
		Publications......	744.25
		Winter Meetings.	705.24
		U. S. Check Tax.	11.44
			$29,662.53
		Net Gain to Surplus..	7,579.66
	$37,242.19		$37,242.19

Statement of Resources and Liabilities

RESOURCES			LIABILITIES		
Permanent Funds (Investment):			Blake Fund:		
Peoples' Sav. Bk.			Principal........	$1,000.00	
(Hadwen) ...	$1,293.47		Income. ...	339.59	
Wor. Five Cts. Sav. Bk.			Dewey Fund:		
(Draper). ...	403.84		Principal`.	1,000.00	
(Eames)..	616.75		Income........	102.69	
(Morse)..... ..	523.32		Draper Fund:		
Wor. Mech. Sav. Bk.			Principal.. . .	300.00	
(Blake).	1,339.59		Income........	103.84	
(Dewey). ..	1,102.69	5,279.66	Eames Fund:		
			Principal.......	500.00	
Investments:			Income........	116.75	
Wor. Five Cts. Sav.			Hadwen Fund:		
Bk...... ..	$2,769.90		Principal . . .	1,000.00	
Wor. Co. Inst. for			Income... .	293.47	
Sav.	2,087.04		Morse Fund:		
Wor. Mechs. Sav.			Principal.......	500.00	
Bk.	2,937.93	7,794.87	Income........	23.32	$5
Worcester Depositors' Corpora-			Mortgage Note Front Street		
tion Class "A" Certificate..		2,315.51	Property.................		215
Membership Fund..........		3,730.00	Surplus:		
Real Estate..		480,000.00	Dec. 7, 1932...	$297,722.80	
Furniture and Fixtures. .		22,671.74	Net Gain 1933...	7,579.66	305
Library.... . . .		2,844.21			
Cash.....................		946.13			
		$525,582.12			$525

Respectfully submitted,

BURT W. GREENWOOD, *Treas*

Auditor's Certificate

I have examined the books of the Treasurer of the Worcester County Horticultural Society, together with vouchers, securities and bank balances, for the year ended December 6, 1933, and find them to be correct.

ADAH B. JOHNSON, *Auditor.*

We have caused an audit of the books of the Treasurer to be made for the year ended December 6, 1933, and the foregoing certificate is hereby approved.

Respectfuly submitted,

H. WARD MOORE, HARRY C. MIDGLEY, ARTHUR S. BELLOWS,
Auditors.

Worcester, Massachusetts
December 6, 1933.

ANNUAL MEETING OF THE COMMITTEE ON ARRANGEMENTS AND EXHIBITIONS

Wednesday, December 21, 1932

Meeting was called to order at 2 P.M. by President Myron F. Converse. Twelve members were present.

On Mrs. Alice M. Forbes' motion, Mr. Allen J. Jenkins was elected chairman.

President Converse read a letter from Mr. James Campbell, who was chosen judge of flowers by the Trustees on December 14, stating that he would be unable to accept but would be glad to assist in case of an emergency.

Mr. Edward W. Breed spoke in favor of having an outside associate judge for our two large exhibitions.

On Mr. Davenport's motion, the President was instructed to appoint a committee of three to select a judge for flowers, plants, etc.

President Converse appointed Messrs. Jenkins, Breed, and Hixon.

Mr. Breed made a motion that "over handle" as applied to baskets be cut out. It was so voted.

The dates set for the Spring Show were March 23, 24, 25, and 26.

There were a few changes in the schedule.

Adjourned.

HERBERT R. KINNEY, *Secretary.*

LIBRARIAN'S REPORT

To the Members of the
Worcester County Horticultural Society:

. As Librarian of the Society, I respectfully submit the following report:

Your Library Committee and Librarian too are pleased to note a keen interest amounting almost to study in both Library and circulation.

There have been several noteworthy additions to our shelves—"Flower Arrangement," "Roses," and "Delphiniums."

The Library Committee in selection has endeavored to foster interest among exhibitors, facilitating exhibition off the beaten path, as well as encouraging study among the younger generation.

The work of binding various periodicals and the Transactions of the Society has been brought up to date.

I would respectfully call the attention of all to the recent addition of new books to our library during the past year, as noted in the schedule of premiums.

I wish to thank the Library Committee and members for the very valuable assistance rendered me as Librarian.

The additions to the Library during the year just closed by purchase or gift will be found in the list herewith given.

Field Museum of |Natural History, Report Series, Vol. IX, No. 2.
Cornell University Agricultural Experiment Station, Memoir 142, 145, 146, 553–557, 560, 564, 566, 567, 569, 570, 572, 575, 576.
Cornell Junior Extension Bulletin, Nos. 46, 244, 246, 250–255, 257, 261.
Cornell Rural School Leaflet, Vol. 26, No. 26.
Massachusetts State College, Leaflets Nos. 7, 20, 60, 99, 103, 109, 116.
The Journal of the Royal Horticultural Society, Vol. LVIII. Part I, Part II.
Massachusetts Fruit Growers Association, 1932.
The National Rose Society, 1933.
The American Rose Annual, 1933.
Annual Report of Parks and Recreation Commissioners of Worcester.
Rose Garden Primer, by Eber Holmes.
American Alpine in the Gardens, by Anderson McCully.
Western American Alpines, by Ira N. Gabrielson.
Sempervivums, by R. Lloyd Praeger, D.Sc.

GARDEN OF BULBS BY IRISTHORPE, MRS. HOMER GAGE, 1933

Flower and Folk-Lore From Far Korea, by Florence Hedleston Crane.
Natural Rock Gardening, by Symons-Jeune.
Delphiniums, by George A. Phillips.
Gardening with Herbs, by Helen Margenthau Fox.
Gardens in America, by Marion Crane.
Lilies for English Gardens, by Gertrude Jekyel.
The Arrangement of Flowers, by Mrs. Walter R. Hine.
Arranging Flowers Throughout the Year, by Katharine T. Cary and Nellie D. Merrell.

PUBLICATIONS AND PERIODICALS

Country Life in America
House and Garden
Guide to Nature
Rhodora
The American City
Horticulture
Florist's Exchange
Gardener's Chronicle
Park and Cemetery
Flower Grower
Market Growers Journal

House Beautiful
The American Home
American Forestry
The New England Homestead
The Rural New Yorker
The Country Gentleman
The National Geographic Magazine
Journal of Economic Entomology
Better Homes and Gardens
The National Horticultural Magazine

ENGLISH PERIODICALS

Homes and Gardens
Gardener's Chronicle

Gardening
The New Flora and Silva

Respectfully submitted,

LUCY M. COULSON, *Librarian*.

December 5, 1933.

REPORT OF THE FINANCE COMMITTEE

Worcester, Massachusetts

To the Members of the
Worcester County Horticultural Society:

The Society's income continues to be sufficient to meet the requirements. The building is still new and the construction is of such a character that no large expenditures have been needed for its proper maintenance. At times there have been occasions to paint and redecorate the walls in parts of the buildings, but no great expense has been involved.

The building serves the Society's needs in a splendid way and enjoys a general usefulness in addition. The item of rental derived from the hall has never been a large one and at the present time is even less, due in part to a reduced demand for such conveniences.

It is recommended that appropriations for premiums and salaries for use during the coming year be provided in the sum of Eighty-Five Hundred Dollars ($8500) to be apportioned by the Trustees.

Respectfully submitted,

MYRON F. CONVERSE,
HERBERT W. ESTABROOK,
Finance Committee.

December 6, 1933.

REPORT OF JUDGE OF FLOWERS

Mr. President and Members of the
  Worcester County Horticultural Society:

The Spring Show, which is always one of the outstanding events of the year, was as usual very fine, and the premiums offered were used in practically all of the classes. By vote of the Committee, the Spring and Fall Shows were to have three judges; therefore, I was ably assisted in awarding the premiums.

Our next Show was that of April 27 with six entries of cut flowers and twelve table decorations. In the plant displays there were four competitors.

On May 11 there were seven good baskets, but no cut flowers. There seems to be a great deal of interest shown in the art of table arrangements, as we had fourteen very excellent table decorations.

June 8. In the first call for standards, eleven were shown, also some very handsome examples of arrangement.

June 15. There was a small show, several classes having only two or three entries in each.

June 22. The Rose Exhibition was very fine with all classes well filled.

June 29. There was a very good showing of dianthus barbatus and delphinium, twelve exhibits of each.

July 6 brought forth cut flowers intended for small growers, with eight exhibitors. Baskets were also called for with ten fine examples.

July 13. Table decorations again were shown with seven entering and eight baskets of sweet peas.

July 20. Table decorations were also a feature of this show, there being twelve, all very good and competition very close.

July 27. The standards were very popular and lend themselves to corners very effectively; ten arrangements were entered. The gladioli this week were very poor, but the annuals were very good with nine in the call.

August 3–13. Fine baskets and ten exhibits of zinnias were noted, with all the other classes well filled.

August 10 was Gladioli Day with some very fine displays and standards.

August 17. Zinnias and dahlias were the leading flowers of the day, also displays of garden flowers with nine exhibits.

August 24. Cut flowers with nine displays and seventeen baskets filled a large part of the hall. One of the best displays of tuberous begonias we have had for years was also shown on this date.

August 31. This was Dahlia Day with part of the hall taken up with some fine displays, also eleven good displays of cut flowers.

September 7. The leading features of the day's exhibition were the baskets of dahlias and cosmos.

September 14. There were fourteen cleverly arranged baskets and ten displays of flower arrangements. The exhibitors deserve great credit for their skill in the arrangements shown in both classes.

September 21. Table decorations again were the leading feature of the show.

October 5. Baskets were the leading feature with twenty in the call. Ferns and hardy chrysanthemums were also shown this week.

The Society also held two Children's Exhibitions on August 12 and September 2 which surely were a credit to the children. The collections of wild flowers was one of the outstanding features on each above-named date.

The year closed with our four-day Chrysanthemum Show which was a credit to the Society as well as the Committee in charge. As in the Spring Show I was assisted in judging by Mr. John Doig and Mr. Percy Veinot.

Respectfully submitted,

ALLYNE W. HIXON, *Judge.*

REPORT OF JUDGE OF VEGETABLES

Mr. President and Members of the
Worcester County Horticultural Society:

Herewith is submitted my 1933 report as Judge of Vegetables:

The past season has been very nearly normal, so far as the Vegetable Department was concerned, both in regard to the quantity and the quality of the vegetables shown and to the fact that they were shown, in nearly all cases, on the dates called for. In only three classes were no exhibits shown on the dates called; namely Alderman Peas on July 6, Bay State Squash on September 21, and Flint Corn on November 9. The peas were shown at a later date, but the squash and corn were not shown at all.

Potatoes, parsnips, tomatoes, sweet corn and peppers— especially the latter which are now a very popular vegetable here—have been shown in large numbers and of excellent quality.

Cauliflower, celery and eggplant were not so good as usual. Squashes were not up to the standard of the past few seasons, with the exception of the Warren Squashes of which we had on exhibition some of the finest it has ever been my privilege to pass judgment upon.

We had two of the largest Children's Exhibitions this past summer that we have ever had since that department was established. Both halls were filled with large and varied displays of flowers and vegetables of really good quality, some of which would compare favorably with those exhibited by their elders at the regular exhibitions.

. In one of the calls for displays of vegetables there were eleven competitors, and in another nine. Competition was keen and the prizes well merited.

Let us hope these young people continue in the good work so that they may some day fill the places left vacant as older exhibitors drop out.

Respectfully submitted,

H. WARD MOORE,
Judge.

At the Annual Meeting of the Worcester County Horticultural Society held at Worcester, Wednesday, December 6, 1933, the following resolution was presented by Mrs. Amy W. Smith and was unanimously adopted by the Society.

IN MEMORIAM

Miss Frances Clary Morse of 57 Chatham Street, Worcester, Massachusetts, became a member of the Worcester County Horticultural Society in 1880. She was a member of the Committee of Arrangements in 1926 and was elected a trustee in 1929.

Born at the above place, 57 Chatham Street, Miss Morse lived there all her life. Naturally she took an active interest in the beautiful old garden on the place with which most of us were familiar. She and her sister helped their mother landscape the estate, and in this way Miss Morse came to know a great deal about plants and flowers.

Her beautiful garden at the "Summit" yielded a vast amount of exquisite bloom, also excellent and interesting fruit and vegetables which she proudly displayed at our Horticultural exhibits.

We marveled at her ambition and tenacity to life in her declining years. One of the last things Miss Morse did was to come to one of our lectures on a stormy Thursday afternoon last winter.

It is a pleasant memory for us all to have known one of the old school so well versed in music, literature, languages, antiques and horticulture, and her death on March 22, 1933, removes from our Society a faithful and valued member.

Resolved that this memorial be placed in the records of our Society.

"THE CALL OF THE NORTH"

Thursday, January 12

Illustrated Lecture

By Mr. Arthur H. Merritt, Boston, Mass.

Canada backs into Alaska, which is the shape of a frying pan with its handle running down the shore. The Japanese current of warm air is felt along the coast where the temperature is somewhat like ours in New England, but more like that of the District of Columbia. As we leave the panhandle and go into the Yukon we come into extremes of temperature where the difference may be 180 degrees. For several months there are twenty to twenty-four hours of sunshine there with the frozen ground underneath.

The first slide was of Jasper National Park where we jump from snow and ice to quite warm weather. Here is seen an attractive log cabin with sixty feet of very beautiful tall delphinium on either side of the main steps. The Government has spent $7,000,000 for this lodge.

Mt. Edith Cavell was pictured in its great beauty with several bears prowling around. A view of Mrs. Merritt on a horse enlivened the picture.

Moline Lake, sixteen miles long, is the most beautiful one in Alaska. The first six miles of it are wide; then it narrows down. Seventeen mountains rise out of the hills. July 23 showed very little snow on the south side of the mountains, but the north side was covered. Thumb Mountain has twelve terraces rolling down to the lake. The slide showed the formation of a glacial valley of ice sliding forward and gradually wearing away. The lake at sunset afforded a most striking picture. Mt. Robinson, 12,972 feet, was shown with beautiful flowers all along the trail. The view of an exquisite waterfall, taken through the car window, was shown on the screen.

Vancouver is a typical American city. A picture of Stanley Park, June 20, presented great cedar trees and many beautiful flowers.

DISPLAY OF CHRYSANTHEMUMS BY CHARLES POTTER, 1933

The lecturer traveled far north and found that the farther north he went the more intensely alluring was the scenery. He traveled on the steamer Prince Henry, inside passage, and declared that next to Norway this affords the most beautiful passage. A map showing the many little islands dotting the way was exhibited and explained. Prince Rupert, the last stop in British Columbia, displays its totem pole; not as a signal of worship but as one of heraldry. Volcanic islands are seen in this section, including four active ones which disappear and reappear.

The Alaskan flag, the subject of a contest in the United States, is an interesting one depicting its history. Its blue background represents the sky; the great bear refers to its former owner, Russia; the north star speaks for itself; and the gold fringe around it bespeaks its gold mines.

Ketchikan, situated high up on a bank, has large warehouses where the halibut, salmon and other products of its industry are stored. Salmon of sixty-five pounds are seen here. The houses are located way up on hills. The blue cast in the ice there is caused by pressure. So the view is better on a cloudy day.

Juneau, the capital of Alaska, recalls the great gold mine. Over a million dollars in 1932 was its production. Baranov Island is on the outskirts. Sitka, nearby, seldom has a temperature of below zero.

At Skaguay where is located Mt. Harding, named in honor of our former president, are many excellent gardens. The lecturer declared he had never seen more beautiful gardens than here and in Victoria. The color and size of the bloom are scarcely believable. Views of many fine gardens were shown, in which figured pansies three to four inches in diameter; delphinium, eight to nine feet high; and particularly fine dahlias.

A narrow gauge train over the mountains with a glimpse of Conductor McCann, a Scotchman who ran the first train over the pass in 1898, was projected on the screen. Over White Pass and up seventeen miles to Inspiration Point a superb view lies before the traveler. An interesting feature of this section is a fine monument to horses at the international boundary. The

Yukon territory is wholly under police control. Men serve until thirty-five, and then find another vocation. Lake Bennett, where stands an old Russian church, was shown, also the very beautiful waterfalls coming down the side of Boundary Island.

One of the many human contacts of interest on this trip was mentioned. Cam Smith, a wealthy real estate dealer of Los Angeles in winter, is seen here summers in the capacity of taxicab driver, located at his attractive home at White Horse.

Miles Canyon is a place of great scenic beauty. The only bridge built across the Yukon was shown. The water here is very swift and the current strong. Views were shown of the docks at White Horse; a splendid Yukon River sunset; Five Finger Rapids and the narrow pass there. From White Horse to Dawson are seen many typical landing places. At Fort Selkirk is a little Episcopal church. Old Chief Isaacs, head of the Indian tribe, is one of the leading supporters of the Methodists. His picture revealed an august personage. The next picture was of a river with caribou passing, coming down to look for food. Six hundred of these were seen in one view. Dawson, like Skagway, is an abandoned city. Slides of all varieties of dogs were seen, an especially fine one being of Bruce, the lead dog. In winter these dogs are all at work.

In 1898 at Henderson's Creek gold was discovered, $11,000 worth in a half-hour. To-day a great deal of gold mining is done in the Klondike. Interesting slides of the gold district were shown, both of former days and now, picturing the washing out of the river and hills. A midnight sun just back from Dawson was one of the most exquisite views. Leaving Dawson, Sentimental Rock, brought by the ice age, is seen, and below there Calico Cliffs with many strange figures in it. Circle City, so named because it was thought to be on the Arctic Circle line, appeared; also a picture of the Arctic Circle.

At Point Barrow were found twelve inches of solidly frozen soil. Fine missionary work has been done here where stands the hospital in which Amundsen's life was saved. Going down from Fort Yukon, one can see Rex Beach's cabin. Here he lived and cut wood, for his health. A rare sight is the midnight sun on the Tanana River. This river has one bridge on which President Harding drove the first spike for the railroad track. Mary Lee Davis's Alaskan home at Fairbanks was shown on the screen. Mrs. Davis planted the only maple trees set out in Alaska. Although there are not over nine weeks of summer here the garden crop is a fine one.

Mt. McKinley Park is our second largest park and will eventually be the largest. The high mountains there are very imposing, Mt. McKinley itself being 20,300 feet. Enormous moose antlers were shown, also a polychrome path road. Across the valley the Sable Mountain peak is seen. Mt. McKinley is so tremendous, one hundred miles long, that it must be seen from the distance. Two hundred and ten hummocks make up the mountain—all larger than Mt. Washington. Many a life has been sacrificed on this mountain.

Beautiful doorways are seen here and there with pots of flowers in bloom. Sweet peas climb to the eaves of the house, and cabbages of three and one-half pounds are common. Passing through Trestle Valley, the lecturer showed a snowslide in mid-summer. Harding's Gateway, an ocean glacier, Bear Creek Canyon where gold was discovered recently, Horse Tail Falls and Bridal Veil Falls, all were pictured on the screen. It was a surprise to see the sign of the New England Fish Co. at the fishing port. Views followed of Cordova Harbor; Iron Tail Bridge; Copper River from which the noise of the ice can be heard twenty miles away; Mt. Rainier, taken from Paradise Inn; a picture of Gordon McKensie, a war ace. From Seattle the views turned to Vancouver where fine parliament buildings are found. The famous Bouchard Garden, sixty-seven acres of flowers, shrubbery and trees afforded much pleasure. The petunia section, pond lily garden and many other excellent views were shown.

A midnight sunset concluded the numerous excellent slides and fine lecture of Alaska, one of the great future places of the United States.

"BEAUTIFUL BERKSHIRES"

Thursday, January 19

Illustrated Lecture

BY MR. S. WALDO BAILEY, PITTSFIELD, MASS.

In the southwest part of the Berkshires the first settlement was made, and it is in this section that the Mt. Everett Reservation lies. There, 2,000 feet up the mountain, is located a little gem—Gilder Lake.

Views of this country carried us along scenes of all seasons depicting the beautiful Berkshires in their every garb. Reference was made to the spirit of Hawthorne which pervades Lenox, where he made his home for a time and wrote his famous "The House of the Seven Gables."

On the first of July the shores of Gilder Lake are aglow with mountain laurel, through which one finds unexcelled trails around the pond. The beautiful paintbrush presents another picture of splendor. Summer and winter contrasts were shown by slides taken of the same views in different seasons, and the great beauty of the section further enhanced.

On moving north on the trail over Mt. Everett one sees several beautiful waterfalls. Views of cascades, dainty falls over the mountain sides, were shown. Bridal Veil Falls with its very dainty spray was shown in summer, then in winter with its contrasting condition of heavy falls and large volume. Going west, almost to the New York boundary we see Berkshire Falls with a wild ravine. Directly east, almost on the Connecticut border is located Campbell's Falls, a state reservation where Connecticut and Massachusetts join forces in preserving scenic beauty. Near Pittsfield, Waconah Falls are seen. This entire section is replete with Indian legends and names.

In the hill country the ox and oxcart may still be seen. Sheep grazing on the hillside is a common sight in this section and a fascinating one. Large numbers of them were seen near the Shaker Settlement at Mt. Lebanon, New York. A wellsweep nearby suggested old times. Substantial farmsteads, always an attraction, are found throughout the section. A colonial doorway, hand-wrought, dating back one hundred to one hundred and fifty years, was shown. Slides of autumn scenery in mid-November showed corn shocks in that region. The Hoosatonic Valley in mild April gave a pleasing picture. Then came a view of the Farmington River waterway, up at the high level, showing shadbush, the first flower to bloom there in spring.

Monument Mountain, 1600 feet high, one of the largest of New England, recalls Bryant's poem of the Indian maid who jumped off the cliff. From the summit, Mt. Everett range in the distance gave a pleasing picture. Several fine views of this mountain, down over the base of the cliff, and the summit of the pulpit were shown on the screen. The face of these cliffs is of so rugged a character that it furnishes almost inaccessible nesting sites, which have been chosen by falcons for raising their brood. The history of such a brood was pictured by stages. A hawk's-eye view of the section furnished a picture of the savage nature of those birds. Monument Mountain is very beautiful in June and July with its abundance of azalea and mountain laurel.

Scattered throughout the valley are numerous farms, the most interesting being that where the Indian first told us how to make maple products. It has remained a great place for these maple delicacies. From autumn sunset of late October we pass to the striking whiteness of the birches with their great purity, especially in the winter season. Little brooks, almost as attractive in their winter garb as in that of spring or summer, pranced here and there. Autumn scenery in Lenox and environs is unsurpassed. Sunsets are always beautiful, but one projected on the screen with tall, straight Lombardy poplars on the border gave an especially inspiring view. Various bodies of water in the Lenox district showed to fine advantage.

A little vista of Greylock with its rugged highlands was seen in winter garb. Chesshire Harbor trail appeared a veritable fairyland in its charm of hoar frost. A carriage road up Greylock showed the sternness and beauty of winter. Then came a picture

JAPANESE GARDEN BY EDWARD W. BREED, 1933

of one of the wildest paths, from which one may look everywhere and see scarcely anything of man's habitat or accomplishment. Yet from the same point, summer conditions showed a miraculous change in a few short weeks. Many other fine slides presented Greylock in its every mood from fields of daisies to frost which does not come off even under strong windy conditions. Memorial Tower, a tribute to World War heroes, is located high up the mountain where it flashes its light across five or six states and is visible at night from the Custom House in Boston and from Wachusett.

The edge of Vermont is seen on a backward glance across the Hoosatonic and several mountain ranges. Hopper Trail up Greylock is a favorite of Williams College students. A view of the Taconic range and of the little brook rumbling down into the valley was very alluring. A recent trail built by the Appalachian Mountain Club and the Green Mountain Club connects Connecticut with New York. Stone Mountain and Katahdin were shown and glimpses of the 2,000 miles of hiking through the Appalachian system. Camps will be constructed along the way later on. People now show a strong inclination to return to the old favorite sport of hiking, to see the country at first hand. Bears are found in the Berkshires; but, for the most part, they are timid.

One great attraction of any region is its trees. The beautiful willow, majestic and rugged, arches many a waterway. Unfortunately, our willows are being attacked and destroyed. A group of these wind-swept trees was shown. Many wild apple trees are seen in this country and a display of apple bloom figured in the slides. On looking westward across New York, we see the Shaker settlement of Mt. Lebanon, located on the post road to Albany and Worcester, with wild gardens showing here and there.

Winter scenery disclosed bunny traces in the snow, and a bunny picture heightened the effect of this scenery. Deer coming down to feast on frozen apples recalled that the number of deer has been greatly reduced, there being perhaps not fifty per cent of the number there four or five years ago. These wild deer do great damage to orchards. An October scene was of the mountain reservation when it belonged to the Whitney family with buffalo, elk, moose and deer much in evidence. Fishermen at the edge of a stream recalled us to reality.

Abandoned farms of the hill towns of former years remind one of the horticulture of an earlier prosperity and denser population. The old rail or Virginia fence is fast disappearing from these country scenes. During the cooler months of the year a beautiful glow of violet is seen on the hills at sunrise and at sunset. Peculiar conditions of light and frost cause this afterglow, which is most marked and beautiful. This condition lasts only a few moments; so that artists have not succeeded in catching it, thought many have tried repeatedly.

The aesthetic side of the mountains was shown by the beauty of wild flower life. Massive displays of early white and yellow daisies, acres of fireweed, and the native rhododendron all showed on the screen. The lady's slipper grows there in abundance and is at its best. Paintbrush is spreading rapidly all over the ranges. Large quantities of mountain laurel add their splendor. The most vivid red in wild flower life is furnished by the cardinal, found there in plenty. Everywhere one looks, all is replete with the great beauty of Nature in the Berkshires.

"RHODODENDRONS AND AZALEAS"

Thursday, February 2

Illustrated Lecture

By Mr. Lorenzo F. Kinney, Jr., Kingston, Rhode Island

Nature is as beautiful as ever despite the depression now confronting us. Especially do the rhododendron and azalea furnish us with the best Nature has to offer from pastel to vivid colors found only in sunrise and sunset.

There are over three hundred kinds of rhododendrons. The varieties we are best acquainted with are man-made; the others are not hardy in this section. Man has not done much to improve them; just brought them together. Those we have here are not native but have been introduced from China, India and other countries; and it has taken us centuries to get what we have.

Views of rhododendron plantations quite near this section were shown. Natural color plates presented excellent pictures of the rhododendron and azalea in their natural forms.

We must determine whether a variety is hardy for this section or not before adopting it. Some disappear around here as they can't stand our severe winters.

The azalea is obtained from all over the world, found everywhere except in Africa. The type we have around here is mainly from India. In the United States the flowers usually come out before the leaves. The Torch Azalea of Japan, one of the most brilliant flowers, is claimed to be one of the first ever brought into the country.

A few of the many varieties of azalea mentioned are the following. Azalea arborescens (Sweet Azalea) has fragrant white flowers; pink stamens appearing after the leaves are nearly full grown. Calendulacea (Flame Azalea) has orange-yellow or red flowers. It is very popular. Azalea canadense or Rhodora canadensis is an attractive dwarf shrub covered in May with rosy-purple flowers. Canescens (Grey Azalea) has fragrant rosy-pink bloom.   Mollis (Chinese Azalea) is of dwarf habit and resembles the rhododendron.   The flowers vary from red to yellow or orange.   It requires a sunny position.   Nudiflora (Pinxter Bloom) has deep pink to reddish-purple blooms in May, a very showy variety.   Viscosa (Swamp Azalea) is the last to bloom.   It has fragrant white flowers in June or July.   It grows better, of course, in moist places.   Poukhanensis (Korean Azalea) is a very choice shrub.   Its purple-lilac flowers which come in May are unique and striking.

A fine mountain view was given of the Flame azalea in North Carolina, its native habitat.   This is the foundation of many of the best varieties.

Rhododendrons, like azaleas, are found all over the world. Some very brilliant ones grow around this section.   Hybridizing was done early in England and Holland, and we are indebted to these countries for many of our fine specimens.

Rhododendron catawbiense is a handsome one.   It has pink and lilac flowers which bloom in early June, and it is very prolific. Maximum, a rosy white, is one of the hardiest, with large and heavy foliage, blossoming in late June or July.   One of the most highly recommended rhododendrons for this section is the Carolina, a very choice early bloomer, hardy, small and compact, with unusually lovely pink flowers and pretty dark green leaves. It is fine for foundation plantings, paths, gardens and shady places.   Rosebay forms a natural background for the smaller Carolina and Catawba.   It has masses of rose-tinted white flowers and its glossy foliage endures frost.   It is used commonly for drives, paths, and underplanting in woods as it is so hardy and beautiful.   Caucassicum is a lovely white and is highly recommended.   President Lincoln, Charles Dickens, Daisy and many others may be had for variety in color and long season. Our native rhododendron from the South is extremely hardy and is good for background effects.   It does very well up North here. Several views of this lovely variety were shown.

Rhododendrons require acid soil and should have plenty of leaf mould and peat.   Never use lime or commercial fertilizer on them.   They should have part shade and in prolonged dry spells should be watered thoroughly. It is wise to pile leaves around their base as they like this arrangement as well in summer as in winter. They grow naturally in the mountains where it is damp and need to be kept watered.

Rhododendrons are the tiniest seed on the market. This seed is sown in flats and the seedlings kept there until they are a year old. They are very difficult to propagate.

Planting for landscape effect requires planning. At the Arnold Arboretum massing of color is extremely attractive. The display of rhododendrons and azaleas there is one of the finest in America. Large planting is effective and a group of large ones makes a fine showing. Roger Williams Park shows the many possibilities in this field. The dark green leaves bring out the color well and are a naturally fine background.

Rhododendrons and azaleas may be used effectively together. The former are two weeks later than the latter and together they are fine in front of evergreens. An unusually fine planting of these together is seen at Roger Williams Park. Both are found in all combinations and positions in parks and cemeteries as they are perfectly hardy. A view of Forest Hills Cemetery displayed a group some fifty years old. In front of hemlocks rhododendrons and azaleas are particularly effective.

Many hybrid forms of these plants are found in all colors. So wide is the choice as to size, color and time of bloom, every home-owner should have a planting of them to increase the beauty of his grounds.

At the conclusion of this most interesting and instructive lecture with fine collection of slides the general desire was to have more and more rhododendrons and azaleas.

"OLD CHINESE GARDENS"

Thursday, February 9

Illustrated Lecture

By Miss Grace M. Boynton, Medford, Mass.

The Chinese are considered the oldest gardeners in the world, for as early as 2200 B.C. China had her gardens. In 600 A.D. this great classic movement developed, spreading through Korea to Japan, Persia and Turkey. In the eighteenth century European contact with China through the priests who located there caused the movement to spread and the Anglo-Chinese garden soon arose in England. Hence, we owe much to China who has made this great contribution to the world of gardens.

The Chinese garden is not public property, for it is found behind high walls of eight to ten feet, and the stranger may pass by without realizing the great beauty behind. Privacy is the key word of the Chinese garden.

A great difference in the technique of sense perception deprives us of full appreciation of the Chinese garden; for, just as the poetry of these people is full of references we do not understand, so, too, is their garden in which the very "dropping of the rose petals" is significant. Their gardens are built out of a system of philosophy alien to our ways of thought.

The conception of the dot is the principle of life, active in passivity, above and beyond the power of man. It is a growth without domination. Nature is beneficent and man is not to interfere; so the virtuous man lives in a state of passivity. The virtuous man is represented as a hermit in a mountain cave, in communion with Nature. Goodness is like water; there is no strife in it. The Chinese do not care for the turmoil of the city. Their egotistic impulse is to retire to the mountain; so they retire, instead, to the garden. The practical person with them is apt to be unrefined. In the West the primary conception is the flowers; but this is not the Chinese view. Their entire landscape is replete with significance; the wood meaning power; the hill, the sacred mountain; and water, goodness and peace.

Their garden is built just as their house is built, every corner serving some definite purpose.

Miss Boynton went to Peiping in 1919 to join the faculty of the newly established Yenching University. When this university was moved outside of Peiping Miss Boynton's home was within the walls of an imperial garden; hence her great study of and interest in Chinese gardens.

The view of the Winter Palace in Peking showed an irregular contour of rocks along the shore, with the proverbial hill and water present. Here are the greatest pleasure grounds in the world. The pleasure gallery shows the use made of color; red typifying young, masculine, strong: yellow, feminine, brooding, the mother quality, this color being used in roofs.

Slides of many scenes were projected, among them a terrace adorned with the silvery pine of North China which grows nowhere else in the world. It is much like our birch. Temples of rare beauty were seen in the mountains. A temple older than Peking figured in the magnificence of the silvery pine with its great height and spread. Black Dragon Pool, well named from the many set-in pools, with its moon gate through which one passes up steps to a brick terrace was a striking view. Plenty of rhododendrons and evergreens adorn the grounds of this temple. A long avenue of cypress and evergreen trees, and beyond, white pines, leads one in the Garden of the Tombs to the resting place of the dead, under the shelter of a mountain.

Lang Jun Yuan, the Garden of Moonlit Fertility, dating back to 1600, well supports the view that the fate of a garden depends upon our moral strength in caring for it. Precaution is taken here, as elsewhere, to preserve privacy. Slides showed running water destined to drive out evil influence of malignant spirits. A chain of artificial lakes surround the palace. Slides of snow pictures showed the entrance to this garden. These snow views displayed well the treatment of tree branches, trained to follow the roof, and other tree designing characteristic of the Chinese garden. Pictures of the inner gate and the Dream of the Red Chamber were also scenes of rare beauty. Attention was called to the use of a hill to shut off one's view from what is beyond, thus prolonging suspense. Then, too, a stone planted in a garden

CHILDREN'S EXHIBITION, 1933

in a conspicuous place bears out the belief that a garden should stimulate all garden reactions. Sinister and grotesque shapes, rocks and the like vary emotional stimulation which a garden contains.

The lecturer's home for four years amid this great beauty and garden influence was shown by many slides, those of early spring being especially entrancing. Gardening is considered by the Chinese one of the greatest arts. Piles of rocks here and there, called rock work by us, mean a false mountain to the Chinese. Lantern windows in the Valley of the Pine Palace formed an impressive picture. Lotus time is a particularly beautiful sight. A slide showed two hundred of these in bloom at once.

The Chinese plan a succession of bloom from spring to mid-June; after that plants in pots are added to the collection. They do not plant in masses, but one plant here and there, or one spray, one bloom is seen for decoration. The scholar is the typical figure in their garden rather than the lover as with us. All these pictures are saturated with literature, woods and subtle implications. It may be the story of a man who sets out in the world to make his fortune. The emperor is an object of veneration—a religion. A synthetic view of The Crystal Spring was shown also. The Let-go Bower, a place of complete relaxation, appeared attractive. Other views shown were rose gardens; the Bower of Philosophy; three old men listening to the song of friendship; the Bower for Awaiting the Fruit, a harbor while waiting for the fruit to ripen. In the last mentioned a man appears in a warm bower; a basket of fruit in absolutely perfect condition is the gift to the emperor.

The Palace of Remembrance representing man's union with Nature was a striking picture. The garden at the Monastery of the Pool and Oak, and the shrine of the Temple of the Mountain Peak were shown and explained. Everywhere this pervading spirit of privacy, reverence and love for the garden was shown.

Many interesting slides showed not only the great beauty of the garden but also the ineffable charm and peace provided by that rare beauty found in the Chinese garden.

"SUNSHINE AND SHADOW IN THE GARDEN"

Thursday, February 16

Illustrated Lecture

BY MR. CARL STANTON, PETERBORO, N. H.

A garden is a picture, a good or poor one according to the artistry expressed in it. A good picture is a combination of sunshine and shadow, a fact too little appreciated by the average gardener. All mountain views, all Nature, prove this statement. Even the mouldings in one's home are tinted in color effects of light and shade.

Many excellent slides were shown depicting this very necessary adherence to the rules of Nature. A view of a woodland in New Jersey showed a small rock garden at the entrance, producing a marked lighting effect. This has a fine lawn as a base, rather than soil, to catch the play of light and shade on it. Much of the beauty of that garden is in that tapestry of green. The owner of this woodland dwells in the city, yet has occasion to camp there by his woodlots now and then and finds great satisfaction in the beauty of his woodland home.

Architects should study light effects, thinking of natural light. Trees, shrubs and flowers are not the only components of a garden; sunshine and shadow must form a part of their scheme. There must be a shady place in the garden as an invitation to enter. Many people remove this condition and spoil the place just to favor some flowers or shrubs.

In Mrs. Abbott's garden in Manchester a play of sunlight and shadow actually makes the small garden the beauty spot it is. It is surrounded by white pines, and a dimmed light brings out real values. Roses of the finest color are there; not in the brilliant sunshine where their glory would fade.

There are two regular ways of dealing with natural light in the garden: first, the entire garden picture as one looks from outside; second, the picture as each detail of the garden comes to the attention. A view of a brook running through a woodland illustrated this point on the screen. This brook was dammed across, thus forming a pool, and an opening was cut at the top of the woodland to obtain space and call attention to the pool not showing before. The ray of light passing through pointed directly at the pool. A picture of a wall in Milton, made of hand-moulded brick, showed that its beauty lies entirely in its shadow. Details may be only the cutting of a limb to show something beyond, or the placing of a large shrub near an extra fine flower group, or the shadow of a lily on the wall. All such details are very important for obtaining the full beauty of the garden. There are two ways of distributing illumination over the entire garden: first, the locating of a garden or a bed in it as seen from the most used points of view; second, the placing of carefully chosen trees or shade-producing devices.

A rose garden in Rockville, Connecticut, shown on the screen, gave a particularly fine effect of lighting to best advantage by fine choice of location. If we place a garden south, southwest or southeast of the point where we should like to go to look at it we gain a much more picturesque effect. A garden is more desirable if we can look down on it; but by looking up sometimes we gain a better shadow effect.

Deciduous trees, such as the dogwood, are quite necessary for desired effect, and these may be chosen for light foliage. A garden must always be associated with a tree or large shrub; trees if possible. Direct force of the sun's rays must be eliminated in some cases and a tree or shrub furnishes this protection. Our plants limit the amount of shade we may have in our garden; but most plants will grow for us without the full glare of the sun, provided we furnish good ventilation for them. Good air circulation is absolutely necessary. A view of a garden in Hartford, Connecticut, illustrated this point well. It is one of good flower culture, with good circulation and just enough sunlight filtering through the elms.

Gardens are of three classes:

1. Botanical garden, for study.

2. Picturesque garden, to be admired for its beautiful coloring, shade and light effects, one especially for show.

3.   Living-room garden, where plants are secondary to our comfort.   In this case one steps from the house into the garden which is always a part of the house. This type is the tendency to-day and is termed often the intimate garden.

A garden path is an attractive feature and useful in general. The brick path with grass joints is a favorite one.   If moss is desired, make a solution of two quarts of molasses and a can of water.   Then water the bricks or stones once every fortnight, and the result will be an effective covering of moss.   Pear trees are often chosen because their foliage is not very dense and the tree is artistic.   Every garden should have a pear tree or old apple tree in its corner for pleasing effect.   We may gain beauty for the garden by aging it as we build it.

Vista cutting is an important subject and such designing requires study.   A vista may be cut through shrubbery forming different types of outline.   A garden path naturally takes the eye into the center of the picture, and a vista may be cut in this way to give a direct view.   Any distance may be designed for the garden.   A false convergence is effected by a long vista, and other lines may falsify distance for the desired effect.

Shrubbery and trees should be trimmed to gain shadows. A park in Rochester, New York, is a good example of this work. The lecturer does not favor surrounding a garden with a hedge as the light is then all the same on one side.   Also, this causes a straight, hard line, whereas a soft line is needed to produce natural effect, the way Nature grows in its wild state, in and out.

Several slides illustrated these points, showing the use of sunlight and shadow for emphasis.   Boundaries may be mysterious, thus doing away with hard lines.   In Berlin, New Hampshire, an ugly looking town, an attempt was made to induce the mill folks to improve conditions there; and after considerable trial and error method the extravagant ideas and poor taste were gradually improved until at least a fair condition was obtained.   A most effective sunlight and shadow garden with no color in it is the Spaulding garden in Peterboro, New Hampshire, located at a quarry, with the quarry little in evidence, thanks to the fine shading device.

Just as architectural work calls for a study of shadows, so the gardener must ponder the best light and shadow effects. In the dark garden emphasis should be placed on the light spot; and in the light garden fine flowers should be placed in the dark spot. Shadow affects our eyes as purple, not as black; and purple paint on a garage will hide it—push it away. All undesirable features should be darkened. A vine covering a fence should be clipped to show shadow and sunlight. Hence, we find that for any location or condition careful study and planning of sunshine and shadow will result in the desired beauty.

DISPLAY OF ROSES BY A. N. PIERSON, INC., 1933

LADIES' DAY
Thursday, February 23

Ladies' Day was held for the first time in several years. A general invitation was extended to all members and to those attending our Winter Meetings.

An interesting program was furnished. Professor Illingworth, of Clark University, gave two groups of readings from the modern poets, those of the nonsense versifiers and the dialect poets being the most entertaining from a humorous point of view.

Mrs. Ethel Sleeper Ruggles, in costume, favored us with two groups of songs. Mr. John Cadieux gave several vocal solos, accompanied by Mrs. Bertha G. Denny.

At the conclusion of this fine entertainment tea was served and a social hour enjoyed by all. The committee in charge consisted of Mrs. Myron F. Converse, Mrs. Burt W. Greenwood, Mrs. Herbert R. Kinney, Miss Lucy M. Coulson, Mrs. Allen J. Jenkins, Mrs. Bertha G. Denny.

"WHAT PLANTS KNOW"

Thursday, March 2

Illustrated Lecture

By Mr. Herbert W. Faulkner, Washington, Conn.

There is a close relationship between animal and plant life. The two kingdoms exist side by side. As we go down in the life stage the life lines approach each other; then fuse and intermingle in the very lowest form, being in this lower order a cell with no distinction. Some animals grow to rocks and bloom like flowers, and it is only as these cells increase that we find a distinction between them.

All plants are composed of cells which act for the good of the whole plant, yet have an independent growth. They are connected by little delicate ribs which really are the nerves. Plants have nutrition, breathing, circulation (for their sap acts the same as our blood), sex, a looking forward and preparation for the future, and procreation is by egg cell—all in common with animal life. A plant must stay put, though, and this has great influence upon its development and psychology. It is just the same with man; he, too, does not become so intelligent a being in a fixed state as if he travels.

The telegraph plant is an interesting case, expressive of worry. At night all leaves are quiet, but when the sun shines they constantly wave up and down. It is not known why they move. This motion takes place through some vital force.

Motion in many plants has a clear purpose, as well expressed by the barberry bush. The six stamens are all charged with pollen, and when an insect reaches into the center for nectar this central mechanism makes possible the seizing of the bee and holding him while the stamens dust him with pollen.

Plants lay up food for their future use and also for their young, their seedling. If a bean is opened, food for the future, for the new life, is seen; clearly an act for the welfare of the race, a looking forward into the future.

Seed is produced not only by pollenation; there is an idealism in it. Nature has developed a marvelous scheme, almost artificial selection, a system of eugenics which accomplishes the breeding of better plants. It is a natural impulse through the whole universe of life to produce better offspring. The young are strong and better able to meet conditions of existence.

An excellent mechanism for cross pollenation exists. When a bee visits a plant he begins at the bottom and goes upward; so all spirals bloom from the bottom up. There is a curious adjustment of habits of the flower to habits of the bee. Mechanism of the bloom insures the bee's getting pollen. This insures cross pollenation as the bee carries away pollen to other flowers. Sage well explains this scheme of cross pollenation.

Plants by mechanical contrivance make sure that their seed is well distributed. A slide well demonstrated this feature by showing lupine pods which have fallen and are ready to explode. The pod explodes and throws out forcibly the seed in all directions. Purple cransfield, a plant highly recommended for our gardens, is an interesting one. The candle, a part of this plant, is equipped with springs which go off, thus scattering the seed. All this deals with the idea of the improvement of the race—with the mind of a plant.

Sensibility of the plant now claims our attention. The sensitive plant is tiny, six to twelve inches, with a long midrib stem. Its leaflets are very sensitive to touch and close instantly when they are touched. Every time it is touched it does the same thing, due to nervous sensibility. At the lower end, if touched, the impulse passes up through the midrib to the place where the center of response is situated.

A plant has a certain sense of life, human impulses. It knows direction up and down. If a geranium is placed in a dark room on its side, in a few days it will begin to turn up its body and continue until it has found the vertical again. It is not necessary to bother placing potato seed with the eye up, for the sprouts follow natural laws regardless of position. A bulb set upside down will eventually come up in a vertical position. Sense of the vertical is a plant sensation.

The above characteristic was proved by an experiment on corn. It was placed on a board to sprout, set in all ways and directions to interfere with natural development. As a result, the little stems shot in all directions. Even if rotated the corn had no sense of direction as the vertical was constantly turning. This upset the mind of the plant and the roots could not go down but went according to the way they were started.

An experiment was performed upon pea seed. Moist cotton was placed in a bag and upon that some pea seed. This sprouted under the moisture and warmth given, as the bag was rolled and fastened. The roots started downward through the bag, down and down in search of the food (the moisture was above). They found a dry condition down below, and so bent upward in search of the water they knew was above. This proved the intelligence of plants.

Venus fly-trap demonstrates the quality of choice in plants. Its leaves possess little sticky fingers, which hold insects. The insect comes down and the sticky fingers close to hold it. This plant grows where there is no nitrogen; so sets a trap for insects to obtain this needed nitrogen. If wood or straw is placed there, the mechanism of the plant does not work, but stays open. This proves that the plant possesses choice.

The amoeba, the lowest form of life, is a mass of protoplasm, almost formless. Yet even this feels around for food. All these intelligences of a plant actually help the plant itself. Cacti in the desert have developed an extraordinary system of spine to keep animals from eating the succulent plants. They have developed a rubber coat to hold in moisture.

There is a power resident in the growing tissue of plants, an innate power under control of the plant system whereby the necessary is done. Apple trees replace limbs. We can't mould the plant to an environment; it must come from within or without. A unity of action is involved, but a plant has no brain. A plant is a little republic; whereas an animal is an empire dominated by the brain.

This great power of plant life is probably something innate—

apparently from within. Or, there may be a more spiritual view of this matter, supported by some. It is a great problem and must remain such, but certain it is that flowers have an intelligence of an indirect sort. The study of this power, the psychology of flowers, has been of great inspiration to the lecturer and is recommended to all.

"THE INTERNATIONAL PEACE GARDEN"
Thursday, March 9

By Mr. Allen J. Jenkins, Shrewsbury, Mass.

At the convention of the National Association of Gardeners in Greenwich, Connecticut, 1928, Mr. H. J. Moore of Islington, Ontario, suggested an international garden as a peace memorial. In 1929 the subject was brought up formally at Toronto, and the National Association of Gardeners accepted the sponsorship of such a garden. This organization, composed principally of private gardeners and some employers, has an active membership of over two thousand. That year a committee of enthusiasts was formed for the purpose and the goal set at $5,000,000.

This committee, boasting such fine representation as Mrs. Pierpont, Mrs. Ford and the late Senator Walsh, reported at the convention in Washington several offers of very fine sites of land around Niagara Falls. These sites were inspected in 1931 but were not accepted, as a water boundary cut our two countries apart. A neutral termination was desired to effect the significance of the garden. Finally, a parcel of 3,000 acres, one-half in the United States and one-half in Canada, in the region of the Province of Manitoba and North Dakota was accepted and was dedicated last July.

The location of this international garden is particularly fortunate since much of it is virgin territory, large forests. Plant life there is about the same as here. The winters are severe but the summers are mild; on the whole, it is quite a favorable climate. There are numerous lakes in this territory, making it a very suitable place. No commercialization is to spoil this property which has been dedicated to the great cause of peace.

During the past two years plans have moved along slowly, due to economic conditions. Then, too, it is desired that this idea be popularized by interesting school children and people in general in it.

A charter has been obtained from the state of New York, but Canada wishes us to have a national charter. A board of twelve trustees will control. No actual work has been done there yet. The desire is to have trees from every state in the Union and from all the provinces of Canada.

July 14, 1932, an international picnic was held and the International Peace Garden dedicated. Many very prominent people were present. An inscribed bronze tablet marks the spot. A letter received from President Hoover at that time will be placed in the cornerstone of the Administration Building when it is laid.

Mr. Jenkins, president of the National Association of Gardeners, epitomized this report to make way for Mr. Gleason, who had been slated for an earlier lecture but, due to illness, had not been able to present it. Mr. Jenkins promised, however, to tell us more about this interesting subject at a later date.

In closing, he surprised us by presenting the screen views taken at the Grafton Garden Club of two of our best loved and most faithful members, Mr. and Mrs. David Fiske of Grafton.

"THE CHARM OF LITTLE GARDENS"
Thursday, March 9

Illustrated Lecture

By Mr. Herbert W. Gleason, Boston, Mass.

Mr. Gleason's twelfth welcome visit to our hall brought an interesting talk on the small gardens, presenting many excellent slides for illustration.

The recent garden movement is one of the most remarkable in our history; in fact, there is nothing else like it in all the world. The great garden movement is world-wide in scope.

The lecturer's own garden, less than a half-acre, has aroused in him a great passion for it. The charm of a garden is known best to him who cultivates it. In it he finds a satisfaction found nowhere else. This charm reflects the degree of interest and skill of the gardener and is an expression of his personality and welcome. Many gardens lack this charm and represent just so much money. Some owners never go into a garden; hence it is not strange that a personal touch of welcome is missing.

A garden to be beautiful does not need to be large, for often it is the little garden that has the rarest charm. But a garden must be closely related to the house, especially the little garden, to have true charm. Many fine slides illustrated this point. Color combinations, if good, add much to the beauty of the garden. Views of elaborate gardens at Newport showed this great charm and informality. The Du Pont garden at Wilmington, Delaware, with its water garden and fountain is one of the most charming gardens ever seen. That of Mr. and Mrs. Lars Anderson of Brookline is large, yet very charming with its bunny scene and gnomes from Bohemia for the enjoyment of young people who visit there.

The Hunnewell garden at Wellesley has the finest exhibit of topiary work in this country, not in exaggerated figures that often border on the hideous, but in the training of trees by which a most pleasing effect is produced. At Santa Barbara, California, this same avoidance of the grotesque is found in the very beautiful clipped trees.   In spite of the formality of a huge and costly garden, it may become one of indefinable charm.

Slides of several gardens illustrating interest and charm were shown.   One of a beautiful garden at Port Arthur, seen thirty-five years ago, was attractive with its little old house in evidence. The Ogden garden at Bar Harbor appeared with its old-fashioned charm and lovely hollyhocks.   At Haverhill, the garden of two elderly ladies with its lovely old flowers proved the effectiveness of the Carolina rhododendron in a little garden.   Other gardens showing skill and appreciation in the handiwork of the owner, succession of bloom, and little garden seats were seen.

At South Duxbury is located the splendid garden of Mrs. Thompson, twenty-five feet square, simple yet of wonderful skill, with an excellent collection of flowers and unusual charm. Other backyard gardens there at Duxbury are attractive.   Mrs. Benedict has a charming garden with its climbing roses in fine combination.   A Long Island garden shows the adoption of restraint in a garden effecting a peculiar charm.   At Cohasset a sun-dial is found in a little garden.   Other gardens there are of great charm, also.   Mrs. Phillip of Swampscott has a garden fifty feet square or less containing a ledge which has been altered and the boulder used for a rock garden.   This garden is quite renowned.   Mrs. John Hussey of Salem has a garden of unusual charm.   Mrs. Goldthwaite of the Marblehead Garden Club has an attractive garden of indefinable charm, wholly her own work.

At Pride's Crossing an Italian well-head filled with water and lilies is a great addition to the Coolidge garden.   Mrs. Agassiz of Canton has a fine garden.   The lecturer recommended Rhododendron Maximum for garden use as it is superior to varieties often used and is one of our best.   At Mrs. Danielson's garden in Medfield a gate at the front of the garden opens into the highway.   Mrs. Howard's garden in Brookline shows a high degree of skill.   At Wood's Hole, Mrs. Whitney has an extensive garden.   A fine one in Milton is the skillful work of the owner, Mrs. McGinley.   A beautiful border, an attractive gate, red flowering dogwood and a succession of bloom furnish the fine picture for this garden.

"A Rose for Every Garden" is the slogan of the American

VEGETABLE DISPLAY, HERBERT R. KINNEY, 1933

Rose Society. It is a good one and should be followed. Every garden requires at least one rose bush. Mrs. Coolidge's garden at North Andover has a fine display of roses around a central basin. Mrs. Crane of Ipswich has one of the most notable rose gardens. One the greatest rose enthusiasts of this country is Mr. Robinson of Bass Rocks whose collection of roses is an excellent one. At North Easton the garden of Mrs. Frothingham has a very beautiful pool surrounded by choice roses.

Many people who have only a limited area to plant prefer a rock garden. Several of these show gardens may be seen at Nahant and all along the North Shore. Mr. Curtis received the highest award at the Horticultural Show of last year, the president's cup. He displayed a large collection of plants, a collection of rare accomplishment. A natural slope affords an excellent position for a rock garden. Mrs. Farrand of Bar Harbor has a beautiful rock terrace garden. An attractive rock garden is owned by Mrs. Houghton of Chestnut Hill. A drift of crocuses, several in one garden, made a pleasing picture.

The cultivation of the wall garden is new and not so well recognized in this section. One may utilize cellar walls of a razed building for this purpose and achieve fine wall planting. Mrs. Francis Thompson of Philadelphia has one of the very best wall gardens in this section of the country and has been awarded a silver medal by the Horticultural Society. Mr. McFadden of Philadelphia has attractive planting in the interstices of stone steps. These plants are not forced out by frost at all there, as they might easily be here in our more severe winters. In time wall gardening will increase in favor and success as has the rock garden in recent years.

The many fine views projected on the screen were a source of great inspiration and well proved Mr. Gleason's contention that there is great charm in the little garden.

ANNUAL REUNION

Thursday, March 16

Following a reception in the library at 6:30 p.m. members and guests marched to the dining hall. Invocation was by the Rev. Dr. Vincent E. Tomlinson.

After a fine dinner served by Mr. Lunt, the president, Mr. Myron F. Converse, extended greetings to all and made a few remarks relative to the successful winter meetings and the coming Spring Show.

Dr. Tomlinson's word to the society was one of praise for its accomplishments and beautiful building. Spare time, he remarked, may well be spent on the soil as it brings fine returns in all directions. This economic depression is reacting in such a way, for many are now seeking country homes and reverting to farm life as a means of subsistence. An account of Dr. Tomlinson's own young life on a farm was very interesting. The conclusion drawn was that we people who love Nature in the garden can well be leaders in showing others the way to enjoy profitable leisure.

Mr. Converse spoke of the days when he and other members of the Worcester Grange used to rehearse with a fellow member, Flora Belcher; and now, there at the head table was sitting Mrs. Flora Belcher Rugg whose son was to be the speaker of the evening. He then presented Mr. Charles Rugg, formerly Assistant Attorney-General of the United States.

Mr. Rugg's talk was "A Trip to Alaska." This trip was made on a government boat but was financed entirely by the individuals themselves. It was a round trip of 7,000 miles and consisted of all inside sailing. The party left Seattle and were gone six weeks.

The island of Vancouver has no shores, no beach, as it rises abruptly and is thickly wooded to the edge. During foggy spells it is necessary for the warning signal to be blown constantly. The first stop in Alaska was Metlakatta where four hundred Indians reside. A wise, alert missionary is accomplishing much there. The first vegetation of the North was seen at this place. Southeastern Alaska is not cold and it is never cold on the water. The temperature was above freezing on New Year's day, even, and there is no frost there after April. Forty degrees is the average temperature in winter and seventy degrees in summer. Long hours of sunlight, in June and July until eleven o'clock, produce a vegetation as rank as in a jungle. It is a physical impossibility to force one's way into the woods. In June raspberry bushes are seen ten feet high, the fruit an inch wide and two inches long.

Journeying northward, the fishing weirs were reached. A curious species of salmon was seen here. These fish have a well-ordered life, staying in the sea four years and the fifth year returning to the original stream where they spawn and die. The Bureau of Fisheries equalizes the supply. Salmon is caught in traps or nets; the same method, in one particular, used two thousand years ago. Mr. Rugg lived in a salmon cannery for several days and is convinced that canned salmon is the best for us to use. No human hand touches the fish, and within fifteen hours from its swimming in the water the salmon is canned and ready for us to eat. The annual value of fish caught in Alaska is $30,000,000. We paid Russia $7,200,000 for Alaska but many times the cost is taken from the country every year.

The glaciers of Alaska are very interesting and seem different from those of Europe. They are the bluest of the blues, a sapphire of most alluring shade.

Gardens of the various cities visited might well be the envy of all. Sweet pea stems eighteen inches to two feet long and dahlias seven to ten feet high with a bloom six to eight inches in diameter apparently come from long ultra violet rays of sunlight. Fruit cannot be grown there, for this year's growth does not get a chance to develop before winter comes. One finds uncomfortable heat inland (Fairbanks was 100 degrees) and these violent changes kill vegetation.

Southwest Alaska is the land of volcanoes with no vegetation other than grass and alders; no trees whatever. The party sailed toward the mountains and out to Bering Sea. The Alaska

Indian is one-fourth Russian, has not much education, and does not thrive on it very well.

Pribilof Islands are situated in mid-ocean. They are volcanic ash or rock and have no soil whatever. This is a famous breeding place for seals. The life of the seal is very interesting. From September to June they live in the water and are never on land during that time. In June the bull seals come to the island, these being seven years or older. They come in tremendous schools, some 200,000 and fight for the best place on the island, that nearest the water, and this becomes their home. July 1st, the cows come, they being three years or older. They select the bull with which they live that year, the bulls having forty to seventy-five cows each. Strict family lines are observed. After the calves are born the cows go for food. Calves are taught to swim by their mother who throws them out in the water, then goes after them. The 1st of September all calves, male and female, go to sea; then the cows go off; the bulls go to sleep on the grass for a month, and then go to sea.

In that country the temperature is never above 50 degrees in summer, so that seed cannot germinate outdoors. There is an extensive wild flora there and several fields were seen blue with lupin, thick and tall and alive with honey bees. Arctic poppies grow there in large numbers.

A bird reservation of five acres, all rock and no soil, harbors four or five different kinds of birds, murre being the most prevalent. They are so numerous that one has to scuff them aside to avoid stepping on them. A quaint, bizarre type of parrot is seen there making its nest in rocks.

The entire trip in and about Alaska was a source of great pleasure and study, and presented this great country in a light never fully appreciated in books.

This interesting talk was followed by dancing and specialty numbers in Horticultural Hall and entertainment for all was provided.

SCHEDULE OF PREMIUMS

Offered by the

Worcester County Horticultural Society

Horticultural Building
30 Elm Street
Worcester, Mass.

For the year

1934

THE ATTENTION OF EXHIBITORS IS PARTICULARLY
CALLED TO THE RULES AND REGULATIONS
GENERAL AND SPECIAL

The Davis Press, Worcester

OFFICERS AND COMMITTEES
of the
WORCESTER COUNTY HORTICULTURAL SOCIETY
For the Year 1934

PRESIDENT
MYRON F. CONVERSE, Worcester, Mass.

VICE-PRESIDENTS
HERBERT A. COOK, Shrewsbury, Mass.   MRS. HOMER GAGE, Worcester, Mass.
S. LOTHROP DAVENPORT, No. Grafton, Mass.

SECRETARY
HERBERT R. KINNEY, of Worcester
Horticultural Hall, 30 Elm Street

TREASURER
BURT W. GREENWOOD, of Worcester

LIBRARIAN
Miss LUCY M. COULSON, of Worcester

TRUSTEES:

Joseph A. Allen	Auburn	Fred L. Chamberlain	Worcester
William Anderson	South Lancaster	James Warr	Worcester
Elizabeth R. Bishop	Sutton	J. Frank Cooper	Worcester
Edward W. Breed	Clinton	Mrs. Bertha G. Denny	Worcester
David L. Fiske	Grafton	Mrs. Alice M. Forbes	Worcester
Richard A. Flagg	Boylston	Harold J. Greenwood	Worcester
Allen J. Jenkins	Shrewsbury	Harry Harrison	Worcester
William McAllister	Whitinsville	Mrs. Leander F. Herrick	Worcester
William E. Morey	Shrewsbury	Allyne W. Hixon	Worcester
Charles Potter	West Boylston	Mrs. Frances A. Kinnicutt	Worcester
Albert W. Schneider	Clinton	H. Ward Moore	Worcester
Mrs. Mary D. White	Holden	Harry I. Randall	Worcester
Chandler Bullock	Worcester	Joseph F. Sherer	Worcester
Willis E. Cary	Worcester	Mrs. Amy W. Smith	Worcester
Fred H. Chamberlain	Worcester	George F. E. Story	Worcester

STANDING COMMITTEE ON FINANCE
Myron F. Converse, *Chairman*, 1934   Herbert W. Estabrook, 1935
Leonard C. Midgley, 1936

NOMINATING COMMITTEE
Willis E. Cary, 1934   Ernest Hansen 1935   Arthur H. Bellows, 1936

ON LIBRARY AND PUBLICATIONS
Edward W. Breed, *Chairman*   Mrs. Amy W. Smith   William Anderson
Herbert R. Kinney, *Secretary*   Lucy M. Coulson, *Librarian*

ON NOMENCLATURE
S. Lothrop Davenport   Mrs. Amy W. Smith   Charles Potter   Herbert R. Kinney
J. Frank Cooper   Allen J. Jenkins   William Anderson   Leonard C. Midgley

ON ARRANGEMENTS AND EXHIBITIONS
Allen J. Jenkins, *Chairman*

Joseph A. Allen	H. Ward Moore	Elizabeth R. Bishop
Mrs. William W. Taft	Edward W. Breed	James Warr
Mrs. Percy G. Forbes	Lucy M. Coulson	S. Lothrop Davenport
Leonard C. Midgley	Allyne W. Hixon	Albert W. Schneider
President, Myron F. Converse	Charles Potter	William E. Morey
	Secretary, Herbert R. Kinney	

AUDITORS
Harry C. Midgley   H. Ward Moore   Arthur H. Bellows

JUDGES
PLANTS AND FLOWERS: William Anderson, South Lancaster
FRUIT: S. Lothrop Davenport, North Grafton
VEGETABLES: H. Ward Moore, Worcester

MEDAL COMMITTEE
Myron F. Converse, *Chairman*   Edward W. Breed   Allen W. Hixon

ON WINTER MEETINGS
Myron F. Converse, *Chairman*   Herbert R. Kinney, *Secretary*
Mrs. Leander F. Herrick   Burt W. Greenwood
Leonard C. Midgley   H. Ward Moore

Office, Library, and Exhibition Hall
30 Elm Street

GENERAL RULES AND REGULATIONS

1. Strict conformity to the Regulations and Rules will be expected and required, as well for the benefit of exhibitors as for the convenience of the Officers of the Society.

2. Every Flower or Plant entered in a class of named varieties should be correctly named.

3. All articles offered for premiums must remain within the Hall throughout the hours of Exhibition, unless special permission for their removal shall be granted by the Committee on Exhibition, etc.

4. No person shall make more than one entry of the same variety or be awarded more than one premium under the same number.

5. The Judges may correct, before the close of any exhibition, awards made by them, if satisfied that such were erroneous.

6. The cards of exhibitors competing for premiums shall be reversed, until after premiums are awarded.

7. Competitors are expected to conform strictly to the conditions under which articles are invited. Evasion or violation of them may be reported to the TRUSTEES for future disqualification of the offender.

8. Articles offered for premiums must be in the Hall by 2 o'clock of the days of Exhibition except when otherwise specified. Between 2 and 3 o'clock the Hall will be in exclusive charge of the Committee on Arrangements and Exhibitions. Open to the public from 3 to 9 o'clock.

9. Competition for premiums is open to all residents of Worcester County, and it is strictly required that all specimens offered for premiums shall have been grown by the competitors, on their own premises, for at least two (2) months previous to the date of exhibition, except where no restriction is stated in schedule.

10. After the articles are arranged they will be under the exclusive charge of the Judges and Committee of Arrangements, and not even the owners will have liberty to remove them until the exhibition is closed, when they will be delivered as the contributors may direct.

11.   Where a certain number or quantity of Plants, Flowers, Fruits or Vegetables is designated in the schedule, there must be neither more nor less than that number or quantity of specimens shown; and in no case can other varieties than those named in the schedule be substituted.

12.   The Judges may exclude from competition all inferior specimens and may correct any errors that they think were without deliberate purpose.

13.   The Committee on Arrangements has power to change the time of exhibition for any article, if an earlier or later season renders such change desirable.

14.   All articles offered for premiums should be correctly named. Indefinite appellations such as "Pippin," "Sweeting," "Greening," etc., will not be considered as names. Any person exhibiting the same variety of Fruit or Vegetable, under different names, or exhibiting as grown by himself Flowers, Fruit or Vegetables grown by another, thereby violating the objects and rules of the Society, shall be debarred from competing for the Society's premiums until reinstated.

15.   Competitors will be required to furnish information as to their mode of cultivation, and to present specimens for trial and examinations, if requested.

16.   In all exhibitions of Cut Flowers for competition, the number of blooms, clusters, sprays or spikes shown is not restricted except that it is expected the exhibitor shall use only a sufficient number to make a well-balanced display. All shall be of one color and of one variety in the same vase, except Displays, Vases, Baskets, Standards, or otherwise specified in the schedule. The use of foliage must be restricted to that of the varieties shown, except with orchids, carnations, gloxinias, sweet peas and displays. The Judge will consider the quality of the flowers rather than the quantity.

17.☞ The Judges are authorized by the Trustees to invite the assistance of competent and discreet persons in the discharge of their duties.

18.   No Judge shall require anything of competitors respecting their exhibits which is not distinctly specified in the schedule.

19. In Table Decorations, collections and displays of Flowers, Fruits, Vegetables, Vases, and Baskets, where the number of exhibits exceeds the number of premiums offered, the Judge *may* award prizes to any worthy exhibits not receiving a premium.

The maximum prize for Vases, Standards, and Baskets shall be two dollars.

20. All premiums that are not claimed within one year after the close of the official year shall be forfeited to the Society.

21. "Downing's Fruits of America," revised edition, will guide the Judge of Fruits in his decisions upon matters at issue.

22. While the Society will take reasonable precautions for the safety of the property of exhibitors, it will be responsible in no case for any loss or damage that may occur.

Scale of Points

Cut Flowers and Wild Flowers.—

Arrangement	30 points
Quality of blooms	40 "
Number of varieties	15 "
Properly named	15

Lilies.—

Size and color of bloom	35 points
Number of perfect flowers and buds on stem	35
Arrangement	15
Properly named	15

Displays.—

Arrangement	40 points
Quality	45 "
Variety	15 "

Collections.—

Quality	45 points
Arrangement	25 "
Variety	30 "

Special Funds

OF THE

WORCESTER COUNTY HORTICULTURAL SOCIETY

The following is a list of the Special Funds of the Worcester County Horticultural Society the income of which is devoted to the purpose stated. The date prefixed to each indicates the year in which the fund was established.

1888.   Francis Henshaw Dewey Fund. $1,000.00.
Income to be used for the purchase of books.

1898.   William Eames Fund. $500.00.
Income to be used in prizes for the promotion of apple culture.

1906.   Frederick A. Blake Fund. $1,000.00.
Income only to be used in providing Medals to be awarded to the originators of new varieties of Fruits or Flowers, preference always being given to residents of Worcester County.

In case that the Worcester County Horticultural Society does not find occasion to award medals for New Fruits or Flowers, the said income may be used in special premiums for Orchids or other choice Greenhouse Plants and Flowers.

1907.   Obadiah Brown Hadwen Fund. $1,000.00.
Income to be used for meritorious exhibits of Flowers, Fruits and Vegetables.

1922.   Edwin Draper Fund. $300.00.
Income to be used in prizes for Horticultural exhibitions held under the direction of said Society.

1924.   Miss Frances Clary Morse Fund. $500.00.
Income to be used in prizes for Flowers.

Flowers, Plants, Fruits and Vegetables

1934

☞THE COMMITTEE ON ARRANGEMENTS AND EXHIBITIONS would direct the earnest attention of the Judge to *Rule 12*.

12. The Judges may exclude from competition all inferior specimens and may correct any errors that they think were without deliberate purpose.

Special Rules

1. EXHIBITORS WILL ADD VALUE TO THEIR EXHIBITS BY HAVING ALL SPECIMENS CORRECTLY AND LEGIBLY NAMED AND THE NUMBER OF VARIETIES WRITTEN ON THE ENTRY CARDS, NOTICE OF WHICH WILL BE TAKEN BY THE JUDGES IN AWARDING THE PREMIUMS.

2. WHILE IT IS EXPECTED THAT EXHIBITORS WILL TAKE PAINS TO CORRECTLY NAME THEIR EXHIBITS, THE JUDGES WILL NOT EXCLUDE AN EXHIBIT FOR MISTAKE IN NOMENCLATURE.

3. IN ALL EXHIBITIONS OF LILIES THE POLLEN MAY BE REMOVED.

By vote of the trustees, all entries must be made to the Secretary and all cards made out by him or his assistants.

Spring Exhibition

Thursday, March 22, 3 to 9 p. m.
Friday, March 23, 9 a. m. to 9 p. m.
Saturday, March 24, 9 a. m. to 9 p. m.
Sunday, March 25, 12 m. to 9 p. m.

All articles for this exhibition must be in the hall and ready for inspection by the judges by 1 o'clock Thursday

Class I	Garden Displays	400.00
Class II	Plant Displays	150.00
Class III	Rock Gardens Not to exceed 100 square feet	100.00
Class IV	Cut Flowers	75.00
Class V	Fruit	75.00
Class VI	Vegetables	75.00

Frederick A. Blake Fund

Class VII	Carnations	25.00

Worcester Garden Club Exhibit

Thursday, April 26

All articles for this exhibition must be in the hall and ready for inspection by the judges by 2 o'clock

This exhibition will be open to the public from 3 to 9 p. m.

Cut Flowers.—
No. 1. Twenty vases   5.00   4.00 3.00
Table Decorations.—
No. 2. For best table decoration, laid
for four covers, no restrictions. Notify the Secretary
two days in advance   7.00 6.00 5.00 4.00 3.00

Scale of Points by Which the Above Class is to be Judged
Arrangement of Flowers and quality.   50 points
Proportion and harmony of flowers
with accessories   30
Accessories   20

Carnations.—
No. 3. Vase or Basket, fifty flowers,
other green permissible   8.00 6.00 4.00
Plant Displays.—
No. 4. Flowering and Foliage Plants.
Sixty dollars may be used in
prizes.
Apple, twelve specimens.—
No. 5. For any variety, eight dollars
may be used for prizes.
Parsnip, twelve specimens.—
No. 6. Hollow Crown   2.00 1.50 1.00   .50
No. 7. Any other variety   2.00 1.50 1.00   .50
Rhubarb, twelve stalks.—
No. 8. Any variety   2.00 1.50 1.00   .50
Lettuce.—
No. 9. Six heads   2.00 1.50 1.00   .50
Radish.—
• No. 10. Two bunches. Six in each bunch   1.50 1.00   .50
Potato, twelve specimens.—
No. 11. Any named variety   2.00 1.50 1.00   .50

May Exhibition
Thursday, May 10

*All articles for this exhibition must be
in the hall and ready for inspection by
the judges by 2 o'clock*

This exhibition will be open to the public from 3 to 9 p. m.

Cut Flowers.—
    No. 12. Twenty vases   3.00 2.50 1.00
    No. 13. Medium basket   3.00 2.50 2.00 1.50 1.00

Spring Bulbs, open culture.—
    No. 14. Display   4.00 3.00 2.50 2.00

Pansy.—
    No. 15.. Twenty vases, one flower
            with foliage in a vase 3.00 2.50 2.00 1.50 1.00 .50

Zonale Geraniums, in bloom.—
    No. 16. Six plants   3.00 2.00 1.00 .50

Table Decorations.—
    No. 17. For best table decoration,
            laid for four covers, no re-
            strictions. Notify the Secre-
            tary two days in advance 7.00 6.00 5.00 4.00 3.00

SCALE OF POINTS BY WHICH THE ABOVE CLASS IS TO BE JUDGED

Arrangement of flowers and quality	50 points
Proportion and harmony of flowers with accessories	30
Accessories	20

Plant Displays.—
    No. 18. For exhibits—no restrictions as
            to where grown, or by whom
            $60.00 may be used for prizes.
            Notify the Secretary two days
            in advance.

Calendula.—
    No. 19. Arranged in Bowl or Basket   3.00 2.00 1.0

Dandelion.—
    No. 20. One-half peck   1.50 1.00 .50

Lettuce.—
    No. 21. Six heads   2.00 1.50 1.00 .50

Spinach.—
    No. 22. One-half peck   1.50 1.00 .50

Radish, two bunches, six in each bunch.—
    No. 23. Globe   1.50 1.00 .50

Rhubarb, twelve stalks.—
    No. 24. Linnæus   2.50 2.00 1.50 1.00 .50

Asparagus, two bunches, twelve specimens each.—
    No. 25. Any variety   3.00 2.50 2.00 1.50 1.00 .50

Onion.—
    No. 26. Two bunches, six in each bunch   1.50 1.00 .50

Thursday, June 7

All articles for this exhibition must be in the hall and ready for inspection by the judges by 2 o'clock

This exhibition will be open to the public from 3 to 9 p. m.

Cut Flowers.—

No. 27. Display	4.00	3.00	2.50	2.00	1.50	1.00
No. 28. Standard		3.00	2.50	2.00	1.50	1.00

Wild Flowers, fifteen vases.—

No. 29. Five stems in a vase. No
duplicates   3.00 2.00 1.50 1.00   .50

Azalea.—

No. 30. Display in vases   3.00 2.00 1.00

Iris, German.—

No. 31. Display   8.00 6.00 4.00 2.00

No. 32. Vase or Basket   3.00 2.50 2.00 1.50 1.00

Rhododendron.—

No. 33. Displays in vases   3.00 2.00

Peonies.—

No. 34. Vase or Basket   3.00 2.50 2.00 1.00

Lupinus.—

No. 35. Vase   3.00 2.00 1.50 1.00

Roses.—

No. 36. Vase of Roses. Five dollars
may be used in prizes.

Zonale Geraniums.—

No. 37. Twenty vases, one truss in each   3.00 2.00 1.00

Strawberries, twenty-four berries.—

No. 38. Five dollars may be used in prizes.

Asparagus, two bunches, twelve specimens each.—

No. 39. Any variety   2.50 2.00 1.50 1.00   .50

Cucumber.—

No. 40. Three specimens   2.00 1.50 1.00   .50

Spinach.—

No. 41. One-half peck   2.50 2.00 1.50 1.00

Rhubarb, twelve stalks.—

No. 42. Monarch   1.50 1.00 .50

No. 43. Victoria   2.50 2.00 1.50 1.00

Beet.—

No. 44. Twelve specimens   2.00 1.50 1.00 .50

Lettuce.—

No. 45. Six heads   2.00 1.50 1.00 .50

Onion.—

No. 46. Two bunches, six each   2.00 1.50 1.00 .50

Thursday, June 14

*All articles for this exhibition must be
in the hall and ready for inspection by
the judges by 2 o'clock*

This exhibition will be open to the public from 3 to 9 p. m.

Cut Flowers.—

No. 47. From hardy plants and shrubs
outdoor culture, *to be named*   5.00 4.00 3.00 2.00

Roses.—

No. 48. Vase H. P. roses, not to exceed
.ten blooms   3.00 2.00 1.00

No. 49. Vase H. T. roses, not exceeding
ten blooms   3.00 2.00 1.00

Peonies.—

No. 50. Best Display of Peonies.
Notify the Secretary two
days in advance   5.00 4.00 3.00 2.00

No. 51. Twenty vases, one flower in
each   4.00 3.00 2.00 1.00 .50

Foxglove.—

No. 52. Vase of twelve spikes   3.00 2.00 1.00 .50

Aquilegia.—

No. 53. Collection   3.00 2.50 2.00 1.00 .50

Begonia.—

No. 54. Four plants in bloom   3.00 2.00 1.00

Cherry, one quart.—

No. 55. For any named variety five
dollars may be used for prizes.

Strawberry, twenty-four berries.—

No. 56. Corsican   1.50 1.00 .50

No. 57. Senator Dunlap   1.50 1.00 .50

No. 58. Howard No. 17   3.00 2.50 2.00 1.50 1.00 .50

No. 59. Any other variety   2.00 1.50 1.00 .50

No. 60. New varieties   2.00 1.50 1.00 .50

Pea, one-half peck.—

No. 61. Any variety.   2.00 1.50 1.00 .50

Rose Exhibition

Thursday, June 21, open from 3 to 9 p. m.

*All articles for this exhibition must be
in the hall and ready for inspection by
the judges by 2 o'clock*

Roses.—
   No. 62. Twelve blooms of distinct named
        varieties of H. P. roses, outdoor
        culture   4.00 3.00 2.00 1.00
   No. 63. Six blooms of distinct named
        varieties of H. P. roses, out-
        door culture   3.00 2.00 1.00 .50
   No. 64. Collection of cut roses. Twelve
        dollars to be used in prizes.
   No. 65. Vase of roses, 12 blooms 3.00 2.50 2.00 1.50 1.00
   No. 66. Vase H. P. roses, not to exceed
        ten blooms   3.00 2.00 1.00
   No. 67. Vase H. T. roses, not exceeding
        ten blooms   3.00 2.00 1.00
   No. 68. Display of cut climbing roses.
        Fifteen dollars may be used in
        prizes.
   No. 69. Basket of roses   3.00 2.50 2.00 1.50

Special Prizes
Miss Frances C. Morse Fund

A. Table decoration of roses. Flowers
     grown by exhibitors   4.00 3.00 2.00 1.00

*   *   *

Peonies.—
   No. 70. Best Display of Peonies.
        Notify the Secretary two days in
        advance   5.00 4.00 3.00 2.00

Aquilegia.—
   No. 71. Bowl   2.50 2.00 1.50 1.00

Special Prizes
Obadiah Brown Hadwen Fund

Hardy Flowers, to be named.—
  B.   Display of outdoor varieties   5.00 4.00 3.00 2.00 1.00

*   *   *

Strawberry, twenty-four berries.—
  No. 72.   Howard No. 17   3.00 2.50 2.00 1.50 1.00   '.50
  No. 73.   Sample   1.50 1.00   .50
  No. 74.   Uncle Joe   2.00 1.50 1.00   .50
  No. 75.   Any other variety   2.00 1.50 1.00   .50
  No. 76.   Collections, not more than six
            varieties   5.00 4.00 3.00 2.00 1.00

Cherry, one quart.—
  No. 77.   Black Tartarian   2.00 1.50 1.00   .50
  No. 78.   Gov. Wood   2.00 1.50 1.00   .50
  No. 79.   Best display, ten dollars may be used for prizes.
  No. 80.   For varieties not scheduled, five dollars may be used
            for prizes.

Pea, one-half peck.—
  No. 81.   Thomas Laxton   2.00 1.50 1.00   .50
  No. 82.   Gradus   2.00 1.50 1.00   .50
  No. 83.   Any other variety   2.00 1.50 1.00   .50

Cabbage, three specimens.—
  No. 84.   Any named variety   2.50 2.00 1.50 1.00

Lettuce.—
  No. 85.   Six heads   2.00 1.50 1.00   .50

Scale of Points

Cut Flowers and Wild Flowers.—

Arrangement	30 points
Quality of blooms	40 "
Number of varieties	15 "
Properly named	15

Lilies.—

Size and color of bloom	35 points
Number of perfect flowers and buds on stem	35
Arrangement	15 "
Properly named	15

Displays.—

Arrangement	40 points
Quality	45 "
Variety	15 "

Collections.—

Quality	45 points
Arrangement	25 "
Variety	30 "

Table Decorations.—

Arrangement of flowers and quality	50 points
Proportion and harmony of flowers with accessories	30
Accessories	20

Thursday, June 28

*All articles for this exhibition must be
in the hall and ready for inspection by
the judges by 2 o'clock*

This exhibition will be open to the public from 3 to 9 p. m.

Cut Flowers.—
No. 86.   Twenty vases   3.00 2.50 2.00 1.50 1.00   .50
Dianthus Barbatus (Sweet William).—
No. 87.   Twelve vases, three clusters
          in a vase   3.00 2.50 2.00 1.50 1.00   .50
Campanula (Canterbury Bells).—
No. 88.   Display   4.00 3.00 2.00 1.00
Delphinium.—
No. 89.   One vase, not more than twelve
          spikes   4.00 3.50 3.00 2.50 2.00 1.50 1.00
Roses.—
No. 90.   Collection of Cut Roses. Ten
          dollars may be used in prizes.
Lilium Candidum.—
No. 91.   Vase   4.00 3.00 2.00 1.00

Special Prizes
Offered by Mr. Herbert R. Kinney

C.   Display of Cut Flowers on round
          tables   3.00 2.50 2.00 1.50 1.00
This number is intended for the growers who do not compete in
the call for twenty vases or displays during the year.

*   *   *

Strawberry, twenty-four berries.—
No. 92.   Downing's Bride   2.00 1.50 1.00   .50
No. 93.   Ten dollars may be used for
          prizes. Preference given to
          worthy varieties of recent
          introduction.
No. 94.   Best display   5.00 4.00 3.00 2.00 1.00

1934

Currant, twenty-four bunches.—

No. 95.   For any variety, five dollars may be used for prizes.

Cherry, one quart.—

No. 96.	Coe's Transparent		1.50	1.00	.50
No. 97.	Elton	2.00	1.50	1.00	.50
No. 98.	Black Eagle		1.50	1.00	.50
No. 99.	Montmorency	2.00	1.50	1.00	.50

Beet, open culture.—

No. 100.	Twelve specimens	2.50	2.00	1.50	1.00	.50

Carrot.—

No. 101.	Two bunches, six in each	2.00	1.50	1.00	.50

Bean, Snap, one-half peck.—

No. 102.	Any named variety	2.50	2.00	1.50	1.00	.50

Pea, one-half peck.

No. 103.	Sutton's Excelsior	2.00	1.50	1.00	.50
No. 104.	Any other variety	2.00	1.50	1.00	.50

Cucumber, three specimens.—

No. 105.	Any variety	1.50	1.00	.50

Thursday, July 5

*All articles for this exhibition must be
in the hall and ready for inspection by
the judges by 2 o'clock*

This exhibition will be open to the public from 3 to 9 p. m.

Cut Flowers.—

No. 106.   Twenty vases   4.00 3.00 2.50 2.00 1.50 1.00
No. 107.   Ten vases   2.50 2.00 1.50 1.00 .50

This number is intended for the growers who do not compete in call for 20 vases and displays during the year.

Basket.—

No. 108.   3.00 2.50 2.00 1.50 1.00

Japanese Iris.—

No. 109.   Display, twenty dollars may be used for prizes.

Delphinium.—

No. 110.   Display, fifteen dollars may be used for prizes.

Wild Flowers, no duplicates.—

No. 111.   Fifteen vases, five stems
          in a vase   2.50 2.00 1.50 1.00 .50

Roses.—

No. 112.   Display of cut climbing roses.   Ten dollars may be
          used in prizes.

Raspberry, Black Cap, one quart.—

No. 113.   Named variety   1.50 1.00 .50

Raspberry, one pint.—

No. 114.   Latham   2.00 1.50 1.00 .50
No. 115.   Varieties not scheduled, five dollars may be used for
          prizes.

Gooseberry, one quart.—

No. 116.   Any named variety   2.00 1.50 1.00 .50

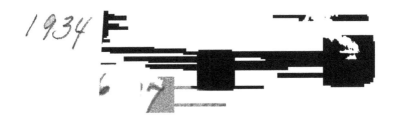

Currant, twenty-four bunches.—

No. 117.	Red Cross	1.50	1.00	.50
No. 118.	Perfection	2.00 1.50	1.00	.50
No. 119.	White Grape	1.50	1.00	.50
No. 120.	Versaillaise	2.00 1.50	1.00	.50
No. 121.	Any other variety	2.00 1.50	1.00	.50

Bean, Snap, one-half peck.—

No. 122.	Wax	2.50	2.00	1.50	1.00
No. 123.	Green Pod	2.50	2.00	1.50	1.00

Pea, one-half peck.—

No. 124.	Alderman	2.00	1.50	1.00	.50
No. 125.	Telephone	2.50	2.00	1.50	1.00
No. 126.	Display		3.00	2.00	1.00

Display of Vegetables.—

No. 127. Not to exceed 24 square feet, $20.00 may be used for prizes. Notify the Secretary two days in advance.

Tomato, twelve specimens.—

No. 128.	Any named variety	2.00	1.50 1.00	.50

Sweet Pea Exhibition

Thursday, July 12

*All articles for this exhibition must be
in the hall and ready for inspection by
the judges by 2 o'clock*

This exhibition will be open to the public from 3 to 9 p. m.

Sweet Peas, annual.—

No. 129. Ten vases, not more than 25
flower stems in a vase   4.00 3.00 2.00

No. 130. Table Decoration—Sweet Peas,
laid for four covers, Gypsophila
may be used. Notify the Secre-
two days in advance   5.00 4.00 3.00 2.00 1.00

SCALE OF POINTS BY WHICH THE ABOVE CLASS IS TO BE JUDGED

Arrangement of flowers and quality   50 points

Proportion and harmony of flowers
with accessories   30   "

Accessories   20

Sweet Peas.—

No. 131. Basket, any green may be used.

4.00 3.00 2.00 1.00

Obadiah Brown Hadwen Fund

D. Collection of Sweet Peas, fifteen dollars may be used in prizes.

*   *   *

Cut Flowers.—

No. 132. Display, not exceeding 30
square feet   4.00 3.00 2.50 2.00 1.50 1.00

Lilium Regale.—

No. 133. Fifteen dollars may be used in prizes.

Centaurea.—

No. 134. Display, Gypsophila may be
used   4.00 3.00 2.50 2.00

Petunia.—
   No. 135. Twenty vases, one flower in
         each   3.00 2.50 2.00 1.00 .50

Apple, twelve specimens.—
   No. 136. Any variety   2.00 1.50 1.00 .50

Blackberry, one quart.—
   No. 137. Any variety   1.50 1.00 .50

Currants, twenty-four bunches.—
   No. 138. Wilder   2.00 1.50 1.00 .50

Cucumber.—
   No. 139. Three specimens   1.50 1.00 .50

Cabbage, three specimens.—
   No. 140. Any variety   2.00 1.50 1.00 .50

Lettuce.—
   No. 141. Twelve heads   2.00 1.50 1.00 .50

Squash, three specimens.—
   No. 142. Summer   2.00 1.50 1.00 .50

Potato, twelve specimens.—
   No. 143. Any variety   2.00 1.50 1.00 .50

Thursday, July 19

*All articles for this exhibition must be
in the hall and ready for inspection by
the judges by 2 o'clock*

This exhibition will be open to the public from 3 to 9 p. m.

Cut Flowers.—
No. 144. Display   4.00 3.00 2.50 2.00 1.50 1.00

Antirrhinum (Snap Dragon).—
No. 145. Fifteen vases, three spikes
      in a vase   3.00 2.00 1.00 .50

Table Decorations.—
No. 146. For best table decoration
      laid for four covers. Flowers
      to be grown by the exhibitor.
      Notify the Secretary two days
      in advance   5.00 4.00 3.00 2.00 1.00

SCALE OF POINTS BY WHICH THE ABOVE CLASS IS TO BE JUDGED

Arrangement of flowers and quality	50 points
Proportion and harmony of flowers with accessories	30
Accessories	20

Sweet Peas, annual.—
No. 147. Five vases, 25 flower stems
      in vase   3.00 2.50 2.00 1.50 1.00

Begonia, tuberous rooted.—
No. 148. Twelve vases   4.00 3.00 2.00 1.00

Apple, twelve specimens.—
No. 149. Yellow Transparent   2.00 1.50 1.00 .50

Blackberry, one quart.—
No. 150. Any variety, five dollars may be used for prizes.

Pear, twelve specimens.—
No. 151. Any named variety, five dollars may be used for
      prizes.

Corn, twelve ears.—
    No. 152. Sweet, any named variety   2.00 1.50 1.00   .50

Tomato, twelve specimens.—
    No. 153. Any named variety   2.00 1.50 1.00   .50

Bean, Shell, one-half peck.—
    No. 154. Any named variety   2.00 1.50 1.00   .50

Potato, twelve specimens.—
    No. 155. Irish Cobbler   2.00 1. 0 1.00   .50
    No. 156. Any other variety   2.00 1.50 1.00   .50

Thursday, July 26

*All articles for this exhibition must be
in the hall and ready for inspection by
the judges by 2 o'clock*

This exhibition will be open to the public from 3 to 9 p. m.

Cut Flowers.—

| No. 157. | Standard | 4.00 | 3.00 | 2.50 | 2.00 | 1.50 | 1.00 |
| No. 158. | Ten vases | | | 2.50 | 2.00 | 1.50 | 1.00 | .50 |

This number is intended for the growers who do not compete
in the call for 20 vases and displays during the year.

Gladiolus.—

No. 159. Twenty vases, one spike in
each   4.00 3.00 2.00 1.00

Phlox, perennial.—

No. 160. Fifteen vases, one cluster
in each   3.00 2.00 1.00 .50

Annuals.—

No. 161. Display   3.00 2.50 2.00 1.50 1.00

Apple, twelve specimens.—

No. 162.	Astrachan	2.00	1.50	1.00	.50
No. 163.	Oldenburg	2.00	1.50	1.00	.50
No. 164.	Yellow Transparent	2.00	1.50	1.00	.50

Blackberry, one quart.—

No. 165. Any varieties, five dollars may be used for prizes.

Pear, twelve specimens.—

No. 166. Any variety   1.50 1.00 .50

Peach, twelve specimens.—

No. 167. Any variety, five dollars may be used for prizes.

Plum, twelve specimens.—

No. 168. Red June   1.50 1.00 .50

Bean, Shell, one-half peck.—

| No. 169. | Dwarf Horticultural | 2.00 | 1.50 | 1.00 | .50 |
| No. 170. | Any other variety | 2.00 | 1.50 | 1.00 | .50 |

Corn, twelve ears.—
   No. 171. Any named variety   2.00 1.50 1.00   .50

Squash, three specimens.—
   No. 172. Summer   2.00 1.50 1.00   .50

Potato, twelve specimens.—
   No. 173. Rose   2.00 1.50 1.00   .50
   No. 174. Varieties not scheduled   2.00 1.50 1.00   .30

Vegetables.—
   No. 175. Display, Round Table, $15.00 may be used for
     prizes. Notify the Secretary two days in advance.

Thursday, August 2

*All articles for this exhibition must be
in the hall and ready for inspection by
the judges by 2 o'clock*

This exhibition will be open to the public from 3 to 9 p. m.

Cut Flowers.—
No. 176.　Basket　　　　　4.00 3.00 2.50 2.00 1.50 1.00

Gladiolus.—
No. 177.　Display　　　　　8.00 6.00 5.00 4.00 3.00

Asters.—
No. 178.　Twenty vases, one bloom in
　　　each　　　　　　　3.00 2.50 2.00 1.00 　.50

Salpiglossis.—
No. 179.　Display　　　　　　　4.00 3.00 2.00

Phlox, perennial.—
No. 180.　Fifteen vases, one cluster
　　.　in each　　　　　3.00 2.00 1.50 1.00 　.50

Zinnia.—
No. 181.　Twenty vases, one flower in
　　　each　　　　　　3.00 2.50 2.00 1.50 1.00 　.50

Wild Flowers, no duplicates.—
No. 182.　Fifteen vases, no duplicates.
　　　Five stems in a vase　　2.50 2.00 1.50 1.00 　.50

Special Prizes
Offered by Mr. Herbert R. Kinney

E.　Table Decorations.　For the best
　　　table decorations　　　3.00 2.50 2.00 1.50 1.00

This call is intended for exhibitors who do not exhibit in other
table decorations during the year. Notify the Secretary two days
in advance.

Apple, twelve specimens.—
No. 183. Oldenburg 2.00 1.50 1.00 .50
No. 184. Williams 2.00 1.50 1.00 .50

Peach, twelve specimens.—
No. 185. Any variety 2.00 1.50 1.00 .50

Cabbage, three specimens.—
No. 186. Copenhagen 2.00 1.50 1.00 .50
No. 187. Any other named variety 2.00 1.50 1.00 .50

Corn, twelve ears.—
No. 188. Yellow, Sweet 2.50 2.00 1.50 1.00 .50

Squash, three specimens.—
No. 189. Any named variety (excepting
summer varieties) 2.00 1.50 1.00 .50

Tomato, open culture, twelve specimens.—
No. 190. Any named variety 2.00 1.50 1.00 .50

Gladiolus Exhibition

Thursday, August 9

*All articles for this exhibition must be
in the hall and ready for inspection by
the judges by 2 o'clock*

This exhibition will be open to the public from 3 to 9 p. m.

Gladiolus.—
    No. 191.   Display. Notify the Secretary two days in advance.
         Forty dollars may be used in prizes.
    No. 192.   Standard of Gladioli   3.00 2.50 2.00 1.00   .50
    No. 193.   Twenty vases, one spike in
         each   4.00 3.00 2.00 1.00   .50

Aster, large flowered, long stem.—
    No. 194.   Vase of 20 blooms   3.00 2.50 2.00 1.00   .50

Salpiglossis.—
    No. 195.   Basket   2.50 2.00 1.00   .50

Phlox Drummondi.—
    No. 196.   Display   2.00 1.50 1.00   .50

Annuals.—
    No. 197.   Display, fifteen dollars may be used in prizes.

Apple, twelve specimens.—
    No. 198.   Williams   2.00 1.50 1.00   .50
    No. 199.   For varieties not scheduled, five dollars may be
         used for prizes.

Apple, crab, twenty-four specimens.—
    No. 200.   Varieties not scheduled   1.50 1.00   .50

Pear, twelve specimens.—
    No. 201.   Clapp's Favorite   3.00 2.50 2.00 1.50 1.00   .50
    No. 202.   For varieties not scheduled, five dollars may be
         used for prizes.

Peach, twelve specimens.—
    No. 203.   Carman   1. 0 1.00   .50
    No. 204.   Any other variety   1.50 1.00   .50

Plum, twelve specimens.—
    No. 205. Washington   1.50 1.00 .50
    No. 206. Japanese varieties, five dollars
               may be used for prizes.

Bean, Shell, one-half peck.—
    No. 207. Dwarf, any variety   2.00 1.50 1.00 .50
    No. 208. Pole, any variety   2.00 1.50 1.00 .50

Bean, String, one-half peck.—
    No. 209. Kentucky Wonder   2.00 1.50 1.00 .50

Corn, Sweet, twelve ears.—
    No. 210. Any named variety   2.50 2.00 1.50 1.00

Tomato, twelve specimens.—
    No. 211. Any named variety   2.50 2.00 1.50 1.00 .50

Mushroom, native.—
    No. 212. Collection of edible varieties, prizes will be awarded.

Cucumber, for pickles.—
    No. 213. One-half peck   2.00 1.50 1.00 .50

Thursday, August 16

*All articles for this exhibition must be
in the hall and ready for inspection by
the judges by 2 o'clock*

This exhibition will be open to the public from 3 to 9 p. m.

Zinnia.—

No. 214. Display, notify the Secretary
two days in advance 4.00 3.00 2.50 2.00 1.50 1.00

Dahlia.—

No. 215. Display. Notify the Secretary
two days in advance   5.00 4.00 3.00 2.00 1.00

Obadiah Brown Hadwen Fund

Display of Garden Flowers.—

F. Not to exceed 24 square feet.
Notify the Secretary two days
in advance   4.00 3.50 3.00 2.50 2.00 1.00

* * *

Aster, single or anemone.—

No. 216. Vase   2.00 1.50 1.00 .50

Plums, twelve specimens.—

No. 217. Bradshaw   3.00 2.00 1.50 1.00 .50

No. 218. Imperial Gage   2.00 1.50 1.00 .50

No. 219. Guiei   1.50 1.00 .50

No. 220. For varieties not scheduled, three
dollars may be used for prizes.

Peach, twelve specimens.—

No. 221. Five dollars may be used in prizes.

Bean, Pole, one-half peck.—

No. 222. Shell   2.50 2.00 1.50 1.00

No. 223. String, any variety   2.50 2.00 1.50 1.00

Corn, twelve ears.—

No. 224. Sweet, not less than twelve rows
2.50 2.00 1.50 1.00

Vegetables.—

No. 225. Display of vegetables from
Home Gardens to cover 12
square feet   6.00 5.00 4.00 3.00 2.00 1.00

Scale of Points

Cut Flowers and Wild Flowers.—

Arrangement	30 points
Quality of blooms	40 "
Number of varieties	15 "
Properly named	15

Lilies.—

Size and color of bloom	35 points
Number of perfect flowers and buds on stem	35
Arrangement	15
Properly named	15 .

Displays.—

Arrangement	40 points
Quality	45 "
Variety	15 "

Collections.—

Quality	45 points
Arrangement	25 "
Variety	30 "

Table Decorations.—

Arrangement of flowers and quality	50 points
Proportion and harmony of flowers with accessories	30 "
Accessories	20

Thursday, August 23

All articles for this exhibition must be
in the hall and ready for inspection by
the judges by 2 o'clock

This exhibition will be open to the public from 3 to 9 p. m.

Cut Flowers.—
No. 226. Display 5.00 4.00 3.50 3.00 2.50 2.00 1.50 1.00
No. 227. Basket   3.00 2.50 2.00 1.50 1.00

Aster, large flowered.—
No. 228. Twenty vases, three blooms
          in each   3.00 2.50 2.00 1.00 .50

Lilies.—
No. 229. Display   5.00 4.00 3.00 2.00
          Notify the Secretary two days
          in advance.

Zinnia, Lilliput variety.—
No. 230. Display   3.00 2.00 1.00 .50

Begonia, tuberous rooted.—
No. 231. Display   5.00 4.00 3.00 2.00 1.00

Verbena.—
No. 232. Basket or Bowl   2.50 2.00 1.50 1.00 .50

Apples, twelve specimens.—
No. 233. Porter   1.50 1.00 .50
No. 234. Gravenstein   2.50 2.00 1.50 1.00 .50
No. 235. For varieties not scheduled, five
          dollars may be used for prizes.

Plum.—
No. 236. Display, no restriction as to
          arrangements   4.00 3.00 2.00 1.00

Peach, twelve specimens.—
No. 237. Any variety   1.50 1.00 .50

Squash, three specimens.—
No. 238. Any named variety   2.50 2.00 1.50 1.00

Pepper, twelve specimens.—
   No. 239. Harris's Early   2.50 2.00 1.50 1.00
   No. 240. Bell Type   2.50 2.00 1.50 1.00

Vegetables.—
   No. 241. Display, not to exceed 24 square feet, $20.00 may
            be used for prizes. Notify the Secretary two days in
            advance.

Dahlia Exhibition

Thursday, August 30

*All articles for this exhibition must be
in the hall and ready for inspection by
the judges by 2 o'clock*

This exhibition will be open to the public from 3 to 9 p. m.

Cut Flowers.—

No. 242. Display   5.00 4.00 3.00 2.50 2.00 1.50 1.00

No. 243. Standard   3.00 2.50 2.00 1.50 1.00 .50

This number is intended for the growers who do not compete in
call for 20 vases and displays during the year.

Dahlia.—

No. 244. Display, thirty-five dollars may be used in prizes.
Notify the Secretary two days in advance.

LARGE FLOWERED.—

No. 245. Twenty vases, one flower in
each   4.00 3.00 2.00 1.50 1.00

Aster.—

No. 246. Vase of large flowered   3.00 2.50 2.00 1.00 .50

No. 247. Display, not exceeding
25 square feet   5.00 4.00 3.00 2.00 1.00

Scabiosa.—

No. 248. Vase   2.50 2.00 1.50 1.00 .50

Apple, twelve specimens.—

No. 249. Gravenstein   3.00 2.50 2.00 1.50 1.00 .50

No. 250. Maiden's Blush   1.50 1.00 .50

No. 251. Wealthy   2.50 2.00 1.50 1.00 .50

Apple, Crab, twenty-four specimens.—

No. 252. Hyslop   2.50 2.00 1.50 1.00 .50

Pear, twelve specimens.—

No. 253. Bartlett   3.00 2.50 2.00 1.50 1.00 .50

No. 254. Varieties not scheduled, five dollars may be used for
prizes.

Peach, twelve specimens.—

No. 255. Champion   1.50 1.00 .50

No. 256. Oldmixon   2.00 1.00 .50

No. 257. Elberta   2.50 2.00 1.50 1.00 .50

No. 258. Seedlings   1.50 1.00 .50
No. 259. Crawford (early)   2.00 1.50 1.00 .50
No. 260. Varieties not scheduled, five dollars may be used
    for prizes.
No. 261. New varieties. Five dollars may be used in prizes.

Plum, twelve specimens.—
No. 262. Golden Varieties   1.50 1. 0 .50
No. 263. Lombard   2.00 1.50 1. 0 .50
No. 264. Quackenboss   1.50 1. 0 .50
No. 265. Burbank   2.00 1.50 1.00 .50
No. 266. Moore's Arctic   1.50 1. 0 .50
No. 267. For Japanese varieties not scheduled, five dollars
    may be used for prizes.
No. 268. Other varieties not scheduled, five dollars may be
    used for prizes.

Grape, three clusters.—
No. 269. Green Mountain   2.00 1.50 1.00 .50
No. 270. Moore's   1.50 1.00 .50

Pepper, twelve specimens.—
No. 271. Squash   2.00 1.50 1.00 .50
No. 272. Any other variety   2.00 1.50 1.00 .50

Tomato, twelve specimens.—
No. 273. Beauty   2.50 2.00 1.50 1.00 .50
No. 274. Any other variety 2.50 2.00 1.50 1.00 .50

Bean, one-half peck.—
No. 275. Dwarf Lima   2.00 1.50 1.00 .50
No. 276. Pole Lima   2.00 1.50 1.00 .50

Cabbage, three specimens.—
No. 277. Any named variety   2.00 1.50 1.00 .50

Celery, blanched (named) six specimens.—
No. 278. Any variety   2.00 1.50 1.00 .50

Carrot, twelve specimens.—
No. 279. Any variety   2.50 2.00 1.50 1.00 .50

Egg Plant.—
No. 280. Three specimens   2.00 1.50 1.00

Mushroom, native.—
No. 281. Collection of edible varieties, prizes will be awarded.

Grape Exhibition

Thursday, September 6

*All articles for this exhibition must be
in the hall and ready for inspection by
the judges by 2 o'clock*

This exhibition will be open to the public from 3 to 9 p. m.

Cut Flowers.—

No. 282. Twenty vases 5.00 4.00 3.50 3.00 2.50 2.00 1.00

Dahlia.—

No. 283. Fifty vases, one flower in each. Twenty-five dollars
may be used for prizes.

No. 284. Twelve vases, one flower in each. This number is
intended for the growers who do not compete in
other classes for Dahlias during the year.

2.50 2.00 1.50 1.00 .50

No. 285. Single varieties, twenty vases 3.00 2.50 2.00 1.00

No. 286. Basket of large flowered 3.00 2.50 2.00 1.00

POMPON.

No. 287. Twenty vases, three sprays in
each 3.00 2.50 2.00 1.00

Cosmos.—

No. 288. Vase or basket 2.50 2.00 1.50 1.00 .50

Apple, twelve specimens.—

No. 289. American Beauty or Sterling 1.50 1.00 .50

No. 290. Twenty-ounce 1.50 1.00 .50

Pear, twelve specimens.—

No. 291. Louise Bonne de Jersey 1.50 1.00 .50

No. 292. Urbaniste 1.50 1.00 .50

No. 293. Varieties not scheduled, five dollars may be used
for prizes.

Peach, twelve specimens.—

No. 294. Crawford (late) 2.00 1.50 1.00 .50

No. 295. Display, no restriction as to
arrangement 8.00 6.00 4.00 3.00

Plum, twelve specimens.—

No. 296. Any variety   2.00 1.50 1.00 .50

Grape, three clusters.—

No. 297. Brighton   1.50 1.00 .50
No. 298. Campbell   1.50 1.00 .50
No. 299. Lindley   1.50 1.00 .50
No. 300. Ontario   1.50 1.00 .50
No. 301. Worden   2.50 2.00 1.50 1.00 .50
No. 302. Concord   2.50 2.00 1.50 1.00 .50
No. 303. Delaware   2.00 1.50 1.00 .50
No. 304. Niagara   2.50 2.00 1.50 1.00 .50
No. 305. Pocklington   1.50 1.00 .50
No. 306. Moore's Diamond   1.50 1.00 .50
No. 307. For other varieties, ten dollars may be used for prizes.
No. 308. Display of Grapes. Ten dollars may be used for prizes.
No. 309. New varieties, five dollars may be used for prizes.

Quince, twelve specimens.—

No. 310. Any variety   2.00 1.50 1.00 .50

Melon, three specimens.—

No. 311. Green Flesh   2.00 1.50 1.00 .50
No. 312. Yellow Flesh   2.00 1.50 1.00 .50
No. 313. Water   2.00 1.50 1.00 .50

Tomato.—

No. 314. Display   4.00 3.00 2.50 2.00 1.00

Vegetables.— .

No. 315. Display to cover 24 square
          feet. Notify the Secretary
          two days in advance   7.00 6.00 5.00 4.00 3.00

Thursday, September 13

*All articles for this exhibition must be
in the hall and ready for inspection by
the judges by 2 o'clock*

This exhibition will be open to the public from 3 to 9 p. m.

Basket.—

No. 316.   4.00 3.00 2.50 2.00 1.50 1.00

Display of Flower Arrangement.—

No. 317.   Twelve receptacles, no restrictions as to kind of tables
used, not to cover more than 24 square feet. Flowers to
be grown by exhibitor. Notify the Secretary two days
in advance. Twenty-five dollars may be used in prizes.

SCALE OF POINTS BY WHICH THE ABOVE CLASS IS TO BE JUDGED

Arrangement of flowers	40 points
Proportion and harmony of flowers with receptacles	35
Quality of flowers	25

Celosia.—

No. 318.   Display   3.00 2.50 2.00 1.50 1.00

Notify the Secretary two days in advance.

Edwin Draper Fund

Begonia, tuberous rooted.—

G.   Display of Potted Plants,   Fifteen dollars may be used in
prizes.   ·   *   *   *

No. 318½.   Cut Flowers in vases.   Ten dollars may be used in
prizes.

Apple, twelve specimens.—

No. 319.   Hubbardston   2.00 1.50 1.00   .50
No. 320.   For other varieties not scheduled, five dollars may be
used for prizes.

Pear, twelve specimens.—

No. 321.   Seckel   3.00 2.50 2.00 1.50 1.00   .50
No. 322.   Any variety, not scheduled   1.50 1.00   .50
No. 323.   Display, no restriction as to
arrangement   6.00 5.00 4.00 3.00 2.00

Notify the Secretary two days in advance.

Quince, twelve specimens.—

No. 324. Orange   2.00 1.50 1.00   .50

Special Prizes
Offered by Miss Frances C. Morse

H.   For most artistic table arrangement of
       Marigolds   4.00 3.00 2.00 1.00

*   *   *

Potato, six varieties (named).—

No. 325.   Twelve specimens of each
                        5.00 4.00 3.00 2.00 1.50 1.00

Squash, three specimens.—

No. 326.   Warren   2.00 1.50 1.00   .50
No. 327.   Golden Hubbard   2.50 2.00 1.50 1.00   .50
No. 328.   For varieties not scheduled, five dollars may be used
             for prizes.

Cabbage, three specimens.—

No. 329.   Red   2.00 1.50 1.00   .50
No. 330.   Savoy   1.50 1.00   .50
No. 331.   Any other variety   2.50 2.00 1.50 1.00   .50

Cauliflower.—

No. 332.   Three specimens   2.50 2.00 1.50 1.00   .50

Turnip.—

No. 333.   Twelve specimens   1.50 1.00   .50

Broccoli.—

No. 334.   Three specimens   2.00 1.50 1.00   .50

Thursday, September 20

*All articles for this exhibition must be
in the hall and ready for inspection by
the judges by 2 o'clock*

· This exhibition will be open to the public from 3 to 9 p. m.

Cut Flowers.—
No. 335. Display, not exceeding 30 square
feet   · 5.00 4.00 3.50 3.00 2.50 2.00 1.50 1.00

Cosmos.—
No. 336. Display. Notify the Secretary
two days in advance   3:00 2.00 1.50 1.00   .50

Table Decorations.—
No. 337. For best table decoration laid
for four covers, no restrictions.
Notify the Secretary two days
in advance
6.00 5.00 4.50 4.00 3.00 2.00 1.50 1.00

SCALE OF POINTS BY WHICH THE ABOVE CLASS IS TO BE JUDGED

Arrangement and quality	50 points
Proportion and harmony of flowers with accessories	30
Accessories	20

Marigold.—
No. 338. Display. ·Notify the Secre-
tary two days in advance   3.00 2.00 1.00   .50

Apple, one standard box.—
No. 339. McIntosh   4.00 3.00 2.00 1.00   .50

Apple, twelve specimens.—
No. 340. Tompkins King   2.00 1.50 1.00   .50
No. 341. McIntosh   ·   3.00 2.50 2.00 1.50 1.00   .50

Pear, twelve specimens.—
No. 342. Sheldon   3.00 2.00 1.50 1.00   .50

Squash, three specimens.—
No. 343. Delicious   2.00 1.50 1.00   .50
No. 344. Any other variety, not scheduled 2.50 2.00 1.50 1.00

Cauliflower, three specimens.—
    No. 345.   2.00 1.50 1.00   .50

Vegetables.—
    No. 346. Collection not to exceed 25
            varieties   10.00 8.00 7.00 6.00 5.00
            Notify the Secretary two days in advance.

Thursday, September 27

All articles for this exhibition must be in the hall and ready for inspection by the judges by 2 o'clock

This exhibition will be open to the public from 3 to 9 p. m.

Basket.—
No. 347.   Twenty dollars may be used in prizes.

Dried Flowers, Statice, Strawflowers, Lunaria (Honesty).—
No. 348.   4.00 3.50 2.00 1.00

Apple, one standard box.—
No. 349.   Any variety not scheduled
                                  4.00 3.00 2.00 1.00   .50

Apple, twelve specimens.—
No. 350.   Sutton Beauty   2.00 1.50 1.00   .50

Display of Fruit.—
No. 351.   Not to exceed 20 square feet. Thirty dollars may be used in prizes.

Pear, twelve specimens.—
No. 352.   Bosc   3.00 2.00 1.50 1.00   .50

Grape, open culture.—
No. 353.   Collection of not less than five varieties, three clusters each.

Table Decorations—Fruit.—
No. 354.   For the best table decoration laid for four covers, no restrictions. Notify the Secretary two days in advance   .   4.00 3.00 2.00 1.00

Pumpkins, three specimens.—
No. 355.   Sweet   2.00 1.50 1.00   .50

Cabbage, three specimens.—
No. 356.   Any named variety   2.50 2.00 1.50 1.00   .50

Parsley.—
No. 357.   One-half peck   2.50 2.00 1.50 1.00   .50

Peppers.—
No. 358. Collection   3.00 2.50 2.00 1.50 1.00

Celery, blanched, six specimens.—
No. 359. Golden   2.50 2.00 1.50 1.00
No. 359½. Other varieties   2.50 2.00 1.50 1.00

Squash, three specimens.—
No. 360. Blue Hubbard   3.00 2.50 2.00 1.50 1.00

Special Prizes
Offered by Mr. Herbert R. Kinney

I. Display of vegetables from
Home Gardens to
cover 16 square feet 5.00 4.00 3.00 2.50 2.00 1.00

Fruit and Vegetable Exhibition
Thursday, October 4

All articles for this exhibition must be
in the hall and ready for inspection by
the judges by 2 o'clock

This exhibition will be open to the public from 3 to 9 p. m.

Ferns.—
No. 361. Display, potted plants, named varieties. Twenty dollars may be used in prizes.

Specimen Fern.—
No. 362. One plant   3.00 2.00 1.00

Cut Flowers.—
No. 363. Display—$40.00 may be awarded in prizes.

Basket.—
No. 364. Fifteen dollars may be used in prizes.

Hardy Chrysanthemum, out-door culture.—
No. 365. Plants. Fifteen dollars may be used in prizes.
No. 366. Cut flowers in vases. Ten dollars may be used in prizes.

Apple, one standard box.—
No. 367. Baldwin   4.00 3.00 2.00 1.00 .50
No. 368. Any other variety except
          McIntosh   4.00 3.00 2.00 1.00 .50

Apple, twelve specimens.—
No. 369. Baldwin   . 3.50 3.00 2.50 2.00 1.50 1.00 .50
No. 370. Bellflower   1.50 1.00 .50
No. 371. Winter Banana   1.50 1.00 .50
No. 372. Peck's   1.50 1.00 .50
No. 373. R. I. Greening   3.00 2.00 1.50 1.00 .50
No. 374. Northern Spy   3.00 2.00 1.50 1.00 .50
No. 375. Palmer   1.50 1.00 .50
No. 376. Roxbury Russet   3.00 2.00 1.50 1.00 .50
No. 377. Cortland   2.00 1.50 1.00 .50
No. 378. Opalescent   1.50 1.00 .50
No. 379. Delicious   2.50 2.00 1.50 1.00 .50
No. 380. Collection, not to exceed
          10 varieties   5.00 4.00 3.00 2.50 2.00
No. 381. New varieties, five dollars may be used in prizes.

No. 382. Sweet varieties not scheduled, five dollars may be used for prizes.

No. 383. For varieties other than sweet not scheduled, fifteen dollars may be used for prizes.

No. 384. For varieties that have been scheduled, fifteen dollars may be used.

Pear, twelve specimens.—

No. 385.	Angouleme		1.50	1.00	.50
No. 386.	Clairgeau		2.00	1.50	1.00 .50
No. 387.	Lawrence	3.00	2.00	1.50	1.00 .50
No. 388.	Winter Nelis		1.50	1.00	.50
No. 389.	Anjou	3.00 2.50	2.00	1.50	1.00 .50
No. 390.	Comice			1.00	.50

No. 391. For varieties not scheduled, ten dollars may be used for prizes.

Grape, open culture.—

No. 392. For any variety, six clusters, ten dollars may be used for prizes.

Peach, twelve specimens.—

No. 393. Any variety, named, ten dollars may be used for prizes.

Quince, twelve specimens.—

No. 394.	Champion	2.00	1.50	1.00	.50

Cauliflower.—

No. 395.	Three specimens	2.50	2.00	1.50	1.00

Celery, blanched, six specimens.—

No. 396.	Golden	2.50	2.00	150	1.00 .50
No. 397.	Any other varieties, not scheduled	2.00	1.50	1.00	.50

Endive.—

No. 398.	Six specimens	1.50	1.00	.50

Leeks.—

No. 399.	Twelve specimens	1.50	1.00	.50

Onion, twelve specimens.—

No. 400. For varieties, five dollars may be used for prizes.

Salsify.—

No. 401.	Twelve specimens	1.50	1.00	.50

Turnip, twelve specimens.—

No. 402.	Purple Top Globe	2.00	1.50	1.00	.50
No. 403.	Any variety, not scheduled	2.00	1.50	1.00	.50

Chrysanthemum Exhibition

Thursday, Nov. 8, 3 to 9 p. m.
Friday, Nov. 9, 9 a. m. to 9 p. m.
Saturday, Nov. 10, 9 a. m. to 9 p. m.
Sunday, Nov. 11, 12 m. to 9 p. m.

*All articles for this exhibition must be
in the hall and ready for inspection by
the judges by 1 o'clock Thursday*

Chrysanthemums.—

No. 404.	Twelve blooms, not less than six varieties, to be named	12.00	10.00	8.00
No. 405.	Collection of twenty-five large blooms, long stems	20.00	15.00	10.00
No. 406.	Pompoms, display in vases	5.00 4.00	3.00	2.00
No. 407.	Single varieties, display in vases	5.00 4.00	3.00	2.00
No. 408.	Anemones, display in vases	5.00 4.00	3.00	2.00
No. 409.	Six specimen plants	10.00	8.00	6.00
No. 410.	One specimen plant	3.00	2.00	1.00

Commercial Growers.—

No. 411.	Chrysanthemums, vase of white	4.00	3.00	2.00
No. 412.	Chrysanthemums, vase of yellow	4.00	3.00	2.00
No. 413.	Chrysanthemums, vase of pink	4.00	3.00	2.00

Note. Six flowers in each, one variety in each vase. Stems not less than two feet.

Non-commercial Growers.—

No. 414.	Chrysanthemums, vase of white	4.00	3.00	2.00
No. 415.	Chrysanthemums, vase of yellow	4.00	3.00	2.00
No. 416.	Chrysanthemums, vase of pink	4.00	3.00	2.00

Note. Six flowers in each, one variety in each vase. Stems not less than two feet.

Chrysanthemums.—

No. 417.	Basket of Pompons	4.00	3.00	2.00	1.00
No. 418.	Basket of Single	4.00	3.00	2.00	1.00
No. 419.	Basket of Anemones	4.00	3.00	2.00	1.00

Frederick A. Blake Fund

J. **Chrysanthemums.**—Best bloom 4.00 3.00 2.00

Obadiah Brown Hadwen Fund

K. **Chrysanthemums.**—Large Flowers. Basket. Fifteen dollars to be awarded in prizes.

Special Prizes
Offered by Mrs. Mabel Knowles Gage

L. **Table Decorations**—Chrysanthemums predominating— Notify the Secretary two days in advance. Fifty dollars to be used in prizes.

* * *

Special Display of Plants.—
>No. 420. Three hundred and fifty dollars may be used for prizes.

Persons competing for these premiums, must notify the Secretary previous to 6 p. m. Monday, November 6.
>No. 421. For exhibits—no restrictions as to where grown, or by whom—$75.00 may be used for prizes.

Fern Globes.—
>No. 422. 3.00 2.00 1.50 1.00

Glass Fernery.—
>No. 423. Other than Fern Globe 4.00 3.00 2.00 1.00

Wild Fruits and Berries.—
>No. 424. Display 5.00 4.00 3.00 2.50 1.50 1.00

Physalis Franchettii (Chinese Lanterns).—
>No. 425. Basket 4.00 3.00 2.00 1.00

Fruit Display.—
>No. 426. No restriction as to arrangement. $40.00 may be used in prizes. Notify the Secretary two days in advance.

Apple, five standard boxes.—
>No. 427. Any variety 15.00 10.00 5.00 4.00

Apples, forty-nine specimens.—

No. 428.	Baldwin	6.00	5.00	4.00	3.00	2.00	1.0
No. 429.	McIntosh	6.00	5.00	4.00	3.00	2.00	1.0
No. 430.	Delicious		5.00	4.00	3.00	2.00	1.00
No. 431.	Any other named variety		5.00	4.00	3.00	2.00	1.00
No. 432.	Fancy Basket of Apples	3.00	2.50	2.00	1.50	1.00
No. 433.	Fancy Basket of Pears	3.00	3.50	2.00	1.50	1.00

Special Exhibition of Apples
William Eames Fund

A. Baldwin, best twelve.—
   Three premiums   1.50 1.00   .50
B. Tompkins King.—
   Three premiums   1.50 1.00   .50
C. Palmer.—
   Three premiums   1.50 1.00   .50
D. Rhode Island Greening.—
   Three premiums   1.50 1.00   .50
E. Roxbury Russet.—
   Three premiums   1.50 1.00   .50
F. Sutton Beauty.—
   Three premiums   1.50 1.00   .50
G. McIntosh.—
   Three premiums   1.50 1.00   .50
H. Any other Variety.—
   Three premiums   1.50 1.00   .50

*   *   *

Brussels Sprouts.—

No. 434.	One-half peck		1.50	1.00	.50

Celery, blanched, six specimens.—

No. 435.	Giant Pascal		2.00	1.50	1.00	.50
No. 436.	Any other variety	2.50	2.00	1.50	1.00	.50

Onion, twelve specimens.—

No. 437.	White Globe			1.50	1.00	.50
No. 438.	Yellow Globe Danvers	2.50	2.00	1.50	1.00	.50
No. 439.	Red Globe		2.00	1.50	1.00	.50
No. 440.	Cracker			1.50	1.00	.50
No. 441.	Any other variety		2.00	1.50	1.00	.50

Cabbage, three specimens.—
No. 442.   2.00 1.50 1.00 .50

Parsnip, twelve specimens.—
No. 443. Hollow Crown   2.00 1.50 1.00 .50
No. 444. Any other variety   2.00 1.50 1.00 .50

Squash, three specimens.—
No. 445. Green Hubbard   2.50 2.00 1.50 1.00 .50

Squash.—
No. 446. Collection   5.00 4.50 4.00 3.00

Gourds.—
No. 447. Display   3.00 2.50 2.00 1.50 1.00 .50

Turnip, twelve specimens.—
No. 448. Purple Top Globe   2.00 1.50 1.00 .50
No. 449. English varieties, not scheduled
                                           2.00 1.50 1.00 .50

Turnip, six specimens.—
No. 450. White Swede   2.00 1.50 1.00 .50
No. 451. Yellow Swede   2.00 1.50 1.00 .50

Potato, twelve specimens.—
No. 452. Green Mountain   2.50 2.00 1.50 1.00
No. 453. Any other variety 2.50 2.00 1.50 1.00

Grains.—
No. 454. Best exhibit, five dollars may be used for prizes.

Field Beans.—
No. 455. Best exhibit, ten dollars may be used for prizes.

———

Annual Meeting, Thursday, December 6, 1934.
Premiums will be paid on or after November 20, 1934.

THE LIBRARY OF THE
WORCESTER COUNTY HORTICULTURAL SOCIETY

The Library Committee wish to call your attention to the Library and Reading Room, where the librarian is always ready to extend every facility possible to those in search of horticultural information.

COMMITTEE ON
LIBRARY AND PUBLICATIONS

EDWARD W. BREED, Chairman　　　　　MRS. AMY W. SMITH
WILLIAM ANDERSON　　　　　　　　HERBERT R. KINNEY
LUCY M. COULSON, Librarian

SOME OF THE RECENT ACCESSIONS TO THE LIBRARY

Rose Garden Primer, by Eber Holmes
American Alpines in the Garden, by Anderson McCully
Western American Alpines, by Ira N. Gabrielson
Sempervivums, by R. Lloyd Praeger, D.Sc.
Flowers and Folk-lore, by Florence Hedleston Crane
Natural Rock Gardening, by B. H. B. Symons-Jeune
Gardens in America, by Marion Cran
Lilies for English Gardens, by Gertrude Jekyll
Gardening with Herbs, by Helen M. Fox
The Arrangement of Flowers, by Mrs. Walter R. Hine
Delphiniums, by George A. Phillips
Arranging Flowers Throughout the Year, by Katherine T. Cary
　and Nellie D. Merrill
Everybody's Garden, by Walter Prichard Eaton
Hortus, by L. H. Bailey and Ethel Zoe Bailey
Pleasures and Problems of a Rock Garden, by Louise Beebe Wilder
Lily Year Book 1932, The Royal Horticultural Society
Practical Carnation Culture, by T. A. Weston
Cactus Culture, by Ellen D. Schulz.
Birds of Massachusetts, Vol. III
How to Grow Roses, by Robert Pyle, J. Horace McFarland and
　G. A. Stevens
Productive Beekeeping, by Frank C. Pellett

Alphabetical Check Iris List, by Mrs. Ethel A. S. Peckham
Rock Garden, by Archie Thornton
Aristocrats of the Trees, by Ernest H. Wilson, M.A., V.M.H.
Rock Garden and Alpine Plants, by Henry Correvon
Our Wild Orchids, by Frank Morris and Edward A. Eames
Principles and Practice in Pruning, by M. G. Kains
Backyard Gardens, by Edward I. Farrington
Commercial Carnation Culture, by J. Harrison Dick
American Rose Annual, 1930
Manual of American Grape Growing, by U. P. Hedrick
The Romance.of Our Trees, by Ernest H. Wilson, M.A., V.M.H.
Plant Culture, by George W. Oliver
Hardy Plants for Cottage Gardens, by Helen R. Albee
Wild Flowers of New York, by Homer D. House
Pages from a Garden Notebook, by Mrs. Francis King
Conifers and Their Characteristics, by Coltman & Rogers
Field Book of American Trees and Shrubs, by F. Schuyler
Gladiolus, by Matthew Crawford
Wild Flowers and Ferns, by Herbert Durand
Making the Grounds Attractive with Shrubbery, by Grace Tabor
The Amateur's Book of the Dahlias, by Mrs. Charles H. Stout
Gardening for Women, by Hon. Frances Wolseley
Insect Pests of Farm, Garden and Orchard, by E. Dwight Sander-
son and Leonard Marion Peairs
Winter Sunshine, by John Burroughs
Wake-Robin, by John Burroughs
Locusts and Wild Honey, by John Burroughs
Plant Breeding, Grafting and Budding, Fruit Improvement,
Small Fruits, Gardening, Useful Plants, Flowers, Trees, Biog-
raphy Index, by Luther Burbank
Commercial Floriculture, by Fritz Bahr
Cyclopedia of Hardy Fruits, by U. P. Hedrick
A Garden of Herbs, by E. S. Rodhe
Textbook of Pomology, by J. H. Gourley
The Rose in America, by J. Horace McFarland
Trees as Good Citizens, by Charles L. Pack
The Fern Lover's Companion, by George Henry Tilton
Color Standards and Color Nomenclature, by Robert Ridgway
Massachusetts Beautiful, by Wallace Nutting

The Book of Hardy Flowers, by H. H. Thomas
Bulbs and Tuberous Rooted Plants, by C. L. Allen
Practical Plant Propagation, by Alfred C. Hottes
The Chrysanthemum, by Arthur Herrington
Commercial Rose Culture, by Eber Holmes
Lists of Plant Types, by Stephen F. Hamblin
Outside the House Beautiful, by Henrietta C. Peabody
Cultivated Evergreens, by L. H. Bailey
American Fruits, by Samuel Fraser
Wall and Water Gardens, by Gertrude Jekyll
Adventures in My Garden, by Louise Beebe Wilder
The Rock Garden, by E. H. Jenkins
The Little Garden for Little Money, by Kate L. Brewster
The Food Supply of New England, Arthur W. Gilbert
The Practical Book of Outdoor Flowers, by Richardson Wright.
Roses for All Climates, by George G. Thomas
American Landscape Architecture, by P. H. Elwood, Jr., A.S.L.A.
Manual of Tree and Shrub Insects, by E. P. Felt
America's Greatest Garden, by Ernest H. Wilson, M.A., V.M.H.
The Principles of Flower Arrangement, by A. White
Flowers for Cutting and Decoration, by Richardson Wright
The Flower Beautiful, by Clarence Moores Weed
Hardy Perennials, by A. J. Macself
The Iris, by John C. Wister
Bulb Gardening, by A. J. Macself
Annuals and Biennials, by Gertrude Jekyll
More Aristocrats of the Garden, by Ernest H. Wilson, M.A., V.M.H.
Garden Cinderellas, by Helen Fox
Lilies, by W. E. Marshall
Lilies and Their Culture in North America, by William N. Craig
A Little Book of Modern Dahlia Culture, by W. H. Waite
Gardening with Peat Moss, by F. F. Rockwell
The Lilac, by Susan Delano McKelvey
Spraying, Dusting and Fumigating of Plants, by A. Freeman
    Mason
Vegetable Forcing, by Ralph L. Watts
Rock Gardening, by Sir James L. Cotter
American Orchid Culture, by Prof. E. A. White
House Plants, by Parker T. Barnes

Lawn Making, by Leonard Barron
Home Flower Growing, by Emil C. Volz
Flower Growing, by Leonard Barron
Flowering Trees and Shrubs, by R. C. Notcutt
Saunders Orchid Guide
Lawns, by F. F. Rockwell
The New Flora and Silva (English)
Garden Lilies, by Isabella Preston
American Rock Gardens, by Stephen F. Hamblin
Productive Soil, by W. W. Weir, M.S.
Tree Crops, by J. Russell Smith
Bush Fruit Production, by Ralph A. Van Meter
The Gladiolus and Its Culture, by A. C. Beal
Spring Flowering Bulbs, by Clark L. Thayer
The Pear and Its Culture, by H. B. Tukey
Muskmelon Culture, by W. J. Wright
Greenhouses, by W. J. Wright
China, Mother of Gardens, by Ernest H. Wilson, M.A., V.M.H.
Lilac Culture, by John C. Wister
Chrysanthemums, by Alex Laurie
Azalias and Camellias, by H. Harold Hume
The Cactus Book, by A. D. Houghton
Garden Pools, by L. W. Ramsey and Charles H. Lawrence
The Book of Water Gardening, by Peter Bisset
Little Book of Climbing Plants, by Alfred C. Hottes
The Book of Shrubs, by Alfred C. Hottes
Japanese Flower Arrangement, by Mary Averill
A History of Garden Art, by Walter P. Wright
Fertilizers for Greenhouses and Garden Crops, by Alex Laurie and
    J. B. Edmond
If I Were to Make a Garden, by Ernest H. Wilson, M.A., V.M.H.

Worcester County Horticultural Society

SCHEDULE OF PRIZES
Offered to
Children of Worcester County

Exhibitions to be held Saturday, August 11
and Saturday, September 1, 1934
Horticultural Building, 30 Elm Street

Worcester, Massachusetts

Saturday, August 11
All articles must be in the hall by 2 o'clock

The exhibits must be the results of individual effort of the
from the time of planting to the arranging of the exhibit.

Open to Children under 14 years of age

Display of Flowers.—

No. 1. Not to exceed fifteen vases

2.00 1.50 1.25 1.00 .50

Zinnia.—

No. 2. Not to exceed 10 vases   .75 .50 .25

Asters.—

No. 3. Not to exceed 10 vases   .75 .50 .25

Petunia.—

No. 4. Not to exceed 10 vases   .75 .50 .25

Calendula.—

No. 5. Not to exceed 10 vases   .75 .50 .25

Wild Flowers.—

No. 6. Not to exceed fifteen vases

1.50 1.25 1.00 .50

No. 7. Vase of Flowers   1.00 .75 .50 .25

Display of Vegetables.—

No. 8. Not to exceed 12 varieties

2.00 1.75 1.50 1.25 1.00 .75

Beets.—

No. 9. Six specimens   .75 .50 .25

Summer Squash.—

No. 10. Two specimens   .75 .50 .25

String Beans.—

No. 11. Two quarts   .75 .50 .25

Potato.—

No. 12 Twelve specimens   1.00 .75 .50

Sweet Corn.—

No. 13. Six ears   1.00 .75 .50

Tomato.—

No. 14. Six specimens   .75 .50 .25

Carrots.—

No. 15. Six specimens   .75 .50 .25

Cucumber.—

No. 16. Two specimens   .75 .50 .25

Open to Children between the ages of 14 and 21

Display of Flowers.—

No. 17. Not to exceed 15 vases 2.50 2.00 1.75 1.00

Asters.—

No. 18. Not to exceed 10 vases 1.00 .75 .50 .25

Petunia.—

No. 19. Not to exceed 10 vases 1.00 .75 .50 .25

Gladiolus.—

No. 20. Basket 1.00 .75 .50 .25

Zinnia.—

No. 21. Not to exceed 10 vases 1.00 .75 .50 .25

Wild Flowers.—

No. 22. Not to exceed 15 vases 1.50 1.25 1.00 .50 .25

No. 23. Vase of Flowers 1.00 .75 .50 .25 .25

Display of Vegetables.—

No. 24. Not over 15 varieties

2.50 2.00 1.75 1.50 1.25 1.00 .50

Potato.—

No. 25. Twelve specimens 1.50 1.00 .75 .50 .25

Beets.—

No. 26. Six specimens 1.00 .75 .50 .25

Carrots.—

No. 27. Six specimens 1.00 .75 .50 .25

Shell Beans.—

No. 28. Two quarts 1.00 .75 .50 .25

String Beans.—

No. 29. Two quarts 1.00 .75 .50 .25

Sweet Corn.—

No. 30. Six ears 1.00 .75 .50 .25

Tomato.—

No. 31. Six specimens 1.25 1.00 .75 .50 .25

Cucumber.—

No. 32 Two specimens 1.00 .75 .50 .25

Summer Squash.—

No. 33. Two specimens 1.00 .75 .50 .25

Saturday, September 1
All articles must be in the hall by 2 o'clock

The exhibits must be the results of individual effort of the child from the time of planting to the arranging of the exhibit.

Display of Flowers.—

No. 34.　Not to exceed 15 vases

2.00	1.50	1.25	1.00	.50	.25

Cosmos.—

No. 35.　Vase	.75	.50	.25	.25

Calendula.—

No. 36.　Not to exceed 10 vases	.75	.50	.25	.25

Petunia.—

No. 37.　Not to exceed 10 vases	.75	.50	.25	.25

Asters.—

No. 38.　Not to exceed 10 vases	.75	.50	.25	.25

Zinnia.—

No. 39.　Not to exceed 10 vases	.75	.50	.25	.25

Marigolds.—

No. 40.　Not to exceed 10 vases	.75	.50	.25	.25

Gladiolus.—

No. 41.　Basket	.75	.50	.25	.25

Wild Flowers.—

No. 42.　Not to exceed 15 vases	1.50	1.25	1.00	.50	.25
No. 43.　Vase of Flowers	1.00	.75	.50	.25	.25

Display of Vegetables.—

No. 44.　Not to exceed 12 varieties

2.00	1.75	1.50	1.25	1.00	.75	.50

Shell Beans.—

No. 45.　Two quarts in pods	.75	.50	.25	.25

Beets.—

No. 46.　Six specimens	1.00	.75	.50	.25	.25

Carrots.—

No. 47.　Six specimens	1.00	.75	.50	.25	.25

Sweet Corn.—

No. 48.　Six ears	1.00	.75	.50	.25	.25

Tomato.—

No. 49.　Six specimens	1.00	.75	.50	.25	.25

Winter Squash.—
    No. 50.   Two specimens   1.00   .75   .25   .25
Potato.—
    No. 51.   Twelve specimens   1.00   .75   .50   .25   .25

Open to Children between the ages of 14 and 21

Display of Flowers.—
    No. 52.   Not to exceed 15 vases   2.50 2.00 1.75 1.50
Petunia.—
    No. 53.   Not to exceed 10 vases   1.00   .75   .50   .25
Dahlias.—
    No. 54.   Not to exceed 10 vases   1.00   .75   .50   .25
Zinnia.—
    No. 55.   Not to exceed 10 vases   1.00   .75   .50   .25
Marigold.—
    No. 56.   Not to exceed 10 vases   1.00   .75   .50   .25
Cosmos.—
    No. 57.   One large vase   1.00   .75   .50   .25
Gladiolus.—
    No. 58.   Basket   1.00   .75   .50   .25
Wild Flowers.—
    No. 59.   Not to exceed 15 vases   1.50 1.25 1.00   .50   .25
    No. 60.   Vase of Flowers   1.00   .75   .50   .25   .25
Dahlia.—
    No. 61.   Vase   1.00   .75   .50   .25
Display of Vegetables.—
    No. 62.   Not to exceed 15 varieties
                          2.50 2.00 1.75 1.50 1.25 1.00   .50
Potato.—
    No. 63.   Twelve specimens   1.50 1.00   .75   .50   .25
Carrots.—
    No. 64.   Six specimens   1.25 1.00   .75   .50   .25
Beets.—
    No. 65.   Six specimens   1.25 1.00   .75   .50   .25
Sweet Corn.—
    No. 66.   Six ears   1.25 1.00   .75   .50   .25

Tomato.—

No. 67. Six specimens	1.25	1.00	.75	.50	.25

Cabbage.—

No. 68. Two specimens   .75 .50 .25

Winter Squash.—

No. 69. Two specimens   1.00 .75 .50 .25

Celery.—

No. 70. Three specimens   .75 .50 .25

Shell Beans.—

No. 71. Two quarts in the pod   1.00 .75 .50 .25

Onion.—

No. 72. Six specimens   1.00 .75 .50 .25

Prizes will be given for other meritorious exhibits.

Competition is open to all children of Worcester County under two classes. Those under 14 years and those between 14 and 21.

Only one child in a family can compete for the same prize.

The exhibits must be the results of individual effort of the child from the time of planting to the arranging of the exhibit.

All exhibits must be in the Hall ready for inspection by the Judges by 2 p. m. Exhibition will close at 4.30 p. m.

Prizes will be paid at the close of the exhibition.

Vases, plates and everything necessary for the exhibition of the flowers and vegetables will be furnished by the Horticultural Society.

Special Prizes Offered
by Secretary Herbert R. Kinney

To the ones receiving the two largest amounts under 14 years of age. $3.00. $2.00.

To the ones receiving the two largest amounts over 14 years of age. $3.00. $2.00.

*   *   *

For further information apply to

HERBERT R. KINNEY,
Secretary.

TRANSACTIONS

OF THE

WORCESTER COUNTY HORTICULTURAL SOCIETY

Reports of the Officers and Lectures

For the year ending December 6, 1934

OFFICERS AND COMMITTEES
of the
Worcester County Horticultural Society
For the Year 1934

PRESIDENT
MYRON F. CONVERSE, Worcester, Mass.

VICE-PRESIDENTS

HERBERT A. COOK   MRS. HOMER GAGE
Shrewsbury, Mass.   Worcester, Mass.

S. LOTHROP DAVENPORT, No. Grafton, Mass.

SECRETARY
HERBERT R. KINNEY, of Worcester
Horticultural Hall, 30 Elm Street

TREASURER
BURT W. GREENWOOD, of Worcester

LIBRARIAN
MISS LUCY M. COULSON, of Worcester

TRUSTEES

Joseph A. Allen	Auburn	Fred L. Chamberlain	Worcester
William Anderson	So. Lancaster	James Warr	Worcester
Elizabeth R. Bishop	Sutton	J. Frank Cooper	Worcester
Edward W. Breed	Clinton	Mrs. Bertha G. Denny	Worcester
David L. Fiske	Grafton	Mrs. Alice M. Forbes	Worcester
Richard A. Flagg	Boylston	Harold J. Greenwood	Worcester
Allen J. Jenkins	Shrewsbury	Harry Harrison	Worcester
William McAllister	Whitinsville	Mrs. Leander F. Herrick	Worcester
William E. Morey	Shrewsbury	Allyne W. Hixon	Worcester
Charles Potter	West Boylston	Mrs. Frances A. Kinnicutt	Worcester
Albert W. Schneider	Clinton	H. Ward Moore	Worcester
Mrs. Mary D. White	Holden	Harry I. Randall	Worcester
Chandler Bullock	Worcester	Joseph F. Sherer	Worcester
Willis E. Cary	Worcester	Mrs. Amy W. Smith	Worcester
Fred H. Chamberlain	Worcester	George F. E. Story	Worcester

STANDING COMMITTEE ON FINANCE

Myron F. Converse, *Chairman*, 1934   Herbert W. Estabrook, 1935
Leonard C. Midgley, 1936

Office, Library, and Exhibition Hall
30 Elm Street

CHARLES POTTER

PRESIDENT'S ADDRESS

To the Members of the
Worcester County Horticultural Society:

We come together at a time when it is pleasant to think rather
more of our interest in horticulture and somewhat less of other
distractions. From early ages it has been said that a man may
be judged by his hobbies and, although this Society has a serious
purpose, yet our interest also fulfills that need.

To my mind a Horticulturist must be a thorough going phil-
osopher. First he should have a fondness for the earth and
green things springing from it. Then he will need more than
a fair amount of patience. Finally, he must be immune to
disappointments. Granting these tastes and qualities, I can think
of no pleasanter occupation than the pursuit of horticulture.

It need not be pointed out that despite the trend of the times
the science of horticulture continues to gain in breadth and
practical importance. Its relation to other sciences is better
established than ever before and we see that its resources have
been only slightly understood. The future is certain to witness
further evolution upon a scale we should not have thought
possible a little while ago.

We may be permitted to take pride in furthering scientific
advancement, as this Society has so ably done in its ninety-four
years of existence. There are only a few organizations of this
character which outnumber us in years and our members may
modestly lay claim to our Society's notable achievement. But
the principal satisfaction comes from observation and study of
the work carried on by our own members.

This year our various shows have reached a high point of
merit and I know that every exhibitor means to try a little
harder during the year ahead, but this is just the challenge to
bring out even finer exhibits.

The details of the Society's work will be best defined in the
various reports which are to be presented to you by the several

officers and committees. They represent the body of workers whose efforts each year bring added distinction to the promotion of horticulture hereabouts.

Respectfully submitted,

MYRON F. CONVERSE, *President.*

Worcester, Massachusetts
December 6, 1934

SECRETARY'S REPORT

Mr. President and Members of the
Worcester County Horticultural Society:

Our first lecture on January 11, was by Dr. Henry R. Rose, of Newark, N. J., on "Washington." He said that one city that every American should see is Washington. George Washington selected the site in 1790. Many of the national buildings were shown and described as well as many of the changes now under way in the City.

January 18. Illustrated lecture, "Sunshine Pictures or Seeing the Invisible," by Mr. Robert Lanning and Miss Marianne Channon, Harpist.

This proved to be a very fine entertainment. The pictures were beautiful and interestingly described and the music soft and low at intervals.

January 25. Illustrated lecture. "Provincetown, Tip o' the Cape," by Mr. Percy A. Brigham, Arlington, Massachusetts. Mr. Brigham showed and described many interesting scenes. He also spoke on some of the early history of the Cape.

February 1. Illustrated lecture. "The Scenic Maritime Provinces," by Mr. Arthur H. Merritt, Boston, Massachusetts.

Mr. Merritt described the very interesting and many beautiful pictures in his easy and entertaining manner.

February 8. Illustrated lecture. "Design and Planting of the Suburban Home Grounds" and "Gardens of Spain," by Miss Harriette W. Patey, of Newtonville, Massachusetts. There were many illustrations of garden plots showing the way to lay out the grounds and others how not to plant them.

These pictures were described in a pleasing and interesting manner.

"Gardens of Spain," shown and described as she saw them on a recent sojourn there.

February 15. Illustrated lecture. "The Glory of the Annuals," by Mr. Arthur Herrington, Madison, New Jersey. It was certainly a pleasure to have Mr. Herrington here again, and to have for his lecture a subject, one of interest to many of our members. He showed many of the newer varieties of the old favorites as well as many not common here. He also left us a list of annuals which we had printed for distribution.

March 1. Ladies' Day. Illustrated lecture. "American Gardens in Comparison with European Gardens," by Mrs. John W. Paris, Trudor City, New York City. She showed many beautiful gardens and described at some length the history of some of them. The Cosmopolitan Garden has assimilated all phases of the European gardens, rather than having one of its own. Following the lecture the ladies furnished light refreshments which proved very popular.

March 8. Illustrated lecture. "Home Life of Our Wild Birds," by Dr. Alfred O. Cross, Brunswick, Maine.

These pictures and the lecturer's easy way of explaining them made this very interesting, especially for bird lovers, and showed many scenes seldom witnessed by the average bird hunter.

He also showed motion pictures of the last Heath Hen.

March 15. Annual Reunion. After a reception in the Library the members and guests assembled in the dining room at 7 P.M.

President Myron F. Converse, extended a welcome to all and remarked upon these reunions as a pleasant family occasion. He called attention to our Spring Show one week hence. He also spoke of the success some members had at the recent Massachusetts Horticultural Society's Exhibition.

He then introduced Prof. Zelotes Coombs who spoke along his usual humorous vein of many of the early organizations in Worcester. He then spoke about many interesting incidents of the organization of our Society and some of its officers and members.

Our Spring Exhibition was satisfactory with classes well filled. The Exhibit of Roses, grown by the A. N. Pierson, Inc., and staged by Randalls Flower Shop, attracted much attention. The Rock Garden Exhibit by W. H. Cross was unique and attractive.

Center, Mrs. Homer Gage. *Stage,* Edward W. Breed, 1934

The Rose Exhibition was the first to show the serious effects of the severe winter, the Climbers being the worst affected.

On June 28, there was a very fine showing of delphinium, but Lilium Candidum was very poor. There was a fine showing of Lilium Regale on July 12th and August 9th. The best showing of Gladiolus of the season, while there were some fine flowers, they were not as a whole up to the average.

It has been suggested that there be some changes in the call for dahlias, calling for the single bloom first and the display the middle of September.

Zinnias have seemed to be popular this year and some of the newer types are very attractive. There were many fine marigolds shown.

Table Decorations have been very popular with 72 tables shown during the year.

The showing of cut flowers, vases, baskets and standards has been the background of most of our Exhibitions and I feel that the arrangement has been better than usual. The baskets have been smaller and the whole arrangement not so heavy. This is probably largely due to our Judges' choice of the lighter arrangement.

Our present Schedule has seemed to give us a good exhibition most every week, but it would seem to be wise to have an occasional new feature and I would suggest that the Committee on Arrangement and Exhibitions consider trying the showing of small vases set on a mirror. This would not only be an attraction but would give our exhibitors a chance to show their skill on a new line.

I had thought of using small vases,—if two calls should be tried that the Society furnish one set of vases and that the Exhibitors supply another, the Society to furnish the mirrors.

The Fruit Exhibit at our Spring Exhibition was one of the best, but during the summer were only fair. There was a very nice showing of grapes on September 6th.

There were no peaches shown during the year. Pears were not shown liberally and much of the fruit was only fair quality.

The Chrysanthemum Exhibition was again a large and attractive one of flowers, fruit and vegetables.

There were not many of the large flowers, but the very liberal showing of the new cascade type seemed to be very much appreciated.

The noticeable change in entering the Auditorium was the placing of all the displays around the outside and stage, while the specimen plants occupied the centre.

Mrs. Gage's exhibit occupied the stage and front with an exhibit largely of Chrysanthemums, many of them standards and the cascade type.

Mr. Breed showed a garden with some very nice chrysanthemum plants.

Mr. Potter's display was largely chrysanthemums. He showed the cascade variety very attractively arranged.

Mr. Campbell showed a large collection of Chrysanthemum plants from the Nathaniel Thayer Estate.

There was a large showing of apples, but the quality was not as good as some years.

The vegetable exhibit was a large one, but the quality was not up to our standard. It would seem as though fruit had suffered from the very severe winter of 1933–1934, more than most things, but roses and many of our flowering shrubs and perennials were badly damaged.

The Children's Exhibitions were very satisfactory. August 11th was not as large as usual, but on September 1st there was a large exhibit of excellent quality.

From Secretary Edward W. Lincoln's Report 1894

"And let it be our fixed, inflexible policy to impress upon the consciousness of the community, that the aim and object of our Society, its reasons for existence—is not the distribution of so much money by way of premiums for specimens exhibited; but rather to ensure that there shall be specimens worthy of exhibition which shall not degenerate from the past floral and pomological rank and reputation of Worcester County."

New Members

WALTER H. CROSS   ORMOND HAMILTON
MISS A. CLAIRE BOWMAN   MRS. DANIEL WALDO LINCOLN
JOHN WALDO HAMILTON   MRS. JOHN W. HIGGINS

Deceased Members

MRS. ABBIE S. JORDAN   GEORGE T. DEWEY
RALPH J. STONE   FRED W. WHITE
LEWIS M. BROOKS   JOHN POLLARD
EVERETT H. WARREN   WILLIAM P. THAYER
MISS AGNES WAITE   CHARLES L. MARSHALL
            HARRY R. SINCLAIR

Respectfully submitted,

HERBERT R. KINNEY, *Secretary.*

TREASURER'S REPORT

For the Year Ending December 5, 1934

Statement of Income and Expenditures

INCOME			EXPENDITURES	
t:			Library	
all ....$	816.00		Winter Meetings.............	
ores	37,499.94	$38,315.94	Periodicals	
			Publications	
manent Funds:			Premiums:	
embership Fund	$121.51		Of 1934.......	$5,344.25
lake Fund.....	27.02		Special	87.50
ewey Fund....	98.02		Children's	
raper Fund....	10.00		Exhibition....	260.90
ames Fund....	23.50		Blake Fund.....	27.00
adwen Fund...	61.02		Draper Fund....	10.00
orse Fund.....	20.02	361.09	Eames Fund.....	23.50
			Hadwen Fund...	61.00
bership Fees............		60.00	Morse Fund.....	20.00
rest Earned:				
rmanent Funds	$172.88		Expense of Exhibitions......	
vestments	255.34	428.22	Office Expense..............	
			Operating Expense...........	
ter Meetings: Tickets.....		154.00	Miscellaneous Expense........	
rance Premium Refund...		5.25	Street Sprinkling...........	
cester Depositors' Corpora-			Furniture and Fixtures.......	
on part payment on a/c of			Maintenance:	
ass "A" Certificate of			Furniture	
terest.		937.51	and Fixtures..	$21.30
kmen's Compensation Ins..		144.00	Real Estate.....	990.15
r Income:				
abel K. Gage..	$50.00		Salaries	
R. Kinney....	37.50	87.50	Interest (Paid).............	⊥
			Interest Added to Permanent	
orary Loan.............		1,000.00	Funds:	
			Income Account..........	
Total..................		$41,493.51	Interest Added to Investments.	
			Insurance	
			Light, Heat, Water and Power.	
			Janitor Service.............	
			United States Check Taxes....	
			Loan Repaid...............	
			Mortgage Note Reduction	
			(Front Street Property)....	1
			Transfer to Membership Fund.	
			Balance of Cash on Hand De-	
as Balance, December 7, 1933		$946.13	cember 5, 1934.............	
		$42,439.64		$4

Statement of Gains and Losses

GAINS

nces of Appropriations:
bi-

...	$39.10	
...	155.75	$194.85
s...........		60.00
manent Funds		361.09
....		87.50
....		38,315.94

$39,019.38

LOSSES

Appropriations	$8.500.0
Depreciations	1,429.
Special and Permanent Fund Premiums................	229.
Expense Accounts........	1,625.
Insurance	820.
Interest	10,269.
Janitor Service.............	2,600.
Light, Heat, Water and Power.	1,225.
Maintenance, Furniture and Fixtures................	21.
Maintenance, Real Estate.. .	990.
Periodicals	96.
Publications	749.
Street Sprinkling...........	5.
United States Check Tax... ..	11.
Winter Meetings......... ...	918.
	$29,494.
Net Gain to Surplus.........	9,525.
	$39,019

Peoples
(Hadwen F
for. Fire Cts.
(Draper Fu.
(Eames Fu.
(Morse Fun.
for. Mech. Sir.
(Blake Fun.
(Dewey Fun.

stments:
for. Fire Cts ...
k............
for. Co. Inst. f :
sr, ...
for. Mech. Sir,
k............
for. Co. Tr. Co.
65 sh. Class A
stk. @ $21.
share ....

bership Fund....
Estate.........
niture and Fixt...
tary ....
t ....

I have ...
Horticult...
for the year ...

We have...
year ending,

Statement of Resources and Liabilities

RESOURCES			LIABILITIES	
nent Funds (Investment):			Blake Fund:	
)les' Savings Bank			Principal	$1,0
Hadwen Fd.)	$1,274.82		Income	3
. Five Cts. Sav. Bk.			Dewey Fund:	
)raper Fund)	407.04		Principal	1,0
]ames Fund)	613.44		Income	
[orse Fund).	520.43		Draper Fund:	
. Mech. Sav. Bk.			Principal	3
]lake Fund).	1,356.45		Income	1
)ewey Fund)	1,040.78	$5,212.96	Eames Fund:	
			Principal	5
nents:			Income	1
. Five Cts. Sav.			Hadwen Fund:	
....	2,860.63		Principal	1,0
. Co. Inst. for			Income	2
....	2,155.41		Morse Fund:	
. Mech. Sav.			Principal	5
....	3,034.17		Income	
. Co. Tr. Co.			Mortgage Note, Front Street	
sh. Class A			Property	203,5
k. @ $21.20			Surplus:	
are	1,378.00	$9,428.21	Dec. 6, 1933.....$305,302.46	
			Net Gain, 1934.. 9,525.32	$314,8
rship Fund...........		3,800.00		
]state................		480,000.00		
ure and Fixtures.......		21,564.75		
....		2,648.01		
....		886.81		
		$523,540.74		$523,

Respectfully submitted,

B. W. GREENWOOD, *Treasu1*

Auditor's Certificate

I have examined the books of the Treasurer of the Worcester County Horticultural Society, together with vouchers, securities and bank balances, for the year ended December 5, 1934, and find them to be correct.

ADAH B. JOHNSON, *Auditor.*

We have caused an audit of the books of the Treasurer to be made for the year ended December 5, 1934, and the foregoing certificate is hereby approved.
Respectfully submitted,

ARTHUR H. BELLOWS, HARRY C. MIDGLEY, H. WARD MOORE,
Auditors.

Worcester, Massachusetts
December 5, 1934.

LIBRARIAN'S REPORT

To the Members of the
Worcester County Horticultural Society:

In presenting to the members my customary Annual Report, it is a pleasure to state that circulation and use of the Library has been far in excess of that of the previous year.

The yearly additions to our Library, which by the way include many of the later and standard reference books pertaining to Horticulture are worthy of more than passing notice.

Too, especially noteworthy, are most helpful bulletins of the various Agricultural Stations.

The usual work of binding and filing of Society records has been continued as formerly.

Now that you are well started in use of your Library may the good work continue, and too much credit cannot be given to the most efficient work of the committee.

The additions to the Library during the year are as follows:

Extension Service, Massachusetts State College, Leaflet Nos. 26, 48, 146.
Cornell Extension Bulletin, Nos. 267, 275–279, 577, 580–586, 589.
Storrs Agricultural Experiment Station, No. 194.
Purdue University Agricultural Society, Circular Nos. 201, 202.
The Journal of the Royal Horticultural Society, Vol. LIX. Parts I, II, III, IV, V.
Massachusetts Fruit Association Report.
The National Rose Society Report, 1934.
The Annual Report of Parks and Recreation Commissioners of Worcester.
The American Rose Annual, 1934.
Climbing Roses, by G. A. Stevens.
Garden Flowers in Color, by G. A. Stevens.
Iris, by William R. Dykes.
Pioneering with Wild Flowers, by George D. Aikin.
Garden Maintenance, by H. Stuart Ortloff.
Gardens in Glass, by Mildred N. Andrews.
Culinary Herbs and Condiments, by M. Grieve, F. R. H. S.
A Field Guide to the Birds, by Roger Tory Peterson.
The Art of Japanese Flower Arrangement, by Alfred Koehn.

PUBLICATIONS AND PERIODICALS

Country Life in America
House and Garden
Guide to Nature
Rhodora
The American City
Horticulture
Florist's Exchange
Gardener's Chronicle
Park and Cemetery
Flower Grower
Market Growers Journal

House Beautiful
The American Home
American Forestry
The New England Homestead
The Rural New Yorker
The Country Gentleman
The National Geographic Magazine
Better Homes and Gardens
Journal of Economic
The National Horticultural Magazine

ENGLISH PERIODICALS

Homes and Gardens
Gardener's Chronicle

Gardening
The New Flora and Silva

Respectfully submitted,

LUCY M. COULSON, *Librarian.*

December 5, 1934.

REPORT OF THE JUDGE OF PLANTS AND FLOWERS

Mr. President and Members of the
Worcester County Horticultural Society:

In reviewing the flower and plant exhibits of the past season, it is gratifying to be able to report that the classes generally were well filled with high grade plants and flowers and competition very keen.

The March Exhibition brought out some very fine garden and plant displays, good Carnations, an exceptionally fine display of Roses from A. N. Pierson, Cromwell, Connecticut.

April 26. Table decorations were the feature of this show and most of the exhibits were very tastefully arranged. Competition in this class was very keen. Foliage and Flowering Plants were shown in good variety and quality.

May 10. Table decorations and plant displays were again the feature. Arrangement and quality very good.

June 7. Rhododendrons and Azaliae called for, but no exhibits of these flowers, presumably on account of the severe winter.

The Rose Show was below the average. Very few good flowers were shown, also on account of the severe winter. Some very fine displays of Paeonias were put up at this Exhibition.

From this time on during the summer the Exhibitions were good. Delphiniums and Sweet Peas were exceptionally fine. Baskets of flowers and standards were also shown in great variety and some of them were very well arranged.

Wonderful Dahlias were shown by several exhibitors; also some very fine Marigolds, Zinnias, Aquilegias, Petunias, Gladiolus, Scabiosa, and Lilies. Asters were very poor.

Plant and Garden displays at the Chrysanthemum Show good, and fine specimen blooms were shown, also many fine varieties of the single and pompom types.

Elmer D. Smith of Adrian, Michigan, exhibited some fine new Anemone flowered varieties.

There was also a fine exhibit of Nerine Fothergillia Major from Albert Schneider, Clinton, and a large vase of the new Carnation E. H. Wilson from S. J. Goddard.

Respectfully submitted,

WILLIAM ANDERSON, *Judge of Plants and Flowers.*

REPORT OF JUDGE OF FRUIT

Mr. President and Members of the
Worcester County Horticultural Society:

In spite of our extreme winter of 1933-34 and the widespread injury to our various kinds of fruit trees and plants, we had throughout the year a fine showing of most all kinds of fruit of good quality.

Cherries and plums were rather light and on June 28 in four classes of cherries only two lots were exhibited. A few plums were shown on each call but at no time were there many.

The extreme low temperatures of last winter with readings frequently 20 degrees below zero not only destroyed practically all of the peach fruit buds, but in many cases killed the trees, consequently not a single peach was shown this season.

Most varieties of strawberries came through good and on June 14th we had twenty-six plates shown, with Howard 17 in the lead.

This was a good currant year, with eleven plates exhibited on June 28th, twenty-five plates and three displays on July 7th and again on the following week, seven plates and two displays were again shown.

Many raspberry varieties received winter injury and on July 5th only one plate was shown, but on July 12th ten were exhibited, and again on the 19th seven more were shown, with Latham the most common variety.

Grapes were a good crop this season, but due to the heavy and frequent rains during the harvesting a large per cent of the crop was lost. The first plate of grapes appeared on August 23rd. This was a new variety, Fredonia, and looks very promising. On September 6th over ninety plates of grapes were shown, with sixteen plates of Concord, followed by Worden, Niagara and Brighton. The Concords in fact were the best shown in many years.

In spite of the severe injury to the pear trees this past winter

WALTER H. CROSS, 1934

we had a good showing of pears, with Seckel in the lead, followed by Anyou, Bartlett and Bosc.

Although apples were a short crop, we had a good showing each week, and the number of boxes, displays and 49's were materially increased this year.   More McIntosh were again shown this year than any other variety but closely followed by Baldwin, Greening, Northern Spy, etc.

On November 8th the fruit exhibits were exceptionally fine with ten fruit displays, twenty-five boxes of apples, mostly McIntosh, 32-49's, the most we have ever had, eleven of which were Baldwins, fourteen baskets of fruit and fifty-six plates.

In fact, although we had a short crop of fruit, the showing on November 8th was the best we have had in years.

Respectfully submitted,

S. LOTHROP DAVENPORT, Judge of Fruit.

REPORT OF JUDGE OF VEGETABLES

Mr. President and Members of the
Worcester County Horticultural Society:

I hereby present the following report for the Vegetable Department

Judging from the number and high quality of the vegetables shown in my department it would seem that the early part of last season was more favorable for their growth than the later part of the season.

The classes were very well filled and on time as per schedule. In only two classes: namely Spinach, called for on May 10, and Brussels Sprouts, called for in November, were none exhibited. On June 14, August 9, and August 16 all classes were filled.

Some of the most noteworthy exhibits were those of Asparagus on May 10 and June 7; Garden Peas on June 14, June 21, June 28, and July 5; Summer Squash on July 26; Tomato displays on September 6; Potatoes (six plates) on September 13; and the collections of Peppers on September 27.

This year Garden Peas have been more abundant and of better quality, generally, than for several years past.

The ''Collection of Peppers'' was a new class on our schedule, an experiment as it were, this year, and the response exceeded our fondest hopes. The center table in the West Hall was nearly filled with bright red, yellow and green peppers arranged in pleasing displays, their vivid coloring and attractive arrangement making them almost as beautiful as the flower displays.

The Collections and Displays of Vegetables were up to the usual high standard throughout the season.

There were also some remarkably fine displays of Mushrooms, some of the best I have ever seen. The two exhibits of Mushrooms in a natural setting of moss, ferns and wild plants, by Mr. Henry Jewett Greene, are deserving of special mention.

The boys and girls, at the two Children's Exhibitions, have

manifested their interest in our society by showing many fine specimens of vegetables arranged in attractive and pleasing displays.

Respectfully submitted,

H. WARD MOORE, *Judge of Vegetables.*

REPORT OF FINANCE COMMITTEE

Worcester, Massachusetts

To the Members of the
Worcester County Horticultural Society:

This Society continues to operate with a balanced budget. Such a situation is one to be preferred at all times, but more especially in these days when financial confusion so generally prevails.

The fixed policy of this Society over the past few years has been based on the simple principle of establishing suitable income and then fixing expenditures which do not exceed the income basis. Our financial circumstances are in a comfortable position because of adherence to this policy, and this fact often gives an exaggerated impression of the Society's financial resources.

The members of this Society are duly grateful and take distinct comfort in the results of this method of management.

Your Committee is of the opinion that Eighty-Five Hundred (8500) Dollars should be appropriated by the Society for distribution by the Trustees for the purpose of awarding premiums and paying salaries during the coming year. Your Committee therefore recommends that such an appropriation be provided at this time.

Respectfully submitted,

MYRON F. CONVERSE,
LEONARD C. MIDGLEY,
HERBERT W. ESTABROOK,
Finance Committee.

December 6, 1934.

At the Annual Meeting of the Worcester County Horticultural Society held at Worcester, December 6, 1934, the following resolution was presented by Mrs. Amy W. Smith and was unanimously adopted by the Society.

IN MEMORIAM

It is with deepest regret that we note the passing of Mrs. Frances A. Kinnicutt on December 28, 1933.

She became a member of the Worcester County Horticultural Society on November 8th, 1906, and a trustee in 1930.

Throughout her life Mrs. Kinnicutt was a flower worshiper. Her love for flowers was manifested in her cultivation of rare greenhouse flowers at her Elm Street residence.

It was a delightful pleasure for passersby to see the display of flowers both inside and outside the house.

She always had interesting exhibitions at our Spring and Fall Horticultural Shows.

Our Society has lost a faithful friend and valued member.

Resolved that this memorial be placed in the records of our Society and a copy of the record be sent to Miss Emily Haynes of 50 Elm Street.

At the Annual Meeting of the Worcester County Horticultural Society held at Worcester, Thursday, December 6, 1934, the following resolution was presented by Mr. Edward W. Breed and was unanimously adopted by the Society.

MR. WILLIAM McALLISTER

In the passing of Mr. McAllister, this Society has lost a very worthy member. During the thirty-five years of his membership with us he showed a keen interest in all of our transactions, and served for a long period on the Board of Trustees.

Mr. McAllister was a gentleman of a rare type, and those of us who were privileged to visit him in his active years when he was gardener at Whitinsville remember the pleasure he afforded us. We shall always think of him in connection with Mr. Mac-Williams who was gardener on an adjoining estate, as both men were expert growers of fruits and flowers, and their contributions to our exhibitions were of unusual excellence.

Resolved that this memorial be placed in the records of this Society.

ANNUAL MEETING OF THE SOCIETY

Wednesday, December 6, 1933

President Myron F. Converse called the meeting to order at 10 o'clock. Thirty-four present.

Secretary read the records of the last Annual Meeting of the Society.

President Converse declared them approved.

President Converse delivered his Annual Address.

The following reports were read:

Secretary, Herbert R. Kinney; Treasurer, Burt W. Greenwood; Librarian, Miss Lucy M. Coulson; Judge on Flowers, Allyne W. Hixon; Judge on Vegetables, H. Ward Moore.

These reports were accepted and referred to the Committee on Library and Publication.

Report of Finance Committee by President Myron F. Converse.

On Mr. Harry Harrison's motion the report was accepted and recommendations adopted. This carried an item of $8500 for premiums and salaries.

Mr. Allen W. Hixon reported for the Nominating Committee.

Mr. H. Ward Moore made a motion "That the report be accepted and that Mr. Hixon cast a yea ballot for the candidates as nominated." So voted.

Mr. Hixon cast the ballot.

President Converse declared them elected.

Resolutions on the death of our late Trustee, Miss Frances Clary Morse, by Mrs. Amy W. Smith, were unanimously adopted.

Mr. Edward W. Breed made a motion that "The Annual Meeting of the Society shall be held on the first Thursday in December."

After discussion by Mr. Harry Harrison and Mr. Burt W. Greenwood the motion was unanimously adopted.

On Mr. Moore's motion the meeting adjourned.

HERBERT R. KINNEY, *Secretary.*

at

the

en-

ers,

tee

on-

and

for

tee.

be

ites

ices

ted.

ual

in

W.

y

R. J. Allen, Holden Street Greenhouses, 1934

ANNUAL MEETING OF THE TRUSTEES

Wednesday, December 13, 1933

President Myron F. Converse called the meeting to order at 2 P.M. Fifteen members present.

Secretary read the records of the last Annual Meeting of the Trustees.

President Converse declared them approved.

President Converse said that this meeting was to name the Committees for next year and the members would find a list of our present Committees in the premium list each of you have.

There was a vacancy on the Committee on Arrangements and Exhibitions caused by the death of Miss Frances C. Morse, and Mrs. William W. Taft had been suggested for the place.

He thought it would be well to have a lady on the Committee on Winter Meetings and would suggest Mrs. Florence C. Herrick in Mr. Davenport's place, if it would meet the approval of the Trustees.

He awaited any recommendations or suggestions.

There being none, Mrs. Homer Gage made a motion "That the Committees with the changes recommended, be elected." So voted.

President Converse appointed Messrs. Jenkin, Schneider and Warr, a committee to prepare a list of Judges.

Mrs. Amy W. Smith and Mrs. Homer Gage spoke on the conservation of wild flowers and suggested that the Committee on Arrangements and Exhibitions consider limiting the exhibits of certain varieties at our regular exhibitions.

Mr. Jenkin's Committee asked for more time to decide on a Judge of Flowers.

On Mrs. Forbes' motion, S. Lothrop Davenport was elected Judge of Fruit and Mr. H. Ward Moore, Judge of Vegetables.

On H. Ward Moore's motion it was voted that the appropriation remain the same as last year.

On Willis E. Cary's motion the Secretary's salary was increased $100.

Mr. Burt W. Greenwood made a motion that the Secretary's Assistant's salary be $100. So voted.

Appropriation $8,500.00

PREMIUMS

Flowers	$2,300.00	
Fruit	1,100.00	
Vegetables	900.00	
Children's Exhibition...........	300.00	
Spring Exhibition.............	800.00	
Chrysanthemum Exhibition......	200.00	
Miscellaneous	200.00	$5,800.00

SALARIES

Treasurer	$ 300.00		
Secretary	900.00		
Librarian	1,100.00		
Judges	300.00		
Assistant Secretary...........	100.00	$2,700.00	$8,500.00

Adjourned,

HERBERT R. KINNEY, *Secretary.*

ANNUAL MEETING OF THE COMMITTEE ON ARRANGEMENTS AND EXHIBITIONS

Thursday, December 21, 1933

Meeting called to order by President Myron F. Converse at 10 A.M. Fifteen present.

President Converse, Mrs. Forbes, Mrs. Taft, Miss Coulson, Miss Bishop, Messrs. Breed, Jenkins, Allen, Warr, Hixon, Schneider, Potter, Morey, Moore, and Kinney.

On Mrs. Forbes' motion, Mr. Jenkins was elected Chairman.

The Exhibition of Wild Flowers was considered at some length and it was voted to make the call.

Not to exceed fifteen vases of five stems each.

For several years there has been no exhibition on the last Thursday in September, on account of the New England Fair.

The Secretary and Librarian were instructed to select from the present schedule exhibits to make an Exhibition on September 27.

There were a few minor changes in the schedule.

The Children's Exhibitions were left with the Secretary.

Adjourned.

HERBERT R. KINNEY, *Secretary.*

"WASHINGTON"

Thursday, January 11

Illustrated Lecture

By Dr. Henry R. Rose, Newark, New Jersey

One city that every American should consider seeing is Washington, the seat of the nation's government. Millions of people journey there yearly and come away with a warmth of meaning and feeling to last a life time. It should be for all a hallowed and inspiring shrine.

We owe the choice of this remarkable site to the farseeing vision of George Washington, who in 1790 made the selection. Otherwise, it would have been located at Philadelphia. It was deemed an advisable location as it was convenient to both North and South and boasted beautiful scenery. Now, of course, it is no longer central, yet still justifies its location, a beauty spot on the famous Potomac, looking toward the home of its founder, George Washington, the Father of his Country in whose honor the city has been named.

The first slide showed one of the city's finest monuments, the figure of Daniel Webster who postponed the Civil War thirty years. The Union Station at Washington gave an interesting view with the great city of distances spread before it. So widespread is its extent nobody thinks of walking.

One of the first views greeting the stranger is that of the mighty Capitol, a tremendous work of art on whose exterior the many inscriptions display a world of philosophy. One never tires of seeing this building which is surpassed in beauty only by the Taj Mahal. At night with the lights playing it is a dazzling sight. Slides revealed the strong resemblance between one view of the Capitol and St. Peter's at Rome. Only one building in this country has an interior surpassing that of the Capitol—the Congressional Library. The gallery of the House of Representatives accommodates 2,000 spectators. The Senate is much smaller, of course.

One of the great scenes in American history showed President Wilson reading the Declaration of War against Germany and Austria. Chief Justice Taft, whose general personality argued equal rights for all and special privileges for none, figured on the screen. Various statues and scenes were depicted: Samuel Adams, Governor Winthrop, the familiar painting of the Signing of the Declaration of Independence.

The Temple of the Scottish Rite of Free-Masonry, with its thirty-six massive columns for support, is another of the city's beautiful buildings. The monument to the memory of Admiral Farragut contains metal from the propeller of his ship, the Hartford, the two thus united forever. Lafayette Circle displays the statue of Andrew Jackson. Lafayette's figure reminds us that France came to our aid in the great conflict and that without the aid of his country Washington and his comrades would not have won.

Washington is a city of many parades, the Army and Navy claiming due place among them. Many views testified to the strong interest of the Americans in marching and watching others march.

The Scott Memorial Home is a commanding structure and surroundings. This home for soldiers, which owes its being to General Winfield Scott, has an endowment of $1,000,000.

Oak Hill Cemetery is a place of reverent and inspiring beauty. Here lies John Howard Payne, author of "Home, Sweet Home," who was first buried in Africa, then in 1883 brought here to rest.

Ford's Theater, where was committed one of the greatest crimes in all history, was shown on the screen. Here, on April 14, 1865, the great Lincoln was assassinated. He was carried across the street to Mr. Ford's house, where today a flag points to the room in which the president died. This house is the Lincoln Memorial House, visited by thousands of school children yearly, as well as by all tourists. It has become one of the most sacred shrines of America, well proving what Stanton said at Lincoln's death: "Now he belongs to the Ages!"

The Post Office, by its many inscriptions, shows its important role as an instrument of public service, for the handling of mail is but one of its many activities in the field of human relationship. The New Willard Hotel is an imposing building where the stranger may find comfort, favor and expense.

A short distance from Pennsylvania Avenue is the Market Place, a street scene of bustle and beauty in its own way. This sidewalk affair is the scene of a Washington tradition, the custom of Washingtonian wives to do their own marketing. This affords them a pleasant walk, the benefit of wise buying and fresh vegetables.

Buildings of prime interest to the sightseer are the Smithsonian Institute, a mine of education, the Patent House and the Pension Building. The Treasury Building has under its wing the control of many phases of life's interest and is not confined to the money problem as is so commonly thought. This department of our government has control over lighthouses, guiding the destiny of millions of travelers. The State War and Navy Building is a massive structure covering four and one-half acres and containing five hundred rooms. The Pan American Building is a fine one of great interest. The National Cathedral of the Protestant Episcopal Church, constructed in 1891, is one of the city's finest buildings.

The Washington Monument, built of Parian marble, is one of the highest monumental statues in the world, being 555 feet, 5½ inches. An army of 12,000 men could be comfortably housed on the inside. Its 900 inside stone steps prove adequate exercise for all brave enough to ascend them. The elevator, which makes the ascent in seven minutes, is always the most popular means of gaining the height. Tablets furnished by the various states adorn the walls of this monument and those walking up are thus furnished with much valuable information.

From the top of the Monument one has an excellent view in all directions. Washington is becoming more and more a great residential city, which fact is realized as the many beautiful homes greet one's view. The Potomac and Potomac Park form a fine picture. The famous Japanese cherry trees, a goodwill offering, adorn the section. In time this will be one of the most wonderful esplanades in all the world. Here and there along the way are seen lovely hedges.

The Lincoln Memorial is a majestic building with an exquisite setting. It was in process of construction for ten years and cost $20,000,000. Its imposing columns, forty-four feet high, are thirty-six in number, representing the thirty-six states in the Union at the time of Lincoln's death. Inside is the Memorial Hall on one wall of which is inscribed the famous Gettysburg Address. This great tribute to Lincoln was pictured looking out upon the city in the way Lincoln might survey it were he with us, proving to us that our destiny is secure as long as we have the spirit of Lincoln with us.

One of Washington's prime interests, of course, is the White House, used for the first time in 1800. In 1814 it was almost destroyed by the British. After this attack it was painted white and has since been known as the White House. The East Room is the one best known to visitors. The Blue Room is the President's reception room, often the scene of a wedding. President Cleveland was the only president to be married there and the Cleveland baby was the only one born in the White House. The State Department dining room is one of grandeur. The White House is of especial interest as it is home as well as an office. Many fine slides acquainted the audience with the interior as well as the exterior of this building.

An impressive tribute was paid to our past presidents, particularly to President Coolidge, a man of quiet force. Theodore Roosevelt was referred to as a vigorous and commanding character; whereas his relative, President Franklin D. Roosevelt, is a man of cool, persuasive force.

The Congressional Library is so remarkable a structure that one cannot explain his conception of its grandeur. Views were shown of the various rooms. The inscriptions in this building are a liberal education in themselves. The Corcoran Art Gallery is a sumptuous building of rare and excellent art. Free instruction is offered there to the budding artist or to any interested

EDWARD W. BREED, 1934

in the field. This Art Gallery has a national and international reputation.

A stay in Washington affords the pleasure of many side trips. Across the river is found the former home of Robert Lee. Here, too, at Arlington, is the great National Cemetery, one of the holiest and most revered shrines in America. The Grave of the Unknown Soldier is a hallowed spot, visited by people from all over the world.

Beyond Arlington, on the Potomac shore, is Mt. Vernon where Washington spent the last years of his life. This fine home has been preserved by the Washington Mt. Vernon Association and the rooms restored to their original splendor. There hangs one of the best paintings of him, showing in true form upon his face the result of small pox. A splendid one of Martha Washington appears there, also. A picture of these early days shows in that home a fine host and hostess. Family life was ideal and Washington was very fond of little Jack and Nellie Custis, his wife's children. Fine gardens show all kinds of roses, an especially fine one being called the Martha Washington. Fruit orchards testify to the owner's love of and interest in farm life. A modest grave at Mt. Vernon marks the passing of this mighty, yet democratic, man.

One of the rare treats of Washington is the Botanical Gardens, containing very valuable and rare specimens of vegetation from all over the world. Views of many fine fruit trees and flowers were shown, also the delightful walk through the gardens to the Capitol. Congress never has wanted to appropriate money for the Botanical Gardens, so the superintendent has to fight hard for their rights.

Slides of picturesque drives and beautiful gardens proved Washington to be a city of outdoor beauty as well as of fine buildings. Rock Creek Park is one of the finest contributions of Nature. Winter scenes of snow and ice gave a pleasing contrast between Washington in its summer glory and its wintry grandeur.

Pennsylvania Avenue, the largest and longest in Washington, is becoming more and more one of exceptional beauty. Business buildings along it are being torn down to make way for finer ones. The plan is to have this avenue a magnificent boulevard. Throughout the city are seen many exquisite scenes: little parks, fountains, monuments of great splendor erected to the memory of our many heroes, presidents, or other famous men.

Numerous slides depicted the city in all her radiant splendor. Old Glory greeted us as the lecturer recited "Sail On, Oh Union." Then followed two slides featuring lilies and chrysanthemums, reflecting the floral beauty of the great city of Washington.

"SUNSHINE PAINTINGS OR SEEING THE INVISIBLE"

Thursday, January 18

Illustrated Lecture

By Mr. Robert S. Lanning, Edgewood, R. I.
Assisted by Miss Marianne Channon, *Harpist*

The mystery of art and wonder of vision was portrayed by the lecturer's slides, all natural color, never touched by the brush. Color photography is a great achievement of recent times. A brief explanation of this process was given.

Throughout this fine lecture and projection of views fine harp music was heard at intervals, often accompanying verse recited by the lecturer. All readings and musical selections were descriptive of the lecture.

Seeing the invisible is a matter for the heart as there is more in the beauty of nature than can be photographed. Its great beauty causes a surge of emotions, quickens our pulses, gives us a feeling that cannot be described. Only the poet or the artist can articulate what we feel, yet cannot say.

Clouds and shadows on the sun in late winter gave a most impressive feeling of beauty and awe, a subtle meaning of mystery unspelled. Melting snow, fast disappearing ice, and the yoke of winter at last thrown off revealed a faint flush and sign of spring. Daffodils soon appeared in their early glory.

Many beautiful garden scenes followed. A lake, and just up from it a fine garden with a sun dial and clusters of lilies waving their lovely bloom gave a series of excellent views. An apple tree in bloom is always a very lovely sight. Several such were shown on the screen. Gardens of pastel tints and shades reflected their worth in color photography.

Springtime has meant much to the poet. A poem on cherry trees was accompanied by harp music, and many fine scenes of cherry trees in their exquisite bloom appeared. A close-up of the bloom would answer any question of why the Japanese make so much of the cherry blossom.

Tulips clustered in a garden gave a pleasing effect in their many colors. Just beyond them in a woodland stood the pale pastel of early spring forming a lovely natural border for the garden.

Nowhere is spring lovelier than in a rock garden. A clearly natural one was shown, a ledge in the cranies of which had been planted fine alpines. Then, by way of contrast, an entirely artificial rock garden was shown. A little stream trickled over the rocks. Pink crushed bricks formed a path. Other views showed Italian influence in decorative gadgets. A border of azaleas and rhododendrons makes a gorgeous display in a garden.

Several views of Roger Williams Park, Providence, some of them close-ups, were shown. This is one of the finest parks in our section and has a notable rose garden.

Rose propagation and cultivation is always a fascinating study. Mr. Burrill's new yellow climber, the first true one to hold its color and prosper in our New England climate, is the Mrs. Curtis James, one of great value and beauty. It will probably be offered for sale by this coming fall.

A group of pictures showed the importance of garden paths. Careful planning and arranging will produce the effect of a large estate, yet it may be only six to eight feet long, an ordinary city back garden. Only two stone steps leading to an opening in a border indicated a gate in a garden wall. A long and interesting path on a very extensive estate showed the need for correct designing in this matter. One path was bordered with columbine, and, leading up a terrace, all flowers, extended to a beautiful scene beyond. This was a lovely garden with seats placed here and there for rest and garden appreciation. A general delicate loveliness of flower and form prevailed.

Autumn, the most gorgeous time of the year, appeared in all its splendor. The spirit of it so well caught by James Whitcomb Riley was reflected in his "When the Frost is on the Punkin."

Many exquisite slides of fall were shown, especially fall in its rugged natural beauty of mountain and woods.

The closing slides were of many glorious sunsets and views of fading day. An old man with great white beard was pictured over in England musing at the close of day upon the great Sea of Eternity—Alfred Tennyson, gazing upon his Sunset and Evening Star. Mr. Lanning then recited that most soulful and precious bit of verse, Tennyson's "Crossing the Bar," to the accompaniment of the harp.

Mr. Lanning's lecture and readings, his excellent slides, and Miss Channon's harp selections afforded much pleasure and inspiration as well as nourishing the mind and soul with that greatest of all beauty—God's hush and flush of Nature.

"PROVINCETOWN, TIP O' THE CAPE"

Thursday, January 25

Illustrated Lecture

By Mr. Percy A. Brigham, Arlington, Mass.

The tendency is to claim any spot well down on the South Shore as Cape Cod, yet, strictly speaking, the Cape does not begin until one has crossed the Canal.

Yet, not to slight one of the leading historical scenes of this country, a stop must be made at Plymouth and a visit paid Plymouth Rock. This granite monument is comparatively small in size for the original rock is set in below it for protection. The whole is now enclosed to avoid further inroads upon it by souvenir seekers. Many points of interest here recall our early history and the steadfast qualities that made it.

Up to 1620 the only visitors to the Cape were explorers who soon sailed away. It was quite different with the Pilgrims. November 11, 1620, they identified the tip of the Cape, Provincetown, and, due to circumstances, spent Sunday there in Thanksgiving and prayer. This was the longest Sunday of their life. Monday all went ashore. Bradford relates the circumstances of this landing on strange soil with no word of greeting or welcome and no house for shelter. At the very tip end of the town is a tablet explaining that the Pilgrims had embarked here on American soil.

Quite a bit inland is a beautiful memorial monument to the Pilgrims. The society raised $25,000 and Massachusetts donated $15,000. Then the Federal Government came forward with an equal amount that this monument might be erected and used as a lookout in case of war. In 1901 the corner stone was laid. The town of Provincetown donated the mound upon which the monument is located. From the top of Provincetown Monument a splendid view is had in all directions. Many of these were projected on the screen.

To establish this new colony the Pilgrims assembled in the cabin of the Mayflower and drew up' the great charter which some declare to be as great as the Magna Carta of England. Mr. Brigham read this charter to the audience.

On the Cape the old and the new are represented with relative charm. The last statue erected there is to the World War soldiers.

The lecturer then showed us Pilgrim Lake and took us up Pilgrim Heights to the spring from which the Pilgrims drank their first New England spring water. Then we journeyed over to Corn Hill. This district was the source of much needed corn for food in those days. Here was an excellent view of Cape Cod Bay.

On the return from Corn Hill a stop was made at a little lake in North Truro. Highland Light, the second most powerful lighthouse on the central Atlantic seaboard, is located here at North Truro. This lighthouse is visited by more people than any other light as it is very accessible and people may park there conveniently. Near it is situated a large radio station. Views from this point are excellent. Many swallows appeared in the views of the cliffs.

Some Pilgrims wanted to remain in Provincetown but others started out across the bay and went ashore at North Eastham. They found signs of an Indian village but camped there for the night, preparing against a surprise from their neighbors. About four o'clock in the morning the Indians did attack, but it was a very light storm. This first encounter with the Indians is recorded on a tablet there.

Several slides gave glimpses of the village: the two principal streets, the Little Garden Shop, the Old House with its ship model, the most photographed house in all New England. This Ship Model House, as it is also called, is a museum containing much of rare interest. The garden around the house is a very attractive one with hollyhocks much in evidence.

Provincetown has many fine gardens. In the olden days loam was brought as a ballast on the return trip by the sailors and

ROLAND K. PARKER, 1934

was deposited in yards; so lovely flowers now flourish in it, with hollyhocks prevailing.

The coming of the Dorothy Bradford is the excitement of the day. Views of this boat, the pier, boys diving for coins (which they seldom miss l), the village from the pier were shown. The ever present indications of the principal industry, fishing, reigned supreme along the front. A typical Cape Cod fisherman was flashed on the screen, not in oilskin, however, as is the Gloucester fisherman. Over one-half the population is Portuguese.

The Artists' Colony is a unique district to visit. The Old Barn has a very interesting history. A large number of playwrights have spent the summer at Provincetown and written plays and produced them here. Notable among these is Eugene O'Neill. No longer is it the famous Play House, however, but only one of the five night clubs of the village.

A million dollar highway leads from the village to Race Point. Interesting sand dunes are seen here. Rows of evergreens keep the sand from blowing around, and the Public Works department is now doing a fine job in that area.

The Matterhorn of the Cape was seen—a sand dune four hundred to five hundred feet high. Several of such dunes were shown. Sand and mosquitoes are everywhere. Not the least beautiful and interesting sight of the Cape are the great combers that come rolling in, every seventh one being larger than the others. Sand was being carried in at such a rapid rate it was decided there soon would be no harbor there, so a breakwater was constructed out to Wood End in 1869 to correct this condition. A life-saving station was deemed necessary, also.

One of the most active coast guard stations on our coast is this at Wood End. Various stations and lighthouses in that section were shown. Chatham originally had twin lights but one was removed to Nauset.

At Orleans is an old house dating back to 1750 with the original timbers and forty-eight panes of glass in the windows. The Old Mill at Brewster was shown, too. Henry Ford tried to purchase this, but failed.

Of all the scenes along the Cape none is more picturesque or interesting than the old windmills. In the early days it was difficult to get a wheelwright to build them. In 1783-4 Thomas Paine built the first mill and his great success became known. He built all the mills for Barnstable, Yarmouth and Truro. He liked Truro so well he decided to remain there and soon became one of its leading citizens. Only a few of these old mills remain but there are many reproductions.

The closing scenes of this most alluring visit to the Tip o' the Cape were views about Provincetown. A sunset taken from the end of Race Point was a sight long to be remembered.

"THE SCENIC MARITIME PROVINCES"

Thursday, February 1

Illustrated Lecture

By Mr. Arthur H. Merritt, Boston, Mass.

As one approaches St. John, New Brunswick, by boat he sees many lighthouses and headlands. This port deals with shipping from all over the world and is quite a little city in itself. Slides of these scenes were shown.

St. John has a very fine Martello Tower. The Reversing Falls are famous and considered one of the high spots of the city. The St. John river runs into the ocean and when the tide rushes in it causes reversing falls. This occurs for twenty minutes twice a day when steamers go up and down the river.

A trip across the river on a ferry, then up to Kingston, brings one to the first church built in New Brunswick. At the time of Mr. Merritt's visit the church was celebrating its anniversary. Inside the church are seen oil lamps and other typical furnishings. The lecturer made his trip up the river on a freight boat, one of the old type Kick Behinds, practically gone today.

At Frederickton are some very fine parliament buildings. Across the river the statue of Bobby Burns claims attention. Streets bear such names as King, Queen, Brunswick. Many of the old covered bridges are seen in that section. The scenery in this district is very beautiful and this the Merritt group enjoyed right from their camp door. Blissfield was their last port of visit. Chatham is an interesting little town and has one of the little shrines found all along the roadside.

Moncton is interesting for its bores. The tide rushes in from eight to ten miles away and can be heard at quite a distance. At Hopewell one has strange views of rocks of many fantastic shapes such as a French heel, animals and the like.

Halifax has an inland harbor about which it extends in the form of arms. Here, troop ships and soldiers gathered for the

World War. This port was one of the busiest war scenes of this continent, and here the great tank explosion occurred, causing vast destruction to the city. Mr. Merritt took the first picture of this location, July 4, 1929, when War Memorial wreaths were placed there. Halifax is a great government home and possesses many fine structures. The Parliament Building is one of the oldest in actual use in the entire British Empire. One of the most frequented spots of the city is the Citadel at the top of a high hill, commanding a sweeping view of the harbor.

Northwest Arms is the location of the great playground of the city and is also a spot of beauty. The Famous War Memorial Tower, guarded by two bronze lions, is an imposing sight and gives forth an influence of awe and veneration. Farther down the coast is scenery which attracts artists in large numbers every summer.

Grand Pré country is in itself a lovely section, and its wealth of associations makes it one of the chief interests in Nova Scotia. Some of the roses and willow trees are the original roots of historic days. Evangeline's well, the chapel, the great Cross, and a bronze statue of Evangeline are all located at Evangeline Park and awaken one's appreciation of Longfellow's immortal poem of Acadia. Several slides of apple blossom time were shown. Old conventions still obtain in this quaint little village.

In Annapolis Valley apple blossom time is very beautiful. Conditions there are highly favorable to good apple culture as the land is moist and rich; consequently the trees are loaded with bloom. Growers are taught to pick and grade apples well. The people are receiving a fine education in ways of making a successful living.

Care of codfish is different from the ordinary method used around here. At 4 P. M. every little pile of fish is covered up; and when the sun comes out in the morning the cover is removed. Massachusetts style is to dry on flakes.

Mr. Merritt and his party had to leave out Annapolis Royal and Digby as the fog was too thick. Chester, the Bar Harbor of the United States, has many New York and New Jersey friends. It is patronized largely by rich Americans who have beautiful homes there. That Sunday happened to be the one before Dominion Day, the Fourth of July of Canada, when historical services are combined with the religious. As Mr. Merritt had been superintendent of a Sunday School in Boston for twenty years, he was called upon to address both the adult and children's services, three in all on that one Sunday.

Many fine views are seen from the train as one proceeds down the south shore, with water in view most of the time. Boats going down the river, sailors, dry codfish in a cart, oxen are all in evidence.

Yarmouth has a fine War Memorial, a tribute to soldiers of the World War. H. H. Raymond, of Brookline, an official of the Eastern Steamship Line, has an attractive home here and one of the best gardens of all Nova Scotia. It is adorned with old-fashioned flowers, the perfect arrangement of which produces an excellent effect. It took Mr. Merritt two hours to go through the entire garden, a great privilege and great treat.

Returning to Halifax by the other shore one sees valleys that remind him of New England. Fine salmon fishing is done here in these various pools. Pretty pastoral scenes are enjoyed along the way. At Sidney is the very pretentious house once occupied by Alexander Graham Bell, and now the home of Mr. Grossman of the National Geographic Society. The oldest house in Sidney is an interesting one. St. George's Church is quite a historical one. Admiral Nelson, while on this side, had to come in here for fuel, and worshiped at this church. A chair was taken from his flagship for the church and is its proudest possession.

About fifteen miles north is 1 B, a soft coal mine out under the ocean. Several views gathered on a visit to this mine were shown. Miners' clothes had to be worn. After a two-mile ride in a car he was taken down in a lift. Horses were working down there, hauling. It seemed strange to find gardens in that place, three and one-half miles out under the ocean. This visit to 1 B was one of the high spots of the whole journey.

Pictou Lodge, where the party stayed, showed an attractive log cabin. From Cape John, the place with the red cliffs, one can see Prince Edward Island on a fair day. The group took a boat across to the island, a beautiful place with many excellent farms. The old Government House is very historic, and counts among its celebrated visitors the Prince of Wales. The fox grounds here are better even than those of Alaska. An excellent potato crop is raised in this section, and hay grows very thick there. Cattle are of the finest breed and condition. Hedges, rather than fences, set a boundary.

A return to Charlottown brings us tide streams. Here, the scenes resemble those of New Hampshire and Vermont.

Throughout this interesting lecture attractive views were shown on the screen, not only of the scenery and general points of interest, but also of Mrs. Merritt and the friends with them.

The closing view was of a glorious sun casting its setting light of beauty over the Scenic Maritime Provinces. Then waved their emblem, the British Flag, and our Old Glory.

"DESIGN AND PLANTING OF THE SUBURBAN HOME GROUNDS" and "GARDENS OF SPAIN"

Thursday, February 8

Illustrated Lecture

By MISS HARRIETTE W. PATEY, NEWTONVILLE, MASS.

Landscape architecture is the art of arranging land and landscape for human use, convenience and enjoyment. If done correctly it is an economy, but costly where mistakes are too evident. In planning a home it is ideal to have the architect and landscape architect work together, for only in this way may the greatest economy, harmony and beauty be achieved. Many fine slides showing the development of this plan from the beginning were shown and carefully explained.

The first plan showed a suburban lot of average size with the house set practically in the middle, a drive to the left leading to the garage in the left rear, then a laundry yard well in back, a pleasure yard leading right to the well-placed house. The dining room and nook, living room and sun porch all faced the sunny side and garden, which formed part of the pleasure yard, having in this setting a most favorable exposure. This was the result of careful planning and wise use of land.

A second view showed the uneconomical use of land, poor arrangement and generally unlivable conditions. In this case the service yard occupied the best part of the land. A third plot plan showed the same position of land with these problems solved, showing the advantage of careful planning.

It is claimed often that the rectangular lot is the only one lending itself to good arrangement, but a lot practically square was shown to have its own charm of position, carefully plotted. A compact arrangement of garage and house intimately connected, with a service yard in between, afforded ample space for a pleasure yard and garden.

EDWARD W. BREED, 1934

Even an extremely irregular lot may be well designed. A slide showed such a place, with the house up near the bank, an interesting terrace leading down from it, the shelf of which formed an outdoor living room, then a grassed terrace, and finally the garden. In this position the house had a commanding view of the lovely slope.

Landscape work showed considerable elevation. In only one case out of one hundred is this elevation properly achieved. Evergreens are beautiful in the right place, but in a short time they grow up and smother the house. Just a row of evergreens may in time produce a most ugly appearance, the tall trees just hiding the house, or, in some cases, completely submerging its importance. Many people insist upon the massed evergreen planting with never a deciduous shrub to soften the effect or provide bloom and color at different seasons. This marked contrast is needed for relief, form, color and general contour. Box tree is good for that purpose in Connecticut but it is not quite hardy in Massachusetts. For this low growing effect clumpy pine or juniper is good. Fillers are needed not only to help fill in spaces here and there but also to vary elevation and soften a more formal line. Careful planning will provide evergreens for winter, flowering shrubs for spring to fall, and berries for the winter, as well as for the autumn.

An interesting slide was of a house on a hillside, the ledge remaining in its own form, planted with natural plant material, thus producing a real glimpse of Nature undisturbed.

Good foundation planting is attractive even in winter. Euonymous is always effective. The dogwood and old wisteria vine all have a place in the picture. Fine spring planting may be had with blossoming dogwood, tall evergreens and the low ground cover of evergreens. Always, of course, planting should be related to the style of the house. This fact is extremely important, yet is far too often overlooked. A little dooryard of a cottage lends itself well to hollyhocks and lilacs.

In winter the dogwood makes a fine appearance, and so do the rhododendron, azalea, cedar, juniper, barberry, cotoneaster, ivy and myrtle. For the deciduous shrub the laburnum is one of the best. Euonymous radicans is the most hardy variety for our winters. A wise choice will provide a garden of shades, foliage and berries which will flourish throughout the winter months.

The general principles controlling any art must be studied and employed by all concerned with landscape architecture. Of first importance is the unity of the whole, especially the joining of the house and the garden. Even a perfectly plain door may be beautified by a covering of grape vine, as evidenced by one slide. A very elaborate out-door living room, a terraced affair, for tea and dining, gave a pleasing view. Even a modest stretch of lawn may furnish this greatly desired out-door room. Europeans live outdoors far more than do we Americans, and most homes have their little private quarters for this ideal nature room. We should so plan our homes and gardens here that we, too, might enjoy more leisure in the garden or out-door living room. One's work, to a certain extent, may be carried on there with greater pleasure and benefit.

In the most carefully planned plot it is difficult to draw a line between the house and garden, so intimate is the connection between them—one large, harmonizing unit. A suggestive walk or pathway, rows of trees, shrubs, or perennial border, all may pave the way to one's garden or out-door home. Stepping stones leading from the house to the desired spot is an effective arrangement. These may be grassed in or may have between them a thyme which will furnish attractive foliage, bloom and a delicate fragrance. Any unsightly post, fence, wall or gateway may have its decoration of clematis or any of the many vines to be had for the purpose.

One slide showed a plot planting of one hundred by seventy-five feet, the out-door living room located on a terrace floor in a sheltered position where late fall and early spring enjoyment may be had. Nearby a smoke bush casts its charm. This shrub is quite hardy here and is extremely decorative; however, it is seldom planted in these parts. A sunken pool is always an attraction in a corner of the garden and garden rock walls are coming more and more into favor.

Regarding the garden furniture, we often find too sophisticated a type in a simple environment. Such incongruity may virtually spoil the scene and should by all means be avoided. Rustic furniture has its own setting; likewise has the more elaborate style of garden furnishings. A woodland scene demands the rustic type, but this has no place in the formal garden. The high brick wall is an excellent boundary for a garden, yet this is so expensive the tendency these days is to have a low brick wall upon which is set an openwork trellis. If the high wall is missing it is well to have a motif, the size and type depending upon the size and nature of the garden. A seat rightly placed will effect the idea of termination. A gate, also, may be used as a terminating feature. ·A type of formal garden was shown in a plot practically symmetrical, with all directed toward a central motif. Again, the symmetry may be the order of left and right leading to some terminal interest.

If the lot adjoining the garden is a wood lot by all means include this wood line in the garden. A pool around which is a semiformal planting of shrubs and plants is always effective. Often an informal garden is the choice as it, also, may be very beautiful and is easier to prepare. It is quite possible to have a good garden on different levels and have a wall way play an important part. Vines, climbers, creepers and hanging varieties are available in large numbers for effecting a most pleasing arrangement. One view was of a wall fountain, the water spraying out from a motif on the wall. Honeysuckle is a favorite for a wall cover.

Standards make good accents in a garden. Flower borders are one of the most successful gardens for the home as they are colorful and inexpensive. It is best to concentrate on some regular color schemes to produce the most desirable effect. Each month has its special offering and these bulbs and plants rightly set will afford constant bloom in the garden from the early spring crocus and other bulbs through the croceum and platycodon. August is the month of phlox, with its excellent coloring. Then, too, the blue salvia is in evidence. Fall has many excellent blooms to offer, the wide choice of chrysanthemums being, perhaps, the most appreciated because of their late visit.

Many people crave a rock garden yet succeed only in a pile of rocks thoroughly distasteful to the eye. If proper conditions for a rock garden are lacking alpines may be planted between flags.

Regardless of the size of a lot, the shape, the contour, the elevation, any home may have an attractive setting as to house and grounds. Careful planning will produce an attractive picture with individual charm.

More thought should be given to the grounds of schools, hospitals and other public buildings. The right surroundings as to landscape beauty may go a long way toward turning a liability into an asset in the case of the problem child.

Spanish Gardens

Sunny Spain is the history of Asiatic derivation—Arabs, Moors and Christians—a conflict of foreign influence and religious strife. The influence of the Moors is still seen in Maorca though they disappeared as a force in the thirteenth century. A typical scene was a long pergola leading down to an olive grove. Fountains in many shapes and positions cast their spray over the gardens, proving of great value to the growth of the garden as well as enhancing its beauty by decoration.

Seville furnished many excellent views. Here, high stucco walls insured privacy and repose. Flowers are not the most important consideration of their gardens, coming second, as they do, to the people's comfort and enjoyment. From the stucco wall comes the well, an indispensable source of welfare for the garden. The use of polychrome tile is a distracting feature of the pagan garden, yet its own attractiveness seemed to them an excuse for its being. Various gardens of roses were seen, and myrtle hedges in profusion. Then came an outside living room dedicated to the memory of Cervantes, windmills and other ornaments recalling the episodes of Don Quixote and his companions. An attractive lagoon figured in the Spanish-American exhibition in Seville in 1929. Gardens laid out as a series of compartments are a unique feature of the Spanish. One patio showed attractive tile seats at the top of steps and dusty miller playing around.

Geraniums are a great favorite in Spain. All gardens display them in one form or another. Even the potted geranium is much in evidence, used as a wall or window decoration. Sometimes they are used as vines, making a very attractive picture with their incessant bloom.

Surprise fountains are used for their cooling influence in the strong sun and heat of these gardens. Everywhere this typical use of tile is seen in fountains, seats here and there, and general decoration. High myrtle hedges are employed to advantage, and the cypress tree, also, is greatly in evidence. Throughout Seville is seen the ever present genius of the Duc of Alba whose influence reigns supreme in the many beauty spots of garden culture.

In southern Spain one continuous hedge of three hundred feet borders a beautiful garden. Wellheads are seen here and there for decoration. All along, typical Moorish scenes come to view. A rock stairway cut by the Moors long ago was shown on the screen. At Cordova the garden of the alcaza figured. Everywhere the alcaza, or castle, furnishes a splendid garden scene with the lovely cypress, porcelain ornaments, pool having always potted plants on its wall or coppice. Even if the garden is lacking, now and then, all Spain has at least window gardens of plants.

Views of Grenada were shown, and the garden created by Rodriguez on the hillside. The Alhambra, the glory of Spain, is still a place of exquisite beauty by day and night. A garden, located up a steep hillside, shaded by great magnolias, was very striking. Throughout this section of the country views reminded us of the inspiration afforded Washington Irving for his works.

After these many fine slides of Spain and her gardens the lecturer left us in lovely Andalusia, breathing the beauty of Spain.

"THE GLORY OF THE ANNUALS"

Thursday, February 15

Illustrated Lecture

By Mr. ARTHUR HERRINGTON, MADISON, NEW JERSEY

Annuals certainly contribute glory to the garden not only because of their beauty but more because they fill up the gap left by perennials. If it were not for annuals gardens would be quite bare during a large part of the season.

The lecturer contrasted briefly the gardens across with our own. Over there in England they are very luxuriant, indeed. The Dorothy Perkins and Hiawatha roses raised here and sent over there did infinitely better across than they did here. The conclusion arrived at was that it is not a question of sunshine over there, but of clouds. The great moisture provides this excellent growth. After this rather discouraging contrast, it is soothing to return to his country and discover that our zinnias are better than theirs. This is due, however, to their coming from Mexico which is a dry section like our own.

We have a great variety of annuals that can be grown well here. They often make the highlights of a garden and provide continuous bloom. They represent a maximum of beauty with a minimum of cost.

It is important, of course, to buy good seed from reliable dealers, and it is advisable to buy the best, highly selective types. Plan ground of moderate size and moisture. Then use ten pounds of fertilizer to two hundred square feet of ground, from one week to ten days before planting. The soil should be dry, too, as wet soil conditions are not favorable. An inch in depth in a drill is the best way of sowing seed. In some sections it is not safe to sow seed before the third week of May, but here in Massachusetts it may be sown earlier. Three weeks after sowing, the seedlings are ready for transplanting. Thin out to one foot apart as room and food are necessary.

There are four families of annuals that can be recommended to the beginner: zinnia, marigold, aster and sweet scabious. Zinnias, a Mexican wild flower, are of many types. Marigolds are bright in color and well worth while. They, too, are Mexican. Asters, so-called, are not true asters. There are hosts of them but the true one is the daisy flower, which is Chinese. Sweet scabious makes the soil hard and should be watered freely.

The zinnia is an old type. All we have now are selective. A slide of the acme showed a zinnia as large as a dahlia of normal size. Now, of course, some dahlias are grown as large as a supper plate and it is a question whether there is any good in this achievement of size. Science has so perfected conditions that some people can now obtain almost any size or type of bloom they wish. A new type of zinnia gradually crept into cultivation a few years ago. The petals are quilted and incurved, and the pastel shades are decidedly different. It grows as high as other types and is exceedingly beautiful. The name of this type is Achievement but in catalogs it is listed under Giant Double Quilled. Another type is the cactus flower zinnia, with very irregular petals. Lilliput zinnias are good for small growth. It is possible to procure perfect color, and the plant blossoms all through the fall to the middle of November. In three rows of zinnias owned by the lecturer not a rogue appeared. Little Mexican ones are tiny. Fine bowl arrangements of zinnias were shown on the screen.

Marigolds, too, are varied in nature. Yellow Africa, a lemon yellow, is very striking. The French marigold is popular, too. A few years ago a new African type appeared, called the Guinea Gold. It has fewer petals and broader ones. This variety is excellent in gardens and offers a wealth of coloring for the fall. It grows large, so plants should be set at least two feet apart. The old type French marigold is smaller.

Asters are very popular but difficult to grow. Soil should be changed every year for them. There are many choices, tall and short. The single aster is very beautiful and is easier to grow than is the double.

Sweet scabious is the best quality and is very fragrant. Many kinds may be procured. It is highly recommended for all gardens.

Snapdragon is an attractive annual in the garden and for cutting. It comes from quite small up to two, three or four feet high. This is not a true annual. It grows wild in southern England and France, and is seen on walls of Normandy. It needs time to develop and should not have too rich or too loose soil.

For all annuals cut faded flowers, do not let them go to seed. Prevent the plant from tiring itself.

Annual larkspur is a weed in its wild state. Every garden should have this annual variety as well as delphinium, as it is very attractive in the garden, is fine for cutting, and may be extended throughout the season by making several sowings. It is not easily transplanted, so the proper plan is to sow the seed and then thin out, as this can be done successfully when the plant is very small. The branching type grows three feet high and is a fine specimen.

Salpiglossis needs to be raised under glass in order to produce good strong plants. Shirley poppy is a good variety of wild poppy. It is very pretty, yet fragile. It should be sown in the open. Cut when the bud is opening; do not wait for full bloom. The South African poppy, Dimorphotheca, comes out quickly and is smothered with flowers. It resents our summer heat so should be raised early and set out in the spring to grow with early bulbs. Nemesia, a South African annual, comes in all shades. It does not like July heat, so should be raised early. It makes a fine plant twelve to eighteen inches high and likes shade.

Calendulas are easily grown, both single and double. This plant likes cold weather, so must be set out early. A July sowing may be made for late fall. The cornflower, or bachelor's button, is better in the early days than in the late. Centaurea is of the same family. It requires a light, free soil. Sweet Sultan is a fine variety of it, fragrant and lovely.

The mallow is single. It does not like the heat. Annual calliopsis or coreopsis grows in the southern states and in Mexico. It is a choice flower but does not transplant well. Chinese pinks, single and double, are well worth cultivating. They can stand a lot of cold and bloom sometimes way into December. The Swan River daisy from South Africa grows well in shade. Cosmos is a good old stand-by, but is rather late here. Fortunately, an early variety is now in use. The double flower is very beautiful. Nigella, or Love-in-a-Mist, is good for a cool, shady spot, if the right type is obtained.

The annual chrysanthemum is a lovely flower developed in recent years. From an old weed it has developed into single and double types of excellent tone. It is easy to raise from seed and should be set two to three feet apart. Sweet peas are always lovely, but they must get an early start around here. South African and Australian straw flowers do not get much moisture. They are very pretty in a garden, and these everlastings make excellent winter bouquets. There is a choice of seven or eight families of these straw flowers. Statice, pink and blue varieties, is good for drying. The California poppy has a range of rich colors, not merely orange and yellow. It grows here well, but the soil must not be too rich or foliage and few flowers will result.

Nasturtiums, both dwarf and climbing varieties, prefer a light, dry soil, not a rich soil. Golden gleam has been out only two years. It is a lovely bloom with delicious fragrance. Other colors of it are coming out this year. Portulaca, also, likes a poor, sandy soil.

Mignonette has a lovely fragrance and is very worth while. It is difficult to establish, but if seeds are sown in a pot and the seedlings set out more can be accomplished with it. It does not like our summer heat, so should get out early. Mathiola bicornis (night scented Stock) is grown chiefly for its delicious fragrance. It doesn't want very rich soil.

Many fine slides illustrated this most interesting and instructive lecture. If the advice given is rightly followed, gardens in Worcester henceforth should be vastly more successful, and more a place of real garden beauty.

Mr. Herrington's chart follows:

Annuals: Selections for Special Purposes

FOR EARLY FLOWERING

Sweet Peas
Nemesia
Dimorphotheca
Cornflower (Centaurea)
Didiscus
Calendulas
Nigella (Love in a Mist)
Poppies, Shirley and Opium

Antirrhinums, Early and Late
Stocks—Mathiold Bicornis
Clarkias
Sweet Sultan Centaurea
Godetias
Nemophila
Phacelia

FOR LATE FLOWERING

Asters
Zinnias
Marigolds
Salpiglossis
Sweet Scabious
Chrysanthemum, Segetum and
    Coronarium
Petunias
Larkspur
Coreopsis

Dianthus (Chinese Pinks)
Phlox Drummondi
Gaillardia
Balsoms
Arctotis
Ageratum
Sunflowers
Cosmos
California Poppies

ANNUALS FOR SHADE

Clarkias
Calendulas
Nemophila
Sweet Sultan
Nemesia

Dianthus
Mignonette
Nicotiana
Mathiola Bicornis (Night Scented
    Stock)

FOR DRY AND LIGHT SOILS

Portulaca
Nasturtiums

California Poppies

ANNUAL VINES

Nasturtium, Climbing Types
Tropoeolum Canariense
Cobea Scandens
Cypress Vine Opomoea
Convolvulous
Dolichos, Hyacinth Bean

Echinocystis Lobata (Mina)
Lophospermum Scandens
Thunbergia
Gourds

"AMERICAN GARDENS IN COMPARISON WITH EUROPEAN GARDENS"

Thursday, March 1

Ladies' Day

Illustrated Lecture

By Mrs. John W. Paris, Trudor City, New York City

Fashions in gardens have passed through many phases since colonial days. All together are the embodiment of America. The cosmopolitan garden has assimilated all phases of European gardens rather than having one of its own.

Italy represents the first of the formal gardens if we except the Ancients, but all modern ideas in this field originated with Italy. With the Renaissance the Italian garden took on more form than it had in Ancient Rome. The first importance was planning of the house and gardens as one, and suiting the garden to the house, its occupants and place. With the exception of roses and potted plants the Italian garden depends very little upon flowers, but on terraces, lawn alleys with box and cypress clipped, trees, all of which give it its charm. The Italian villa garden was the most wonderful type the world has ever had.

England in the nineteenth century fell under the Victorian influence, and the garden was an ugly affair. Annuals were allowed to grow to only eight or ten inches, Mr. William Robinson was the one who had the garden emerge from the Victorian type to take on the present beautiful form. He preached and talked for forty years before this change was brought about. Then others fell in line.

The English garden seems to fit our type of landscape and general conditions better than any other, such as Italy. The history of the English garden is short but one of progress and achievement. Various types were adapted in diversified conditions. According to many, the suburbs of Philadelphia, the

IRISTHORPE, MRS. HOMER GAGE, 1934

north shore of Long Island and the suburbs of Boston have the most beautiful gardens of this country.

Henry Middleton of South Carolina went to England to study landscape gardening. Middleton Gardens, 1850, were shown on the screen, with the first azaleas and lovely pleated alleys. A place nearby has pools and a wealth of azaleas. A short distance from Middleton Place is a beautiful magnolia garden. In 1843 an order was sent from Philadelphia to the Orient for some azaleas, and this consignment was sent to the Magnolia Gardens. Japonicas have a long season and thrive here in abundant glory. A notice posted at Kew Gardens indicates that azaleas in their greatest glory are to be seen at Charleston, South Carolina, in the United States of America.

At Lake Como in Italy are beautiful azaleas, but not quite comparable to those of our South. There they are sheared, but here they are allowed to grow to their natural height.

The first settlement in this country was at St. Augustine, August 28, 1565. Spanish influence is noted here. The Spanish style of garden is well adapted to Florida and California for their tropical seasons produce the very best effects. The Spanish renaissance of gardens and architecture came into being. Many typical Spanish scenes were shown.

The Singing Tower, gift of the late Mr. Edward Bok, is a remarkable conception. He stipulated that it must equal in beauty the Tower of Belgium, and it surely does. The surroundings are as fine as the tower. It is a sanctuary, a place of rest for both humans and birds. It is all beauty and compared by many travelers with the Taj Mahal.

Lookout Mountain, Chattanooga, has charming gardens. Some three thousand acres are devoted to a National Parks system.

Gardens in and near Washington, D. C., were mentioned. Going down the Potomac, fine gardens are seen by the traveler. Mrs. Pierre DuPont's gardens are beautiful. A great feature of the estate is Mr. DuPont's garden of six acres under glass. A fine box border adorns the DuPont garden and a wealth of peonies. Numerous slides of Philadelphia gardens were shown, also.

Mr. William Robinson's home and magnificent gardens in Sussex were shown. Greensward is used for a path. English gardens have masses of gaiety and masses of green to relieve the coloring. St. John's College, Oxford, has the well known pleated alley so popular in England. Grotesque figures are a heritage from the Roman days in England. Not many of such figures are seen here as we prefer to let Nature run her course. A few specimens of the spiral effect were shown. This is worked in between levels and is a most difficult type of topiary work to achieve.

Mr. William Cole's garden in Long Island is the most beautiful one in this country. It contains two hundred acres beautifully arranged. Mrs. Ward was the first woman of Long Island to take a personal interest in the garden. Now two-thirds of the gardens are cared for by women. The remarkably fine gardens of Mrs. Frances H. Burnett, Mrs. Whitney, Dr. Satterthwaite, Mrs. Robert Bacon and John D. Rockefeller, Sr., were shown. From Mr. Rockefeller's garden the outlook over the Hudson is like looking out at a river in Italy. It is one of the most gorgeous views in the world. Mrs. Jay Gould's garden is a splendid one. All through the Catskills and around the Hudson are seen exquisite ones of every type.

Gardens of the Pacific coast greatly resemble those of Spain and Italy. Olive trees are a fine contribution. A tropical charm flourishes throughout these far western gardens much as in Florida.

The United States has made rapid strides in garden culture during these recent years and the movement continues to spread. We have vision, and much more to contribute to the garden.

After Mrs. Paris's finely illustrated talk Ladies' Day was observed. A social hour followed with tea. The committee in charge were: Mrs. Leander F. Herrick, Chairman; Mrs. Myron F. Converse, Mrs. Burt W. Greenwood, Mrs. Herbert R. Kinney, Miss Lucy M. Coulson, Mrs. Arthur E. Denny, Mrs. Allen J. Jenkins. This annual affair was well attended and greatly enjoyed by all.

"HOME LIFE OF OUR WILD BIRDS"

Thursday, March 8

Illustrated Lecture

By Dr. Alfred O. Gross, Brunswick, Maine

The coast of Maine with its rough, rugged lines was shown in the first slide. Landing at this far point was difficult, but once ashore an abundance of bird life was in evidence as a reward for one's trouble. Gulls flourished here, their nests open and exposed to the elements.

In the interior many were seen, quite oblivious to the group of people watching them. One just out of the egg showed his protective coloring. Gulls have webbed feet and swim almost as well as ducks. Two perched on a log near the water were ready for another swim. As many as twenty-five to thirty of these birds were seen on a single spruce tree.

Mt. Desert Island and a lively view of these birds furnished a fine motion picture. Two sitting against the bright light of evening sunset afforded an unusual scene. A male bird going through his courtship performance all for the benefit of his mate was both interesting and amusing. After this exhibition she returned to her nest only to be pulled off forcibly by the male.

When Dr. Gross and his friends approached, the mother bird gave a call of warning and her little one settled down unnoticed. When the light in use was gone the little one came out again and nestled. Oftentimes a bird goes twelve miles or so to get food for the young. A picture of an entire family was shown, one little one an albino. This character of albinism is transmitted to the young.

The island has many petrels. This bird comes out only at night as it does not see in the daytime. It lays a single white egg. Pictures of this bird had to be taken by means of a flashlight.

Views of pheasants, their nests, eider ducks, and a nest of seven eggs were shown. A look the following day disclosed empty eider shells, the little ones all out.

One of the best ways to reach these outlying islands is by aeroplane. Views from the air proved highly interesting. Col. Charles Lindbergh's summer home was one of them. Osprey on the rocky islands gave a rugged picture, showing nests where the young had just hatched. There is a great similarity between the young osprey and eaglets.

Eider ducks arrive at Kent's Island in April. At one time they were scarce in that region but Dr. Gross reported over one hundred nests there at his visit. Some of these nests were located near those of the petrel, others among the iris. Hatching time is always interesting in the life of the eider. Great precaution is taken to conceal the young. One can do a great deal with ducks on a reservation. Views showed wild black ducks feeding out of the hand in a manner of barnyard fowl.

Martha's Vineyard, the home of the last heath hen was shown next. The State spent over $70,000 to keep this bird, but it became extinct. Although extinct for a long time on the mainland it lasted for some years on the island. In 1916 two thousand of these birds were destroyed by a fire which swept their reservation. In 1921 only five birds remained, two of them females. In 1928 only the three males survived. This bird is very similar to the prairie chicken in many ways. Poultry disease played a large part in its disappearance. The heath hen had a peculiar courtship performance, going through many antics and uttering queer sounds.

A picture of the blind, six feet in all directions, in which Dr. Gross and Mr. Thornton Burgess took their position to study the last heath hen, was projected on the screen. These men often spent a whole day waiting for results. One rainy day the bird appeared and was held captive for a time. This picture was the last taken of the last heath hen in the world.

Now, the rough grouse is in danger of extinction. These birds are used for a study of parasites and diseases. The bird feeds upon berries of the false Solomon's-seal. Hatching time in one view showed two eggs just hatching. These young birds hide under leaves and are hard to find.

The prairie chicken is closely related to the heath hen of Martha's Vineyard. Wisconsin affords a splendid hiding place for this bird. Motion pictures showed its courtship performance to be very similar to that of the heath hen. The male's whole self is put into this courtship.

Slides showed a blind being placed in position near the nest of a prairie chicken. It was let stand there a day or two before Dr. Gross and his companion entered it, then the bird paid no attention to it. In this way the observers could study the bird at close range without disturbing its natural movements.

The black crowned night heron is active chiefly at night, when it builds its nest and builds well, too. Some trees seen contained nine to twelve of these nests. They are homely birds looking more like a monkey than a bird. One was just coming out on a cliff, and another was shown at eight days.

Slides of the red-eyed vireo, with a nest in construction, followed. These young developed into handsome birds. The chimney swift was seen, also. The Baltimore oriole builds a lovely nest, one of the finest specimens of all bird architecture. The rose-breasted grosbeak was shown delivering a bit of food down the beak of one of the young birds while four other open mouths were waiting to be fed. The blue jay is a beautiful bird, but preys on the nests and eggs of other birds, thus proving quite a terror. The cedar waxwing is a fine bird.

One slide revealed a hermit thrush and a cowbird in the same nest. The mother thrush accepted the young cowbird as her own and this little one was fed by its foster parents.

Views of a bird trip to New Hampshire, with Dr. Potter of Clark University, showed many familiar birds of our section. The white throated sparrow was in the spruce woods. It is found only in the higher altitudes. The white breasted mountain hatch appeared on the screen.

Mrs. Webster's home at Holderness is the scene of birds of many varieties. Feeding shelves and boxes, houses are everywhere, all for the birds. Mrs. Webster was shown feeding birds

CHARLES POTTER, 1934

in close contact; so tame have her little friends become they eat from and on her finger. A pair of yellow warblers appeared in the lilac bushes where their nest was located. So young were their offspring they had to thrust the worm into their mouth to feed them.

Dr. Gross has seen birds feeding at Brunswick, Maine, when the temperature was fifteen below zero. These little feathered friends are with us always. No matter what the climate, temperature or section of the country, some bird will greet us in its own habitat or season.

Dr. Gross's motion pictures of bird life were unusually interesting and helpful. They were bound to arouse further interest in the study of feathered life.

ANNUAL REUNION

March 15

The annual reunion opened with a reception in the library at 6:30 p.m. Dinner was served at 7:00. The Rev. Lester C. Holmes, pastor of the Pleasant Street Baptist Church pronounced the invocation.

The president, Mr. Myron F. Converse, extended a welcome to all. He announced that two of the society's most loyal members, Mr. and Mrs. David L. Fiske of Grafton, could not be with us but had sent their greetings and good wishes. Mr. Converse requested the secretary, Mr. Herbert R. Kinney, to have flowers sent from the society to these good friends, whose presence was greatly missed by all. Mr. Converse remarked upon the value of these reunions as a pleasant family occasion, saying that at the dinner twenty-five years ago Chief Justice Arthur P. Rugg was the speaker, having for his subject "Flowers in Window Boxes."

Attention was called to our Spring Show only one week away. The Boston Flower Show was highly spoken of and cognizance taken of our members who were successful exhibitors at it. Mrs. Homer Gage's exhibit had taken first prize in its class, also a gold medal. Here, Mr. Jenkins was extended special greeting and complimented on his success in winning such fame for Mrs. Gage's exhibit. The Worcester Garden Club (Mrs. Gage, president) had a fine set-up. Mrs. William Thayer gained two prizes. It is gratifying to hear of our members extending their interest by exhibiting elsewhere, thus winning fame for Worcester County.

In 1928 a large number of members assembled at the reunion which was practically the dedication of our new Horticultural Hall. One of the speakers at that occasion was virtually edged out, deeming it wise, owing to pressure of time and lengthy speeches of others, to make his talk a brief one. So, for this present occasion he had kindly agreed to favor the group with that speech. Professor Zelotes Coombs, a fellow member, was then presented.

Prof. Coombs' address was on "Work and Activities of the Society during the Ninety-four Years since its Organization." His own membership in the society boasts forty years, and his practical interest is evidenced by a farm in Auburn. The speaker reviewed briefly the history of organizations in Worcester from the appointment of a committee by the General Court, in 1665. This section of the state possessed fine chestnut trees and four hundred acres of meadow land. In 1674 the first settlement was made here, these settlers being primarily an agricultural people. Here we find the real foundation of our Worcester County Horticultural Society.

For a great many years there was no strong inclination to organize, then Old South Church appeared on practically the site of our Common. In 1722 the town of Worcester was incorporated. The Unitarian Church was organized in 1783. Clearly, these early settlers were independent individuals and enjoyed playing a lone hand, but all the while settlement progressed. In 1793 the Worcester Fire Society was formed, the first real organization here.

In 1818 our fellow organization, the Worcester County Agricultural Society, was formed, due to a certain real need among the citizens. At first, meetings were held on the Common, then fair grounds were purchased on Highland Street, and more recently, the present fine site in Greendale. The population was then less than 3,000. Most of the prominent men of the town joined this organization. Too much emphasis was placed on hogs and other livestock to please some of the members, so they decided to withdraw from this group and start an organization more to their liking and advantage.

As a result, in September, 1840, the Worcester County Horticultural Society was founded, its aim being to draw special attention to vegetables, fruits and flowers. Among these men of outstanding influence in the community was Dr. John Green, one of the pioneers, the leading physician of the time, the founder of our Public Library, a relative of the more recent benefactor who willed Green Hill Park to the city. Then there were Benjamin Heywood, John Milton Earle, John Davis and Isaac Davis.

In March, 1842, the society was incorporated and it progressed steadily, due to careful planning. Regular exhibitions were held. Soon a desire arose for possessing a building of their own. Before long Horticultural Hall was erected on Front Street, with a mortgage of $12,000 attached. People were inclined to look askance at this bold undertaking and expected to have the society bankrupt, yet, in thirty-one years that mortgage was lifted and the ownership cleared.

For years exhibitions were held in the society's own room, sometimes in Brinley Hall and a number of times in Mechanics Hall. At first an admission fee was charged and over $200 was raised in so doing; but in 1880 the society decided to make no charge for admission. (Here the speaker congratulated the society for throwing its doors open to all, declaring it to be a powerful civic influence that is bound to be far-reaching in scope.) By careful management the society prospered yet never grew rich. At one time it was a question of holding the property on Front Street.

The first president was Dr. John Green. Isaac Davis, the leading lawyer, a man interested in every phase of civic life, one of the founders of Worcester Academy, followed. Then came John Milton Earle, editor of the Massachusetts Spy, Postmaster, a Senator, and the one really responsible for the charter of Worcester.

These men were all greatly interested in horticulture but had not so great an interest in the mechanical world. Some of the leading men, however, had this interest and organized the Mechanics Association. One of the founders was Ichabod Washburn, active in the cause in 1840-41. In 1842 the Mechanics Association was started and in 1854 it boasted a new building of its own. An interesting parellelism may be drawn between these two societies claiming as they did the attention and influence of all the great men of the day.

The fourth president was John Davis. Daniel Waldo Lincoln's name is one always close to the society. The organization owes a lot to the Lincoln family who have ever taken a keen interest in it. There was a strong desire on the part of these great men in the early days to raise pears, and over three hundred varieties were propagated by Daniel Waldo Lincoln. Ultimately, the pear craze died out. Another president was William Merrifield. George Jaques, founder of the Worcester City Hospital, served in 1863-64. Other fine workers for our cause were Senator George Frisbie Hoar, Emery Washburn, J. Henry Hill, Henry L. Parker, the Salisburys, father and son.

Lives of the men who founded this society were always closely entwined with civic life. All were interested in a certain line of horticulture. They built for us a foundation better than they realized and left a wonderful heritage for us to carry on.

Compared with the Massachusetts Horticultural Society ours impresses favorably. We have our own beautiful building, well set up and perfectly appointed, a place of beauty in itself and an excellent setting for our flower shows. It is becoming more and more a civic center for all organizations and is registering strong civic interest. The work of our society has an elevating and culturizing influence which, we trust, will continue for all time. Such is the spirit which has come down to us from the garden.

In conclusion, the speaker paid a fine tribute to our executive, Mr. Converse, to whom the society owes a great debt of gratitude for his careful and effective guidance. Portraits of the earlier workers of this society reflect the great work of these pioneers who still cast their influence as they gaze upon us from the walls. Work such as ours cannot but make people feel better for having passed this way.

After this inspirational address by Prof. Coombs members and guests adjourned to the Auditorium where dancing followed. Intermissions were given over to specialty acts by a professional troupe of Boston and selections by the Kiwanis Glee Club. This varied program provided enjoyment for all.

INDEX

SCHEDULE OF PREMIUMS

Offered by the

Worcester County Horticultural Society

Horticultural Building
30 Elm Street
Worcester, Mass.

For the year

1935

THE ATTENTION OF EXHIBITORS IS PARTICULARLY
CALLED TO THE RULES AND REGULATIONS
GENERAL AND SPECIAL

The Davis Press, Worcester

OFFICERS AND COMMITTEES
of the
WORCESTER COUNTY HORTICULTURAL SOCIETY
For the Year 1935

PRESIDENT
MYRON F. CONVERSE, Worcester, Mass.

VICE-PRESIDENTS
HERBERT A. COOK, Shrewsbury, Mass.　　　MRS. HOMER GAGE, Worcester, Mass.
S. LOTHROP DAVENPORT, No. Grafton, Mass.

SECRETARY
HERBERT R. KINNEY, of Worcester
Horticultural Hall, 30 Elm Street

TREASURER
BURT W. GREENWOOD, of Worcester

LIBRARIAN
Miss LUCY M. COULSON, of Worcester

TRUSTEES:

Joseph A. Allen	Auburn	Fred L. Chamberlain	Worcester
William Anderson	Wellesley	J. Frank Cooper	Worcester
Miss Elizabeth R. Bishop	Sutton	Mrs. Bertha G. Denny	Worcester
Edward W. Breed	Clinton	Mrs. Alice M. Forbes	Worcester
David L. Fiske	Grafton	Harold J. Greenwood	Worcester
Richard A. Flagg	Boylston	Harry Harrison	Worcester
Allen J. Jenkins	Shrewsbury	Mrs. Florence C. Herrick	Worcester
William E. Morey	Shrewsbury	Allen W. Hixon	Worcester
Charles Potter	West Boylston	Allyne W. Hixon	Worcester
Albert W. Schneider	Clinton	Mrs. Anna N. W. Hobbs	Worcester
Myron S. Wheeler	Berlin	H. Ward Moore	Worcester
Mrs. Mary D. White	Holden	Harry I. Randall	Worcester
Chandler Bullock	Worcester	Joseph F. Sherer	Worcester
Willis E. Cary	Worcester	Mrs. Amy W. Smith	Worcester
Fred H. Chamberlain	Worcester	George F. E. Story	Worcester

STANDING COMMITTEE ON FINANCE
Herbert W. Estabrook, 1935　　　　　　　　　　　Leonard C. Midgley, 1936
Myron F. Converse, *Chairman*, 1937

NOMINATING COMMITTEE
Ernest Hansen 1935　　　　Arthur H. Bellows, 1936　　　　Charles B. Rugg, 1937

ON LIBRARY AND PUBLICATIONS
Edward W. Breed, *Chairman*　　　Mrs. Amy W. Smith　　　William Anderson
Herbert R. Kinney, *Secretary*　　　　　　　Lucy M. Coulson, *Librarian*

ON NOMENCLATURE
S. Lothrop Davenport　Mrs. Amy W. Smith　Charles Potter　　Herbert R. Kinney
J. Frank Cooper　　　Allen J. Jenkins　　William Anderson　Leonard C. Midgley

ON ARRANGEMENTS AND EXHIBITIONS
Allen J. Jenkins, *Chairman*

Joseph A. Allen	H. Ward Moore	Elizabeth R. Bishop
Mrs. William W. Taft	Edward W. Breed	Allen W. Hixon
Mrs. Percy G. Forbes	Lucy M. Coulson	S. Lothrop Davenport
Leonard C. Midgley	Allyne W. Hixon	Albert W. Schneider
President, Myron F. Converse	Charles Potter	William E. Morey

Secretary, Herbert R. Kinney

AUDITORS
Harry C. Midgley　　　　　H. Ward Moore　　　　　Arthur H. Bellows

JUDGES
PLANTS AND FLOWERS: William Anderson, South Lancaster
FRUIT:　　　　　　　S. Lothrop Davenport, North Grafton
VEGETABLES:　　　　H. Ward Moore, Worcester

MEDAL COMMITTEE
Myron F. Converse, *Chairman*　　　Edward W. Breed　　　　Allen W. Hixon

ON WINTER MEETINGS
Myron F. Converse, *Chairman*　　　Herbert R. Kinney, *Secretary*
Mrs. Leander F. Herrick　　　　　Mrs. Anna N. W. Hobbs
Leonard C. Midgley　　　　　　　H. Ward Moore

Office, Library, and Exhibition Hall
30 Elm Street

GENERAL RULES AND REGULATIONS

1. Strict conformity to the Regulations and Rules will be expected and required, as well for the benefit of exhibitors as for the convenience of the Officers of the Society.

2. Every Flower or Plant entered in a class of named varieties should be correctly named.

3. All articles offered for premiums must remain within the Hall throughout the hours of Exhibition, unless special permission for their removal shall be granted by the Committee on Exhibition, etc.

4. No person shall make more than one entry of the same variety or be awarded more than one premium under the same number.

5. The Judges may correct, before the close of any exhibition, awards made by them, if satisfied that such were erroneous.

6. The cards of exhibitors competing for premiums shall be reversed, until after premiums are awarded.

7. Competitors are expected to conform strictly to the conditions under which articles are invited. Evasion or violation of them may be reported to the TRUSTEES for future disqualification of the offender.

8. Articles offered for premiums must be in the Hall by 2 o'clock of the days of Exhibition except when otherwise specified. Between 2 and 3 o'clock the Hall will be in exclusive charge of the Committee on Arrangements and Exhibitions. Open to the public from 3 to 9 o'clock.

9. Competition for premiums is open to all residents of Worcester County, and it is strictly required that all specimens offered for premiums shall have been grown by the competitors, on their own premises, for at least two (2) months previous to the date of exhibition, except where no restriction is stated in schedule.

10. After the articles are arranged they will be under the exclusive charge of the Judges and Committee of Arrangements, and not even the owners will have liberty to remove them until the exhibition is closed, when they will be delivered as the contributors may direct.

11. Where a certain number or quantity of Plants, Flowers, Fruits or Vegetables is designated in the schedule, there must be neither more nor less than that number or quantity of specimens shown; and in no case can other varieties than those named in the schedule be substituted.

12. The Judges may exclude from competition all inferior specimens and may correct any errors that they think were without deliberate purpose.

13. The Committee on Arrangements has power to change the time of exhibition for any article, if an earlier or later season renders such change desirable.

14. All articles offered for premiums should be correctly named. Indefinite appellations such as "Pippin," "Sweeting," "Greening," etc., will not be considered as names. Any person exhibiting the same variety of Fruit or Vegetable, under different names, or exhibiting as grown by himself Flowers, Fruit or Vegetables grown by another, thereby violating the objects and rules of the Society, shall be debarred from competing for the Society's premiums until reinstated.

15. Competitors will be required to furnish information as to their mode of cultivation, and to present specimens for trial and examinations, if requested.

16. In all exhibitions of Cut Flowers for competition, the number of blooms, clusters, sprays or spikes shown is not restricted except that it is expected the exhibitor shall use only a sufficient number to make a well-balanced display. All shall be of one color and of one variety in the same vase, except Displays, Vases, Baskets, Standards, or otherwise specified in the schedule. The Judge will consider the quality of the flowers rather than the quantity.

17. ☞ The Judges are authorized by the Trustees to invite the assistance of competent and discreet persons in the discharge of their duties.

18. No Judge shall require anything of competitors respecting their exhibits which is not distinctly specified in the schedule.

19. In Table Decorations, collections and displays of Flowers Fruits, Vegetables, Vases, and Baskets, where the number of exhibits exceeds the number of premiums offered, the Judge may award prizes to any worthy exhibits not receiving a premium.

The maximum prize for Vases, Standards, and Baskets shall be two dollars.

20. All premiums that are not claimed within one year after the close of the official year shall be forfeited to the Society.

21. "Downing's Fruits of America," revised edition, will guide the Judge of Fruits in his decisions upon matters at issue.

22. **While the Society will take reasonable precautions for the safety of the property of exhibitors, it will be responsible in no case for any loss or damage that may occur.**

Scale of Points

Cut Flowers and Wild Flowers.—

Arrangement	30 points
Quality of blooms	40 "
Number of varieties	15 "
Properly named	15 "

Lilies.—

Size and color of bloom	35 points
Number of perfect flowers and buds on stem	35 "
Arrangement	15 "
Properly named	15 "

Displays.—

Arrangement	40 points
Quality	45 "
Variety	15 "

Collections.—

Quality	45 points
Arrangement	25 "
Variety	30 "

Special Funds

OF THE

WORCESTER COUNTY HORTICULTURAL SOCIETY

The following is a list of the Special Funds of the Worcester County Horticultural Society the income of which is devoted to the purpose stated. The date prefixed to each indicates the year in which the fund was established.

1888.   Francis Henshaw Dewey Fund. $1,000.00.
Income to be used for the purchase of books.

1898.   William Eames Fund. $500.00.
Income to be used in prizes for the promotion of apple culture.

1906.   Frederick A. Blake Fund. $1,000.00.
Income only to be used in providing Medals to be awarded to the originators of new varieties of Fruits or Flowers, preference always being given to residents of Worcester County.

In case that the Worcester County Horticultural Society does not find occasion to award medals for New Fruits or Flowers, the said income may be used in special premiums for Orchids or other choice Greenhouse Plants and Flowers.

1907.   Obadiah Brown Hadwen Fund. $1,000.00.
Income to be used for meritorious exhibits of Flowers, Fruits and Vegetables.

1922.   Edwin Draper Fund. $300.00.
Income to be used in prizes for Horticultural exhibitions held under the direction of said Society.

1924.   Miss Frances Clary Morse Fund. $500.00.
Income to be used in prizes for Flowers.

Flowers, Plants, Fruits and Vegetables

1935

☞THE COMMITTEE ON ARRANGEMENTS AND EXHIBITIONS would direct the earnest attention of the Judge to *Rule 12.*

12. The Judges may exclude from competition all inferior specimens and may correct any errors that they think were without deliberate purpose.

Special Rules

1. EXHIBITORS WILL ADD VALUE TO THEIR EXHIBITS BY HAVING ALL SPECIMENS CORRECTLY AND LEGIBLY NAMED AND THE NUMBER OF VARIETIES WRITTEN ON THE ENTRY CARDS, NOTICE OF WHICH WILL BE TAKEN BY THE JUDGES IN AWARDING THE PREMIUMS.

2. WHILE IT IS EXPECTED THAT EXHIBITORS WILL TAKE PAINS TO CORRECTLY NAME THEIR EXHIBITS, THE JUDGES WILL NOT EXCLUDE AN EXHIBIT FOR MISTAKE IN NOMENCLATURE.

3. IN ALL EXHIBITIONS OF LILIES THE POLLEN MAY BE REMOVED.

By vote of the trustees, all entries must be made to the Secretary and all cards made out by him or his assistants.

Spring Exhibition

Thursday, April 4, 3 to 9 p. m.
Friday, April 5, 9 a. m. to 9 p. m.
Saturday, April 6, 9 a. m. to 9 p. m.
Sunday, April 7, 12 m. to 9 p. m.

All articles for this exhibition must be in the hall and ready for inspection by the judges by 1 o'clock Thursday

Class I	Garden Displays	300.00
Class II	Plant Displays	250.00
Class III	Rock Gardens	
	Not to exceed 100 square feet	100.00
Class IV	Cut Flowers	75.00
Class V	Fruit	75.00
Class VI	Vegetables	75.00

Frederick A. Blake Fund

Class VII	Carnations	25.00

Worcester Garden Club Exhibit

May Exhibition
Thursday, May 9

All articles for this exhibition must be in the hall and ready for inspection by the judges by 2 o'clock

This exhibition will be open to the public from 3 to 9 p. m.

Cut Flowers.—
    No. 1. Twenty vases   3.00 2.50 1.00
    No. 2. Medium basket   3.00 2.50 2.00 1.50 1.00

Spring Bulbs, open culture.—
    No. 3. Display   4.00 3.00 2.50 2.00

Pansy.—
    No. 4. Twenty vases, one flower with foliage in a vase 3.00 2.50 2.00 1.50 1.00 .50

Zonale Geraniums, in bloom.—
    No. 5. Six plants   3.00 2.00 1.00 .50

Table Decorations.—
    No. 6. For best table decoration, laid for four covers, no restrictions. Notify the Secretary two days in advance 7.00 6.00 5.00 4.00 3.00

SCALE OF POINTS BY WHICH THE ABOVE CLASS IS TO BE JUDGED

Arrangement	40 points
Quality	25 "
Proportion and harmony of flowers with accessories	20
Accessories	15

Plant Displays.—
    No. 7. For exhibits—no restrictions as to where grown, or by whom $60.00 may be used for prizes. Notify the Secretary two days in advance.

Calendula.—
    No. 8. Arranged in Bowl or Basket   3.00 2.00 1.00

Dandelion.—
    No. 9. One-half peck   1.50 1.00   .50

Lettuce.—
    No. 10. Six heads   2.00 1.50 1.00   .50

Spinach.—
    No. 11. One-half peck   1.50 1.00   .50

Radish, two bunches, six in each bunch.—
    No. 12. Globe   1.50 1.00   .50

Rhubarb, twelve stalks.—
    No. 13. Linnæus   2.50 2.00 1.50 1.00   .50

Asparagus, two bunches, twelve specimens each.—
    No. 14. Any variety   3.00 2.50 2.00 1.50 1.00   .50

Onion.—
    No. 15. Two bunches, six in each bunch   1.50 1.00   .50

Thursday, June 13

All articles for this exhibition must be
in the hall and ready for inspection by
the judges by 2 o'clock

This exhibition will be open to the public from 3 to 9 p. m.

Cut Flowers.—
No. 16.   From hardy plants and shrubs
outdoor culture, *to be named*   5.00 4.00 3.00 2.00

Wild Flowers.—
No. 17.   Five stems in a vase.
No duplicates   3.00 2.00 1.50 1.00 .50

Roses.—
No. 18.   Vase H. P. roses, not to exceed
ten blooms   3.00 2.00 1.00

No. 19.   Vase H. T. roses, not exceeding
ten blooms   3.00 2.00 1.00

Peonies.—
No. 20.   Best Display of Peonies.
Notify the Secretary two
days in advance   5.00 4.00 3.00 2.00

No. 21.   Twenty vases, one flower in
each   4.00 3.00 2.00 1.00 .50

Foxglove.—
No. 22.   Vase of twelve spikes   3.00 2.00 1.00 .50

Aquilegia.—
No. 23.   Display   3.00 2.50 2.00 1.00 .50

Begonia.—
No. 24.   Four plants in bloom   3.00 2.00 1.00

Cherry, one quart.—
No. 25.   For any named variety five
dollars may be used for prizes.

Strawberry, twenty-four berries.—
No. 26.   Senator Dunlap   1.50 1.00 .50
No. 27.   Howard No. 17   3.00 2.50 2.00 1.50 1.00 .50
No. 28.   Any other variety   2.00 1.50 1.00 .50
No. 29.   New varieties   2.00 1.50 1.00 .50

Pea, one-half peck.—
No. 30.   Any variety   2.00 1.50 1.00 .50

Rhubarb, twelve stalks.—
No. 31.   Victoria   2.50 2.00 1.50 1.00 .50

Rose Exhibition

Thursday, June 20, open from 3 to 9 p. m.

*All articles for this exhibition must be
in the hall and ready for inspection by
the judges by 2 o'clock*

Roses.—

No. 32. Twelve blooms of distinct named
varieties of H. P. roses, outdoor
culture   4.00 3.00 2.00 1.00

No. 33. Six blooms of distinct named
varieties of H. P. roses, out-
door culture   3.00 2.00 1.00 .50

No. 34. Collection of cut roses. Twelve
dollars to be used in prizes.

No. 35. Vase of roses, 12 blooms   3.00 2.50 2.00 1.50 1.00

No. 36. Vase H. P. roses, not to exceed
ten blooms   3.00 2.00 1.00

No. 37. Vase H. T. roses, not exceeding
ten blooms   3.00 2.00 1.00

No. 38. Display of cut climbing roses.
Fifteen dollars may be used in
prizes.

No. 39. Basket of roses   3.00 2.50 2.00 1.50

Special Prizes
Miss Frances C. Morse Fund

A. Table decoration of roses, laid for
four covers. Flowers grown by
exhibitors   4.00 3.00 2.00 1.00

*   *   *

Peonies.—

No. 40. Best Display of Peonies.
Notify the Secretary two days in
advance   5.00 4.00 3.00 2.00

Aquilegia.—

No. 41. Bowl   2.50 2.00 1.50 1.00

Special Prizes
Obadiah Brown Hadwen Fund

Hardy Flowers, to be named.—

B.   Display of outdoor varieties   5.00 4.00 3.00 2.00 1.00

*   *   *

Strawberry, twenty-four berries.—

No. 42.	Howard No. 17	3.00	2.50	2.00	1.50	1.00	.50
No. 43.	Sample				1.50	1.00	.50
No. 44.	Uncle Joe			2.00	1.50	1.00	.50
No. 45.	Any other variety			2.00	1.50	1.00	.50
No. 46.	Collections, not more than six varieties	5.00	4.00	3.00	2.00	1.00

Cherry, one quart.—

No. 47.   Black Tartarian   2.00 1.50 1.00   .50
No. 48.   Gov. Wood   2.00 1.50 1.00   .50
No. 49.   Best display, ten dollars may be used for prizes.
No. 50.   For varieties not scheduled, five dollars may be used for prizes.

Pea, one-half peck.—

No. 51.   Thomas Laxton   2.00 1.50 1.00   .50
No. 52.   Gradus   2.00 1.50 1.00   .50
No. 53.   Any other variety   2.00 1.50 1.00   .50

Cabbage, three specimens.—

No. 54.   Any named variety   2.50 2.00 1.50 1.00

Lettuce.—

No. 55.   Six heads   2.00 1.50 1.00   .50

Scale of Points

Cut Flowers and Wild Flowers.—

Arrangement	30 points
Quality of blooms	40 "
Number of varieties	15 "
Properly named	15

Lilies.—

Size and color of bloom	35 points
Number of perfect flowers and buds on stem	35
Arrangement	15 "
Properly named	15 "

Displays.—

Arrangement	40 points
Quality	45 "
Variety	15 "

Collections.—

Quality	45 points
Arrangement	25 "
Variety	30 "

Table Decorations.—

Arrangement	40 points
Quality	25 "
Proportion and harmony of flowers with accessories	20
Accessories	15

Thursday, June 27

*All articles for this exhibition must be
in the hall and ready for inspection by
the judges by 2 o'clock*

This exhibition will be open to the public from 3 to 9 p. m.

Cut Flowers.—
    No. 56. Twenty vases   3.00 2.50 2.00 1.50 1.00   .50

Dianthus Barbatus (Sweet William).—
    No. 57. Twelve vases, three clusters
           in a vase   3.00 2.50 2.00 1.50 1.00   .50

Campanula.—
    No. 58. Display   4.00 3.00 2.00 1.00

Delphinium.—
    No. 59. One vase, not more than twelve
           spikes   4.00 3.50 3.00 2.50 2.00 1.50 1.00

Roses.—
    No. 60. Collection of Cut Roses. Ten
           dollars may be used in prizes.

Lilium Candidum.—
    No. 61. Vase   4.00 3.00 2.00 1.00

Special Prizes
Offered by Mr. Herbert R. Kinney

C. Display of Cut Flowers on round
        tables   3.00 2.50 2.00 1.50 1.00
This number is intended for the growers who do not compete in
the call for twenty vases or displays during the year.

*   *   *

Strawberry, twenty-four berries.—
    No. 62. Downing's Bride   2.00 1.50 1.00   .50
    No. 63. Ten dollars may be used for
           prizes. Preference given to
           worthy varieties of recent
           introduction.
    No. 64. Best display   5.00 4.00 3.00 2.00 1.00

Currant, twenty-four bunches.—
No. 65.   For any variety, five dollars may be used for prizes.

Cherry, one quart.—

No. 66. Coe's Transparent		1.50	1.00	.50
No. 67. Black Eagle		1.50	1.00	.50
No. 68. Montmorency	2.00	1.50	1.00	.50
No. 69. Any other variety	2.00	1.50	1.00	.50

Beet, open culture.—

No. 70. Twelve specimens	2.50	2.00	1.50	1.00	.50

Carrot.—

No. 71. Two bunches, six in each	2.00	1.50	1.00	.50

Bean, Snap, one-half peck.—

No. 72. Any named variety	2.50	2.00	1.50	1.00	.50

Pea, one-half peck.

No. 73. Sutton's Excelsior	2.00	1.50	1.00	.50
No. 74. Any other variety	2.00	1.50	1.00	.50

Cucumber, three specimens.—

No. 75. Any variety	1.50	1.00	.50

Friday, July 5
(Instead of Thursday, which is a holiday)
All articles for this exhibition must be in the hall and ready for inspection by the judges by 2 o'clock

This exhibition will be open to the public from 3 to 9 p. m.

Cut Flowers.—

No. 76.   Twenty vases   4.00 3.00 2.50 2.00 1.50 1.00
No. 77.   Ten vases   2.50 2.00 1.50 1.00 .50

This number is intended for the growers who do not compete in call for 20 vases and displays during the year.

Basket.—

No. 78.   3.00 2.50 2.00 1.50 1.00

Japanese Iris.—

No. 79.   Display, twenty dollars may be used for prizes.

Delphinium.—

No. 80.   Display, fifteen dollars may be used for prizes.

Wild Flowers, no duplicates.—

No. 81.   Fifteen vases, five stems
in a vase   2.50 2.00 1.50 1.00 .50

Roses.—

No. 82.   Display of cut climbing roses.   Ten dollars may be used in prizes.

Raspberry, Black Cap, one quart.—

No. 83.   Named variety   1.50 1.00 .50

Raspberry, one pint.—

No. 84.   Early varieties   2.00 1.50 1.00 .50
No. 85.   Varieties not scheduled, five dollars may be used for prizes.

Gooseberry, one quart.—

No. 86.   Any named variety   2.00 1.50 1.00 .50

Currant, twenty-four bunches.—

No. 87.	Red Cross		.50 1.00	.50
No. 88.	Perfection	2.00	.50 1.00	.50
No. 89.	White Grape		.50 1.00	.50
No. 90.	Versaillaise	2.00	1.50 1.00	.50
No. 91.	Any other variety	2.00	.50 1.00	.50

Bean, Snap, one-half peck.—

No. 92.	Wax	2. 0	2.00 1.50 1.00
No. 93.	Green Pod	2.50	2.00 1.50 1.00

Pea, one-half peck.—

No. 94.	Alderman	2. 0	1.50 1.00 .50
No. 95.	Telephone	2.50	2.00 .50 1.00
No. 96.	Display		3.00 2.00 1.00

Display of Vegetables.—

No. 97.   Not to exceed 24 square feet, $20.00 may be used for prizes. Notify the Secretary two days in advance.

Tomato, twelve specimens.—

No. 98.	Any named variety	2.00 1.50 1.00	.50

Sweet Pea Exhibition

Thursday, July 11

All articles for this exhibition must be in the hall and ready for inspection by the judges by 2 o'clock

This exhibition will be open to the public from 3 to 9 p. m.

Sweet Peas, annual.—
    No. 99. Ten vases, not more than 25
           flower stems in a vase   4.00 3.00 2.00
    No. 100. Table Decoration—Sweet Peas,
           laid for four covers, Gypsophila
           may be used. Notify the Secre-
           two days in advance   5.00 4.00 3.00 2.00 1.00

SCALE OF POINTS BY WHICH THE ABOVE CLASS IS TO BE JUDGED

Arrangement	40 points
Quality	25 "
Proportion and harmony of flowers with accessories	20
Accessories	15

Sweet Peas.—
    No. 101. Basket, any green may be used.
                         4.00 3.00 2.00 1.00

Obadiah Brown Hadwen Fund

D. Collection of Sweet Peas, fifteen dollars may be used in prizes.

*   *   *

Cut Flowers.—
    No. 102. Display, not exceeding 30
           square feet   4.00 3.00 2.50 2.00 1.50 1.00

Lilium Regale.—
    No. 103. Fifteen dollars may be used in prizes.

Centaurea.—
    No. 104. Display, Gypsophila may be
           used   4.00 3.00 2.50 2.00

Petunia.—
No. 105. Twenty vases, one flower in
      each   3.00 2.50 2.00 1.00 .50

Raspberry, one pint.—
No. 106. Latham   2.00 1.50 1.00 .50
No. 107. Cuthbert   1.50 1.00 .50

Apple, twelve specimens.—
No. 108. Any variety   2.00 1.50 1.00 .50

Blackberry, one quart.—
No. 109. Any variety   1.50 1.00 ..50

Currants, twenty-four bunches.—
No. 110. Wilder   2.00 1.50 1.00 .50

Cucumber.—
No. 111. Three specimens   1.50 1.00 .50

Cabbage, three specimens.—
No. 112. Any variety   2.00 1.50 1.00 .50

Lettuce.—
No. 113. Twelve heads   2.00 1.50 1.00 .50

Squash, three specimens.—
No. 114. Summer   2.00 1.50 1.00 .50

Potato, twelve specimens.—
No. 115. Any variety   2.00 1.50 1.00 .50

Thursday, July 18

*All articles for this exhibition must be
in the hall and ready for inspection by
the judges by 2 o'clock*

This exhibition will be open to the public from 3 to 9 p. m.

Cut Flowers.—
No. 116. Display   4.00 3.00 2.50 2.00 1.50 1.00

Antirrhinum (Snap Dragon).—
No. 117. Display   3.00 2.00 1.00 .50

Table Decorations.—
No. 118. For best table decoration
laid for four covers. Flowers
to be grown by the exhibitor.
Notify the Secretary two days
in advance   5.00 4.00 3.00 2.00 1.00

SCALE OF POINTS BY WHICH THE ABOVE CLASS IS TO BE JUDGED

Arrangement	40 points
Quality	25 "
Proportion and harmony of flowers with accessories	20
Accessories	15

Sweet Peas, annual.—
No. 119. Five vases, 25 flower stems
in vase   3.00 2.50 2.00 1.50 1.00

Begonia, tuberous rooted.—
No. 120. Twelve vases   4.00 3.00 2.00 1.00

Apple, twelve specimens.—
No. 121. Yellow Transparent   2.00 1.50 1.00 .50

Blackberry, one quart.—
No. 122. Any variety, five dollars may be used for prizes.

Corn, twelve ears.—
No. 123. Sweet, any named variety   2.00 1.50 1.00 .50

Tomato, twelve specimens.—
   No. 124. Any named variety   2.00 1.50 1.00   .50

Bean, Shell, one-half peck.—
   No. 125. Any named variety   2.00 1.50 1.00   .50

Potato, twelve specimens.—
   No. 126. Irish Cobbler   2.00 1.50 1.00   .50
   No. 127. Any other variety   2.00 1.50 1.00   .50

Thursday, July 25

All articles for this exhibition must be in the hall and ready for inspection by the judges by 2 o'clock

This exhibition will be open to the public from 3 to 9 p. m.

Cut Flowers.—
No. 128. Standard	4.00	3.00	2.50	2.00	1.50	1.00
No. 129. Ten vases		2.50	2.00	1.50	1.00	.50

This number is intended for the growers who do not compete in the call for 20 vases and displays during the year.

Gladiolus.—
No. 130. Twenty vases, one spike in
each   4.00   3.00   2.00   1.00

Phlox, perennial.—
No. 131. Fifteen vases, one cluster
in each   3.00   2.00   1.00   .50

Annuals.—
No. 132. Display   3.00   2.50   2.00   1.50   1.00

Apple, twelve specimens.—
No. 133. Astrachan   2.00   1.50   1.00   .50
No. 134. Yellow Transparent   2.00   1.50   1.00   .50

Blackberry, one quart.—
No. 135. Any varieties, five dollars may be used for prizes.

Pear, twelve specimens.—
No. 136. Any variety   1.50   1.00   .50

Peach, twelve specimens.—
No. 137. Any variety, five dollars may be used for prizes.

Plum, twelve specimens.—
No. 138. Red June   1.50   1.00   .50

Bean, Shell, one-half peck.—
No. 139. Dwarf Horticultural   2.00   1.50   1.00   .50
No. 140. Any other variety   2.00   1.50   1.00   .50

Corn, twelve ears.—
No. 141.   Any named variety   2.00 1.50 1.00   .50

Squash, three specimens.—
No. 142.   Summer   2.00 1.50 1.00   .50

Potato, twelve specimens.—
No. 143.   Rose   2.00 1.50 1.00   .50
No. 144.   Varieties not scheduled   2.00 1.50 1.00   .30

Vegetables.—
No. 145.   Display, Round Table, $15.00 may be used for
prizes.   Notify the Secretary two days in advance.

Thursday, August 1

*All articles for this exhibition must be
in the hall and ready for inspection by
the judges by 2 o'clock*

This exhibition will be open to the public from 3 to 9 p. m.

Cut Flowers.—
No. 146. Basket   4.00 3.00 2.50 2.00 1.50 1.00

Flower Arrangement for Living Room.—
No. 147. Pottery container to be furnished
by exhibitor   3.00 2.50 2.00 1.50 1.00 .50

Gladiolus.—
No. 148. Display   8.00 6.00 5.00 4.00 3.00

Asters.—
No. 149. Twenty vases, one bloom in
each   3.00 2.50 2.00 1.00 .50

Salpiglossis.—
No. 150. Display   4.00 3.00 2.00

Phlox, perennial.—
No. 151. Fifteen vases, one cluster
in each   3.00 2.00 1.50 1.00 .50

Zinnia.—
No. 152. Twenty vases, one flower in
each   3.00 2.50 2.00 1.50 1.00 .50

Wild Flowers, no duplicates.—
No. 153. Fifteen vases, no duplicates.
Five stems in a vase   2.50 2.00 1.50 1.00 .50

Special Prizes
Offered by Mr. Herbert R. Kinney

E. Table Decorations. For the best
table decorations   3.00 2.50 2.00 1.50 1.00

This call is intended for exhibitors who do not exhibit in other
table decorations during the year. Notify the Secretary two days
in advance.

Apple, twelve specimens.—
No. 154.   Oldenburg   2.00 1.50 1.00   .50
No. 155.   Williams   2.00 1.50 1.00   .50

Peach, twelve specimens.—
No. 156.   Any variety   2.00 1.50 1.00   .50

Cabbage, three specimens.—
No. 157.   Copenhagen   2.00 1.50 1.00   .50
No. 158.   Any other named variety   2.00 1.50 1.00   .50

Corn, twelve ears.—
No. 159.   Yellow, Sweet   2.50 2.00 1.50 1.00   .50

Squash, three specimens.—
No. 160.   Any named variety (excepting
              summer varieties)   2.00 1.50 1.00   .50

Tomato, open culture, twelve specimens.—
No. 161.   Any named variety   2.00 1.50 1.00   .50

Gladiolus Exhibition
Thursday, August 8

All articles for this exhibition must be in the hall and ready for inspection by the judges by 2 o'clock

This exhibition will be open to the public from 3 to 9 p. m.

Gladiolus.—
No. 162. Display. Notify the Secretary two days in advance. Forty dollars may be used in prizes.
No. 163. Standard of Gladioli   3.00 2.50 2.00 1.00   .50
No. 164. Twenty vases, one spike in
    each   4.00 3.00 2.00 1.00   .50

Aster, large flowered, long stem.—
No. 165. Vase of 20 blooms   3.00 2.50 2.00 1.00   .50

Salpiglossis.—
No. 166. Basket   2.50 2.00 1.00   .50

Phlox Drummondi.—
No. 167. Display   2.00 1.50 1.00   .50

Annuals.—
No. 168. Display, fifteen dollars may be used in prizes.

Display of Flowers on a Mirror.—
No. 169. Small vase to be shown on a mirror. Vase and mirror to be furnished by the society. Ten dollars may be used in prizes. Highest award not to exceed $1.50. One entry for each exhibitor.

Apple, twelve specimens.—
No. 170. Williams   2.00 1.50 1.00   .50
No. 171. For varieties not scheduled, five dollars may be used for prizes.

Apple, crab, twenty-four specimens.—
No. 172. Varieties not scheduled   1.50 1.00   .50

Pear, twelve specimens.—
No. 173. Clapp's Favorite   3.00 2.50 2.00 1.50 1.00   .50
No. 174. For varieties not scheduled, five dollars may be used for prizes.

Peach, twelve specimens.—
    No. 175. Carman   1.50 1.00 .50
    No. 176. Any other variety   1.50 1.00 .50

Plum, twelve specimens.—
    No. 177. Washington   1.50 1.00 .50
    No. 178. Japanese varieties, five dollars
                 may be used for prizes.

Bean, Shell, one-half peck.—
    No. 179. Dwarf, any variety   2.00 1.50 1.00 .50
    No. 180. Pole, any variety   2.00 1.50 1.00 .50

Bean, String, one-half peck.—
    No. 181. Kentucky Wonder   2.00 1.50 1.00 .50

Corn, Sweet, twelve ears.—
    No. 182. Any named variety   2.50 2.00 1.50 1.00

Tomato, twelve specimens.—
    No. 183. Any named variety 2.50 2.00 1.50 1.00 .50

Mushroom, native.—
    No. 184. Collection of edible varieties, prizes will be awarded.

Cucumber, for pickles.—
    No. 185. One-half peck   2.00 1.50 1.00 .50

Thursday, August 15

*All articles for this exhibition must be
in the hall and ready for inspection by
the judges by 2 o'clock*

This exhibition will be open to the public from 3 to 9 p. m.

Zinnia.—
    No. 186. Display, notify the Secretary
             two days in advance 4.00 3.00 2.50 2.00 1.50 1.00

Dahlia.—
    No. 187. Twenty vases, one flower in
             each vase   4.00 3.00 2.00 1.00

Obadiah Brown Hadwen Fund

Display of Garden Flowers.—
    F. Not to exceed 24 square feet.
       Notify the Secretary two days
       in advance   4.00 3.50 3.00 2.50 2.00 1.00

*   *   *

Aster, single or anemone.—
    No. 188. Vase   2.00 1.50 1.00   .50

Apples, twelve specimens.—
    No. 189. Any variety   2.00 1.50 1.00   .50

Plums, twelve specimens.—
    No. 190. Bradshaw   3.00 2.00 1.50 1.00   .50
    No. 191. Imperial Gage   2.00 1.50 1.00   .50
    No. 192. Guiei   1.50 1.00   .50
    No. 193. For varieties not scheduled, three
             dollars may be used for prizes.

Peach, twelve specimens.—
    No. 194. Five dollars may be used in prizes.

Bean, Pole, one-half peck.—
    No. 195. Shell   2.50 2.00 1.50 1.00
    No. 196. String, any variety   2.50 2.00 1.50 1.00

Corn, twelve ears.—
    No. 197. Sweet, not less than twelve rows
                       2.50 2.00 1.50 1.00

Vegetables.—

No. 198. Display of vegetables from
Home Gardens to cover 12
square feet   6.00 5.00 4.00 3.00 2.00 1.00

Scale of Points

Cut Flowers and Wild Flowers.—

Arrangement	30 points
Quality of blooms	40 "
Number of varieties	15 "
Properly named	15

Lilies.—

Size and color of bloom	35 points
Number of perfect flowers and buds on stem	35 "
Arrangement	15
Properly named	15

Displays.—

Arrangement	40 points
Quality	45 "
Variety	15 "

Collections.—

Quality	45 points
Arrangement	25 "
Variety	30 "

Table Decorations.—

Arrangement	40 points
Quality	25 "
Proportion and harmony of flowers with accessories	20
Accessories	15

Thursday, August 22

All articles for this exhibition must be in the hall and ready for inspection by the judges by 2 o'clock

This exhibition will be open to the public from 3 to 9 p. m.

Cut Flowers.—

No. 199. Display 5.00 4.00 3.50 3.00 2.50 2.00 1.50 1.00

No. 200. Basket   3.00 2.50 2.00 1.50 1.00

Aster, large flowered.—

No. 201. Twenty vases, three blooms
in each   3.00 2.50 2.00 1.00 .50

Lilies.—

No. 202. Display   5.00 4.00 3.00 2.00
Notify the Secretary two days
in advance.

Dahlia.—

LARGE FLOWERED.—

No. 203. Twenty vases, one flower in
each   4.00 3.00 2.00 1.50 1.00

Zinnia, Lilliput variety.—

No. 204. Display   3.00 2.00 1.00 .50

Begonia, tuberous rooted.—

No. 205. Display   5.00 4.00 3.00 2.00 1.00

Verbena.—

No. 206. Basket or Bowl   2.50 2.00 1.50 1.00 .50

No. 207. Display. A group of five miniature vases, not to exceed 4 inches in height. Vases to be owned by exhibitors. Six dollars may be used for prizes. Highest award not to exceed $1.50.

Apples, twelve specimens.—

No. 208. Porter   1.50 1.00 .50

No. 209. Gravenstein   2.50 2.00 1.50 1.00 .50

No. 210. For varieties not scheduled, five
dollars may be used for prizes.

Plum.—

No. 211. Display, no restriction as to
arrangements   4.00 3.00 2.00 1.00

Peach, twelve specimens.—

No. 212.   Any variety   1.50 1.00   .50

Squash, three specimens.—

No. 213.   Any named variety   2.50 2.00 1.50 1.00

Pepper, twelve specimens.—

No. 214.   Harris's Early   2.50 2.00 1.50 1.00

No. 215.   Bell Type   2.50 2.00 1.50 1.00

Vegetables.—

No. 216.   Display, not to exceed 24 square feet, $20.00 may
be used for prizes. Notify the Secretary two days in
advance.

Thursday, August 29

All articles for this exhibition must be in the hall and ready for inspection by the judges by 2 o'clock

This exhibition will be open to the public from 3 to 9 p. m.

Cut Flowers.—

No. 217.	Display	5.00	4.00	3.00	2.50	2.00	1.50	1.00
No. 218.	Standard		3.00	2.50	2.00	1.50	1.00	.50

This number is intended for the growers who do not compete in call for 20 vases and displays during the year.

Dahlia.—

No. 219. Fifty vases, one flower in each. Twenty-five dollars may be used in prizes. Notify the Secretary two days in advance.

Aster.—

No. 220.	Vase of large flowered	3.00	2.50	2.00	1.00	.50
No. 221.	Display, not exceeding 25 square feet	5.00	4.00	3.00	2.00	1.00

Scabiosa.—

No. 222.	Vase	2.50	2.00	1.50	1.00	.50

Apple, twelve specimens.—

No. 223.	Gravenstein	3.00	2.50	2.00	1.50	1.00	.50
No. 224.	Maiden's Blush				1.50	1.00	.50
No. 225.	Wealthy		2.50	2.00	1.50	1.00	.50

Apple, Crab, twenty-four specimens.—

No. 226.	Hyslop	2.50	2.00	1.50	1.00	.50

Pear, twelve specimens.—

No. 227.	Bartlett	3.00	2.50	2.00	1.50	1.00	.50

No. 228. Varieties not scheduled, five dollars may be used for prizes.

Peach, twelve specimens.—

No. 229.	Champion			1.50	1.00	.50
No. 230.	Oldmixon			2.00	1.00	.50
No. 231.	Elberta	2.50	2.00	1.50	1.00	.50
No. 232.	Seedlings			1.50	1.00	.50
No. 233.	Crawford (early)		2.00	1.50	1.00	.50

No. 234. Varieties not scheduled, five dollars may be used for prizes.

No. 235. New varieties. Five dollars may be used in prizes.

Plum, twelve specimens.—

No. 236.	Golden Varieties	1.50	1.00	.50
No. 237.	Lombard	2.00 1.50	1.00	.50
No. 238.	Quackenboss	1.50	1.00	.50
No. 239.	Burbank ·	2.00 1.50	1.00	.50
No. 240.	New varieties	1.50	1.00	.50

No. 241. For Japanese varieties not scheduled, five dollars may be used for prizes.

No. 242. Other varieties not scheduled, five dollars may be used for prizes.

Grape, three clusters.—

No. 243.	Green Mountain	2.00 1.50	1.00	.50
No. 244.	Moore's	1.50	1.00	.50
No. 245.	Ontario	1.50	1.00	.50

Pepper, twelve specimens.—

No. 246.	Squash	2.00 1.50	1.00	.50
No. 247.	Any other variety	2.00 1.50	1.00	.50

Tomato, twelve specimens.—

No. 248.	Beauty	2.50 2.00	1.50	1.00	.50
No. 249.	Any other variety	2.50 2.00	1.50	1.00	.50

Bean, one-half peck.—

No. 250.	Dwarf Lima	2.00 1.50	1.00	.50
No. 251.	Pole Lima	2.00 1.50	1.00	.50

Cabbage, three specimens.—

No. 252.	Any named variety	2.00 1.50	1.00	.50

Celery, blanched (named) six specimens.—

No. 253.	Any variety	2.00 1.50	1.00	.50

Carrot, twelve specimens.—

No. 254.	Any variety	2.50 2.00	1.50	1.00	.50

Egg Plant.—

No. 255.	Three specimens	2.00	1.50	1.00

Mushroom, native.—

No. 256. Collection of edible varieties, prizes will be awarded.

Dahlia Exhibition

Thursday, September 5

All articles for this exhibition must be in the hall and ready for inspection by the judges by 2 o'clock

This exhibition will be open to the public from 3 to 9 p. m.

Cut Flowers.—

No. 257. Display   5.00 4.00 3.50 3.00 2.50 2.00 1.00

Dahlia.—

No. 258. Display. Thirty-five dollars may be used for prizes. Notify the secretary two days in advance.

No. 259. Twelve vases, one flower in each. This number is intended for the growers who do not compete in other classes for Dahlias during the year.

2.50 2.00 1.50 1.00 .50

No. 260. Single varieties, twenty vases 3.00 2.50 2.00 1.00

No. 261. Basket of large flowered 3.00 2.50 2.00 1.00

POMPON.

No. 262. Twenty vases, three sprays in each 3.00 2.50 2.00 1.00

Cosmos.—

No. 263. Vase or basket   2.50 2.00 1.50 1.00 .50

No. 264. Metal container of cut flowers, container to be furnished by exhibitor 3.00 2.50 2.00 1.00

Apple, twelve specimens.—

No. 265. American Beauty or Sterling   1.50 1.00 .50

No. 266. Twenty-ounce   1.50 1.00 .50

Pear, twelve specimens.—

No. 267. Louise Bonne de Jersey   1.50 1.00 .50

No. 268. Urbaniste   1.50 1.00 .50

No. 269. Varieties not scheduled, five dollars may be used for prizes.

Peach, twelve specimens.—

| No. 270. | Crawford (late) | 2.00 | 1.50 | 1.00 | .50 |
| No. 271. | Display, no restriction as to arrangement | 8.00 | 6.00 | 4.00 | 3.00 |

Plum, twelve specimens.—

| No. 272. | Any variety | 2.00 | 1.50 | 1.00 | .50 |

Grape, three clusters.—

No. 273.	Brighton		1.50	1.00	.50
No. 274.	Campbell		1.50	1.00	.50
No. 275.	Lindley		1.50	1.00	.50
No. 276.	Worden	2.50	2.00	1.50	1.00	.50
No. 277.	Concord	2.50	2.00	1.50	1.00	.50
No. 278.	Delaware		2.00	1.50	1.00	.50
No. 279.	Niagara	2.50	2.00	1.50	1.00	.50
No. 280.	Pocklington		1.50	1.00	.50
No. 281.	Moore's Diamond		1.50	1.00	.50
No. 282.	For other varieties, ten dollars may be used for prizes.
No. 283.	Display of Grapes. Ten dollars may be used for prizes.
No. 284.	New varieties, five dollars may be used for prizes.

Quince, twelve specimens.—

| No. 285. | Any variety | 2.00 | 1.50 | 1.00 | .50 |

Melon, three specimens.—

No. 286.	Green Flesh	2.00	1.50	1.00	.50
No. 287.	Yellow Flesh	2.00	1.50	1.00	.50
No. 288.	Water	2.00	1.50	1.00	.50

Tomato.—

| No. 289. | Display | 4.00 | 3.00 | 2.50 | 2.00 | 1.00 |

Vegetables.—

| No. 290. | Display to cover 24 square feet. Notify the Secretary two days in advance | 7.00 | 6.00 | 5.00 | 4.00 | 3.00 |

Thursday, September 12

*All articles for this exhibition must be
in the hall and ready for inspection by
the judges by 2 o'clock*

This exhibition will be open to the public from 3 to 9 p. m.

Basket of Cut Flowers.—

No. 291. 3.00 2.50 2.00 1.50 1.00 .50

Display of Flower Arrangement.—

No. 292. Twelve receptacles, no restrictions as to kind of tables used, not to cover more than 24 square feet. Flowers to be grown by exhibitor. Receptacles to be furnished by the exhibitors. Notify the Secretary two days in advance. Twenty-five dollars may be used in prizes.

SCALE OF POINTS BY WHICH THE ABOVE CLASS IS TO BE JUDGED

Arrangement of flowers 40 points
Proportion and harmony of flowers with
receptacles 35
Quality of flowers 25

Celosia.—

No. 293. Display 4.00 3.00 2.50 2.00 1.50 1.00
Notify the Secretary two days in advance.

Edwin Draper Fund

Begonia, tuberous rooted.—

G. Display of Potted Plants. Fifteen dollars may be used in prizes.

*   *   *

No. 294. Cut Flowers in vases. Ten dollars may be used in prizes.

Apple, twelve specimens.—

No. 295. Hubbardston 2.00 1.50 1.00 .50
No. 296. For other varieties not scheduled, five dollars may be used for prizes.

Pear, twelve specimens.—
No. 297. Seckel   3.00 2.50 2.00 1.50 1.00 .50
No. 298. Any variety, not scheduled   1.50 1.00 .50
No. 299. Display, no restriction as to
        arrangement   6.00 5.00 4.00 3.00 2.00
        Notify the Secretary two days in advance.

Quince, twelve specimens.—
No. 300. Orange   2.00 1.50 1.00 .50

Special Prizes
Offered by Miss Frances C. Morse

H. For most artistic table arrangement of
        Marigolds, laid for four covers   4.00 3.00 2.00 1.00

                    *   *   *

Potato, six varieties (named).—
No. 301. Twelve specimens of each
                5.00 4.00 3.00 2.00 1.50 1.00
Squash, three specimens.—
No. 302. Warren   2.00 1.50 1.00 .50
No. 303. Golden Hubbard   2.50 2.00 1.50 1.00 .50
No. 304. For varieties not scheduled, five dollars may be used
        for prizes.
Cabbage, three specimens.—
No. 305. Red   2.00 1.50 1.00 .50
No. 306. Savoy   1.50 1.00 .50
No. 307. Any other variety   2.50 2.00 1.50 1.00 .50
Cauliflower.—
No. 308. Three specimens   2.50 2.00 1.50 1.00 .50
Turnip.—
No. 309. Twelve specimens   1.50 1.00 .50
Broccoli.—
No. 310. Three specimens   2.00 1.50 1.00 .50

Thursday, September 19

*All articles for this exhibition must be
in the hall and ready for inspection by
the judges by 2 o'clock*

This exhibition will be open to the public from 3 to 9 p. m.

Cut Flowers.—
No. 311. Display, not exceeding 30 square
feet   5.00 4.00 3.50 3.00 2.50 2.00 1.50 1.00

Cosmos.—
No. 312. Display. Notify the Secretary
two days in advance   3.00 2.00 1.50 1.00 .50

Table Decorations of Flowers.—
No. 313. For best table decoration laid
for four covers, no restrictions.
Notify the Secretary two days
in advance
6.00 5.00 4.50 4.00 3.00 2.00 1.50 1.00

SCALE OF POINTS BY WHICH THE ABOVE CLASS IS TO BE JUDGED

Arrangement   40 points
Quality   25   "
Proportion and harmony of
flowers with accessories   20
Accessories   15

Marigold.—
No. 314. Display. Notify the Secretary two days in advance   3.00 2.00 1.00 .50

Apple, one standard box.—
No. 315. McIntosh   4.00 3.00 2.00 1.00 .50

Apple, twelve specimens.—
No. 316. Tompkins King   2.00 1.50 1.00 .50
No. 317. McIntosh   3.00 2.50 2.00 1.50 1.00 .50

Pear, twelve specimens.—
No. 318. Sheldon   3.00 2.00 1.50 1.00 .50

Squash, three specimens.—

| No. 319. | Delicious | 2.00 | 1.50 | 1.00 | .50 |
| No. 320. | Any other variety, not scheduled | 2.50 | 2.00 | 1.50 | 1.00 |

Cauliflower, three specimens.—

| No. 321. | | 2.00 | 1.50 | 1.00 | .50 |

Vegetables.—

No. 322. Collection not to exceed 25
varieties   10.00 8.00 7.00 6.00 5.00
Notify the Secretary two days in advance.

Thursday, September 26

*All articles for this exhibition must be
in the hall and ready for inspection by
the judges by 2 o'clock*

This exhibition will be open to the public from 3 to 9 p. m.

Standard of Cut Flowers.—
No. 323.   Twenty dollars may be used in prizes.

Dried Flowers, Statice, Strawflowers, Lunaria (Honesty).—
No. 324.   Display.   4.00 3.50 2.00 1.00

Apple, one standard box.—
No. 325.   Any variety not scheduled
                              4.00 3.00 2.00 1.00   .50

Apple, twelve specimens.—
No. 326.   Sutton Beauty   2.00 1.50 1.00   .50

Display of Fruit.—
No. 327.   Not to exceed 20 square feet. Thirty dollars may be
           used in prizes.

Pear, twelve specimens.—
No. 328.   Bosc   3.00 2.00 1.50 1.00   .50

Grape, open culture.—
No. 329.   Collection of not less than five varieties, three clusters
           each.   3.00 2.50 2.00 1.50 1.00

Table Decorations—Fruit.—
No. 330.   For the best table decoration
           laid for four covers, no restric-
           tions. Notify the Secretary two
           days in advance   4.00 3.00 2.00 1.00

Pumpkins, three specimens.—
No. 331.   Sweet   2.00 1.50 1.00   .50

Cabbage, three specimens.—
No. 332.   Any named variety 2.50 2.00 1.50 1.00   .50

Parsley.—
No. 333.   One-half peck   2.50 2.00 1.50 1.00   .50

Peppers.—
No. 334.   Display   3.00 2.50 2.00 1.50 1.00

Celery, blanched, six specimens.—
No. 335.   Golden   2.50 2.00 1.50 1.00
No. 336.   Other varieties   2.50 2.00 1.50 1.00

Squash, three specimens.—
No. 337.   Blue Hubbard   3.00 2.50 2.00 1.50 1.00

Special Prizes
Offered by Mr. Herbert R. Kinney

I.   Display of vegetables from
       Home Gardens to
       cover 16 square feet   5.00 4.00 3.00 2.50 2.00 1.00

Fruit and Vegetable Exhibition
Thursday, October 3
All articles for this exhibition must be in the hall and ready for inspection by the judges by 2 o'clock

This exhibition will be open to the public from 3 to 9 p. m.

Ferns.—

No. 338. Display, potted plants, named varieties. Twenty dollars may be used in prizes.

Specimen Fern.—

No. 339. One plant   3.00 2.00 1.00

Cut Flowers.—

No. 340. Display—$40.00 may be awarded in prizes.

Basket.—

No. 341. Fifteen dollars may be used in prizes.

Hardy Chrysanthemum, out-door culture.—

No. 342. Plants. Fifteen dollars may be used in prizes.

No. 343. Cut flowers in vases. Ten dollars may be used in prizes.

Apple, one standard box.—

No. 344.	Baldwin	4.00	3.00	2.00	1.00	.50
No. 345.	Any other variety except McIntosh	4.00	3.00	2.00	1.00	.50

Apple, twelve specimens.—

No. 346.	Baldwin	3.50	3.00	2.50	2.00	1.50	1.00	.50
No. 347.	Bellflower					1.50	1.00	.50
No. 348.	Winter Banana					1.50	1.00	.50
No. 349.	Peck's					1.50	1.00	.50
No. 350.	R. I. Greening				3.00	2.00	1.50	1.00	.50
No. 351.	Northern Spy				3.00	2.00	1.50	1.00	.50
No. 352.	Palmer					1.50	1.00	.50
No. 353.	Roxbury Russet				3.00	2.00	1.50	1.00	.50
No. 354.	Cortland					2.00	1.50	1.00	.50
No. 355.	Opalescent					1.50	1.00	.50
No. 356.	Delicious				2.50	2.00	1.50	1.00	.50
No. 357.	Collection, not to exceed 10 varieties			5.00	4.00	3.00	2.50	2.00

No. 358. New varieties, five dollars may be used in prizes.

No. 359.   Sweet varieties not scheduled, five dollars may be used for prizes.

No. 360.   For varieties other than sweet not scheduled, fifteen dollars may be used for prizes.

No. 361.   For varieties that have been scheduled, fifteen dollars may be used.

Pear, twelve specimens.—

No. 362.   Angouleme   1.50 1.00   .50

No. 363.   Clairgeau   2.00 1.50 1.00   .50

No. 364.   Lawrence   3.00 2.00 1.50 1.00   .50

No. 365.   Anjou   3.00 2.50 2.00 1.50 1.00   .50

No. 366.   For varieties not scheduled, ten dollars may be used for prizes.

No. 367.   For new varieties, five dollars may be used in prizes.

Grape, open culture.—

No. 368.   For any variety, six clusters, ten dollars may be used for prizes.

Peach, twelve specimens.—

No. 369.   Any variety, named, ten dollars may be used for prizes.

Quince, twelve specimens.—

No. 370.   Champion   2.00 1.50 1.00   .50

Cauliflower.—

No. 371.   Three specimens   2.50 2.00 1.50 1.00

Celery, blanched, six specimens.—

No. 372.   Golden   2.50 2.00 150 1.00   .50

No. 373.   Any other varieties, not
            scheduled   2.00 1.50 1.00   .50

Endive.—

No. 374.   Six specimens   1.50 1.00   .50

Leeks.—

No. 375.   Twelve specimens   1.50 1.00   .50

Onion, twelve specimens.—

No. 376.   For varieties, five dollars may be used for prizes.

Salsify.—

No. 377.   Twelve specimens   1.50 1.00   .50

Turnip, twelve specimens.—

No. 378.   Purple Top Globe   2.00 1.50 1.00   .50

No. 379.   Any variety, not scheduled   2.00 1.50 1.00   .50

Chrysanthemum Exhibition

Thursday, Nov. 7, 3 to 9 p. m.
Friday, Nov. 8, 9 a. m. to 9 p. m.
Saturday, Nov. 9, 9 a. m. to 9 p. m.
Sunday, Nov. 10, 12 m. to 9 p. m.

All articles for this exhibition must be in the hall and ready for inspection by the judges by 1 o'clock Thursday

Chrysanthemums.—

No. 380.	Twelve blooms, not less than six varieties, to be named	12.00	10.00	8.00
No. 381.	Collection of twenty-five large blooms, long stems	20.00	15.00	10.00
No. 382.	Pompoms, display in vases	5.00 4.00	3.00	2.00
No. 383.	Single varieties, display in vases	5.00 4.00	3.00	2.00
No. 384.	Anemones, display in vases	5.00 4.00	3.00	2.00
No. 385.	Six specimen plants	10.00	8.00	6.00
No. 386.	One specimen plant	3.00	2.00	1.00

Commercial Growers (Standard Varieties).—

No. 387.	Chrysanthemums, vase of white	4.00	3.00	2.00
No. 388.	Chrysanthemums, vase of yellow	4.00	3.00	2.00
No. 389.	Chrysanthemums, vase of pink	4.00	3.00	2.00

Note. Six flowers in each, one variety in each vase. Stems not less than two feet.

Non-commercial Growers.—

No. 390.	Chrysanthemums, vase of white	4.00	3.00	2.00
No. 391.	Chrysanthemums, vase of yellow	4.00	3.00	2.00
No. 392.	Chrysanthemums, vase of pink	4.00	3.00	2.00

Note. Six flowers in each, one variety in each vase. Stems not less than two feet.

Chrysanthemums.—

No. 393.	Basket of Pompons	4.00	3.00	2.00	1.00
No. 394.	Basket of Single	4.00	3.00	2.00	1.00
No. 395.	Basket of Anemones	4.00	3.00	2.00	1.00

Frederick A. Blake Fund

J. Chrysanthemums.—Best bloom   4.00 3.00 2.00

Obadiah Brown Hadwen Fund

K. Chrysanthemums.—Large Flowers. Basket. Fifteen dollars
to be awarded in prizes.

Special Prizes
Offered by Mrs. Mabel Knowles Gage

L. Table Decorations—Laid for four covers, Chrysanthemums
predominating. Notify the Secretary two days in advance.
Fifty dollars to be used in prizes.

*   *   *

Special Display of Plants.—
> No. 396. Three hundred and fifty dollars may be used for
> prizes.

Persons competing for these premiums, must notify the Secretary previous to 6 p. m. Monday, November 4.
> No. 397. For exhibits—no restrictions as to where grown,
> or by whom—$75.00 may be used for prizes.

Fern Globes.—
> No. 398.   3.00 2.00 1.50 1.00

Glass Fernery.—
> No. 399. Other than Fern Globe   4.00 3.00 2.00 1.00

Wild Fruits and Berries.—
> No. 400. Display   5.00 4.00 3.00 2.50 1.50 1.00

Physalis Franchettii (Chinese Lanterns).—
> No. 401. Basket   4.00 3.00 2.00 1.00

Fruit Display.—
> No. 402. No restriction as to arrangement. $40.00 may be used
> in prizes. Notify the Secretary two days in advance.

Apple, five standard boxes.—
> No. 403. Any variety   15.00 10.00 5.00 4.00

Apples, forty-nine specimens.—

No. 404.	Baldwin	6.00	5.00	4.00	.0	2.00	1.00
No. 405.	McIntosh	6.00	5.00	4.00	.0	2.00	1.00
No. 406.	Delicious		5.00	4.00	3.00	2.00	1.00
No. 407.	Any other named variety						
			5.00	4.00	3.00	2.00	1.00
No. 408.	Fancy Basket of Apples	3.00	2.50	2.00	1.50	1.00
No. 409.	Fancy Basket of Pears	3.00	3.50	2.00	1.50	1.00

Special Exhibition of Apples
William Eames Fund

A. **Baldwin, best twelve.—**
   Three premiums   1.50 1.00   .50
B. **Northern Spy.—**
   Three premiums   1.50 1.00   .50
C. **Delicious.—**
   Three premiums   1.50 1.00   .50
D. **Rhode Island Greening.—**
   Three premiums   1.50 1.00   .50
E. **Roxbury Russet.—**
   Three premiums   1.50 1.00   .50
F. **Sutton Beauty.—**
   Three premiums   1.50 1.00   .50
G. **McIntosh.—**
   Three premiums   1.50 1.00   .50
H. **Any other Variety.—**
   Three premiums   1.50 1.00   .50

                    *   *   *

Brussels Sprouts.—

| No. 410. | One-half peck | | 1.50 | 1.00 | .50 |

Celery, blanched, six specimens.—

| No. 411. | Giant Pascal | | 2.00 | 1.50 | 1.00 | .50 |
| No. 412. | Any other variety | 2.50 | 2.00 | 1.50 | 1.00 | .50 |

Onion, twelve specimens.—

No. 413.	White Globe			1.50	1.00	.50
No. 414.	Yellow Globe Danvers	2.50	2.00	1.50	1.00	.50
No. 415.	Red Globe		2.00	1.50	1.00	.50
No. 416.	Cracker			1.50	1.00	.50
No. 417.	Any other variety		2.00	1.50	1.00	.50

Cabbage, three specimens.—
No. 418.   2.00 1.50 1.00   .50

Parsnip, twelve specimens.—
No. 419.   Hollow Crown   2.00 1.50 1.00   .50
No. 420.   Any other variety   2.00 1.50 1.00   .50

Squash, three specimens.—
No. 421.   Green Hubbard   2.50 2.00 1.50 1.00   .50

Squash.—
No. 422.   Collection   5.00 4.50 4.00 3.00

Gourds.—
No. 423.   Display   3.00 2.50 2.00 1.50 1.00 .50

Turnip, twelve specimens.—
No. 424.   Purple Top Globe   2.00 1.50 1.00   .50
No. 425.   English varieties, not scheduled
                                       2.00 1.50 1.00   .50

Turnip, six specimens.—
No. 426.   White Swede   2.00 1.50 1.00   .50
No. 427.   Yellow Swede   2.00 1.50 1.00   .50

Potato, twelve specimens.—
No. 428.   Green Mountain   2.50 2.00 1.50 1.00
No. 429.   Any other variety   2.50 2.00 1.50 1.00

Grains.—
No. 430.   Best exhibit, five dollars may be used for prizes.

Field Beans.—
No. 431.   Best exhibit, ten dollars may be used for prizes.

———

Annual Meeting, Thursday, December 5, 1935.
Premiums will be paid on or after November 20, 1935.

THE LIBRARY OF THE
WORCESTER COUNTY HORTICULTURAL SOCIETY

The Library Committee wish to call your attention to the Library and Reading Room, where the librarian is always ready to extend every facility possible to those in search of horticultural information.

COMMITTEE ON
LIBRARY AND PUBLICATIONS

EDWARD W. BREED, Chairman   MRS. AMY W. SMITH
WILLIAM ANDERSON   HERBERT R. KINNEY
                  LUCY M. COULSON, Librarian

SOME OF THE RECENT ACCESSIONS TO THE LIBRARY

Rose Garden Primer, by Eber Holmes
American Alpines in the Garden, by Anderson McCully
Western American Alpines, by Ira N. Gabrielson
Sempervivums, by R. Lloyd Praeger, D.Sc.
Flowers and Folk-lore, by Florence Hedleston Crane
Natural Rock Gardening, by B. H. B. Symons-Jeune
Gardens in America, by Marion Cran
Lilies for English Gardens, by Gertrude Jekyll
Gardening with Herbs, by Helen M. Fox
The Arrangement of Flowers, by Mrs. Walter R. Hine
Delphiniums, by George A. Phillips
Arranging Flowers Throughout the Year, by Katherine T. Cary
    and Nellie D. Merrill
Everybody's Garden, by Walter Prichard Eaton
Hortus, by L. H. Bailey and Ethel Zoe Bailey
Pleasures and Problems of a Rock Garden, by Louise Beebe Wilder
Lily Year Book 1932, The Royal Horticultural Society
Practical Carnation Culture, by T. A. Weston
Cactus Culture, by Ellen D. Schulz.
Birds of Massachusetts, Vol. III
How to Grow Roses, by Robert Pyle, J. Horace McFarland and
    G. A. Stevens
Productive Beekeeping, by Frank C. Pellett

Alphabetical Check Iris List, by Mrs. Ethel A. S. Peckham
Rock Garden, by Archie Thornton
Aristocrats of the Trees, by Ernest H. Wilson, M.A., V.M.H.
Rock Garden and Alpine Plants, by Henry Correvon
Our Wild Orchids, by Frank Morris and Edward A. Eames
Principles and Practice in Pruning, by M. G. Kains
Backyard Gardens, by Edward I. Farrington
Commercial Carnation Culture, by J. Harrison Dick
American Rose Annual, 1930
Manual of American Grape Growing, by U. P. Hedrick
The Romance of Our Trees, by Ernest H. Wilson, M.A., V.M.H.
Plant Culture, by George W. Oliver
Hardy Plants for Cottage Gardens, by Helen R. Albee
Wild Flowers of New York, by Homer D. House
Pages from a Garden Notebook, by Mrs. Francis King
Conifers and Their Characteristics, by Coltman & Rogers
Field Book of American Trees and Shrubs, by F. Schuyler
Gladiolus, by Matthew Crawford
Wild Flowers and Ferns, by Herbert Durand
Making the Grounds Attractive with Shrubbery, by Grace Tabor
The Amateur's Book of the Dahlias, by Mrs. Charles H. Stout
Gardening for Women, by Hon. Frances Wolseley
Insect Pests of Farm, Garden and Orchard, by E. Dwight Sander-
    son and Leonard Marion Peairs
Winter Sunshine, by John Burroughs
Wake-Robin, by John Burroughs
Locusts and Wild Honey, by John Burroughs
Plant Breeding, Grafting and Budding, Fruit Improvement,
    Small Fruits, Gardening, Useful Plants, Flowers, Trees, Biog-
    raphy Index, by Luther Burbank
Commercial Floriculture, by Fritz Bahr
Cyclopedia of Hardy Fruits, by U. P. Hedrick
A Garden of Herbs, by E. S. Rodhe
Textbook of Pomology, by J. H. Gourley
The Rose in America, by J. Horace McFarland
Trees as Good Citizens, by Charles L. Pack
The Fern Lover's Companion, by George Henry Tilton
Color Standards and Color Nomenclature, by Robert Ridgway
Massachusetts Beautiful, by Wallace Nutting

The Book of Hardy Flowers, by H. H. Thomas
Bulbs and Tuberous Rooted Plants, by C. L. Allen
Practical Plant Propagation, by Alfred C. Hottes
The Chrysanthemum, by Arthur Herrington
Commercial Rose Culture, by Eber Holmes
Lists of Plant Types, by Stephen F. Hamblin
Outside the House Beautiful, by Henrietta C. Peabody
Cultivated Evergreens, by L. H. Bailey
American Fruits, by Samuel Fraser
Wall and Water Gardens, by Gertrude Jekyll
Adventures in My Garden, by Louise Beebe Wilder
The Rock Garden, by E. H. Jenkins
The Little Garden for Little Money, by Kate L. Brewster
The Food Supply of New England, Arthur W. Gilbert
The Practical Book of Outdoor Flowers, by Richardson Wright.
Roses for All Climates, by George G. Thomas
American Landscape Architecture, by P. H. Elwood, Jr., A.S.L.A.
Manual of Tree and Shrub Insects, by E. P. Felt
America's Greatest Garden, by Ernest H. Wilson, M.A., V.M.H.
The Principles of Flower Arrangement, by A. White
Flowers for Cutting and Decoration, by Richardson Wright
The Flower Beautiful, by Clarence Moores Weed
Hardy Perennials, by A. J. Macself
The Iris, by John C. Wister
Bulb Gardening, by A. J. Macself
Annuals and Biennials, by Gertrude Jekyll
More Aristocrats of the Garden, by Ernest H. Wilson, M.A.,V.M.H.
Garden Cinderellas, by Helen Fox
Lilies, by W. E. Marshall
Lilies and Their Culture in North America, by William N. Craig
A Little Book of Modern Dahlia Culture, by W. H. Waite
Gardening with Peat Moss, by F. F. Rockwell
The Lilac, by Susan Delano McKelvey
Spraying, Dusting and Fumigating of Plants, by A. Freeman
    Mason
Vegetable Forcing, by Ralph L. Watts
Rock Gardening, by Sir James L. Cotter
American Orchid Culture, by Prof. E. A. White
House Plants, by Parker T. Barnes

Lawn Making, by Leonard Barron
Home Flower Growing, by Emil C. Volz
Flower Growing, by Leonard Barron
Flowering Trees and Shrubs, by R. C. Notcutt
Saunders Orchid Guide
Lawns, by F. F. Rockwell
The New Flora and Silva (English)
Garden Lilies, by Isabella Preston
American Rock Gardens, by Stephen F. Hamblin
Productive Soil, by W. W. Weir, M.S.
Tree Crops, by J. Russell Smith
Bush Fruit Production, by Ralph A. Van Meter
The Gladiolus and Its Culture, by A. C. Beal
Spring Flowering Bulbs, by Clark L. Thayer
The Pear and Its Culture, by H. B. Tukey
Muskmelon Culture, by W. J. Wright
Greenhouses, by W. J. Wright
China, Mother of Gardens, by Ernest H. Wilson, M.A., V.M.H.
Lilac Culture, by John C. Wister
Chrysanthemums, by Alex Laurie
Azalias and Camellias, by H. Harold Hume
The Cactus Book, by A. D. Houghton
Garden Pools, by L. W. Ramsey and Charles H. Lawrence
The Book of Water Gardening, by Peter Bisset
Little Book of Climbing Plants, by Alfred C. Hottes
The Book of Shrubs, by Alfred C. Hottes
Japanese Flower Arrangement, by Mary Averill
A History of Garden Art, by Walter P. Wright
Fertilizers for Greenhouses and Garden Crops, by Alex Laurie and
     J. B. Edmond
If I Were to Make a Garden, by Ernest H. Wilson, M.A., V.M.H.

Worcester County Horticultural Society

SCHEDULE OF PRIZES
Offered to
Children of Worcester County

Exhibitions to be held Saturday, August 17
and Saturday, September 7, 1935
Horticultural Building, 30 Elm Street

Worcester, Massachusetts

Saturday, August 17

All articles must be in the hall by 2 o'clock

The exhibits must be the results of individual effort of the child from the time of planting to the arranging of the exhibit.

Open to Children under 14 years of age

Display of Flowers.—

No. 1.   Not to exceed fifteen vases

2.00	1.50	1.25	1.00	.50	.25

Zinnia.—

No. 2.   Not to exceed 10 vases

.75	.50	.25	.25

Asters.—

No. 3.   Not to exceed 10 vases

.75	.50	.25	.25

Petunia.—

No. 4.   Not to exceed 10 vases

.75	.50	.25	.25

Calendula.—

No. 5.   Not to exceed 10 vases

.75	.50	.25	.25

Wild Flowers.—

No. 6.   Not to exceed fifteen vases

1.50	1.25	1.00	.50	.25

No. 7.   Vase of Flowers

1.00	.75	.50	.25	.25

Display of Vegetables.—

No. 8.   Not to exceed 12 varieties

2.00	1.75	1.50	1.25	1.00	.75	.50

Beets.—

No. 9.   Six specimens

.75	.50	.25	.25

Summer Squash.—

No. 10.   Two specimens

.75	.50	.25	.25

String Beans.—

No. 11.   Two quarts

.75	.50	.25	.25

Potato.—

No. 12   Twelve specimens

1.00	.75	.50	.25

Sweet Corn.—

No. 13.   Six ears

1.00	.75	.50	.25

Tomato.—

No. 14.   Six specimens

.75	.50	.25	.25

Carrots.—

No. 15.   Six specimens

.75	.50	.25	.25

Cucumber.—

No. 16.   Two specimens

.75	.50	.25	.25

Open to Children between the ages of 14 and 21

Display of Flowers.—
No. 17.   Not to exceed 15 vases   2.50 2.00 1.75 1.00

Asters.—
No. 18.   Not to exceed 10 vases   1.00 .75 .50 .25

Petunia.—
No. 19.   Not to exceed 10 vases   1.00 .75 .50 .25

Gladiolus.—
No. 20.   Basket   1.00 .75 .50 .25

Zinnia.—
No. 21.   Not to exceed 10 vases   1.00 .75 .50 .25

Wild Flowers.—
No. 22.   Not to exceed 15 vases   1.50 1.25 1.00 .50 .25
No. 23.   Vase of Flowers   1.00 .75 .50 .25 .25

Display of Vegetables.—
No. 24.   Not over 15 varieties
                     2.50 2.00 1.75 1.50 1.25 1.00 .50

Potato.—
No. 25.   Twelve specimens   1.50 1.00 .75 .50 .25

Beets.—
No. 26.   Six specimens   1.00 .75 .50 .25

Carrots.—
No. 27.   Six specimens   1.00 .75 .50 .25

Shell Beans.—
No. 28.   Two quarts   1.00 .75 .50 .25

String Beans.—
No. 29.   Two quarts   1.00 .75 .50 .25

Sweet Corn.—
No. 30.   Six ears   1.00 .75 .50 .25

Tomato.—
No. 31.   Six specimens   1.25 1.00 .75 .50 .25

Cucumber.—
No. 32   Two specimens   1.00 .75 .50 .25

Summer Squash.—
No. 33.   Two specimens   1.00 .75 .50 .25

Saturday, September 7
All articles must be in the hall by 2 o'clock

The exhibits must be the results of individual effort of the child from the time of planting to the arranging of the exhibit.

Open to Children under 14 years of age

Display of Flowers.—

No. 34. Not to exceed 15 vases

2.00	1.50	1.25	1.00	.50	.25

Cosmos.—

No. 35. Vase .75 .50 .25 .25

Calendula.—

No. 36. Not to exceed 10 vases .75 .50 .25 .25

Petunia.—

No. 37. Not to exceed 10 vases .75 .50 .25 .25

Asters.—

No. 38. Not to exceed 10 vases .75 .50 .25 .25

Zinnia.—

No. 39. Not to exceed 10 vases .75 .50 .25 .25

Marigolds.—

No. 40. Not to exceed 10 vases .75 .50 .25 .25

Gladiolus.—

No. 41. Basket .75 .50 .25 .25

Wild Flowers.—

No. 42. Not to exceed 15 vases 1.50 1.25 1.00 .50 .25

No. 43. Vase of Flowers 1.00 .75 .50 .25 .25

Display of Vegetables.—

No. 44. Not to exceed 12 varieties

2.00	1.75	1.50	1.25	1.00	.75	.50

Shell Beans.—

No. 45. Two quarts in pods .75 .50 .25 .25

Beets.—

No. 46. Six specimens 1.00 .75 .50 .25 .25

Carrots.—

No. 47. Six specimens 1.00 .75 .50 .25 .25

Sweet Corn.—

No. 48. Six ears 1.00 .75 .50 .25 .25

Tomato.—

No. 49. Six specimens 1.00 .75 .50 .25 .25

Winter Squash.—
No. 50. Two specimens   1.00 .75 .25 .25
Potato.—
No. 51. Twelve specimens   1.00 .75 .50 .25 .25

Open to Children between the ages of 14 and 21

Display of Flowers.—
No. 52. Not to exceed 15 vases   2.50 2.00 1.75 1.50
Petunia.—
No. 53. Not to exceed 10 vases   1.00 .75 .50 .25
Dahlias.—
No. 54. Not to exceed 10 vases   1.00 .75 .50 .25
Zinnia.—
No. 55. Not to exceed 10 vases   1.00 .75 .50 .25
Marigold.—
No. 56. Not to exceed 10 vases   1.00 .75 .50 .25
Cosmos.—
No. 57. One large vase   1.00 .75 .50 .25
Gladiolus.—
No. 58. Basket   1.00 .75 .50 .25
Wild Flowers.—
No. 59. Not to exceed 15 vases 1.50 1.25 1.00 .50 .25
No. 60. Vase of Flowers 1.00 .75 .50 .25 .25
Dahlia.—
No. 61. Vase   1.00 .75 .50 .25
Display of Vegetables.—
No. 62. Not to exceed 15 varieties
    2.50 2.00 1.75 1.50 1.25 1.00 .50
Potato.—
No. 63. Twelve specimens 1.50 1.00 .75 .50 .25
Carrots.—
No. 64. Six specimens 1.25 1.00 .75 .50 .25
Beets.—
No. 65. Six specimens 1.25 1.00 .75 .50 ·.25
Sweet Corn.—
No. 66. Six ears 1.25 1.00 .75 .50 .25

Tomato.—
No. 67.   Six specimens   1.25 1.00 .75 .50 .25

Cabbage.—
No. 68.   Two specimens   .75 .50 .25

Winter Squash.—
No. 69.   Two specimens   1.00 .75 .50 .25

Celery.—
No. 70.   Three specimens   .75 .50 .25

Shell Beans.—
No. 71.   Two quarts in the pod   1.00 .75 .50 .25

Onion.—
No. 72.   Six specimens   1.00 .75 .50 .25

Prizes will be given for other meritorious exhibits.

Competition is open to all children of Worcester County under two classes. Those under 14 years and those between 14 and 21.

Only one child in a family can compete for the same prize.

The exhibits must be the results of individual effort of the child from the time of planting to the arranging of the exhibit.

All exhibits must be in the Hall ready for inspection by the Judges by 2 p. m. Exhibition will close at 4.30 p. m.

Prizes will be paid at the close of the exhibition.

Vases, plates and everything necessary for the exhibition of the flowers and vegetables will be furnished by the Horticultural Society.

Special Prizes Offered
by Secretary Herbert R. Kinney

To the ones receiving the two largest amounts under 14 years of age. $3.00. $2.00.

To the ones receiving the two largest amounts over 14 years of age. $3.00. $2.00.

*   *   *

For further information apply to

HERBERT R. KINNEY,
Secretary.

TRANSACTIONS

OF THE

WORCESTER COUNTY
HORTICULTURAL
SOCIETY

Reports of the Officers and Lectures

For the year ending December 6, 1935

OFFICERS AND COMMITTEES
of the
Worcester County Horticultural Society
For the Year 1935

PRESIDENT

MYRON F. CONVERSE, Worcester, Mass.

VICE-PRESIDENTS

HERBERT A. COOK   MRS. HOMER GAGE
Shrewsbury, Mass.   Worcester, Mass.
S. LOTHROP DAVENPORT, No. Grafton, Mass.

SECRETARY

HERBERT R. KINNEY, of Worcester
Horticultural Hall, 30 Elm Street

TREASURER

BURT W. GREENWOOD, of Worcester

LIBRARIAN

MISS LUCY M. COULSON, of Worcester

TRUSTEES

Joseph A. Allen	Auburn	Fred L. Chamberlain	Worcester
William Anderson	Wellesley	J. Frank Cooper	Worcester
Miss Elizabeth R. Bishop	Sutton	Mrs. Bertha G. Denny	Worcester
Edward W. Breed	Clinton	Mrs. Alice M. Forbes	Worcester
David L. Fiske	Grafton	Harold J. Greenwood	Worcester
Richard A. Flagg	Boylston	Harry Harrison	Worcester
Allen J. Jenkins	Shrewsbury	Mrs. Florence C. Herrick	Worcester
William E. Morey	Shrewsbury	Allen W. Hixon	Worcester
Charles Potter	West Boylston	Allyne W. Hixon	Worcester
Albert W. Schneider	Clinton	Mrs. Anna N. W. Hobbs	Worcester
Myron S. Wheeler	Berlin	H. Ward Moore	Worcester
Mrs. Mary D. White	Holden	Harry I. Randall	Worcester
Chandler Bullock	Worcester	Joseph F. Sherer	Worcester
Willis E. Cary	Worcester	Mrs. Amy W. Smith	Worcester
Fred H. Chamberlain	Worcester	George F. E. Story	Worcester

STANDING COMMITTEE ON FINANCE

Herbert W. Estabrook, 1935   Leonard C. Midgley, 1936
Myron F. Converse, *Chairman*, 1937

Office, Library, and Exhibition Hall
30 Elm Street

DAVID LUTHER FISKE
1840–1935

PRESIDENT'S ADDRESS

To the Members of the
Worcester County Horticultural Society:

Events move rapidly, as indicated by the fact that we have come to the end of another year's work in the history of this Society—a year which has culminated in the usual amount of the pleasure of accomplishment, and yet saddened by the passing from our circle of some of our associates whose friendships and services seem irreparable.

The year has witnessed a program of activities which included a Lecture Course conducted each Thursday afternoon, beginning in January and continuing until the Reunion which was held on the evening of Thursday, March 28, 1935. The lecturers were persons well informed on their chosen subjects and presented to us in an interesting manner much information pertinent to the subject of horticulture.

The Reunion, an annual event, included dinner, followed by an address entitled "The Geographic Backgrounds of Our Western European Civilization," delivered by Dr. W. Elmer Ekblaw of Clark University. His knowledge and pleasing delivery gained for him a warm place in the hearts of his fellow members. The evening's program was interspersed with music by the Unity Male Quartette of Boston.

The Spring Show, in quality, arrangement, and design, offered a new and charming conception of floral beauty and preceded the weekly exhibits of flowers, fruits, and vegetables held during the summer months, which were of the usual high quality, and displayed the results of the work of some one hundred fifty-six exhibitors whose efforts are an indication of their devotion to the promotion of horticulture.

November brought its bounty of chrysanthemums for the Fall Show, which has so long distinguished the Society's yearly program, and with them came other varieties of plants and flowers, products of the season, which added grandeur to the scene.

The Horticultural Society of New York sponsored a party, including the following members of our Society—Mrs. Leander F. Herrick and her mother, Mrs. Charles H. Ellsworth, Mrs. Converse and myself—that journeyed to Holland during the month of May to visit the Floral Show held at Heemstede, where acres of land were devoted to the exhibition of tulips and other bulbous plants. The tulip finds in Holland a friendly soil and an atmosphere not unlike its native Asia, and thus it thrives under the skilled cultivation of the Dutch people.

The Chelsea Flower Show, conducted in London under the auspices of the Royal Horticultural Society, was in progress during the journey and afforded the travelers an opportunity to visit another of the world's famous exhibitions. It was a pleasure to accompany our New York friends as well as to share in the reception which awaited us abroad.

Turning, for the moment, to our membership, one finds a group united in their efforts to promote the welfare of the Society, and these contacts have developed friendships of the richest character. Intrusion on this circle through the passing of any of its number brings sadness likened only to a family bereavement. Such has been our fate during the past season, for we have witnessed the close of the careers of a number of our members, including Miss Lucy M. Coulson, Librarian for a quarter of a century; David L. Fiske, Esquire, past President; and Mr. Fred L. Chamberlain, Trustee. To each one may be ascribed a large place in the Society's affairs, as will be more particularly chronicled in memorials to be presented at this meeting.

In closing this, my twelfth annual message, I extend in behalf of myself and those with whom I am closely associated our heartfelt thanks for the generous support which you have given to this work and for the assurances for the future.

Respectfully submitted,

MYRON F. CONVERSE, President.

Worcester, Massachusetts
December 5, 1935

SECRETARY'S REPORT

Mr. President and Members of the
Worcester County Horticultural Society:

The first change in the Secretary's office during the last twenty years came the first of January of this year when Miss Coulson went to the Hospital.

On November 2, 1910, Miss Coulson was elected Librarian and Assistant Secretary. She had exclusive charge of the clerical work of the Society for five years before I was elected Secretary. As I had been Vice-President and Chairman of the Committee of Arrangements during that time we were used to working together and feel that we got along as well as could be expected. She was never in the office but once after she went to the hospital.

For the first three months Mr. Huey and I looked after the Library. When it became necessary to have some one here regularly, it was only natural that, as we were just substituting for Miss Coulson, I should think of her friend of long standing and who had many times come into the office when she wished to be away for a few hours or a day. I asked Mrs. Field if she would like to take over Miss Coulson's work until she was able to return. She has been here since early in April. I feel that she has filled the position in a courteous, efficient, and dignified manner and if this meeting votes to continue her services in the same capacity, it will make no mistake.

Our activities for the year have been carried on along the lines long followed by the Society of having lectures and exhibitions. We scheduled ten lectures and every lecturer was here on time. The attendance was very good. At the last six lectures, there were shown, in the west room, some very interesting plants that proved to be a real attraction. All the lectures were illustrated.

January 17, "Philippine Life," by Dr. Forman T. McLean, New York Botanical Gardens. As the lecturer had spent several years on the Islands, his pictures and lecture represented conditions as they really existed there.

January 24, "Roses and Rose Gardens," by Dr. G. Griffin Lewis, Syracuse, N. Y.

He said that it is not true that only skilled people can grow roses; nor is there any place in the country where roses will not grow, if one picks the right species for the place. After considering roses, he showed pictures of some of the best rose gardens in the world.

January 31, "The Gaspé Peninsula," by Mr. Arthur H. Merritt, Boston, Mass. He showed this newly opened northern summer vacation trip with his very real pictures and explained them in his own clever way.

February 7, "The March of the Seasons through the White Mountains," by Albert Leonard Squire, Newton, Mass. This was beautifully illustrated and his descriptions were such as to make his audience feel that he not only enjoyed the mountains, but loved to describe them.

February 14, "Something Old and Something New," by Mrs. Ethel N. S. Peckham, Sterlington, N. Y. She spoke of the flower show in the other room as "An innovation which proved well worth while." Old things are considered only a joke by many who are always looking for something new, little realizing that the new are only modified old. She showed and described many interesting pictures.

February 21, "Preservation of Beautiful and Historic Places in Massachusetts," by Mr. Bradford Williams, Boston, Mass. The pictures represented many scenes from Cape Cod to the Berkshires; some have been improved, others are in more or less natural condition. Some have real beauty while others show more of a rugged nature. They were very interestingly described by the lecturer.

February 28, "Charleston, South Carolina," by Miss Dorothy Emmons, Newton, Mass. This was our first lecture from this section of the country and showed conditions very different from those in New England. The pictures, many of them beautiful, were described in a pleasing way.

March 7, "A Garden Travelogue," by Mrs. Harriette W. Long, Cambridge, Mass. There were shown many Gardens in England, France, Spain, and Italy, some of them of the newer type but more of the older ones.

IRISTHORPE, MRS. HOMER GAGE, 1935

March 14, "Flowers for the Home," by Mrs. Georgiana R. Smith, Dedham, Mass. This lecture was not illustrated by pictures, but with real flowers and accessories. Flowers in relation to the container is a common subject, but we should think of flowers in relation to the container and both in relation to the home. Her many contributions were displayed to show that this could be done. The lecture was very much enjoyed.

March 21, "The Importance of Birds in Your Garden," by Lawrence B. Fletcher, Cohasset, Mass. This lecture not only showed what birds did to hold insects in check, but many very interesting things about their habits and some of the things learned from the banding of many different classes of birds.

March 28, Annual Reunion. Reception in the Library at 6.30 p. m. was followed by a dinner at 7 o'clock. The invocation was pronounced by the Rev. Dr. Samuel B. Ayres, Acting Pastor of the First Universalist Church. Response was chanted by the Unity Male Quartette of Boston.

At the close of a fine dinner, served by Mr. Lunt, a welcome was extended by President Converse. After selections by the Quartette we adjourned to the Auditorium where President Converse introduced Dr. W. Elmer Ekblaw, the speaker of the evening. His address dealt with some of the geographical elements of our culture which seemed to have begun in central Asia and worked slowly westward. Several fine selections by the Quartette followed this interesting and informative talk.

Dancing was enjoyed during the evening.

Our Spring Exhibition was again very attractive, with the stage turned into a woodland scene. The path leading from the west room took you into the woods and to the pool on the stage, which was a very realistic opening in the woods. When you turned, you saw a beautifully arranged exhibit of spring gardens.

The rock gardens in the west room were excellent.

When we consider the date of this exhibition, April 4–7, the exhibits of both fruits and vegetables were good.

I have thought for several years that while cut flowers are one of our main features during the summer and fall, there should be some better way of dividing the premiums. If there could be two classes there would be more of the blue and red and less of the pink prizes.

Table decoration is another large class that is worthy of consideration, as it is used when the exhibitions promise to be small.

Our new calls brought out large entries.

Flower arrangement for the living room. Pottery containers to be furnished by the exhibitor. Six entries.

Small vase of flowers on a mirror. Vase and mirror furnished by the Society. Twenty-five entries.

Group of five miniature vases. Vases owned by the exhibitor. Sixteen entries.

Metal container of cut flowers. Containers furnished by exhibitor. Thirteen entries.

All of these exhibits seemed to be very interesting and should be tried again.

The calls for Dahlias were too early.

The Grafton Garden Club made a fine exhibit in the lower vestibule.

The Fruit and Vegetables were fully up to standard.

Our Children's Exhibitions were both good. While there were not as many entries as sometimes, the quality was better. I think we have never had two Children's Exhibitions before when the quality and arrangement was as good. There were 202 entries under 14 years and 190 over.

Several years ago I called your attention to what seemed to be an excessive use of boxes at our exhibitions, and was accused of not liking them, but that is not so. It is possible to overdo a good thing. If it is desirable to use so many, there must be more provided so that anyone coming in after 10 a. m. may get one.

Our Fruit Exhibits have not been as good during the summer as usual, with the exception of strawberries which were behind our schedule. Cherries, raspberries, blackberries, and plums were light and of only fair quality. There were some very fine peaches shown. Mr. Davenport showed an excellent plate of Hale. I think we call for many of the standard varieties of both apples and pears too early. That is particularly so when we call for them only once. There were some very nice displays.

Our vegetable exhibits were good and most classes, after the early summer, were well filled. The collections were better than the average.

Our Chrysanthemum Exhibition proved to be very satisfactory; while there were not so many really superior exhibits as
sometimes, there was a very dignified and pleasing layout.

Mr. Edward W. Breed had the center and Iristhorpe the stage.
Mr. Charles Potter, the right side, and Mr. Robert J. Allen and
Holmes' Greenhouses, the left.

Mrs. Homer Gage's call for table decorations in the lecture
room made a very attractive showing.

New Members

Mr. Robert J. Allen	Miss Lucinda Kinney
Mr. Alton R. Anderson	Mrs. Violet S. Merritt
Miss Katherine A. Bigelow	Mrs. Gertrude C. Olson
Mrs. Dorothy W. Bowker	Mrs. Winifred A. Scarlet
Dr. W. Elmer Ekblaw	Miss G. Hazel Trask
Mrs. Florence E. Field	Mr. Thomas R. Wentzell
Mr. Reginald H. Fox	Miss Lucy M. Wheeler
Mrs. Katherine Homka	Mr. Lester E. Winter

Members Deceased in 1935

Mr. Charles E. Burbank	Mrs. Serena L. Dewar
Mrs. Elizabeth F. P. Chamberlain	Mr. David L. Fiske
Mr. Fred L. Chamberlain	Mr. Charles David Kendall
Miss Lucy M. Coulson	Miss Alice Scott
Dr. Thomas J. Cronin	Miss Annie M. Lincoln

Respectfully submitted,

Herbert R. Kinney, *Secretary.*

December 5, 1935

TREASURER'S REPORT

For the Year Ending December 4, 1935

Statement of Income and Expenditures

INCOME			EXPENDITURES		
Rnt:			Library......................		
Hall............	$770.00		Winter Meetings............		
Stores..........	39,999.96	$40,769.96	Periodicals.................		
			Publications................		
Pmanent Funds:			Premiums:		
Membership Fund	$114.18		Of 1935.........	$5,578.00	
Blake Fund.....	32.00		Special.........	85.50	
Dewey Fund....	62.96		Children's		
Draper Fund....	10.00		Exhibition....	259.05	
Eames Fund....	24.00		Blake Fund.....	32.00	
Hadwen Fund...	55.00		Draper Fund....	10.00	
Morse Fund.....	20.00	318.14	Eames Fund....	24.00	
			Hadwen Fund...	55.00	
mbership Fees...........		150.00	Morse Fund.....	20.00	
erest Earned:			Children's Garden, City Hospital		
Permanent Funds	$157.49		Expense:		
nvestments.....	243.29	400.78	Exhibitions..............		
			Office....................		
ter Meetings: Tickets.....		4.00	Operating................		
urance Premium Refund...		2.72	Miscellaneous.............		
er Income:			Street Sprinkling............		
Mabel K. Gage..	$50.00		Furniture and Fixtures.......		
Herbert R. Kinney	35.50		Maintenance:		
Premium of 1934			Furniture		
refused.......	15.00	100.50	and Fixtures...	$176.31	
			Real Estate.....	329.90	
estments:			Salaries....................		
Light, Heat—Discount re-			Interest (Paid).............		
ceived on coal bill........	2.04		Interest Added to Permanent		
Premium Unclaimed 1934...	.50		Funds...................		
ment on account of retire-			Interest Added to Investments		
ment price of Worcester			Insurance...................		
County Trust Co. Class A			Light, Heat, Water and Power.		
tock....................		78.00	Janitor Service.............		
			United States Check Tax.....		
		$41,826.64	Mortgage Note Reduction		
			(Front Street Property).....		
			Transfer to Membership Fund.		
			Returned to Investments.....		
Cah Balance, December 6, 1934		886.81	Balance of Cash on Hand, December 4, 1935...........		
		$42,713.45			$

Statement of Gains and Losses

GAINS		
Unexpended Balances of Appropriations:		
Children's Exhibitions........	$40.95	
Salaries........	160.34	$201.29
Membership Fees............		150.00
Income from Permanent Funds		318.14
Unclaimed Premiums.........		.50
Rents.....................		40,769.96
Other Income..............		100.50

LOSSES	
Appropriations..............	
Depreciation...............	
Special and Permanent Fund Premiums................	
Excess of Premiums Awarded over Appropriation.........	
Expense Accounts...........	
Children's Garden...........	
Insurance..................	
Interest....................	
Janitor Service.............	
Light, Heat, Water and Power.	
Maintenance Accounts........	
Periodicals.................	
Publications................	
Street Sprinkling............	
United States Check Tax.....	
Winter Meetings.............	

Net Gain to Surplus..........

$41,540.39

Statement of Resources and Liabilities

RESOURCES			LIABILITIES	
ient Funds (Investment):			Blake Fund:	
iles' Savings Bank			Principal.................	$1,0
:adwen Fund) $1,258.33			Income..................	3
Five Cts. Sav. Bk.			Dewey Fund:	
iraper Fund). 409.35			Principal.................	1,0
ames Fund). 607.97			Income..................	
Iorse Fund). 516.15			Draper Fund:	
Mech. Sav. Bk.			Principal.................	3
lake Fund).. 1,365.43			Income..................	1
iewey Fund). 1,009.26	$5,166.49		Eames Fund:	
			Principal	5
nents:			Income..................	1
Co. Inst. for			Hadwen Fund:	
v.......... $2,298.55			Principal	1,0
Five Cts. Sav.			Income..................	2
:.......... 2,947.08			Morse Fund:	
Mech. Sav.			Principal.................	5
:.......... 3,125.87			Income..................	
Co. Trust			Mortgage Note, Front Street	
). 65 sh. Class			Property.................	190,0
Stk. at $20			Surplus:	
r share...... 1,300.00	9,671.50		Dec. 5, 1934....$314,827.78	
			Net Gain, 1935.. 12,781 45	327,6
iership Fund..........	3,950.00			
state...............	480,000.00			
ire and Fixtures.......	20,514.80			
/....................	2,439.87			
....	1,033.06			
	$522,775.72			$522,7

Respectfully submitted,

B. W. GREENWOOD, *Treasu*

Auditor's Certificate

I have examined the books of the Treasurer of the Worcester County Horticultural Society, together with vouchers, securities and bank balances, for the year ended December 4, 1935, and find them to be correct.

ADAH B. JOHNSON, *Auditor.*

We have caused an audit of the books of the Treasurer to be made for the year ended December 4, 1935, and the foregoing certificate is hereby approved.

Respectfully submitted,

H. WARD MOORE, ARTHUR H. BELLOWS, HARRY C. MIDGLEY,
Auditors.

Worcester, Massachusetts
December 4, 1935

LIBRARIAN'S REPORT

Mr. President and Members of the
  Worcester County Horticultural Society:

Since early in April of this year, it has been a pleasure for me to substitute in the Library of your Society for my dear friend Miss Coulson, and at this time I want to express my gratitude to your very efficient Library Committee and all members of this Society who have helped to make my experience most pleasant.

From the records of the Library for previous years, I find the circulation and use of the Library has been most gratifying, with a noticeable increase in the number of books taken out.

Many valuable bulletins on varied horticultural and agricultural subjects have been received from Cornell and Purdue Universities.

The usual publications and periodicals for reading in the Library have been continued.

It is with deep appreciation that we acknowledge the recent gift of the following books from the Library of the late Dr. Leonard P. Kinnicutt:

Roses and Rose Growing, Rose G. Kingsley, 1908.
The Gypsy Moth, Edward H. Forbush, Charles H. Fernald, 1896.
1906 Edition Bailey's Cyclopedia of American Horticulture, 4th ed., 6 vols., 1906.
Scottish Gardens, Sir Herbert Maxwell, London, 1911.
The Practical Book of Out-door Rose Growing, George C. Thomas, Jr., 1914.
Nature's Garden, Neltje Blanchan, 1900.
America's Greatest Garden, E. H. Wilson, 1925.
The Wonders of Instinct, J. H. Fabre, London, 1918.
The Amateur Orchid Cultivator's Guide Book, H. A. Burberry, London, 1895.
Everyman's Garden Every Week, Charles A. Selden, 1914.

Although some are duplicates, they are valuable, and it is an advantage to have more than one copy.

Also, we appreciate and have acknowledged the gift of *The Century Supplement to the Dictionary of Gardening* by George Nicholson from the Library of William McAllister of Whitinsville.

New books added to the Library this year are as follows:

Manual of Cultivated Trees and Shrubs, Alfred Rehder.
Mexican Plants for American Gardens, Cecil Hulse Matschat.
The Gladiolus Book, McLean, Clark and Fischer, 1927.
Dwarf and Slow Growing Conifers, Murray Hornibrook, 1923.
Our American Maples and Some Others, Margaret Curtis Finley, 1934.
Our Native Cacti, Edith Bailey Higgins, 1931.
Succulents, A. J. van Laren, 1934.
House Plants, Marjorie Morrell Sulzer, 1935.
The 1935 American Rose Annual.
Herbs and the Earth, Henry Beston, 1935.
Old Roses, Mrs. Frederick Love Keays, 1935.
Plants of the Vicinity of New York, Dr. H. A. Gleason, 1935.
Flower and Table Arrangements, Esther Longyear Murphy.
Garden Design, Marjorie Sewell Caufley.
Tuberous-Rooted Begonias and Their Culture, George Otten, 1935.
Flower Arrangement, F. F. Rockwell and Esther C. Grayson.
American Ferns, Edith A. Roberts and Julia R. Lawrence.
Also the 1929–30–31–32–33 and 34 Yearbooks of the New England Gladiolus
Society.

Respectfully submitted,

MRS. FLORENCE E. FIELD, *Acting Librarian.*

REPORT OF CHAIRMAN OF THE LIBRARY COMMITTEE

Mr. President and Members of the
  Worcester County Horticultural Society:

During the past year, our Library has lost its faithful librarian, Miss Lucy M. Coulson, and the Society will greatly miss her genial manner which added so much to the pleasure of our members.

Our Library has been thoroughly overhauled the past season and catalogued in a very systematic manner, enabling one to find the exact location of books on any subject. Another feature adopted by libraries has been added to our own plan. It is now arranged to have the date the book is to be returned to fall due on Thursdays, the day of our meetings and exhibitions. In the past some of our patrons have kept books an unreasonable length of time, thus depriving others of the use of them.

Mrs. Florence E. Field has been a great help to us in the work referred to above, and the Library Committee sincerely hope that you will endorse her as librarian in the election that follows.

We are constantly adding new books to our collection, and the Committee is ready at all times to make such additions as the members may suggest or desire.

Respectfully submitted,

EDWARD W. BREED, *Chairman Library Committee.*

REPORT OF THE JUDGE OF PLANTS AND FLOWERS

Mr. President and Members of the
Worcester County Horticultural Society:

In presenting my report as Judge of Plants and Flowers, it is a pleasure to state that during the past year the exhibits compared favorably with similar exhibits in other years.

Many of the shows were featured by fine exhibits of the standard varieties.

During the early summer, peonies, roses, and delphiniums were shown in great variety and excellent quality.

July brought out sweet peas, lilies and iris. In late summer, fine exhibits of gladioli and dahlias were put up. Of these there were many of great merit. Popular features during the summer were the table decorations and the class calling for a small vase of flowers shown on a mirror.

Standards and baskets of flowers were exhibited at most of the shows and added greatly to the attractiveness of the hall.

The Spring and Autumn Exhibitions were both beautifully planned and executed; fine groups of plants and vases of very fine cut chrysanthemums were on exhibition; also well arranged fern globes and glass ferneries and interesting exhibits of wild fruits and berries.

Respectfully submitted,

WILLIAM ANDERSON, *Judge of Plants and Flowers.*

REPORT OF JUDGE OF FRUIT

Mr. President and Members of the
Worcester County Horticultural Society:

As our seasons vary from year to year, so do our exhibits of fruit vary in variety, quantity, and quality. Although there were some entries in almost every class, we had this year rather light showing of cherries and plums.

Peaches were again a light crop due to the severe winter, although many more were exhibited than had been anticipated, some of which were exceptionally fine. There were several new varieties of peaches shown, which originated at the New Jersey Experiment Station, such as Cumberland, Golden Jubilee, and Eclipse, and these seemed to be much hardier than such standards as our Elberta, and I believe are going to be valuable varieties.

In general, the showings of small fruits were good, although they were at their best about a week after the call, so that in case of the strawberries the schedule was moved back one week.

Howard 17 still seems to be the most popular berry; and in fact on June 13 there were as many Howard 17 shown as all other varieties put together. Several new ones were shown this season such as Fairfax, Dorsett, etc., which looked quite promising.

Some fine raspberries and blackberries were shown over a very long period. In fact, the last plate of raspberries was shown on August 8, and the last blackberry on August 29.

Grapes were somewhat behind the schedule. although we had a fair display on September 5, and later about twenty-five plates on September 26, some of which were exceptionally fine.

Although the pear crop was short this year, we had exceptionally fine showings of Bosc, Sechel, Anjou, and Bartlett, with more Bosc than any other variety; and on September 26, fifteen plates were exhibited.

McIntosh, Baldwin, Wealthy, and Spy were the most important varieties of apples shown with about an equal division

EDWARD W. BREED, 1935

between Baldwin and McIntosh. The past season has been a
most difficult one in which to grow good fruit due to the ravages
of apple scab.   Nevertheless, we had some fine showings of
apples, both on October 3 and November 7, with well-filled classes
of exceptionally good fruit. The forty-nine classes were again
very popular, with thirty lots at the November Show, making a
most attractive way in which to show good fruit. At this show,
Baldwins again took the lead as we had more shown than any
other variety, and they were of exceptionally fine quality,
indicating that Baldwins are still one of our best varieties.

Respectfully submitted,

S. LOTHROP DAVENPORT, *Judge of Fruit.*

REPORT OF JUDGE OF VEGETABLES

Mr. President and Members of the
Worcester County Horticultural Society:

I herewith submit my report as Judge of Vegetables for 1935.

At this time I wish to pay tribute to the memory of those two sterling members of our Society who have so recently passed away, and who aided so much in the improvements that have taken place in the exhibitions in our Vegetable Department, Messrs. David L. Fiske and Fred L. Chamberlain.

Only a few members of our Society are privileged to contribute to the success of our exhibitions for as many years as Messrs. Fiske and Chamberlain were. Their exhibits of high quality vegetables, always tastefully displayed, will be sadly missed by the Vegetable Department.

The Spring Exhibition brought out a goodly showing of both hothouse and well-kept, cellar-stored vegetables.

At the May Exhibition no spinach was shown and only one exhibit of asparagus which is rather unusual, but due, no doubt, to the rather late, cold spring.

Among the other vegetables of which none were shown when called for were: peas on June 13, string beans on June 27, sweet corn on July 18, and shell beans (one class) on July 25. All of these, but especially beans, were shown in abundance on later dates. Early carrots, some varieties of peas and beans, and early winter squashes were not very plentiful.

Some of the outstanding exhibits in the Vegetable Department during the past season were the fine showing of iceberg lettuce on July 11, the two exhibitions of mushrooms on August 8 and 29 respectively, the displays of tomatoes on September 5 and of peppers on September 26, both of which displays nearly filled the center table in the West Hall and, which, with their bright colors and neat arrangements, were very attractive.

The cauliflowers, shown October 3, were as fine as I have ever seen, and the displays of gourds at the November Show claimed much attention and received well-deserved praise.

Respectfully submitted,

H. WARD MOORE, *Judge of Vegetables.*

REPORT OF FINANCE COMMITTEE

To the Members of the
Worcester County Horticultural Society:

In reviewing the affairs of the Society, the members of this Committee are pleased to report that through the exercise of prudence the usual satisfactory financial condition has been maintained and that the work has been conducted with the purpose of rendering a real service through the promotion of the Art of Horticulture.

The splendid character of the exhibits of the past year, which we believe will be maintained, has led us to a recommendation that ten thousand dollars be appropriated at this meeting for distribution by the Trustees for payment of premiums and salaries for the ensuing year. This amount, fifteen hundred dollars in excess of last year's appropriation, will permit of a deserved increase in the Department of Plants and Flowers, special mention being given to the Spring Show and the Chrysanthemum Exhibition.

Respectfully submitted,

MYRON F. CONVERSE,
LEONARD C. MIDGLEY,
H. W. ESTABROOK,
Finance Committee.

Worcester, Massachusetts
December 5, 1935

MEMORIAL TO DAVID LUTHER FISKE

As a man, David Luther Fiske was one of "Nature's noblemen." He came of distinguished lineage of which he was justly proud. His respect for his forbears was of more than ordinary feeling, and it was always a delight to hear him speak of them. He was born on July 19th, in the year 1840, and quietly passed on at his home on October 17th, 1935, thus rounding out ninety-five years of a life of varied interests, and usefulness.

As a citizen, he was most loyal to his native town, serving it in many ways and filling the various offices in a faithful manner, so that the title, "The Grand Old Man of Grafton," was worthily bestowed.

As an horticulturist, Mr. Fiske was, for more than half a century, connected with, and an active supporter of, this Society. He served on numerous committees, and in the years 1922 and 1923 was our president. He was considered an authority on fruits and vegetables, and his exhibits in these classes were always of a high order, as the many awards would testify. Not only here in Worcester, but also in Boston at the Massachusetts Horticultural Society, he was a frequent exhibitor, and naturally received suitable recognition, sometimes taking the sweepstakes premium.

He was a member of Worcester Grange for more than fifty years, having received a gold badge to commemorate that event. He was connected with The Fruit Growers' Association and the Massachusetts Harvest Club. He also belonged to the Sons of the American Revolution, and was a member of the National Geographic Society, and an honorary member of the Grafton Garden Club. In all of these affiliations he was highly honored by the service which he rendered.

As a friend, there was none truer than Mr. Fiske. His Christian character, his loyal devotion to his family, his daily contact with others, and his interest in the high ideals of life, were characteristic of his career.

Resolved that, in the passing of Mr. Fiske, this Society has lost one of its most valued members, that horticulture will miss his contributions, and that we all will cherish his memory.

Resolved that this memorial be placed in the records of our Society, and copy of the record be sent to the family of Mr. Fiske.

November 20, 1935

MEMORIAL TO FRED L. CHAMBERLAIN

It is with the deepest regret that we note the passing of Mr. Fred L. Chamberlain, on November 10, 1935.

He became a member of the Worcester County Horticultural Society in 1898 and was elected a trustee in 1917.

He was a very quiet member, but was always on hand to be counted on at our meetings.

He was one of our best exhibitors in the vegetables and fruit classes.

While not a large producer, he lived through the time of the greatest enthusiasm in agricultural and horticultural exhibitions this county has ever known.

Our Society was increasing its vegetable and fruit activities and the agricultural exhibitions in the county were at the apex of their activities.

He became one of the best exhibitors in the county.

His judgment in the selecting and arranging of his exhibits was always a credit to him and won him many first prizes. While of late he had been dropping from the commercial to the amateur class, his two displays of vegetables this year were evidence that he had not lost his knack in the growing and arranging of vegetables.

Resolved that this memorial be placed in the records of this Society and a copy be sent to his widow.

Respectfully submitted,

HERBERT R. KINNEY.

December 5, 1935.

Lucy M. Coulson

MEMORIAL TO LUCY M. COULSON

In these busy, ever-changing days, few people stop to re-member the past. But to those of us who knew Lucy Coulson, it is difficult to accustom ourselves to her absence from these familiar walls.

For over thirty years Lucy Coulson stood for all that was best in our Worcester County Horticultural Society. She be-came a member on December 30, 1905.

On November 2, 1910, she was elected Librarian and Assistant Secretary of this Society and filled these offices faithfully. She inherited from her English ancestry a clean-cut and logical intellect.

No matter what information on any sort of horticultural subject anyone wished, Lucy Coulson was able to help. She could turn to any book of our very complete library and help with the desired information.

She was a constant contributor to our Society's exhibitions, and her wisdom, artistic temperament, and sense of justice led us to depend upon her judgment.

She was an excellent gardener and raised almost all of the annuals and perennials she exhibited.

Her willingness at all times to assist any member of the Society regarding the Library and helping with their exhibitions made her an important factor in our Society.

Her death on September 20, 1935, removed from our midst a faithful and valuable member.

Resolved that this memorial be placed in the records of this Society and copies be sent to her sisters and brother.

Respectfully submitted,

AMY W. SMITH.

December 5, 1935

ANNUAL MEETING OF THE SOCIETY

Thursday, December 6, 1934

President Myron F. Converse called the meeting to order at 10 a. m.   Thirty-six present.

Secretary read the call for the meeting

Secretary read the records of the last Annual Meeting of the Society.

President Converse declared them approved.

President Myron F. Converse delivered his Annual Address. The following reports were read:

Secretary, Herbert R. Kinney; Treasurer, Burt W. Greenwood; Librarian, Miss Lucy M. Coulson; Judge of Flowers, William Anderson by Miss Coulson; Judge of Fruit, S. Lothrop Davenport; Judge of Vegetables, H. Ward Moore.

On Mr. George F. E. Story's motion these reports were accepted and referred to the Committee on Library and Publication.

President Myron F. Converse read the Finance Committee's report.

On Mr. H. Ward Moore's motion the report was accepted and adopted.

Mr. Edward W. Breed presented a Memorial on our late Trustee, Mr. William McAllister.   Accepted by a rising vote.

Mrs. Amy W. Smith presented a Memorial on our late Trustee, Mrs. Frances A. Kinnicutt which was accepted by a rising vote.

Mr. Willis E. Cary reported for the Nominating Committee.

Mr. George F. E. Story made a motion that the report be accepted and that the Secretary cast a year ballot for the candidates as nominated.

Secretary cast the ballot.

President declared them elected.

Mr. Harry Harrison, after some very apt remarks in which he spoke of the long and very valuable services our President had rendered our Society for many years, presented him with a copper plaque from the Society.

ROBERT J. ALLEN, 1935

He then presented him with a wrist watch, also from the Society.

These gifts were accepted very gracefully by President Converse.

On Mr. Jenkins' motion the meeting adjourned.

HERBERT R. KINNEY, *Secretary.*

ANNUAL MEETING OF THE TRUSTEES

Thursday, December 13, 1934

Meeting called to order at 2 p. m. by President Myron F. Converse. Seventeen present.

Secretary read the records of the last Annual Meeting of the Trustees.

President Converse declared them approved.

President Converse read the last year's appropriation and said that it had been quite satisfactory.

Mr. Burt W. Greenwood made a motion, "That the appropriations be the same as last year." So voted.

President Converse said that this meeting appointed the committees for the year, and that members would find a list of the present members in the premium list they had.

Mr. Burt W. Greenwood resigned from the Committee on Winter Meetings.

Mrs. Anna N. W. Hobbs was nominated to fill the vacancy.

There was a vacancy on the Committee on Arrangements and Exhibitions caused by Mr. Warr leaving the city.

Mr. Allen J. Jenkins nominated Mr. Allen W. Hixon to fill the vacancy.

President Converse asked if there were any other changes.

There being none, Mr. Harry Harrison made a motion "That the committees with the changes recommended be elected." So voted.

President Converse said that he had understood that the judging the past season had been fully as satisfactory as usual, and if there was no objection we appoint the same ones for the coming year.

There being no objection, Mr. Hixon made a motion "That the same judges serve another year." So voted.

Appropriations for Premiums and Salaries...................$8,500.00

PREMIUMS

Flowers......................	$2,300.00	
Fruit........................	1,100.00	
Vegetables.....	900.00	
Children's Exhibition...........	300.00	
Spring Exhibition..............	800.00	
Chrysanthemum Exhibition.....	200.00	
Miscellaneous..	200.00	$5,800.00

SALARIES

Treasurer.....................	$300.00		
Secretary.	900.00		
Librarian....................	1,100.00		
Judges.......................	300.00		
Assistant to Secretary..........	100.00	$2,700.00	$8,500.00

Adjourned.

HERBERT R. KINNEY, *Secretary.*

"PHILIPPINE LIFE"

Thursday, January 17

Illustrated Lecture

By Dr. Forman T. McLean, New York Botanical Garden

This lecture on Philippine life was especially valuable as Dr. McLean lived in the Philippines several years and is thoroughly acquainted with these people who live half way round the world from us. A map of their country was superimposed on a map of eastern United States, showing the relation it bears to us in size. Throughout, the Islands are strictly tropical.

Manila, on the fortified isle of Carrigador, is thoroughly well fortified, yet extensive coastline leaves the place subject to attack for all that. Shipping is its most important feature. Sampans, for loading and unloading, were shown. On going into Manila from the waterfront one sees the old Spanish city of Manila, the same as it was centuries ago. Built in solid stone and masonry, the interior of this walled city shows the great conservatism of old Spain. The habit of renting the first floor for a shop and living up over it is still prevalent. The cool patio, a walled-in garden, all shrubs and trees, no lawn, is characteristic.

Back from the business section are some grand old houses. Windows there are never glazed, but are always made of thin shell, to withstand earthquakes which are severe and frequent. These gardens were built more after the American plan by natives who came here and returned with new ideas. Hedges of hibiscus in bloom give a pleasing sight.

Women of that country were shown dressed in the court costume of the seventeenth century Spain, for at that time a Filipino was first taken to Spain, liked the dress and returned to pass on the Spanish style. The long train is used even for street dress. The men's costume of that time was typical Chinese. This difference has continued to the present time. The people move along slowly in an average temperature of 82°. The children are good-natured, but do not measure up to our idea of honesty.

There are one hundred different kinds of bananas and Dr. McLean had fifteen kinds in his garden. Filipinos cook this fruit, preserve it, and use it for oiling the face.

A pretentious suburban home was shown with a picket fence around it for protection against robbers. The Spaniards built good roads and walls. The curves to the road and buttresses served as a protection for the soldiers. A home made entirely of bamboo with a palm leaf roof is a common type. Typhoons ruin elaborate houses, so many who could have better places build these flimsy affairs. The bamboo was taken there from Indo-China, where it blooms. It does not bloom in the Philippines, fortunately, so keeps on growing and producing cane. It is the fastest growing plant in the world. Some pink flowered lotus, whose seeds are edible, were seen growing near a lake.

These people live a very restricted life in many ways. Their diet is quite largely hulled rice and fish. Bamboo traps are used for catching fish.

The Philippine Islands are one-half mountains. The road winds along the sides of the mountains through the forest. Lumber is an important business there. The tropical plum has hard wood and is used for house supports. The orchid thrives there as some rain falls practically every day. A fine type of acacia is seen there, also.

Life itself is based largely on the Malay plan. The mortar and pestle are used practically every meal. Their rice gets mouldy and goes bad, while in the hull it lasts indefinitely, so has to be kept in that form. Cooking is very primitive, indeed. A fire is built right under the pots, or sometimes a packing box is used and the pot set over it. Rice is never fully cooked, usually only one-half so. This swells up and gives the feeling of a full meal.

During the dry season the caribou is turned out to pasture. He is tended and driven by one man as he does not like strangers. A man drives one pony, only; if there are two ponies, two men are required. The caribou, or water buffalo, enjoys the water and likes to take a bath in the middle of the day, then rest. He is used for plowing.

Roland K. Parker, Iristhorpe, Eugene Parsons, Philip P. Warren and Walter R. Cross, 1935

Slides depicting the culture of rice were shown. Women were seen setting new rice plants, for these people believe that the productivity of the land is connected with women. Some sections grow two crops of rice a season. Flailing was shown, the process by which rice is separated from straw, which is then spread out to dry and used for hats and baskets. Yams are grown there in abundance, too. In the real sense they are not sweet potatoes at all; they are entirely different, in fact, only taste like sweet potatoes. The guava was introduced in the early days when the Philippines were a sub-province of Mexico. A West India plant, avocada, or alligator pear, is very nutritious, rich in oil, and is eaten with lemon as it is flat by itself.

A typical village, with no sanitation whatever, was shown. Americans have accomplished a great deal for the Filipino, but much is yet to be done. Artesian wells have done away with disease contracted from the poor water supply, but malaria is still rampant and claiming attention.

The dry season is the season of blooming for many plants. The silk cotton tree is a lovely sight in May when it comes into bloom. The full leaf comes later. An excellent view from the rear porch of the lecturer's home was seen, patches of woodland everywhere, and his large banana patch.

The hat industry is very important. Hats of the tough fiber of the fan palm are superior to the Panama. A substantial native home was shown with roof made of sugar palm thatch, very durable, lasting from thirty to forty years.

The coconut industry is one of the largest and best in the world. The best planting for them is twenty feet apart. They begin to bear in seven years and are in full bearing in ten years. A person may set out one thousand trees when young, rent out, and have an income for the rest of his life. Most of the fruit is used for coconut oil, soaps, and the like. The process of floating coconuts down the river was shown. A primitive oil press was shown. This fruit yields a high quality of oil. Manila hemp, a strong tough fiber, is next to the coconut industry.

The yield of the forests is about the same as that of our great forests. Views were shown of rotten underbrush, climbing palm covered with thorns, a badly tangled natural jungle with one of the native figs three times the size of our own. A jungle in the forests was seen with a heavy gathering of vines all over the trees; ferns hanging from the tree tops; mossy forests in which the trees are covered with moss all through the season.

When we talk of freeing the Islands, we talk of freeing three different races as different as Italian from German, who cannot understand one another except in English or Spanish. American occupation has helped by giving them a common language. At the college, established in 1911, students must specialize in English. The United States has been trying to build the Philippines into an independent nation. Very few there understand even common arithmetic.

The Negritos, the first people to settle there, are like the pigmies of Africa, four feet high, people of primitive agriculture and hunting. Women are very small, much smaller than the men. This race is dying out as it cannot help itself.

The closing scenes were of natural scenery and gardens. Giant trees, one hundred fifty feet tall in a forest of five different levels of trees, made a fine picture. Shrubs and the herbaceous level were down below. The straggling fig is worshipped by these people. Lovely moss draped in festoons gave a pleasing feeling. Handsome pitcher plants grow there, an ornamental plant that captures insects. Pretty ferns and fragrant jungles were shown. Hibiscus is very brilliant in that country and the wild orchid is a lovely sight. Everywhere one sees the great charm of nature, so different in the various countries.

"ROSES AND ROSE GARDENS"

Thursday, January 24

Illustrated Lecture

By G. Griffin Lewis, Syracuse, New York

There is no more healthful environment than that of a rose garden where one experiments, acquires skill, and becomes a successful out-door grower. It is not true that only skilled people can grow roses. Nor is there any place in the country where roses will not grow if one only picks the right species for the place.

The following list of rules is given for people who would have good rose gardens:

Do not commence with too many varieties.

Purchase from a reliable dealer who will enumerate faults.

Do not buy potted roses. Constricted pot roots do not send out feeders.

Do not buy year-old roses.

Do not buy own root roses. They do not thrive as well or live as long. A budded rose already has a root system.

Do not buy monstrous dormant bushes, such as sold in a department store, for as a rule they have been forced.

Order early. It is preferable to plant in the fall. Then the ground is still pliable and sometimes warm. Better roses may be had in the fall than in the spring as they come fresh from the fields then.

Do not buy foreign grown roses, as the roots are dry and never do very well.

A few well cared for will furnish more bloom. Add to the number as you grow in experience.

Do not plant in the shade of trees as the roots of the tree will rob the roots of the roses of nourishment, and the bushes will be shaded from the sun's rays.

Do not plant on the north side of buildings.   At least six hours of sunshine is required.

Do not plant too early in the fall, for if too warm underneath, the bushes will sprout.   The latter part of November and first of December is all right.

Do not plant too late in the spring.   This is a great mistake as the sap will flow into the canes and the roots will not get a proper start.

Do not plant too far apart.   Close planting keeps the ground cool and moist.   Dwarf polyanthas may be set twelve inches apart; hybrid teas, eighteen inches; hybrid perpetuals, two feet; tree and rugosas, three feet; climbers, five feet.

Do not plant too shallow.   One to one and one-half inches below the hump is good.   The surface of the soil will protect the budded part from freezing and avoid suckers.

Do not plant too deep or roots will start from canes and it will have own roots.

Prune canes to two to four or five eyes, never over five.   Also prune roots as well as canes, especially large roots.   Small feeding roots draw nourishment from the soil.   After planting do not neglect to hill the rose up, whether in spring or fall.   This is to protect growth at the top until it gets a start.

Do not plant tall with low varieties.

Do not do any fall pruning other than is necessary and do this before severe frost sets in.

Do not prune new wood on small clusters such as Excelsa and Hiawatha.   Prune them after blooming and leave only new growth.

Do not prune old wood on the Silver Moon or Van Fleet, for it is the two-year-old wood that will bloom next year.

Do not fail to cut bloom with good long stems as this is the only summer pruning we have.   Burn all prunings, leaves, etc. to avoid spread of all germs.

Do not overfeed your roses.   Part bone meal, sheep phosphate and wood ash is best.

Do not use green manure.

Do not water or spray on hot days, especially while the sun is shining.

Spray the undersurface of foliage as that is the most vulnerable to disease.

Watch for suckers at all times during the growing season. If shoots come a little distance from the plant they are suckers and should be cut off from below the surface.

Do not neglect disbudding for good bloom. Leave only the center one.

Do not mulch too early as this will delay the blooming season. Even in August it is not good. Peat moss is excellent material to mix with soil if it is heavy wet soil.

Do not encourage field mice by covering roses with leaves or straw. Pine boughs are the best and field mice are not so likely to get in. The lecturer hills up, then places manure between the bushes. Out of three hundred bushes he lost only three bushes and a climber. He leaves climbers just as in summer, does not cover them. Get the right kind and all will be well. He never lays down climbers any more. The Los Angeles must be covered.

Do not place manure next to the rose when you hill up as it retains moisture and freezes.

The Empress Josephine had three hundred roses in her garden, which was the first public garden exclusively roses. There are twelve thousand now. English, French, and Germans have had public rose gardens for many years. Elizabeth Park at Hartford, established in 1904, was the first one here. In 1907 Lyndell Park in Minneapolis had a rose garden. We have now one hundred nine public rose gardens with fifteen to twenty more on the way. This is probably more than all other countries in the world. The lecturer predicted that eventually every city will have its public rose garden.

Mrs. Harriet Foote of Marblehead is probably the greatest rose garden architect of this country. Views of her place and gardens she had planned were shown. Mrs. Crane of Ipswich has one of the Foote gardens. The late Thomas Lawson estate has lovely Dorothy Perkins roses. The garden of Mrs. Frothingham of North Easton has a splendid rose display. The late Mr. Walsh of Woods Hole was interested in rose propagation. Hillcrest, at Weston, where twenty boys are taken on each summer to work on the place, was shown. Pillar roses at the Charles H. Hobson place were seen. The Mary Wallace garden at Franklin Park, Boston, is a lovely one.

In 1925 the lecturer's own rose garden was started. The annual exhibit of the Syracuse Rose Society held that same year was pictured. Dr. Huey has the most thrifty character and is the most prolific of any climbing rose. The blossom is very dark. This is by far the best climber. An individual blossom was shown to be almost as black as the Negrette rose. The Mills garden, Delaware Park rose garden, and that of Helen Gould were seen on the screen.

In 1925 the Catholic chaplain at Sing Sing purchased tools and advised the lifers to get out in the garden and dig. Now there are over two thousand bushes there in the lovely garden. A greenhouse has been constructed, too.

At Tacoma, Washington, Fort Defense Park has large rose arbors and a splendid display of bloom. Seattle, Washington, also, has a lovely rose garden. Santa Barbara, Los Angeles, and Pasadena uphold the rose standard of California with their public gardens and private estates. Pageants throughout this section speak for their great love of roses.

Elizabeth Park has fine tree roses. These will not stand winter cold or hot weather, so are hard to care for and not so commonly grown. At Arlington, Virginia, is the first test garden under the American Rose Society. The Dr. Van Fleet is propagated there. The late Edward Bok of Pennsylvania planted thousands of rosebushes. The late Captain Thomas of Germantown, Pennsylvania, had a fine garden there, then went out to Beverly Hills, California, where he had a magnificent one.

Mrs. Henry Ford's garden at Dearborn, Michigan, is well known. This elaborate garden was constructed by Mrs. Foote. Breeze Hill, the home of Dr. Horace MacFarlane, president of the American Rose Society, was shown. He has a fine display of Excelsas.

Some foreign rose gardens were pictured. Niagara Falls, Canada, has roses. A Bulgarian rose field, for commercial purposes, was seen. Single roses are grown, two hundred pounds of petals being required for one teaspoonful of attar of roses. At

Christ's Church in New Zealand is a long public rose garden. The climate there is very satisfactory for rose growing. Peace Palace at the Hague was seen with its lovely roses. Kew Rose Garden, near London, was shown with the Dorothy Perkins reflected in the water. South Africa, Ireland, France, Germany, all figured with their fine rose gardens, too numerous to mention. The oldest rosebush in the world is a briar rose planted in 818 by Louis, son of Charlemagne. It is still blooming.

Roses do better together than with other plants. The best yellow rambler roses for around here are Gardenia, a lovely climber, also the New Darwin, but all yellow climbers fade to white. A yellow rose with an orange center which does not fade is Pe Lilie d'Or. Climbing American Beauty comes out a few blooms at a time, so is not satisfactory. Zephyr Andromache surpasses it in every way. It hasn't a thorn on the bush and does not change color. That and Dr. Huey are highly recommended.

Edward W. Breed, 1935

"THE GASPÉ PENINSULA"

Thursday, January 31

Illustrated Lecture

By Mr. Arthur S. Merritt, Boston, Mass.

Four hundred years ago Cartier landed here and flew his flag of ownership. But the British also claimed the territory and there was constant warfare until by treaty Gaspicia fell into British hands.

For two hundred years the Gaspé has been shut away from the rest of the country by mountains, with no roads over which to travel. This little peninsula of fishermen has been content to live apart, having only the steamship as a means of communication with the outside world. Until six years ago, when the new Perron Highway was built, these people had the customs of over two hundred years ago. The north side speaks pure French, the southern, more Canadian and quite a little fairly good English.

The traveler should wait until after the fogs are over in June, then for eight or ten weeks fairly good weather is enjoyed. He has several ways to choose from: by train from the North Station; by plane to Montreal or Quebec and from there by the excellent bus system installed last summer; or in his own automobile it makes a splendid trip. An ideal way would be by plane, then a return by auto. Two weeks should be allowed for full appreciation and comfort. The lecturer's trip lasted seventeen days.

Accommodations are fine and very reasonable. If one is counting on a hotel stop he should engage ahead. Tourist homes run by fishermen and certified by the Government are spotlessly clean and the expense is only one dollar a night. There is a monotony of food there, of course. The system of modern cabins is a fine one, ranging from the log cabin to the more fancy one, some having shower baths. Everything is thoroughly wholesome. The lecturer's party of four had supper, a night's lodging and breakfast, all for the ridiculously low price of from $6.00 to $8.50.

The first slide showed Mrs. Merritt standing at the East Boston Airport. Their plane, carrying nine passengers, made its first stop at Burlington, Vermont. Views over Lake Champlain, the Adirondacks and Mt. Royal were shown. Then came St. Hubert's Field, the landing place just outside Montreal and the barouche to Mt. Royal.

A fine section of summer resorts such as Rivière-du-Loup where the splendid cathedral is, Trois Pistoles, St. Simon and Rimouski were shown. Only one road is open into the interior and drivers are cautioned to take the course followed by the lecturer's party rather than come from the opposite direction which is the outside of the road and very dangerous, indeed.

The real Gaspé Trail starts at Ste. Flavie. Just beyond are Metis Beach, and Sandy Bay. Travelers usually stop at either of these beaches.

Road signs are carefully placed and mean exactly what they say. If they are followed a safe drive is the reward. The road and traction are good, but curves are dangerous and require great care.

The traveler passes through about one hundred covered bridges, built partly to keep the autos from being blown off into the water. Many of these bridges extend from one hill to another and are not over water at all.

Cap Chat, a little village, is finally reached. It was given and named by Champlain, a founder of Quebec. Here is the longest covered bridge in this part of Quebec. Cod and salmon fishing is prevalent here.

Ste. Anne des Monts is the first village of the second section of the route. Its scenery is most beautiful, with large mountains serving as a background for fields, rivers and valley, down to the shore of the St. Lawrence. A cathedral church graces this village, also. Of the sixty-eight parishes in the Gaspé only one is without a church. The cream of the scenery is found from this point on, the road winding along the river through the hills, in and out, up and down, for one hundred and twenty miles.

Waterfalls are seen after a time; the water is so clear that the rocks can be seen through it.

Mont St. Pierre is a real fishing village where the traveler may hire a boat, fisherman and all,. for $5.00 for the entire morning. Mont Louis, Madeleine, Grande Valle come next; then down around Cap des Rosiers the road winds by Cap aux Os to the Gaspé, the real landing place of the French. Sunsets are excellent here. From the various lighthouses on the way, excellent views are enjoyed. Wild flowers are abundant and are especially lovely at Cap Gaspé. The cliffs and the field daisies are larger and more beautiful here than anywhere else. Cap Gaspé Light is an interesting and historic place, where exercises in honor of the great Cartier were held last summer. Ralph's Beach is all American. Its many cabins bear such familiar names as Amos 'n' Andy and cost only seventy-five cents a night.

At the foot of Percé a large rock is torn, giving the place its name, and here is located General Logan Park. Many fine views of the rock and of the little town were shown. This great rock of Percé is beautifully colored in places, and never twice looks alike, due to fog, sunshine or atmospheric conditions. It is twelve hundred feet high, two hundred eighty feet long, and 300 feet thick. The Three Sisters is a peculiar piece of shore line. It is very picturesque, large cliffs, caves and archways causing many peculiar formations.

About three miles from Percé lies Bonaventure Island where the largest bird reservation in the country is located. Eleven kinds of birds inhabit this island, along the high cliffs, every speck of shore rock being covered with them. They were shown flying close to the water, screaming and swishing, to be heard miles away.

English towns are located along this section: Chandler, Newport, Port Daniel, New Carlisle. Fishing is prevalent and the civilization much more advanced. A stop was made at Cascapedia. Carleton is an interesting lumber town. A grass-grown road leads to the old zinc mines, abandoned since the depression. Only one train a day passes through this country and the traveler may play tag with it for hours. Restigouche is the scene of famous salmon clubs whose members are largely

American millionaires.   Matapedia is a very beautiful valley with over forty miles of the best scenery.

Down through Maine, Holton, Sherman, along the rugged shores excellent scenery was displayed.   Mt. Desert section has a fine system of roads, and the land bordering them is left as near the natural state as possible.   A boulevard leads to the top of Cadillac Mountain where a wonderful view is disclosed.

The closing slides were sunset with its gorgeous afterglow, a mass of color fitting for a benediction.   Then came the great emblem waving over this fine land of ours—Old Glory.

"THE MARCH OF THE SEASONS THROUGH THE WHITE MOUNTAINS"

Thursday, February 7

Illustrated Lecture

By ALBERT LEONARD SQUIER, NEWTON, MASS.

The excellent slides illustrating this lecture were selected from nearly ten thousand pictures made by the speaker in the White Mountains during the past twenty-five years. All were painted by him with a brush no larger than the point of a pin. For nearly thirty years Mr. Squier has been experimenting on lantern transparency.

The march of the seasons through the White Mountains is an interesting study best appreciated by actual contact. This gradual transition from season to season is one of the most striking features of the mountain, showing, as it does, the full beauty of mountain nature in all her variety of dress.

What the White Mountains lack in altitude they make up for in friendliness. It is not necessary to have altitude to have a garden; and these mountains, though not the highest, form their own fine garden view.

Nature is never more lovely than in her robe of white, especially in the mountains where the great white stillness reigns. To see and feel this splendor at close range one must veer from the beaten paths. A snowshoe trip through the mountains satisfies this desire for closer mountain scenery.

Perhaps no one knows the great winter miracle of the mountain as well as the woodman and the country doctor. The former by very nature is a part of the mountains, in steady contact with trees. The latter may be seen trudging along over unbeaten mountain passes, breaking the way through snowdrifts as he goes on his errand of mercy. Nature lovers, too, must wend their snowy way through the mountains if they would appreciate not only that great white beauty, but also the awakening of spring. Mountain roads are becoming more and more passable and it is hoped that conditions may still further improve so more people may visit the section in the winter months.

Sleighing through the woods and over the hills affords pleasure for many. A view of the old covered bridge spanning the Pemigewassett and leading to the Flume was shown. Then came the Flume with its December coating of ice just forming. The water had stopped exactly where it fell, a winter prisoner of ice. A little later, as one looked up the ravine, he saw a mass of ice throughout, a frozen waterfall, a miniature Niagara. Next came its covering of snow. No ice appeared on the east wall but the west was covered. This formation of ice resembled a beautiful clear sunburst.

In 1914 the lecturer first saw the Flume. The east wall, caressed by the sun, was entirely free of ice which always covers the opposite wall. An ice organ appeared in the Flume, the formation resembling pipes of a great organ. Six miles from North Woodstock is Lost River, truly named, because there is no trace of a river.

Gradually the twelve to fifteen feet of snow thinned out and the melting ice and snow showed winter leaving and spring coming along. Rivers, bordered with the color of early flowers, rushed along merrily.

June is blossom time in the mountains. Early in the season nature lovers are seen dotting the landscape, glad of the free air after perhaps spending the winter in an apartment. If one can go to the mountains only once a year he should go in June. Fields of daisies, white and brown-eyed, abound along the hillsides, and no beauty can surpass the lovely New England laurel. The wild rose, a universal favorite, is seen everywhere. Goldenrod lights up the mountains with its sunny glow. A stretch of four miles of this golden beauty was seen by many, appreciated by most, but slighted by some who drove by at the rate of fifty miles per hour.

Franconia Notch has a charm of its own. Slides showed this section in its varied beauty. Lafayette, on which the ashes of the late Professor Carpenter were strewn, stood out in its glory. Lost River, arising from under great rocks, the Cave of Lost

Souls, named by Professor Carpenter, and the Cave of the Bull were shown. A fernland near Plymouth, valleys and woods up the Pemigewasett, all in their summer glory, together with Georgiana Fall, various lakes and farms throughout this fine country were pictured. The Notch and Flume were shown at various periods, also Old Man's Foot and Profile Lake. Then came the famous Old Man on the Mountain, composed of four ledges, forty feet across the profile. When one of these ledges was in danger of slipping off it was anchored by an expert quarry-man, held fast to the others again. Here is the most finely chiseled face on any mountain anywhere.

Throughout this country are seen deer in large numbers, adding their share to the beauty of the mountains. Big game may still be found here. Echo Lake is another attractive sight.

From here the views took us to a different range, entirely distinct, where more shade was found, a section, Alpine in character. Bethlehem appeared with sheep and shepherd. One little black sheep figured. A good shepherd had brought in all his sheep; not one was lost. Washington, Adams, Madison, and Jefferson ranges and peaks appeared. The Elephant's Head and other fanciful slopes loomed here and there. Views along the Saco, Willard Notch, Bridal Veil Falls, were shown. Scenes of Indian legends were described and projected on the screen.

Chicorua in early morning is a place of beauty and inspiration. It is well worth losing part of one's sleep to arise in the wee hours and glimpse the world from this high point. The lake is a sea of heavenly blue. Along the shores are many fine camps for boys and girls, where nature lore and water sports may be studied and enjoyed. One picture caught a boy diving forty feet from the cliff into the lake.

By this time fall is appearing and the scenery takes on a different phase. Dixville Notch is seen in its splendor. Sun shining on the goldenrod cast a new light of fall. Near by, fancy shows in the calm and sacred stillness of the mountain, a procession of mountain priests chanting a hymn, followed by choir boys dressed some in gold and others in silver. The many peaks are decked in a new beauty. Saddle, the fifth notch, Pinkham

TABLE DECORATIONS, NOVEMBER 1935, SPONSORED BY MRS. HOMER GAGE

Notch, the old trail along Crawford Notch, falls in this vicinity, and the pastoral Saco valley were all shown.

The mountains are a marvelous spectacle in October, color setting in by late September or early October. Many consider this the most beautiful time of the year in which to visit the mountains, and it surely is the most colorful. Many of these mountain scenes were again shown in their fall garb of bright colors, duller browns, and grays. Indian summer is a delightful season, a sort of afterglow of beauty and hope.

Soon fall has lost her radiant beauty and the woods are brown, but still a lovely sight with its varied russet tones. Fall is passing and winter is again with us, back with all its fairy wonderland in the endless march of the seasons.

> "God gave the field to the farmer,
> To the sailor he gave the sea;
> But God gave me the mountains
> For they last eternally."

"SOMETHING OLD AND SOMETHING NEW"

Thursday, February 14

Illustrated Lecture

By Mrs. Ethel N. S. Peckham, Sterlington, New York

Mrs. Peckham praised the Flower and Vegetable Show held in the adjoining room, an innovation which proved well worth while. She complimented the Potter, Breed, and Iristhorpe exhibits, and declared Mr. Kinney's display of golden rhubarb as lovely as any plants or flowers. So pleased was she with these handsome long stalks of rhubarb that she planned to take some home with her.

The title of her talk was taken from the saying

"Something old and something new,
Something borrowed and something blue."

Old things and ideas are considered jokes by many who are always after the new, little realizing that the new is only a modified old, or that the old often wears better than the new. Many old tools are seen as religious symbols of long ago. The Roman cistern, filled with water coming from high mountains, is still needed in modified form in the garden. We should not use very cold water on plants when they are hot, that of the temperature of the air is best.

Old things of attractive shapes are noted, such as the basket of pioneer times made in the Roman style, suitable for oranges and tangerines. There are some like it today, that are modified adaptations.

A good garden will always be a good garden if it suits the purpose for which it was made. It must have the proper proportion even as to walks, so that after many years it will still be a beautiful thing.

A book of 1300 showed shallow digging, not spading down, but on the slant. People who sell tools should show the correct ways of using them, Mrs. Peckham believes. In these old books are found the names of many of our so-called modern plants, and we learn that these plants are not new at all, but discovered long ago. About 1597–1660 frittilarias are mentioned. Iris Susiana is first mentioned as sold for a garden in the time of Elizabeth. Iris Azuria came out in 1812, a real true sky blue. Daffodils are mentioned in a 1557 book, also jonquils, and narcissus, which was odorous. Fine old plots should not be neglected to make way for new ones, as some old ones are far better.

The Forum at Rome was adorned with lovely wistaria. In recent years we have been growing the light blue from China. As for things borrowed, we have the coconut palm which came to us by being washed ashore. Other plant life has been brought by birds, ships, and other means. Some plants have been taken from this country across, only to be brought back later.

Scenes in France were shown. People were gathering violets for the perfume industry. Olives there in combination suggested a fine idea. It is well to have together bloom for spring and for fall.

Many try out things before a club. This is very beneficial and is sure to reap a harvest of ideas. A flower show made to look like a real garden in which the plants are actually growing is an ideal one. A view of one at Columbus, Ohio, was seen. Special plant societies are represented, and experts on the plot for judges. The amount of the prize does not necessarily stand for the quality; it is the successful growing that counts. Ghost iris, a white bloom, is a fine Florida iris. Many good old varieties will not grow here. African and Dutch iris are hardy now. Silene, another white bloom, is a fine grower. Rubro does well in California. Brahmin is a gorgeous dark blue and is still good after being rained on.

Many fine crocuses of the old type are good growers today. Martican lilies are found in a great variety. Michaelmas daisies in all colors and sizes are fine in a garden. Saxifraga longiflora is good, Falling Waters being a splendid new English variety shown recently at a flower show. Daffodils are always in favor. Moonshine is a lovely white, triangular type. Harvest Moon, a pale cream, eight inches high, is good for a rock garden. Medusa is a gorgeous red color, white outside, and is late. Golden Harvest is a lovely one and drew a prize recently. King Alfred is early. Wheel of Fortune, Fortune's Cheer, and Fortune's Life are all good. Crucible is one of the new ones. Sparkhall and Poeticus are favorites. Silver Chimes is not hardy here, but will do well in Washington, D. C. There are quite a few double varieties. Daphne is a splendid double white narcissus.

New York Botanical Garden has millions of bulbs which look as if they were growing wild. There are many ways of planting a garden, but the rule always is to fit the garden to the land.

Gardening should begin when one is two years of age, if only training consists in picking up stones. In this way love of nature, interest in gardening and appreciation of the gardens of others may be fostered and promoted. Many fine slides were shown, but perhaps the best of all had one of life's greatest blossoms in it—a little child.

"PRESERVATION OF BEAUTIFUL AND HISTORIC PLACES IN MASSACHUSETTS"

Thursday, February 21

Illustrated Lecture

By Bradford Williams, Boston, Mass.

Of late years people have been appreciating more the great beauty of nature and have slowly developed a desire to preserve these spots. Much of this awakening, perhaps, is due to the strong influence of Henry David Thoreau, the great lover of nature, a student, and a writer. His essays have attracted attention to New England's beauty and have set people to exploring the landscape.

Charles Eliot, son of the late president of Harvard University, called together a number of like-minded nature lovers, people desirous of acquiring and holding beautiful and historic places in Massachusetts. This group petitioned the State for exemption from taxation of such acquired sections and won a favorable reply. The Trustees of Public Reservations called together the chairmen of several clubs in and near Boston, and it was proposed to the Legislature that there be a Metropolitan Park Commission in the Boston area. This bill was passed and $5,000,000 was expended to buy beautiful sections along the Charles River, the Fells, and in Milton. Since that time the two groups have been co-operating.

Various beauty spots owned by the State were shown. An area at Brewster, Cape Cod, the gift to the Board of Trustees of Mrs. Roland Dickerson, is now a public reservation. A wooded tract outside Boston, where some men camped week-ends, is now the property of the Commission.

People come from all parts of the country to see an old town or city. Chestnut Street, Salem, a memory of the merchant trade of long ago, was shown with its well-known doorways and colonial gardens. The home of Miss Mabel Choate of Stockbridge, containing early American furniture rivaling that of the Metropolitan Museum of New York, and ever lovely colonial garden were shown. A large tract in Westfield and Chesterfield, in the gorge of the Berkshires, was pictured. The Board holds one half of this territory while the rest is privately owned. The private owner has spoiled his section by improving it. Steps for visitors and other changes have detracted from the beauty of nature. Unfortunately, this happens here and there, largely for commercial purposes. Sign boards, refreshment stands and the like should not be set up in the wrong place. The State Department of Conservation provides many places for camping accommodations.

The Massachusetts Landscape Survey is to determine about outstanding scenery, and workers are sent into the field to examine such places as suggested. These workers are sent to women's clubs and other organizations to lecture and gain support.

Plum Island is one of the characteristic views of Massachusetts. An early law of this State is a peculiar one. It states that when the tide goes out the public has no right to walk on the beach. Between high water and low water the beach belongs to adjoining land and the owner. The Old Colony law specifies that when fishing, fowling, or approaching in a boat, one is safe here.

Horseneck Beach is a good example of a fine tract of beach unguided. This is a nice section, only the cottages erected there spoil it. Telegraph poles through the dunes destroy the natural flavor, and the houses are not at all attractive. They are a sort of paper box structure, and are not permanent looking. A garage is proper enough in the city but has no place here in a spot of great naturalness. Signs, too, spoil the true beauty of natural surroundings

Another division is the moor and seaside upland. The outside of Cape Cod at Truro was shown. Here the sea beats in and the top line of the moor changes every year. Sometimes the station has to be moved back. There are miles of rolling grassland without houses, and only occasional trees as great gales ruin them. Cape Ann has perfect headlands. The sea breaks on the gate block along the shore. The Board has purchased a section of Rockport where nothing has been done to spoil it.

Views of the Taconic Trail, coming from New York, were shown, also Greylock and a bit of that beautiful section. Fine roads run through the Berkshires, Route 8 being one of the best. The road through the valley gives lovely upland views. A typical New England scene showed some fine old elms. We worry over the future of the elm as many of our fine old trees are being ruined by pests and abuses. The old New England stone wall and farmhouse were a treat to see. Winter furnishes quite a different view along the scenic highways, always beautiful.

The gorge of Deerfield Valley, west of Greenfield, most nearly resembles Switzerland. The Mohawk Trail through this section is a very popular one, with its long display of exquisite scenery. The Boston and Maine Railroad route along the trail and through this lovely section was shown. The views from the train and from the automobile offer different phases of the same spots through quite a long stretch of scenery. The river bed offers fine scenes. Without question, our Massachusetts Switzerland is the Deerfield Gorge. The heights of Greylock were shown. A war memorial has been placed on the top. It is a good looking memorial, effectively placed. Mt. Everett, with numerous waterfalls, was seen (the one at Sage's Ravine was particularly beautiful), and Diana's Pool. New York has built a fine trail over which Massachusetts people go to look at their own falls from the park in New York.

Another series of views dealt with the woodland areas. A section covered with trees may not be a forest, but it is at least a woodland. Fall is the most beautiful time in the forest whether the colored leaves are still on the trees or are forming a carpet of grandeur. October and November are the two months of glory in a wooded area. One must really be alone in the heart of a forest to fully appreciate its great beauty and sacred stillness.

A few foreign slides were introduced: the Lorna Doone country with its scarce wild deer; a stretch of moorland in Devonshire; the Lake Region—all of which have been donated and are being preserved for their historic and literary value, to be used and enjoyed, with restrictions, by home folks and visitors as well.

In this State the Board of Trustees have been donated various tracts of especial value and beauty, such as a section in Monu ment Mountain, by Miss Helen Butler; Petticoat Hill, in honor of Edward Nash; Halibut Point in Rockport. Nineteen miles from the State House, near Medfield, is a tract of rhododendrons, . a carpet of lady's slipper, owned by the Trustees.

Thoreau suggested that all such places of natural beauty be preserved; and that it would be wise to have a committee look out for this matter, as places of rare beauty should belong to all.

The Massachusetts Trustees of Public Reservations is a busy organization, trying to interest people in preservation work and in donating desirable places privately owned to be preserved for the good of all.

"CHARLESTON, SOUTH CAROLINA"

Thursday, February 28

Illustrated Lecture

By Miss Dorothy S. Emmons, Newton, Mass.

Charleston is the type of place one intends to stop at for a few days yet leaves reluctantly at the end of a month. The charm of this city has been registered in song and story, but nothing, not even the pictures of it, can truly portray the grandeur and quaint charm of this lovely old city.

After the Edict of Nantes, 1680, the Huguenots came over to this section of the country and were followed by others. Their influence is felt throughout the city. Many slides depicted the various styles of architecture, types of influence pervading the place, and the fine ironwork of the city. Charleston has been called the City of Lavender and Old Lace, probably because of this fine lacy ironwork, some of which was imported from England, but most of it was made here.

Seeing the flush of dawn through some of these fine gardens is a beautiful sight. The large iron gate and wall cast their impressive shadow throughout. A walk down to the Garden Club with a view of the shining old buildings of Church Street and their splendid iron doorways is a pleasant one. Everywhere one sees these gateways of iron with their intricate and highly diversified designs. They, alone, convey to the visitor much of the wonder and charm of the city and awaken in him a desire for the past, a look at the days when all this beauty reigned in its prime.

St. Philip's Church, the oldest Episcopal church in the South was shown, an imposing building breathing the atmosphere of early religious worship. Everywhere churches stand out as some of the best examples of architecture. St. Michael's is another fine old church. Its bells, made in England, crossed the ocean five times, back and forth, records of warfare, then were recast in England and sent to Charleston. Such historic possessions enhance the value as well as the beauty and interest in this Carolina city.

One section has remained primarily a British district. Here the planters settled. Even today the speech and customs of these people are decidedly English.

The people of Charleston are as charming today as their city. Everywhere is reflected a truly gentlemanly and ladylike quality. They are very cordial, highly social and appreciative of everything cultural and artistic. They are a loyal and patriotic people, the many patriotic slabs expressing this feeling of respect and loyalty. Fifty-two wars have been waged in and around here, ranging from regular strife to a struggle with the forces of nature such as tidal waves, fires, and earthquakes. The old Powder House of 1704–05 is now the home of the Colonial Dames. Another old building of 1765 days, the headquarters during the Revolution, is still occupied by a member of the family. Great people such as Washington and Lafayette have been there.

After the Revolution, Charleston College was started in a lovely pink limestone building. Ashley Hall, the home of a rich planter, now a girls' school, is typical of the early homes. Most of the houses of that period had street or service entrances of ironwork, some with charming porticos. These gateways and fences are beautiful and worthy of study.

The Russell House has an interesting history. Mr. Russell made his own plans and took them to England, stipulating that the house must be built just that way. He rejected any advice. The builder came over and constructed the house as ordered, and to the owner's amazement there was no stairway. Mr. Russell regretted his not listening to reason and had a spiral stairway added.

A unique type of architecture was developed at this time, and many stone buildings were erected. The Smythe House with its stunning gateway was shown as a sample of the entire street. The gateway of sword design made a formidable entrance. The old unwrought iron used in this period never rusted. The painted iron is cast iron. Many gateways of all types of design were shown. One had a lyre for its central motif. Lace motifs were very popular and effective. Seldom are two identical gateways seen. Arched gateways were quite elaborate. The lovely Villa Marguerite was pictured, also a row of fine houses at East Bay. Church Street, with lichens and mosses on the walls, archways and balconies, was shown in all its beauty and majesty.

One of the great interests of Charleston is the Negro section. The music of these people in its various forms is a rare treat, one not to be missed by the visitor. Views were shown of the little Negro farms, the people working, and the general life of the plantation. Everywhere is echoed Negro music, weird and beautiful, quite typical of the African jungle.

Throughout Charleston and vicinity, the landscape is one of great natural beauty, mosses hanging gracefully flap in the wind and afford many light effects in different weather conditions and at different times of the day and night. The cypress gardens have a charm different from anything else ever seen. An old rice field has been turned into a beautiful garden by Mr. Kittredge. In these one hundred and fifty years, great cypress trees have grown up there. One may walk for miles through this garden and canoe around much of it. In the moonlight it is an enchanting scene, "grave with the sense of fate, a mystical foreshadow," as has been written of it.

Ashley River district, Medway Plantation, with its early house still standing at the end of three terraces, gave a fine picture. The front approach to all these plantations is from the river side. Medway is now used by the family as a hunting lodge. The entrance to Magnolia Plantation showed sheep grazing there. The influence of this section is decidedly English. Azalea gardens of this place show a great variety, more than can be imagined, some are ten to fourteen feet high. One may walk over twenty-five acres of this garden.

Middleton Place was shown in all its glory. Here was achieved the first great landscape garden of America. The old house stood through the American Revolution but was burned eventually, only one wing partially surviving. This place has been restored and is now occupied by Mr. Smith. André Michaud of France came over here to help Mr. Middleton establish his gardens. After one hundred and fifty years the japonicas are still

GRAFTON GARDEN CLUB, 1935

living there.   The river, house, and garden are all in the same
axis. Terraces sweep along for a quarter of a mile. Butterfly
lakes and the old rice mill were shown.   Middleton Place winds
along like a delicate necklace.   A peacock made a fine picture as
he sat up in a tree.   The forest and lake section of the garden is
very imposing.   Amy Lowell and others have well described this
magnificent estate in verse.

"A GARDEN TRAVELOGUE"

Thursday, March 7

Illustrated Lecture

By Mrs. Harriette W. Long, Cambridge, Mass.

Very few records of old English gardens survive, but we do
know that they had walls around them for seclusion, and a moat
outside the wall for protection. The garden had a rectangular
plan and was subdivided into compartments. Arbors were there
in that place of rest and recreation. Frequently a maize and
topiary work were seen. In some gardens swans were swimming
in the moat, and peacocks were there, sometimes used, it is said,
for watchdogs. It is claimed that they would cry out when
strangers appeared, but that feature is questioned.

Penhurst Place garden is the reproduction of a medieval garden. Views of it were seen, with a tennis court and orchard on
one side. Yew walks or alleys were popular. Outside the wall,
in many cases, is one of these walks or alleys. Montacute is a
famous old place recently given to the State. It has a large garden and kitchen garden, and outside the balustrade cows graze.
Longheath is one of the finest gardens, where many old-fashioned
favorites may be seen. Roses and pink pentstemon are lovely
there. Three feet above the general level is a walk.

Newplace, Stratford-on-Avon, has a lovely garden, compartments of bright bloom where tulips are in evidence. At West-
moreland is a fine Dutch garden designed by a Frenchman.
During the reign of William and Mary topiary work was very
popular. A great hedge walls in this garden, on either side of
which is the orchard, and the service yard. Near Banbury is
seen the ancestral home of the Washington family, restored by
interested Americans and English. It is an interesting relic and
the gardens are fine. The Queen's own lovely rose garden at
Windsor, set against a stone wall, was shown.

The cottage garden is typical of the English and has done much for the person of small means. No plot is too small to be planted there. One of the most elaborate gardens in England is Selworthy, in Somerset. All through England are famous and beautiful gardens, each interesting in its own way.

In France quite formal gardens are seen among the medieval forms. In the seventeenth century all French gardens were under one strong influence. Parterre gardens, clipped hedges, statuary, pools, fountains, large water theater were the result of this influence. At Versailles hundreds of trees were set out every year. Everything here was done on a large scale, for the garden covered many miles, and had cool running pools in shady walks. Ornamental lattice work is typical.

In Paris, there is one very modern garden. Small formal gardens on various levels, three dimensions, are seen here occasionally. Villa Florentine at Cannes shows English influence with its border of cineraria and arches of roses. All along the French Riviéra are many fine expansive gardens of varied style.

Spanish gardens are seen to advantage on the island of Majorca. There geraniums grow luxuriantly by the roadside. Pottery is much in evidence. Courtyards and old seaside gardens are interesting and lovely everywhere. Large fountains and long pergolas down the side of the garden are effective. The color scheme changes often. At Palma, the capital, are especially beautiful scenes. Even humble peasants have their gardens. The Spanish enjoy living out of doors more than any other people. Here and there is seen a loggia with tile decorating the Spanish shrine. Near Barcelona is a classical garden with Moorish influence, traced to Moorish domination from the eighth to the fifteenth century. The true Spanish garden shows Asiatic influence. A pool with swans floating in it is a common sight. A labyrinth here and there, making one's journey a difficult one, may have a pool in the center.

Seville is more Spanish than Spain. The garden patio is square or rectangular, enclosed by a hedge. Water is seen and heard flowing in these gardens. Polychrome tile made into steps, walls, statuary, and the like, rather than the flowers themselves, provide the garden coloring. Intimate outdoor living rooms are a common luxury. Trees in a Cordova section were shown in their glory. These were owned by an American. Andalusia has many flat or hillside gardens. The home of a Moorish king at Ronda was seen. The garden here is terraced down abruptly to three hundred feet below. Stairs led down here to the bed of the river in the old days.

The Alhambra, the palace of the Moorish kings, is surrounded by a wooded hillside, and its garden is a series of walled enclosures. A canal, with jets of water here and there, is seen in many gardens. These water devices cool the garden living rooms and make them comfortable in the extreme temperature of Spain.

The Italian garden is beautiful in aspect at any time of year. Its design is in harmony with the house and surrounding landscape. These gardens are meant to be lived in comfortably in the unbearable heat conditions. At any time of year the Italian garden has its mountain view. A lovely sight are the terraces with villa above. In a Roman garden is seen the Fountain of the Dragons, backed by cypress trees. Terraces of the hundred fountains are above—a great sight. Throughout this garden is a prolific use of water. Mussolini has promoted the use of public gardens. Everywhere in these old gardens pools and cascades are seen.

Florence has her share of beautiful gardens, rolling countryside, and water scenes. Walled-in gardens look out in the distance. The Medici garden, one of the best, had its fine loggia and other attractions. The royal gardens with their pools were very intriguing. The region about Lake Como is very lovely. Maggiore's terrace upon terrace and fine villa adorning the top, orange and lemon trees in abundance, gave a rare picture.

Goethe's walled garden at Frankfort is a mecca for all visitors. German gardens at Dresden were shown. At Berlin were seen many flowers of one kind in clumps instead of a variety. At tulip and iris time the suburban section is very popular. Intimacy of garden and house is in complete harmony, producing much of the garden charm.

Each country has its own garden charm and characteristics, yet gardens are gardens in whatever country, much alike in their difference, all beautiful in their own right the world over.

"FLOWERS FOR YOUR HOUSE"

Thursday, March 14

Illustrated Lecture

By Mrs. Georgiana R. Smith, Dedham, Mass.

March is generally conceded to be the most uninteresting month of the year as it is a hang-over from winter, yet begrudging of spring. A promise of the new season is all about us yet discernible, for the most part, only in our homes. Our everlastings, however beautiful, seem already to have served their purpose, and we are impatient for real green life or fresh nature. Richardson Wright has remarked that the only thing he has against everlastings is that they are everlasting.

At this time we enjoy a forward look to the early flower shows. Unfortunately, we tend to lose sight of the real purpose of a flower show which is, in part, a lesson in appreciating flower arrangement. But scale, proportion and study of things in relation to their background are not an end in themselves; they must serve to emphasize the beauty of flowers themselves by displaying them to their best advantage.

The flower arrangement of Mrs. Smith's lecture was not that for a flower show but one to be followed in beautifying the home. In this matter design is important, yet too much emphasis is placed upon rules. We must learn to see with our eyes. to feel color, rhythm and harmony, as no set rules will ever bring this about.

Flowers in relation to the container is a common subject, but we should think of flowers in relation to the container and both in relation to the home. "More perfect than a perfect rose is that rose in a perfect setting."

For design, the first principle is unity. The picture must be complete as a whole. It is an important factor, but not enough in itself. Interest is held by variety. Order is our plan. Rhythm of color and form furnishes poise and rest.

Effective flower arrangement in terms of home decoration in harmony with the furnishings of one's home was demonstrated. Various chintzes and other fine materials were employed to bring before the audience a picture of the typical home of today, with its variety of tone. Chintzes of warm color are greatly favored. In spring we may have a little touch of yellow to liven up the place; thus we may come from a dull house to a bright one. Flowers bring life to inanimate objects in our home.

Several backgrounds suggesting general color and character of a room were shown. A pleasing one was the sort of room where inherited old things are mixed with modern furniture, a natural combination, often found these days. On the wall was placed an old picture. On a table just beneath it stood an old egg boiler with a rock inside, a square, solid affair in which were arranged red tulips on one side and calendulas on the other, in a balance of color. Modernists are using this asymmetrical plan rather than the former order of symmetry.

Another effect was arranged, this time showing a room belonging to a person who has old things, but wishes to be classed as modern. The chintz was gray with cream color and yellow blending, then dark brown was used and deep yellow. This contrast was very effectively given. A piece of framed needlework hung on the wall. An attractive bit of flower arrangement was set on the table beneath it.

Next came a room with a blue background and a bit of rather exotic color—purple mixed with yellow. Flower arrangement was a deep purple and yellow, setting off the room excellently.

A pinkish chintz was very pleasing to the eye, but brought forth the criticism that the quietest things are best to live with, then other light effects may be had from flowers and such. This pink mixture was used with a clear pink fabric. Such a combination called for a tall vase with deep pink tulips, some white flowers, and green foliage mixed in. The appearance of this room was dainty, yet one that might become monotonous.

An entirely different type of room was placed in suggestion, perhaps an old barn made over into a room. In this studio appeared a little mauve water color blending with the orange scheme of the room. A small low arrangement of flowers added character in a little peasant pottery pitcher from Carolina. Something white should always be placed in such pottery.

An almost monotonous gray and brown scheme was shown. This is a modern tendency. An aluminum container held white flowers with green foliage, grass collected by the lecturer last fall.

A study in brown and green was very attractive. Snapdragons set off this room. Nature provides so many greens one can always find just the right one for desired effect. The California eucalyptus is a lovely green with yellow and red in the stem. Flowers are always set off to advantage by their foliage, often as lovely as the bloom itself.

A house belonging to someone who possesses a great many Chinese effects was shown. These furnishings in themselves are a lovely pattern. Painting on rice paper, the background of Chinese, the paper painted green and glazed, was set off by a fabric with soft colors such as rose or, perhaps, gold. The flower arrangement in this case was yellow and white. There is quite an affinity between old Chinese and some modern gadgets.

Heather is useful at this time of year and not expensive. It is a good filler and works in well with most flowers. To obtain good flowers one should go to the grower.

The blending of modern fabrics in color schemes is very pleasing, indeed. Such room plans were shown on the chart. Brown with cream effects, used with plain dark brown, showed a bronze container with white flowers, pale yellow daffodils, dark wall flowers and yellow primroses—a very striking arrangement bringing out the tones of the fabrics.

Magenta is interesting if we know how to use it. A deep rose magenta chintz combined with rose and cream calls for deep blue. A container of tall grass will set this off well.

It has been claimed that all people are either the green and rust or the blue and mulberry variety, but this, we hope, is not true. We are all, however, too much afraid of color and lose much charm that might be effected in the home. We should experiment with color, play with it until we have learned to exercise our faculty and choose wisely. The beauty of home decoration lies chiefly in artistic form, which may be accomplished by study and feeling of color, harmony and rhythm.

"THE IMPORTANCE OF BIRDS IN YOUR GARDEN"

Thursday, March 21

Illustrated Lecture

By Lawrence B. Fletcher, Cohasset, Mass.

Mr. Fletcher, secretary of the Federation of Bird Clubs of New England, is a staunch defender of the presence of birds in our garden.

In summer the gypsy moth lays five to six hundred eggs which are dormant all winter. Then early in the spring five hundred small caterpillars go to the tree top to destroy the leaves. In the adult stage they come down and soon lay five hundred more eggs apiece. The second year, if nothing prevents, there are 250,000 eggs, and this steady multiplication goes on.

Chickadees, nuthatches, and woodpeckers go up and down the trees all winter and take these eggs, in this way ridding us of so many pests. All summer these birds come along from South America, take caterpillars and other pests, and so protect the trees from destruction.

Nowadays an extensive study of bird migration is being made by placing an aluminum identification band on the leg of each bird. In this way the history of birds is studied and it is now possible to know what country they come from, at what time, when they return, and the like. Some five to six thousand people are now banding, recording the time of arrival and departure, and general behavior of these birds.

Mr. Fletcher maintains a bird sanctuary at Cohasset, and handles about one thousand birds of some thirty-seven species a year, with only one man to help him. Twenty birds nesting there are insectivorous birds. Last year there were forty-five blue-birds in his garden. They live on the corn borer, green worm, and canker worm, if just supplied with proper nesting homes and food.

The biological aspect of these feathered friends is important, and their every behavior is carefully watched to furnish this information. One box in the catalpa tree has been occupied by the same bird three years in succession. All but four birds have a different husband each year. Only the goose, dove, ostrich, and swan have a husband for life.

The digestion of young birds is rapid and the appetite great. One of the lecturer's neighbors fed her young for five days, then a male bird appeared with a band by which it was known that he was the husband of last year. Her present husband had failed her for some reason, so her former mate rallied to her aid. The tendency of all species to bring up their young·is the one outstanding feature of bird life. Perhaps the lesson taught by the foster father is stick to your first mate!

Many fine slides depicting this bird sanctuary and other gardens inhabited by birds followed. A rose garden at Cohasset boasting eleven pairs of bluebirds was shown. Nest boxes, costing only seventy-five cents, adorned a pergola, providing homes for several pairs of bluebirds. The very lovely hanging rose garden of Mr. and Mrs. Edward Webster, at Falmouth, will soon have many bird boxes placed there. The Oswood Howe estate in Brookline is the home of many feathered friends.

The house wren is easy to secure for a tenant and is the first to come. He feeds on the green caterpillar. Warblers come along anywhere from April 15 to May 30. Many of these birds inhabit the lovely garden of Mrs. Wallace at Wellesley Hills. Even for esthetic joy, regardless of their great benefit, birds are certainly a prime factor in a garden. The cuckoo feeds caterpillars to her young. The bobolink lives entirely on insects. The purple finch is a good friend, also. A chickadee is a permanent resident of Mr. Fletcher's garden, working all winter and all summer. She feeds her young on sunflower seed, which they adore.

Throughout the gardens of Mr. and Mrs. Endicott of Danvers may be seen many families of birds. The red start, Indigo-bunting, tree swallow, nuthatch and woodpecker are all insectivorous birds, the last named being very important. The starling takes insectivorous food to his young, thereby being given a clean bill of health as to his status. One objection to this bird is that he drives out all others so Mr. Fletcher does not give him quarters, but the starling in the long run really does more good than harm, as he lives eight months of the year on insects.

A trap is inexpensive and takes thirty to forty birds at a time. It is predatory proof and does not harm the birds any. It is quite easy to take seed-eating birds, but not so easy to capture the insectivorous type. Some birds do not mind being trapped, and return time and again to the same place of captivity, showing also that banding does not bother them.

Views of bands and banded birds were shown. Discoverers of these banded birds report to the Biological Survey in Washington, D. C., and 210,151 letters were received from all over the world. The process of holding a bird while the band is being slipped on was shown. The size of the band is according to the size of the leg. A bird is placed on his back for this purpose, and he usually lies there in that position for sixty seconds or so before leaving with the band. Mrs. Herrick of Toppsfield banded 690 birds the first year.

The little junco or snowbird eats noxious weeds and seeds. He comes about January 10 and remains until April 27. The little fellow at Mr. Fletcher's has been taken out of the trap about twenty-two times during that period. At one time six of the nine of the previous year were taken again from the same trap. The little song sparrow arrives in early March, the vanguard of spring.

Mrs. Hamel of Worcester does great banding. She finds, as many others, that sons and daughters come back and build nests on almost the identical spot where they were hatched.

Excellent views of Mr. Fletcher's lovely place at Cohasset were shown. One looks from the veranda into a pond with an old-fashioned garden on the shore where he does his banding. He has taken one song sparrow out of a trap here for the seventh time and knows her seven husbands.

Mrs. Morgan, widow of the late Professor Morgan, wished to do her bit, so set a trap in her second floor apartment and banded 900 birds the first year. Humming birds are attracted to delphinium and bee balm, so, for a substitute, her device was a pill bottle of sweetened water, with a red flannel spread around it. In this way she succeeded in banding fourteen humming birds by using an old embroidery hoop with baskets attached to it for traps.   These little birds go down to Argentina when they leave here, but return to the little pill bottle.   Purple finches visit her loft in large numbers.

The humming bird is the smallest bird we have.   He makes a long pendulum swing and is the only side swinger.   The ruby-throated humming bird eats the bee balm.   She sits on her nest twenty-one days.   The little ones are no larger than a thumb nail.   They become very friendly and sit in one's hand when acquainted with a person.   One of these birds was shown taking a sip of honey from a medicine dropper.   Another one lit on Dr. Parson's eyeglasses, then took a sip of honey from his lip.

Walter Dean, the late professor of botany at Harvard and a noted ornithologist, was in very close intimacy with birds.   They would feed near his face and willingly become banded.   They would depart for South America, then return the next year to his place at Franklin, New Hampshire.

Sixty per cent of our birds leave us and go via Florida and the Antilles to Argentina.   All insectivorous birds do this.   Then there is a great migration to Buzzard's Bay for hatching.   There is no such thing as an early or a late season with birds; they come to us from Argentina in time to destroy insect pests.

Views were shown of the crested flycatcher at a box.   Duxbury beach gallinaceous birds, the woodcock and the partridge, were shown.   The females of these birds will feign illness or a broken leg to take attention away from the nest.   A vast flock of Canadian geese were seen migrating.   A bird sanctuary at Lake Erie was an interesting sight.   Wild geese by the thousands were migrating to Hudson Bay.   The banding of these birds is a help to hunters who obtain information as to the best fields for hunting.

The night hawk, a beautiful bird, comes from central South America.   It builds no nest, but just locates on roofs of houses. One landed on the roof of Bowdoin College where Dr. Gross, the ornithologist, is located.   She has been back five years in succession with five different husbands.   A study of conditions shows a great difference in husbands, even in bird life.

The Payne place at Chatham, a great breeding place for tern, was shown.   This bird comes here from South America, the middle of April. Cape Cod would be nothing without sea gulls or terns. These birds feed their young in the air. Although there are ten to fifteen thousand in the air a young bird knows his mother. October 15 these birds go to Cape Horn for the winter.

The migration of birds is extremely interesting and quite surprising. They may be seen in Alaska, then a short time later may be discovered in Africa. In thirty-four days they have traveled nine thousand miles.

Massachusetts has fourteen bird sanctuaries, that at Plum Island, off Newburyport, being the best of all. Almost all of the island has been purchased for this purpose. A permanent warden is in charge. Many fine views of this sanctuary, which is open all year round, were shown. Several memorial paths have been dedicated to supporters and bird lovers, past and present, that to Claire N. Brown, dedicated to the memory of a true lover of nature, being the most impressive.

In all this study of bird life the economic value is a strong one, but the scientific value, also, is of prime importance. Aside from these two objects, the esthetic value, the sheer joy will repay the bird lover for banding his little feathered friends.

ANNUAL REUNION

March 28

A reception in the library at 6:30 p.m. was followed by a dinner at 7:00. The invocation was pronounced by the Rev. Dr. Samuel B. Ayres, acting pastor of the First Universalist Church. Response was chanted by the Unity Male Quartette of Boston.

At the close of a fine dinner served by Mr. Lunt a welcome was extended by the president, Mr. Myron F. Converse. Attention was called to the Spring Show. Mr. Converse requested the secretary to have roses and greetings sent two of our loyal members, Mr. and Mrs. Fiske of Grafton, who were unable to be with us. After selections by the Unity Male Quartette we adjourned to the main hall where the speaker of the evening was presented.

Dr. W. Elmer Ekblaw delivered the following address: "The Geographic Backgrounds of Our Western Civilization."

Dr. Ekblaw first complimented the Society on its successful career and outstanding good to the community, saying that such organizations as ours have made America what it is today— combinations of utilities and esthetics. He also spoke of the fine music just presented by the Quartette.

Charts and maps were used by the speaker to trace the development of peoples in the world in relation to their land. This address dealt not at all with race (about which very little is known), but with some of the geographical elements of our culture, which are much more easily traced.

It is generally agreed that our culture began in Mesopotamia, in the great mountain group of central Asia. Here is the old ancestral home of the sheep, camel, horse, ass, and ox. Here we find the beginning of stock raising and domestication of animals. The district had very fertile soil. Rainfall averaged less than fifteen inches, in some places less than ten, so it was favorable for grass land and stock raising. Agriculture would have been impossible but for the mountain land which sent out innumerable streams. Steady, fresh water bearing a mixed content was relatively easily utilized for irrigation the year round. This sedentary agriculture necessitated people's working shoulder to shoulder, sacrificing individual interest to the good of the group— community living.

Thus, this early period was characterized by

1. Presence of wild animals.
2. Fertile soils.
3. Community interest—working for the common group.

This territory was also the region of many of the fruits and plants of the garden: pear, apple, pomegranate, possibly the peach, and some of the small fruits. Here also was the region of the wheat fields. Wheat has been found growing wild in northern Arabia. Oats from Abyssinia and from southern Turkestan contributed to the supply.

Excavations in Mesopotamia, worked in layers, showed at the bottom about 4,200 years B. C. indications of law. Many artifacts were uncovered, proving this section the origin of culture. As early as 2,600 years B. C. Mesopotamia had developed considerable international training. Currency had already been established, and even then there was a question of the content of gold and silver. Early tablets in cuneiform script reveal much of interest at this time. Here has been discovered the oldest deed to land in the world, a tract on the Tigris River passed from father to son, and this land can be almost definitely located. In 2,400 B. C. there was a system of land measurement, as we have today. Registration of land titles with the stamp of government on it has been noted. So, also, was found the oldest marriage contract in the world between husband and wife in which he is to support her and her family for ten years, and if agreeable at the end of that time the contract might be renewed.

A seal to a mail bag dating back to 4,200 B. C. shows that culture had developed to that extent, and presupposes a long period of culture antedating that time. The clock has been put back to 6,000 B. C., showing a high degree of culture achieved in Mesopotamia by 4,000 B. C.

The spread of culture was discontinuous, not a sudden transfer, but probably only gradual, and was carried westward across the barriers. An opportunity was afforded for individuality and independence between these various sections. This culture spread across the Mediterranean, across Rome to Carthage, having the sea for a great barrier to conquer. The same intermittent and discontinuous culture advanced gradually with an independent and individual object, always retaining certain fundamental characteristics of origin.

All this progress was characterized by a scarcity of arable land of which there were no large areas, all relatively small in extent. Hence, food was difficult to obtain. Early in the evolution of our culture land was precious. All peoples have had to face scarcity of land and production. At an early stage, with the privacy of the home, a high value of land was felt as private personal property.

The Mediterranean climate was very unfavorable with its summer drouth and winter rainfall. It was a question of irrigation and farming done by very careful methods. There was an adaptation of the whole life to that unfavorable summer season. This brought about a development of foresight and thrift.

The Orientals have not had to develop these qualities. The Chinese and Indian literature and history indicate that their culture came from the same center—from the West. This movement was not discontinuous, but always from less favorable to more favorable conditions. They had great fertile river valleys. Population developed fast, but stagnation came after a time as the great excess of population pressed on the resources of the land. Kipling's poem is indeed true as regards East and West for the two do not understand each other much.

Northwest Europe had much the same kind of conditions, a relatively small area of fertile soil. This scarcity of land throughout resulted in a pastoral character of industry and led to religion, the high ideal of our Christian religion from Judea.

The development of navigation on the Mediterranean is interesting. There were comparatively few storms, sunshine and clear sky prevailing. The sea was calm and the many harbors along it, with ridges and islands, made it easy to land by day, or by night when the course might be set by the stars. So, early existed here a veritable nursery of navigation. The Greeks today monopolize the Mediterranean. The scarcity of land forced the people out to sea to trade with other people. In this way a high development of navigation came about.

Such lands made the most progress. The policy of segregation makes for stagnation. There must be an impetus, and widest trade brings about the widest culture. The Eskimo is still primitive, not touched by civilization, as he is in an isolated state.

This culture spread to northwest Europe where the same conditions obtained as in the Mediterranean, so we look at their life in much the same way.

Here the lecturer remarked that we of the United States are likely to lose some of this development of our culture, and to stagnate, if we don't guard against disparagement of our American ideals and habits. No people is more kindly charitable and hospitable. There is no reason why we should be ashamed of ourselves. We must safeguard this great heritage of ours and preserve the unity of the people. We are so diversified here in America, yet are essentially one people. This democracy of ours is the greatest and richest, so the heritage of our religion. We stand today on the threshold of the greatest renaissance the world has ever known. Institutions and ideals are our safeguard and we need not worry about the future. This difficulty is the clearing away of old traditions and the building up of new.

We feel a note of encouragement for the future. Our western European culture is destined for better things today. Ideals such as the Worcester County Horticultural Society holds make for a better world. All this is an outcome of western European culture which is the product of many thousand years of environment.

Several fine selections by the Quartette followed this interesting and informative talk. Dancing was enjoyed for the remainder of the evening.

INDEX

SCHEDULE OF PREMIUMS

Offered by the

Worcester County Horticultural Society

Horticultural Building
30 Elm Street
Worcester, Mass.

For the year

1936

THE ATTENTION OF EXHIBITORS IS PARTICULARLY
CALLED TO THE RULES AND REGULATIONS
GENERAL AND SPECIAL

The Davis Press, Worcester

OFFICERS AND COMMITTEES
of the
WORCESTER COUNTY HORTICULTURAL SOCIETY
For the Year 1936

PRESIDENT
MYRON F. CONVERSE, Worcester, Mass.

VICE-PRESIDENTS
HERBERT A. COOK, Shrewsbury, Mass.   MRS. HOMER GAGE, Worcester, Mass
S. LOTHROP DAVENPORT, No. Grafton, Mass.

SECRETARY
HERBERT R. KINNEY, of Worcester
Horticultural Hall, 30 Elm Street

TREASURER
BURT W. GREENWOOD, of Worcester

LIBRARIAN
MRS. FLORENCE E. FIELD, of Worcester

TRUSTEES:

Joseph A. Allen	Auburn	Willis E. Cary	Worcester
William Anderson	Wellesley	Frederick H. Chamberlain	Worcester
Miss Elizabeth R. Bishop	Sutton	J. Frank Cooper	Worcester
Edward W. Breed	Clinton	Mrs. Bertha G. Denny	Worcester
Ralph C. Breed	Clinton	Mrs. Alice M. Forbes	Worcester
Richard A. Flagg	Boylston	Harold J. Greenwood	Worcester
Allen J. Jenkins	Shrewsbury	Harry Harrison	Worcester
William E. Morey	Shrewsbury	Mrs. Florence C. Herrick	Worcester
Eugene O. Parsons	Auburn	Allen W. Hixon	Worcester
Charles Potter	West Boylston	Allyne W. Hixon	Worcester
Albert W. Schneider	Clinton	Mrs. Anna N. W. Hobbs	Worcester
Myron S. Wheeler	Berlin	H. Ward Moore	Worcester
Mrs. Mary D. White	Holden	Harry I. Randall	Worcester
Ernest P. Bennett	Worcester	Mrs. Amy W. Smith	Worcester
Chandler Bullock	Worcester	George F. E. Story	Worcester

STANDING COMMITTEE ON FINANCE
Leonard C. Midgley, 1936   Herbert W. Estabrook, 1938
Myron F. Converse, 1937

NOMINATING COMMITTEE
Arthur H. Bellows, 1936   Charles B. Rugg, 1937   Harold S. Bowker, 1938

ON LIBRARY AND PUBLICATIONS
Edward W. Breed, *Chairman*   Mrs. Amy W. Smith   William Anderson
Herbert R. Kinney, *Secretary*   Florence E. Field *Librarian*

ON NOMENCLATURE
S. Lothrop Davenport   Mrs. Amy W. Smith   Charles Potter   Herbert R. Kinney
J. Frank Cooper   Allen J. Jenkins   William Anderson Leonard C. Midgley

ON ARRANGEMENTS AND EXHIBITIONS
Allen J. Jenkins, *Chairman*

Joseph A. Allen	H. Ward Moore	Elizabeth R. Bishop
Mrs. William W. Taft	Edward W. Breed	Allen W. Hixon
Mrs. Percy G. Forbes	Mrs. Florence E. Field	S. Lothrop Davenport
Leonard C. Midgley	Allyne W. Hixon	Mrs. Bertha G. Denny
President, Myron F. Converse	Charles Potter	William E. Morey
	Secretary, Herbert R. Kinney	

AUDITORS
Harry C. Midgley   H. Ward Moore   Arthur H Bellows

JUDGES
PLANTS AND FLOWERS: William Anderson, Wellesley
FRUIT: S. Lothrop Davenport, North Grafton
VEGETABLES: H. Ward Moore, Worcester

MEDAL COMMITTEE
Myron F. Converse, *Chairman*   Edward W. Breed   Allen W. Hixon

ON WINTER MEETINGS
Myron F. Converse, *Chairman*   Herbert R. Kinney, *Secretary*
Mrs. Leander F. Herrick   Mrs. Anna N. W. Hobbs
Leonard C. Midgley   H. Ward Moore

Office, Library, and Exhibition Hall
30 Elm Street

GENERAL RULES AND REGULATIONS

1. Strict conformity to the Regulations and Rules will be expected and required, as well for the benefit of exhibitors as for the convenience of the Officers of the Society.

2. Every Flower or Plant entered in a class of named varieties should be correctly named.

3. All articles offered for premiums must remain within the Hall throughout the hours of Exhibition, unless special permission for their removal shall be granted by the Committee on Exhibition, etc.

4. No person shall make more than one entry of the same variety or be awarded more than one premium under the same number.

5. The Judges may correct, before the close of any exhibition, awards made by them, if satisfied that such were erroneous.

6. The cards of exhibitors competing for premiums shall be reversed, until after premiums are awarded.

7. Competitors are expected to conform strictly to the conditions under which articles are invited. Evasion or violation of them may be reported to the TRUSTEES for future disqualification of the offender.

8. Articles offered for premiums must be in the Hall by 2 o'clock of the days of Exhibition except when otherwise specified. Between 2 and 3 o'clock the Hall will be in exclusive charge of the Committee on Arrangements and Exhibitions. Open to the public from 3 to 9 o'clock.

9. Competition for premiums is open to all residents of Worcester County only, and it is strictly required that all specimens offered for premiums shall have been grown by the competitors, on their own premises, for at least two (2) months previous to the date of exhibition, except where no restriction is stated in schedule.

10. After the articles are arranged they will be under the exclusive charge of the Judges and Committee of Arrangements, and not even the owners will have liberty to remove them until the exhibition is closed, when they will be delivered as the contributors may direct.

11.   Where a certain number or quantity of Plants, Flowers, Fruits or Vegetables is designated in the schedule, there must be neither more nor less than that number or quantity of specimens shown; and in no case can other varieties than those named in the schedule be substituted.

12.   The Judges may exclude from competition all inferior specimens and may correct any errors that they think were without deliberate purpose.

13.   The Committee on Arrangements has power to change the time of exhibition for any article, if an earlier or later season renders such change desirable.

14.   All articles offered for premiums should be correctly named. Indefinite appellations such as "Pippin," "Sweeting," "Greening," etc., will not be considered as names. Any person exhibiting the same variety of Fruit or Vegetable, under different names, or exhibiting as grown by himself Flowers, Fruit or Vegetables grown by another, thereby violating the objects and rules of the Society, may be debarred from competing for the Society's premiums until reinstated.

15.   Competitors will be required to furnish information as to their mode of cultivation, and to present specimens for trial and examinations, if requested.

16.   In all exhibitions of Cut Flowers for competition, the number of blooms, clusters, sprays or spikes shown is not restricted except that it is expected the exhibitor shall use only a sufficient number to make a well-balanced display. All shall be of one color and of one variety in the same vase, except Displays, Vases, Baskets, Standards, or otherwise specified in the schedule. The Judge will consider the quality of the flowers rather than the quantity.

17. ☞ The Judges are authorized by the Trustees to invite the assistance of competent and discreet persons in the discharge of their duties.

18.   No Judge shall require anything of competitors respecting their exhibits which is not distinctly specified in the schedule.

19. In Table Decorations, collections and displays of Flowers, Fruits, Vegetables, Vases, and Baskets, where the number of exhibits exceeds the number of premiums offered, the Judge *may* award prizes to any worthy exhibits not receiving a premium.

The maximum prize for Vases, Standards, and Baskets shall be two dollars.

20. All premiums that are not claimed within one year after the close of the official year shall be forfeited to the Society.

21. "Downing's Fruits of America," revised edition, will guide the Judge of Fruits in his decisions upon matters at issue.

22. While the Society will take reasonable precautions for the safety of the property of exhibitors, it will be responsible in no case for any loss or damage that may occur.

Scale of Points

Cut Flowers and Wild Flowers.—

Arrangement	30 points
Quality of blooms	40 "
Number of varieties	15 "
Properly named	15

Lilies.—

Size and color of bloom	35 points
Number of perfect flowers and buds on stem	35 "
Arrangement	15
Properly named	15 "

Displays.—

Arrangement	40 points
Quality	45 "
Variety	15 "

Collections.—

Quality	45 points
Arrangement	25 "
Variety	30 "

Table Decoration.—

Artistic perfection of arrangement of whole	45 points
Quality	30 "
Proportion and harmony of flowers with accessories	25

Special Funds

OF THE

WORCESTER COUNTY HORTICULTURAL SOCIETY

The following is a list of the Special Funds of the Worcester County Horticultural Society the income of which is devoted to the purpose stated. The date prefixed to each indicates the year in which the fund was established.

1888.   Francis Henshaw Dewey Fund. $1,000.00.
Income to be used for the purchase of books.

1898.   William Eames Fund. $500.00.
Income to be used in prizes for the promotion of apple culture.

1906.   Frederick A. Blake Fund. $1,000.00.
Income only to be used in providing Medals to be awarded to the originators of new varieties of Fruits or Flowers, preference always being given to residents of Worcester County.

In case that the Worcester County Horticultural Society does not find occasion to award medals for New Fruits or Flowers, the said income may be used in special premiums for Orchids or other choice Greenhouse Plants and Flowers.

1907.   Obadiah Brown Hadwen Fund. $1,000.00.
Income to be used for meritorious exhibits of Flowers, Fruits and Vegetables.

1922.   Edwin Draper Fund. $300.00.
Income to be used in prizes for Horticultural exhibitions held under the direction of said Society.

1924.   Miss Frances Clary Morse Fund. $500.00.
Income to be used in prizes for Flowers.

Flowers, Plants, Fruits and Vegetables

1936

☞ THE COMMITTEE ON ARRANGEMENTS AND EXHIBITIONS would direct the earnest attention of the Judge to *Rule 12*.

12. The Judges may exclude from competition all inferior specimens and may correct any errors that they think were without deliberate purpose.

Special Rules

1. EXHIBITORS WILL ADD VALUE TO THEIR EXHIBITS BY HAVING ALL SPECIMENS CORRECTLY AND LEGIBLY NAMED AND THE NUMBER OF VARIETIES WRITTEN ON THE ENTRY CARDS, NOTICE OF WHICH WILL BE TAKEN BY THE JUDGES IN AWARDING THE PREMIUMS.

2. WHILE IT IS EXPECTED THAT EXHIBITORS WILL TAKE PAINS TO CORRECTLY NAME THEIR EXHIBITS, THE JUDGES WILL NOT EXCLUDE AN EXHIBIT FOR MISTAKE IN NOMENCLATURE.

3. IN ALL EXHIBITIONS OF LILIES THE POLLEN MAY BE REMOVED.

By vote of the trustees, all entries must be made to the Secretary and all cards made out by him or his assistants.

Spring Exhibition

Thursday, March 12, 3 to 9 p. m.

Friday, March 13, 9 a. m. to 9 p. m.

Saturday, March 14, 9 a. m. to 9 p. m.

Sunday, March 15, 12 m. to 9 p. m.

All articles for this exhibition must be in the hall and ready for inspection by the judges by 1 o'clock Thursday

Class I	Garden Displays	800.00
Class II	Plant Displays	350.00
Class III	Rock Gardens Not to exceed 100 square feet	125.00
Class IV	Cut Flowers	75.00
Class V	Fruit	75.00
Class VI	Vegetables	75.00

Frederick A. Blake Fund

Class VII	Carnations	25.00

Worcester Garden Club Exhibit

Thursday, April 23

*All articles for this exhibition must be
in the hall and ready for inspection
by the judges by 2 o'clock*

This exhibition will be open to the public from 3 to 9 p. m.

Cut Flowers.—
No. 1.   Twenty vases   4.00 3.00 2.00

Table Decorations.—
No. 2.   Table decoration, laid for four
covers, no restrictions.
Round table   5.00 4.00 3.00 2.50 2.00
Oblong table   5.00 4.00 3.00 2.50 2.00
Notify the Secretary two
days in advance.

Carnations.—
No. 3.   Vase or Basket, fifty flowers,
.   other green permissible   6.00 5.00 4.00

Plant Displays.—
No. 4.   Plants in Bloom with Foliage
Plants. Sixty dollars may be
used in prizes.

Apple, twelve specimens.—
No. 5.   For any variety, eight dollars
may be used for prizes.

Parsnip, twelve specimens.—
No. 6.   Hollow Crown   2.00 1.50 1.00 .50
No. 7.   Any other variety   2.00 1.50 1.00 .50

Rhubarb, twelve stalks.—
No. 8.   Any variety   2.00 1.50 1.00 .50

Lettuce.—'
No. 9.   Six heads   2.00 1.50 1.00 .50

Radish.—
No. 10.   Two bunches. Six in each bunch   1.50 1.00 .50

Potato, twelve specimens.—
No. 11.   Any named variety   2.00 1.50 1.00 .50

May Exhibition

Thursday, May 14

*All articles for this exhibition must be
in the hall and ready for inspection by
the judges by 2 o'clock*

This exhibition will be open to the public from 3 to 9 p. m.

Cut Flowers.—

No. 12.   Twenty vases   3.00 2.50 1.00
No. 13.   Medium basket   3.00 2.50 2.00 1.50 1.00

Spring Bulbs, open culture.—

No. 14.   Display   4.00 3.00 2.50 2.00

Pansy.—

No. 15.   Twenty vases, one flower
          with foliage in a vase 3.00 2.50 2.00 1.50 1.00 .50

Zonale Geraniums, in bloom.—

No. 16.   Six plants   3.00 2.00 1.50 1.00

Table Decorations, Spring Flowers.—

No. 17.   Table decoration, laid for
          four covers. Roses restricted.
          Notify the Secretary two days
          in advance   5.00 4.00 3.00 2.00 1.00

Plant Displays.—

No. 18.   For exhibits—no restrictions as
          to where grown or by whom,
          $60.00 may be used for prizes.
          Notify the Secretary two days
          in advance.

Calendula.—

No. 19.   Arranged in Bowl or Basket   3.00 2.00 1.00

1.50 1.00 .50

2.00 1.50 1.00 .50

1.50 1.00 .50

each bunch.—
1.50 1.00 .50

2.50 2.00 1.50 1.00 .50

elve specimens each.—
3.00 2.50 2.00 1.50 1.00 .50

each bunch 1.50 1.00 .50

Iris Exhibition
Thursday, June 4
*All articles for this exhibition must be
in the hall and ready for inspection by
the judges by 2 o'clock*

This exhibition will be open to the public from 3 to 9 p. m.

Cut Flowers.—

No. 27.	Display	4.00 3.00 2.50 2.00 1.50 1.00
No. 28.	Standard	3.00 2.50 2.00 1.50 1.00

Wild Flowers, fifteen vases.—

No. 29. Five stems in a vase. No
    duplicates   3.00 2.00 1.50 1.00 .50

Azalea.—

No. 30. Display in vases   3.00 2.00 1.00

Iris, German.—

No. 31.	Display	8.00 6.00 4.00 2.00
No. 32.	Vase or Basket	3.00 2.50 2.00 1.50 1.00

Rhododendron.—

No. 33. Displays in vases   3.00 2.00

Peonies.—

No. 34. Vase or Basket   3.00 2.50 2.00 1.00

Lupinus.—

No. 35. Vase   3.00 2.00 1.50 1.00

Roses.—

No. 36. Vase of Roses. Five dollars
    may be used in prizes.

Zonale Geraniums.—

No. 37. Twenty vases, one truss in each   3.00 2.00 1.00

Strawberries, twenty-four berries.—

No. 38. Five dollars may be used in prizes.

Asparagus, two bunches, twelve specimens each.—

No. 39. Any variety   2.50 2.00 1.50 1.00 .50

2.00 1.50 1.00 .50

2.50 2.00 1.50 1.00

      1.50 1.00 .50
2.50 2.00 1.50 1.00

2.00 1.50 1.00 .50

2.00 1.50 1.00 .50

ch   2.00 1.50 1.00 .50

Thursday, June 11

*All articles for this exhibition must be
in the hall and ready for inspection by
the judges by 2 o'clock*

This exhibition will be open to the public from 3 to 9 p. m

Cut Flowers.—

No. 47.   From hardy plants and shrubs
outdoor culture, **to be named**   5.00 4.00 3.00

Wild Flowers.—

No. 48.   Five stems in a vase.
No duplicates   3.00 2.00 1.50 1.00

Roses.—

No. 49.   Vase H. P. roses, not to exceed
ten blooms   3.00 2.00

No. 50.   Vase H. T. roses, not exceeding
ten blooms   3.00 2.00

Peonies.—

No. 51.   Best Display of Peonies.
Notify the Secretary two
days in advance   5.00 4.00 3.00

No. 52.   Twenty vases, one flower in
each   4.00 3.00 2.00 1.00

Foxglove.—

No. 53.   Vase of twelve spikes .   3.00 2.00 1.00

Aquilegia.—

No. 54.   Display   3.00 2.50 2.00 1.00

Begonia.—

No. 55.   Four plants in bloom   3.00 2.00

Strawberry, twenty-four berries.—

No. 56.   Any variety   1.50 1.00

Pea, one-half peck.—

No. 57.   Any variety   2.00 1.50 1.00

Rhubarb, twelve stalks.—

No. 58.   Victoria   2.50 2.00 1.50 1.00

Rose Exhibition
Thursday, June 18, open from 3 to 9 p. m.

*All articles for this exhibition must be
in the hall and ready for inspection by
the judges by 2 o'clock*

Roses.—

No. 59. Twelve blooms of distinct named
varieties of H. P. roses, outdoor
culture   4.00 3.00 2.00 1.00

No. 60. Six blooms of distinct named
varieties of H. P. roses, out-
door culture   3.00 2.00 1.00 .50

No. 61. Collection of cut roses. Twelve
dollars to be used in prizes.

No. 62. Vase of roses, 12 blooms   3.00 2.50 2.00 1.50 1.00

No. 63. Vase H. P. roses, not to exceed
ten blooms   3.00 2.00 1.00

No. 64. Vase H. T. roses, not exceeding
ten blooms   3.00 2.00 1.00

No. 65. Display of cut climbing roses.
Fifteen dollars may be used in
prizes.

No. 66. Basket of roses   3.00 2.50 2.00 1.50

Special Prizes
Miss Frances C. Morse Fund

A. Table decoration of roses, laid for
four covers. Flowers grown by
exhibitors   4.00 3.00 2.50 1.00 .50

*   *   *

Peonies.—

No. 67. Best Display of Peonies.
Notify the Secretary two days in
advance   5.00 4.00 3.00 2.00

Aquilegia.—

No. 68. Bowl   2.50 2.00 1.50 1.00

Special Prizes
Obadiah Brown Hadwen Fund

Hardy Flowers, to be named.—

B.   Display of outdoor varieties   5.00 4.00 3.00 2.00 1.00

*   *   *

Strawberry, twenty-four berries.—

No. 69.	Senator Dunlap			1.50 1.00	.50
No. 70.	Howard No. 17	3.00 2.50	2.00	1.50 1.00	.50
No. 71.	Culver		2.00	1.50 1.00	.50
No. 72.	Any other variety		2.00	1.50 1.00	.50
No. 73.	New varieties		2.00	1.50 1.00	.50

Cherry, one quart.—

No. 74.   For any named variety, five dollars may be used for prizes.

Pea, one-half peck.—

No. 75.	Thomas Laxton	2.00 1.50	1.00	.50
No. 76.	Gradus	2.00 1.50	1.00	.50
No. 77.	Any other variety	2.00 1.50	1.00	.50

Cabbage, three specimens.—

No. 78.   Any named variety   2.50 2.00 1.50 1.00

Lettuce, six heads.—

No. 79.   Big Boston Type   2.00 1.50 1.00   .50

Thursday, June 25

*All articles for this exhibition must be
in the hall and ready for inspection by
the judges by 2 o'clock*

This exhibition will be open to the public from 3 to 9 p. m.

Cut Flowers.—
No. 80.	Twenty vases	3.00	2.50	2.00	1.50	1.00	.50
No. 81.	Basket		2.50	2.00	1.50	1.00	.50

Dianthus Barbatus (Sweet William).—
No. 82. Twelve vases, three stems
in a vase   3.00 2.50 2.00 1.50 1.00 .50

Campanula.—
No. 83. Display   4.00 3.00 2.00 1.00

Delphinium.—
No. 84. One vase, not more than twelve
spikes   4.00 3.50 3.00 2.50 2.00 1.50 1.00

Roses.—
No. 85. Collection of Cut Roses. Ten
dollars may be used in prizes.

Special Prizes
Offered by Mr. Herbert R. Kinney

C. Display of Cut Flowers on round
tables   3.00 2.50 2.00 1.50 1.00

This number is intended for the growers who do not compete in
the call for twenty vases or displays during the year.

*   *   *

Strawberry, twenty-four berries.—
No. 86.	Howard No. 17	3.00	2.50	2.00	1.50	1.00	.50
No. 87.	Sample				1.50	1.00	.50
No. 88.	Dorset			2.00	1.50	1.00	.50
No. 89.	Any other variety			2.00	1.50	1.00	.50
No. 90.	Collections, not more than six varieties	5.00	4.00	3.00	2.00	1.00	

Currant, twenty-four bunches.—
No. 91. For any variety, five dollars may be used for prizes.

Cherry, one quart.—

No. 92.	Black Tartarian	2.00 1.50 1.00 .50
No. 93.	Gov. Wood	2.00 1.50 1.00 .50
No. 94.	Best display, ten dollars may be used for prizes.	
No. 95.	For varieties not scheduled, five dollars may be used for prizes.	

Beet, open culture.—

| No. 96. | Twelve specimens | 2.00 1.50 1.00 .50 |

Carrot.—

| No. 97. | Two bunches, six in each | 2.00 1.50 1.00 .50 |

Pea, one-half peck.

| No. 98. | Sutton's Excelsior | 2.00 1.50 1.00 .50 |
| No. 99. | Any other variety | 2.00 1.50 1.00 .50 |

Cucumber, three specimens.—

| No. 100. | Any variety | 1.50 1.00 .50 |

Thursday, July 2

All articles for this exhibition must be in the hall and ready for inspection by the judges by 2 o'clock

This exhibition will be open to the public from 3 to 9 p. m.

Cut Flowers.—
No. 101. Twenty vases   4.00 3.00 2.50 2.00 1.50 1.00
No. 102. Ten vases   2.50 2.00 1.50 1.00 .50

This number is intended for the growers who do not compete in call for 20 vases and displays during the year.

Basket.—
No. 103.   3.00 2.50 2.00 1.50 1.00

Japanese Iris.—
No. 104. Display, twenty dollars may be used for prizes.

Delphinium.—
No. 105. Display, fifteen dollars may be used for prizes.

Lilium Candidum.—
No. 106. Vase   4.00 3.00 2.00 1.00

Wild Flowers, no duplicates.—
No. 107. Fifteen vases, five stems
in a vase   2.50 2.00 1.50 1.00 .50

Roses.—
No. 108. Display of cut climbing roses. Ten dollars may be used in prizes.

Strawberry, twenty-four berries.—
No. 109. Downing's Bride   2.00 1.50 1.00 .50
No. 110. Ten dollars may be used for prizes. Preference given to worthy varieties of recent introduction.
No. 111. Best display   5.00 4.00 3.00 2.00 1.00

Raspberry, Black Cap, one quart.—
No. 112. Named variety   1.50 1.00 .50

Raspberry, one pint.—
No. 113. Early varieties   2.00 1.50 1.00 .50
No. 114. Varieties not scheduled, five dollars may be used for prizes.

Gooseberry, one quart.—

No. 115.   Any named variety   2.00 1.50 1.00   .50

Cherry, one quart.—

No. 116.   Coe's Transparent   1.50 1.00   .50
No. 117.   Montmorency   2.00 1.50 1.00   .50
No. 118.   Any other variety   2.00 1.50 1.00   .50

Currant, twenty-four bunches.—

No. 119.   For any variety, five dollars may be used for prizes.

Bean, Snap, one-half peck.—

No. 120.   Any named variety   2.00 1.50 1.00   .50

Pea, one-half peck.—

No. 121.   Alderman   2.00 1.50 1.00   .50
No. 122.   Telephone   2.00 1.50 1.00   .50
No. 123.   Display   3.00 2.50 2.00 1.00

Display of Vegetables.—

No. 124.   Not to exceed 24 square feet, $20.00 may be used
for prizes. Notify the Secretary two days in advance.

Tomato, twelve specimens.—

No. 125.   Any named variety   2.00 1.50 1.00   .50

Sweet Pea Exhibition
Thursday, July 9

*All articles for this exhibition must be
in the hall and ready for inspection by
the judges by 2 o'clock*

This exhibition will be open to the public from 3 to 9 p. m.

Sweet Peas, annual.—
No. 126. Ten vases, not more than 25
    flower stems in a vase   4.00 3.00 2.00
No. 127. Table Decoration—Sweet Peas,
    laid for four covers, Gypsophila
    may be used. Notify the Secre-
    two days in advance   4.00 3.00 2.50 2.00 1.00

Sweet Peas.—
No. 128. Basket, any green may be used.
    3.00 2.00 1.50 1.00

Obadiah Brown Hadwen Fund

D. Collection of Sweet Peas, fifteen dollars may be used in prizes.

* * *

Cut Flowers.—
No. 129. Display, not exceeding 30
    square feet   4.00 3.00 2.50 2.00 1.50 1.00

Lilium Regale.—
No. 130. Fifteen dollars may be used in prizes.

Centaurea.—
No. 131. Display, Gypsophila may be
    used   4.00 3.00 2.50 2.00

Petunia.—
No. 132. Twenty vases, one flower in
    each   3.00 2.50 2.00 1.00 .50

Raspberry, one pint.—
No. 133. Latham   2.00 1.50 1.00 .50
No. 134. Cuthbert   1.50 1.00 .50
No. 135. Any other variety   1.50 1.00 .50

Apple, twelve specimens.—

No. 136.   Any variety   2.00 1.50 1.00   .50

Currant, twenty-four bunches.—

No. 137.   Red Cross   1.50 1.00   .50
No. 138.   Perfection   2.00 1.50 1.00   .50
No. 139.   White Grape   1.50 1.00   .50
No. 140.   Versaillaise   2.00 1.50 1.00   .50
No. 141.   Any other variety   1.50 1.00   .50

Bean, Snap, one-half peck.—

No. 142.   Wax   2.00 1. 0 1.00   .50
No. 143.   Green Pod   2.00 1.50 1.00   .50

Cucumber.—

No. 144.   Three specimens   1.50 1.00   .50

Cabbage, three specimens.—

No. 145.   Any variety   2.00 1.50 1.00   .50

Lettuce, Iceberg.—

No. 146.   Twelve heads   2.00 1.50 1.00   .50

Squash, three specimens.—

No. 147.   Summer   2.00 1.50 1.00   .5

Thursday, July 16

*All articles for this exhibition must be
in the hall and ready for inspection by
the judges by 2 o'clock*

This exhibition will be open to the public from 3 to 9 p. m.

Cut Flowers.—
No. 148. Display   4.00 3.00 2.50 2.00 1.50 1.00

Antirrhinum (Snap Dragon).—
No. 149. Display   3.00 2.00 1.00 .50

Table Decorations.—
No. 150. Table decoration laid for
four covers. Flowers to be
grown by the exhibitor. Notify the Secretary two days in
advance   5.00 4.00 3.00 2.50 2.00 1.50 1.00

Sweet Peas, annual.—
No. 151. Five vases, 25 flower stems
in vase   3.00 2.50 2.00 1.50 1.00

Begonia, tuberous rooted.—
No. 152. Twelve vases   4.00 3.00 2.00 1.00

Apple, twelve specimens.—
No. 153. Yellow Transparent   2.00 1.50 1.00 .50

Raspberry.—
No. 154. Any variety   1.50 1.00 .50

Blackberry, one quart.—
No. 155. Any variety, five dollars may be used for prizes.

Currants, twenty-four bunches.—
No. 156. Wilder   2.00 1.50 1.00 .50

Corn, twelve ears.—
No. 157. Sweet, any named variety   2.00 1.50 1.00 .50

Tomato, twelve specimens.—
No. 158. Any named variety   2.00 1.50 1.00 .50

Potato, twelve specimens.—
No. 159. Any variety   2.00 1.50 1.00 .50

Lettuce, twelve heads.—
No. 160. Any variety   2.00 1.50 1.00 .50

Thursday, July 23

All articles for this exhibition must be in the hall and ready for inspection by the judges by 2 o'clock

This exhibition will be open to the public from 3 to 9 p. m.

Cut Flowers.—

No. 161. Standard	4.00	3.00	2.50	2.00	1.50 1.00
No. 162. Ten vases		2.50	2.00	1.50	1.00 .50

This number is intended for the growers who do not compete in the call for 20 vases and displays during the year.

Gladiolus.—

No. 163. Twenty vases, one spike in
each   4.00 3.00 2.00 1.00

Phlox, perennial.—

No. 164. Fifteen vases, one cluster
in each   3.00 2.00 1.00 .50

Annuals.—

No. 165. Display   3.00 2.50 2.00 1.50 1.00

Apple, twelve specimens.—

No. 166. Astrachan	2.00	1.50	1.00	.50
No. 167. Yellow Transparent	2.00	1.50	1.00	.50

Blackberry, one quart.—

No. 168. Any varieties, five dollars may be used for prizes.

Raspberry.—

No. 169. Any variety   1.50 1.00 .50

Plum, twelve specimens.—

No. 170. Red June   1.50 1.00 .50

Bean, Shell, one-half peck.—

No. 171. Any named variety 2.00 1.50 1.00 .50

Corn, twelve ears.—

No. 172. Any named variety 2.00 1.50 1.00 .50

Squash, three specimens.—

No. 173. Summer 2.00 1.50 1.00 .50

Potato, twelve specimens.—

No. 174. Irish Cobbler 2.00 1.50 1.00 .50
No. 175. Any other variety 2.00 1.50 1.00 .50

Vegetables.—

No. 176. Display, Round Table, $20.00 may be used for prizes. Notify the Secretary two days in advance.

Thursday, July 30

All articles for this exhibition must be
in the hall and ready for inspection by
the judges by 2 o'clock

This exhibition will be open to the public from 3 to 9 p. m.

Cut Flowers.—
No. 177.   Basket   4.00 3.00 2.50 2.00 1.50 1.00

Flower Arrangement for Living Room.—
No. 178.   Pottery container to be furnished
by exhibitor   3.00 2.50 2.00 1.50 1.00   .50

Gladiolus.—
No. 179.   Display   8.00 6.00 5.00 4.00 3.00

Larkspur, annual.—
No. 180.   Display   3.00 2.50 2.00 1.00

Salpiglossis.—
No. 181.   Display   4.00 3.00 2.00 1.00

Phlox, perennial.—
No. 182.   Fifteen vases, one cluster
in each   3.00 2.00 1.50 1.00   .50

Zinnia.—
No. 183.   Twenty vases, one flower in
each   3.00 2.50 2.00 1.50 1.00   .50

Wild Flowers, no duplicates.—
No. 184.   Fifteen vases, no duplicates.
Five stems in a vase   2.50 2.00 1.50 1.00   .50

Special Prizes
Offered by Mr. Herbert R. Kinney

E.   Table Decorations. For the best
table decorations   3.00 2.50 2.00 1.50 1.00

This call is intended for exhibitors who do not exhibit in other table decorations during the year. Notify the Secretary two days in advance.

Apple, twelve specimens.—

No. 185.	Oldenburg	2.00	1.50	1.00	.50
No. 186.	Astrachan	2.00	1.50	1.00	.50

Peach, twelve specimens.—

No. 187.	Any variety	2.00	1.50	1.00	.50

Bean, Shell, one-half peck.—

No. 188.	Dwarf Horticultural	2.00	1.50	1.00	.50
No. 189.	Any other variety	2.00	1.50	1.00	.50

Cabbage, three specimens.—

No. 190.	Copenhagen	2.00	1.50	1.00	.50
No. 191.	Any other named variety	2.00	1.50	1.00	.50

Corn, twelve ears.—

No. 192.	Yellow, Sweet	2.50	2.00	1.50	1.00	.50

Potato, twelve specimens.—

No. 193.	Rose	2.00	1.50	1.00	.50
No. 194.	Varieties not scheduled	2.00	1.50	1.00	.50

Tomato, open culture, twelve specimens.—

No. 195.	Any named variety	2.00	1.50	1.00	.50

Gladiolus Exhibition
Thursday, August 6

*All articles for this exhibition must be
in the hall and ready for inspection by
the judges by 2 o'clock*

This exhibition will be open to the public from 3 to 9 p. m.

Gladiolus.—
No. 196. Display. Notify the Secretary two days in advance.
Forty dollars may be used in prizes.
No. 197. Standard of Gladioli   3.00 2.50 2.00 1.00   .50
No. 198. Twenty vases, one spike in
each   4.00 3.00 2.00 1.00   .50

Aster, large flowered, long stem.—
No. 199. Vase of 20 blooms   3.00 2.50 2.00 1.00   .50

Salpiglossis.—
No. 200. Bowl   2.50 2.00 1.00   .50

Phlox Drummondi.—
No. 201. Display   2.00 1.50 1.00   .50

Annuals.—
No. 202. Display, fifteen dollars may be used in prizes.

Flowers on a Mirror.—
No. 203. Small vase to be shown on a mirror. Vase and mirror
to be furnished by the society. Ten dollars may be
used in prizes. Highest award not to exceed $1.50.
One entry for each exhibitor.

Apple, twelve specimens.—
No. 204. Williams   2.00 1.50 1.00   .50
No. 205. For varieties not scheduled, five dollars may be
used for prizes.

Apple, crab, twenty-four specimens.—
No. 206. Varieties not scheduled   1.50 1.00   .50

Peach, twelve specimens.—
No. 207. Carman   1.50 1.00   .50
No. 208. Any other variety   1.50 1.00   .50

936

97

Plum, twelve specimens.—

No. 209. Washington	1.50	1.00	.50

No. 210. Japanese varieties, five dollars
may be used for prizes.

Squash, three specimens.—

No. 211. Any named variety (excepting
summer varieties)   2.00   1.50   1.00   .50

Bean, Shell, one-half peck.—

No. 212. Dwarf, any variety   2.00   1. 0   1.00   .50
No. 213. Pole, any variety   2.00   1.50   1.00   .50

Bean, String, one-half peck.—

No. 214. Kentucky Wonder   2.00   1.50   1.00   .50

Corn, Sweet, twelve ears.—

No. 215. Any named variety   2.00   1.50   1.00   .50

Tomato, twelve specimens.—

No. 216. Any named variety   2.50   2.00   1.50   1.00   .50

Mushroom, native.—

No. 217. Collection of edible varieties. Twenty dollars to be
used for prizes.

Cucumber, for pickles.—

No. 218. One-half peck   2.00   1.50   1.00   .50

Thursday, August 13

*All articles for this exhibition must be
in the hall and ready for inspection by
the judges by 2 o'clock*

This exhibition will be open to the public from 3 to 9 p. m

Gladiolus.—
No. 219. Basket. Fifteen dollars to be used in prizes.

Zinnia.—
No. 220. Display, notify the Secretary
two days in advance 4.00 3.00 2.50 2.00 1.50

Dahlia.—
No. 221. Display. Single, pompom,
and miniature 3.00 2.50 2.00

Obadiah Brown Hadwen Fund

Display of Garden Flowers.—
F. Not to exceed 24 square feet.
Notify the Secretary two days
in advance 4.00 3.50 3.00 2.50 2.00

*   *   *

Flowers on Mirror.—
No. 222. Small vase to be shown on a mirror. Exhibitors
use own containers. Ten dollars may be used in p
Highest award not to exceed $1.50. One entry for
exhibitor.

Aster, single or anemone.—
No. 223. Vase 2.00 1.50 1.00

Apples, twelve specimens.—
No. 224. Any variety 2.00 1.50 1.00

Plums, twelve specimens.—
No. 225. Bradshaw 3.00 2.00 1.50 1.00
No. 226. Imperial Gage 2.00 1.50 1.00
No. 227. Guiei 1.50 1.00
No. 228. For varieties not scheduled, three
dollars may be used for prizes.

936

97

Peach, twelve specimens.—
No. 229. Five dollars may be used in prizes.

Pear, twelve specimens.—
No. 230. Clapp's Favorite   3.00 2.50 2.00 1.50 1.00 .50
No. 231. For varieties not scheduled, five dollars may be used for prizes.

Bean, Pole, one-half peck.—
No. 232. Shell   2.00 1.50 1.00 .50
No. 233. String, any variety   2.00 1.50 1.00 .50

Corn, twelve ears.—
No. 234. Sweet, not less than twelve rows
                                   2.00 1.50 1.00 .50
Vegetables.—
No. 235. Display of vegetables from
          Home Gardens to cover 12
          square feet   5.00 4.00 3.00 2.00 1.00

Thursday, August 20

*All articles for this exhibition must be
in the hall and ready for inspection by
the judges by 2 o'clock*

This exhibition will be open to the public from 3 to 9

Cut Flowers.—

No. 236.	Display.	Class 1		5.00 4.00
		Class 2	4.00	3.50 3.00
No. 237.	Basket		3.00	2.50 2.00

Aster, large flowered.—

No. 238. Twenty vases, three
blooms in a vase 3.00 2.50 2.00

Lilies.—

No. 239. Display 5.00 4.00
Notify the Secretary two days
in advance.

Dahlia.—

LARGE FLOWERED.—

No. 240. Twenty vases, one flower in
each 4.00 3.00 2.00

Zinnia, Lilliput variety.—

No. 241. Display 3.00 2.00

Begonia, tuberous rooted.—

No. 242. Display 5.00 4.00 3.00

Verbena.—

No. 243. Basket or Bowl 2.50 2.00 1.50

Five Miniature Vases.—

No. 244. Display. A group of five miniature va
exceed 4 inches in height. Vases to be
exhibitors. Ten dollars may be used
Highest award not to exceed $1.50.

Apples, twelve specimens.—

No. 245. Porter 1.50
No. 246. Gravenstein 2.50 2.00 1.50
No. 247. For varieties not scheduled, five
dollars may be used for prizes.

n as to

4.00 3.00 2.00 1.00

1.50 1.00   .50

2.50 2.00 1.50 1.00

2. 0 2.00 1. 0 1.00
2.50 2..00 1.50 1.00

.

ed 24 square feet, $20.00 may
otify the Secretary two days in

Thursday, August 27

*All articles for this exhibition must be
in the hall and ready for inspection by
the judges by 2 o'clock*

This exhibition will be open to the public from 3 to 9 p. m

Cut Flowers.—

No. 254.	Display. Class 1		5.00	4.00	3.50
	Class 2	4.00	3.50	3.00	2.50
No. 255.	Standard	3.00	2.50	2.00	1.50	1.00

This number is intended for the growers who do not compe
call for 20 vases and displays during the year.

Dahlia.—

No. 256. Twenty vases, one flower in
each   4.00   3.00   2.00   1.50

Gladiolus.—

No. 257. Basket   3.00   2.50   2.00   1.00

Aster.—

No. 258. Display, not exceeding
25 square feet   5.00   4.00   3.00   2.00

Scabiosa.—

No. 259. Vase   2.50   2.00   1.50   1.00

Apple, twelve specimens.—

No. 260.	Gravenstein	3.00	2.50	2.00	1.50	1.00
No. 261.	Maiden's Blush				1.50	1.00
No. 262.	Wealthy		2.50	2.00	1.50	1.00

Apple, Crab, twenty-four specimens.—

No. 263. Hyslop   2.50   2.00   1.50   1.00

Peach, twelve specimens.—

No. 264.	Champion		1.50	1.00
No. 265.	Oldmixon		2.00	1.00
No. 266.	Golden Jubilee	2.00	1.50	1.00
No. 267.	Seedlings		1.50	1.00
No. 268.	Crawford (early)	2.00	1.50	1.00

No. 269. Varieties not scheduled, five dollars may be used for prizes.

No. 270. New varieties. Five dollars may be used in prizes.

Plum, twelve specimens.—

No. 271. Golden Varieties		1.50	1.00	.50
No. 272. Lombard	2.00	1.50	1.00	.50
No. 273. Quackenboss		1.50	1.00	.50
No. 274. Burbank	2.00	1.50	1.00	.50
No. 275. New varieties		1.50	1.00	.50

No. 276. For Japanese varieties not scheduled, five dollars may be used for prizes.

No. 277. Other varieties not scheduled, five dollars may be used for prizes.

Grape, three clusters.—

No. 278. Green Mountain	2.00	1.50	1.00	.50
No. 279. Moore's		1.50	1.00	.50
No. 280. Ontario		1.50	1.00	.50
No. 281. Varieties not scheduled		1.50	1.00	.50

Pepper, twelve specimens.—

No. 282. Squash	2.00	1.50	1.00	.50
No. 283. Any other variety	2.00	1.50	1.00	.50

Tomato, twelve specimens.—

No. 284. Beauty	2.50	2.00	1.50	1.00	.50
No. 285. Any other variety	2.50	2.00	1.50	1.00	.50

Bean, one-half peck.—

No. 286. Dwarf Lima	2.00	1.50	1.00	.50
No. 287. Pole Lima	2.00	1.50	1.00	.50

Cabbage, three specimens.—

No. 288. Any named variety	2.00	1.50	1.00	.50

Celery, blanched (named) six specimens.—

No. 289. Any variety	2.00	1.50	1.00	.50

Carrot, twelve specimens.—

No. 290. Any variety	2.50	2.00	1.50	1.00	.50

Egg Plant.—

No. 291. Three specimens	2.00	1.50	1.00	.50

Mushroom, native.—

No. 292. Collection of edible varieties. Twenty dollars to be used for prizes.

Thursday, September 3

All articles for this exhibition must be in the hall and ready for inspection by the judges by 2 o'clock

This exhibition will be open to the public from 3 to 9 p. m

Cut Flowers.—
No. 293.	Display. Class 1			5.00	4.00	3.50
	Class 2		4.00	3.50	3.00	2.50
No. 294.	Metal container of cut flowers, container to be furnished by exhibitor			3.00	2.50	2.00

Dahlia.—
No. 295.	Twenty vases, one flower in each vase	4.00	3.00	2.00

Cosmos.—
No. 296.	Vase or basket	2.50	2.00	1.50	1.00

Apple, twelve specimens.—
No. 297.	New varieties	2.00	1.50	1.00

Pear, twelve specimens.—
No. 298.	Bartlett	3.00	2.50	2.00	1.50	1.00
No. 299.	Louise Bonne de Jersey				1.50	1.00
No. 300.	Urbaniste				1.50	1.00
No. 301.	Varieties not scheduled, five dollars may be for prizes.					

Peach, twelve specimens.—
No. 302.	Crawford (late)	2.00	1.50	1.00
No. 303.	Elberta	2.00	1.50	1.00
No. 304.	Display, no restriction as to arrangement	8.00	6.00	4.00

Plum, twelve specimens.—
No. 305.	Any variety	2.00	1.50	1.00

Grape, three clusters.—
No. 306.	Brighton	1.50	1.00
No. 307.	Campbell	1.50	1.00
No. 308.	Lindley	1.50	1.00

No. 309.	Worden	2.50	2.00	1.50	1.00	.50
No. 310.	Concord	2.50	2.00	1.50	1.00	.50
No. 311.	Delaware		2.00	1.50	1.00	.50
No. 312.	Niagara	2.50	2.00	1.50	1.00	.50
No. 313.	Pocklington			1.50	1.00	.50
No. 314.	Moore's Diamond			1.50	1.00	.50
No. 315.	For other varieties, ten dollars may be used for prizes.					
No. 316.	New varieties, five dollars may be used for prizes.					

Quince, twelve specimens.—

No. 317.	Any variety	2.00	1.50	1.00	.50

Melon, three specimens.—

No. 318.	Green Flesh	2.00	1.50	1.00	.50
No. 319.	Yellow Flesh	2.00	1.50	1.00	.50
No. 320.	Water	2.00	1.50	1.00	.50

Tomato.—

No. 321. Display. Fifteen dollars may be used for prizes.

Vegetables.—

No. 322. Display to cover 24 square feet. Notify the Secretary two days in advance   7.00 6.00 5.00 4.00 3.00

Dahlia Exhibition

Thursday, September 10

*All articles for this exhibition must be
in the hall and ready for inspection by
the judges by 2 o'clock*

This exhibition will be open to the public from 3 to 9 p. m.

Dahlia.—

No. 323. Fifty vases, one flower in each. Twenty-five dollars may be used in prizes. Notify the Secretary two days in advance.

No. 324. Twelve vases, one flower in each. This number is intended for the growers who do not compete in other classes for Dahlias during the year.

2.50 2.00 1.50 1.00 .50

No. 325. Single varieties, twenty vases   3.00 2.50 2.00 1.00

No. 326. Basket of large flowered   3.00 2.50 2.00 1.00

POMPON.

No. 327. Twenty vases, three sprays in each   3.00 2.50 2.00 1.00

Basket of Cut Flowers.—

No. 328.   3.00 2.50 2.00 1.50 1.00 .50

Display of Flower Arrangement.—

No. 329. No restrictions as to kind of tables used, not to cover more than 24 square feet. Flowers to be grown by exhibitor. Receptacles to be furnished by the exhibitors. Notify the Secretary two days in advance. Twenty-five dollars may be used in prizes. No baskets.

SCALE OF POINTS BY WHICH THE ABOVE CLASS IS TO BE JUDGED

Arrangement of flowers	40 points
Proportion and harmony of flowers with receptacles	35
Quality of flowers	25

Celosia.—

No. 330. Display   4.00 3.00 2.50 2.00 1.50 1.00
Notify the Secretary two days in advance.

Begonia, tuberous rooted.—

No. 331. Cut flowers in vases. Ten dollars may be used in prizes.

Edwin Draper Fund

Begonia, tuberous rooted.—
　　G.　Display of Potted Plants.　Fifteen dollars may be used in
　　　　prizes.　　　　　　　*　　*　　*

Apple, twelve specimens.—
　　No. 332.　American Beauty or Sterling　　1.50　1.00　.50
　　No. 333.　Twenty-ounce　　　　　　　　　1.50　1.00　.50
Pear, twelve specimens.—
　　No. 334.　Seckel　　　　　3.00　2.50　2.00　1.50　1.00　.50
　　No. 335.　Any variety, not scheduled　　1.50　1.00　.50
　　No. 336.　Display, no restriction as to
　　　　arrangement　　　　6.00　5.00　4.00　3.00　2.00
　　　　Notify the Secretary two days in advance.
Peach.—
　　No. 337.　Any variety　　　　　　　　1.50　1.00　.50
Quince, twelve specimens.—
　　No. 338.　Orange　　　　　　　　2.00　1.50　1.00　.50
Grapes.—
　　No. 339.　Display of Grapes. Ten dollars may be used for prizes.
Potato, six varieties (named).—
　　No. 340.　Twelve specimens of each
　　　　　　　　5.00　4.00　3.00　2.00　1.50　1.00
Squash, three specimens.—
　　No. 341.　Warren　　　　　　　　2.00　1.50　1.00　.50
　　No. 342.　Golden Hubbard　　2.50　2.00　1.50　1.00　.50
　　No. 343.　For varieties not scheduled, five dollars may be used
　　　　for prizes.
Cabbage, three specimens.—
　　No. 344.　Red　　　　　　　　　2.00　1.50　1.00　.50
　　No. 345.　Savoy　　　　　　　　　　1.50　1.00　.50
　　No. 346.　Any other variety　　2.50　2.00　1.50　1.00　.50
Cauliflower.—
　　No. 347.　Three specimens　　2.50　2.00　1.50　1.00　.50
Turnip.—
　　No. 348.　Twelve specimens　　　　　1.50　1.00　.50
Broccoli.—
　　No. 349.　Three specimens　　　　2.00　1.50　1.00　.50

Thursday, September 17

*All articles for this exhibition must be
in the hall and ready for inspection by
the judges by 2 o'clock*

This exhibition will be open to the public from 3 to 9 p. m.

Dahlia.—

No. 350. Display. Thirty-five dollars may be used for prizes.
Notify the secretary two days in advance.

Cut Flowers.—

No. 351. Display, not exceeding 30 square
feet   5.00 4.00 3.50 3.00 2.50 2.00 1.50 1.00

Cosmos.—

No. 352. Display. Notify the Secretary
two days in advance   3.00 2.00 1.50 1.00   .50

Table Decorations of Flowers.—

No. 353. Table decoration laid for
four covers. Flowers grown by
exhibitor. Notify the Secretary two days in advance.
6.00 5.00 4.50 4.00 3.00 2.00 1.50 1.00

Marigold.—

No. 354. Display. Notify the Secretary two days in advance   3.00 2.00 1.00   .50

Apple, one standard box, standard pack.—

No. 355. McIntosh   4.00 3.00 2.00 1.00   .50

Apple, twelve specimens.—

No. 356. Hubbardston   2.00 1.50 1.00   .50
No. 357. Tompkins King   2.00 1.50 1.00   .50
No. 358. McIntosh   3.50 3.00 2.50 2.00 1.50 1.00   .50
No. 359. For other varieties not scheduled, five dollars may be
used for prizes.

Pear, twelve specimens.—

No. 360. Sheldon   3.00 2.00 1.50 1.00   .5

1936

97

Squash, three specimens.—

No. 361. Delicious   2.00 1.50 1.00   .50

No. 362. Any other variety, not scheduled 2.50 2.00 1.50 1.00

Cauliflower, three specimens.—

No. 363.   2.00 1.50 1.00   .50

Vegetables.—

No. 364. Collection not to exceed 25

varieties   '10.00 8.00 7.00 6.00 5.00

Notify the Secretary two days in advance.

Thursday, September 24

*All articles for this exhibition must be
in the hall and ready for inspection by
the judges by 2 o'clock*

This exhibition will be open to the public from 3 to 9 p. m.

Cut Flowers.—

No. 365.　Display　　　　　5.00 4.00 3.00 2.00 1.00

Standard of Cut Flowers.—

No. 366.　Twenty dollars may be used in prizes.

Dried Flowers, Statice, Strawflowers, Lunaria (Honesty).—

No. 367.　Display.　　　　　4.00 3.50 2.00 1.00

Apple, one standard box, standard pack.—

No. 368.　Any variety not scheduled

　　　　　　　　　　4.00 3.00 2.00 1.00　.50

Apple, twelve specimens.—

No. 369.　Sutton Beauty　　　2.00 1.50 1.00　.50

Display of Fruit.—

No. 370.　Not to exceed 20 square feet. Thirty dollars may be
　　　　　used in prizes.

Pear, twelve specimens.—

No. 371.　Bosc　　　3.00 2.50 2.00 1.50 1.00　.50

Grape, open culture.—

No. 372.　Collection of not less than five varieties, three clusters
　　　　　each.　　　　　3.00 2.50 2.00 1.50 1.00

Table Decorations—Fruit.—

No. 373.　Table decoration laid for
　　　　　four covers, no restrictions.
　　　　　Notify the Secretary two days
　　　　　in advance　　　4.00 3.00 2.00 1.00

Pumpkins, three specimens.—

No. 374.　Sweet　　　　2.00 1.50 1.00　.50

936

9 7

Cabbage, three specimens.—
　No. 375.　Any named variety　.2.50　2.00　1.50　1.00　.50

Parsley.—
　No. 376.　One-half peck　　2.50　2.00　1.50　1.00　.50

Peppers.—
　No. 377.　Display. Fifteen dollars to be used for prizes.

Celery, blanched, six specimens.—
　No. 378.　Golden　　　　2.50　2.00　1.50　1.00
　No. 379.　Other varieties　2.50　2.00　1.50　1.00

Squash, three specimens.—
　No. 380.　Blue Hubbard　3.00　2.50　2.00　1.50　1.00

Special Prizes
Offered by Mr. Herbert R. Kinney

I.　Display of vegetables from
　　　　Home Gardens to
　　　　cover 16 square feet　5.00　4.00　3.00　2.50　2.00　1.00

Fruit and Vegetable Exhibition
Thursday, October 1

*All articles for this exhibition must be
in the hall and ready for inspection by
the judges by 2 o'clock*

This exhibition will be open to the public from 3 to 9 p. m.

Ferns.—
No. 381. Display, potted ferns, named varieties. Twenty dollars may be used in prizes.

Specimen Fern.—
No. 382. One plant   3.00 2.00 1.00

Cut Flowers.—
No. 383. Display—$40.00 may be awarded in prizes.

Basket.—
No. 384. Fifteen dollars may be used in prizes.

Hardy Chrysanthemum, out-door culture.—
No. 385. Plants. Fifteen dollars may be used in prizes.
No. 386. Cut flowers in vases. Ten dollars may be used in prizes.

Apple, one standard box, standard pack.—

No. 387.	Baldwin	4.00 3.00 2.00 1.00	.50
No. 388.	Any other variety except McIntosh	4.00 3.00 2.00 1.00	.50

Apple, twelve specimens.—

No. 389.	Baldwin	3.50 3.00 2.50 2.00 1.50 1.00	.50
No. 390.	Bellflower	1.50 1.00	.50
No. 391.	Winter Banana	1.50 1.00	.50
No. 392.	Peck's	1.50 1.00	.50
No. 393.	R. I. Greening	3.00 2.00 1.50 1.00	.50
No. 394.	Northern Spy	3.00 2.00 1.50 1.00	.50
No. 395.	Palmer	1.50 1.00	.50
No. 396.	Roxbury Russet	3.00 2.00 1.50 1.00	.50
No. 397.	Cortland	2.00 1.50 1.00	.50
No. 398.	Opalescent	1.50 1.00	.50
No. 399.	Delicious	2.50 2.00 1.50 1.00	.50
No. 400.	Collection, not to exceed 10 varieties	5.00 4.00 3.00 2.50 2.00
No. 401.	New varieties, five dollars may be used in prizes.

No. 402. Sweet varieties not scheduled, five dollars may be used for prizes.

No. 403. For varieties other than sweet not scheduled, fifteen dollars may be used for prizes.

No. 404. For varieties that have been scheduled, fifteen dollars may be used.

Pear, twelve specimens.—

No. 405.	Angouleme			1.50 1.00	.50
No. 406.	Clairgeau		2.00 1.50	1.00	.50
No. 407.	Lawrence	2.50 2.00	1.50	1.00	.50
No. 408.	Anjou	3.00 2.50 2.00	1.50	1.00	.50

No. 409. For varieties not scheduled, ten dollars may be used for prizes.

No. 410. For new varieties, five dollars may be used in prizes.

Grape, open culture.—

No. 411. For any variety, six clusters, ten dollars may be used for prizes.

Peach, twelve specimens.—

No. 412. Any variety, named, ten dollars may be used for prizes.

Quince, twelve specimens.—

No. 413.	Champion	2.00 1.50 1.00	.50

Cauliflower.—

No. 414.	Three specimens	2.50 2.00 1.50 1.00	.50

Celery, blanched, six specimens.—

No. 415.	Golden	2.50 2.00 1.50 1.00	.50
No. 416.	Any other varieties, not scheduled	2.00 1.50 1.00	.50

Endive.—

No. 417.	Six specimens	1.50 1.00	.50

Leeks.—

No. 418.	Twelve specimens	1.50 1.00	.50

Onion, twelve specimens.—

No. 419. For varieties, five dollars may be used for prizes.

Salsify.—

No. 420.	Twelve specimens	1.50 1.00	.50

Turnip, twelve specimens.—

No. 421.	Purple Top Globe	2.00 1.50 1.00	.50
No. 422.	Any variety, not scheduled	2.00 1.50 1.00	.50

Chrysanthemum Exhibition

Thursday, Nov. 5, 3 to 9 p. m.
Friday, Nov. 6, 9 a. m. to 9 p. m.
Saturday, Nov. 7, 9 a. m. to 9 p. m.
Sunday, Nov. 8, 12 m. to 9 p. m.

*All articles for this exhibition must be
in the hall and ready for inspection by
the judges by 1 o'clock Thursday*

Chrysanthemums.—

No. 423.   Twelve blooms, not less than
    six varieties, to be named   12.00 10.00 8.00
No. 424.   Collection of twenty-five large
    blooms, long stems   20.00 15.00 10.00
No. 425.   Pompoms, display in vases   5.00 4.00 3.00 2.00
No. 426.   Single varieties, display in vases
                              5.00 4.00 3.00 2.00
No. 427.   Anemones, display in vases   5.00 4.00 3.00 2.00

Commercial Growers.—

No. 428.   Chrysanthemums, vase of white   4.00 3.00 2.00
No. 429.   Chrysanthemums, vase of yellow   4.00 3.00 2.00
No. 430.   Chrysanthemums, vase of pink   4.00 3.00 2.00

Note. Six flowers in each, one variety in each vase. Stems not less than two feet.

Non-commercial Growers.—

No. 431.   Chrysanthemums, vase of white   4.00 3.00 2.00
No. 432.   Chrysanthemums, vase of yellow   4.00 3.00 2.00
No. 433.   Chrysanthemums, vase of pink   4.00 3.00 2.00

Note. Six flowers in each, one variety in each vase. Stems not less than two feet.

Chrysanthemums.—

No. 434.   Basket of Pompons   4.00 3.00 2.00 1.00
No. 435.   Basket of Single   4.00 3.00 2.00 1.00
No. 436.   Basket of Anemones   4.00 3.00 2.00 1.00

Special Display of Plants.—

No. 437. Seven hundred dollars may be used for prizes.

Persons competing for these premiums, must notify the Secretary previous to 6 p. m. Monday, November 2.

No. 438. For exhibits—no restrictions as to where grown, or by whom—$150.00 may be used for prizes.

No. 439. Six specimen plants   10.00 8.00 6.00

No. 440. One specimen plant   3.00 2.00 1.00

Frederick A. Blake Fund

J. Chrysanthemums.—Best bloom   4.00 3.00 2.00

Obadiah Brown Hadwen Fund

K. Chrysanthemums.—Large Flowers. Basket. Fifteen dollars to be awarded in prizes.

Special Prizes
Offered by Mrs. Mabel Knowles Gage

L. Table Decorations.—A Thanksgiving table. No restrictions. Laid for four covers. Notify the Secretary two days in advance. Fifty dollars to be used in prizes.

Fern Globes.—

No. 441.   3.00 2.00 1.50 1.00

Glass Fernery.—

No. 442. Other than Fern Globe   4.00 3.00 2.00 1.00

Wild Fruits and Berries.—

No. 443. Display   5.00 4.00 3.00 2.50 1.50 1.00

Physalis Franchettii (Chinese Lanterns).—

No. 444. Basket   4.00 3.00 2.00 1.00

Fruit Display.—

No. 445. No restriction as to arrangement. $40.00 may be used in prizes. Notify the Secretary two days in advance.

Apple, three standard boxes, standard pack.—

No. 446. Any variety   10.00 8.00 7.00 5.00 4.00

Apples, forty-nine specimens.—

No. 447.	Baldwin	6.00	5.00	4.00	3.00	2.00	1.00
No. 448.	McIntosh	6.00	5.00	4.00	3.00	2.00	1.00
No. 449.	Delicious		5.00	4.00	3.00	2.00	1.00
No. 450.	Any other named variety		5.00	4.00	3.00	2.00	1.00
No. 451.	Fancy Basket of Apples	3.00	2.50	2.00	.50	1.00	
No. 452.	Fancy Basket of Pears	3.00	2.50	2.00	1.50	1.00	

Special Exhibition of Apples
William Eames Fund

A. Baldwin, best twelve.—
Three premiums   1.50   1.00   .50

B. Northern Spy.—
Three premiums   1.50   1.00   .50

C. Delicious.—
Three premiums   1.50   1.00   .50

D. Rhode Island Greening.—
Three premiums   1.50   1.00   .50

E. Roxbury Russet.—
Three premiums   1.50   1.00   .50

F. Sutton Beauty.—
Three premiums   1.50   1.00   .50

G. McIntosh.—
Three premiums   1.50   1.00   .50

H. Any other Variety.—
Three premiums   1.50   1.00   .50

*   *   *

Brussels Sprouts.—

No. 453.	One-half peck	2.00	1.50	1.00	.50

Celery, blanched, six specimens.—

No. 454.	Giant Pascal	2.00	1.50	1.00	.50
No. 455.	Any other variety	2.50	2.00	1.50	1.00	.50

Onion, twelve specimens.—

No. 456.	White Globe		2.00	1.50	1.00	.50
No. 457.	Yellow Globe Danvers	2.50	2.00	1.50	1.00	.50
No. 458.	Red Globe		2.00	1.50	1.00	.50
No. 459.	Cracker			1.50	1.00	.50
No. 460.	Any other variety	2.50	2.00	1.50	1.00	.50

Cabbage, three specimens.—

No. 461.   2.00 1.50 1.00 .50

Parsnip, twelve specimens.—

No. 462. Hollow Crown   2.00 1.50 1.00 .50
No. 463. Any other variety   2.00 1.50 1.00 .50

Squash, three specimens.—

No. 464. Green Hubbard   2.50 2.00 1.50 1.00 .50

Squash.—

No. 465. Collection   5.00 4.50 4.00 3.50 3.00

Gourds.—

No. 466. Display. Twelve dollars to be used for prizes.

Turnip, twelve specimens.—

No. 467. Purple Top Globe   2.00 1.50 1.00 .50
No. 468. English varieties, not scheduled

                                       2.00 1.50 1.00 .50

Turnip, six specimens.—

No. 469. White Swede   2.00 1.50 1.00 .50
No. 470. Yellow Swede   2.00 1.50 1.00 .50

Potato, twelve specimens.—

No. 471. Green Mountain   2.50 2.00 1.50 1.00
No. 472. Any other variety   2.50 2.00 1.50 1.00

Grains.—

No. 473. Best exhibit, five dollars may be used for prizes.

Field Beans.—

No. 474. Best exhibit, ten dollars may be used for prizes.

Annual Meeting, Thursday, December 3, 1936.
Premiums will be paid on or after November 20, 1936.

THE LIBRARY OF THE
WORCESTER COUNTY HORTICULTURAL SOCIETY

The Library Committee wish to call your attention to the Library and Reading Room, where the librarian is always ready to extend every facility possible to those in search of horticultural information.

COMMITTEE ON
LIBRARY AND PUBLICATIONS

EDWARD W. BREED, Chairman . MRS. AMY W. SMITH
WILLIAM ANDERSON HERBERT R. KINNEY
FLORENCE E. FIELD, Librarian

SOME OF THE RECENT ACCESSIONS TO THE LIBRARY

Mexican Plants for American Gardens, by Cecile Hulse Matschat
The Gladiolus Book, by Forman T. McLean
Dwarf and Slow Growing Conifers, by Murray Hornibrook
Our American Maples and Some Others, by Margaret Curtin Finley
Manual of Cultivated Trees and Shrubs, by Alfred Rehder
Our Native Cacti, by Edith Bailey Higgins
Cacti, by A. J. van Laren
Succulents, by A. J. van Laren
House Plants, by Marjorie Norrell Sulzer
The American Rose Annual—1935
Herbs and the Earth, by Henry Beston
Old Roses, by Mrs. Frederick Love Keays
Plants of the Vicinity of New York, by H. A. Gleason, Ph.D.
Flower and Table Arrangements, by Esther Longyear Murphy
Flower Arrangement, by F. F. Rockwell and Esther C. Grayson
Garden Design, by Marjorie Sewell Caufley
Tuberous-Rooted Begonias and their Culture, by George Otten
American Ferns, by Edith A. Roberts and Julia R. Lawrence.
Vegetable Crops, by Dr. Homer C. Thompson
The Gardener's How Book, by Chesla C. Sherlock
How to Arrange Flowers, by Dorothy Biddle
Azaleas and Camellias, by H. Harold Hume

The Rose Manual, by J. H. Nicolas
Gardening with Herbs, by Helen Morgenthau Fox
The 1929–1930–1931–1932–1933– and 1934 Year Books of the New England Gladiolus Society
Western American Alpines, by Ira N. Gabrielson
Pioneering with Wildflowers, by George D. Aiken
Japanese Flower Arrangement, by Mary Averill
Gardening for the Small Place, by Leonard Barron
The Gladiolus and its Culture, by Alvin C. Beal, Ph.D.
Adventures in Dish Gardening, by Patten Beard
Rock Garden and Alpine Plants, by Henry Correvon
Gardens in America, by Marion Cran
Our Wild Orchids, by Edward A. Eames
American Orchid Culture, by Prof. E. A. White
Spring Flowering Bulbs, by Clark L. Thayer
The Book of Shrubs, by Alfred C. Hottes
Garden Pools, by L. W. Ramsey and Charles H. Lawrence
The Cactus Book, by A. D. Houghton
Patio Gardens, by Helen Morgenthau Fox
Fruits and Vegetables under Glass, by William Turner
The Book of Water Gardening, by Peter Bisset
Little Book of Climbing Plants, by Alfred C. Hottes
Rose Garden Primer, by Eber Holmes
Flowering Trees and Shrubs, by R. C. Notcutt •
Chrysanthemums, Under Glass and Outdoors, by Alexander Laurie
Fertilizers for Greenhouses and Garden Crops, by Alexander Laurie
Flowers for Cutting and Decoration, by Richardson Wright
The Arrangement of Flowers, by Mrs. Walter R. Hine
Agriculture, Soils and How to Treat Them, by William P. Brooks
Productive Bee-Keeping, by Frank C. Pellet
A Field Guide to the Birds, by Roger Tory Peterson .
Roses for all Climates, by George C. Thomas
Cultivated Evergreens, by L. H. Bailey
The Amateur's Book of the Dahlia, by Mrs. Charles H. Stout
Delphiniums, Their History and Cultivation, by George A. Phillips
Lilies and Their Culture in North America, by William N. Craig

Worcester County Horticultural Society

SCHEDULE OF PRIZES
Offered to
Children of Worcester County

Exhibitions to be held Saturday, August 22
and Saturday, September 12, 1935
Horticultural Building, 30 Elm Street

Worcester, Massachusetts

Saturday, August 22

All articles must be in the hall by 1 o'clock

The exhibits must be the results of individual effort of the c
from the time of planting to the arranging of the exhibit.

Open to Children under 14 years of age

Display of Flowers.—
  No. 1. Not to exceed fifteen vases

                  2.00 1.50 1.25 1.00   .50

Zinnia.—
  No. 2 Not to exceed 10 vases   .75   .50   .25

Asters.—
  No. 3. Not to exceed 10 vases   .75   .50   .25

Petunia.—
  No. 4. Not to exceed 10 vases   .75   .50   .25

Calendula.—
  No. 5. Not to exceed 10 vases   .75   .50   .25

Wild Flowers.—
  No. 6. Not to exceed fifteen vases

                      1.50 1.25 1.00   .50
  No. 7. Vase of Flowers   1.00   .75   .50   .25

Display of Vegetables.—
  No. 8. Not to exceed 12 varieties

              2.00 1.75 1.50 1.25 1.00   .75

Beets.—
  No. 9. Six specimens   .75   .50   .25

Summer Squash.—
  No. 10. Two specimens   .75   .50   .25

String Beans.—
  No. 11. Two quarts   .75   .50   .25

Potato.—
  No. 12 Twelve specimens   1.00   .75   .50

Sweet Corn.—
  No. 13. Six ears   1.00   .75   .50

Tomato.—
  No. 14. Six specimens   .75   .50   .25

Carrots.—
  No. 15. Six specimens   .75   .50   .25

Cucumber.—
  No. 16. Two specimens   .75   .50   .25

Open to Children between the ages of 14 and 21

Display of Flowers.—
No. 17.   Not to exceed 15 vases   2.50 2.00 1.75 1.00

Asters.—
No. 18.   Not to exceed 10 vases   1.00   .75   .50   .25

Petunia.—
No. 19.   Not to exceed 10 vases   1.00   .75   .50   .25

Gladiolus.—
No. 20.   Basket   1.00 .75   .50   .25

Zinnia.—
No. 21.   Not to exceed 10 vases   1.00   .75   .50   .25

Wild Flowers.—
No. 22.   Not to exceed 15 vases   1.50 1.25 1.00   .50   .25
No. 23.   Vase of Flowers   1.00   .75   .50   .25   .25

Display of Vegetables.—
No. 24.   Not over 15 varieties
                    2.50 2.00 1.75 1.50 1.25 1.00   .50

Potato.—
No. 25.   Twelve specimens   1.50 1.00   .75   .50   .25

Beets.—
No. 26.   Six specimens   1.00   .75   .50   .25

Carrots.—
No. 27.   Six specimens   1.00   .75   .50   .25

Shell Beans.—
No. 28.   Two quarts   1.00   .75   .50   .25

String Beans.—
No. 29.   Two quarts   1.00   .75   .50   .25

Sweet Corn.—
No. 30.   Six ears   1.00   .75   .50   .25

Tomato.—
No. 31.   Six specimens   1.25 1.00   .75   .50   .25

Cucumber.—
No. 32   Two specimens   1.00   .75   .50   .25

Summer Squash.—
No. 33.   Two specimens   1.00   .75   .50   .25

Saturday, September 12
All articles must be in the hall by 1 o'clock

The exhibits must be the results of individual effort of the child from the time of planting to the arranging of the exhibit.

Open to Children under 14 years of age

Display of Flowers.—

No. 34. Not to exceed 15 vases

2.00	1.50	1.25	1.00	.50	.25

Cosmos.—

No. 35. Vase		.75	.50	.25	.25

Calendula.—

No. 36. Not to exceed 10 vases   .75   .50   .25   .25

Petunia.—

No. 37. Not to exceed 10 vases   .75   .50   .25   .25

Asters.—

No. 38. Not to exceed 10 vases   .75   .50   .25   .25

Zinnia.—

No. 39. Not to exceed 10 vases   .75   .50   .25   .25

Marigolds.—

No. 40. Not to exceed 10 vases   .75   .50   .25   .25

Gladiolus.—

No. 41. Basket   .75   .50   .25   .25

Wild Flowers.—

No. 42. Not to exceed 15 vases   1.50 1.25 1.00 .50 .25

No. 43. Vase of Flowers   1.00 .75 .50 .25 .25

Display of Vegetables.—

No. 44. Not to exceed 12 varieties

2.00 1.75 1.50 1.25 1.00 .75 .50

Shell Beans.—

No. 45. Two quarts in pods   .75 .50 .25 .25

Beets.—

No. 46. Six specimens   1.00 .75 .50 .25 .25

Carrots.—

No. 47. Six specimens   1.00 .75 .50 .25 .25

Sweet Corn.—

No. 48. Six ears   1.00 .75 .50 .25 .25

Tomato.—

No. 49. Six specimens   1.00 .75 .50 .25 .25

Winter Squash.—
  No. 50. Two specimens   1.00 .75 .25 .25

Potato.—
  No. 51. Twelve specimens   1.00 .75 .50 .25 .25

Open to Children between the ages of 14 and 21

Display of Flowers.—
  No. 52. Not to exceed 15 vases   ⁄ 2.50 2.00 1.75 1.50

Petunia.—
  No. 53. Not to exceed 10 vases   1.00 .75 .50 .25

Dahlias.—
  No. 54. Not to exceed 10 vases   1.00 .75 .50 .25

Zinnia.—
  No. 55. Not to exceed 10 vases   1.00 .75 .50 .25

Marigold.—
  No. 56. Not to exceed 10 vases   1.00 .75 .50 .25

Cosmos.—
  No. 57. One large vase   1.00 .75 .50 .25

Gladiolus.—
  No. 58. Basket   1.00 .75 .50 .25

Wild Flowers.—
  No. 59. Not to exceed 15 vases   1.50 1.25 1.00 .50 .25
  No. 60. Vase of Flowers   1.00 .75 .50 .25 .25

Dahlia.—
  No. 61. Vase   1.00 .75 .50 .25

Display of Vegetables.—
  No. 62. Not to exceed 15 varieties
               2.50 2.00 1.75 1.50 1.25 1.00 .50

Potato.—
  No. 63. Twelve specimens   1.50 1.00 .75 .50 .25

Carrots.—
  No. 64. Six specimens   1.25 1.00 .75 .50 .25

Beets.—
  No. 65. Six specimens   1.25 1.00 .75 .50 .25

Sweet Corn.—
  No. 66. Six ears   1.25 1.00 .75 .50 .25

Tomato.—
No. 67.   Six specimens   1.25 1.00 .75 .50 .25

Cabbage.—
No. 68.   Two specimens   .75 .50 .25

Winter Squash.— .
No. 69.   Two specimens   1.00 .75 .50 .25

Celery.—
No. 70.   Three specimens   .75 .50 .25

Shell Beans.—
No. 71.   Two quarts in the pod   1.00 .75 .50 .25

Onion.—
No. 72.   Six specimens   1.00 .75 .50 .25

Prizes will be given for other meritorious exhibits.

Competition is open to all children of Worcester County under two classes. Those under 14 years and those between 14 and 21.

Only one child in a family can compete for the same prize.

The exhibits must be the results of individual effort of the child from the time of planting to the arranging of the exhibit.

All exhibits must be in the Hall ready for inspection by the Judges by 1 p. m. Exhibition will close at 4.30 p. m.

Prizes will be paid at the close of the exhibition.

Vases, plates and everything necessary for the exhibition of the flowers and vegetables will be furnished by the Horticultural Society.

Special Prizes Offered
by Secretary Herbert R. Kinney

To the ones receiving the two largest amounts under 14 years of age. $3.00. $2.00.

To the ones receiving the two largest amounts over 14 years of age. $3.00. $2.00.

*   *   *

For further information apply to

HERBERT R. KINNEY,
Secretary.

TRANSACTIONS

OF THE

WORCESTER COUNTY
HORTICULTURAL
SOCIETY

Reports of the Officers and Lectures

For the year ending December 3, 1936

OFFICERS AND COMMITTEES
of the
Worcester County Horticultural Society
For the Year 1936

PRESIDENT
MYRON F. CONVERSE, Worcester, Mass.

VICE-PRESIDENTS
HERBERT A. COOK   MRS. HOMER GAGE
Shrewsbury, Mass.   Worcester, Mass.
S. LOTHROP DAVENPORT, No. Grafton, Mass.

SECRETARY
HERBERT R. KINNEY, of Worcester
Horticultural Hall, 30 Elm Street

TREASURER
BURT W. GREENWOOD, of Worcester

LIBRARIAN
MRS. FLORENCE E. FIELD, of Worcester

TRUSTEES

Joseph A. Allen	Auburn	Willis E. Cary	Worcester
William Anderson	Wellesley	Frederick H. Chamberlain	Worcester
Miss Elizabeth R. Bishop	Sutton	J. Frank Cooper	Worcester
Edward W. Breed	Clinton	Mrs. Bertha G. Denny	Worcester
Ralph C. Breed	Clinton	Mrs. Alice M. Forbes	Worcester
Richard A. Flagg	Boylston	Harold J. Greenwood	Worcester
Allen J. Jenkins	Shrewsbury	Harry Harrison	Worcester
William E. Morey	Shrewsbury	Mrs. Florence C. Herrick	Worcester
Eugene O. Parsons	Auburn	Allen W. Hixon	Worcester
Charles Potter	West Boylston	Allyne W. Hixon	Worcester
Albert W. Schneider	Clinton	Mrs. Anna N. W. Hobbs	Worcester
Myron S. Wheeler	Berlin	H. Ward Moore	Worcester
Mrs. Mary D. White	Holden	Harry I. Randall	Worcester
Ernest P. Bennett	Worcester	Mrs. Amy W. Smith	Worcester
Chandler Bullock	Worcester	George F. E. Story	Worcester

STANDING COMMITTEE ON FINANCE
Leonard C. Midgley, 1936   Myron F. Converse, *Chairman*, 1937
Herbert W. Estabrook, 1938

NOMINATING COMMITTEE

Arthur H. Bellows, 1936   Charles B. Rugg, 1937
                    Harold S. Bowker, 1938

ON LIBRARY AND PUBLICATIONS

Edward W. Breed, *Chairman*   Mrs. Amy W. Smith
                    William Anderson
    Herbert R. Kinney, *Secretary*   Mrs. Florence E. Field, *Librarian*

ON NOMENCLATURE

S. Lothrop Davenport	Charles Potter
J. Frank Cooper	William Anderson
Mrs. Amy W. Smith	Herbert R. Kinney
Allen J. Jenkins	Leonard C. Midgley

ON ARRANGEMENTS AND EXHIBITIONS

Allen J. Jenkins, *Chairman*

Joseph A. Allen	Allyne W. Hixon
Mrs. William W. Taft	Charles Potter
Mrs. Percy G. Forbes	Elizabeth R. Bishop
Leonard C. Midgley	Allen W. Hixon
H. Ward Moore	S. Lothrop Davenport
Edward W. Breed	Mrs. Bertha G. Denny
Mrs. Florence E. Field	William E. Morey

President, Myron F. Converse
Secretary, Herbert R. Kinney

AUDITORS

Harry C. Midgley   H. Ward Moore
                    Arthur H. Bellows

JUDGES

PLANTS AND FLOWERS: William Anderson, Wellesley Hills
FRUIT: S. Lothrop Davenport, North Grafton
VEGETABLES: H. Ward Moore, Worcester

MEDAL COMMITTEE

Myron F. Converse, *Chairman*   Edward W. Breed
                    Allen W. Hixon

ON WINTER MEETINGS

Myron F. Converse, *Chairman*
Herbert R. Kinney, *Secretary*

Mrs. Leander F. Herrick	Mrs. Anna N. W. Hobbs
Leonard C. Midgley	H. Ward Moore

Office, Library, and Exhibition Hall
30 Elm Street

Florence E. Field, Librarian

PRESIDENT'S ADDRESS

To the Members of the
Worcester County Horticultural Society:

The widespread attention which the art of horticulture is receiving prompts the members of this Society to increased activity in this their chosen field. It is the belief of your officers and the members of your various committees that much insight and stimulation emanates from the lectures which are conducted each week during the winter season. This year's course was an example of the good material which is available for such a program. We are encouraged by the attention which is accorded to this part of the Society's work.

The weekly seasonal shows have been favored with an abundance of entries, and the exhibits produced on these occasions have been most acceptable—with rare exceptions—while in many instances the specimens were of unusually high quality.

The Children's Exhibits always are a source of much interest, and the accomplishments of that group of little workers are a matter of much satisfaction. Isn't it possible that some of these young people, on whom this Society's future may depend, can be aided with advice of the more experienced gardeners of today? It may be that the members of the Committee on Arrangements and Exhibitions can organize such an undertaking in a simple and effective manner.

E. L. D. Seymour, B. S. A., editor of the *Gardeners' Encyclopedia* published during the year, was the guest speaker at our annual reunion held on the evening of March 5, 1936, and from his fund of information, he brought pertinent facts which were of special interest to our members. The privilege of holding these pleasant gatherings in our suitable surroundings furnishes another bright spot in our yearly program. Each member should avail himself of the privilege of these annual gatherings.

The Library has continued as one of our important departments, and Mrs. Florence E. Field, during this her first year as Librarian, has demonstrated her ability and fitness for the position.

Many of our members likewise are associated with the Massachusetts Horticultural Society and delight in the success of that pioneer organization. We read its publication—*Horticulture*—and wish that more details of our schedules were presented to its readers.

Your President's message would be incomplete without a word of commendation of the Spring Show held in March and the Chrysanthemum Show held in November, which mark the beginning and end of the season's schedule. In all respects, these events clearly reflect the intelligent and faithful work performed by the committee members and by the exhibitors who so grandly aid in these undertakings as well as in the numerous other activities which enter into the year's work.

Respectfully submitted,

MYRON F. CONVERSE, *President.*

Worcester, Massachusetts
December 3, 1936

SECRETARY'S REPORT

Mr. President and Members of the
Worcester County Horticultural Society:

Our activities for the year have been carried on along lines followed by the Society for many years, having lectures during January and February, with a four-day Spring Show in March and exhibitions Thursday afternoons and evenings during June, July, August, and September.

We usually have a one-day exhibition in April and May and one or two in October and a four-day Chrysanthemum Show in November.

This year we had a small plant and flower exhibition in the West Room at the time of each of our lectures which seemed well worth while.

Our lectures began January 9, with "Miracles in Nature," by Mr. Arthur Pillsbury, Berkeley, Calif.

This lecture was in many ways very different from his earlier ones, as it was largely given to describing new methods of growing plants in water and the modern machinery used in taking pictures.

January 16, "Flora of Western Scotland," by Dr. J. R. Jack, Cambridge, Mass.

After describing some of its geography, he showed and explained many beautiful pictures and told some very interesting anecdotes making it a very interesting lecture.

January 23, "Our Island Kingdom in the Pacific," by Charles H. Tozier, Boston, Mass.

This lecture goes back to the discovery of these islands in 1778 by Captain Cook and describes some of the early conditions.

The main features of the lecture and pictures represent present-day life and the strange and beautiful things to be seen there now. A fine lecture beautifully illustrated.

January 30, "The Use of Flowers in the Home and in Design Work," by Donald White and two assistants.

"In all art the first thing we must have is some conception in our minds of that which we want to produce."

"The second rule is to keep your composition as natural as possible."

"The third rule is not to overdo the units in flower arrangements."

This report is well worth reading by those interested in flower arrangements.

February 6, "Rock Gardens, Their Location and Construction," by Carl Stanton, Peterborough, N. H.

This lecture was illustrated by many fine pictures and described in an interesting manner. It featured improving unpleasant conditions rather than making entirely new ones.

February 13, "The Gardens of Russia," by Mrs. Cyrus Winslow Merrell, New Canaan, Conn.

In Leningrad she found three types of public parks and they were beautifully planted. It also has a Botanical Garden which was established in 1680 and was landscaped in 1724 by an English gardener.

Mrs. Merrell did not see a lawn mower in Russia.

February 20, "Prize Gardens and Plant Exhibits," by Mr. Edward I. Farrington, Secretary of the Massachusetts Horticultural Society. He showed pictures of many beautiful gardens and plant displays, some in the making; and his descriptions of them were very interesting making it one of our best lectures.

February 27, "The Hardy Garden in Continuous Bloom," by Mrs. Katherine L. Rice, Grand Rapids, Mich.

"The first prerequisite is to know what plants to use and what they need. Then see that they are planted under proper conditions." She showed and explained many apt pictures. She also listed many varieties and recommended many combinations. It was a very satisfactory lecture.

On March 5, the Annual Reunion was held.

The Library was attractively decorated with palms, ferns, yellow roses, snapdragons, and white sweet peas.

Reception was at 6.30. In the receiving line were, Mr. and Mrs. Myron F. Converse, Mrs. Homer Gage, Mr. and Mrs. S. Lothrop Davenport, and Mr. E. L. D. Seymour of New York City.

The ushers were, Mr. Malcolm Midgley, Mr. H. Ward Moore, Mr. Harrison G. Taylor, Mr. Burt W. Greenwood, Mr. Allen Hixon and Mr. Leonard C. Midgley.

The receiving line led the march to the dining room, where the tables were decorated with red roses.

The invocation was by Dr. Tomlinson.

President Converse spoke of the death of ex-President David L. Fiske who had passed away during the last year.

After a fine dinner, served by Mr. Lunt, the Unity Quartette sang "Swing Along," and the meeting adjourned to the Auditorium to a lecture by Mr. E. L. D. Seymour who spoke on "The Gardens of Tomorrow."

He said, "The three factors that are going to contribute most to the gardens of tomorrow are

1. Design and element
2. Element, called materials and methods
3. Human element, the gardener, himself."

After this lecture there was dancing and a social time.

The Spring Exhibition, while perhaps not quite up to our best, was good. There were five gardens, twelve plant displays, and two rock gardens.

Mrs. Gage's display on the stage was very attractive.

Mr. Breed's display in the center attracted a great deal of attention as did Mr. Allen's wild garden in the corner.

Mr. Potter's and Sunnyside Greenhouses were good.

There was an excellent exhibit of fruit and vegetables down stairs.

June 4: This was a very nice exhibition. There was a large showing of cut flowers and there were eleven displays and twelve baskets of iris. No rhododendron or azaleas were shown. There was only one display of geranium, but four good peonies. There were seven plates of strawberries.

June 11: There was a nice showing of wild flowers. The peonies were good. There were fourteen exhibits of strawberries.

The Rose Exhibit on June 18 was not up to standard, although there were some nice roses. There were some good strawberries.

June 25: There was only one fine vase of delphinium.

There were some nice Japanese iris and wild flowers shown July 2.

There was a very large showing of sweet peas on July 9, as well as two nice displays of regal lilies.

July 30: The recent call for Flower Arrangement for the Living Room brought out a large and interesting exhibit.

Gladiolus Exhibition, August 6.

This was a real gladiolus show. There were nine displays, eight standards and nine, twenty vases.

There was also an entry of twenty-six, small vase on a mirror, which attracted much attention.

Our new call for displays of Cut Flowers on August 20, 27, and September 3 making two classes was well received.

Dahlia Exhibition, September 10.

This was one of our best Dahlia Exhibitions, showing several different varieties in separate classes. The flowers being in their prime.

The display of Flower Arrangement seemed to have much improved since the number of containers was not limited; it gives a wider range and a chance for a more artistic arrangement, especially of the more delicate flowers.

Mr. Edward W. Breed made a fine showing of potted tuberous rooted begonias.

September 17: The display of Dahlias certainly proved that, this year, this date was right for this exhibit. There were eight entries and five of them were fine.

The collections of vegetables were especially good.

September 24: The displays of Fruit were not up to standard although as a whole they made a nice showing.

The display of Vegetables from home gardens was excellent.

October 1, Fruit and Vegetable Exhibition.

There was an excellent showing of flowers for this time of year.

The showing of both Fruit and Vegetables was light and much of it not up to standard in quality.

The Chrysanthemum Exhibition was again a very successful one. While many of those attending thought that perhaps the Auditorium was not quite as beautiful as sometimes, there were no doubts about the West Room being the best ever.

There was considerable falling off in the Fruit exhibit both in quality and amount, due largely to the short crop of apples.

IRISTHORPE, MRS. HOMER GAGE, SPRING 1936

Vegetables were good, but only a small exhibit, with the exception of squashes which were liberally shown and of good quality.

Mrs. Homer Gage's call for a "Thanksgiving Table Decoration'" brought an entry of fifteen tables which made a fine showing in the Lecture Hall.

The exhibition in the Conference Room of various wild exhibits seemed a real attraction.

The Children's Exhibitions this year were probably the best the Society ever held.

This was partially due to our calling for the exhibits to be in place by 1 o'clock p.m., giving more time to get the judging done and some changes made.

The classes were well filled and the quality was good.

Some of the exhibitors showed real skill in their arrangements, and they all showed keen interest in their exhibits.

I believe there is no line of our endeavor that is more worthy than these exhibitions.

The Entry Blank has proved to be a new feature that has helped all along the line. The cards can be made out the day before and we know something about what is coming and the exhibitors can get their cards quicker.

During the last few years the Committee on Arrangement and Exhibitions has been increasing the number of calls where a certain amount of money was designated for prizes rather than premiums, and I feel that has been a very satisfactory arrangement, especially when there is liable to be considerable difference in the exhibits.

Our practice has been under this condition to use our prize stickers with the amount of the prize put on the card.

This has been quite satisfactory to the exhibitors but the public is interested in who gets the blue, and it was sometimes difficult to hunt up the order in which the judge had awarded the amount, and it would seem as though we might just as well use our regular premium stickers on these exhibits.

Table decorations have been a feature of our exhibitions for a long time and still are a real attraction.

We have always, until this year, used round tables. This year we have used some oblong ones.

As we had only six of the new ones, it was necessary to use some of the round and oblong ones at the same time, which may have caused the feeling that they should not be used together.

It is possible that the new tables are not large enough or that perhaps they would be better if laid for two rather than four covers.

Respectfully submitted,

HERBERT R. KINNEY, *Secretary*

December 3, 1936

TREASURER'S REPORT

For the Year Ending December 2, 1936

Statement of Income and Expenditures

INCOME			EXPENDITURES		
Rent:			Library..................		
Hall............	$660.00		Winter Meetings...........		
Stores..........	39,999.96	$40,659.96	Periodicals................		
			Publications...............		
			Premiums:		
Permanent Funds:			Of 1936........	$6,665.50	
Membership Fund	$108.26		Special..........	85.00	
Blake Fund......	19.00		Children's		
Dewey Fund.....	37.20		Exhibitions.....	277.65	
Draper Fund....	15.00		Blake Fund......	19.00	
Eames Fund.....	22.00		Draper Fund....	15.00	
Hadwen Fund....	66.50		Eames Fund.....	22.00	
Morse Fund.....	11.00	278.96	Hadwen Fund....	66.50	
			Morse Fund.. ..	11.00	
Membership Fees...........		100.00			
			Expense:		
Interest Earned:			Exhibitions..............		
Permanent Funds.	$142.99		Office....................		
Investments.....	230.78	373.77	Operating................		
			Miscellaneous............		
			Street Sprinkling...........		
Winter Meetings: Tickets....		141.00	Furniture and Fixtures.......		
Other Income:			**Maintenance:**		
Mabel K. Gage...	$50.00		Furniture		
H. R. Kinney....	35.00	85.00	and Fixtures....	$294.49	
			Real Estate......	1,019.90	
Light, Heat, Etc.:					
Discount received on Coal			Salaries..................		
Bill....................		2.00	Interest Paid..............		
Payments on account of Re-			Interest Added to Permanent		
tirement Price of Worcester			Funds...................		
County Trust Company Class			Interest Added to Investments		
A Stock.................		195.00	Insurance................		
			Light, Heat, Water, etc......		
		$41,835.69	Janitor Service.............		
			Mortgage Note Reductions		
			(Front Street Property).....		
			Transfer to Membership Fund		
			Returned to Investments.....		
Cash Balance, December 4, 1935	1,033.06		Cash Balance, December 2, 1936		
	$42,868.75				

₂ment of Gains and Losses

	LOSSES	
·iations:	Appropriations..............	$10,000.00
	Premiums in excess of appro-	
	priation.................	65.50
	Depreciation...............	1,302.93
$317.35	Special and Permanent Fund	
	Premiums................	218.50
100.00	Expense Accounts...........	1,811.46
278.96	Insurance.................	767.51
40,659.96	Interest...................	9,052.85
85.00	Janitor Service.............	2,617.80
	Light, Heat, Water, etc......	1,312.87
	Maintenance Accounts.......	1,314.39
	Periodicals................	85.50
	Publications........	829.60
	Street Sprinkling......	5.70
	Winter Meetings...........	1,248.16
		$30,632.74
	Net Gain to Surplus.........	10,808.53
$41,441.27		$41,441.27

Statement of Resources and Liabilities

RESOURCES			LIABILITIES
Permanent Funds (Investment):			Blake Fund:
Peoples' Savings Bank			Principal................
(Hadwen Fund) $1,226.66			Income.................
Wor. Five Cts. Sav. Bk.			Dewey Fund:
(Draper Fund) 405.68			Principal................
(Eames Fund). 602.79			Income.................
(Morse Fund). 519.43			Draper Fund:
Wor. Mech. Sav. Bk.			Principal................
(Blake Fund).. 1,384.22			Income.................
(Dewey Fund). 1,000.00	$5,138.78		Eames Fund:
			Principal................
Investments:			Income.................
Wor. Co. Inst.			Hadwen Fund:
for Sav....... $2,556.20			Principal................
Wor. Five Cts.			Income.................
Sav. Bk....... 3,028.68			Morse Fund:
Wor. Mech. Sav.			Principal................
Bk... ...... 3,212.40			Income.................
Wor. Co. Trust			Mortgage Note, Front Street
Co. Class A			Property................
stk. 65 sh. at			Surplus:
$17 per share.. 1,105.00	9,902.28		Dec. 4, 1935....$327,609.23
			Net Gain, 1936. 10,808.53
Membership Fund.........	4,050.00		
Real Estate...............	480,000.00		
Furniture and Fixtures......	19,940.31		
Library..................	2,280.99		
Cash....................	1,244.18		
	$522,556.54		

Respectfully submitted,

B. W. GREENWOOD, *T*

Auditor's Certificate

I have examined the books of the Treasurer of the Worcester Coun
Horticultural Society, together with vouchers, securities, and bank balanc
for the year ended December 2, 1936, and find them to be correct.

ADAH B. JOHNSON, *Accountant.*

Worcester, December 1, 1936

We have caused an audit of the books of the Treasurer to be made f
the year ended December 2, 1936, and the foregoing certificate is here
approved.

Respectfully submitted,

H. WARD MOORE, ARTHUR H. BELLOWS, HARRY C. MIDGLEY,
Auditors.

Worcester, Massachusetts

LIBRARIAN'S REPORT

Mr. President and Members of the
Worcester County Horticultural Society:

During the year 1936, the use of the Library has been gratifying.
The circulation of books and periodicals exceeded the number of
three hundred and twenty-eight against last year's figure of two
hundred and ninety-seven.

Through the generous efforts of your Library Committee in
selecting and purchasing books on subjects of particular interest in
horticulture today, we have a very complete and modern Library,
and would emphasize the fact that we look forward to the time
when every member of this Society will be upon its active list.

Many valuable bulletins on varied horticultural and agricultural
subjects have been received, and the usual publications and periodicals
for reading in the Library have been continued.

Some work has been done in the repair and preservation of bind-
ings.

It is with deep appreciation that we acknowledge the gift of the
book, *Rhododendrons and Azaleas*, by Clement Gray Bowers, from
the Worcester Garden Club. It has been in constant circulation
since we received it.

Other new books added to the Library this year are as follows:

Vegetable Crops, Dr. Homer C. Thompson, 1931.

Cactus, A. J. van Laren, 1935.

The Gardener's How Book, Chesla C. Sherlock, 1935.

Insect Enemies of Shade Trees, Glenn W. Herrick, 1935.

The 1936 Gladiolus Year Book, New England Gladiolus Society.

How to Know the Mosses, Elizabeth Marie Dunham, 1916.

Ferns of the Vicinity of New York, John Kunkel Small, 1935.

Bigger and Better Roses for Garden, House and Exhibition, G. F. Mappin, London, 1935.

Lilies: Their Culture and Management, H. Drysdale Woodcock, J. Coutts,
London, 1935.

A Year in the Rose Garden, J. H. Nicholas, 1936.

Rhododendrons and Azaleas, Clement Gray Bowers, 1935.

California Cactus, E. M. Baxter, 1935.

The Garden Encyclopedia, Edited by E. L. D. Seymour, 1936.
Clematis, The Large and Small Flowered, Ernest Markham, London, 1935.
Rock Gardens: How to Make and Maintain Them, Lewis B. Meredith, 1913.
Plant Hunting on the Edge of the World, F. Kingdon Ward, London, 1930.
The 1936 American Rose Annual, The American Rose Society.
New Flower Arrangements, Mrs. Walter R. Hine, 1936.
The Book of Perennials, Alfred C. Hottes, 1933.
Gentians, David Wilkie, London, 1936.
Fertilizers and Crop Production, L. L. Van Slyke, 1932.
Daylilies, Dr. A. B. Stout, 1934.
The Flowering Plants, Grasses, Sedges and Ferns of Great Britain, 6 vols., Ann Pratt, London.
Plant Propagation, Alfred C. Hottes, 1934.
The Living Garden, E. J. Salisbury, London, 1936.
Weeds, W. C. Muenscher, 1935.
First Gourd Book, Helen M. Tillinghast, 1935.
Adventures with Hardy Bulbs, Louise Beebe Wilder, 1936.

Respectfully submitted,

FLORENCE E. FIELD, *Librarian*

December 3, 1936

REPORT OF THE JUDGE OF PLANTS AND FLOWERS

Mr. President and Members of the
Worcester County Horticultural Society:

The Spring Show which is the most important of the season brought out some very fine exhibits. The garden and plant displays were good, the largest of which were arranged in the Main Hall and gave it the appearance of one large flower garden. There were fine displays of cactus, succulents, and herbs. Cut flowers were good, among which were fine vases of antirrhinums, calla lilies, gerberas, anemones, and sweet peas.

April 23. Noteworthy on this date were the table decorations and a fine display of flowering plants from Charles Potter, and a group of well grown French hydrangeas showing the newest varieties exhibited by R. J. Allen.

May 14. Table decorations were again the feature with several very good plant exhibits.

At the Iris Exhibition on June 4 there were fine displays of German iris and wild flowers. Standards of cut flowers were largely shown.

On June 11 large displays of peonies were in competition, also good exhibits of roses.

From this date on during the summer at the regular weekly exhibitions the class for 20 vases of cut flowers was well filled with flowers of a high grade and great variety and exhibits of Japanese iris, delphiniums, lilies, sweet peas, and roses. Extensive exhibits of gladioli and annuals were shown on August 6. The class for small vase of flowers shown on a mirror proved to be popular, there being 25 exhibits, and again on August 13, 30 exhibits were in competition.

August 27 was one of the best shows of the season. There were fine displays of cut flowers, dahlias, and asters. A large number of standards and baskets were exhibited. There is a tendency on the part of many exhibitors in these two classes to crowd too much material into their exhibits. This detracts greatly from the artistic effect.

Early September brought out fine displays of dahlias, tuberous rooted begonias and table decorations.

Chrysanthemum Show. The plant and garden exhibits were good, some vases of large flowered cut chrysanthemums were exceptionally fine. The displays of hardy fruits and berries, fern globes, and ferneries were good.

In the upper hall there were 15 table decorations in competition for Special Prizes offered by Mrs. Gage and a fine display of carnations exhibited by the Worcester County members of the New England Carnation Society. This was one of the finest and most tastefully arranged exhibits in the Show and was arranged by Harry Randall.

In connection with the Chrysanthemum Exhibition, it is my opinion, that in addition to the special display of plants, provision ought to be made for garden arrangements which would not be in competition with the plant displays. I suggest that the Exhibition Committee give this their consideration.

Respectfully submitted,

WILLIAM ANDERSON, *Judge of Plants and Flowers*

December 3, 1936

EDWARD W. BREED, SPRING 1936

, tuberous

ibits were
ere excep-
rn globes,

ompetition
of carna-
New Eng-
and most
by Harry

s my opin-
sion ought
in compe-
tion Com-

Flowers

REPORT OF JUDGE OF FRUIT

Mr. President and Members of the
Worcester County Horticultural Society:

The season of 1936 will be recorded as one of many extremes. First the spring flood which did so much damage in many sections of Worcester County, and then the period of drought which was the longest and most severe that this section has experienced for years, and last the extreme cold weather early in the fall.

The fruit season also experienced many extremes. The spring opened with practically a full bloom of most varieties of fruit, and yet at harvest time we had one of the smallest crops of apples this section has harvested in about twenty years, due to the poor set of fruit, drought, disease, damage, and severe storms.

In spite of these extremes the showing of fruit this season has been up to the usual standard of quality and quantity, and throughout the season most classes were well filled.

The most important varieties of fruit as shown by the exhibits this season are as follows: Strawberries, Howard No. 17; raspberries, Lathan; grapes, Worden, Concord and Niagara; pears, Bartlett, Clapp's Favorite, Seckel and Bosc; peaches, Elberta; and apples, Baldwin, McIntosh and Northern Spy. Many of these varieties have been standard for some time, but we also had exhibited many new varieties of fruit some of which are sure to become standard as Fredonia grape, Golden Jubilee peach, etc.

Some of our older varieties of fruits, especially apples, peaches, and plums, are gradually disappearing and in a few years will be out of the market.

Blueberries are being shown in increasing numbers and possibly we should have a call for this delicious fruit.

This season the displays of fruit have increased in number and improved in quality and have added considerably to our exhibits.

We have not, however, had many exhibitors in the standard box classes, and I would suggest that we supplement this class for one season with flats of apples.

Respectfully submitted,

S. Lothrop Davenport, *Judge of Fruit*

December 3, 1936

REPORT OF JUDGE OF VEGETABLES

Mr. President and Members of the
Worcester County Horticultural Society:

I hereby submit my report as Judge of Vegetables for 1936.

The Spring Show, March 12 to 15 inclusive, saw a fine exhibition of vegetables, both of the fresh hothouse grown ones and the cellar stored ones.

The past season was one in which at least some specimens were shown on the day scheduled in all but three instances; namely, peas, any variety on June 11; peas, Sutton's Excelsior on June 25, and sweet corn, any variety on July 16. In ten classes, however, there was only one exhibit of the variety shown on the day scheduled. Most of these instances were in the early part of the season.

Out of a total of 636 exhibits in all classes during the year, exclusive of the Spring Show, cabbages lead in the number of exhibits with 58, closely followed by potatoes and squash with 55 and 54 exhibits, respectively. The other vegetables were shown in the following quantities: onions 42; shell beans 38; tomatoes 37; displays of vegetables 29; string beans 26; peas and rhubarb 22 each; sweet corn 20; celery, parsnips, and peppers 18 each; turnips 16; lettuce 15; asparagus 11; carrots 10; cauliflower, field beans, and mushrooms 9 each; parsley, pumpkins, beets, and gourds 8 each; melons, pepper display, and spinach 7 each; broccoli, and tomato display 6 each; dandelions, cucumbers, and radishes 5 each; pickling cucumbers, salsify, and squash collections 4 each; eggplants 3; grains 2; and brussels sprouts, endive, and leeks 1 each.

Onions lead in the largest number of exhibits of any one kind at a single exhibition with 23 at our November show. Among the other larger ones were cabbage and tomatoes with 20 exhibits each at our August 27 and September 10 shows, respectively, and potatoes with 19 exhibits at our November show.

The various displays of vegetables, both of the single kind and of an assortment of kinds, are still one of the most attractive features of our exhibitions; peppers and gourds being especially colorful and do much to make the vegetable exhibits almost as beautiful and pleasing as the fruit or flower exhibitions are.

The children made two very creditable exhibitions this year, with several newcomers in their ranks, showing that they are not losing interest in our Society.

Several of the children exhibitors of past years have graduated from that class and have become exhibitors in the adult classes with very gratifying results, showing that the training received as children has proved of value both to themselves and to the Society.

We hope this interest will continue for years to come, as no doubt it will.

Respectfully submitted,

H. WARD MOORE, *Judge of Vegetables*

December 3, 1936

REPORT OF FINANCE COMMITTEE

To the Members of the
Worcester County Horticultural Society:

The financial status of the Society is evidenced in the Treasurer's report and, as you may observe, indicates a satisfactory outcome of the year's transactions.

The main source of income is from the real estate located on Front Street, formerly used in part as the Society's headquarters. The present lease of the property in its entirety was made with the F. W. Woolworth Company, effective as of June 1, 1924, at which time our present location (30 Elm Street) was purchased. The new building, which is free of debt, serves our purposes in an adequate way, and because of its modern construction, but little outlay is required for its maintenance. It is advisable, therefore, in these days of opportunity, to clear the indebtedness from the Front Street property and thus be the better prepared for future requirements.

The last annual meeting granted an appropriation of $10,000 to be distributed by the Trustees for the purpose of awarding premiums and paying salaries during the year of 1936. The members of your Finance Committee recommend like action for the coming year.

Since the election of Herbert W. Estabrook on December 1, 1920, to membership on the Finance Committee, there had been no change in its personnel until his death on April 28, 1936. During his term of service, there arose many questions of policy vitally affecting the future of the Society. Always, and with utmost fidelity, he gave freely of his time to the consideration of these problems, and his discussion of them reflected the benefit of his wide business experience. His associates on the committee extol his virtues and miss him from their councils.

It is the recommendation of the undersigned that this tribute to his memory be adopted by the Society, to be entered upon the records, and that a copy with our sympathy be forwarded to his family.

Respectfully submitted,

MYRON F. CONVERSE,
LEONARD C. MIDGLEY,
Finance Committee

Worcester, Massachusetts
December 3, 1936

The following tribute to the memory of Herbert W. Estabrook is contained in the report of the Finance Committee of the Worcester County Horticultural Society submitted at the annual meeting held in Worcester, December 3, 1936.

IN MEMORIAM

"Since the election of Herbert W. Estabrook on December 1, 1920, to membership on the Finance Committee, there had been no change in its personnel until his death on April 28, 1936. During his term of service, there arose many questions of policy vitally affecting the future of the Society. Always, and with utmost fidelity, he gave freely of his time to the consideration of these problems, and his discussion of them reflected the benefit of his wide business experience. His associates on the committee extol his virtues and miss him from their councils.

"It is the recommendation of the undersigned that this tribute to his memory be adopted by the Society, to be entered upon the records, and that a copy with our sympathy be forwarded to his family."

Respectfully submitted,

MYRON F. CONVERSE,
LEONARD C. MIDGLEY,
Finance Committee

Adopted by the Society.
Herbert R. Kinney,
Secretary
December 3, 1936

ANNUAL MEETING OF THE SOCIETY

Thursday, December 5, 1935

President Myron F. Converse called the meeting to order at 10 a.m. "by his wrist watch." Forty-four present.

Secretary read the call for the meeting.

Secretary read the records of the last Annual Meeting of the Society.

President Converse declared them approved.

President Myron F. Converse delivered his Annual Address.

The following reports were read:

Secretary, Herbert R. Kinney; Treasurer, Burt W. Greenwood; Librarian, Mrs. Florence E. Field; Judge of Flowers, William Anderson; Judge of Fruits, S. Lothrop Davenport; Judge of Vegetables, H. Ward Moore.

These reports were accepted and referred to the Committee on Library and Publication.

Report of the Finance Committee by Mr. Leonard C. Midgley. This report recommended an appropriation of ten thousand dollars for premiums and salaries for the coming year.

On Mr. Harry Harrison's motion this report was accepted and adopted.

Memorials for our late Trustees were presented by Mrs. Amy W. Smith for Miss Lucy M. Coulson, Mr. Edward W. Breed for Mr. David L. Fiske, and Herbert R. Kinney for Fred L. Chamberlain.

These memorials were each accepted by a rising vote.

Mr. Ernest Hansen reported for the Nominating Committee.

President Myron F. Converse asked if there were any more nominations.

There being none, he asked Mr. John Bowker to cast a yea ballot for the candidates as nominated.

He cast the ballot, and President Converse declared them elected.

There being no further business, the meeting dissolved.

HERBERT R. KINNEY, *Secretary*

ANNUAL MEETING OF THE TRUSTEES

Thursday, December 12, 1935

Meeting called to order at 10 a.m. by President Myron F. Converse. Twenty-three present.

Secretary read the records of the last Annual Meeting of the Trustees.

President Converse declared them approved.

President Converse said that the first business was the selecting of the committees; that the Trustees would find a list of the present committees in the premium lists you have.

There was a vacancy on the Library Committee caused by Miss Coulson's death and he would suggest that our present Librarian, Mrs. Florence E. Field, fill her place.

He would suggest that Mrs. Bertha G. Denny be a member of the Committee on Arrangements and Exhibitions.

He had no suggestions for changes of Auditors, Judges, Medal, or Winter Meetings. He awaited suggestions.

There being no other changes recommended, he declared the committees with the changes recommended elected.

President Converse read a list of the appropriations for the coming year.

Mr. Allen J. Jenkins made a motion "That the schedule as read be adopted." So voted.

Appropriation for 1936.................. .... $10,000.00

PREMIUMS

Flowers..................	$1,800.00	
Fruits....................	1,000.00	
Vegetables.............	800.00	
Children's Exhibition........	300.00	
Spring Exhibition..........	1,600.00	
Chrysanthemum Exhibition..	1,400.00	
Miscellaneous.............	225.00	$7,125.00

SALARIES

Treasurer...	$350.00		
Secretary..................	1,000.00		
Librarian..........	1,000.00		
Assistant to Secretary.......	125.00		
Judges....................	400.00	$2,875.00	$10,000.00

Mrs. Homer Gage recommended that the Society have some oblong tables.

Adjourned.

HERBERT R. KINNEY, *Secretary*

ANNUAL MEETING OF THE COMMITTEE C
ARRANGEMENTS AND EXHIBITIONS

December 19, 1935

President Myron F. Converse called the meeting to order at 9 a.m. Seventeen present.

On Mrs. Percy G. Forbes's motion, Mr. Allen J. Jenkins was chosen chairman.

On Mr. Midgley's motion, it was voted to enforce rule 8.

Rule 9. It was voted to insert the word "only" after "County" in the second line.

Rule 14. It was voted to substitute "May" for "Shall" be debarred from competition for the Society's premiums until reinstated.

On Mrs. Denny's motion, it was voted to cut out the scale of points for Table Decorations in the call and place them with the other scales of points.

Chairman Jenkins appointed Mrs. Forbes, Miss Bishop, Mrs. Taft, Mrs. Denny, and Mrs. Field a committee to revise the scale of points and the schedule for Table Decorations.

It was voted to hold the Spring Exhibition March 12, 13, 14 and 15.

It was voted to put back in the schedule the April and the first June Exhibition that were dropped last year with a few minor changes.

August 20 and 27 and September 3—Two classes of cut flowers.

The dahlia premiums were carried forward.

Some slight changes in the arranging of prizes for the Chrysanthemum Exhibition.

The Children's Exhibitions were left with the Secretary.

Adjourned.

HERBERT R. KINNEY, *Secretary*

"MIRACLES IN NATURE"

Thursday, January 9

Illustrated Lecture

By Mr. Arthur Pillsbury, Berkeley, Cal.

Most remarkable results have been obtained recently by a method of growing vegetables and flowers without soil. For over one hundred and thirty years this method has been used, but it is only within the last two years that it has been considered practical for commercial purposes. It is still in the experimental stage; but it is hoped that within a year or two most of the so-called "city dwellers" can raise all the vegetables and flowers they need in the small areas available to them.

Anyone wishing to experiment with this method should proceed as follows:

Over a tank of water six inches deep place wire netting, similar to mosquito wire. Cover this with excelsior or straw, adding sawdust if planting seeds. Secure a bottle having a cork with two glass tubes going through it; fill the bottle with a chemical—the formula of which can be obtained from Mr. Pillsbury—and place the bottle on its side in the water.

On the screen, Professor Gary was shown weighing out the eleven essential elements plants must have. He put them into a one-pound bottle and placed the bottle in the tank of water. No water or chemical will need to be added during the growth of the plants.

The same chemical formula is being used for growing everything at the present time, but experimental work is being done with different formulas for different things.

In planting potatoes by this method, cut them up the same as in planting them in the soil; but, instead of planting them in hills and rows, you place the pieces in the excelsior about six inches apart. Tomato plants should be twelve inches apart either way. When planting seeds be sure to add sawdust to the excelsior.

Results obtained by growing potatoes and tomatoes in this tank method would indicate the great commercial value of this way. Experiments show that from two thousand to three thousand bushels of potatoes can be raised to the acre and from $50,000 to $75,000 worth of tomatoes, basing the selling price at 15 cents a pound, the wholesale price during March when the tomatoes ripened.

The plants grown by the tank method are much larger than those grown in the soil. Potato plants grow to a height of four feet and some tomato plants in a greenhouse grew twenty-five feet. The size and the flavor of the tomatoes are the same as those grown by the soil method, indeed they cannot be told apart. Potatoes look the same as those grown in the soil, but do not attain the size of the large Idaho potatoes. There is no difference in the flavor.

In answer to a question, Mr. Pillsbury stated that the plants grow so much more rapidly in the tank method, they are not apt to be infected by disease or to be bothered by insects.

Extensive experiments are also being made with other vegetables, especially cucumbers. On the screen, Mr. Pillsbury was shown picking a squash plant out of a tank and putting it back again. All sorts of things were growing in this same tank, including some very beautiful begonias, gladioli, chrysanthemums, radishes, and carrots. The tank was about two feet wide and ten feet long, made of a light framework of wood, plastered with cement.

In growing flowers by this method, the seeds may be put into excelsior and sawdust in a small basket, which can be set in the tank. When the plants blossom, the baskets can be lifted out and put in a container in the house.

Most of the experiments of growing flowers by this method were made with wild flowers. Technicolor motion pictures were shown of flowers growing in their natural habitat, some of them having the beautiful Yosemite Valley for a background. Flowers which seldom grow more than twelve or fifteen inches high in their natural habitat grew four feet high in the tank method and the blossoms were much larger. Thus, many wild flowers can be developed into wonderful house plants. Natural color pictures of these flowers, taken over long periods, showed them opening and closing. Some wild flowers are so regular in opening and closing that one might build a clock out of them. Lapsed time pictures showed plants growing.

R. J. Allen, Spring 1936

Flowers from all over the country have been used in experiments and pictures shown include the following flowers: cactus, star cactus, nightblooming cereus, chrysanthemums, woolly bears, yellow daisies, Johnny jump-ups, oxalis, California poppy, milkweed, thistle, scarlet bugler, iris or blue flag, leopard lily, regal lily, tiger lily, verbena, and sea daisy.

If Mr. Burbank had used this tank method for his experiments, he could have accomplished in a little space that which took many acres.

Experiments with flowers by putting them in different chemicals made interesting pictures and showed that almost the same sort of reaction took place in plant life that took place in animal life. Flowers in aspirin died in six hours, flowers in strychnine and digitalis lived somewhat longer; but those in water lasted three days. Flowers put into bootleg also died very quickly.

Mr. Pillsbury's laboratory is in the basement of his home and contains five different units, all of which can be running at one time or only one at a time. It represents an investment of $45,000 in cameras and microscopes. In addition, the cameras used for taking lapsed time pictures are rented from the moving picture studios, as they cannot be bought. They are worth $10,000 each.

Pictures of the tandem microscopic cameras and the manner in which they work were shown. Pictures taken with these cameras showed the action of two different kinds of mold on two pieces of bread and also the quickness with which bacteria destroyed the mold, illustrating the constant war by one form of life on another.

Many difficulties have yet to be overcome in combining technicolor with microscopic camera.

From pictures taken with these tandem microscopic cameras it has been definitely shown that protoplasm does go from one cell to another, which has been disputed among scientists for years. Mr. Pillsbury said, "Protoplasm is life," and quoted Huxley as terming protoplasm the basis of life. The enormous activity of protoplasm was shown by moving pictures taken with these cameras.

The story of the spirillum, which is found on stagnant water, was told and pictured. Technicolor moving pictures showed it being gathered from the water. It is yellowish on the surface and greenish underneath. At night it sinks to the bottom of the water. When the sun shines on it, it manufactures oxygen. We were next shown pictures taken under the microscopic cameras of the conjugating stage, which occurs in the spring. These pictures showed that the actual passing of the male cell takes fifteen minutes and that it takes five or six hours, as it runs into the spores, to form fertile spores.

We also saw the X-ray motion picture camera with which some of the pictures were made. It does not use a lense and is a very expensive process to use. It is believed this method of taking pictures will open up many fields of experimental research work. A rosebud, which was used as a subject for pictures in this camera, lasted many days longer than it ordinarily would last.

The second miracle is the story of the green leaf. There are three classes of leaves, leaves that resemble the oak leaf, the blade of grass, and the pine needle.

The enormous energy and power of cells in one layer of a leaf were pictured by the microscopic X-ray camera. Multiply the number of cells by all the leaves in the world and you can see how much power is developed. More power is developed by these cells than there is in all the locomotives in the world. We may harness that power sometime.

There are more complications in the movements of cells of a leaf than in any instrument made.

There are so many things going on in life all the time, one cannot be a student of life and an atheist.

"FLORA OF WESTERN SCOTLAND"

Thursday, January 16

Illustrated Lecture

By Dr. J. R. Jack, Cambridge, Mass.

The flora of any country depends largely on two factors: the geological construction of the country and the climate. In both of these Scotland is rather peculiar.

Although small, Scotland is divided into two almost equal parts by what is known as the "Great Highland Fault." To the north of that fault are the Highlands—rough, sharp mountains with deep valleys; while to the south are the lowlands, much "flatter" country.

The fairly mild climate is very remarkable when we consider the latitude. However, this is governed to a large extent by the fact that the Gulf Stream flows right up the west coast and the prevailing winds are southwest, so that usually there is a good deal of moisture.

Many visitors to Scotland are surprised at some of the plants growing there. In one garden there was some Mountain Laurel growing between two palm trees. The palm trees blossomed but the laurel did not. Rhododendrons particularly thrive there, better than anywhere else, except in their native land.

In the past botanists studied dried plants. While the study of dried plants is necessary, yet they are only mummies. Now botanists study living plants and measure them up with their associates.

Very beautiful colored slides of the various flowers of Scotland were shown, among which are the following: dog violet, which is about the earliest of the spring flowers; harebell, which is claimed by scientists as the "bluebell of Scotland" and which blossoms by thousands after the longest day of the year is past; wild hyacinth, which is claimed by common people as the "bluebell of Scotland" and which blossoms by millions; and yellow iris, which is not as beautiful as the blue iris of New England. In the slide showing the dog violet, there were lichens growing. They flourish only in a clear atmosphere.

Some interesting facts were told about gorse, which has a beautiful yellow flower with a faint but sweet perfume. When the plant is young the leaves are soft; but very quickly it seems to find this a "hard world," as it turns its leaves into spikes. There is a saying that "Kissing goes out of fashion when the gorse goes out of bloom." This is literally and absolutely true. However, the plant does its best to live up to its responsibilities by blossoming from the first of January until the thirty-first of December.

It is difficult to know just which plants are native and indigenous and which escape from gardens. Some think the lily of the valley is an escape.

A picture of the English mayflower, which is the hawthorn, showed one mass of white flowers with lovely red anthers.

Scenes of Scotland taken in the springtime included a picture of a stone cottage with thatched roof in a state of decay. The older folks of Scotland lived in such houses. Oftentimes the thatched roof would be covered with a mass of flowers.

"Nature's method of taking care of a bad season" is illustrated by the seeds of the snow gentian, an annual, whose seeds have vitality for a number of years. This flower takes the place of the fringed gentian of North America.

The mountain Alpine forget-me-not is found on only one mountain in Scotland. Unlike many Alpine plants it can be grown in a Lowland garden.

A piece of parsley fern, covering four acres on the side of a hill, can be seen five miles away in clear weather. This fern looks a great deal like parsley, but does not have the strong scent of it.

Club moss is a plant which grows half way up the mountainside; Swedish dogwood is an arctic plant with purple flowers and silvery white bracts, growing only in the northern part of Scotland; Sedum Angelicum grows only on the driest rocks; chickweed wintergreen only grows where there are pine needles; and Epilobiums are very nice as wild flowers, but are undesirable for gardens.

Colored time photographs can be utilized for photographing other forms of nature. A butterfly was shown sleeping on a branch with head down, when a cloud obscured the sun, and a female ghost moth was shown just as she emerged from a chrysalis to dry her wings.

It was proved that Nature is just as expert as the best artist in arranging color schemes by a slide showing several different colored flowers.

Among other flowers shown by slides were yellow sedum, marsh marigold, cow wheat, purple gentian, white gentian, waterlily, Drosera Angelica, Drosera Rotundifolia, wood sage, sow thistle, dandelion, wild heath, heather, veronica, honeysuckle, marsh aster, wild geranium or cranesbill, Hypericum or St. John's-wort, autumn crocus, and flowering rush.

Many interesting stories were told about various flowers. A miner in Ayrshire sowed some seeds of Vipers-Bugloss in a pile of black bing, a residue from coal mining, and transformed it into a mass of beautiful blue.

In the long ago the devil's foot plant was celebrated for its many cures of difficult diseases. Tradition says that whenever anyone was cured of a disease by this plant, he became an adherent to the Church. The devil did not like this at all, so he sent his imps to cut off the roots of the flower. When the plant found itself dying, it called out to Heaven for aid. It was enabled to send out many roots above where it was cut off and was thus enabled to live. This plant has a great mass of roots surrounding a center root which looks as though it had been cut off.

Several entertaining things were told about the thistle, the emblem of Scotland. During a surprise attack by the Danes when they were trying to conquer the Scots, a Dane stepped on a thistle. He made such a clamor that it woke the Scots and the Danes were defeated.

The honey of the thistle very often ferments and the bees become intoxicated. Frogs seem to understand this, and you will often see a fat frog sitting at the bottom of a plant waiting for the bees to fall off. The same thing happens in New England and did even during prohibition.

An American told Dr. Jack that America has three grievances against England: first, the English sparrow; second, the orange hockweed; and third, the Irish voter. The orange hockweed is one of the wild flowers of Scotland.

Most people are not aware that ivy has a flower. It is a most attractive bait for moths.

Dr. Jack claims "Poverty has its advantages." Scotland, having only one kind of goldenrod, does not become embroiled in discussions over the various species as this country does.

The yew tree in this country does not have fruit, but in Scotland it does. The fruit is not considered to be dangerous, although the root and tree are poisonous. No one, however, seems willing to prove the edibility of the fruit. The fruit of the blackthorn has a bloom which is very like that found on grapes.

In the pictures of holly that were shown, the berry was white. The berries begin to show color by November and are at their best at Christmas time.

Several pictures of fungus, showed both the poisonous and the edible varieties.

Beautiful pictures of wonderful Highland scenery portrayed mountains, rivers and autumn scenes. It was interesting to note that the maple leaves turned to a dull russet instead of the brilliant hues that we have in the autumn in New England.

Because the lecture was being given before a Horticultural Society, several slides of garden scenes were shown.

The final picture, taken in the fall, showed the "Bonny, bonny banks of Loch Lomond" with a snow-capped mountain in the background.

"OUR ISLAND KINGDOM IN THE PACIFIC"

Thursday, January 23, 1936

Illustrated Lecture

By CHARLES H. TOZIER, BOSTON, MASS.

The Hawaiian Islands were discovered by Captain James Cook in 1778. When he reported the discovery in England, he was unable to adequately describe their beauty and unusualness.

The dawn of civilization in these islands came in the year 1820, when a band of twenty-two missionaries sailed from Boston. There is standing today in Honolulu a replica of Park Street Church, Boston, built in memory of this band of missionaries. Colored slides of the exterior showed the only difference between the two churches was the absence of a clock on the tower of the Honolulu Church. The interior is finished in white stucco with mahogany trim and fixtures—a typical New England Colonial church.

By way of the moving picture camera, we sailed aboard the *Empress of Japan,* the largest and finest boat on the Pacific, into the harbor of Honolulu. We noticed how well the harbor was sheltered by the surrounding mountains, were told that "Diamond Head" was so well fortified that it was known as the Gibraltar of the Pacific, were welcomed by "Aloha Tower" and a band of musicians, were entertained by boys diving for coins tossed into the water, and were greeted by friends with bouquets of beautiful flowers and by natives selling them.

We saw the sandy beach on which Captain Cook landed and a memorial to the first Christian service held on the Island. This was the burial service of a seaman which took place January 28, 1779.

We were shown the ancient palace, which housed the former kings and queens and, by way of contrast, a building of modern architecture.

The statue of the king who received the first missionaries was surrounded by beautiful flowers and trees; in fact, we saw so many marvelous flowers and such magnificent foliage that our eyes became drugged with beauty. In scenes along the coast were all kinds of palm trees, bushes of beautiful poincianas, with both red and yellow blossoms, and banyan trees covering large areas.

The homes of the natives are huts of straw with only one door and no windows. In front of the hut are generally all the possessions of a native. A "well-to-do" native may possess a dug-out canoe, a fishing net, a surf board and some water bottles.

In front of one hut we saw a boy making flower chains and his sister splitting reeds which the mother wove into mats for the floor. In order to get a drink, the boy walked up a very tall palm tree, with the greatest of ease, picked some cocoanuts and threw them down to the ground. After descending, he split open the husks by pounding the cocoanuts on a pick stuck in the ground with the point upwards. Then he made a hole in the shell and proceeded to drink the milk.

In front of another hut we saw a one-man band, consisting of father rapping on a gourd and singing, and mother doing the Hula Hula. This is a religious dance which shows the traditions of the tribe and is also done to appease the wrath of the gods. The natives are very serious about doing this dance and each action has a meaning. We saw four very beautiful girls dance by moonlight the dance of the sea, the gourd dance or harvest dance, the cocoanut or fruit dance, and the fire or volcano dance.

Some of the natives make a living by selling coral. The white coral sells for less than the colored. We wondered where such marvelous colors came from, and upon investigation found mother and daughter very busy with paint brushes.

Even though the native huts seemed very primitive in comparison with the bungalow homes of the more prosperous people, still both were surrounded by the same beauties of nature.

A more startling contrast even than these were shown by the breath-taking beauty of the estates of two very wealthy men.

Several roads leading into the first one we saw were lined with cocoanut and royal palms. We might almost say the house was embedded in gorgeous flowers and foliage. A most magnificent indoor tree fern was growing on an arched piazza, and all the plants and flowers in and around the house were the finest specimens of their kinds.

The Japanese garden on this estate is one of the most beautiful anywhere, and compares favorably with any of the fine gardens in Japan.

In addition to many of the flowers which grow in our own gardens, such as delphiniums, dahlias, roses, petunias, begonias, etc. the various gardens on this estate had red poincianas, godetias, passion flowers, yellow allamandas, poinsettias, fuchsias, red pepper bushes, apple cactus, star cactus, bougainvillea, many varieties of orchids, and many trees and flowers which Dr. Tozier did not name. As Dr. Tozier said, there are no words to describe the beauties of these gardens which require the care of one hundred Japanese laborers.

The second home belongs to a man with an income of $30,000 a month. The most interesting thing on this estate was an aquarium in a beautiful setting of trees, vines and flowers. Movies taken of a devilfish in one of the tanks showed the fascinating movements of this repulsive fish and his ability to change his color to match his background. It is hard to conceive why the natives consider the eyes of this fish a great delicacy, nevertheless we saw them dive for a devilfish, bring it up and bite out the eyes.

It was interesting to see the water for this aquarium being aerated by trickling it through vines. Some of the roses in the surroundings of this aquarium were eight inches in diameter and were very beautiful.

Some interesting contrasts were also shown in the paintings of a French artist, done in 1800, of his conceptions of the natives of Hawaii and the natives' conceptions of themselves.

We also saw the magnificent robes, head dresses, etc. which the early kings and queens wore, made of the feathers of brilliant colored birds. It took 150,000 to 200,000 birds to make one cape. These are preserved in the Bishop Museum in Honolulu and are the finest specimens of feather work in the world.

In the garden surrounding the Mormon Temple were daisies ten inches across. They have very light yellow centers and are a Japanese variety. There was a large plot of very deep red single begonias, also some wonderful dahlias, twelve inches and fourteen inches across, and in the loveliest colors.

We saw many peculiar trees—monkey trees, trees which had fruit looking exactly like hot dogs or bologna sausages, date palm

CHARLES POTTER, ALBERT W. SCHNEIDER, SPRING 1936

trees on which the dates do not mature, and paw-paw trees. There was also a very fine specimen of an out-door tree fern, twenty-five feet high.

The night-blooming cereus, a cactus plant whose blossoms last only one night and wilt about 5:00 o'clock in the morning, makes us wonder why nature grows such a beautiful flower for so short a duration of time.

It is hard to realize the years of training which are needed to perfect one in the art of surf-board riding as we watched the ease with which the boys and men engaged in this difficult sport.

The "flowers of the sea," as Dr. Tozier would say, that one catches when he goes fishing are very unusual to say the least. We have our suspicions that many fishermen would like to catch the porcupine fish which has what looks like a corkscrew growing out of his head just above the eye. There is also the fish which has what looks like two mouths. The story goes that if he gets a hook in his mouth he simply discards the inner mouth and gets away. At least a fisherman would have some proof for his story of the fish that got away.

We also saw three specimens of the star flower cactus, called the silver sword. There is a single stock with hundreds of white stems on the ends of which are yellow star flowers. These were growing right out of rocks in the center of a crater of a volcano with no other green thing in sight.

The most awe-inspiring part of the trip was seeing the volcano "Killauea" in full action. It was hard to believe that this moving mass could be rock, although we were told it was molten rock with a temperature of from 900° to 1000° and would destroy everything before it.

The effect at night was one of even more grandeur. A spatter of red, flaring up in the black night, reminded Dr. Tozier of the mud geysers at Yellowstone National Park. Two streams of lava flowing towards each other seemingly disappeared right down into the earth. Fountains of red lava threw fragments of rock twenty-five feet high. We can hardly wonder that the natives worship such a manifestation of nature and live in fear of it.

With a look at one of God's great pictures—a sunset—we end a perfect day in the Island Kingdom of the Pacific.

"THE USE OF FLOWERS IN THE HOME AND IN DESIGN WORK"

THURSDAY, January 30

Illustrated Lecture

By Donald White and Two Assistants, Wakefield, Mass.

In flower arrangement we take the principles of design and apply them to the things which flowers possess.

In all art the first things we must have is some conception in our own minds of that which we wish to produce. Many people take flowers and try an arrangement merely hoping that the result will be what they like to see. The result is always disappointing.

The second rule is to keep your composition as natural as possible.

The third rule is not to overdo the use of units in a flower arrangement.

The three principles which art imposes upon us are first, rhythm; second, balance; and third, harmony.

It is rather difficult to always clearly sense the distinction between rhythm and harmony, because many arrangements have both principles very highly developed.

We may think of rhythm as force in motion, or, as applied to color, a flow of color or movement. Generally we think of harmony as a static force. Sometimes we have harmony that is really kinetic in form, but in the concept of our minds is static.

To illustrate this point Mr. White took the composition which Miss Goldwaithe had been making and which was designed to show tone rhythm. A bouquet of pink sweet peas, starting on the left with a very light pink, shading towards a medium pink in the center, with darker pink on the right, showing a horizontal flow of color. This flow of color may be horizontal or vertical and may travel the entire spectral scale, but this is unnecessary in the average composition. In addition to the flow of color or rhythm in this arrangement, we have a common unit and accord in color. Now if we took these same flowers and mixed them up, we would lose the rhythm, but would still have harmony, but a concept of harmony which remains static. It will not be in motion.

We have in flowers three qualities; tone or color shade, measure or size of the units, and shape. In most American decoration color has been emphasized to the almost total exclusion of both size and shape.

There are certain other qualities to flowers such as odor, etc., which are personal matters and will not be discussed here.

When we have tone rhythm, the next principle with which we have to deal is tone balance. We can most easily obtain balance with symmetry; that is, take an element and balance one on each side. Balace should inspire a feeling of rest or response. If there is anything in a composition to disturb that feeling, you may be sure that the composition is not correct.

The receptacle used very often influences this principle. If a receptacle is too small at the base, it gives a feeling of fear that it may tip over, or a feeling of instability and we lose the feeling of balance.

We have in the second composition, consisting of King Alfred narcissus and William Copeland tulips, the question of applying to color or tone the principle of balance.

The simpler types of arrangements in flowers are much more satisfactory and we may take a lesson in this from the Japanese. We cannot, however, take Japanese art as it is practiced in Japan and make it American art. It is Oriental and can never be American. The Japanese, however, have taught us many things.

It is very interesting to see how Japanese floral art was developed. At the time Columbus discovered America it was at its height. In the very early days when the Japanese wanted to give votive offerings to the Gods, they brought green twigs. As time went on they started bringing flowers. The increasing influence of ancestor worship gradually led them to give flowers to parents and gradually developed into the giving of flowers to friends. We have then a very strong religious background, and even today in Japan the question of floral arrangement is a formal and social occasion. For this reason we must be very careful how we interpret their art in connection with ours. The Japanese art in floral arrangement is very largely one of simplicity.

Our floral art today is something very different from that of twenty-five years ago. Grandmother's' bouquet was a symbol of something which we admired, but from an artistic point of view something was lacking.

To illustrate the applying to tone the principle of harmony, we take the carnation. It is a peculiar flower in many ways and is much maligned. It has lost favor for a number of years as a flower for home decoration. People have decided it is obsolete. Something seems to be wrong. The reason for this is so obvious, it seems strange we have not found the trouble before. We put green asparagus fern or some other fern with them, in which the green is a yellow green, thereby effectively killing the carnations. The carnation must be judged by its own foliage which is a blue-green.

Then we must study the arrangement of carnations. In the first place lay an inconspicuous piece of arbor vitae or spruce as a holder in the top of the receptacle. This enables us to place the flower in the position desired. Then we should take another lesson from the Japanese. Take the stem of a carnation between the forefingers and thumbs of both hands and give a breaking motion in the direction in which you desire the stem to curve. In this manner you will discover that you may do anything you desire with your flowers and make them bend any way in which you want them to.

The next thing to consider is rhythm of size, that is flowers ranging from buds to fully opened flowers. This was illustrated by a bouquet of calendulas with the buds at the top and graduating in size from half opened flowers in the center of the bouquet to fully opened blossoms at the base, showing vertical rhythm. This is most easily shown with one kind of flower rather than with two or more kinds.

The next composition showed another way of having rhythm of balance with units of different size. The smaller units were bunched at one side toward the base, thereby giving us a mass effect which takes away the difference in size of the units, so that neither detracts from the other, leaving a sense of balanced arrangement. This can be done much easier by simply putting the larger units at the base.

Generally to obtain measure or size harmony, we use sizes that are closely alike. In the next composition acacias and gerberas or

African daisies were used. They are very different in size, but were successfully combined. The failure or success in arranging these is determined by the way in which the size of either one stands out from the other.

Art is a question of the eye. An arrangement of flowers that pleases one person may not please another. If that were not so, how would some of our modern artists escape the guillotine?

This point was illustrated by the two large compositions Miss Callahan had arranged. Some of the audience liked the first arrangement, while the majority preferred the second. It is a matter of personal preference.

In making this arrangement Miss Callahan used one of the hardest flowers known to use, the calla. This plant belongs to the Arum family which includes the weirdest flowers. She was faced in the beginning with three things, the long stem, the size, and the shape of the calla. She combined with the calla the narcissus, in which we have something of the same motive in shape as the calla, then groups of sweet peas in lavender pink shades carrying out the motive of color and heather also in lavender shades. We should not mass callas too much, but must keep them to the central part.

Three sprays of umbrella palm, which is not a palm, but is sedge, much like sedge growing in our own fields and meadows, were arranged to show the Japanese motive. This was an all green composition with units the same shape and size, but arranged at different heights.

The next composition illustrated shape balance and was formed by a bouquet of snapdragons in a tall blue receptacle. In general, the height of the flowers above the receptacle should be, roughly, about one and one-half times the height of the container. With lower holders, however, that proportion increases rapidly. Choose a container whose lines will melt into the lines of the arrangement, one that will follow down from the flowers. Containers should not be noticeable. They should, as a rule, be darker in tone or color than the flowers, although occasionally there are instances where light yellow and some other types do fit, a gray container being the best of all.

The final arrangement showed shape harmony, and was what is called an old-fashioned bouquet. In a composition of this type the ultimate shape of the individual flower must approximate the shape of all the other flowers, regardless of size or color. You can put a great many colors and sizes together and get shape harmony, if you use the same shapes throughout the composition.

In a mixed bouquet of this type there are various points of interest and many people like this type. If a person is sick he will enjoy picking out the various flowers he recognizes.

We should not lose sight of individual choices. Many people like to use blue and silver at Christmas time. Mr. White, however, feels that as a foil to the darkness, to the clouds, to snow, and to nature when it is quiescent, we need color that is radiant. Blue and silver, while being a correct combination from an artistic point of view, act as a damper to the spirit of some people.

In closing Mr. White suggested that we take more time, not only in making floral arrangements but in doing all the other things we do. Americans rush too much. We are trying to get too many things in too short a time and we are getting nowhere. If we took more time to do things, we as a people would be happier and more contented, if not wealthier.

"ROCK GARDENS: THEIR LOCATION AND CONSTRUCTION"

Thursday, February 6

Illustrated Lecture

By CARL STANTON, PETERBOROUGH, N. H.

One can have more fun creating a Rock Garden than working with any other type of garden, because of the chance to use originality in design, different types of rocks and many varieties of plants.

There are two ways to approach the making of a Rock Garden, first, to make use of available locations and, second, to build to suit certain types of flowers that you desire to use.

If outcropping ledges can be made a part of a Rock Garden, they are a great aid to the designer in making the garden seem at home in its surroundings. A scene from a garden which was built around a ledge illustrated this most effectively. A few rocks of the same texture as the ledge were added around the base and up one side, forming uneven steps to the top. The stones added were carefully placed so that the stratification of the stones followed the same direction as that of the ledge.

Sometimes we have the problem of too much ledge showing with the added difficulty of the ledge not being very beautiful. Then we have to use great care in partially covering it with earth, so that plants will seem to be growing naturally and the added stones will seem to belong there.

Rock Gardens can be made very useful wholly aside from their artistic value. They may be constructed to act as screens for garages, drives and neighboring buildings.

We were shown pictures of the way in which an ugly view can be transformed into a beauty spot that may be made to be one of the features of the grounds. Flat rocks were imbedded in a bank where a roadway was cut through; bayberry, ferns, and ground juniper were planted among them, and a necessary evil was converted into a lovely landscape.

Often on estates which are extremely well developed there occurs one or more apparently useless and often untidy spaces that make ideal Rock Garden locations instead of being more or less a nuisance. One corner, where a gardener kept his mulch pile of leaf mold, was transformed into a lovely enclosed Rock Garden with a tiny pool surrounded by artificial banking that looked extremely natural. Rocks jutted out of the banking; the water trickled down over them and the plants and flowers looked "right at home" in the surroundings. A stream of water about a foot wide ran across the path at one point, so that you had to step over the "brooklet" in walking through the garden.

Rock Gardens are difficult things to handle and it is not easy to make them artistic and in harmony with the rest of the landscape. It is a real task to tie the informality of a Rock Garden up to the formality of the house. Ordinarily the greater the distance from the house, the easier it is to mold it into its surroundings and not have it look like a "sore thumb" or as out of place as an automobile tire painted white, filled with earth, and planted with purple geraniums. Occasionally, however, the house is built on a ledge or is surrounded by ledges. Even then, unless great care is taken, a Rock Garden planted on such a ledge will always seem to stand out instead of being part of the landscape. Several pictures illustrated this point.

To secure the right effect in a Rock Garden, it is well to exaggerate everthing. In planning one garden, Mr. Stanton visualized a scene in the White Mountains and then made an exaggerated miniature likeness to the cliffs, chasms and ledges of the mountain scene. Slopes on a site are a real help in this regard. In this particular garden, the house stood on one corner of a city block on a little knoll. By making a more decided slope so that the lawn became a valley, he made a path down into the woods which occupied the rest of the lot. It was hard to realize you were looking at a city garden, so well had the effect of a rustic scene been achieved.

It is well sometimes to know what not to do. The pictures, showing what not to do, disclosed a Rock Garden with the stones placed "any which way," giving a most untidy appearance. A Rock Garden that is not restful is vastly more untidy than any other kind of a garden.

Because a Rock Garden does not require much formality of de-

sign, it can be tied to the rest of the landscape in many queer little ways. One of these is by the use of stepping stones. If you want to call attention to your Rock Garden, make a gracefully curved stepping-stone path leading to it and build the simulated ledges to follow the same curve to the center or nucleus of your Rock Garden, which may be a little pool.

In one scene taken in a Connecticut garden, water trickled from a small fountain, followed a line of stepping stones down to a very small pool from which it flowed down into a second pool.

We were shown the actual work being done in the construction of a Rock Garden on a flat piece of ground. When excavating for the pool, the earth was thrown up around it to make a ragged appearance. Nothing was made even or formal. Flat rocks were embedded in the banking and uneven steps were built to the top, some of them being one and one-half feet to four feet wide, with a rise of from four inches to a foot. One may dispense with monotony by making the steps more or less steep and tortuous and of various grades and widths, with exaggerated ups and downs.

It is very important to secure the right kind of stones in building a Rock Garden. It is much easier to achieve a natural effect if the rocks are well weather worn. Flat type rocks are easiest to use, but occasionally other types may be added for accent. In the bank of one pool, one rock was left standing upright alongside the waterfall, to call attention to it.

It is not absolutely necessary to have water in a Rock Garden, but it does put life and sparkle into it. If striving for naturalness, be careful to see that the water issues out from between the rocks and not from the very top of the hill.

In the scene of a waterfall in New Hampshire, our attention was called to the way the water started near the top in a single stream, struck a little ledge and divided into two streams, when it disappeared behind another ledge and came out in four different streams.

This same idea was carried out in a Rock Garden with a very small amount of water being used over and over again. It was more effective than a large amount of water used incorrectly. A shady spot was selected for the waterfall. The water trickled over the stones, part of it falling directly into the pool, the rest of it following the rocks down a little further before falling into the pool, in different places.

We were shown several pictures of this particular garden, built near the house which was on a rocky ledge near the ocean. The pool was very shallow in one end, but by using black stones under the water and white ones on top, an appearance of depth was secured.

In constructing a pool be careful not to have too much of the cement work showing. Where cement work is shown, an artificial man-made effect, rather than a natural rustic effect, is the result. The bottom of the pool may be of cement with rocks added if desired, but the sides should look as though built of stones. Pile the stones, leaving about six inches behind them so the cement can be poured in back of them and can then be covered with earth.

If a pool begins to leak, it may be well to try the scheme of dumping a bag of cement into the water of the leaky pool and stirring it up once an hour during the day. As the cement hardens, it may repair the leak.

Somewhere in your Rock Garden design a seat. It is better to have the benches of a rustic type in keeping with the informality of a Rock Garden rather than a stiff, formal, cut-stone bench, or a well-made bench painted white. If there is a waterfall, place the bench nearby, so the music which it makes may be enjoyed.

A platform of stones can be called a Rock Garden. One scene showed such a garden with a planted wall as a background. In building a wall be sure to rest the stones on top of one another, filling in the cracks with loam and plenty of fertilizer. Limestone chips put in such a wall, also help give nourishment to the plants. In this particular garden, a pipe with small holes at intervals was buried in back of the wall, so the plants could be easily watered.

Big evergreens are a great help in making a Rock Garden. In the winter time they are especially attractive. They make a vertical accent which is very good with horizontal stones. Deciduous trees may also be used. Be sure the foundations of your garden are strong enough to support heavy planting if you plan to use them. To secure the effect of having a tree look as though it was growing out of a six-inch crack, plant the tree well down in the ground and then pile the rocks up around it.

If your Rock Garden has rather dry soil, common juniper, some of the jack pines, or some of the shrubby oaks will do well. The little plants we call hens and chickens will also thrive in a dry place.

Laurel, rhododendrons, andromeda, azaleas, are all good Rock Garden plants. All kinds of ferns make excellent material to be used.

It is very easy to overplant a Rock Garden, and one must watch this carefully. It is foolish to pay a lot for rocks and to spend a lot of time and effort placing them properly, and then cover them all over with plants.

It is well to have some of your planting material on hand when you start building your garden, so that it will be readily available when needed.

It is very difficult to obtain appropriate architectural features for a Rock Garden. One garden had a very charming group made of stone. It featured four gnomes seated around a table playing cards, and was screened with plants so that it made a delightful surprise when you suddenly came upon it. At night it was illuminated with a red light. All architectural features should be chosen for compatibility and fitness as well as for usefulness and then should be absolutely subordinate to both plants and material surrounding them.

good Roc
erial to be

ust watch
spend a lo
r them all

and when
y available

atures for
p made of
ying cards,
ul surprise
nated with
for com-
should be
ding them.

IRISTHROPE, MRS. HOMER GAGE, FALL 1936

"THE GARDENS OF RUSSIA"

Thursday, February 13

Illustrated Lecture

By Mrs. Cyrus Winslow Merrell

There is no doubt that everyone is more or less interested in what is going on in Russia, no matter what opinion they may hold regarding it. However, no one will deny that it is the greatest experiment in a design for living that the world has even seen.

Many contradictory stories are brought back regarding conditions in Russia. When Mrs. Merrill heard one man say there is nothing whatever going on in Russia in the horticultural line—old gardens being neglected and no new ones being made—she decided to see for herself.

On her arrival in Leningrad she was taken for a two and one-half hour ride for information and orientation, and during that time saw many evidences of gardening, although they were very different from what exists in our country. Of course, not much is known regarding horticulture in Russia before the Revolution; but it is safe to assume that the poor people knew nothing about gardens, the aristocrats being the only ones who had the time, the money, or the opportunity to enjoy this luxury.

In Leningrad there are three types of public parks and those are beautifully planted. The first type of park is the "Park of Cultural Rest." Courses of some kind are actually given there and many people take them. As everyone has one day in five free from work, there is always a large group of people free to listen to the lectures and to enjoy life. One of these parks accommodates 200,000 people. These parks also have beautiful nurseries and kindergartens where one can leave the children.

The second type of park has been made in memory of heroes of the Revolution. One of these parks was once a great parade ground and contains twenty or thirty acres. Around a center plot there is a wall of polished granite. Within that wall are buried the most honored dead, while just outside the wall are buried those next honored. The rest of the ground is made into a playground for the children. It was toward the end of June when Mrs. Merrill was there and she saw them taking the last of the tulips out of one bed in this park and replanting it with fuchsias.

The third type of park is much like our parks and, undoubtedly, existed before the Revolution. These are well kept up.

In addition to these three types of parks which exist in most of the cities, Leningrad has a fine Botanic Garden, which was established in 1680 and landscaped in 1724 by an English gardener. The general plan of the garden still follows that design, but just before the Revolution a modern looking Rock Garden and a Bog Garden were added.

The large estates belonging to the wealthy aristocrats of Russia all had beautiful gardens, but the poor people never saw these before the Revolution. Now these large estates are made into sanitariums where the workers may spend their one month's vacation free and the workers who do very difficult work may spend their two months' vacation free. As little is done for the individual in Russia, much is done for the many.

Railroad stations, public buildings, churches, theaters, etc. are more or less surrounded with flowers. You may also see phlox, marigolds and such ordinary flowers to us, planted in narrow borders about ten inches wide along the streets. As you approach the railroad station, the streets grow wider.

As no one is allowed to take pictures of railroad stations or near tracks, Mrs. Merrill was unable to show us any scenes of the beds of flowers surrounding the station. We did, however, see pictures of the Astoria Hotel and scenes around it, including St. Isaac's Cathedral, said to be the richest cathedral in Russia. At the time the pictures were taken, nothing was growing in the carefully prepared gardens near these buildings.

Mrs. Merrill did not see a lawn mower in Russia and thinks there can be none, because of the ragged, unkempt appearance of the grass. The grass is allowed to grow six or eight inches high and then is cut with a sickle.

The season for growing flowers in this part of Russia is very short and when hot weather does come, it is extremely hot.

The shrubs are very ordinary and are mostly lilacs, snowberry and common varieties of spirea.

Most of the statues have some sort of planting around them, generally, red geraniums.

The roads outside the city are very bad, nevertheless a trip of twenty-five miles was made in order to see the palace which Peter the Great built, and where all the Czars and Czarinas lived. On the way out of the grounds, one saw the palace where the last Czar lived.

In great contrast to this magnificence, the tiny village houses where the poor people live were shown. Some effort is made at planting around some of these. Of course, in this section of the country frosts come in September, so the season for flowers is very short.

In a few of the cottages one could see pots of geraniums and nasturtiums on the window-sills. Evidently these could stand the bitter cold of winter. The houses are not well built, as were the first houses our forefathers built in this country, neither are the new buildings well built. This is probably due to the lack of skilled and trained workers.

The first thing you see in Moscow is the emblem of the Star and the Hammer and Anvil in bright red, and below it is a gigantic statue of Lenin. He is looking down a long aisle of palms.

Moscow is a much more elaborate city than Leningrad and the "Parks of Cultural Rest" much nicer. There are long beds of red geraniums and coleus and much shrubbery. The Children's Village is very fine. The smallest children have the latest type of blocks to play with, such as are used in our more advanced schools. Constructive toys of all kinds are available to the older children. All kinds of gymnastic apparatus is provided.

The smallest children were shown having a good time sailing boats on a rather shallow pool, while the older children were learning to row small boats, not over four or five feet long, on a larger and deeper pond. Some effort has been made to surround these two ponds with flowers, but the beds of pansies, forget-me-nots, etc. did not have a well kept appearance.

A little planting had been started around one of the new apartment houses for workers. These apartment houses are painted very drab colors and do not lend the color to the landscape that we are prone to think of as belonging to Russia. They do, however, provide nice places for the children to play, with nurses to take care of them.

No one is allowed to have more space at home than a room approximately ten square feet. In all the homes Mrs. Merrill saw, there was a bed in every room but the kitchen.

An old historic convent, where, in the old days, wealthy husbands confined their wives when they became tired of them, is surrounded by a magnificent wall. Crowded against this wall, both inside and outside the enclosure, are "shanty" buildings in which workers live.

Very seldom is a tourist allowed out alone in Russia, so that Mrs. Merrill had a difficult time trying to study the horticulture of Russia, because other tourists were not interested in this phase of Russian life. One afternoon, however, she did manage to get a taxi all to herself and managed to take many interesting pictures of children playing in the parks and elderly people quietly enjoying the beauty of both the flowers and the children.

From Moscow Mrs. Merrill went to Sebastopol. She was not allowed to take any pictures there. In the region around Sebastopol, the flowers are perfectly enchanting. There are choice varieties of all kinds of flowers including daisies, chicory, lemon yellow mulleins, gilia, scabiosa, borage, lavender asters, spikes of blue and magenta orchids, pink mallow, gypsophila, larkspur, violets, lilies, feverfew, salvia, hollyhocks, sweet alyssum, sedums, and purple and yellow scrophularia.

The district around Sebastopol is a great deal like the Riviera, although not as beautiful. Much of the plant material is the same, however.

From Sebastopol Mrs. Merrill went to Yalta. Here she found a park that was established about 1823 and the beds of flowers are still laid out in the original manner. This park is quite well kept up.

In the hills near Yalta, Alexander the Third built a hunting lodge, as he was told he could be cured of his illness if he would live there awhile. It has now been made into a tubercular sanitarium. The grounds were most attractive and were planted with both deciduous and evergreen trees. One statue near the lodge was surrounded by beds of foxgloves and hollyhocks.

As the Russians are not particular about taking tourists to a place when something is going on, Mrs. Merrill did not see a Collective Farm in operation. She showed us a few slides of pictures she had taken on one. The little houses are quite attractive and are well kept up. There is a very good schoolhouse on this farm and also a fine recreation house for the children.

Another house built by Alexander the Third has been made into a sanitarium for workers. The grounds are laid out after the grand manner with palms, cacti, cypress trees, and beautiful evergreens of all kinds. A beautiful arbor, covered with vines and flowers and built on a sloping hillside, leads down to the Black Sea. In the distance are the mountains. It would be very difficult to adequately describe the great beauty of these grounds, as shown by the slides.

The famous Botanic Gardens of Russia are also very beautiful. Gardeners are constantly at work to find flowers, fruits and vegetables that can be grown in Russia. Eight hundred varieties of roses are grown there. The Bog Garden is the loveliest Mrs. Merrill has ever seen. The views we saw were very lovely.

It took twenty-seven hours for the boat trip across the Black Sea to Odessa. The passengers were landed at the foot of the famous steps of Odessa which lead from the sea level to the esplanade on the cliff overlooking the sea. This esplanade is most attractively planted with evergreens and flowers.

One street in Odessa called "Boulevard of the Proletariat" is lined for two miles with beautiful estates which have now been turned into sanitariums where workers may spend their vacations.

One of the estates, with a house worth around $200,000 had to have a dining room added to take care of the two hundred workers who would be there at one time. There is quite a noticeable difference in the architecture of the original house and the addition which is of very cheap construction.

With one exception, the gardens and parks of Kiev certainly look as if they had been there many years, and are of a very formal type. On a bank a modernistic garden was so planted that portraits of Lenin, Karl Marx, and Stalin were plainly visible.

On returning to Leningrad, Mrs. Merrill took a ride into the country to see another palace built by Peter the Great. The architecture is very like that of a French Chateau, and it is known as the

Versailles of Russia because of the many fountains in front of the terrace. The planting also is suggestive of Versailles.

There is no evidence that any of the beautiful surroundings of the palace had ever been destroyed.

Looking from the terrace in front of this palace you can see ships in the distance sailing on the Gulf of Finland. Looking in another direction, you can see an exquisite formal garden with two arbors or summer houses, with a pond in which are islands with statuary. In another direction, there are trees in long rows exactly like those in the Luxembourg Gardens. In the past all this beauty was enjoyed by the few, but now great crowds of people flock here to share it.

Even though it is not being done in our way, certainly something is being done in the way of gardening in Russia. If the people of Russia would develop their native flowers and perennials instead of so many annuals, their gardens would be more interesting.

"PRIZE GARDENS AND PLANT EXHIBITS"

Thursday, February 20, 1936

Illustrated Lecture

EDWARD I. FARRINGTON, BOSTON, MASS.

A garden of unusual interest in New Hampshire is one having a long vista down the centre with trees and hedges on either side. Through small openings in the hedges one may step into small gardens, each complete in itself, and completely hidden from every other garden. One of these small gardens is of the English type and is planted wholly with begonias; another is entirely of heliotrope, and so on.

The most pretentious rose garden on the Atlantic Coast, or at least in New England, is on the James estate at Newport, R. I., and was planned by Mrs. Harriett Foote, of Marblehead, the best rosarian in the United States. It is laid out right next to the ocean and is on several different terraces or levels. One slide showed a broad expanse of roses, covering perhaps an acre. Mrs. Foote has one unbreakable rule regarding her work with roses, and that is, that no blooms shall be cut until they have faded. She wants all the strength of the plant to go into the wood. If a client fails to observe this rule, she will no longer care for the garden.

If you should visit the garden of Mrs. Foote at Marblehead next June, you will be amazed at the size and extent of the roses you find there. Practically every new specie may be seen, and the blossoms grow to such a size that they frequently have to be held up. The rose bushes that grow two or three feet high in the ordinary garden grow five or six feet high for her. Every fall the bushes are taken down and partly buried, or else covered with leaves or some other protection.

A garden which received the Gold Medal of the Massachusetts Horticultural Society is one on the Endicott place in Danvers. Three different periods in this country's history are represented. One portion is of the Revolutionary period, one of the Civil War period, and another is of the modern period. There is a very unique summer house in the Revolutionary garden, which almost makes one think of a small New England church.

From the large well-kept garden of the Anderson estate in Chestnut Hill, one may have a view of the entire city of Boston. Mr. Larz Anderson was at one time Minister from this country to Japan, and one of the features of his grounds is a Japanese garden. Among the interesting things in it are some trained dwarf evergreens which are very old, one 300 years, and of course these are very valuable. This is one of the choice and skilled arts of the Japanese.

Another of the Gold Medals of the Massachusetts Horticultural Society was given to the Stone estate in Marion, with its many attractive paths and drives. This garden has numerous rhododendrons and azaleas, although most of the flowers are annuals.

A terraced garden in Nahant, showing the three levels, with the first garden on the same level as the house, makes it possible for one to step out of the house directly into the garden "living-room," a most desirable feature. This shows what splendid results may be obtained with careful planning and moderate expenditure.

A garden near Fall River is completely surrounded by a privet hedge six or eight feet high. After this picture was taken, the hedge was completely frozen back to the ground, so that the next spring it was only a few inches high. The California privet hedge is not sufficiently hardy to endure the extreme cold of New England winters.

Among other Gold Medal gardens is that of Mrs. M. L. Gardner of Manchester. Here is a water garden, a large center pool surrounded by smaller pools, filled with lilies and aquatic plants. Also, the Hunnewell Gold Medal was given to Mr. Winthrop for his garden in Lenox. This estate covers fifty or sixty acres, and is very unique in that no flowers are grown on it. One corner of the grounds has a rock garden, but most of the estate is planted with evergreens and shrubbery surrounding and intersecting the beautiful lawns. Many are already familiar with the lovely doorway of Mrs. Gage's summer home in Shrewsbury which is framed with roses, and the rose arbor which shelters the pathway to the door.

Many people are not as interested in large gardens as they are in smaller plots where they may try out their special favorites or make some certain type of garden. A tiny courtyard may suggest part of Europe rather than America. Again it is the rock garden. One of the most successful of these in Massachusetts belongs to Mrs. Isaac Sprague of Wellesley. Another type somewhat in favor is the wall garden. This, however, requires just-right conditions and great skill in building. A section of garden in Chestnut Hill adds to its charm by a bit of well-chosen sculpture. One of the few topiary gardens in this country is on the Hunnewell estate in Wellesley.

The Arnold Arboretum, "America's Greatest Garden," is full of beautiful and unusual as well as familiar plants, mostly trees and shrubs, and also offers some very fine examples of landscape gardening. All who have seen them will remember the azaleas which cover the hillside with their bright flame in early spring. Here, too, is splendid mountain laurel, a typical American plant which does not thrive as well anywhere else in this country, and should be the national flower of the United States.

In Boston, the Municipal Rose Garden at Franklin Park and the one at the Fenway are worthy of note and contain many of the newer roses.

Leaving New England, the estate of Pierre S. Dupont in Delaware is one of the most elaborate to be found in the world, and was awarded a medal. A part of this estate is an electrical garden, where its many pools and fountains sparkling with myriad lights transform it into a veritable fairyland. Mr. Dupont plans to leave this entire estate to the public to become a great public park.

It is of interest to know that the Massachusetts Horticultural Society was formed in 1829 and began holding shows before the Civil War. When this occurred, it found itself without a home and held some of the shows in tents. Then the Music Hall was utilized for this purpose. Next a new place was found on Tremont Street where shows were held continuously. Then came an opportunity to sell the old hall, so it was decided to build a new structure. A storm of protest arose over the choice of a site, but time has proved that the choice was well made. The difference in flower shows and exhibitions, held in those early beginnings and the present time, are very marked, not only in the style and type of show, but in their artistic and educational values as well; and, from the carefully planned

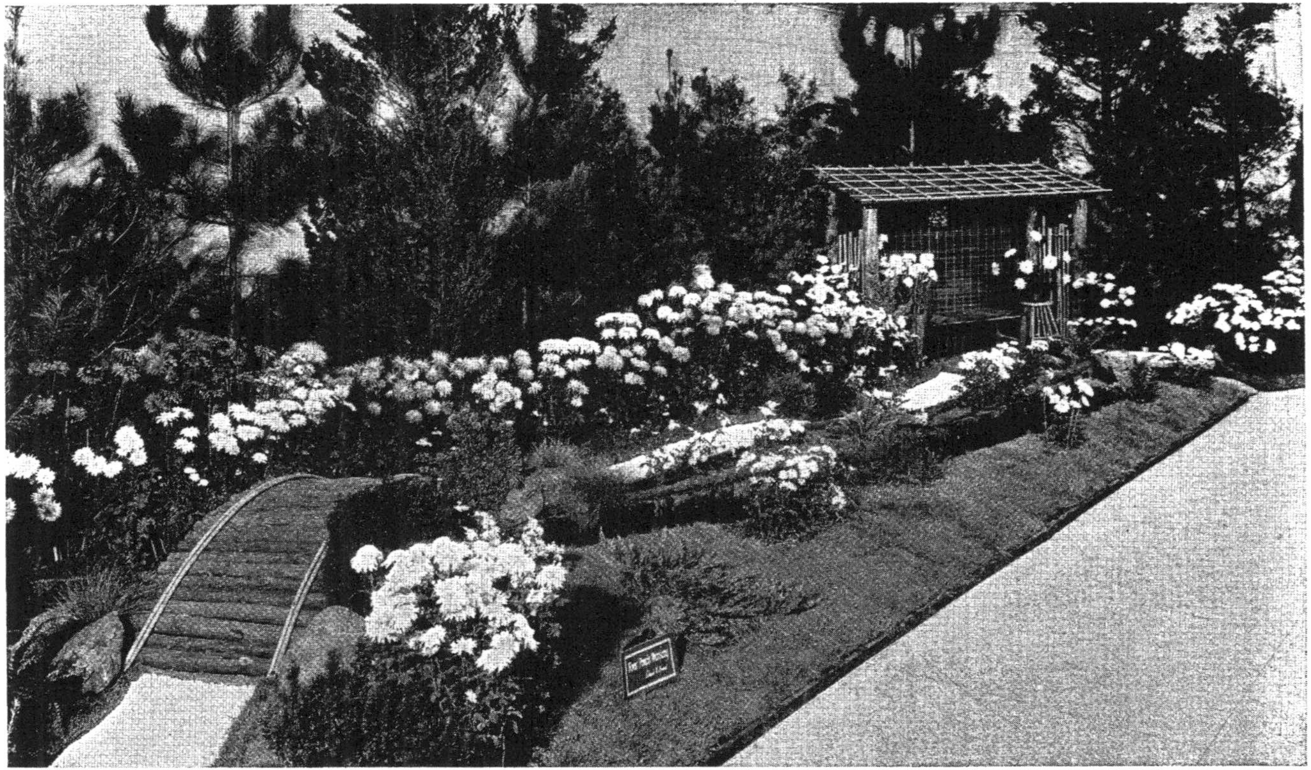

Edward W. Breed, Fall 1936

arrangements of today, one can readily see the great progress which
has been made by exhibitors.

Some excellent shows have been staged in Boston. Those of Mr.
Burrage's day were outstanding, particularly an exhibit of orchids
which filled the entire hall. Exceedingly tall palm trees were brought
from the South and hung with tropical moss, truly an amazing piece
of work. Orchid exhibits have received a tremendous impetus from
these put up by Mr. Burrage. They are probably the finest to be
found anywhere in this country. On another occasion he filled the
entire hall with wild flowers collected from all over New England
and arranged in a very naturalistic setting. The exhibits of Mr.
Roland of Nahant, with his wonderful Acacias, have never been
surpassed and will never be forgotten.

The Centennial Exhibit was the first big show to be held in
Mechanics Building, which included a desert garden brought from
California in three freight cars. This was later established as a
permanent part of the Kew Gardens in England.

Garden Clubs have played an extremely important part in developing shows throughout the United States. They are, on the whole,
of the modern type, with much real artistic effect, showing originality
and revealing a great amount of thought and work. The exhibits
of the Audubon Society also prove appealing, interesting, and most
instructive.

The New York Annual Exhibition is the outstanding show of the
country, with attendance well over 100,000. Here they have gone
a long way in the development of horticultural interest, even in the
city itself. At Rockefeller Center an amazing series of gardens
have been built upon the roof, where tons and tons of earth have
been carried to make these gardens possible.

Cleveland and Philadelphia have particularly fine buildings for
their exhibitions. They both employ landscape architects who plan
the entire layout, a method found most helpful in giving uniformity.
The large building in Atlantic City has the largest unbroken floor
area, not always the best for pleasing exhibits. Chicago has a very
long building. St. Louis is fortunate in having a Botanic Garden
with an endowment and some skilled and expert gardeners. Nearer
by, Providence is also trying to build up a large and successful show;
and in each case, the individual problems of the different societies

have been painstakingly worked out.   Here, too, in Worcester, splendid progress been made in recent years.

The planning of a flower show is a big job and involves a tre dous amount of work from start to finish, for plans must be c fully made, studied, and started into operation for weeks, mo and years ahead of the time it was ready for the public to see enjoy.

"A garden is earth's greatest hymn of praise to heaven."

"THE HARDY GARDEN IN CONTINUOUS BLOOM"

Thursday, February 27

Illustrated Lecture

By Mrs. Katherine L. Rice, Grand Rapids, Mich.

The hardy garden can be kept in bloom all summer quite easily if proper provision is made. The first prerequisite is to know what plants to use and what they need. Then we must see they are planted under the right conditions and we must give them the particular care they require.

There are seven families of plants that will follow through in close succession: jonquils and tulips, the irises, the peonies, canterbury bells and foxgloves, delphiniums and lilies, phlox, and hardy asters and chrysanthemums.

Foxgloves, of course, are not considered a hardy plant, but they help to fill in so nicely that we take a little leeway and include them in our garden.

It is essential to use a few annuals to supplement the perennials and bi-ennials in a hardy garden.

If you want your hardy garden to last for a long time, you need great depth of soil with good drainage. Start three feet down with coal ashes, sand, humus and fertilizer, so that by top dressing the plants will be amply fed. It is astonishing the way plants will send down and down for their food. Of course, very few plants will grow down three feet, but by means of their capillary attraction they can coax the food up to their roots. Also, if soil is very deep the plants will go down for food instead of crowding other plants.

We must remember also that we cannot have a good garden without background and skyline, something that will lead the eyes off to vistas. Every vista must be preserved. They all enter into the composition of the garden.

The first slide showed the plan of the grounds around the cottage home of the speaker. There are a series of gardens here on a relatively small area of about two acres, so planned that, while the whole is unified, there can be certain portions out of bloom without taking away effect of the whole.

You enter a small attractive gate and go through the spring garden to reach the cottage door. The hardy garden is seen across a stretch of lawn and is arranged in a semi-circle effect with a background of evergreen trees. It measures about 100 feet from tip to tip. The end portions are about 18 feet wide and the center portion is about 12 feet wide. The background for the hardy garden also forms the background for the formal garden. Then come the peony and iris gardens and beyond them is a rock garden with a still pool.

There are several paths through the grounds, so that you can go around the garden in different ways without retracing your steps.

Except in very early spring before the leaves come out on the trees, the pathway from the gate to the house is quite shady. A view of this section of the path, taken in early spring, showed jonquils and grape hyacinths in bloom. Early varieties of jonquils are bulbocodium, conspicuus and citrinus, and campernelles are used with grape hyacinths.

A view taken from the doorway shows path opening out and vista to be seen through an opening in the background of white pines and white lilacs. The pathway goes between beautiful evergreen trees, weeping willow trees, cactus and hills of juniper, giving one a feeling of being in the country, and gradually leads one into the mood for flowers. We pass the running pool near the house, and follow the pathway down to the hardy garden where the lilacs are in blossom, forming a background with white pines and spruces for the tulips and intermediate irises, which are kept near the edge. After a few years the lilacs grow pretty tall, so it is wise to put in a few new ones each year. The lilacs used in this garden are as follows:

White, double: Mme. Lemoine, Miss E. Wilmott, Edith Cavell.
White, single: Jan von Tol, Vestale.
Dark, double: My Favorite, Charles Joly, Mrs. Edward Harding.
Dark, single: Ludwig Spaeth, Reumur, Congo, Paul Thirion.
Bluest: President Lincoln and President Grevy.
Pinkest, single: Macrostachya and Lucie Baltet.
Pinkest double: Belle de Nancy.
Rosy lilac, double: Leon Gambetta.

Azure lilac, double: Rene Jarry Des-Loges.
Purple lilac, double: Capitaine Baltet.
Cobalt lilac, double: Katharine Havemeyer.

Tulips will give a better effect in a garden if they are planted in clumps rather than in rows. Then when the peony foliage begins to leaf out, it will quickly cover them up. Tulips to be used in lilac time with intermediate irises are: Georgia, Bluet, American Black Prince, Moonlight and Yellow Moon.

Species peonies come very early and are nice to plant with tulips. It is better to starve these than to give them too much manure. A few of them in a hardy border is enough. The recommended kinds are:

Pink shades: Russi Major, Avante Garde, Arietaina, Northern Glory, Bakeri, Witmaniana, Macrocarpa and hybrids.
Light Yellow: Mlokoswitschi and Macrophylla.
Red tones: Ophia and Lucida.
Yellow-red: Labata and Sunbeam.

The tree peonies come after the species and give another type of foliage.

Peony Officinalis is the earliest to bloom and is called the peony of our grandmothers' gardens. It comes in red and pink foliage and is not very good in hot summer, so be sure to place it where foliage will be covered. The two varieties are Rosea and Rubra.

The next question to be decided is whether to have irises and poppies. If you use both, you can use the irises in only the blue and purple shades, as the salmon color of the poppies is very hard to use with other colors. Mrs. Rice uses poppies in other places, but not in her hardy garden.

Poppies suited to the hardy garden:

Salmon: Mrs. Perry and similar shades.
Cherry: Mrs. Strobart.
Mauve to Lavender: Masterpiece and Enchantress.
Wine: Mahony.

We saw several views of her poppy garden with garden heliotrope growing between the poppies.

We followed a primrose path around to the tea house where we saw two large clumps of yellow irises on either side of the steps.

We also saw other views of irises. Lupins are the very best foil for irises.

It is a lot of fun to group irises. One group which makes an interesting combination is the tall Claret Cup with Bruno, Jacqueline Guillot, and Jubilee.

Sometimes a combination of flowers will make a most pleasing effect. The Duke of Bedford iris and the early single peony, Madaline Gauthier, are stunning with pink lupins.

We were shown a scene from a garden in Fort Wayne, Ind., showing a wall built of Indiana limestone with lilacs blooming in iris time. Lilacs generally bloom in tulip time, but these are species lilacs and bloom after other kinds are all through blooming. They are in bloom for about a month. Another excellent shrub to have with irises is the Paul's Scarlet thorn.

The species lilacs recommended are Josikae, Villosa Reflexa, Lutece, and Sweginzoi.

The varieties of white irises which give accent in the garden are: Wambliska, LaNeiga, Shasta, Sophronia, Taj Mahal, Michaline, and Charraire.

A new type of iris which is much larger than old type are the Sibiricas and the recommended varieties are: Kingfisher Blue, Papillon, Emperor, King Caesar, Periwinkle, Turquoise Cup, and Snow Queen.

These are needed in the hardy garden to bring out peonies which are now coming into bloom.

The earliest blooming single peony is Thurlow's Helen, and it is not only the earliest to bloom, but it continues to bloom for a long time. One of the two best white single peonies to bloom is Marguerite Dessert. This has a little "airy-fairy" blossom with a center which looks like the center of a rose. You can tell the difference between Chinese and single peonies because the single peonies have a center more like a rose, while the Chinese peonies have a center more like a chrysanthemum. Other single peonies shown are Snow Sprite, L'Etincelante, Vera, and Mischief.

Going along the peony path to the pool, we find the peonies are interplanted, some early, some midseason, and some late, so that this path is quite colorful for a long time. There are twelve or fourteen kinds of double peonies, but some of the blooms are so heavy they do not hold up well and most storms batter them to pieces. If the peonies are selected with strong stems in mind, we can have our peonies without tieing them to stakes. August Dessert is one of the best double peonies. The blossoms are loosely built and are not heavy. Another thing to watch for in peonies is how well does the blossom hold its color during its lifetime. Many peonies, which begin with a very beautiful color, fade quickly and it is therefore well to plant them where they can have some shade. The Primvere and Mme. Jules Dessert hold color well, but the Walter Faxon needs a little protection from the sun. The Walter Faxon has a very distinctive blossom—a beautiful loose shape, in a fluffy pink with double heart. There are very few peonies that are as pure a pink as this one is, but there is another, Souvenir de Louis Bigot, which is a much later blossoming peony. In the picture showing this peony in bloom the delphiniums are beginning to blossom.

The blossom of the Lillian Gumm peony has a very formal shape and is not at all heavy. Mrs. Rice told about meeting the Mr. Gumm who originated this peony at the National Peony Show. He asked Mrs. Rice what she thought about advertising his peony under the caption: "Better Peonies by Gumm."

The Isani-Guidi is the most beautiful of all the white Japanese peonies. The Ama-no-sode No. 2 is not nearly as good as the No. 1, which is a tall, big, glorious pink, Japanese peony, probably as good in its class as Helen of the singles. The stem is strong and while it bends out a little, it will not break easily. When you do find strong stems, you find a good peony. By giving peonies a small amount of wood ashes you can strengthen the stems. The spirea palmata elegans is a valuable aid in softening effect of peonies.

Mrs. Rice is always glad when the season of irises and peonies is over because it keeps her so "keyed-up."

Next come the foxgloves and canterbury bells. They help a great deal in filling in and supplementing the other flowers. The form of the foxgloves especially helps to take the eye upward. Delphiniums used in groups give a better pictorial effect to the hardy garden. And now our garden is alive with blue!

With delphiniums we have the lilies. Regal lilies are the best bet for the hardy garden. It is watering the garden that spoils the bulbs of the lilies, as they do not need as much water as the rest of the garden. The sulphuria lily was brought from Tibet and is not as hardy as the regal. However, if you put the sulphuria in pots and bury the pots in the garden when it is time for it to blossom, you will find that it will do very well. A cross between the sulphurium and regal lilies is being developed, and it is hoped to obtain as strong a lily as the regal.

Himalayan lilies need a little shade and they give a more spectacular effect with a background of evergreen. The mother bulb never blooms twice and it takes two years for new bulbs to develop, so it is well to plant a few each year in order to have blossoms every year.

When the delphiniums have gone out of bloom, there comes a time when you have to work rather hard to get good distribution of bloom. Then is when the annuals, such as snapdragon and petunias add color through the border of the hardy garden. The annual peony—pink double poppy—also should be ready by now. Three sowings should be made, two in the spring and one in the fall.

The Japanese irises begin to bloom the last of June. These vary greatly, some being tall, some being short, some having three petals, some six petals, and some nine petals, and some being light in tone and some dark. The general run of tones is very dark and rich, so we must remember to use quite a lot of light to secure proper accent.

The Japanese iris Celeste is stippled, streaked, and pied. It has only three petals and has great variety of shape, size, and height. A hybridrized iris called Shelford Giant is as noble in the iris class as the Himalayan lily is in the lily class and is still relatively rare. It has very upstanding foliage and the blossom is light yellow with a white blotch. Yellow is essential to the gayety of a garden, but only the light yellows are acceptable.

Do not buy Hemerocallis Hyperion unless the foliage is upstanding. This plant blooms for six weeks and measures as much as the regal lily. These are most effective planted between peonies.

The slide showing the garden at the very height of the hot summer season shows hollyhocks blooming in the background, the phlox getting ready to blossom and innumerable other plants on the way to blossoming—daisies, snapdragons, ageratum, sweet alyssum, sweet williams, etc. It is in the hot summer time when you begin to treasure the edge most. The yellow of the verbascum is cool in the heat of summer. This is a glorified mullein. The perpendicular line of the verbascum repeated at intervals helps to give rhythm in the border.

Then phlox time comes. The new phloxes are very lovely and very much improved over the old types.

Mrs. Rice has discovered that white is the strongest color in the garden and so if she were planting her garden over, she would not use it in front, but would bring other colors to front. Many of the new phloxes are coming in a new rose shade: Asa Gray, Rigoletto, William Tell, Jean Bart, Louise Gann, Champs Elysees, Ethel Pritchard.

Artimesia Silver King and Physostegia Gigantea give high accent in the garden at this time.

Other recommended types of phlox are:

Salmon combinations: Lillian, Enchantress, Evangeline, Rising Sun, Evelyn, Daily Sketch, Jules Sandeau, George Mendel, Morgenrood, Traviata.

Red tones which combine well with salmons: Camilla Schneider, E. I. Farrington, Robin Hood, Mrs. Schoulton, Debs, Hauptmann Koehl.

Delicate shades for either group: Ann Cook, Mt. Laurel, Daybreak, Mme. Paul Detrie, Guy Moore, Mrs. Pfitzer, Mrs. Livingston Farrand, Milly von Hoboken, Special French, Pink Beauty.

Blends for either group: Hanny Pfleiderer, Wanadis, Crepescule.

Rose reds for either group: Africa, Billiant, September Glow.

Purple shades especially desirable with rose shades: Fantome, Royal Purple, Border Gem, Iris, Minerva, Le Mahdi, Dr. Charcot, Blue Hill, Wm. Ramsey, Widar.

When the phlox has gone by, the zinnias can be brought forward. Mrs. Rice grows the zinnias in the background and when ready to blossom brings them out in clumps and puts them in the places left vacant by the removal of the canterbury bells.

Sedum spectabile, called "live forever" when we were children, has a beautiful colored foliage. Sedum maximum has wine flower and wine foliage.

The edge of hardy garden becomes alive with petunias of a lovely blue shade. To get the best effect at this time, keep the edge soft.

Some day late in August, the Halls amaryllis planted in the spring will bloom with a beautiful, pinkish lavender colored blossom and will make a delightful picture against the evergreen.

SUNNYSIDE GREENHOUSES, R. J. ALLEN, A. E. CONTI, FALL 1936

...s rhythm i...

...ery lovely and...

...st color in th...
...she would no...
    Many of th...
...ray, Rigoletto...
...Elysees, Eth...

...ve high accen...

..., Rising Sun...
..., Morgenrood...

...Schneider, E. I...
...mann Koehl...
...Daybreak, Mme...
...ngton Farrand...

...psule.
...ow.
...ne, Royal Pur...
...oot, Blue Hill...

...ught forward...
...when ready t...
...the places left...

...were children...
...s wine flowe...

...nias of a lovel...
...p the edge sof...
...ed in the sprin...
...d blossom and...

Gladioli are another supplementary feature for the hardy garden and are most effective when planted in groups. They will bloom astonishingly late.

The hardy aster, Frikarti, a good deal like an alpine aster, will begin to bloom in July and will bloom all the rest of the season. The Luteus aster is a light yellow aster. When the great season of blooming is past, the hardy aster will keep up the soft bloom through October. In the spring, divide the hardy asters, leaving only three little roots in one spot, and fertilize them. Then when other flowers have gone by, they will spread out and fill in the hardy border.

Among the newcomers in the hardy asters are: Red Rover, Countess, Ethel Ballard, Louvain, Blue Gem, Little Boy Blue, Anita Ballard, Freedom, Skyland Queen, Gray Lady, Maggie Perry, Joan Baughan.

Dahlias take up too much room in a hardy garden. A good way to handle them is top plant them in small tubs and develop them out back somewhere. When they begin to bloom, bring them out into the hardy garden, tub and all.

The acid test of a hardy garden is whether it is a good garden in winter, the time when we begin to look at the design and we are not distracted by color.

It is hard work, but it is creative work. Mrs. Rice's husband, who is a horticulturist by the gift of God, painted a few lines on the tool shed door:

> "Late to bed, early to rise,
> Work like the devil and fertilize."

ANNUAL REUNION

March 5

The Library was most attractively decorated with palms, ferns, yellow roses, snapdragons, and white sweet peas, making one forget the snow storm outside. In the receiving line were Mr. and Mrs. Myron F. Converse, Mrs. Homer Gage, Mr. and Mrs. S. Lothrop Davenport, and Mr. E. L. D. Seymour, of New York City. Music was furnished by the orchestra during the reception. The ushers were: Mr. Malcolm C. Midgley, Mr. H. Ward Moore, Mr. Leonard C. Midgley, Mr. Harrison G. Taylor, Mr. Allen W. Hixon, and Mr. Burt W. Greenwood.

Those in the receiving line led the march to the dining room, where the tables looked most inviting with red roses for decoration. The invocation was given by Dr. Tomlinson.

At the conclusion of dinner, served by Mr. Lunt, the President spoke briefly of the work of the Society, mentioning the shows held every week during the summer months, the Spring Show held for four days beginning March 12 this year, and the Chrysanthemum Exhibit held for four days in November, and the lectures which are given each Thursday afternoon during January and February. He also called attention to the splendid work done by the Vice Presidents, two of whom were present, Mrs. Gage and Mr. Davenport. Mr. Cook was unable to attend because of the inclement weather.

Mr. Converse thanked Dr. Tomlinson for "coming once each year to pray for us"; whereupon Dr. Tomlinson responded, "If that is all the praying that is done, I will have to make a longer prayer next year."

The President also spoke of the death of Mr. David L. Fiske, which occurred during the past year, and suggested that it would be fitting to send flowers to Mrs. Fiske.

The Unity Quartette, of Boston, sang "Swing Along!" and the meeting adjourned to go upstairs for the lecture. Preceding the lecture the Quartette sang two numbers, "I Love Life" and "My Heart Is a Silent Violin," and responded with an encore.

The speaker, Mr. E. L. D. Seymour, was introduced by President

Converse as editor of the "Garden Column" of the *Herald Tribune,* of New York, and editor of *The Garden Encyclopedia,* the most complete volume of this type, Mr. Converse remarked, that he had seen, a copy of which is in the library.

The subject of Mr. Seymour's address was "The Garden of Tomorrow."

The Worcester County Horticultural Society is to be congratulated on its splendid achievements during the many years it has been in existence. It adds luster to a magnificent part of the Commonwealth, the progressive and enterprising City of Worcester. The importance and status of Worcester in the public eye and mind are shown by the attitude of a certain tourist. On his arrival in Los Angeles he was asked by another tourist where he was from. "Boston," was the reply. "What route did you take to get here?" was the next question. "Oh, the one that goes through Worcester!"

As much as one likes flowers, in order to grow them, one must have some knowledge about them. The attempts of Mr. Seymour's mother to have a garden were not very successful because no one in the family knew anything about gardening.

In Mr. Seymour's childhood the family collected a little pile of stones with which his Mother intended to make what was then known as a "rockery." After being away from home for some years, he returned and found this pile of stones partly buried under grass, a mute evidence of that desire of his mother's which was never fulfilled. For this reason, he is desirous of helping anyone who wants flowers to have them.

In creating the gardens of tomorrow, it will be necessary to have very specific knowledge if we are to accomplish the results desired, and we must know where we are headed. We still have a long way to go yet in gardening, for no matter how very beautiful the effects we achieve now, there are still greater beauties for which to strive.

Perhaps you have heard of the expression "green hand" or "green thumb," referring to the knack of making things grow. The speaker first heard the expression from an English woman, who mentioned "green thumb," and now there is a book published which mentions "green fingers." It is an individual trait or gift which most of us do not have, hence the necessity for most of us to give the best of care and attention that we can in producing plants.

1. Design element.
2. Element called materials and methods.
3. Human element—the gardener himself.

Garden design grows largely out of environment, that is, it is influenced by natural conditions that man cannot change, such as climate and weather, and including even trends of living. Human habits vary from time to time and garden habits vary with them. The formal gardens of the past gave way to informal designs and now the formal garden is coming back under the name "modernistic."

We have seen the front yard gardens, with ornate ornaments, pick up and move to the back yard and now we see them developing into specific types of garden. For instance, at Rockefeller Center in New York, there is a rock garden, a water garden, a cactus garden, and an African garden with plants from South Africa, etc. The effect of today's news also affects garden habits, as is shown by a very active interest in the African garden at the present time.

As we see this constant change of interest we wonder if we are making progress or whether we are like Rastus, whose wife gave him twenty-five cents to spend at the circus. He spent it all in riding on the merry-go-round. When he finished riding Mandy asked, "Yo' all done spent yo' money, but where yo' been?"

However, we are moving forward as is shown by a new appreciation of the fitness of things—the fitness of plants to one another and of plantings to one another, the fitness of all of the garden elements to surroundings, and the desires of the people who are supposed to enjoy them. We are also approaching something of a different social aspect; an aspect in which the rights of others play a larger part than they used to.

We are thinking more about roadside plantings, parks, and open countryside, as a result of the theory that the landscape belongs to everyone. Of course, the increased speed with which the automobile is driven may necessitate a different form of planting. One man has suggested it might be well to have very narrow borders about a mile long of the same kind of flowers, so the motorist could see the flower!

There are many factors to be taken into consideration in regard to the choosing of plants for tomorrow's garden. Rarity and variety of form and color and other peculiarities will influence our choice.

Scientists are doing marvelous things to aid the horticulturist. Consider the experimenting that is carried on with the plants explorers bring back; consider the use of the X-ray to find out what is causing disease; consider the experimenting with plants to create something new.

Burpee's activities in creating a new and very beautiful nasturtium necessitated making 58,000 different crosses. When they found what they were after, they grew two more generations before selling the seeds. They have not only created a beautiful blossom, but a more sturdy plant that can withstand disease. This developing of plants that can withstand disease is a remarkable development by the scientist.

The progress which scientists are making in developing new methods of growing plants is enough to amaze one. In New Jersey they are experimenting with growing flowers in sand by watering them with carefully prepared solutions. It will not be very long before you can grow plants in the home in pots of sand by giving a plant certain drops of some kind of diet. It sounds almost to good to be true, but, nevertheless, very successful experiments have been made along this line.

They are now perfecting a new type of greenhouse. By having only one part of one side of glass and by insulating the rest, by using electrical lights instead of sun's rays and utilizing the light for heat also, the florists are producing very nice crops more easily and simply than with the old type of greenhouse. They are even talking about making this new type of greenhouse two or three stories high.

Cornell University, in reporting experiments with the black spot on roses, claim they have worked out a method of controlling it in the greenhouse. If this proves true, we will have one more enemy in the rose garden conquered.

They are using electricity in another interesting way. Modern insect traps to attract all insects are being put around gardens and electricians are experimenting with colors to find out what colors attract the various insects.

New knowledge is constantly producing finer, more beautiful

vegetables and flowers. Mr. Seymour is convinced that tomorrow's gardens depend mostly perhaps on the men and women who are going to care for those gardens.

In looking over a report of Mr. Edward W. Lincoln for the year 1879, which Mr. Seymour considers a splendid literary achievement, he noticed the aim of the Worcester County Horticultural Society was to advance the science and improve the practice of horticulture and to develop and improve the public taste. The successful career of this society can be traced back to the high idealism of the men and women who founded it and who would tolerate nothing but absolute excellence in their achievements.

There is need for a greater, more general appreciation of what horticulture really means, an appreciation by the world at large—by legislature, by government, by people who are not interested in horticulture, but who are, after all, very much affected by it. We must work for a more general appreciation of what horticulture means, so that institutions of learning will offer classes in appreciation of horticulture, just as they do in appreciation of the arts. No other art contributes any more to our daily life than the practice or influence of horticulture.

Those who do gardening know that they work for the joy that is in it, but others cannot comprehend this joy. There are quite a few alphabetical relief projects in the City of New York which give a splendid opportunity for workers to exercise. The boss on one of these projects couldn't comprehend why one of the men was complaining about not having a shovel, and tried to tell him he would't have to work hard if he had nothing to work with. Then the man explained that the other men all had shovels or something to lean on and so he wanted one.

The gardens of tomorrow, like the gardens of yesterday and today are going to be beautiful and fruitful. They are going to bring joy, as well as an occasional lame back, to those who make them and joy to those who behold them. They are going to typify all that is noble and good from the splendid International Peace Garden down to the smallest little plot in some child's garden. And all this will be brought about by the activities of this society and other enthusiasts in this country.

Those who continue to rejoice and take pride in horticulture be worthy of the degree B.E.—Beautifiers of Earth.

In closing this address, Mr Seymour read a very beautiful p entitled "Song of Horticulture," written by Cy Tannhauser.

The Quartette sang two numbers "Lift Thine Eyes" and "I Takes a Thousand Years."

INDEX

SCHEDULE OF PREMIUMS

Offered by the

Worcester County Horticultural Society

Horticultural Building
30 Elm Street
Worcester, Mass.

For the year

1937

THE ATTENTION OF EXHIBITORS IS PARTICULARLY
CALLED TO THE RULES AND REGULATIONS
GENERAL AND SPECIAL

The Davis Press, Worcester

GENERAL RULES AND REGULATIONS

1. Strict conformity to the Regulations and Rules will be expected and required, as well for the benefit of exhibitors as for the convenience of the Officers of the Society.

2. Every Flower or Plant entered in a class of named varieties should be correctly named.

3. All articles offered for premiums must remain within the Hall throughout the hours of Exhibition, unless special permission for their removal shall be granted by the Committee on Exhibition, etc.

4. No person shall make more than one entry of the same variety or be awarded more than one premium under the same number.

5. The Judges may correct, before the close of any exhibition, awards made by them, if satisfied that such were erroneous.

6. The cards of exhibitors competing for premiums shall be reversed, until after premiums are awarded.

7. Competitors are expected to conform strictly to the conditions under which articles are invited. Evasion or violation of them may be reported to the TRUSTEES for future disqualification of the offender.

8. Articles offered for premiums must be in the Hall by 2 o'clock of the days of Exhibition except when otherwise specified. Between 2 and 3 o'clock the Hall will be in exclusive charge of the Committee on Arrangements and Exhibitions. Open to the public from 3 to 9 o'clock.

9. Competition for premiums is open to all residents of Worcester County only, and it is strictly required that all specimens offered for premiums shall have been grown by the competitors, on their own premises, for at least two (2) months previous to the date of exhibition, except where no restriction is stated in schedule.

10. After the articles are arranged they will be under the exclusive charge of the Judges and Committee of Arrangements, and not even the owners will have liberty to remove them until the exhibition is closed, when they will be delivered as the contributors may direct.

11. Where a certain number or quantity of Plants, Flowers, Fruits or Vegetables is designated in the schedule, there must be neither more nor less than that number or quantity of specimens shown; and in no case can other varieties than those named in the schedule be substituted.

12. The Judges may exclude from competition all inferior specimens and may correct any errors that they think were without deliberate purpose.

13. The Committee on Arrangements has power to change the time of exhibition for any article, if an earlier or later season renders such change desirable.

14. All articles offered for premiums should be correctly named. Indefinite appellations such as "Pippin," "Sweeting," "Greening," etc., will not be considered as names. Any person exhibiting the same variety of Fruit or Vegetable, under different names, or exhibiting as grown by himself Flowers, Fruit or Vegetables grown by another, thereby violating the objects and rules of the Society, may be debarred from competing for the Society's premiums until reinstated.

15. Competitors will be required to furnish information as to their mode of cultivation, and to present specimens for trial and examinations, if requested.

16. In all exhibitions of Cut Flowers for competition, the number of blooms, clusters, sprays or spikes shown is not restricted except that it is expected the exhibitor shall use only a sufficient number to make a well-balanced display. All shall be of one color and of one variety in the same vase, except Displays, Vases, Baskets, Standards, or otherwise specified in the schedule. The Judge will consider the quality of the flowers rather than the quantity.

17. The Judges are authorized by the Trustees to invite the assistance of competent and discreet persons in the discharge of their duties.

18. No Judge shall require anything of competitors respecting their exhibits which is not distinctly specified in the schedule.

19. In Table Decorations, collections and displays of Flowers, Fruits, Vegetables, Vases, and Baskets, where the number of exhibits exceeds the number of premiums offered, the Judge *may* award prizes to any worthy exhibits not receiving a premium.

The maximum prize for Vases, Standards, and Baskets shall be two dollars.

20. All premiums that are not claimed within one year after the close of the official year shall be forfeited to the Society.

21. "Downing's Fruits of America," revised edition, will guide the Judge of Fruits in his decisions upon matters at issue.

22. While the Society will take reasonable precautions for the safety of the property of exhibitors, it will be responsible in no case for any loss or damage that may occur.

Scale of Points

Cut Flowers and Wild Flowers.—

Arrangement	30 points
Quality of blooms	40 "
Number of varieties	15 "
Properly named	15

Lilies.—

Size and color of bloom	35 points
Number of perfect flowers and buds on stem	35
Arrangement	15
Properly named	15

Displays.—

Arrangement	40 points
Quality	45 "
Variety	15 "

Collections.—

Quality	45 points
Arrangement	25 "
Variety	30 "

Table Decoration.—

Artistic perfection of arrangement of whole	45 points
Quality	30 "
Proportion and harmony of flowers with accessories	25

Special Funds

OF THE

WORCESTER COUNTY HORTICULTURAL SOCIETY

The following is a list of the Special Funds of the Worcester County Horticultural Society the income of which is devoted to the purpose stated. The date prefixed to each indicates the year in which the fund was established.

1888.   Francis Henshaw Dewey Fund. $1,000.00.
Income to be used for the purchase of books.

1898.   William Eames Fund. $500.00.
Income to be used in prizes for the promotion of apple culture.

1906.   Frederick A. Blake Fund. $1,000.00.
Income only to be used in providing Medals to be awarded to the originators of new varieties of Fruits or Flowers, preference always being given to residents of Worcester County.

In case that the Worcester County Horticultural Society does not find occasion to award medals for New Fruits or Flowers, the said income may be used in special premiums for Orchids or other choice Greenhouse Plants and Flowers.

1907.   Obadiah Brown Hadwen Fund. $1,000.00.
Income to be used for meritorious exhibits of Flowers, Fruits and Vegetables.

1922.   Edwin Draper Fund. $300.00.
Income to be used in prizes for Horticultural exhibitions held under the direction of said Society.

1924.   Miss Frances Clary Morse Fund. $500.00.
Income to be used in prizes for Flowers.

Flowers, Plants, Fruits and Vegetables

1937

☞The Committee on Arrangements and Exhibitions would direct the earnest attention of the Judge to *Rule 12*.

12.   The Judges may exclude from competition all inferior specimens and may correct any errors that they think were without deliberate purpose.

Special Rules

1.   Exhibitors should have all specimens correctly and legibly named and the number of varieties written on the entry cards, notice of which will be taken by the judges in awarding the premiums.

2.   While it is expected that exhibitors will take pains to correctly name their exhibits, the judges will not exclude an exhibit for mistake in nomenclature.

3.   In all exhibitions of lilies the pollen may be removed.

By vote of the trustees, all entries must be made to the Secretary and all cards made out by him or his assistants.

Spring Exhibition

Thursday, March 4, 3 to 9 p. m.
Friday, March 5, 9 a. m. to 9 p. m.
Saturday, March 6, 9 a. m. to 9 p. m.
Sunday, March 7, 12 m. to 9 p. m.

*All articles for this exhibition must be
in the hall and ready for inspection
by the judges by 1 o'clock Thursday*

Class I	Garden Displays	1150,
Class II	Plant Displays	
Class III	Rock Gardens	
	Not to exceed 100 square feet	125.
Class IV	Cut Flowers	75.
Class V	Fruit	75.
Class VI	Vegetables	75.

Frederick A. Blake Fund

Class VII	Carnations	25.

Worcester Garden Club Exhibit

Thursday, April 22

*All articles for this exhibition must be
in the hall and ready for inspection
by the judges by 2 o'clock*

This exhibition will be open to the public from 3 to 9 p. m.

Cut Flowers.—

No. 1. Twenty vases   4.00 3.00 2.00

Table Decorations.—

No. 2. Round table laid for
        four covers.   5.00 4.00 3.00 2.50 2.00
        Oblong table for two covers 5.00 4.00 3.00 2.50 2.00
        Notify the Secretary two
        days in advance.

Carnations.—

No. 3. Vase or Basket, fifty flowers,
        other green permissible   6.00 5.00 4.00

Plant Displays.—

No. 4. Plants in Bloom with Foliage
        Plants. Sixty dollars may be
        used in prizes.

Apple, twelve specimens.—

No. 5. For any variety, eight dollars
        may be used for prizes.

Parsnip, twelve specimens.—

No. 6. Hollow Crown   2.00 1.50 1.00   .50
No. 7. Any other variety   2.00 1.50 1.00   .50

Rhubarb, twelve stalks.—

No. 8. Any variety   2.00 1.50 1.00   .50

Lettuce.—

No. 9. Six heads   2.00 1.50 1.00   .50

Radish.—

No. 10. Two bunches. Six in each bunch   1.50 1.00   .50

Potato, twelve specimens.—

No. 11. Any named variety   2.00 1.50 1.00   .50

May Exhibition

Thursday, May 13

*All articles for this exhibition must be
in the hall and ready for inspection by
the judges by 2 o'clock*

This exhibition will be open to the public from 3 to 9 p.

Cut Flowers.—

No. 12.	Twenty vases			3.00	2.50
No. 13.	Medium basket	3.00	2.50	2.00	1.50

Wild Flowers, fifteen vases.—

No. 14. Five stems in a vase. No
duplicates   3.00 2.00 1.50 1.00

Spring Bulbs, open culture.—

No. 15. Display   4.00 3.00 2.50

Pansy.—

No. 16. Twenty vases, one flower
with foliage in a vase 3.00 2.50 2.00 1.50 1.00

Zonale Geraniums, in bloom.—

No. 17. Six plants   3.00 2.00 1.50

Table Decorations, Spring Flowers.—

No. 18. Table decoration, laid for
two or four covers. Roses prohibited. Notify the Secretary
two days in advance   5.00 4.00 3.00 2.00

Plant Displays.—

No. 19. For exhibits—no restrictions as
to where grown or by whom,
$60.00 may be used for prizes.
Notify the Secretary two days
in advance.

Calendula.—

No. 20.   Arranged in Bowl or Basket   3.00 2.00 1.00

Dandelion.—

No. 21.   One-half peck   1.50 1.00   .50

Lettuce.—

No. 22.   Six heads   2.00 1.50 1.00   .50

Spinach.—

No. 23.   One-half peck   1.50 1.00   .50

Radish, two bunches, six in each bunch.—

No. 24.   Globe   1.50 1.00   .50

Rhubarb, twelve stalks.—

No. 25.   Linnæus   2.50 2.00 1.50 1.00   .50

Asparagus, two bunches, twelve specimens each.—

No. 26.   Any variety   3.00 2.50 2.00 1.50 1.00   .50

Onion.—

No. 27.   Two bunches, six in each bunch   1.50 1.00   .50

Iris Exhibition

Thursday, June 3

*All articles for this exhibition must be
in the hall and ready for inspection by
the judges by 2 o'clock*

This exhibition will be open to the public from 3 to 9 p. m

Iris, German.—
No. 28.   Display   8.00 6.00 4.00 2.
No. 29.   Twenty vases, three stems in
   a vase preferably named   3.00 2.50 2.00 1.50 1.
No. 30.   Basket   2.50 2.00 1.50 1.

Cut Flowers.—
No. 31.   Display   4.00 3.00 2.50 2.00 1.50 1.

Azalea.—
No. 32.   Display in vases   3.00 2.00 1.

Rhododendron.—
No. 33.   Displays in vases   3.00 2.

Peonies.—
No. 34.   Vase or Basket   3.00 2.50 2.00 1.

Lupinus.—
No. 35.   Vase   3.00 2.00 1.50 1.

Roses.—
No. 36.   Vase of Roses. Five dollars
   may be used in prizes.

Zonale Geraniums.—
No. 37.   Twenty vases, one truss in each   .   3.00 2.00 1.

Asparagus, two bunches, twelve specimens each.—
No. 38.   Any variety   2.50 2.00 1.50 1.00   .

Cucumber.—
No. 39.   Three specimens   2.00 1.50 1.00   .

Spinach.—
No. 40.   One-half peck   2.50 2.00 1.50 1.

2.50 2.00 1.50 1.00 .50

2.00 1.50 1.00 .50

2.00 1.50 1.00 .50

ch 2.00 1.50 1.00 .50

Thursday, June 10

*All articles for this exhibition must be
in the hall and ready for inspection by
the judges by 2 o'clock*

This exhibition will be open to the public from 3 to 9 p. m.

Cut Flowers.—

No. 45. From hardy plants and
shrubs outdoor culture,
to be named 4.00 3.00 2.50 2.00 1.50 1.

Wild Flowers, fifteen vases.—

No. 46. Five stems in a vase.
No duplicates 3.00 2.50 2.00 1.50 1.00 .

Siberian Iris.—

No. 47. Medium basket 2.00 1.50 1.00 .

Roses.—

No. 48. Vase H. P. roses, not to exceed .
ten blooms 3.00 2.00 1.

No. 49. Vase H. T. roses, not exceeding
ten blooms 3.00 2.00 1.

Peonies.—

No. 50. Display of Peonies. Notify
the Secretary two days in
advance 5.00 4.00 3.00 2.

No. 51. Twenty vases, one flower in
each 4.00 3.00 2.00 1.00 .

Foxglove.—

No. 52. Vase of twelve spikes 3.00 2.00 1.00 .

Aquilegia.—

No. 53. Display 3.00 2.50 2.00 1.00 .

Begonia.—

No. 54. Four plants in bloom 3.00 2.00 1.

Strawberry, twenty-four berries.—

No. 55. Any variety, five dollars may be used in prizes.

Rhubarb, twelve stalks.—

No. 56. Victoria 2.50 2.00 1.50 1.00 .

Rose Exhibition

Thursday, June 17, open from 3 to 9 p. m.

*All articles for this exhibition must be
in the hall and ready for inspection by
the judges by 2 o'clock*

Roses.—

No. 57. Twelve blooms of distinct named
varieties of H. P. roses, outdoor
culture   4.00   3.00   2.00   1.00

No. 58. Six blooms of distinct named
varieties of H. P. roses, out-
door culture   3.00   2.00   1.00   .50

No. 59. Twelve blooms of distinct named
varieties of H. T. roses, outdoor
culture   4.00   3.00   2.00   1.00

No. 60. Six blooms of distinct named
varieties of H. T. roses, outdoor
culture   3.00   2.00   1.00   .50

No. 61. Collection of cut roses. Twelve
dollars to be used in prizes.

No. 62. Vase of roses, 12 blooms   3.00   2.50   2.00   1.50   1.00

No. 63. Vase H. P. roses, not to exceed
ten blooms   3.00   2.00   1.00

No. 64. Vase H. T. roses, not exceeding
ten blooms   3.00   2.00   1.00

No. 65. Display of cut climbing roses.
Fifteen dollars may be used in
prizes.

No. 66. Basket of roses   3.00   2.50   2.00   1.50

Special Prizes
Miss Frances C. Morse Fund

A. Table decoration of roses, laid for
two or four covers. Flowers
grown by exhibitors   4.00   3.00   2.50   1.00   .50

Peonies.—
    No. 67. Display of Peonies. Notify
           the Secretary two days in
           advance   5.00 4.00 3.00

Aquilegia.—
    No. 68. Bowl   2.50 2.00 1.50

Special Prizes
Obadiah Brown Hadwen Fund

Hardy Flowers, to be named.—
    B. Display of outdoor varieties   5.00 4.00 3.00 2.00

*　　*　　*

Strawberry, twenty-four berries.—

No. 69.	Senator Dunlap		1.50	1.00
No. 70.	Howard No. 17	3.00 2.50 2.00	1.50	1.00
No. 71.	Culver	2.00	1.50	1.00
No. 72.	Any other variety	2.00	1.50	1.00
No. 73.	New varieties	2.00	1.50	1.00

Cherry, one quart.—
    No. 74. For any named variety, five
           dollars may be used for prizes.

Pea, one-half peck.—
    No. 75. Thomas Laxton   2.00 1.50 1.00
    No. 76. Any other variety   2.00 1.50 1.00

Cabbage, three specimens.—
    No. 77. Any named variety   2.50 2.00 1.50

Lettuce, six heads.—
    No. 78. Big Boston Type   2.00 1.50 1.00

Thursday, June 24

All articles for this exhibition must be in the hall and ready for inspection by the judges by 2 o'clock

This exhibition will be open to the public from 3 to 9 p. m.

Cut Flowers.—
No. 79. Twenty vases   3.00 2.50 2.00 1.50 1.00 .50
No. 80. Basket   2.50 2.00 1.50 1.00 .50

Dianthus Barbatus (Sweet William).—
No. 81. Twelve vases, three stems
in a vase   3.00 2.50 2.00 1.50 1.00 .50

Campanula.—
No. 82. Display   4.00 3.00 2.00 1.00

Delphinium.—
No. 83. One vase, not more than twelve
spikes   4.00 3.50 3.00 2.50 2.00 1.50 1.00

Roses.—
No. 84. Collection of Cut Roses. Ten
dollars may be used in prizes.

Special Prizes
Offered by Mr. Herbert R. Kinney

C. Display of Cut Flowers on round
tables   3.00 2.50 2.00 1.50 1.00

This number is intended for the growers who do not compete in the call for twenty vases or displays during the year.

* . * *

Strawberry, twenty-four berries.—
No. 85. Howard No. 17   3.00 2.50 2.00 1.50 1.00 .50
No. 86. Sample   1.50 1.00 .50
No. 87. Dorset   2.00 1.50 1.00 .50
No. 88. Any other variety   2.00 1.50 1.00 .50
No. 89. Collections, not more than six
varieties   5.00 4.00 3.00 2.00 1.00

Currant, twenty-four bunches.—
No. 90. For any variety, five dollars may be used for prizes.

Cherry, one quart.—

| No. 91. | Black Tartarian | 2.00 | 1.50 | 1.00 | .50 |
| No. 92. | Gov. Wood | 2.00 | 1.50 | 1.00 | .50 |

No. 93.   Best display, ten dollars may be used for prizes.

No. 94.   For varieties not scheduled, five dollars may be used for prizes.

Beet, open culture.—

| No. 95. | Twelve specimens | 2.00 | 1.50 | 1.00 | .50 |

Carrot.—

| No. 96. | Two bunches, six in each | 2.00 | 1.50 | 1.00 | .50 |

Pea, one-half peck.

| No. 97. | Gradus | 2.00 | 1.0 | 1.00 | .50 |
| No. 98. | Any other variety | 2.00 | 1.50 | 1.00 | .50 |

Cucumber, three specimens.—

| No. 99. | Any variety | | 1.50 | 1.00 | .50 |

Thursday, July 1

*All articles for this exhibition must be
in the hall and ready for inspection by
the judges by 2 o'clock*

This exhibition will be open to the public from 3 to 9 p. m.

Cut Flowers.—
No. 100. Twenty vases   4.00 3.00 2.50 2.00 1.50 1.00
No. 101. Ten vases   2.50 2.00 1.50 1.00 .50
This number is intended for the growers who do not compete
in call for 20 vases and displays during the year.

Basket.—
No. 102.   3.00 2.50 2.00 1.50 1.00

Japanese Iris.—
No. 103. Display, twenty dollars may be used for prizes.
No. 104. Ten vases, one stem in a vase,
          preferably named   2.00 1.50 1.00   .50

Delphinium.—
No. 105. Display, fifteen dollars may be used for prizes.

Lilium Candidum.—
No. 106. Vase   4.00 3.00 2.00 1.00

Wild Flowers, no duplicates.—
No. 107. Fifteen vases, five stems
          in a vase   2.50 2.00 1.50 1.00   .50

Roses.—
No. 108. Display of cut climbing roses. Ten dollars may be
          used in prizes.

Strawberry, twenty-four berries.—
No. 109. Downing's Bride   2.00 1.50 1.00   .50
No. 110. Ten dollars may be used for
          prizes. Preference given to
          worthy varieties of recent
          introduction.
No. 111. Best display   5.00 4.00 3.00 2.00 1.00

Raspberry, Black Cap, one quart.—
No. 112. Named variety   1.50 1.00   .50

Raspberry, one pint.—

No. 113. Early varieties   2.00 1.50 1.00   .50

No. 114. Varieties not scheduled, five dollars may be used for
          prizes.

Gooseberry, one quart.—

No. 115. Any named variety   2.00 1.50 1.00   .50

Cherry, one quart.—

No. 116. Coe's Transparent   1.50 1.00   .50

No. 117. Montmorency   2.00 1.50 1.00   .50

No. 118. Any other variety   2.00 1.50 1.00   .50

Currant, twenty-four bunches.—

No. 119. For any variety, five dollars may be used for prizes.

Bean, Snap, one-half peck.—

No. 120. Any named variety   2.00 1.50 1.00   .50

Pea, one-half peck.—

No. 121. Sutton's Excelsior   2.00 1.50 1.00   .50

No. 122. Alderman   2.00 1.50 1.00   .50

No. 123. Display   3.00 2.50 2.00 1.00

Display of Vegetables.—

No. 124. Not to exceed 24 square feet, $20.00 may be used
          for prizes. Notify the Secretary two days in advance.

Tomato, twelve specimens.—

No. 125. Any named variety   2.00 1.50 1.00   .50

Sweet Pea Exhibition
Thursday, July 8
*All articles for this exhibition must be
in the hall and ready for inspection by
the judges by 2 o'clock*

This exhibition will be open to the public from 3 to 9 p. m.

Sweet Peas, annual.—
No. 126.   Ten vases, not more than 25
    flower stems in a vase   4.00 3.00 2.00
No. 127.   Table Decoration—Sweet Peas,
    laid for two or four covers, Gyp-
    sophila may be used.   Notify the
    Secretary two days in advance
         4.00 3.00 2.50 2.00 1.00

Sweet Peas.—
No. 128.   Basket, any green may be used.
         3.00 2.00 1.50 1.00

Obadiah Brown Hadwen Fund

D.   Collection of Sweet Peas, fifteen dollars may be used in prizes;

*   *   *

Cut Flowers.—
No. 129.   Display, not exceeding 30
    square feet   4.00 3.00 2.50 2.00 1.50 1.00

Lilium Regale.—
No. 130.   Fifteen dollars may be used in prizes.

Centaurea.—
No. 131.   Display, Gypsophila may be
    used   4.00 3.00 2.50 2.00

Petunia.—
No. 132.   Twenty vases, one flower in
    each   3.00 2.50 2.00 1.00 .50

Raspberry, one pint.—
No. 133.   Latham   2.00 1.50 1.00 .50
No. 134.   Cuthbert   1.50 1.00 .50
No. 135.   Any other variety   1.50 1.00 .50

Apple, twelve specimens.—

No. 136. Any variety   2.00 1.50 1.00

Currant, twenty-four bunches.—

No. 137. Red Cross   1.50 1.00
No. 138. Perfection   2.00 1.50 1.00
No. 139. White Grape   1.50 1.00
No. 140. Versaillaise   2.00 1.50 1.00
No. 141. Any other variety   1.50 1.00

Pea, one-half peck—

No. 142. Telephone   2.00 1.50 1.00

Bean, Snap, one-half peck.—

No. 143. Wax   2.00 1. 0 1.00
No. 144. Green Pod   2.00 1.50 1.00

Cucumber.—

No. 145. Three specimens   1.50 1.00

Cabbage, three specimens.—

No. 146. Any variety   2.00 1.50 1.00

Lettuce, Iceberg.—

No. 147. Twelve heads   2.00 1.50 1.00

Squash, three specimens.—

No. 148. Summer   2.00 1.50 1.00

Thursday, July 15

All articles for this exhibition must be in the hall and ready for inspection by the judges by 2 o'clock

This exhibition will be open to the public from 3 to 9 p. m.

Cut Flowers.—

| No. 149. | Display | 4.00 | 3.00 | 2.50 | 2.00 | 1.50 | 1.00 |
| No. 150. | Standard | 3.00 | 2.50 | 2.00 | 1.50 | 1.00 | .50 |

Antirrhinum (Snap Dragon).—

| No. 151. | Display | | | 3.00 | 2.00 | 1.00 | .50 |

Table Decorations.—

No. 152. Table decoration laid for two or four covers. Flowers to be grown by the exhibitor. Notify the Secretary two days in advance   4.00 3.50 3.00 2.50 2.00 1.50 1.00

Sweet Peas, annual.—

No. 153. Five vases, 25 flower stems in vase   3.00 2.50 2.00 1.50 1.00

Begonia, tuberous rooted.—

| No. 154. | Twelve vases | 4.00 | 3.00 | 2.00 | 1.00 |

Apple, twelve specimens.—

| No. 155. | Yellow Transparent | 2.00 | 1.50 | 1.00 | .50 |

Raspberry.—

| No. 156. | Any variety | 1.50 | 1.00 | .50 |

Blackberry, one quart.—

No. 157. Any variety, five dollars may be used for prizes.

Blueberry.—

| No. 158. | One quart | 1.50 | 1.00 | .50 |

Currants, twenty-four bunches.—

| No. 159. | Wilder | 2.00 | 1.50 | 1.00 | .50 |

Corn, twelve ears.—

| No. 160. | Sweet, any named variety | 2.00 | 1.50 | 1.00 | .50 |

Tomato, twelve specimens.—

| No. 161. | Any named variety | 2.00 | 1.50 | 1.00 | .50 |

Potato, twelve specimens.—

| No. 162. | Any variety | 2.00 | 1.50 | 1.00 | .50 |

Lettuce, twelve heads.—

| No. 163. | Any variety | 2.00 | 1.50 | 1.00 | .50 |

Thursday, July 22

*All articles for this exhibition must be
in the hall and ready for inspection by
the judges by 2 o'clock*

This exhibition will be open to the public from 3 to 9

Cut Flowers.—

| No. 164. | Display | 4.00 3.00 2.50 2.00 |
| No. 165. | Ten vases | 2.50 2.00 1.50 |

This number is intended for the growers who do n
in the call for 20 vases and displays during the year.

Gladiolus.—

No. 166. Twenty vases, one spike in
each   4.00 3.00

Phlox, perennial.—

No. 167. Fifteen vases, one cluster
in each   3.00 2.00

Annuals.—

No. 168. Display   3.00 2.50 2.00

Apple, twelve specimens.—

| No. 169. | Astrachan | 2.00 1.50 |
| No. 170. | Yellow Transparent | 2.00 1.50 |

Blackberry, one quart.—

No. 171. Any varieties, five dollars may be used for

Blueberry, one quart.—

No. 172.   1.50

Raspberry.—

No. 173. Any variety   1.50

Plum, twelve specimens.—

No. 174. Red June   1.50

Bean, Shell, one-half peck.—

No. 175. Any named variety   2.00 1.50

Corn, twelve ears.—

    No. 176. Any named variety   2.00 1.50 1.00   .50

Squash, three specimens.—

    No. 177. Summer   2.00 1.50 1.00   .50

Potato, twelve specimens.—

    No. 178. Irish Cobbler   2.00 1.50 1.00   .50
    No. 179. Any other variety   2.00 1.50 1.00   .50

Vegetables.—

    No. 180. Display, Round Table, $20.00 may be used for prizes. Notify the Secretary two days in advance.

Thursday, July 29

All articles for this exhibition must be in the hall and ready for inspection by the judges by 2 o'clock

This exhibition will be open to the public from 3 to 9 p. m.

Cut Flowers.—
No. 181. Basket   3.00 2.50 2.00 1.50 1.00

Flower Arrangement for Living Room.—
No. 182. Pottery container to be furnished
          by exhibitor   3.00 2.50 2.00 1.50 1.00 .50

Gladiolus.—
No. 183. Display   8.00 6.00 5.00 4.00 3.00

Larkspur, annual.—
No. 184. Display   3.00 2.50 2.00 1.00

Salpiglossis.—
No. 185. Display   4.00 3.00 2.00 1.00

Phlox, perennial.—
No. 186. Fifteen vases, one cluster
          in each   3.00 2.00 1.50 1.00 .50

Zinnia.—
No. 187. Twenty vases, one flower in
          each   3.00 2.50 2.00 1.50 1.00 .50

Wild Flowers.—
No. 188. Fifteen vases, no duplicates.
          Five stems in a vase   2.50 2.00 1.50 1.00 .50

Special Prizes
Offered by Mr. Herbert R. Kinney

E. Table Decorations. For the best
    table decorations   3.00 2.50 2.00 1.50 1.00

This call is intended for exhibitors who do not exhibit in other table decorations during the year. Notify the Secretary two days in advance.

Blueberry, one quart.—
No. 189. Cultivated   2.00 1.50 1.00

Apple, twelve specimens.—
No. 190. Oldenburg   2.00 1.50 1.00 .50
No. 191. Astrachan   2.00 1.50 1.00 .50

Peach, twelve specimens.—
No. 192. Any variety   2.00 1.50 1.00 .50

Bean, Shell, one-half peck.—
No. 193. Dwarf Horticultural   2.00 1.50 1.00 .50
No. 194. Any other variety   2.00 1.50 1.00 .50

Cabbage, three specimens.—
No. 195. Copenhagen   2.00 1.50 1.00 .50
No. 196. Any other named variety   2.00 1.50 1.00 .50

Corn, twelve ears.—
No. 197. Yellow, Sweet   2.50 2.00 1.50 1.00 .50

Potato, twelve specimens.—
No. 198. Rose   2.00 1.50 1.00 .50
No. 199. Varieties not scheduled   2.00 1.50 1.00 .50

Tomato, open culture, twelve specimens.—
No. 200. Any named variety   2.00 1.50 1.00 .50

Gladiolus Exhibition
Thursday, August 5

*All articles for this exhibition must be
in the hall and ready for inspection by
the judges by 2 o'clock*

This exhibition will be open to the public from 3 to 9 p. m.

Gladiolus.—

No. 201. Display. Notify the Secretary two days in advance.
Forty dollars may be used in prizes.

No. 202.	Standard of Gladioli	3.00	2.50	2.00	1.00	.50
No. 203.	Twenty vases, one spike in each	4.00	3.00	2.00	1.00	.50

Aster, large flowered, long stem.—

No. 204.	Vase of 20 blooms	3.00	2.50	2.00	1.00	.50

Salpiglossis.—

No. 205.	Bowl	2.50	2.00	1.00	.50

Phlox Drummondi.—

No. 206.	Display	2.00	1.50	1.00	.50

Annuals.—

No. 207. Display, fifteen dollars may be used in prizes.

Flowers on a Mirror.—

No. 208. Small vase to be shown on a mirror. Vase and mirror
to be furnished by the society. Ten dollars may be
used in prizes. Highest award not to exceed $1.50.
One entry from each exhibitor.

Apple, twelve specimens.—

No. 209.	Williams	2.00	1.50	1.00	.50

No. 210. For varieties not scheduled, five dollars may be
used for prizes.

Apple, crab, twenty-four specimens.—

No. 211.	Varieties not scheduled	1.50	1.00	.50

Peach, twelve specimens.—

No. 212.	Carman	1.50	1.00	.50
No. 213.	Any other variety	1.50	1.00	.50

Plum, twelve specimens.—
No. 214.   Japanese varieties, five dollars
may be used for prizes.

Squash, three specimens.—
No. 215.   Any named variety (excepting
summer varieties)   2.00 1.50 1.00   .50

Bean, Shell, one-half peck.—
No. 216.   Dwarf, any variety   2.00 1. 0 1.00   .50
No. 217.   Pole, any variety   2.00 1.50 1.00   .50

Bean, String, one-half peck.—
No. 218.   Kentucky Wonder   2.00 1.50 1.00   .50

Corn, Sweet, twelve ears.—
No. 219.   Any named variety   2.00 1.50 1.00   .50

Tomato, twelve specimens.—
No. 220.   Any named variety   2.50 2.00 1.50 1.00   .50

Mushroom, native.—
No. 221.   Collection of edible varieties. Twenty dollars to be
used for prizes.

Cucumber, for pickles.—
No. 222.   One-half peck   2.00 1.50 1.00   .50

1937]

Peach.

No. 2

No. 2

No. 2
No. 2

No. 2

No. 2

Thursday, August 12

*All articles for this exhibition must be
in the hall and ready for inspection by
the judges by 2 o'clock*

This exhibition will be open to the public from 3 to 9 p. m.

Gladiolus.—
No. 223.   Basket.   Fifteen dollars to be used in prizes.

Zinnia.—
No. 224.   Display, notify the Secretary
two days in advance   4.00 3.00 2.50 2.00 1.50 1.00

Dahlia.—
No. 225.   Display. Single, pompon,
and miniature   3.00 2.50 2.00 1.00

Obadiah Brown Hadwen Fund

Display of Garden Flowers.—
F.   Not to exceed 24 square feet.
Notify the Secretary two days
in advance   4.00 3.50 3.00 2.50 2.00 1.00

*   * .   *

Flowers on Mirror.—
No. 226.   Small container to be shown on a mirror. Exhibitors
may use own containers. Ten dollars may be used in
prizes. Highest award not to exceed $1.50. One entry from
each exhibitor.

Aster, single or anemone.—
No. 227.   Vase   2.00 1.50 1.00   .50

Apples, twelve specimens.—
No. 228.   Any variety   2.00 1.50 1.00   .50

Plums, twelve specimens.—
No. 229.   Washington   1.50 1.00   .50
No. 230.   Bradshaw   3.00 2.00 1.50 1.00   .50
No. 231.   Imperial Gage   2.00 1.50 1.00   .50
No. 232.   For varieties not scheduled, three
dollars may be used for prizes.

Peach, twelve specimens.—

No. 233.   Five dollars may be used in prizes.

Pear, twelve specimens.—

No. 234.   For varieties not scheduled, five dollars may be used for prizes.

Bean, Pole, one-half peck.—

No. 235.   Shell   2.00 1.50 1.00   .50
No. 236.   String, any variety 2.00 1.50 1.00   .50

Corn, twelve ears.—

No. 237.   Sweet, not less than twelve rows

2.00 1.50 1.00   .50

Vegetables.—

No. 238.   Display of vegetables from
Home Gardens to cover 12
square feet   5.00 4.00 3.00 2.00 1.00

Thursday, August 19

*All articles for this exhibition must be
in the hall and ready for inspection by
the judges by 2 o'clock*

This exhibition will be open to the public from 3 to 9 p. m.

Cut Flowers.—

No. 239.	Display. Class 1	5.00	4.00	3.50	3.00	
	Class 2	4.00	3.50	3.00	2.50	2.00
No. 240.	Basket	3.00	2.50	2.00	1.50	1.00

Aster, large flowered.—

No. 241.	Twenty vases, three blooms in a vase	3.00	2.50	2.00	1.00	.50

Lilies.—

No. 242.	Display	5.00	4.00	3.00	2.00

Notify the Secretary two days
in advance.

Dahlia.—

LARGE FLOWERED.—

No. 243.	Twenty vases, one flower in each	4.00	3.00	2.00	1.50	1.00

Zinnia, Lilliput variety.—

No. 244.	Display	3.00	2.00	1.00	.50

Begonia, tuberous rooted.—

No. 245.	Display	5.00	4.00	3.00	2.00	1.00

Verbena.—

No. 246.	Basket or Bowl	2.50	2.00	1.50	1.00	.50

Five Miniature Containers.—

No. 247. Display. A group of five miniature containers, not to exceed 4 inches in height. Containers to be owned by exhibitors. Ten dollars may be used for prizes. Highest award not to exceed $1.50.

Apples, twelve specimens.—

No. 248.	Porter		1.50	1.00	.50	
No. 249.	Red Gravenstein	2.50	2.00	1.50	1.00	.50

No. 250. For varieties not scheduled, five
dollars may be used for prizes.

Plum.—

No. 251.　Display, no restriction as to
arrangements　　　　　　　　　4.00 3.00 2.00 1.00

Peach, twelve specimens.—

No. 252.　Any variety　　　　　　　1.50 1.00　.50

Pear, twelve specimens.—

No. 253.　Clapp's Favorite　3.00 2.50 2.00 1.50 1.00　.50

Squash, three specimens.—

No. 254.　Any named variety　　　2.50 2.00 1.50 1.00

Pepper, twelve specimens.—

No. 255.　Harris's Early　　　　　2.50 2.00 1.50 1.00
No. 256.　Bell Type　　　　　　　2.50 2.00 1.50 1.00

Vegetables.—

No. 257.　Display, not to exceed 24 square feet, $20.00 may
be used for prizes. Notify the Secretary two days in
advance.

Thursday, August 26

All articles for this exhibition must be in the hall and ready for inspection by the judges by 2 o'clock

This exhibition will be open to the public from 3 to 9 p. m.

Cut Flowers.—

No. 258. Display. Class 1   5.00 4.00 3.50 3.00

               Class 2   4.00 3.50 3.00 2.50 2.00

No. 259. Pair Mantel vases. Vases to be owned by exhibitor. Ten dollars may be used for prizes.

Dahlia.—

No. 260. Standard—Dahlias
predominating   2.50 2.00 1.50 1.00 .50

Gladiolus.—

No. 261. Basket   3.00 2.50 2.00 1.00 .50

Aster.—

No. 262. Display, not exceeding
25 square feet   5.00 4.00 3.00 2.00 1.00

Scabiosa.—

No. 263. Vase   2.50 2.00 1.50 1.00 .50

Apple, twelve specimens.—

No. 264. Gravenstein   3.00 2.50 2.00 1.50 1.00 .50

No. 265. Maiden's Blush   1.50 1.00 .50

No. 266. Wealthy   2.50 2.00 1.50 1.00 .50

Apple, Crab, twenty-four specimens.—

No. 267. Hyslop   2.50 2.00 1.50 1.00 .50

Peach, twelve specimens.—

No. 268. Champion   1.50 1.00 .50

No. 269. Oldmixon   2.00 1.00 .50

No. 270. Golden Jubilee   2.00 1.50 1.00 .50

No. 271. Seedlings   1.50 1.00 .50

No. 272. Crawford (early)   2.00 1.50 1.00 .50

No. 273. Varieties not scheduled, five dollars may be used for prizes.

No. 274. New varieties. Five dollars may be used in prizes.

Plum, twelve specimens.—

No. 275. Golden Varieties	1.50	1.00	.50
No. 276. Lombard	2.00 1.50	1.00	.50
No. 277. Burbank	2.00 1.50	1.00	.50
No. 278. New varieties	1.50	1.00	.50

No. 279. For Japanese varieties not scheduled, five dollars may be used for prizes.

No. 280. Other varieties not scheduled, five dollars may be used for prizes.

Grape, three clusters.—

No. 281. Green Mountain	2.00 1.50	1.00	.50
No. 282. Moore's	1.50	1.00	.50
No. 283. Ontario	1.50	1.00	.50
No. 284. Varieties not scheduled	1.50	1.00	.50

Pepper, twelve specimens.—

No. 285. Squash	2.00 1.50	1.00	.50
No. 286. Any other variety	2.00 1.50	1.00	.50

Tomato, twelve specimens.—

No. 287. Beauty	2.50 2.00	1.50	1.00	.50
No. 288. Any other variety	2.50 2.00	1.50	1.00	.50

Bean, one-half peck.—

No. 289. Dwarf Lima	2.00 1.50	1.00	.50
No. 290. Pole Lima	2.00 1.50	1.00	.50

Cabbage, three specimens.—

No. 291. Any named variety	2.00 1.50	1.00	.50

Celery, blanched (named) six specimens.—

No. 292. Any variety	2.00 1.50	1.00	.50

Carrot, twelve specimens.—

No. 293. Any variety	2.50 2.00	1.50	1.00	.50

Egg Plant.—

No. 294. Three specimens	2.00 1.50	1.00	.50

Mushroom, native.—

No. 295. Collection of edible varieties. Twenty dollars to be used for prizes.

Thursday, September 2

*All articles for this exhibition must be
in the hall and ready for inspection by
the judges by 2 o'clock*

This exhibition will be open to the public from 3 to 9 p. m.

Cut Flowers.—
No. 296.　Display. Class 1　　　　5.00 4.00 3.50 3.00
　　　　　　　　Class 2　　　4.00 3.50 3.00 2.50 2.00

No. 297.　Metal container of cut flowers,
　　　　　container to be furnished by
　　　　　exhibitor　　　3.00 2.50 2.00 1.50 1.00　.50

Dahlia.—
No. 298.　Twenty vases, one flower in
　　　　　each vase　　　　4.00 3.00 2.00 1.00

Cosmos.—
No. 299.　Vase or basket　　2.50 2.00 1.50 1.00　.50

Celosia.—
No. 300.　Display　　4.00 3.00 2.50 2.00 1.50 1.00
　　　　　Notify the Secretary two days in advance.

Apple, twelve specimens.—
No. 301.　New varieties　　2.00 1.50 1.00　.50
No. 302.　Wealthy　　　　2.00 1.50 1.00　.50

Pear, twelve specimens.—
No. 303.　Louise Bonne de Jersey　　1.50 1.00　.50
No. 304.　Urbaniste　　　　　1.50 1.00　.50
No. 305.　Varieties not scheduled, five dollars may be used
　　　　　for prizes.

Peach, twelve specimens.—
No. 306.　Crawford (late)　　2.00 1.50 1.00　.50
No. 307.　Elberta　　　　　2.00 1.50 1.00　.50
No. 308.　Display, no restriction as to
　　　　　arrangement　　　8.00 6.00 4.00 3.00

Plum, twelve specimens.—
No. 309.　Any variety　　　2.00 1.50 1.00　.50

Grape, three clusters.—

No. 310.	Brighton			1.50	1.00	.50
No. 311.	Campbell			1.50	1.00	.50
No. 312.	Lindley			1.50	1.00	.50
No. 313.	Worden	2.50	2.00	1.50	1.00	.50
No. 314.	Concord	2.50	2.00	1.50	1.00	.50
No. 315.	Delaware		2.00	1.50	1.00	.50
No. 316.	Niagara	2.50	2.00	1.50	1.00	.50
No. 317.	Pocklington			1.50	1.00	.50
No. 318.	Moore's Diamond			1.50	1.00	.50

No. 319. For other varieties, ten dollars may be used for prizes.

No. 320. New varieties, five dollars may be used for prizes.

Quince, twelve specimens.—

No. 321.	Any variety	2.00	1.50	1.00	.50

Melon, three specimens.—

No. 322.	Green Flesh	2.00	1. 0	1. 0	.50
No. 323.	Yellow Flesh	2.00	1. 0	1.00	.50
No. 324.	Water	2.00	1.50	1.00	.50

Tomato.—

No. 325. Display. Fifteen dollars may be used for prizes.

Vegetables.—

No. 326. Display to cover 24 square
feet. Notify the Secretary
two days in advance   7.00 6.00 5.00 4.00 3.00

Dahlia Exhibition

Thursday, September 9

*All articles for this exhibition must be
in the hall and ready for inspection by
the judges by 2 o'clock*

This exhibition will be open to the public from 3 to 9 p. m.

Dahlia.—

No. 327.   Fifty vases, one flower in each. Twenty-five dollars
may be used in prizes. Notify the Secretary two
days in advance.

No. 328.   Twelve vases, one flower
in each   2.50 2.00 1.50 1.00   .50

This number is intended for the growers who do not compete
in other classes for Dahlias during the year.

No. 329.   Single varieties, twenty vases 3.00 2.50 2.00 1.00

No. 330.   Basket of large flowered   3.00 2.50 2.00 1.00

POMPON.

No. 331.   Twenty vases, three sprays in
each   3.00 2.50 2.00 1.00

Display of Flower Arrangement.—

No. 332.   No restrictions as to kind of tables used, not to cover
more than 24 square feet. Flowers to be grown by
exhibitor. Receptacles to be furnished by the exhibitors.
Notify the Secretary two days in advance. Twenty-five
dollars may be used in prizes. No baskets.

SCALE OF POINTS BY WHICH THE ABOVE CLASS IS TO BE JUDGED

Arrangement of flowers   40 points
Proportion and harmony of flowers with
· receptacles   35
Quality of flowers   25

Begonia, tuberous rooted.—

No. 333.   Cut flowers in vases. Ten dollars may be used in
prizes.

Edwin Draper Fund

Begonia, tuberous rooted.—

G. Display of Potted Plants. Fifteen dollars may be used in prizes.

* * *

Apple, twelve specimens.—

No. 334. Varieties not scheduled, five dollars may be used for prizes.

Pear, twelve specimens.—

No. 335.	Bartlett	3.00	2.50	2.00	1.50	1.00	.50
No. 336.	Seckel	3.00	2.50	2.00	1.50	1.00	.50
No. 337.	Any variety, not scheduled				1.50	1.00	.50
No. 338.	Display, no restriction as to arrangement		6.00	5.00	4.00	3.00	2.00

Notify the Secretary two days in advance.

Peach.—

No. 339. Any variety   1.50 1.00 .50

Quince, twelve specimens.—

No. 340. Orange   2.00 1.50 1.00 .50

Grapes.—

No. 341. Display of Grapes. Ten dollars may be used for prizes.

Squash, three specimens.—

No. 342. Warren   2.00 1.50 1.00 .50
No. 343. Golden Hubbard   2.50 2.00 1.50 1.00 .50
No. 344. For varieties not scheduled, five dollars may be used for prizes.

Cabbage, three specimens.—

No. 345. Red   2.00 1.50 1.00 .50
No. 346. Savoy   1.50 1.00 .50
No. 347. Any other variety   2.50 2.00 1.50 1.00 .50

Cauliflower.—

No. 348. Three specimens   2.50 2.00 1.50 1.00 .50

Turnip.—

No. 349. Twelve specimens   1.50 1.00 .50

Broccoli.—

No. 350. Three specimens   2.00 1.50 1.00 .50

Thursday, September 16

All articles for this exhibition must be
in the hall and ready for inspection by
the judges by 2 o'clock

This exhibition will be open to the public from 3 to 9 p. m.

Dahlia.—
No. 351. Display. Fifty dollars may be used for prizes.
Notify the secretary two days in advance.
No. 352. Basket   2.50 2.00 1.50 1.00 .50
This number is intended for growers who do not compete in
other classes for Dahlias during the year.

Cosmos.—
No. 353. Display. Notify the Secretary
two days in advance   3.00 2.00 1.50 1.00 .50

Marigold.—
No. 354. Display. Notify the Secretary two days in advance   3.00 2.00 1.00 .50

Apple, one standard box, standard pack.—
No. 355. McIntosh   4.00 3.00 2.00 1.00 .50

Apple, twelve specimens.—
No. 356. Hubbardston   2.00 1.50 1.00 .50
No. 357. Tompkins King   2.00 1.50 1.00 .50
No. 358. McIntosh   3.50 3.00 2.50 2.00 1.50 1.00 .50
No. 359. For other varieties not scheduled, five dollars may be
used for prizes.

Pear, twelve specimens.—
No. 360. Sheldon   3.00 2.00 1.50 1.00 .50

Potato, six varieties (named).—
No. 361. Twelve specimens of each
5.00 4.00 3.00 2.00 1.50 1.00

Squash, three specimens.—

No. 362.   Green Delicious   2.00 1.50 1.00   .50
No. 363.   Any other variety, not scheduled 2.50 2.00 1.50 1.00

Cauliflower, three specimens.—

No. 364.   2.00 1.50 1.00   .50

Vegetables.—

No. 365.   Collection not to exceed 25
           varieties   10.00 8.00 7.00 6.00 5.00
           Notify the Secretary two days in advance.

Thursday, September 23

*All articles for this exhibition must be
in the hall and ready for inspection by
the judges by 2 o'clock*

This exhibition will be open to the public from 3 to 9 p. m.

Cut Flowers.—

No. 366.　Display　　　4.00　3.50　3.00　2.50　2.00　1.50　1.00

Standard of Cut Flowers.—

No. 367.　Twenty dollars may be used in prizes.

Dried Flowers, Statice, Strawflowers, Lunaria (Honesty).—

No. 368.　Display.　　　　　　　4.00　3.50　2.00　1.00

Apple, one standard box, standard pack.—

No. 369.　Any variety not scheduled

　　　　　　　　　　　　4.00　3.00　2.00　1.00　.50

Apple, twelve specimens.—

No. 370.　Sutton Beauty　　　　2.00　1.50　1.00　.50

Display of Fruit.—

No. 371.　Not to exceed 20 square feet. Thirty dollars may be
　　　　　used in prizes.

Pear, twelve specimens.—

No. 372.　Bosc　　　　　3.00　2.50　2.00　1.50　1.00　.50

Grape, open culture.—

No. 373.　Collection of not less than five varieties, three clusters
　　　　　each.　　　　　　　3.00　2.50　2.00　1.50　1.00

Table Decorations of Flowers.—

No. 374.　Table decoration laid for
　　　　　two or four covers. Flowers
　　　　　grown by exhibitor. Notify
　　　　　the Secretary two days in
　　　　　advance　6.00　5.00　4.50　4.00　3.00　2.00　1.50　1.00

Pumpkins, three specimens.—

No. 375.　Sweet　　　　　　　2.00　1.50　1.00　.50

Cabbage, three specimens.—
No. 376. Any named variety   2.50 2.00 1.50 1.00 .50

Parsley.—
No. 377. One-half peck   2.50 2.00 1.50 1.00 .50

Peppers.—
No. 378. Display. Fifteen dollars to be used for prizes.

Celery, blanched, six specimens.—
No. 379. Golden   2.50 2.00 1.50 1.00
No. 380. Other varieties   2.50 2.00 1.50 1.00

Squash, three specimens.—
No. 381. Blue Hubbard   3.00 2.50 2.00 1.50 1.00

Special Prizes
Offered by Mr. Herbert R. Kinney

I. Display of vegetables from
Home Gardens to
cover 16 square feet   5.00 4.00 3.00 2.50 2.00 1.00

Fruit and Vegetable Exhibition
Thursday, September 30

*All articles for this exhibition must be
in the hall and ready for inspection by
the judges by 2 o'clock*

This exhibition will be open to the public from 3 to 9 p. m.

Cut Flowers.—
No. 382.   Display—$40.00 may be awarded in prizes.

Hardy Chrysanthemum, out-door culture.—
No. 383.   Cut flowers in vases. Ten dollars may be used in prizes.

Apple, one standard box, standard pack.—

McIntosh	4.00	3.00	2.00	1.00	.50

Apple, twelve specimens.—

No. 384.	Baldwin	3.50	3.00	2.50	2.00	1.50	1.00	.50
No. 385.	Bellflower					1.50	1.00	.50
No. 386.	Winter Banana					1.50	1.00	.50
No. 387.	Peck's					1.50	1.00	.50
No. 388.	R. I. Greening				3.00	2.00	1.50	1.00	.50
No. 389.	Northern Spy				3.00	2.00	1.50	1.00	.50
No. 390.	Palmer					1.50	1.00	.50
No. 391.	Roxbury Russet				3.00	2.00	1.50	1.00	.50
No. 392.	Cortland					2.00	1.50	1.00	.50
No. 393.	Opalescent					1.50	1.00	.50
No. 394.	Delicious				2.50	2.00	1.50	1.00	.50

No. 395.   New varieties, five dollars may be used in prizes.
No. 396.   Sweet varieties not scheduled, five dollars may be used for prizes.
No. 397.   For varieties other than sweet not scheduled, fifteen dollars may be used for prizes.
No. 398.   For varieties that have been scheduled, fifteen dollars may be used.

Pear, twelve specimens.—

No. 399.	Angouleme			1.50	1.00	.50
No. 400.	Clairgeau		2.00	1.50	1.00	.50
No. 401.	Lawrence	2.50	2.00	1.50	1.00	.50

No. 402.　Anjou　　　　　　3.00　2.50　2.00　1.50　1.00　.50
No. 403.　For varieties not scheduled, ten dollars may be used for prizes.
No. 404.　For varieties that have been scheduled, ten dollars may be used for prizes.

Grape, open culture.—
No. 405.　For any variety, six clusters, ten dollars may be used for prizes.

Peach, twelve specimens.—
No. 406.　Any variety, named, ten dollars may be used for prizes.

Quince, twelve specimens.—
No. 407.　Champion　　　　　　2.00　1.50　1.00　.50

Cauliflower.—
No. 408.　Three specimens　　　2.50　2.00　1.50　1.00　.50

Celery, blanched, six specimens.—
No. 409.　Golden　　　　　　　2.50　2.00　1.50　1.00　.50
No. 410.　Any other varieties, not
　　　　　scheduled　　　　　　2.00　1.50　1.00　.50

Endive.—
No. 411.　Six specimens　　　　　　1.50　1.00　.50

Leeks.—
No. 412.　Twelve specimens　　　　1.50　1.00　.50

Onion, twelve specimens.—
No. 413.　For varieties, five dollars may be used for prizes.

Salsify.—
No. 414.　Twelve specimens　　　　1.50　1.00　.50

Turnip, twelve specimens.—
No. 415.　Purple Top Globe　　　2.00　1.50　1.00　.50
No. 416.　Any variety, not scheduled　2.00　1.50　1.00　.50

Thursday, October 7

*All articles for this exhibition must be
in the hall and ready for inspection by
the judges by 2 o'clock*

This exhibition will be open to the public from 3 to 9 p. m.

Ferns.—

No. 417. Display, potted ferns, named varieties. Twenty
dollars may be used in prizes.

Specimen Fern.—

No. 418. One plant   3.00 2.00 1.00

Hardy Chrysanthemum, out-door culture.—

No. 419. Plants. Twenty dollars may be used in prizes.

Cut Flowers.—

No. 420. Basket. Ten dollars may be used in prizes.

Apple, one standard box, standard pack.—

No. 421. Baldwin   4.00 3.00 2.00 1.00   .50

No. 422. Any other variety except
McIntosh   4.00 3.00 2.00 1.00   .50

No. 423. Collection, not to exceed
10 varieties   5.00 4.00 3.00 2.50 2.00 1.00

No. 424. Three flats, any
variety   8.00 7.00 6.00 5.00 4.00 3.00

Apples, forty-nine specimens.—

No. 425. McIntosh   5.00 4.00 3.00 2.00 1.00

No. 426. Any other named variety
               5.00 4.00 3.00 2.00 1.00

Table Decorations—Fruit.—

No. 427. Table decoration laid for
two or four covers, no restrictions. Notify the Secretary
two days in advance   4.00 3.00 2.00 1.00

Onion, twelve specimens.—

No. 428. Yellow Globe Danvers   2.50 2.00 1.50 1.00   .50

Parsnip, twelve specimens.—

No. 429. Any variety   2.00 1.50 1.00   .50

Squash.—

No. 430.　Collection　　　　　5.00　4.50　4.00　3.50　3.00

Turnip, twelve specimens.—

No. 431.　English varieties, not scheduled　2.00　1.50　1.00　.50

Celery, blanched, six specimens.—

No. 432.　Any variety　　　　2.50　2.00　1.50　1.00　.50

Grains.—

No. 433.　Best exhibit, five dollars may be used for prizes.

Field Beans.—

No. 434.　Best exhibit, ten dollars may be used for prizes.

Chrysanthemum Exhibition

Thursday, Nov. 4, 3 to 9 p. m.
Friday, Nov. 5, 9 a. m. to 9 p. m.
Saturday, Nov. 6, 9 a. m. to 9 p. m.
Sunday, Nov. 7, 12 m. to 9 p. m.

*All articles for this exhibition must be
in the hall and ready for inspection by
the judges by 1 o'clock Thursday*

Chrysanthemums.—

No. 435.	Twelve blooms, not less than six varieties, to be named	12.00	10.00	8.00
No. 436.	Collection of twenty-five large blooms, long stems	20.00	15.00	10.00
No. 437.	Pompons, display in vases	5.00 4.00	3.00	2.00
No. 438.	Single varieties, display in vases	5.00 4.00	3.00	2.00
No. 439.	Anemones, display in vases	5.00 4.00	3.00	2.00
No. 440.	Six specimen plants	10.00	8.00	6.00
No. 441.	One specimen plant	3.00	2.00	1.00

Standard Commercial Varieties.—

No. 442.	Chrysanthemums, vase of white	4.00	3.00	2.00
No. 443.	Chrysanthemums, vase of yellow	4.00	3.00	2.00
No. 444.	Chrysanthemums, vase of pink	4.00	3.00	2.00

Note. Six flowers in each, one variety in each vase. Stems not less than two feet.

Exhibition Varieties.—

No. 445.	Chrysanthemums, vase of white	4.00	3.00	2.00
No. 446.	Chrysanthemums, vase of yellow	4.00	3.00	2.00
No. 447.	Chrysanthemums, vase of pink	4.00	3.00	2.00

Note. Six flowers in each, one variety in each vase. Stems not less than two feet.

Chrysanthemums.—

No. 448.	Basket of Pompons	4.00	3.00	2.00	1.00
No. 449.	Basket of Single	4.00	3.00	2.00	1.00
No. 450.	Basket of Anemones	4.00	3.00	2.00	1.00

Garden Displays } A
Plant Displays } B   775.00

Persons competing for these premiums must notify the Secretary three weeks before date of Exhibition.

Special Exhibits.—
Seventy-five dollars may be used for prizes.

Frederick A. Blake Fund

J. **Chrysanthemums.**—Best bloom   4.00 3.00 2.00

Obadiah Brown Hadwen Fund

K. **Chrysanthemums.**—Large Flowers. Basket. Fifteen dollars to be awarded in prizes.

Special Prizes
Offered by Mrs. Mabel Knowles Gage

L. **Table Decorations.**—A Thanksgiving table. No restrictions. Laid for two or four covers. Notify the Secretary two days in advance. Fifty dollars to be used in prizes.

Fern Globes.—
No. 451.   3.00 2.00 1.50 1.00

Glass Fernery.—
No. 452. Other than Fern Globe   4.00 3.00 2.00 1.00

Wild Fruits and Berries.—
No. 453. Display   5.00 4.00 3.00 2.50 1.50 1.00

Physalis Franchettii (Chinese Lanterns).—
No. 454. Basket   4.00 3.00 2.00 1.00

Fruit Display.—
No. 455. No restriction as to arrangement. $40.00 may be used in prizes. Notify the Secretary two days in advance.

Apples, forty-nine specimens.—

No. 456.	Baldwin	6.00	5.00	4.00	3.00	2.00	1.00
No. 457.	Delicious		5.00	4.00	3.00	2.00	1.00
No. 458.	Any other named variety		5.00	4.00	3.00	2.00	1.00
No. 459.	Fancy Basket of Apples	3.00	2.50	2.00	1.50	1.00
No. 460.	Fancy Basket of Pears	3.00	2.50	2.00	1.50	1.00

Special Exhibition of Apples
William Eames Fund

A. Baldwin, best twelve.—
Three premiums   1.50 1.00 .50

B. Northern Spy.—
Three premiums   1.50 1.00 .50

C. Delicious.—
Three premiums   1.50 1.00 .50

D. Rhode Island Greening.—
Three premiums   1.50 1.00 .50

E. Roxbury Russet.—
Three premiums   1.50 1.00 .50

F. Sutton Beauty.—
Three premiums   1.50 1.00 .50

G. McIntosh.—
Three premiums   1.50 1.00 .50

H. Any other Variety.—
Three premiums   1.50 1.00 .50

*   *   *

Brussels Sprouts.—
No. 461. One-half peck   2.00 1.50 1.00 .50

Celery, blanched, six specimens.—
No. 462. Giant Pascal   2.00 1.50 1.00 .50
No. 463. Any other variety   2.50 2.00 1.50 1.00 .50

Onion, twelve specimens.—

No. 464. White Globe		2.00 1.50 1.00	.50
No. 465. Red Globe		2.00 1.50 1.00	.50
No. 466. Cracker		1.50 1.00	.50
No. 467. Any other variety	2.50 2.00 1.50 1.00		.50

Cabbage, three specimens.—

No. 468.   2.00 1.50 1.00   .50

Parsnip, twelve specimens.—

No. 469. Hollow Crown   2.00 1.50 1.00   .50

Squash, three specimens.—

No. 470. Green Hubbard   2.50 2.00 1.50 1.00   .50

Gourds.—

No. 471. Display. Twelve dollars to be used for prizes.

Turnip, twelve specimens.—

No. 472. Purple Top Globe   2.00 1.50 1.00   .50

Turnip, six specimens.—

No. 473. White Swede   2.00 1.50 1.00   .50
No. 474. Yellow Swede   2.00 1.50 1.00   .50

Potato, twelve specimens.—

No. 475. Green Mountain   2.50 2.00 1.50 1.00
No. 476. Any other variety   2.50 2.00 1.50 1.00

Annual Meeting, Thursday, December 2, 1937.
Premiums will be paid on or after November 20, 1937.

THE LIBRARY OF THE
WORCESTER COUNTY HORTICULTURAL SOCIETY

The Library Committee wish to call your attention to the Library and Reading Room, where the librarian is always ready to extend every facility possible to those in search of horticultural information.

COMMITTEE ON
LIBRARY AND PUBLICATIONS

EDWARD W. BREED, Chairman   MRS. AMY W. SMITH
WILLIAM ANDERSON   HERBERT R. KINNEY
FLORENCE E. FIELD, Librarian

SOME OF THE RECENT ACCESSIONS TO THE LIBRARY

Cactus, by A. J. van Laren—1935

California Cactus, by E. M. Baxter—1935

The Gardener's How Book, by Chesla C. Sherlock—1935

Insect Enemies of Shade Trees, by Glenn W. Herrick—1935

1936 Gladiolus Year Book, New England Gladiolus Society

How to Know the Mosses, by Elizabeth Marie Dunham—1916

Ferns of the Vicinity of New York, by John Kunkel Small—1935

Bigger and Better Roses for Garden, House and Exhibition
(English), by G. F. Mappin—1935

Lilies: Their Culture and Management, by H. Drysdale Woodcock
and J. Coutts (London, 1935)

Rhododendrons and Azaleas, by Clement Gray Bowers—1935

A Year in the Rose Garden, by J. H. Nicolas—1936

The Garden Encyclopedia, Edited by E. L. D. Seymour—1936

Clematis (The Large and Small Flowered), by Ernest Markham
(London, 1935)

Rock Gardens: How to Make and Maintain Them, by Lewis B.
Meredith—1923

Plant Hunting on the Edge of the World, by F. Kingdon Ward
(London, 1930)

The 1936 American Rose Annual, The American Rose Society

New Flower Arrangements, by Mrs. Walter R. Hine—1936

The Book of Perennials, by Alfred C. Hottes—1933

Gentians, by David Wilkie, (London, 1936)

Daylilies, by Dr. A. B. Stout—1934

The Flowering Plants, Grasses, Sedges and Ferns of Great Britain,
by Ann Pratt, 6 vols.

Plant Propagation, by Alfred C. Hottes—1934

The Living Garden, by E. J. Salisbury (London, 1936)

First Gourd Book, by Helen M. Tillinghast—1935

Adventures with Hardy Bulbs, by Louise Beebe Wilder—1936

Vegetable Crops, by Dr. Homer C. Thompson—1931
Fertilizers and Crop Production, by Dr. L. L. Van Slyke—1932
Weeds, by W. C. Muenscher—1935
Mexican Plants for American Gardens, by Cecile Hulse Matschat
The Gladiolus Book, by Forman T. McLean
Our Native Cacti, by Edith Bailey Higgins
Succulents, by A. J. van Laren
House Plants, by Marjorie Norrell Sulzer
Herbs and the Earth, by Henry Beston
Old Roses, by Mrs. Frederick Love Keays
Flower and Table Arrangements, by Esther Longyear Murphy
Flower Arrangement, by F. F. Rockwell and Esther C. Grayson
Tuberous-Rooted Begonias and their Culture, by George Otten
American Ferns, by Edith A. Roberts and Julia R. Lawrence
Azaleas and Camellias, by H. Harold Hume
Gardening with Herbs, by Helen Morgenthau Fox
The Gladiolus and its Culture, by Alvin C. Beal, Ph.D.
American Orchid Culture, by Prof. E. A. White
Spring Flowering Bulbs, by Clark L. Thayer
The Book of Shrubs, by Alfred C. Hottes
Garden Pools, by L. W. Ramsey and Charles H. Lawrence
Fruits and Vegetables under Glass, by William Turner
The Book of Water Gardening, by Peter Bisset
Little Book of Climbing Plants, by Alfred C. Hottes
Flowering Trees and Shrubs, by R. C. Notcutt
Chrysanthemums, Under Glass and Outdoors, by Alexander Laurie
Flowers for Cutting and Decoration, by Richardson Wright
The Arrangement of Flowers, by Mrs. Walter R. Hine
Roses for all Climates, by George C. Thomas
Cultivated Evergreens, by L. H. Bailey
Delphiniums, Their History and Cultivation, by George A. Phillips
Lilies and Their Culture in North America, by William N. Craig

Worcester County Horticultural Society

SCHEDULE OF PRIZES
Offered to
Children of Worcester County

Exhibitions to be held Saturday, August 21
and Saturday, September 11, 1937
Horticultural Building, 30 Elm Street

Worcester, Massachusetts

Saturday, August 21
All articles must be in the hall by 1 o'clock

> The exhibits must be the results of individ-
> ual effort of the child from the time of
> planting to the arranging of the exhibit.

Open to Children under 14 years of age

Display of Flowers.—

No. 1. Not to exceed fifteen vases

2.00	1.50	1.25	1.00	.50

Zinnia.—

No. 2. Not to exceed 10 vases   .75 .50 .25

Asters.—

No. 3. Not to exceed 10 vases   .75 .50 .25

Petunia.—

No. 4. Not to exceed 10 vases   .75 .50 .25

Calendula.—

No. 5. Not to exceed 10 vases   .75 .50 .25

Wild Flowers.—

No. 6. Not to exceed fifteen vases 1.50 1.25 1.00 .50

No. 7. Vase of Flowers   1.00 .75 .50 .25

Display of Vegetables.—

No. 8. Not to exceed 12 varieties

2.00	1.75	1.50	1.25	1.00	.75

Beets.—

No. 9. Six specimens   .75 .50 .25

Summer Squash.—

No. 10. Two specimens   .75 .50 .25

String Beans.—

No. 11. Two quarts   .75 .50 .25

Potato.—

No. 12 Twelve specimens   1.00 .75 .50

Sweet Corn.—

No. 13. Six ears   1.00 .75 .50

Tomato.—

No. 14. Six specimens   .75 .50 .25

Carrots.—

No. 15. Six specimens   .75 .50 .25

Cucumber.—

No. 16. Two specimens   .75 .50 .25

Open to Children between the ages of 14 and 21

Display of Flowers.—

No. 17. Not to exceed 15 vases — 2.50 2.00 1.75 1.00

Asters.—

No. 18. Not to exceed 10 vases — 1.00 .75 .50 .25

Petunia.—

No. 19. Not to exceed 10 vases — 1.00 .75 .50 .25

Gladiolus.—

No. 20. Basket — 1.00 .75 .50 .25

Zinnia.—

No. 21. Not to exceed 10 vases — 1.00 .75 .50 .25

Wild Flowers.—

No. 22. Not to exceed 15 vases — 1.50 1.25 1.00 .50 .25

No. 23. Vase of Flowers — 1.00 .75 .50 .25 .25

Display of Vegetables.—

No. 24. Not over 15 varieties

2.50 2.00 1.75 1.50 1.25 1.00 .50

Potato.—

No. 25. Twelve specimens — 1.50 1.00 .75 .50 .25

Beets.—

No. 26. Six specimens — 1.00 .75 .50 .25

Carrots.—

No. 27. Six specimens — 1.00 .75 .50 .25

Shell Beans.—

No. 28. Two quarts — 1.00 .75 .50 .25

String Beans.—

No. 29. Two quarts — 1.00 .75 .50 .25

Sweet Corn.—

No. 30. Six ears — 1.00 .75 .50 .25

Tomato.—

No. 31. Six specimens — 1.25 1.00 .75 .50 .25

Cucumber.—

No. 32 Two specimens — 1.00 .75 .50 .25

Summer Squash.—

No. 33. Two specimens — 1.00 .75 .50 .25

Saturday, September 11

All articles must be in the hall by 1 o'clock

> The exhibits must be the results of individual effort of the child from the time of planting to the arranging of the exhibit.

Open to Children under 14 years of age

Display of Flowers.—

No. 34. Not to exceed 15 vases 2.00 1.50 1.25 1.00 .50 .25

Cosmos.—

No. 35. Vase .75 .50 .25 .25

Calendula.—

No. 36. Not to exceed 10 vases .75 .50 .25 .25

Petunia.—

No. 37. Not to exceed 10 vases .75 .50 .25 .25

Asters.—

No. 38. Not to exceed 10 vases .75 .50 .25 .25

Zinnia.—

No. 39. Not to exceed 10 vases .75 .50 .25 .25

Marigolds.—

No. 40. Not to exceed 10 vases .75 .50 .25 .25

Gladiolus.—

No. 41. Basket .75 .50 .25 .25

Wild Flowers.—

No. 42. Not to exceed 15 vases 1.50 1.25 1.00 .50 .25

No. 43. Vase of Flowers 1.00 .75 .50 .25 .25

Display of Vegetables.—

No. 44. Not to exceed 12 varieties

2.00 1.75 1.50 1.25 1.00 .75 .50

Shell Beans.—

No. 45. Two quarts in pods .75 .50 .25 .25

Beets.—

No. 46. Six specimens 1.00 .75 .50 .25 .25

Carrots.—

No. 47. Six specimens 1.00 .75 .50 .25 .25

Sweet Corn.—

No. 48. Six ears 1.00 .75 .50 .25 .25

Tomato.—
    No. 49. Six specimens   1.00 .75 .50 .25 .25

Winter Squash.—
    No. 50. Two specimens   1.00 .75 .25 .25

Potato.—
    No. 51. Twelve specimens   1.00 .75 .50 .25 .25

Open to Children between the ages of 14 and 21

Display of Flowers.—
    No. 52. Not to exceed 15 vases   2.50 2.00 1.75 1.50

Petunia.—
    No. 53. Not to exceed 10 vases   1.00 .75 .50 .25

Dahlias.—
    No. 54. Not to exceed 10 vases   1.00 .75 .50 .25

Zinnia.—
    No. 55. Not to exceed 10 vases   1.00 .75 .50 .25

Marigold.—
    No. 56. Not to exceed 10 vases   1.00 .75 .50 .25

Cosmos.—
    No. 57. One large vase   1.00 .75 .50 .25

Gladiolus.—
    No. 58. Basket   1.00 .75 .50 .25

Wild Flowers.—
    No. 59. Not to exceed 15 vases 1.50 1.25 1.00 .50 .25
    No. 60. Vase of Flowers   1.00 .75 .50 .25 .25

Dahlia.—
    No. 61. Vase   1.00 .75 .50 .25

Display of Vegetables.—
    No. 62. Not to exceed 15 varieties
                  2.50 2.00 1.75 1.50 1.25 1.00 .50

Potato.—
    No. 63. Twelve specimens   1.50 1.00 .75 .50 .25

Carrots.—
    No. 64. Six specimens   1.25 1.00 .75 .50 .25

Beets.—
    No. 65. Six specimens   1.25 1.00 .75 .50 .25

Sweet Corn.—
    No. 66. Six ears   1.25 1.00 .75 .50 .25

Tomato.—
No. 67.   Six specimens   1.25 1.00 .75 .50 .25

Cabbage.—
No. 68.   Two specimens   .75 .50 .25

Winter Squash.—
No. 69.   Two specimens   1.00 .75 .50 .25

Celery.—
No. 70.   Three specimens   .75 .50 .25

Shell Beans.—
No. 71.   Two quarts in the pod   1.00 .75 .50 .25

Onion.—
No. 72.   Six specimens   1.00 .75 .50 .25

Prizes will be given for other meritorious exhibits.

Competition is open to all children of Worcester County under two classes. Those under 14 years and those between 14 and 21.

Only one child in a family can compete for the same prize.

The exhibits must be the results of individual effort of the child from the time of planting to the arranging of the exhibit.

All exhibits must be in the Hall ready for inspection by the Judges by 1 p. m. Exhibition will close at 4.30 p. m.

Prizes will be paid at the close of the exhibition.

Vases, plates and everything necessary for the exhibition of the flowers and vegetables will be furnished by the Horticultural Society.

Special Prizes Offered
by Secretary Herbert R. Kinney

To the ones receiving the two largest amounts under 14 years of age. $3.00. $2.00.

To the ones receiving the two largest amounts over 14 years of age. $3.00. $2.00.

*   *   *

For further information apply to

HERBERT R. KINNEY,
Secretary.

TRANSACTIONS

OF THE

WORCESTER COUNTY
HORTICULTURAL
SOCIETY

Reports of the Officers and Lectures

For the year ending December 3, 1937

Office, Library, and Exhibition Hall
30 Elm Street

BERTHA G. DENNY, Assistant to Secretary

PRESIDENT'S ADDRESS

To the Members of the
Worcester County Horticultural Society:

The fundamental purpose of this Society, namely, the promotion of the Art of Horticulture, expressed by its founders at the time of its organization in 1840, has continued to be its aim and objective throughout the succeeding years.

The Society's appropriation each year provides funds to be awarded as premiums to exhibitors who have merited recognition, the merit having been first established by judges chosen annually by the Trustees for such purpose. A set of rules and regulations, established by the Committee on Arrangements and Exhibitions, and amended from time to time, provides a foundation on which all competition is based. It is only through the observance of these rules and regulations that we can hope for the attainment of just awards. Likewise, such observance by the management is necessary to preserve the dignity of the occasion.

The children's exhibits have been numbered among the outstanding accomplishments of the year. It is gratifying to note the interest of these young people, some of whom have been with us for several years and give promise of becoming exhibitors in the "big shows" of the future. We are pleased to note their zeal and hope for their continued interest in horticulture as well as in the activities of the Society.

In the résumé of a year's work, we are accustomed to give emphasis to the feature shows of the season, namely, the Spring Show held in March and the November Chrysanthemum Show. These exhibits this year were of the usual high standard and reflect credit to the Society and, in turn, to the numerous participants who made the success possible.

The schedule of exhibits also includes a program of seasonal shows conducted on Thursday of each week during the summer months. These weekly exhibitions contribute a real and sustaining influence to the Society's work and bridge the long period between spring and fall. The weekly attendance is expressive of the genuine interest in horticulture which exists in this community. It is hoped that in the future more attention will be focused on these weekly shows, thereby giving encouragement to the exhibitors while, at the same time, the public will derive much benefit from the consequent diffusion of ideas relating to plant life.

A course of lectures was conducted on Thursday afternoons during the winter months, concluding with the Annual Reunion held Thursday evening, February 25, 1937. The reception accorded to the lecturers was indicative of general approval. The coming winter audiences should find an equally attractive program in store.

It was my privilege recently, while in Washington, to attend a chrysanthemum plant exhibit conducted for a week or so under government auspices in the conservatories of the Department of Agriculture. An amazing number of varieties was displayed to thousands of visitors who attended. Many people, especially students, were observed taking notes and providing themselves with the information which was easily obtainable from labels attached to each plant.

Thus we find ourselves on the threshold of another year with a vigorous organization happy to undertake the work ahead.

Respectfully submitted,

MYRON F. CONVERSE, *President.*

Worcester, Massachusetts
December 2, 1937

SECRETARY'S REPORT

Mr. President and Members of the
Worcester County Horticultural Society:

Our lecture course for 1937 was along our usual lines with all lectures illustrated.

January 7, "Roses of Yesterday and Today," by Mr. Leonard Barron, New York City.

President Converse introduced the speaker who has been distinguished in horticultural activities for many years.

He said, "The American people must like roses because they kill ten million plants every year and then replace them."

He showed and described many of the older and some more recent varieties.

January 14, "The Arnold Arboretum, America's Greatest Garden," by Donald Wyman, Ph.D. Horticulturalist, Jamaica Plain, Mass.

The library at the Arboretum has 43,000 volumes and an Herbarium of 410,000 specimens. There are 6,500 woody trees and shrubs and about 600 different species of hawthorns.

January 21, "Lakes and Gardens of Ontario," by Mr. Arthur H. Merritt, Boston, Mass.

About 110 miles north of Toronto is the beautiful Muskoka Lake Region. Here are found the island homes and gardens of wealthy people from Cleveland, Pittsburgh, Chicago, and the middle west. These people buy an island outright. Often in modest homes, they live in the midst of expensive gardens.

He showed many beautiful pictures, especially of gardens.

January 28, "New, Interesting and Desirable Hardy, Herbaceous and Bulbous Plants," by Mr. William N. Craig, Weymouth, Mass.

He showed and described many varieties, some of them new, of hardy garden plants with special emphasis on those that can be used for late summer and fall.

February 4, "Color in the Garden," by Mr. Donald D. Wyman, North Abington, Mass.

He said that a well-planned garden should have points of interest in spring, summer, fall and winter.

He showed and explained many beautiful groups and combinations.

February 11, "Spring and Autumn in the Garden," by Mrs. Preston Rice, Grand Rapids, Mich.

She believes combination of plantings and distribution of colors are things to be considered in the spring garden.

"The handling of color is not so much a matter of what the color is, but, rather how much there is of it." She could not think of spring without Iris.

February 18, "What I Saw in Japan," by Dr. Frank A. Waugh, Amherst, Mass.

Dr. Waugh spent considerable time in Japan under very favorable conditions and saw many things that the average traveler would not be privileged to see and was permitted to take many beautiful pictures; this combined with his being a keen observer and fine lecturer gave us one of our best entertainments.

In connection with each of our lectures there were exhibited a few plants in the West Room. I think it well worth while.

February 25, Annual Reunion was held.

The Library was decorated with palms and yellow roses.

Reception at 6:30. In the receiving line were President and Mrs. Converse and Vice-Presidents Mrs. Homer Gage and Mr. Herbert A. Cook.

At 7 o'clock the line formed to march to the dining room which was decorated with red roses on each table. Reverend Clifton Wheeler offered prayer.

A roast beef dinner was served by Mr. Lunt.

Before settling for the evening entertainment, President Converse suggested that a rising greeting be given Mr. Herbert A. Cook, who recently celebrated his ninetieth birthday.

The Unity Male Quartet furnished the music.

After the dinner Mr. Charles Murray of Boston furnished the entertainment which seemed to be well received.

We then adjourned to the Auditorium for dancing.

The Spring Exhibition was up to our average or a little better. In the Auditorium Mr. Potter had the center, Mr. Breed the stage,

Mr. Allen the southeast corner, the Sunnyside Greenhouses the north end; west side, Hixon's Greenhouses with Mr. Schneider in the center and Mr. Conti on the south.

Iristhorpe used the West Room with a Tulip Garden.

Downstairs the Worcester florists had the west section and the exhibit was hardly up to standard. The center section was given up to plant displays.

The north vestibule was occupied by Mr. Schneider, south by Holmes' Greenhouses, and the east section by fruit and vegetables, both of which were good with some excellent apples. There were three rock gardens in the main vestibule.

Mr. Davenport showed a very fine basket of Virginia carnations. There was a fine showing of a carnation "Puritan" from Mr. Axel C. Sorensen, of Lexington, Mass.

The outstanding feature of the Exhibition was the new double snapdragon shown by Meadowcroft Greenhouses, Lexington, Mass. The flowers were a delicate pink on straight stalks, and the flowers lasted much longer than the usual snapdragon. The Society awarded it a silver medal.

April Exhibition: There were five fine plant displays, twelve table decorations, and three baskets of carnations. Fruit and vegetables were light.

May Exhibition: Wild flowers were good. There was a large exhibit of pansies, some very fine, ten table decorations and only three plant displays. There was a light showing of vegetables, except rhubarb which was fine.

.. June 3, Iris Exhibition: There were five displays, five twenty vases, and seven baskets of iris, eight displays of cut flowers, and six vases of roses. Rhubarb was again good.

June 10: There were eight exhibits of cut flowers and seven of wild flowers and seven of Siberian iris. There was a good showing of Aquilegia.

June 17, Rose Exhibition: There was a fine showing of roses except the H. P. classes which were light. The H. T. were fine. Table decorations were good. Peonies were fair, hardy flowers good. There was a fine showing of Howard 17 strawberries, other varieties fair to good; cherries poor; vegetables light.

June 24: There was a fine showing of Dianthus Barbatus of

fair quality; four good tables; a very light showing of strawberries and currants; cherries poor.

July 1: Cut flowers good; baskets fine; Japanese Iris good.
Delphinium and Lilium Candidum were good, but only a few
entries. Wild flowers and strawberries were light, and there
were three good collections of vegetables.

July 8, Sweet Pea Exhibition: There was a very good showing—four, ten vases, seven tables, four baskets, and seven displays. There were only three displays of Lilium Regale. Vegetables were good.

July 15: There were nine displays, ten standards of cut flowers,
eleven table decorations, and five displays of sweet peas; a fine
showing of raspberries, no blackberries or corn, but four plates
of potatoes.

July 22: Three exhibits of gladiolus, eight of perennial
phlox, seven displays of annuals, six plates of apples and two
of corn, five exhibits of summer squash, and four collections
of vegetables.

July 29: There were twenty entries in the class for Flower
Arrangement for the Living Room; four displays of gladiolus.
The vegetable entries were light.

August 5, Gladiolus Exhibition: There were six displays,
five standards and five, twenty vases of gladiolus. Fifteen
displays of annuals, twenty-two entries "Flowers on Mirror."
There was one fine plate of peaches. Some fine corn and tomatoes and three collections of mushrooms.

August 12: Seventeen baskets of gladiolus, fourteen displays of garden flowers and twenty-five displays of "Flowers
on a Mirror." There was a nice showing of shell beans and
three good exhibits from home gardens.

August 19: Eleven exhibits of cut flowers and eleven baskets.
Only three displays of lilies and four of tuberous rooted begonias.
There was a showing of nineteen miniature vases.

August 26: There were ten cut flowers and seventeen pairs
mantle vases. Seven fine vases of Scabiosa. There were seven
calls for peaches and only three plates shown. Green Mountain
grapes were better than usual. It was the best showing of vegetables this season.

WORCESTER COUNTY HORTICULTURAL SOCIETY, 30 ELM ST., WORCESTER, MASS.

September 2: Metal container of cut flowers was again popular with seventeen entries and twelve entries of cosmos. There was a large showing of grapes—eight entries of Concord and Niagara. Three collections of vegetables and five of tomato were exhibited. Some were very nice. Some very fine yellow flesh melons were shown.

September 9: Dahlia Exhibition: While there were not so many entries of dahlias as last year, the quality was good. There were four, fifty vases, two, twelve vases, two singles, three pompons, and three large baskets shown.

The display of flower arrangement was fine with ten entries. Tuberous rooted begonias were not up to standard. There were eleven entries of Bartlett and ten of Seckel pears and four good collections of vegetables were shown.

September 16: Six displays of dahlias, but not as good as last year were shown. There was a nice display of potatoes and the first good cauliflower to be shown this year.

September 23: Thirteen table decorations, some of them excellent, five good fruit displays, and three Home Gardens were exhibited.

September 30: Apples were not shown as liberally as usual, but the quality was good. There were nine plates of Baldwins and six of Northern Spy. There was a large showing of grapes. Pears were only fair. Vegetables were not up to average.

October 7: There were nineteen baskets of flowers, some fine. Not many apples were shown; and there were nine table decorations of fruit. Some nice collections of squash and dry beans were displayed.

November 4–7, Chrysanthemum Exhibition: Auditorium—West side, north end, Mr. Potter; south end, Iristhorpe; stage, Mr. Schneider; south side, south end, Hixon's Greenhouses; center, Mr. Breed; north end, Sunnyside Greenhouses. West room—North end, west side, Mr. Bostock; south end, Mr. Allen; south side, north end, Mr. Conti; center, Rainbow Gardens; specimen plants south end. Main vestibule downstairs—Vegetables. Southeast vestibule—Vases of chrysanthemums. Dining room—West section fruit; center, vegetables; south, chrysanthemums. Southeast vestibule—An exhibit of Cacti.

again

·: Conco
·:-e of
·:-y fine yell

·: were not
:: good. Th
:-:s, thre

·:-h ten en
::. There
·: and four

·: : as good
:-:v of potato

·:-: of them e
: Gardens we

:-:lly as u
·:-: of Bal
·.:-g of gr
a·.·erage.
·: ·:s, some
·-: :able de
: and drv

·:: Auditor
·:-horpe;
·: Greenh
·-h uses.

· Rainbow Gai-
·:-: downstairs-
·-:vsanthemums
·:-:ables; south
·-:-it of Cact:

There was a very attractive exhibit of wild fruit and nuts ferneries and an exhibit from The Natural History Society i the Conference Room.

Mrs. Homer Gage's call for table decorations brought ou an entry of fourteen tables which made a fine showing in th Lecture Room.

Our Children's Exhibitions were again very satisfactory Classes were well filled with the exception of a few varieties o flowers at the September show.

It was very interesting to see the real interest the childre took in the arranging of their exhibits. They worked ver quietly and while they did not have the variety and quantit to work with that our regular exhibitors have, they used wha they did have well.

There were 322 entries in the classes called for and there wer quite a number of other entries in both exhibitions.

Respectfully submitted,

HERBERT R. KINNEY, *Secretary*

December 2, 1937

TREASURER'S REPORT
For the Year Ending December 1, 1937

Statement of Income and Expenditures

INCOME

Rent:
Hall............	$420.00	
Stores..........	39,999.96	$40,419.96

Permanent Funds:
Membership Fund	$101.58	
Blake Fund......	15.00	
Dewey Fund.....	25.15	
Draper Fund.....	6.00	
Eames Fund.....	23.50	
Hadwen Fund....	60.00	
Morse Fund......	11.00	242.23

Membership Fees............	80.00

Interest Earned:
Permanent Funds.	$129.20	
Investments......	220.03	349.23

Winter Meetings: Tickets....	182.00

Other Income:
Mabel K. Gage...	$50.00	
H. R. Kinney....	30.00	80.00

Payments on account of Retirement Price of Worcester County Trust Company Class A Stock................	195.00

George McWilliam Fund: Received from Estate of George McWilliam (Income to be used for purposes of Society)................	100.00

$41,648.42

Cash Balance, December 3, 1936   1,244.18

EXPENDITURES

Library....................		
Winter Meetings.............		
Periodicals.................		
Publications................		
Premiums:		
Of 1937.........	$6,459.00	
Special.........	80.00	
Children's Exhibitions..........	246.50	
Blake Fund......	15.00	
Draper Fund.....	6.00	
Eames Fund.....	23.50	
Hadwen Fund....	60.00	
Morse Fund......	11.00	

Medals....................		
Expense:		
Exhibitions..............		
Office...................		
Operating................		
Miscellaneous............		
Street Sprinkling............		
Maintenance:		
Furniture and Fixtures..........	$432.01	
Real Estate......	907.28	

Salaries....................	
Interest Paid...............	
Interest Added to Permanent Funds....................	
Interest Added to Investments	
Insurance..................	
Light, Heat, Water, etc.......	
Janitor Service..............	
Mortgage Note Reductions (Front Street Property)....	
Transfer to Membership Fund	
Returned to Investments.....	
Investment of McWilliam Fund —Worcester Mechanics Savings Bank................	

Cash Balance, December 1, 1937

Statement of Gains and Losses

GAINS			LOSSES	
Balances of Appropriations:			Appropriations..............	$10,000.00
Exhibi-			Depreciation................	1,228.68
....	$53.50		Special and Permanent Fund	
....	70.00		Premiums.................	195.50
Appro-			Expense Accounts...........	1,637.11
....	366.00	$489.50	Insurance...................	738.59
			Interest....................	8,320.11
			Janitor Service.............	2,622.00
Fees............	80.00		Light, Heat, Water..........	1,283.38
Permanent Funds	242.23		Maintenance Accounts.......	1,339.29
....	40,419.96		Medals.....................	10.10
c...............	80.00		Periodicals.................	82.45
			Publications................	853.25
		$41,311.69	Street Sprinkling............	5.70
			Winter Meetings	1,139.69
				$29,455.85
			Net Gain to Surplus........	11,855.84
				$41,311.69

Statement of Resources and Liabilities

RESOURCES			LIABILITIES	
Permanent Funds (Investment):			Blake Fund:	
Peoples' Savings Bank			Principal...............	
(Hadwen Fund) $1,197.50			Income.................	
Wor. Five Cts. Sav. Bk.			Dewey Fund:	
(Draper Fund)	409.87		Principal...............	
(Eames Fund)	594.45		Income.................	
(Morse Fund)	521.48		Draper Fund:	
Wor. Mech. Sav. Bk.			Principal.............	
(Blake Fund).	1,404.03		Income.................	
(Dewey Fund)	1,000.00		Eames Fund:	
(McWilliam			Principal...............	
Fund).....	100.00	$5,227.33	Income......	
Investments:			Hadwen Fund:	
Wor. Co. Inst.			Principal...............	
for Sav......	$2,814.25		Income.................	
Wor. Five Cts.			Morse Fund:	
Sav. Bk......	3,104.86		Principal...............	
Wor. Mech. Sav.			Income.................	
Bk.........	3,293.20		McWilliam Fund:	
Wor. Co. Trust			Principal...............	
Co. Class A			Income................	
stk. 65 shs. at			Mortgage Note, Front Street	
$14 per share.	910.00	10,122.31	Property...............	1
			Surplus:	
Membership Fund.........		4,130.00	Dec. 3, 1936...$338,417.76	
Real Estate...............		480,000.00	Net Gain, 1937. 11,855.84	3
Furniture and Fixtures......		18,943.29		
Library..................		2,084.92		
Cash....................		993.08		
		$521,500.93		$5

Respectfully submitted,

B. W. GREENWOOD, *Tr*

Auditor's Certificate

I have examined the books of the Treasurer of the Worcester County Horticultural Society, together with vouchers, securities and bank balances, for the year ended December 1, 1937, and find them to be correct.

ADAH B. JOHNSON, *Accountant*

We have caused an audit of the books of the Treasurer to be made for the year ended December 1, 1937, and the foregoing certificate is hereby approved.

Respectfully submitted,

H. WARD MOORE, HARRY C. MIDGLEY, ARTHUR H. BELLOWS,
Auditors

Worcester, Massachusetts
December 1, 1

REPORT OF THE LIBRARY COMMITTEE

Mr. President and Members of the
Worcester County Horticultural Society:

This branch of the Society's activity is busily engaged in catering to the demands of members for literature that is helpful.

It is a great problem to select books that are of outstanding value because there are so many popular books that give but a general idea of gardening. We try, however, to choose volumes that have a real practical value, chiefly those written by specialists in their own respective lines.

Then, too, the popular American magazines of today are so filled with advertising of various kinds that relatively little remains of horticultural value that is worth binding or preserving. I am pleased to say there are a few exceptions.

Your Committee is always ready to purchase any books that may be especially worth while.

We are also pleased to note the increasing call for books in our library, and in a few instances we have had to procure more than one copy.

Edward W. Breed, Chairman

December 1, 1937

LIBRARIAN'S REPORT

Mr. President and Members of the
Worcester County Horticultural Society:

The Library is in its customary good condition.

As your Librarian I am privileged to inform you of a gratifying increase in the circulation of the many valuable books and periodicals owned by our Society.

The card index and index by authors made in 1935 and 1936 have proved of great benefit to the patrons of our Library.

In the judgment of your Librarian some of the most beneficial information on horticultural subjects may be found in the serial publications available on the tables in the Library. I wish more of our members would avail themselves of the opportunity which this literature affords.

The books purchased by our Library committee this year are as follows:

Pioneering with Fruits and Berries, by George D. Aiken, 1936.
Roses of the World in Color, by J. Horace McFarland, 1936.
Succulent Plants, by H. Jacobsen, 1935.
The Identification of Trees and Shrubs, by F. K. Makins, 1937.
Japanese Flower Arrangement for Modern Homes, by Margaret Preininger, 1936.
Your City Garden, by Margaret McKenny and E. L. D. Seymour, 1937.
The Royal Horticultural Society Lily Year-Book for 1936.
The 1937 American Rose Annual, Edited by J. Horace McFarland.
American Delphinium Society Year Book for 1936.
Design in Flower Arrangement, by John Taylor Arms and Dorothy Noyes Arms, 1937.
The Book of Bulbs, by F. F. Rockwell, 1932.
The Complete Book of Gardening, Edited by Leonard Barron, 1936.
The Book of Shrubs, by Alfred C. Hottes, 1937.
The Mushroom Handbook, by Louis C. C. Krieger, 1936.
How to Grow Roses, (Revised and rewritten), by McFarland and Pyle, 1937.

Grateful acknowledgment is due Mrs. Frank C. Smith for the gift of *Wild Gardens of New England*, by Walter Prichard Eaton, dedicated to Mrs. Smith by the author.

Respectfully submitted,

FLORENCE E. FIELD, *Librarian*

December 2, 1937

gratifying
and peri-

and 1936
rary.
beneficial
the serial
wish more
 ity which

this year

Preininger,

our, 1937

land.

othy Noye

6.

Pyle, 193;

Smith for
Prichar

brarian

CHARLES POTTER AND EDWARD W. BREED, SPRING 1937

REPORT OF THE JUDGE OF PLANTS AND FLOWERS

Mr. President and Members of the
Worcester County Horticultural Society:

The Spring Show, which is the outstanding exhibition of the year, compared favorably with those of former years. There was strong competition for all the premiums offered, with many special exhibits, among which were fine exhibits of cacti, succulents, and herbs. There were also fine vases of calla lilies, antirrhinums, and sweet peas. A fine vase of the new double flowering antirrhinums was exhibited by the originator, C. H. Lothrop of Lexington. This is a fine, strong growing variety with perfect double flowers of a beautiful salmon pink color.

Table decorations were the feature of the April and May Exhibitions, with good displays of wild flowers and potted plants.

The Iris Exhibition on June 3 was good. In addition to the very fine displays of iris, there was strong competition in the class for cut flowers. Azaleas and rhododendrons were shown for the first time in several years.

On June 10 wild flowers and Aquilegias were the feature of the show. Some fine displays of both were on exhibition.

The Rose Show on June 17 was good. Fine roses were shown in many of the best varieties. Peonies were also shown on this date.

The June 24 show was noteworthy for the fine displays of roses and dianthus. The delphiniums and campanulas were not as good as usual.

On July 1 splendid Japanese iris and delphiniums were featured, and four fine displays of roses.

Presumably on account of the hot, dry weather, the exhibits during the month of July, with the exception of the class for twenty vases of cut flowers, were below the usual standard.

On August 5 there were fine displays of gladiolus and annuals; also twenty-six exhibits of "a small vase of flowers shown on a mirror."

On August 12 zinnias were largely shown.

On August 19 the display of cut flowers and lilies was ver good.

On August 26 a class calling for a pair of mantel vases prove to be interesting and popular and competition was keen. Ther were also some very fine standards of dahlias.

The September Exhibitions were poor. The usual fine dis plays of dahlias were missing, presumably on account of exten sive damage done by the corn borer. At·the end of the mont there were some fine displays of roses, and the class for twent vases of cut flowers was good. Indeed, the exhibits in this clas throughout the summer were of fine quality and competitio was very close, as many as eleven competitors appearing·a some of the exhibitions.

The Chrysanthemum Show, November 5, was notable fo the attractive garden arrangements in the main hall and fo the large number of cut and potted chrysanthemums on exhibi tion. The upper hall contained attractively arranged exhibit of wild fruits and berries; also glass ferneries and globes in grea variety.

Respectfully submitted,

WILLIAM ANDERSON, Judge of Plants and Flowers

December 2, 1937

REPORT OF JUDGE OF FRUIT

Mr. President and Members of the
Worcester County Horticultural Society:

Another season has passed leaving its records in the many
fields of agriculture. On the fruit pages we find that the season
of 1937 was one of the most difficult years in which to grow good
fruit. Insect pests were very abundant due probably to our
mild winter, curculio were one of the worst pests heavily dam-
aging peaches, plums, pears, and apples. The season was also
most favorable to the development of apple scab and very few
varieties escaped without some injury from this pest. Many
of the smaller growers lost their McIntosh crop this past season.
Black-rot of grapes was also very severe and in some cases destroyed the entire grape crop. These pests all had a marked
effect on the number and quality of fruit shown this season.
In the spring the prospects were for a most bountiful crop of all
kinds of fruits, but due to the heavy losses caused by the severe
infestations of various pests many of the fruit crops were rather
light.

We did, however, have a fine display of fruit at the Spring
Show with three displays, seven, forty-nine, and seventeen
plates.

Many of the calls this year, especially for strawberries, raspberries, peaches, apples, etc., were too early for the season and
many of those classes were only partly filled with immature fruit.
In fact we had a rather light showing this season of cherries,
plums, peaches, early apples, the older varieties, and even Mc-
Intosh did not make its usual showing.

We did, however, on June 17 have a good showing of strawberries, with Howard 17 still in the lead. Many of the new
varieties of strawberries were also shown. On July 15 we had
a fine showing of raspberries with ten entries in one class. Currants made a fine showing this season with many plates of good
fruit.

In spite of the severe damage from black-rot, grapes made

a fine showing with Concords and Niagaras in the lead.   Th
Concords in fact were exceptionally fine, the best we have ha
in years.

The calls for Bartlett, Seckel and Bosc pears were well fille
with some exceptionally fine fruit.

The Fruit Exhibit of September 30 brought out some fin
apples and pears with fourteen plates of grapes.   Baldwins thi
year took the lead from McIntosh in the number of plates show
with McIntosh, Spy, and Delicious following along with Cour
land as the most popular new variety.

At the Chrysanthemum Exhibition the showing of fruit wa
exceptionally good for this season and made a most fitting en
ing for our 1937 exhibits.

Respectfully submitted,

S. LOTHROP DAVENPORT, *Judge of Fruit*

December 2, 1937

REPORT OF JUDGE OF VEGETABLES

Mr. President and Members of the
Worcester County Horticultural Society:

Again it is my privilege to submit the annual report for the department of vegetables and to bring to your attention therein some of the outstanding features of our season's exhibitions.

All through the season we have noticed that both the quantity and the quality of many of the vegetables shown were not up to the usual high standard. This was due, in part at least, to the weather conditions.

At the April exhibition we had only one exhibit of rhubarb, while at the May exhibition lettuce and asparagus were not shown in the usual abundance, nor were they of as high quality as usual.

At the regular weekly shows in June we had only a small showing of asparagus and no beets nor cucumbers until the June 24 show. Peas were not at all abundant at any time and were rather inferior in quality.

During July the vegetable exhibits became more abundant and of better quality, with the exception of sweet corn.

August exhibitions showed still more improvement. We then had excellent exhibits of summer squash, sweet corn, peppers, tomatoes, shell beans, and carrots. We also had many fine collections of mushrooms at the two exhibitions in which they were shown.

The exhibits of melons, winter squash, celery and cauliflower, especially the latter two, were far below their usual standard generally. Seldom do we see so few and such poor specimens of cauliflower at our shows as were shown this year. Not all the celery, however, was poor, as we had some very good celery shown on September 23.

The displays of gourds at our November show, of which there were seven, were of very fine quality. Great interest was shown in these exhibits by the visitors to this show and much favorable comment passed upon them, thus attesting to the growing popularity of this vegetable.

The displays and collections of vegetables have been of very good quality and fairly numerous. In this class we have sadly missed the extraordinarily fine exhibits which we have had for so many years from our veteran exhibitor, our worthy Secretary, Mr. Herbert R. Kinney. For reasons best known to himself he has deemed it best to curtail his exhibitions in this department.

While none of our other exhibitors have quite attained the heights of perfection that Mr. Kinney has in this department they are improving each year and will, no doubt, maintain the high standard we have always enjoyed.

Two exhibitions of the products of the children's gardens were held with the usual fine individual plates and displays shown. These exhibitions speak well for the continued growth and prosperity of the Society.

Respectfully submitted,

H. WARD MOORE, *Judge of Vegetables*

December 2, 1937

REPORT OF FINANCE COMMITTEE

To the Members of the
Worcester County Horticultural Society:

The Society's work for the year has been completed with results which seem to meet with general satisfaction. The income, likewise, has been maintained on a satisfactory basis and has permitted continuance of the various activities. The Treasurer's report will disclose the results in detail, and your attention is invited thereto.

On April 14, 1937, the Treasurer received a gift of $100 from Mrs. J. D. McQueen to be held in memory of George McWilliam, a former trustee who, in the years past, served the Society as an exhibitor and also as a judge. This gift was made in accordance with directions given by Mrs. Belle McWilliam before her death.

It is hereby recommended that the gift be accepted as a fund to be known as the George and Belle McWilliam Fund. It is further recommended that the Treasurer be authorized and directed to add $100 from the Society's funds to this account as a token of appreciation.

This Committee recommends that $10,000 be appropriated for use as the Trustees may direct for the payment of premiums and salaries during the coming year.

Respectfully submitted,

MYRON F. CONVERSE,
LEONARD C. MIDGLEY,
HARRY HARRISON,
Finance Committee

Worcester, Massachusetts
December 2, 1937

ted with
The in-
...asis and
...e Treas-
attention

...00 from
William,
...ociety as
...a accord-
...efore her

...as a fund
d. It is
...ized and
account

...ropriated
...remiums

RSE,
LEY,

...mittee

ALBERT W. SCHNEIDER, SPRING 1937

ANNUAL MEETING OF THE SOCIETY

Thursday, December 3, 1936

President Myron F. Converse called the meeting to order at 10 o'clock a.m. Thirty present.

Secretary read the call for the meeting.

Secretary read the records of the last Annual Meeting of the Society.

President Converse declared them approved.

President Converse delivered his Annual Address.

The following reports were read:

Secretary, Herbert R. Kinney; Treasurer, Burt W. Greenwood; Librarian, Mrs. Florence E. Field; Judge of Flowers, William Anderson; Judge of Fruits, S. Lothrop Davenport; Judge of Vegetables, H. Ward Moore.

On Mr. Allen J. Jenkins' motion, these reports were accepted and referred to the Committee on Library and Publication.

President Myron F. Converse read the report of the Finance Committee. This report recommended an appropriation of ten thousand dollars for premiums and salaries.

On Mr. Harry Harrison's motion this report was accepted and adopted.

In the absence of the Nominating Committee the President read their report.

President Converse asked if there were other nominations.

There being none, Mr. H. Ward Moore made a motion that the candidates as nominated be elected. It was so voted.

President Converse declared them elected.

The resolutions on the death of our late member of the Finance Committee, Herbert W. Estabrook, were unanimously adopted by a rising vote.

Mrs. Homer Gage said she would continue her appropriation for the Fall Show table decorations another year.

Adjourned.

HERBERT R. KINNEY, *Secretary*

ANNUAL MEETING OF THE TRUSTEES

Thursday, December 10, 1936

President Myron F. Converse called the meeting to order at 10 o'clock a.m. Seventeen present.

Secretary read the records of the last Annual Meeting of the Trustees.

President Converse declared them approved.

President Converse said that this meeting appointed the committees and judges. He spoke highly of the satisfactory handling of the Society's business this year by the present committees and judges. He read a list of the present committees and judges and asked if there were any changes desired.

There being none, Mr. Allen J. Jenkins made a motion that the same committees and judges serve another year. It was so voted.

Mrs. Homer Gage and Mrs. Percy G. Forbes spoke in favor of having ladies judge table decorations.

Appropriation for Premiums and Salaries................ $10,000.00

PREMIUMS

Flowers...................	$1,800.00	
Fruits....................	1,000.00	
Vegetables................	800.00	
Children's Exhibition.......	300.00	
Spring Exhibition.	1,600.00	
Chrysanthemum Exhibition..	1,400.00	
Miscellaneous.............	225.00	$7,125.00

SALARIES

Treasurer.................	$350.00		
Secretary.................	1,000.00		
Librarian.................	1,000.00		
Assistant to Secretary.......	125.00		
Judges...................	400.00	$2,875.00	$10,000.00

Adjourned.

HERBERT R. KINNEY, *Secretary*

ANNUAL MEETING OF THE COMMITTEE ON ARRANGEMENTS AND EXHIBITIONS

Thursday, December 10, 1936

Meeting called to order in the Library, immediately after the Trustees adjourned, by President Myron F. Converse. Fourteen present.

On Mrs. Percy G. Forbes's motion, Mr. Allen J. Jenkins was unanimously elected chairman.

The whole morning was given up to discussing the By-Laws.

The only change made was in Special Rule 1, which was changed to read,

"1. Exhibitors should have all specimens correctly and legibly named and the number of varieties written on the entry card, notice of which will be taken by the judges in awarding the premiums."

Other changes made in the schedule were as follows:

SPRING EXHIBITION

Class 1		Garden Display ⎫ $1,150.00	
Class 2		Plant Display ⎭	
April	22	Table Decorations	
		Round table laid for four covers	
		Oblong table laid for two covers	
May	13	Wild Flowers from June 3	
		Table Decorations laid for two or four covers	
		Roses prohibited	
June	10	Add Siberian Iris, medium basket	
June	17	Add Six and Twelve H. T. roses with same premiums as offered for H. P. roses	
		Gradus peas to next week	
June	24	Sutton peas to next week	
July	1	Telephone peas to next week	
July	15	Add blueberries	
July	29	Add cultivated blueberries	
August	13	Clapp's favorite pears to August 19	
September	2	Bartlett pears to September 9	
September	2	Celosia from September 10	
September	9	Collection of potatoes, September 16	

September 24   Table Decorations to October 7
From October 1 to October 7
     Display of potted and specimen ferns
     Hardy chrysanthemum plants
     Apples
     One standard box of Baldwins
     One standard box, any other variety
     Collection of apples
From November 4 to October 7
     Onions, Yellow Globe Danvers
     Parsnips, any variety
     Display of grains
     Display of beans
     Collection of squash

 Adjourned.

          HERBERT R. KINNEY, *Secretary*

"ROSES OF YESTERDAY AND TODAY"

Thursday, January 7, 1937

Illustrated Lecture

By Mr. Leonard Barron, New York City

President Myron F. Converse introduced the speaker, who has been distinguished in horticultural activities for many years. He was at one time Editor of *The Garden Magazine*; Horticultural Editor of *The American Home*; President of the American Rose Society; President of the Long Island Horticultural Society; former Secretary and now Director of the Horticultural Society of New York; Fellow of the American Association for Advancement of Science; member of the American Society for Horticultural Science; Fellow of the Royal Horticultural Society and Chapter Associate of New York Chapter; member American Society of Landscape Architects; and former President of the American Delphinium Society.

He is well known on the lecture platform and among garden club members and for his radio talks on gardening. He is an occasional lecturer at Columbia; and his writings are familiar through his magazine contributions. He has several books to his credit: *Lawns and How to Make Them*, *Roses and How to Grow Them*, *Flower Growing*, and *Gardening for the Small Place*. He has lately been made Editor-in-Chief of *Flower Grower*.

"The American people must like roses because they kill ten million rose plants each year, and then replace them."

Importance is attached to this most largely appreciated of flowers because people like color. The rose presents color in a most magnificent style. It is for this reason that work is continually going on in an attempt to secure new and finer combinations of colors.

The rose of yesterday was very different from that of today. In the early days of rose culture, before our generation, some of the roses which are so popular in our gardens of today were not known. The feeling of idealism which persists has lead us to the kind of rose that we have today.

In the middle of the nineteenth century, Hybrid Perpetual Roses were popular for every purpose. Hybrid Perpetuals are husky bushes which bear a great crop of big, double, fragrant roses in early summer and occasionally throughout the summer and autumn. They are characterized by the richest colorings, ranging from white to darkest red. These blossoms have continued in their popularity because we insist on asking that the life of a rose be a continuous performance. We expect it to bloom through the summer and fall—nearly into winter.

Perhaps the chief exponent of this group is the Frau Karl Druschki. This is a well-known variety with large white blossoms of exquisite beauty. It is beautifully shaped and has light solid green foliage. One of the problems of this rose is universal adaptation. It will not bloom in the Middle West.

Among the first of the old roses is the Cabbage or Provence Rose, sometimes called the Hundred Leaf Rose, as it is distinguished by its fullness of petals. This flower is a light rosy pink in color and has a hardy globular bloom. It is very brilliant and fragrant.

From the white York and the Lancaster Rose which is red, a student obtained a variegated Damask Rose. This red and white flower would be accepted today as a modernistic rose. Perhaps no other flower has a greater historical significance than the York and Lancaster. Representative of two famous English houses of the same names, it will be recalled how important a part the "War of Roses" played in the shaping of British history.

Always a favorite has been the Tea Rose, which won its name because of its peculiar fragrance. Its color varies in shades of pale yellow and pink. Introduced from China, this flower has undergone myriads of variations.

One of the most common of the older roses is the Double-Brier, which is not infrequently found in old gardens. The Harrison Yellow, which is a soft golden yellow and very fragrant, the extremely hardy Persian Yellow, which is a deep golden color, and the Austrian Copper, with a clear bright yellow blossom, are varieties of semi-double briers.

Another important, although somewhat unpopular, flower is the Bourbon Rose, named for the Isle of Boar. It is a cross of the common China Rose and Red Rose. This plant blooms best and most abundantly in autumn. It has few spines or thorns, does not open well, and is hard to raise if the weather is not highly favorable. Its unpopularity is primarily due to its thinness and flatness in shape.

Other old favorites have been the extremely hardy Moss Roses. These flowers are not seen on the eastern coast of America, but are often seen growing wild over old cabins. Their prickly stalks grow upright, branching to five feet and bearing a free bloom. Although these flowers have a delightful fragrance, they are subject to powdery mildew. A mossy substance grows about the foot and calyx of these flowers. From the above, the Yellow Moss, or Golden Moss, represents a new combination of color.

The British counterpart of this is the European Dog Rose, which is often seen along the edge of English roads in midsummer. This rose seems well adapted to expanse, as it spreads very rapidly. It does not seem to fit American climate.

Rambler Roses are very hardy and are characterized by vigorous growth, although the small double blossoms fade. They resent coal smoke or drafts.

The Memorial or Wichuraiana Rose is also extremely hardy. It is a creeping rose sometimes seen in cemeteries. Its blossom is fragrant and very glossy foliage is characteristic. This plant climbs particularly well if supported. Many of the climbing clustered roses were blended and the climax was the Silver Moon, which has a very large open flower of pure waxy white. This rose is also very vigorous and has rich glossy foliage.

As the name implies, the native Prairie Rose is not a coastal flower, but is native to inland America. This very interesting flower climbs naturally. Deep red in color, it flowers in large clusters. In the fall it has a profusion of round scarlet berries which last all winter.

Another valuable rose has been the Rugosa, which was developed from the red and white wild Japanese Roses, thriving in Eastern Siberia and Northern Japan. This plant is a rugged, thorny, and rough leaved shrub. As it is almost frost-proof and very poor for cutting, it serves excellently for hedges.

The Rose Ecae is also native of Central Asia. It was found by a man named E. C. Aitchison. The name Ecae was made from

IRISTHORPE, MRS. HOMER GAGE, SPRING 1937

his initials. The wood is part of the beauty of this rose and it has pale yellow flowers, which turn to white.

Many of the new roses have been derived, in one way or another, from the President Herbert Hoover Rose, which is somewhat like the Talisman. This very popular rose has well formed fragrant blooms, and it was the forerunner of the brilliant modern colors. Some of its more common variances are Autumn, Texas Gold, Texas Centennial, and Emily Hillock.

The Dixon's Centennial is a rose of sublime beauty, combining a magnificent color with vigorous growth. This flower is very fragrant and features a long stem.

The Leonard Barron Rose (named for the lecturer) seems to thrive on the northern Pacific coast, although it will not grow well here. Mr. Barron is unable to grow them at all, while his son, who lives not far away, raises them by the armful. A possible cause for this illogical difference may be under-drainage of soil.

Good form is found in the Carrie Jacobs Bond, which has a very small stem and large flowers. In color, it is a rich deep red with a coral sheen. Although this flower is characterized by good balance, it is not a productive bloomer.

The Crimson Glory is a well branched compact bush. Its flower is an intensely deep vivid crimson, mellowed by a velvety nap.

The Etoile de Holland is the most reliable red rose of today. It is the greatest triumph; its brilliant red bloom is very fragrant and the plant is a vigorous grower.

Two small roses are worthy of mention. The Rouletti is only four inches high. This plant is so small that it can be planted in a thimble and still grow! It has tiny pink flowers less than one inch in diameter. The Tom Thumb is so tiny that the plant and pot can be carried in the palm of the hand. The flower is a dark crimson, shading to white at the base of the petals.

A new rose to be introduced this season is the Eclipse, a hybrid tea rose of interesting character. This flower has won prizes in Rome, Paris, and Portland, and its popularity is rapidly sweeping the country. This upright, narrow plant has a bud two inches long. In full bloom it has over twenty-five petals. This American creation derived its name through being discovered at the moment of a solar eclipse.

In conclusion, the following general observations may be found helpful: It has been very difficult, even with the American Rose Society, to convince those exhibiting roses of the difference between rose bud and rose bloom. A bud is not a bloom. Although it is very hard to tell the difference between the two, a rose must be one half to three quarters open to be a bloom, and to be permitted on the exhibit table. Things that count there are purity of form and color.

We Americans do not give much consideration to form in roses; the important things for us are new shades and healthy plants. We do not care whether the petals are notched, scalloped or smooth, but desire constant bloomers. In Europe, on the contrary, more attention is given to form in the growing of roses. Even if they get but one bloom, they are content provided that bloom is perfectly proportioned. Rose literature should be read with this understanding.

In crossing different species of roses, it is the third generation cross that gives real achievement. In this connection, it is well to remember that all good features are not to be had in one crossing. For instance, combinations of yellow in the middle of a bloom and red on the outside, are very rare; in fact they are difficult to obtain at all.

Attention is also drawn to the caution that should be exercised in indorsing any particular rose to another person. The difficulty arises in the fact that what will grow well in your garden may not grow at all in another person's. Moreover, people's tastes do not coincide. A safe procedure is to try them all and retain that which is good, as there is no rose that will grow everywhere.

By and large, roses are getting better and better. New goals are being achieved; we are on the threshold of progress in American rose culture. The future has all before it.

"THE ARNOLD ARBORETUM: AMERICA'S GREATEST GARDEN"

Illustrated Lecture

By Donald Wyman, Ph.D., Horticulturist, Jamaica Plain, Massachusetts

Thursday Afternoon, January 14, 1937

Historically, the Arnold Arboretum was first established in 1872, as the result of a will left by one of the farsighted men of that day, who was interested in growing trees in this vicinity.

Professor Charles Sprague Sargent, a young man at Harvard, was the first Director. He found himself with a worn-out farm and $3,000 with which to run it. This was not very much to be sure, but as a result of Professor Sargent's energy, hope, and enthusiasm, the Arnold Arboretum has grown to what it is today.

Outstanding at the Arnold Arboretum is its library of 43,000 volumes, written in 35 languages and dialects. Due largely to Professor Sargent's findings, it is the best of its kind in the country.

Many people find the Herbarium, a garden of living plants, with its 410,000 specimens in cases, indispensable as a source of information. This garden contains many strange plants from all over the world. If an unknown plant is sent to the Herbarium, it can be compared with those classified at the garden, and its name returned.

At the Arboretum, there are 6,500 woody trees and shrubs. Of these there are 137 different kinds of maples, 48 kinds of dogwood, and about 600 different species of hawthorns; 126 kinds of crab apples and 320 kinds of lilacs. In order to have a plant testing garden, these growing plants are essential, so that what is good may be distinguished from what is bad.

Using this testing garden to its fullest advantage, it has been found that it is not necessary to go to China and other countries to get plants with beautiful flowers. For instance, it has been discovered that the flowering dogwood is the best all-round plant for garden use. It opens early and has good flowers. Its foliage, which is not subject to the ravages of insects or disease, its red fruit in the fall, and rich autumn coloring, make this plant interesting all year round.

A trip through the Arnold Arboretum, from the Jamaica Plain gate, would begin at the Administration Building. The first thing to be seen would be the magnolia collection, then the lindens and next 1,000 different kinds of shrubs.

Beside shaded walks and brooks, the visitor would see, one after the other, the lilacs, then Wilson's Chinese collection, the rhododendrons, two blocks of mountain laurel which is particularly beautiful in June, and finally, a magnificent display of crab apples. From atop the highest hill in the Arboretum, one can see downtown Boston.

A few of the most commonly available plants at the Arnold Arboretum should be described briefly. One of these plants, of which the Arboretum is very proud, is the climbing hydrangea. It grows all the way to the roof on the north wall of the Administration Building. The hydrangea was introduced prior to the founding of the Arboretum and the original plants are still in existence. This slow growing shrub blooms late in June and has a great deal of character. It is something to be proud of. The common hydrangea will grow nearly anywhere and under almost any conditions. It is considered among the coarse plants.

Azaleas have been very extensively planted in the Arboretum, and from the end of April until mid-July, they produce a gorgeous display of color. Although the very hardy Japanese azaleas have a bad odor, not unlike that of a skunk, they are very useful in crossing with non-hardy azaleas, having a pleasant fragrance. The result is a hardy, pleasant scented plant, having reddish colored flowers. The Kaempferi azaleas have been planted by the thousands all over the Arboretum, so that by the third week in May, the landscape looks as though it were on fire. This plant is the common mountain azalea of Japan.

The Persian lilac is wrongly named, as it seems to be of Chinese origin, from which place it was introduced to Persia. It is a broad shrub of moderate height with slender, drooping wide-spreading branches, narrow leaves, and small, fragrant, lavender-colored flowers borne hundreds together in compact clusters. This shrub flowers profusely and when the common lilac is past its best.

The Japanese dogwood was introduced by the Arnold Arboretum. Its petal tips are pointed and the flowers open after the leaves are fully opened. It represents beauty of a native type. The leaves detract and hide the flowers. For garden use, this flower should be planted down, so that the blooms will show.

The Laburnum (goldenchain) is native to Southern Europe. It has long pendulous clusters of yellow flowers in May and June. The Laburnum alpinum, the Scotch Laburnum, is also native to Southern Europe, as well as Scotland. It is the hardiest laburnum, and blooms in May.

The Viburnum tomentosum is the first cousin of the Japanese snowball that blooms in May and June. It does not have the round clusters of the Japanese snowball, but flat clusters of sterile and fertile flowers, which are two to four inches across, and so placed that they are opposite and face upward. The fruit is small, oval, red, changing to blue-black. The Japanese snowball is made up of sterile flowers entirely.

Although the Chionanthus (fringetree) is native of Virginia and the Carolinas, it grows perfectly hardy here. Blooming in June, this large, treelike shrub usually grows ten feet tall, but sometimes attains a height of thirty feet. The flowers are greenish-white with narrow drooping petals, and are arranged in drooping clusters. This is a very interesting plant, as the sexes are separate. The female only bears fruit.

Introduced by E. H. Wilson, the Kolkwitzia (Beautybush) has an interesting story connected with it. In the summer of 1901, Mr. Wilson found it on the high mountains of Northern Hupeh, and in the autumn secured the seeds. He did not see the wild plant in blossom until June, 1910, when it flowered for the first time. So, Mr. Wilson, who has traveled thousands of miles, had to come to the Arnold Arboretum to see this plant in bloom. It is related to the honeysuckle and resembles it somewhat. It grows six feet tall. The flowers are bell-shaped and are pale pink with orange veins in the throat, the buds are deeper colored. The flowers bloom in June and are produced in pairs, forming a cluster of about twenty-five flowers.

Of the fifteen good types of rhododendrons available at the Arboretum, there are variations in color to pink, white and light lavender. This does not include a number of species. One of the most adaptable to this climate is the Charles Dickens, which has a good red blossom. There is one kind of rhododendron that can be grown on the Cape, but cannot be grown in Boston. The Rhododendron fortunei cannot be grown in Boston, but is being grown at Sandwich. It has the largest flower of all rhododendrons. The Rhododendron minus is good for rock gardens. It is about three feet tall, and blooms late.

Only a few of the large variety of Philadelphus found at the Arboretum can be mentioned here. The virginal—Philadelphus —Mock orange (Syringa) is the finest large flowered variety, having blossoms about two and one half inches in diameter. This shrub is very good to look at, but its lovely white fragrant flowers are its only ornamental characteristic. As a plant, there are better, for it does not face to the ground well. Splendens-philadelphus is a very showy and large plant, having an arching habit. This plant has dense clusters of very lovely, creamy white flowers. Blooming about the middle of June, the late lilac (Syringa villosa) has an odor of rubber. Pale pink, it has almost semi-double flowers of character.

There is no duplicate in the country of the Silk tree at the Arnold Arboretum, introduced by Mr. Wilson. Seen in Korea, seed of this plant was sent to the Arboretum. One seedling proved to be hardy. It has the finest foliage of any northern woody plant, and it sometimes yields hardy seed. It is hoped that with the use of chemicals hardy plants will be grown that can produce more of these trees. Blooming nearly all summer, it is just as pretty in September as in July.

A large variety of heathers have been found which will grow perfectly in Massachusetts. These plants have a nestlike habit and flower in colors of white, pink, and light blue.

Bottlebrush buckeye is seen commonly in Louisiana and the Mississippi Valley. Related to the horse chestnut, it grows to a height of from three to ten feet, producing tiny white flowers in long candlelike clusters.   The flowers bloom in July and August.

The Buddleia davidi (orange-eye butterfly bush) plants are compact in their growth—often as tall as eight feet.   The flowers are lilac and have an orange-yellow throat, produced in terminal clusters.   They bloom from July until late autumn.   There are a number of varieties.

Just pride is felt toward the Sargent's Cherry at the Arnold Arboretum.   It is the hardiest and tallest of all cherries.   Raised from seeds sent from Japan in 1890, it has rose-pink flowers, each about one inch across.   The Cherry elaeagnus (elaeagnus longipes) has tiny flowers of exquisite fragrance and its red berries are very attractive in the summer time.

Although not native, Barberry grows in profusion at the Arnold Arboretum.   The Berberis thunbergi (Japanese barberry) has yellow flowers, tinged with red on the outside.   Its bright red, oval fruit is attractive, even until spring.   This makes a good hedge plant.   The common Barberry bears its flowers and fruit in long pendulous clusters, against a rich background of dark green foliage.   Unfortunately, this plant carries wheat rust.

The Cedar of Lebanon is interesting because of its biblical interest.   The hardy strain of this tree was discovered in Asia Minor where the climate is harsh and snow lays several feet on the ground for five months of the year.   The director of the Arnold Arboretum commissioned Walther Siehe, a collector living in Smyrna, to secure its seeds.   Ripe cones were received from other sources prior to 1904, but they failed to grow hardily.   Professor Sargent introduced the hardy strain into the Northern United States.   This very fine conifer is now growing from forty to fifty feet tall in the Arboretum.   Peculiarly enough, the cones are so hard that they have to be drilled before the seeds can be reached.

Excellent use is made of the Crab Apple at the Arboretum. The Cherry Crab Apple, having apples which are red on the side the sun strikes and yellow on the shaded side, varies as to size and color.   Blooming very early, this tree is valuable both for its flowers and fruit.   The Arnold Crab Apple originated at the

lants are
e flowers
terminal
ere are a

e .Arnold
Raised -
flowers,
laeagnus
d berries

ı at the
ese bar-
ide. Its
g. This
bears its
ch back-
t carries

. biblical
in Asia
l feet on
r of the
collector
received
hardily.
Northern
om forty
he cones
eeds can

boretum.
. the side
s to size
both for
ed at the

EDWARD W. BREED, SPRING 1937

Arboretum. It has rose-colored flowers which fade white. It bears yellow fruit.

Mr. Wilson has introduced a late Honeysuckle which fruits late. It begins to ripen in October and its leaves remain on the plant longer than they do on other plants. This is the tallest growing of all Honeysuckles.

The Smoke bush makes a very good showing. There is a red fruiting form and gives the appearance of a cloud of smoke or mist.

Originating in the Adams Nursery, in Springfield, is the dense growing compact form of the Burning Bush. Although six years old at the Arboretum, one plant there is only four feet tall and has never been sheared. It holds its good red color in autumn for ten days and is one of the most outstanding plants in the fall because of this fact.

Not very common is the Beauty berry. Its pinkish flowers are not very conspicuous, but are followed by clusters of violet berries which ripen in September and October.

A conspicuous lack of roses at the Arboretum will be immediately apparent to the visitor. The reason is that with twelve men caring for the two hundred and sixty-five acres under cultivation, time cannot be afforded for the attention the roses need; also, in near-by Franklin Park there is a very good rose garden, with several hundred rose varieties in it.

"LAKES AND GARDENS OF ONTARIO"

Illustrated Lecture

By Mr. Arthur H. Merritt, Boston, Mass.

Thursday, January 21, 1937

This is the fourth time that Mr. Merritt has lectured before the Worcester County Horticultural Society. The lecture was something in the nature of a travel talk, covering a vacation trip in the summer of 1936 into the lakes of Ontario where some unusual pictures were made of the garden homes and islands of the summer residents.

About 110 miles north of Toronto is the beautiful Muskoka Lake Region, consisting of Lakes Muskoka, Rosseau, and Joseph. Here are found the island homes and gardens of wealthy people from Cleveland, Pittsburgh, Chicago, and the Middle West. Instead of buying a lot of land to build on, these people buy outright an island, small or large. Often in modest homes these people live in the midst of expensive gardens. Flowers and shrubs often cover an entire island and as the Ontario climate is quite similar to that of New England these garden flowers are not unlike those found in our New England gardens.

The Muskoka Navigation Company owns a fleet of fine steamers which in the summer time make accessible each and every island. One steamer, the Sagamo, makes a daily 100-mile trip through the lakes, and carries thousands of tourists who come there to enjoy the beautiful scenery. Most of the island homes have cable connection with the mainland, carrying both telephone and electric light wires, while a daily supply boat will call at any island on signal and the owner may purchase both supplies and merchandise as well as gasolene and oil for their motor boats. It is said there are over 1,000 expensive motor boats on the Muskoka Lakes. Many of these people own their private airplanes and on a Friday night in the summer it is a common sight to see a plane land which left Pittsburgh, Cleveland, Chicago, or even New York a few hours before, making it possible for business men to spend a week-end with their family. On Sunday evening, or early Monday morning these planes are seen returning the owners to their places of business far away.

Most of the shore line of the Muskoka Lakes is heavily wooded right down to the shore. There have been few or no forest fires to destroy the natural beauty and there are a few beautiful rocky cliffs. The lakes cover a territory about 50 miles long, and one could easily imagine they were at Moosehead Lake or Rangeley Lakes in Maine.

Most gorgeous cloud effects are to be found in the Muskoka Region as often cold air from the north country meets the warmer air from the Great Lakes creating sunsets of glorious colorings and magnificent reflections in the water. In the midst of this natural splendor are found convenient hotels and camps. One of these is the noted Elgin House, where a guest may have his room in a separate building like the annex with a private piazza and garden of flowers which he may enjoy during his stay. Another hotel with a beautiful outlook over the lake is the Windemere, boasting of its $15,000 kitchen outfit. The most expensive and stylish hotel in the region is the Royal Muskoka Hotel, situated on a high point of land reached by a five minute walk from a steamship wharf, this walk being bordered the entire length with beautiful flowers and rockery effects. There is an 18-hole golf course with beautiful scenery and picturesque summer furniture for those who care to rest, read, or enjoy the lake scenery.

On the Lake of Bays, just north of the Muskoka Lakes, is a lake of beauty which has a shore line of 300 miles, yet the lake itself is only 18 miles long. On this lake is located the famous Bigwin Inn where a rather novel arrangement of buildings allows the guest to register at the central administration building but his room is assigned to a distant building reached by long covered walks and assuring quiet and restful sleep. These covered walks also extend to the dining room, seating 600 people, and the convention hall, seating 1200 people, and the recreation hall, where over 600 people may dance at one time.

Coming back to the Muskoka Lake region, Mr. Merritt called particular attention to the treatment of the shore line of the lake by the summer residents who often make this shore into one continuous garden. The boathouse is often more elaborate than the residence and in many places the upper part of the boathouse is made into a dining room, and sometimes even sleeping quarters. The residences are difficult to photograph as they are usually hidden away in the woods. "No trespass" signs are naturally rather plentiful, but Mr. and Mrs. Merritt found the people most gracious and hospitable and when it was learned that they desired to photograph these garden homes, every coöperation was extended, and perhaps for the first time a real New England outsider enjoyed miles of walks through these beautiful gardens of cultivated wild flowers.

One family from Pittsburgh has been enjoying a very beautiful summer home. A visitor suggested that they ought to have a large stone fireplace, so last summer the erection of this was begun. Large stones were secured from a distance and brought in on scows, while derricks had to be brought from distant Toronto. The shelf stone alone measured 11 feet 4 inches long, 3 feet wide and was 18 inches thick, and required great skill in being put in place. It was discovered that these stones were too large to put in the summer home, so the owner most conveniently had the fireplace built out doors and a new summer home built around the fireplace, thus all were made happy.

One of the choicest islands is that owned by Mr. Silverwood, the president of the famous Silverwood Dairies of Canada. His entire island is a flower garden, with a mile of gravel walks, these so extensive that the renewal of gravel this last spring was only at an expense of $900. Small summerhouses dot the walks to make it possible to enjoy all the scenic beauty of both garden and lake. Mr. Silverwood has specialized in rock gardens with rare flowers, and he has a most artistic manner of retaining natural beauty with cultivated ideas. Beautiful outdoor furniture makes attractive resting places for the visitor. As usual the boathouse is placed on the back side of the island, out of sight and sound of the home.

Perhaps the most extensive gardens of the Muskoka Lakes are found on Lake Rosseau at the summer home of Lady Eaton, the owner of the famous Eaton Department stores of Canada.

Permission is seldom given to anyone to visit these gardens, but this last summer through the courtesy of the head gardener, Mr. and Mrs. Merritt were able to visit and photograph her magnificent gardens. In the midst of these she has her own race track and stables and in the season her famous trotting horses are seen daily. Everywhere one goes it is along a walk beautiful with flowers. An artistic tennis building nestles close to the courts and a tea room is conveniently close by where afternoon tea may be served when desired. No matter by which entrance one approaches the main residence it is always along a walk bordered with flowers and shrubs. The gardener's home is a rustic log cabin, and it requires two or three hours to properly visit and enjoy these Eaton gardens.

Mr. Merritt then called to the attention of the audience the fact that as the climate of Ontario is similar to New England, that the Ontario wild flowers greet the New Englander on every side. Beautifully colored slides were shown of the pussy willow, painted trillium, lady slipper, columbine, dandelion, red clover, mountain laurel, thistle, golden rod, pond lily, and black-eyed susan. A particularly choice plate was an arrangement consisting of a tiny blueberry bush showing the leaf, the blossom, the red unripe berry and the deep blue ripe berry.

Mr. Merritt then stated that as there was time, he would like to show the audience just a slide or two of many other Canadian gardens he had photographed. Starting with the noted Raymond Gardens of Yarmouth, N. S., slides covering other points in Canada were quickly shown. The beautiful gardens of the Jasper Park Lodge, Alberta, showed delphinium growing 6 to 8 feet high with rows fifty feet long of this beautiful flower enriching the walk to the main doorway of the Lodge. At Skagway, Alaska, the flower gardens were visited where pansies 3½ inches in diameter were picked by Mrs. Merritt, also a dahlia 11½ inches in diameter and where sweet peas grow so tall that a step ladder is needed to pick the blossoms, and where delphinniums 8 feet high were photographed. At Dawson and in the Klondike Yukon River flowers were shown in profusion. Here Mr. Merritt stated that flowers were often grown in the sod roof of the houses and cabins, one man having his lettuce garden on his roof. Fireweed grows in great profusion and a slide showed a mass over 6 feet high. Wild cotton plants are found on every hand. After three or four slides covering the beautiful gardens at Anchorage, Alaska, Mr. Merritt closed his lecture with pictures of the world famous Butchard Gardens, near Victoria, B. C. Here Mr. Butchard has turned the old quarries into magnificent series of flower gardens. Flowers from all over the world are found growing here. Rose walks cause exclamations of delight from the visitor and words fail to describe portions of the garden such as an embankment 250 feet long, 40 feet high, covered with rare blossoms. There are three high spots in the Butchard Gardens: first, the Italian Gardens where trimmed boxwood trees and rambler rose archways reflect into the water; second, the most artistically arranged back yard of the home; and third, a particular rose arbor so situated that Mrs. Merritt was able to stand in the arbor and look out on one of those rare Pacific Coast sunsets covered by a gorgeous slide which Mr. Merritt used in closing his lecture.

"NEW, INTERESTING AND DESIRABLE HARDY HERBACEOUS AND BULBOUS PLANTS"

By Mr. William N. Craig, Weymouth, Mass.

Thursday Afternoon, January 28, 1937

Presented here, in outline form, is a brief discussion of herbaceous and bulbous plants, that are hardy in this part of Massachusetts, for garden use.

Chrysanthemums are very fine things to grow. The Korean variety is the hardiest type. Last year was the first time any double Korean variety Chrysanthemums were shown. One was named Indian Summer, a vivid glowing orange, which blooms in October. Another was called Romany; this is an orange carmine red, and also blooms in October. These Chrysanthemums should be given room to properly spread, as they require more space than the old ones. Several varieties that were tried out started blooming about September 15. Some of these were Thalia, Fortuna, Psyche, and Vesta. Some of the old ones are Early Bronze, much better than Aladdin, the very popular Jean Treadway, which is a very excellent pink, September Queen, and Amelia, which is a low-cushioned type, pink in color, very compact and free flowering.

Esther Reed is a new double snow white Shasta Daisy, the best novelty in hardy plants.

There are about ninety very fine hybrids of Hemerocallis or Day Lilies. A few outstanding ones were shown in England last year. The finest of all varieties is Hyperion, pure rich yellow. A good one flowering in July is Mikado—showy, round, clear gold flower with a tawny splash across each petal. Within the last two or three years, Hemerocallis Lilies have increased rapidly in favor. They are good garden plants for this locality and have no insect pests or diseases.

Poppies are good things if the right colors are found. There are several other good colors besides red. For instance, Apricot Queen, which is a single deep apricot color, Perry's Pink, Perry's White, Princess Ena and Parkmanni.

SUNNYSIDE GREENHOUSES, FALL 1937

DY

erba-
lassa-

orean
e any
One
looms
range
nthe-
quire
tried
were
ones
pular
ueen,
very

, the

lis or
land
vel-
und,

ased
ality

here
ricot
rry's

There are quite a few types in the Anemone family. The Japanese (Japonica) is not as hardy as other varieties but is very striking. It blooms from August to frost. The Sylvestris Anemone grows nine or ten inches high and blooms in May and June.

The Pulsatilla Anemone (Pasque Flower) blooms in April with flowers of lavender, white, and ruby colors.

The Phlox has good flowers from late June onward. The best white in existence is the rather dwarf, Diplomat. Columbia is one of the good patented varieties, although it is no better than some others which are unpatented. The particularly fine salmon-pink Enchantress is even better. It has as good color and is more widely grown. A good Phlox also is Jules Sandeau. It is a free flowering salmon-pink with large blossoms. The finest of all pink varieties is Daily Sketch. The flowers are immense. The Divaricata is a native species and is worthy of extensive planting. It begins to bloom early in April and continues through May. It has large flowers which are very freely produced and lavender in color.

Scabiosa Caucasica blooms over a long period. It lasts longer when cut than any other perennial plant. Abroad every shop window is full of Scabiosa through the entire summer months. The long stemmed ones in Great Britain cost six pence per dozen. They are good things to grow and are quite hardy, if planted properly. The lecturer had some sent to Liverpool on August 15 and eight days later took them home. They are very attractive.

There are one or two Lilium additions worth mentioning. Lilium Regale (Regal Lily) is ivory-white, shaded pink on the outside and yellow in the throat. This blooms in July.

Formosanum, from Formosa, has long trumpet-like, fragrant, white blooms. The Elegans Lilium is a very interesting dwarf Japanese species for rock garden planting. It grows one to two feet high, with large showy trumpetlike blooms of rich coloring, during June and July. Speciosum Rubrum is a very fine lily, having rosy white blooms heavily spotted with crimson. It grows three to four feet tall. The Lilium Rubellum blooms in early June. It grows nine inches tall and carries pure pink trumpets.

Hardy asters are seen along our roadsides and are very charming in the fall. Little Pink Lady and Burbank's Charming Asters bloom late in October and will stand freezing without injury. Some good dwarf type Hybrid Border Asters are Nancy, Marjorie, Ronald, and Lilac Time. These are compact subjects. One of the finest Asters is the Charles Wilson, which is a reddish purple, growing two and one-half feet high. It blooms late in September and is well worth while.

Sidalcea is not grown as much here as abroad. It comes in three heights: dwarf, twelve to fifteen inches; medium, two and one-half feet high; and tall, four to six feet. It will bloom the first year if sown early.

Eupatorium Coelestinum (Mistflower) blooms in the middle of October with clusters of blue flowers. This is a very useful flower.

Royal Lady's Slippers grow best in the shade in mossy soil.

Sweet Wivelsfield is a cross between Sweet William and the hardy spice plant. It resembles a large flowering Sweet William, and is good for cutting. It grows about twelve inches high.

The Echinops (Globe Thistle) grows tall, three to five feet, and has very attractive foliage and steel blue heads of flowers.

The Gaillardias (Blanket Flowers) are very showy plants, their colorful flowers in red and gold bloom from July until frost. Sungold is a beautiful yellow variety.

Gypsophila (Baby's Breath), Bristol Fairy, grows two and one-half feet high here. (In Europe this flower grows four to six feet.) It flowers more or less continuously throughout the summer. It has great panicles of pure white double flowers. Bodgeri is a grand double continuous blooming white 12 inches high.

Delphiniums are very popular subjects in the hardy border. They are very attractive, they require a sweet soil, a lot of lime and good drainage. Fine bone is a safe fertilizer for them.

Anchusa Myosotideflora has flowers like a Forget-me-not, grows about one foot high and blooms in March and April.

The Primula Cashmeriana is a lovely species with large purplish rose blooms. It flowers the first week in April and onwards.

The Arabis (Rock Cress) Alpina is a favorite for borders and rock gardens. This hardy and long-lived plant has pure white flowers soon after snow disappears, the double form is much the best.

The early blooming Helleborus Niger (Christmas Rose) is quite hardy here. Its large, artistically formed flowers are white, lightly flushed with purple. This flowers from late October until March.

There have been many new Tulips introduced and of these the majority have been Darwins. Perhaps the best known breeder is the giant Louis XIV variety, blending a nice pastel purple with a golden brown edge. A good Cottage Tulip is the John Ruskin, a charming apricot rose with a shading of mauve and a margin of pale yellow. Another good Cottage Tulip is Sirene. This is a cherry colored flower with a large white base. It has almost a lily-like appearance.

An improved type of Narcissus Poeticus is Thelma. This very colorful and large-sized flower has *substantial* overlapping snow-white petals and a broad, light yellow cup, margined with deep scarlet. Another good Narcissus is Olympia, which has a large yellow blossom. The Poetaz Narcissus Helios is a pure beauty of deep yellow. It is large and free flowering. The Orchid Narcissus is also very good; its botanical name is Triandrus Thalia.

Jonquilla Simplex is the sweet scented Jonquil, having grass like foliage. Queen of Spain is a soft yellow color and grows about twelve inches high.

Of the several species of Iris, the Spanish Iris should be planted four inches deep. The Dutch Iris blooms earlier. Better coloring is to be had in the lovely English Iris. The Japanese Iris is quite hardy here and blooms early in July. It has very large flowers in many lovely colors and is well worth growing.

Fritillaria Meleagris, the Guinea Hen Flower should be planted three or four inches deep in the fall. This flower is quite lovely early in May.

A nice hardy plant is the Spring Snowflake, Leucojum Vernum, growing about nine inches high. It flowers in May.

A good fall flowering crocus is Sativus (Saffron Crocus). The plant has large, pleasing, fragrant blooms of a beautiful purple-lilac color, feathered with white. The anthers are bright orange.

Fresh manure should be kept away from the Gold Banded Lily of Japan (Lilium Auratum). This is a large, graceful, fragrant ivory-white flower with chocolate-crimson spots and striped through the center with golden yellow. The improved Tiger Lily, Tigrinum Splendens, has bright orange-red blossoms with shining black spots. It grows to five feet tall and blooms in September.

A good climbing Rose is Mermaid. This has beautiful, single, creamy-white flowers. Austrian Copper Rose is rather weak growing, but is a striking color. One of the oldest roses is York and Lancaster. There are some sixty new Roses each year. One of the best is McGredy's Yellow. Carrie Jacobs Bond is one of the prominent roses of recent introduction. It is an entrancing deep rose with a coral sheen. It has graceful form and is pleasingly fragrant.

Most bulbous plants come from the continents of Europe, North America, and Asia. Those from Australia or Africa are not hardy in this part of the country. There has been a great deal of controversy over the treatment of bulbs coming from abroad. It is possible that all imported bulbs will have to be hot water treated about six hours as a safeguard against some insects that have come into this country on bulbs. One of the most common of these pests is the eel-worm. In order to determine what is to be done about this situation, a meeting was held in Washington, about six weeks ago. The results of this conference have not as yet been published.

The flower grower cannot exercise too much care in the purchase of his bulbs. Although it is common practice in Japan to cut the roots off bulbs, the lecturer has found, through experience, that they will mold if treated in this way. If bulbs are to live actively, the roots must be left on.

"COLOR IN THE GARDEN"

Illustrated Lecture

By Mr. Donald D. Wyman, North Abington, Mass.

Thursday Afternoon, February 4, 1937

Many of us, it seems, are prone to believe that the "merry month of May" is the only time that gardens are colorful. But there can be color every season of the year and a well planned garden should have points of interest in fall, winter, spring and summer. If well planned, the following can be used in gardens to good advantage.

Magnolias are very welcome in early spring. Two kinds which seem to be useful in this part of the country are Stellata (Star Magnolia) whose pure white, scented flowers are the earliest to bloom, and the Pink Saucer Magnolia (Soulangeana), which is seen so abundantly along Commonwealth Avenue in Boston.

With Azaleas it is highly possible to have a successive bloom from April to July. The soft coloring of native Pink Shell Azaleas blends well with other things. This plant not only is hardy, but artistic and graceful. Although the Amoena (Evergreen Azalea) cannot be grown successfully in Boston or Worcester, it flourishes on the Cape, in Rhode Island, and Connecticut. One of our good contributions from China has been the Chinese Azalea, Azalea Mollis, whose flowers express variations from yellow to orange. This plant has rough foliage and can be grown successfully. The Kaempferi (Japanese Azalea) has nice salmon-pink blossoms which appear the latter part of May. As these shrubs sometimes grow to a height of four to five feet, they appear best when used with a background. There is nothing prettier than the delicate coloring of the Sweet Azalea. The fragrance of this hardy flower which is not unlike that of new mown hay, lends a splendid touch to the garden.

By using different varieties of Rhododendrons, a continuous bloom can be had from May to July. Of the many available

kinds, the Carolina Rhododendron is one of the most satisfactory. Blooming very early, these blossoms make up in number what they lack in size. The Rhododendron Maximum, if
placed where a shade-loving plant is necessary, gives a glorious
effect. Large, broad, evergreen type leaves are characteristic
of this shrub. Blooming in June and July its pink-tinged white
flowers give a delightful effect which is not too showy. The
Hybrid Rhododendron is not propagated as readily as many
other varieties of trees and shrubs. This bush has to be grafted
in order to assure sameness of color. In making use of Rhododendrons in the garden, it should be remembered that while
Rhododendrons give a good display of color, they need shade,
particularly in the month of March, when warm days and cold
nights are not infrequent.

There is a wide variety of flowering trees and shrubs that can
be used to distinct advantage in the garden. For example, there
is a delicacy about the blossoms of the Flowering Cherries.
These trees should be planted with more thought and care than
any other flowering tree. These trees must be planted for good
root drainage and a good circulation of air is essential. The
Cercis (Judas Tree), flowers in early spring long before other
things are in bloom. The Pink Flowering Dogwood is good in
fall as well as spring. The Chinese Dogwood has beautiful fall
coloring. Originally seen in the prairies of Illinois, the Flowering
Crab Apple has been grown in American nurseries for many
years. There are many very satisfactory kinds available. One
of the first trees to assume autumn foliage is the Native Oxy-
dendron, whose small whitish flowers look a bit like lilies-of-the-
valley. Very conspicuous, with its yellow foliage in fall, is the
Shagbark Hickory (some other trees having yellow foliage in
fall are the Birch and Sugar Maple). A very shapely shade tree
is the Sweet Gum, which looks like Maple at first glance. This
tree grows particularly well in Pennsylvania and New Jersey
where it is native. The native Washington Hawthorn has nice
flowers in spring and an abundance of berries in the fall. Another "fall" tree which is not so showy in summer, is the native
Tupelo, whose gnarled branches grow almost at right angles.
Black Alder, the fragrant Sumac, along with others, are an important part of a well planned garden.

Introduced by the Arnold Arboretum was the large growing
Kolkwitza (Beauty Bush). This very attractive plant should
have abundant space. Its soft bell-shaped pink flowers are to
be seen in June. Flowering later in the spring than most others,
is the very fragrant Syringa Japonica. This shrub has nice
dark green foliage and its creamy white flowers bloom from
June 20 to July 10. A well grown Viburnum Tomentosum forms
a compact round bush. The Viburnum Sieboldii, with its rich
foliage and white flowers, although not new, is very satisfactory.
The fruit is pinkish red, changing to blue-black when fully ripe.
The Virginal Philadelphus Mock Orange has been commercially
offered for the past ten or twelve years. Although not hand-
somely shaped, this bush has dark green foliage and good flowers
(semi-double in late June) in such profusion that it looks almost
like a snowstorm. The fragrant blossoms of this shrub to a great
measure compensate for its lack of shape. The perennial Spiraea
is good planted as a border. It has substance, vigor and does
not have to be replanted. It can be used in combination with
flowering shrubs.

One of the most interesting of all is the Euonymus yedoensis.
This shrub has small yellow flowers in spring and its pinkish
husks are quite striking in the fall. The Winged Burning Bush
is good every season of the year. It has scarlet seed pods with
orange colored berries.

Japanese Yews are being used more and more for hedges.
Increasing use for this purpose is predicted, because of its apparent immunity to weather conditions.

Very interesting backgrounds can be obtained in a number
of ways. A good suggestion is the graceful Hemlock or White
Pine, which is hard to duplicate as a background for Azaleas, etc.
White Birch brings out the beauty of the background in a garden.

Vines are very useful in softening architectural features. It
is generally believed that increasing use will be made during the
next few years of Clematis. The Sweet Autumn Clematis (purple
Clematis) blooms earlier than the Japanese Clematis. Large
flowered Clematis come in several different colors. Wisteria
Vines should not be planted against a house, but rather in a
place where they will not interfere with construction. The

EDWARD W. BREED, FALL 1937

flower clusters should be given plenty of room to hang down. It is suggested that grafted ones be obtained as they start sooner. It sometimes takes as long as twenty-one years before Wisteria blooms and even then, they do not necessarily bloom each year. Climbing Hydrangeas give a softening touch and they are one of the few vines that will adhere to masonry. As they are notoriously slow-growing, they may be substituted by the rapid growing Polygonum Auberti (Silver Lace Flower). However the Climbing Hydrangeas are well worth waiting for. The Turquoise Berry has robin's egg blue berries, which are very ornamental and a good foliage.

In this part of the country, we are very fortunate in having a good opportunity for rock gardens. Get old weather-beaten moss-covered rocks that will give the appearance of age. As one's eye goes first to those things that are unattractive, never get rocks that are new looking or colorful.

Several popular varieties of Lilies have earned a well deserved place in the garden. Hybrid Lilies are hardy and free-flowering. Their colorful blossoms range from white, pink, into blue and rich rosy-purple. Regal Lilies, introduced by Dr. E. H. Wilson, of the Arnold Arboretum, grow five, six, and seven feet tall. They sometimes have thirty-five to forty large trumpet-shaped blossoms in a single clump. These sweet scented flowers are a shaded pink on the outside and tinged with canary yellow at the base. The Candidum (Madonna Lily) has pure white flowers on a stately stem, which bloom during May and June. The Auratum (Gold Banded Lily of Japan) has large graceful ivory-white flowers with chocolate crimson spots, and striped through the center with golden yellow.

Great strides have been made in climbing roses in the past twenty years. Some good ones are: Dr. W. Van Fleet, Golden Climber, Silver Moon, and Paul's Scarlet Climber. There are very few flowers that bloom over so long a period as the roses do. Yellow, in roses, is the weakest of all colors. It is genuinely hoped that someone will find a good hardy yellow in the not too far distant future.

There are many things at hand with which to make our gardens. If the beauty of a garden is to be determined by color, fragrance, and form, a number of suggestions as to garden-planning should be observed. When a person goes into a garden and, after a brief glance around, begins to wonder when they are going to serve the ginger-ale, that garden is not properly made. If it were, everything could not have been seen at once. Little walks and paths are not only intriguing, but they provide charm. Through proper arrangement, a small place can be made to seem spacious and vice versa. The same individuality can be expressed in the planning of a garden as in the furnishing of a home.

It is well to remember that a great deal of the natural beauty is taken away when plants are pruned too closely. Further, if the cut is made late in the spring, the new growth will cover it up. Plant a lot of white in the garden. Let this be the yardstick by which you measure your color scheme. Beware of the ever-present danger of over-planting. There is nothing that gives a better appearance and is more effective, than a good piece of turf. Above all, strive for privacy in your garden.

In retrospect, let it be said that although a tremendous amount of interest is shown new things, it is, at the same time, possible that some of the old things are planted far less than they should be. Yet, rightly, styles are changing. There are many worth while things being added, and there is still need for more.

"SPRING AND AUTUMN IN THE GARDEN"

Illustrated Lecture

By Mrs. Preston Rice, Grand Rapids, Mich.

Thursday Afternoon, February 11, 1937

If a person has time to work in autumn and plan the spring garden, there is any number of flowers blooming throughout the spring season readily available. He is a very poor gardener who cannot get good spring flowers, as nature is with us at that time in giving many lovely flowers with which to work out spring gardens. Combination of plantings and distribution of colors are things to be considered in the spring garden. It is advisable to start planning as far back as fall, so that a great quantity of these lovely things will be coming up just after the snow starts to melt. It is most natural at this time of year for the garden to show a profusion of yellow.

Hedges are suggested for outlining the drive. The Canadian Hemlock is very good for this purpose. As it will not grow where there is a great deal of sun, it is suggested that the shrub be underhung by tall evergreens.

Crocuses are always nice things to have in the early spring. One of the earliest and best Crocuses is Susianus, the Cloth of Gold Crocus. This is a lovely shade of yellow and is much better than the Dutch Crocus.

The Kaufmanniana Tulip is always lovely. This flower blooms in April. Two other nice botanical Tulips are Greigi, which blooms in April and May, and Sprengeri, which is the latest to bloom. The Munstead strain of Primroses comes only in shades of yellow. These are good used along with Tulips.

Bulbocodium Conspicuus, the Hoop-Petticoat Jonquil, grows only about six inches high. It has dainty golden blooms as early as the middle of March. Good bouquets may be made with either Jonquils or Narcissus if they are arranged properly.

It is easy to get a permit from Washington to import good

species Peonies. They bloom before the others. These should be imported by individuals, since the nurserymen cannot afford to do this on a wholesale basis.

Tulips in yellow, orange and brown are good used with Doronicum Excelsum. Doronicum Excelsum is very fragile looking, but is a nice spring plant.

Columbine is nice, but usually has to be put in each year.

The Lily Umbellatum grows from one and a half to two and a half feet in height. It will grow well in the shade. Sometimes it has as many as eighteen flowers in one clump. Lilium Tenuifolia is a very nice lily. It has fine slender stalks. It never seems to be in the way, and is not ugly in ripening. It takes very little room. Of the Yellow Lilies, Pardalinum giganteum (Sunset Lily) is a very lovely thing. It is only when Lily bulbs are planted quite deeply that they live the year round. By planting them deeply, the water is able to get at them during the summer and keep them alive. The Superbum Lily is very hardy and good. Hemerocallis Lilies, if well planned, have a succession of blooms during May, June, July, August, and the early part of September. Some very good ones are Hyperion, which is the most gorgeous of any of the Day Lilies, Ophir, George Yeld, and Achillea Eupatorium.

Hugonis Roses are very good for background. However, they are subject to borers. Rosa Xanthina is recommended as being superior to Hugonis. It is just as hardy and better all around.

Oriental Poppy Oroflamme seems to fight with everything, due to its color. The handling of a color is not so much a matter of what the color is, but rather how much there is of it. The Oriental Poppy is very lovely when placed entirely by itself in a pocketlike place, surrounded by evergreens. Never use it along with any other flowers.

We couldn't think of spring without Iris. The following are some of the better kinds which should be grown. Jubilee, Coppersmith, Valencia, Ophelia, Pluie d'Or, Helios, Besant, Goldilocks, G. P. Baker, Chromylla, Vesper Gold, Desert Gold and Citronella. Citronella was introduced by Mr. Bliss at England. This Iris seems to be always in tune, as it is good for furnishing a transition in coloring. Cristata is also quite good, although it does not have the character of Verna. The latter requires shade and sour soil. In planting Iris, much attention should be given to the spacing of the bulbs. The dark Iris are valuable for emphasis, if too many of them are not used. Dominion is the father Iris, which introduced endurance of petals. Work out different levels in planting Iris.

Never must we, as gardeners, cultivate only those things that are most spectacular, but should spend some time on the lower and gentler things. Things that will grow up underneath or around taller things and form a tapestry, are always well worth while and make the garden more attractive.

Of the Azaleas, the Chinese Azalea, Azalea mollis, seems to be worthy of mention. Its blossoms are principally shades of yellow and orange. At the Cabin Gardens of Mr. and Mrs. Rice, in Grand Rapids, Mich., they do not have as good luck with Azaleas as we do in this part of the country.

Yellow Yarrow is splendid in any garden, as it blooms over a long period of time. Senecio gives a dash of color. Marigolds and Zinnias are also good things to have. They are very colorful.

Laburnum Vossi (Goldenchain) is very fine, although rather easily winter-killed. However, it will come back in the spring.

Viburnum Horosee is good to employ in making transition from color to color, since its gray leaves are very much desired. This plant should have good drainage, and protection from the winds.

Pools in gardens are very good for shadows and reflection. They make a quiet retreat.

Walls are also nice, provided they are not entirely covered with vegetation. As rock gardens do not seem to thrive in Michigan, more attention is paid to walls.

The Daphne Cneorum is often over-fertilized. If this is done, it will bloom itself to death. This plant is best in spring.

The Anemone Pulsatilla (cousin of the Pasque Flower) has a beautiful seed pod which is as good as the flower.

Lilacs are very valuable spring material. The species Lilacs are good. They grow almost to the size of a tree and bloom one month after the French Hybrids.

IRISTHORPE, MRS. HOMER GAGE, FALL 1937

although
requires
hould be
valuable
ninion is
. Work

ings that
he lower
neath or
ell worth

seems to
hades of
nd Mrs.
ood luck

ms over
larigolds
colorful.
h rather
e spring.
ransition
desired.
from the

eflection.

covered
hrive in

is done,
ng,
er) has a

es Lilacs
loom one

Primroses come in many colors: yellow, blue, purple, wine, and lavender. They are very hardy. Primula denticulata is a good perennial. It grows about ten inches high and when in bloom looks like rosettes. It should be divided rather often, as it has a tendency to become crowded.

A good shrub is Prunus Niedzwetzkyana. It is a beautiful Japanese-like thing. The blossoms appear before the leaves.

In planting Tulips, it is well to plant them more or less in clumps. Some people prefer to plant them more or less by themselves and others have an undergrowth. The latter is believed by the lecturer to be the better. It is well to have some other plant coming along, such as Phlox, to cover after they are through blooming. Scilla Companulata is very good with Tulips, as are the early Azaleas.

Tree Peonies are very pretty things. The named varieties are still very expensive, but you can buy some very lovely unnamed ones at reasonable prices. They bloom about ten days to two weeks before the Chinese. They have nice woody stalks, a suedelike leaf, and very good colors.

Paul's Scarlet Thorn is excellent in Iris time. As it doesn't clash with anything else, it is suggested that you have one in the vicinity of your Iris.

The Malus Floribunda is not good when not in bloom and is, therefore, grown for beauty of flowers alone.

Robina Hispida (Rose Acacia) blooms at Locust time. It is not so brilliant as Malus Floribunda, but is hardy and has good foliage.

Do not be discouraged if Florida Dogwood does not bloom right off. Often it takes six or seven years after planting before it blooms. When it does start to bloom, however, it will be covered. Even one will add great joy to any place.

The best early Peony is Helen. It is the earliest of the single peonies. Pride of Langport Peony is not quite so good, but is less expensive to buy.

When buying bulbs, get the best you can get, even if you can only get a few instead of getting many of the cheaper ones.

In spite of many attempts to secure a good yellow Peony, there are no really good ones yet, but there are so many other good yellow flowers that we can enjoy Peonies in their original shades. One good attempt is Flashlight, but even this is not a perfect yellow. Japanese Peonies seem to literally flash color across the garden. A good imported one is Masterpiece. Some good Japanese Peonies are Cathedral, Goldmine, which is not very tall but beautiful in combination with everything, Alliance, Dawn, which is the formal type of Japanese Peony, and Jishikukeni. All hybridizers are working to get a good yellow Peony. Until this is found, we shall have to depend on the yellow-centered Peonies. Good Peonies should have a stiff enough stem to support the bloom, and it should not be necessary to have to tie up the stems. Such a Peony is Phyllis Kelway.

White Delphiniums are of no garden value. There are so many other good white flowers for the garden that one should not bother with the white Delphiniums. As there are few really good blues in the garden outside of the Delphiniums, the most should be made of Delphinium blue.

Long before the Delphiniums are cut down, the Shelford Giant Iris comes. This is a cross between two species, Ochraleucha and Aurea. Sometimes this marvelous flower grows six feet tall. It is one of the purest colored flowers.

Phlox is one of the things that will bring out new colors. Silver King is a nice white, finding popular use. This flower must not be allowed to become bushy.

A second blooming of Phlox can be had in the fall. Native Veronica Virginica may be used at this time to add height. If Zinnias are planted to fill in, a delightful fall color is added.

Sedum Spectabile and Sedum Magnificum are both splendid in combination with Zinnias. Sedum Sieboldi is also very good. It can be used to advantage in rock planting.

The colors seem to change in autumn from yellows to deeper copperlike shades.

When all the flowers have ceased to bloom, even the fungus growths and poison mushrooms with their white caps are lovely to look at. They add a great deal of interest to late gardens.

The Tree Lantana is not often thought of in summer, but if it is placed in a strategic place, it will rejuvenate the garden.

It is better to buy Sassafras at a nursery than to try to cultivate the wild. When the first frost comes, they will show good color.

European Mountain Ash is good along a back line. It has lovely berries in fall which come quite early, and it has very graceful branches.

The Oriental Lenten Rose comes in several colors and is very good.

The Pyracantha Lalandi is another of the late native plants. It has Azalea-like foliage and berries similar to European Mountain Ash, except for the fact that the birds will not eat them. These berries usually persist through the winter.

"WHAT I SAW IN JAPAN"

Illustrated Lecture

By Dr. Frank A. Waugh, Amherst, Mass.

Thursday Afternoon, February 18, 1937

When a professor takes six months to go abroad, it is usually for some profound research. He is undoubtedly going to investigate something and write a book about it. Professor Waugh went to Japan just for the enjoyment of the trip, and to see his son, who then lived there.

Having his son at hand, facilitated his seeing many things which would not be seen by the average stranger, traveling in Japan. For instance, he received an invitation from the Mikado and Empress to attend their Garden Party to see the cherry blossoms. This was due to the fact that his son was friendly, in a business way, with a high official of the Japanese Government, and he had put the lecturer's name on the invitation list.

It seems to be a well-known fact among travelers, that it is nearly impossible to take any pictures in Japan, since this is forbidden in many places. Professor Waugh carried three cameras all around Japan and had no difficulty taking pictures. For instance, he attended a public procession in Tokyo which was magnificent. He hoped to get some pictures of it, but there were so many people that it seemed impossible. Finally, he shinnied half-way up a light pole to get some pictures, and was getting along nicely when he looked up and saw a policeman coming toward him. He began to think of some alibis, and was much surprised when the officer moved some of the people and made room for him to take his pictures. The above is typical of the way Dr. Waugh was treated during his entire stay in Japan.

Japan has many mountains, all of which are grand. The island is also famous for its temples. Only about 20 per cent of Japan is cultivated and most of the cultivated land is irrigated.

Professor Waugh found it interesting to note the way the Japanese grew their strawberries. There are ditches two feet or more deep along both sides of the plants, and these ditches are filled with water. Professor Waugh had some of the berries and they were very fine, but he does not think they would keep as well for shipping, as those planted in the American way. Rice is always irrigated.

Another kind of farming in Japan is Noodle Farming. These noodles are made mostly of rice flour. One section of the country is devoted to this type of farming alone. The natives hang the noodles outside their homes on racks, until they are dry and ready to sell. If, while the noodles are hung on their racks drying, it starts to rain, one sees the mother and children come out and take them inside, then as soon as it clears, they hang them all out again.

Azaleas in Japan remind one of our mountain laurel. They may be seen along paths through the woods, by the thousands, and are very striking. There are also some very lovely roses growing in Japan.

After the famous cherry blossoms have gone by, the iris comes on. Tokyo has a very gorgeous park where there is a lovely iris garden. Dr. Waugh went to see this garden one Sunday afternoon when it was open. The park opened at two o'clock, and over 200,000 persons visited the park on that afternoon, just to see the iris. This shows the Japanese feeling for lovely things. The iris was planted along the water's edge, and the shore line was shored up with bamboo rip-rap.

At the Kora Ku-en, which was laid out by a Chinese landscape architect 300 years ago, the Japanese have established an arsenal, and parts of the garden are filled with munition factories. Although it is almost impossible to get permission to enter this garden, Professor Waugh was invited to visit it with a friend; while looking over the great garden, there appeared a Japanese with tea for them.

During the latter part of Dr. Waugh's stay in Japan, he visited the Japanese National Morning Glory Society's Annual Exhibition, which was very beautiful. Every day the morning glories were replaced with fresh, and people came from quite a

way the Jap-
two feet or
ditches are
the berries and
would keep as
way. Rice

ming. These
of the coun-
natives hang
are dry and
racks drying,
come out and
hang them all

laurel. They
the thousands,
lovely roses

the iris comes
a lovely iris
Sunday after-
o'clock, and
noon, just to
lovely things.
the shore line

landscape
lished an ar-
factories
to enter the
with a friend
a Japanese

pan, he visited
Annual Ex
the morning
from quite a

CHARLES POTTER, FALL 1937

distance just to see this Exhibition, which shows further their love for beauty.

In order to appreciate the Japanese garden, one is supposed to know the Buddhist religion. Dr. Waugh does not believe that a knowledge of this religion is necessary for anyone to recognize beauty, and believes that he appreciated the beauty of these gardens even though he did not know the religious background of the garden.

Much use is made of rocks in Japanese gardens. They are used for walks, waterfalls, etc. Azaleas are used in some of the gardens, although many gardens contain rocks alone, and no blossoms, and in some not even grass is allowed to grow. To accomplish this, the soil is raked twice a day. Many of the gardens have lovely bridges cut out of stone, and stone water basins are common. The waterfalls are usually a rectangular upright stone. One is supposed to use the imagination, as there is no water going over the waterfall or in the stream beds. These stones are washed each day by the gardener. The foundation of Japanese architecture is the stones. Trees and flowers come second. In one Temple Garden there was a total of fifteen stones, which were placed by a Chinese landscape architect long ago. He arranged these fifteen stones so that one could not stand in any single place in the garden and see all fifteen stones at once. While looking over a very beautiful garden, Dr. Waugh wandered down to the edge of the garden, where he spied what looked like an American rock garden. There were scattered rocks with flowers growing up between them. He was admiring this when the guide who was showing him through the garden found him, and told him to come away from that "dump." This was where they had thrown away all the stones which they did not want, and the wild flowers had sprung up and made, what we would consider, a very lovely rock garden, but this would not be a Japanese idea of a garden at all. Most of the stones have a religious background with which the Japanese are very familiar. The stones are very choice and have beautiful lines. There are stepping stones going up the side of a hill, with little ferns all along the way, which makes a very natural looking picture. In one place, a Chinese moon bridge, made over six hundred years ago by a Chinese monk, has withstood all the earthquakes, some of which have killed thousands of people.

Japanese people seem to value trees in proportion to the amount of scaffolding they can put under them. The Japanese ideal tree is a tree which is made to represent a dragon.

There are some very lovely little dwarf trees which can be bought at the expensive flower shops in Japan. These little trees are put into a "harness" to make them dwarfed and are tended for fifteen years, after which time they are put into a very lovely flower pot and sold. Professor Waugh bought a very lovely tree and pot which cost him, complete, 2¾c. It is customary there to have only one plant in your house at a time. When you tire of this plant and want a change you can go to what they call a "reserve garden" and exchange this plant for another.

There is one kind of tree in Japan, however, which is not shored up with bamboo. This tree, the Cryptomeria, often grows two hundred feet high, and is hundreds of years old. When the temples were being built, one of the daimios who was very poor, said he had no money, but a lot of trees which he would be willing to donate. Of the million given away in this manner, there are twenty miles of them still growing.

Many Japanese customs seem a bit unusual to the average American tourist. For example, tea is offered you at every turn. Again, you can't go into any Japanese home or hotel without first removing your shoes. If you want to go into the garden, there are wooden shoes which are furnished for this purpose. Since the Japanese never use chairs, the hotel rooms, like all others, are furnished with cushions on which to sit. There is always a beautiful view of a garden from the hotel room window. The walls slide open in summer, opening upon a narrow porch with polished floors.

At the entrance to the temples, one always finds a water basin at the door, with a dipper. Before going into the temple, one is supposed to wash his mouth out, thus washing his sins away.

Most of the Japanese gardens are enclosed. These enclosures are made by placing bamboo poles closely together. Although some of them have a stone foundation, most of them are just bamboo fences.

In Japan there are some beautiful old castles, representing very lovely old architecture. Most of these old castles are entirely uninhabited; not even a caretaker is present. However, just the other side of these castles are modern stores, much like our own department stores.

There are thousands of temples and shrines all over Japan. The Dai-butsu of Kamakura is an example. The bronze figure at this shrine stands fifty feet above its pedestal. It is very impressive to see the people walking up the steps to worship at this shrine. Many tourists laugh at these folks who worship an idol, but Dr. Waugh does not believe it makes very much difference what the name is that you have for deity, and looks upon this as a very impressive ceremony.

ANNUAL REUNION

The annual reunion of the Worcester County Horticultural Society took place on February 25, 1937. In the receiving line, which formed in the library before the grandfather's clock, were President and Mrs. Myron F. Converse, Vice-Presidents Mrs. Homer Gage and Mr. Herbert A. Cook, of Shrewsbury, who recently celebrated his ninetieth birthday.

The dining room downstairs was gaily decorated for the occasion and on each table was a large centerpiece of red roses. When all had gathered, at seven o'clock, Rev. Clifton Wheeler offered prayer. A delicious dinner was served, consisting of fruit cup, cream of celery soup, celery and pickles, roast beef, creamed potatoes, squash, banana fritters, ice cream in flower designs with cake, and coffee.

Before settling for the entertainment of the evening, which was furnished in part by the Unity Male Quartet, of Boston, President Myron F. Converse suggested that a rising greeting be shown Mr. Herbert A. Cook.

The speaker of the evening was introduced as Sir Lord Gray, who chose for his subject, "A Glimpse of Floriculture from Abroad." After several minutes there were only a few who began doubting the authenticity of the vague generalities about bulbs emanating from the speaker's platform. But before these doubts could be resolved into downright suspicion, the speaker suddenly finished. Sir Gray was scarcely seated when it was suggested that since there were so many in the audience who had visited England, he tell what part he came from. Carefully removing his pince-nez, Mr. Charles Murray gravely admitted that he was not from England at all, but Boston, and that the only bulbs he knew anything about were electric light bulbs. The deception over, he swung into his stride of impersonator and provided a hilarious evening of fun.

Dancing followed in the auditorium, which was beautifully decorated with spring flowers. Music was furnished by Harry Felton's Orchestra.

INDEX

SCHEDULE OF PREMIUMS

Offered by the

Worcester County Horticultural Society

Horticultural Building
30 Elm Street
Worcester, Mass.

For the year

1938

THE ATTENTION OF EXHIBITORS IS PARTICULARLY
CALLED TO THE RULES AND REGULATIONS
GENERAL AND SPECIAL

The Davis Press, Worcester

GENERAL RULES AND REGULATIONS

1. Strict conformity to the Regulations and Rules will be expected and required, as well for the benefit of exhibitors as for the convenience of the Officers of the Society.

2. Every Flower or Plant entered in a class of named varieties should be correctly named.

3. All articles offered for premiums must remain within the Hall throughout the hours of Exhibition, unless special permission for their removal shall be granted by the Committee on Exhibition, etc.

4. No person shall make more than one entry of the same variety or be awarded more than one premium under the same number.

5. The Judges may correct, before the close of any exhibition, awards made by them, if satisfied that such were erroneous.

6. The cards of exhibitors competing for premiums shall be reversed, until after premiums are awarded.

7. Competitors are expected to conform strictly to the conditions under which articles are invited. Evasion or violation of them may be reported to the TRUSTEES for future disqualification of the offender.

8. Articles offered for premiums must be in the Hall by 2 o'clock of the days of Exhibition except when otherwise specified. Between 2 and 3 o'clock the Hall will be in exclusive charge of the Committee on Arrangements and Exhibitions. Open to the public from 3 to 9 o'clock.

9. Competition for premiums is open to all residents of Worcester County only, and it is strictly required that all specimens offered for premiums shall have been grown by the competitors, on their own premises, for at least two (2) months previous to the date of exhibition, except where no restriction is stated in schedule.

10. After the articles are arranged they will be under the exclusive charge of the Judges and Committee of Arrangements, and not even the owners will have liberty to remove them until the exhibition is closed, and no sale of Fruit, Flowers or Vegetables shall be made in the building.

11.   Where a certain number or quantity of Plants, Flowers, Fruits or Vegetables is designated in the schedule, there must be neither more nor less than that number or quantity of specimens shown; and in no case can other varieties than those named in the schedule be substituted.

12.   The Judges may exclude from competition all inferior specimens and may correct any errors that they think were without deliberate purpose.

13.   The Committee on Arrangements has power to change the time of exhibition for any article, if an earlier or later season renders such change desirable.

14.   All articles offered for exhibition should be correctly named. Indefinite appellations such as "Pippin," "Sweeting," "Greening," etc., will not be considered as names. Any person exhibiting the same variety of Fruit or Vegetable, under different names, or exhibiting as grown by himself Flowers, Fruit or Vegetables grown by another, thereby violating the objects and rules of the Society, may be debarred from competing for the Society's premiums until reinstated.

15.   Competitors will be required to furnish information as to their mode of cultivation, and to present specimens for trial and examinations, if requested.

16.   In all exhibitions of Cut Flowers for competition, the number of blooms, clusters, sprays or spikes shown is not restricted except that it is expected the exhibitor shall use only a sufficient number to make a well-balanced display. All shall be of one color and of one variety in the same vase, except Displays, Vases, Baskets, Standards, or otherwise specified in the schedule. The Judge will consider the quality of the flowers rather than the quantity.

17.☞The Judges are authorized by the Trustees to invite the assistance of competent and discreet persons in the discharge of their duties.

18.   No Judge shall require anything of competitors respecting their exhibits which is not distinctly specified in the schedule.

19.   In Table Decorations, collections and displays of Flowers, Fruits, Vegetables, Vases, and Baskets, where the number of exhibits exceeds the number of premiums offered, the Judge *may* award prizes to any worthy exhibits not receiving a premium.

The maximum prize for Vases, Standards, and Baskets shall be two dollars.

20.   All premiums that are not claimed within one year after the close of the official year shall be forfeited to the Society.

21.   U. P. Hendrick's "Fruits of New York," and S. A. Beach's "The Apples of New York," will guide the Judge of Fruits in his decisions upon matters at issue.

22.   While the Society will take reasonable precautions for the safety of the property of exhibitors, it will be responsible in no case for any loss or damage that may occur.

Scale of Points

Cut Flowers and Wild Flowers.—

Arrangement	30 points
Quality of blooms	40 "
Number of varieties	15 "
Properly named	15

Lilies.—

Size and color of bloom	35 points
Number of perfect flowers and buds on stem	35
Arrangement	15 "
Properly named	15 "

Displays.—

Arrangement	40 points
Quality	45 "
Variety	15 "

Collections.—

Quality	45 points
Arrangement	25 "
Variety	30 "

Table Decoration.—

Quality of Flowers	50 points
Proportion and harmony of flowers with accessories	30
Artistic arrangement of whole	20

Special Funds

OF THE

WORCESTER COUNTY HORTICULTURAL SOCIETY

The following is a list of the Special Funds of the Worcester County Horticultural Society the income of which is devoted to the purpose stated. The date prefixed to each indicates the year in which the fund was established.

1888.   Francis Henshaw Dewey Fund. $1,000.00.
Income to be used for the purchase of books.

1898.   William Eames Fund. $500.00.
Income to be used for prizes for the promotion of apple culture.

1906.   Frederick A. Blake Fund. $1,000.00.
Income only to be used in providing Medals to be awarded to the originators of new varieties of Fruits or Flowers, preference always being given to residents of Worcester County.

In case that the Worcester County Horticultural Society does not find occasion to award medals for New Fruits or Flowers, the said income may be used for special premiums for Orchids or other choice Greenhouse Plants and Flowers.

1907.   Obadiah Brown Hadwen Fund. $1,000.00.
Income to be used for meritorious exhibits of Flowers, Fruits and Vegetables.

1922.   Edwin Draper Fund. $300.00.
Income to be used for prizes for Horticultural exhibitions held under the direction of said Society.

1924.   Miss Frances Clary Morse Fund. $500.00.
Income to be used for prizes for Flowers.

1937.   George and Belle McWilliam Fund.
Income to be used for prizes for Flowers.

Flowers, Plants, Fruits and Vegetables

1938

☞The Committee on Arrangements and Exhibitions would direct the earnest attention of the Judge to *Rule 12*.

12. The Judges may exclude from competition all inferior specimens and may correct any errors that they think were without deliberate purpose.

Special Rules

1. Exhibitors should have all specimens correctly and legibly named and the number of varieties written on the entry cards, notice of which will be taken by the judges in awarding the premiums.

2. While it is expected that exhibitors will take pains to correctly name their exhibits, the judges will not exclude an exhibit for mistake in nomenclature.

3. In all exhibitions of lilies the pollen may be removed.

By vote of the trustees, all entries must be made to the Secretary and all cards made out by him or his assistants.

Spring Exhibition

Thursday, March 10, 3 to 9 p. m.

Friday, March 11, 9 a. m. to 9 p. m.

Saturday, March 12, 9 a. m. to 9 p. m.

Sunday, March 13, 12 m. to 9 p. m.

Notify Secretary four weeks in advance
for space

*All articles for this exhibition must be
in the hall and ready for inspection
by the judges by 1 o'clock Thursday*

Class I	Garden Displays	
		1150.00
Class II	Plant Displays	
Class III	Rock Gardens	
	Not to exceed 100 square feet	125.00
Class IV	Cut Flowers	75.00
Class V	Fruit	75.00
Class VI	Vegetables	75.00

Frederick A. Blake Fund

Class VII	Carnations	25.00

Worcester Garden Club Exhibit

Thursday, April 28

*All articles for this exhibition must be
in the hall and ready for inspection
by the judges by 2 o'clock*

This exhibition will be open to the public from 3 to 9 p. m.

Cut Flowers.—
No. 1.   Display, 24 square feet   4.00 3.00 2.00

Table Decorations.—
No. 2.   Oblong table laid for
four covers   5.00 4.50 4.00 3.00 2.50 2.00 1.00
No restrictions.
Notify the Secretary two
days in advance.

Carnations.—
No. 3.   Vase or Basket, fifty flowers,
other green permissible   6.00 5.00 4.00

150.00 **Plant Displays.—**
No. 4.   Plants in Bloom with Foliage
Plants. Sixty dollars may be
125 00   used for prizes.

Apple, twelve specimens.—
No. 5.   For any variety, eight dollars
may be used for prizes.

75 00 **Parsnip, twelve specimens.—**
75 00   No. 6.   Hollow Crown   2.00 1.50 1.00   .50
No. 7.   Any other variety   2.00 1.50 1.00   .50

Rhubarb, twelve stalks.—
No. 8.   Any variety   2.00 1.50 1.00   .50

25.00 **Lettuce.—**
No. 9.   Six heads   2.00 1.50 1.00   .50

Radish.—
No. 10.   Two bunches. Six in each bunch   1.50 1.00   .50

Potato, twelve specimens.—
No. 11.   Any named variety   2.00 1.50 1.00   .50

May Exhibition

Thursday, May 12

*All articles for this exhibition must be
in the hall and ready for inspection by
the judges by 2 o'clock*

This exhibition will be open to the public from 3 to 9 p. m.

Cut Flowers.—

No. 12.	Display, 24 square feet		3.00	2.50	1.00
No. 13.	Medium basket	3.00 2.50	2.00	1.50	1.00

Wild Flowers, fifteen vases.—

No. 14. Not more than five stems
in a vase. No duplicates   3.00 2.00 1.50 1.00   .50

Spring Bulbs, open culture.—

No. 15. Display   4.00 3.00 2.50 2.00

Pansy.—

No. 16. Twenty vases, one flower
with foliage in a vase 3.00 2.50 2.00 1.50 1.00   .50

Zonale Geraniums, in bloom.—

No. 17. Six plants   3.00 2.00 1.50 1.00

Table Decorations, Spring Flowers.—

No. 18. Round table, laid for four
covers. Roses prohibited.
No other restrictions. Notify the Secretary two
days in advance   5.00 4.00 3.00 2.00 1.00

Plant Displays.—

No. 19. For exhibits—no restrictions as
to where grown or by whom,
$60.00 may be used for prizes.
Notify the Secretary two days
in advance.

Calendula.—
No. 20. Arranged in Bowl or Basket   3.00 2.00 1.00

Dandelion.—
No. 21. One-half peck   1.50 1.00 .50

Lettuce.—
No. 22. Six heads   2.00 1.50 1.00 .50

Spinach.—
No. 23. One-half peck   1.50 1.00 .50

Radish, two bunches, six in each bunch.—
No. 24. Globe   1.50 1.00 .50

Rhubarb, twelve stalks.—
No. 25. Linnæus   2.50 2.00 1.50 1.00 .50

Asparagus, two bunches, twelve specimens each.—
No. 26. Any variety   2.50 2.00 1.50 1.00 .50

Onion.—
No. 27. Two bunches, six in each bunch   1.50 1.00 .50

Iris Exhibition

Thursday, June 9

*All articles for this exhibition must be
in the hall and ready for inspection by.
the judges by 2 o'clock*

This exhibition will be open to the public from 3 to 9 p. m.

Iris, German.—

No. 28.	Display				8.00	6.00	4.00	2.00	
No. 29.	Twenty vases, three stems in								
	a vase preferably named	3.00	2.50	2.00	1.50	1.00			
No. 30.	Basket			2.50	2.00	1.50	1.00		

Cut Flowers.—

No. 31.	Display	4.00	3.00	2.50	2.00	1.50	1.00

Azalea.—

No. 32.	Display in vases	3.00	2.00	1.00

Rhododendron.—

No. 33.	Displays in vases	3.00	2.00

Peonies.—

No. 34.	Vase or Basket	3.00	2.50	2.00	1.00

Lupinus.—

No. 35.	Vase	3.00	2.00	1.50	1.00

Roses.—

No. 36.	Vase of Roses. Five dollars
	may be used for prizes.

Zonale Geraniums.—

No. 37.	Twenty vases, one truss in each	3.00	2.00	1.00

Asparagus, two bunches, twelve specimens each.—

No. 38.	Any variety	2.50	2.00	1.50	1.00	.50

Cucumber.—

No. 39.	Three specimens	2.00	1.50	1.00	.50

Spinach.—

No. 40.	One-half peck	2.50	2.00	1.50	1.00

Rhubarb, twelve stalks.—
>No. 41.   Any variety   2.50 2.00 1.50 1.00   .50

Beet.—
>No. 42.   Twelve specimens   2.00 1.50 1.00   .50

Lettuce.—
>No. 43.   Six heads   2.00 1.50 1.00   .50

Onion.—
>No. 44.   Two bunches, six each   2.00 1.50 1.00   .50

ATTENTION IS DIRECTED TO THE

RULES AND REGULATIONS APPEARING ON PAGES 3 AND 4,

GIVING SPECIAL EMPHASIS TO THE FOLLOWING:

9.   Competition for premiums is open to all residents of Worcester County only, and it is strictly required that all specimens offered for premiums shall have been grown by the competitors, on their own premises, for at least two (2) months previous to the date of exhibition, except where no restriction is stated in schedule.

10.   After the articles are arranged, they will be under the exclusive charge of the Judges and Committee of Arrangements, and not even the owners will have liberty to remove them until the exhibition is closed, and no sale of Fruit, Flowers or Vegetables shall be made in the building.

14.   All articles offered for exhibition should be correctly named. Indefinite appellations such as "Pippin," "Sweeting," "Greening," etc., will not be considered as names. Any person exhibiting the same variety of Fruit or Vegetables, under different names, or exhibiting as grown by himself Flowers, Fruit or Vegetables grown by another, thereby violating the objects and rules of the Society, may be debarred from competing for the Society's premiums until reinstated.

Thursday, June 16

*All articles for this exhibition must be
in the hall and ready for inspection by
the judges by 2 o'clock*

This exhibition will be open to the public from 3 to 9 p. m.

Cut Flowers.—
No. 45. From hardy plants and
shrubs outdoor culture,
to be named   4.00 3.00 2.50 2.00 1.50 1.00

Wild Flowers, fifteen vases.—
No. 46. Not more than five
stems in a vase. No
duplicates   3.00 2.50 2.00 1.50 1.00   .50

Siberian Iris.—
No. 47. Medium basket   2.00 1.50 1.00   .50

Roses.—
No. 48. Vase H. P. roses, not to exceed
ten blooms   3.00 2.00 1.00
No. 49. Vase H. T. roses, not exceeding
ten blooms   3.00 2.00 1.00

Peonies.—
No. 50. Display of Peonies. Notify
the Secretary two days in
advance   5.00 4.00 3.00 2.00
No. 51. Twenty vases, one flower in
each   4.00 3.00 2.00 1.00   .50

Foxglove.—
No. 52. Vase of twelve spikes   3.00 2.00 1.00   .50

Aquilegia.—
No. 53. Display   3.00 2.50 2.00 1.00   .50

Begonia.—
No. 54. Four plants in bloom   3.00 2.00 1.00

Strawberry, twenty-four berries.—
No. 55. Any variety, five dollars may be used for prizes.

Rhubarb, twelve stalks.—
No. 56. Victoria   2.50 2.00 1.50 1.00 .50

Rose Exhibition

Thursday, June 23, open from 3 to 9 p. m.

All articles for this exhibition must be in the hall and ready for inspection by the judges by 2 o'clock

oses.—

No. 57. Twelve blooms of distinct named varieties of H. P. roses, outdoor culture 4.00 3.00 2.00 1.00

No. 58. Six blooms of distinct named varieties of H. P. roses, outdoor culture 3.00 2.00 1.00 .50

No. 59. Twelve blooms of distinct named varieties of H. T. roses, outdoor culture 4.00 3.00 2.00 1.00

No. 60. Six blooms of distinct named varieties of H. T. roses, outdoor culture 3.00 2.00 1.00 .50

No. 61. Collection of cut roses. Fifteen dollars to be used for prizes.

No. 62. Vase of roses, 12 blooms 3.00 2.50 2.00 1.50 1.00

No. 63. Vase H. P. roses, not to exceed ten blooms 3.00 2.00 1.00

No. 64. Vase H. T. roses, not exceeding ten blooms 3.00 2.00 1.00

No. 65. Display of cut climbing roses. Fifteen dollars may be used for prizes

No. 66. Basket of roses 3.00 2.50 2.00 1.50

Special Prizes
Miss Frances C. Morse Fund

Table decoration of roses, oblong table laid for four covers. Flowers grown by exhibitors 4.00 3.00 2.50 1.00 .50

Peonies.—

No. 67. Display of Peonies. Notify
the Secretary two days in
advance   5.00 4.00 3.00 2.00

Aquilegia.—

No. 68. Bowl   2.50 2.00 1.50 1.00

Special Prizes
Obadiah Brown Hadwen Fund

Hardy Flowers, to be named.—

B. Display of outdoor varieties   5.00 4.00 3.00 2.00 1.00

*   *   *

Strawberry, twenty-four berries.—

No. 69. Senator Dunlap   1.   1.00   .50
No. 70. Howard No. 17   3.00 2.50 2.00 1.   1.00   .50
No. 71. Culver   2.00 1.50 1.00   .50
No. 72. Any other variety   2.00 1.00 1.00   .50
No. 73. New varieties not scheduled 2.00 1.50 1.00   .50

Cherry, one quart.—

No. 74. For any named variety, five
dollars may be used for prizes.

Pea, one-half peck.—

No. 75. Thomas Laxton   .00 1.00 1.00   .50
No. 76. Any other variety   2.00 1.50 1.00   .50

Cabbage, three specimens.—

No. 77. Any named variety   2.00 1.50 1.00 .50

Lettuce, six heads.—

No. 78. Big Boston Type   2.00 1.50 1.00   .50

Thursday, June 30

*All articles for this exhibition must be
in the hall and ready for inspection by
the judges by 2 o'clock*

This exhibition will be open to the public from 3 to 9 p. m.

Cut Flowers.—

| No. 79. | Display | 3.50 | 3.00 | 2.50 | 2.00 | 1.50 | 1.00 |
| No. 80. | Basket | | 2.50 | 2.00 | 1.50 | 1.00 | .50 |

Dianthus Barbatus (Sweet William).—

No. 81. Twelve vases, three stems
in a vase   3.00   2.50   2.00   1.50   1.00   .50

Campanula.—

No. 82. Display   4.00   3.00   2.00   1.00

Delphinium.—

No. 83. One vase, not more than twelve
spikes   4.00   3.50   3.00   2.50   2.00   1.50   1.00

Roses.—

No. 84. Collection of cut roses. Fifteen
dollars may be used for prizes.

Peonies.—

No. 85. Vase   3.00   2.00   1.00

Special Prizes
Offered by Mr. Herbert R. Kinney

C. Display of Cut Flowers on round
tables   3.00   2.50   2.00   1.50   1.00

This number is intended for the growers who do not compete in
the call for twenty vases or displays during the year.

*   *   *

Strawberry, twenty-four berries.—

No. 86.	Howard No. 17	3.00	2.50	2.00	1.50	1.00	.50
No. 87.	Sample				1.50	1.00	.50
No. 88.	Dorset			2.00	1.50	1.00	.50
No. 89.	Any other variety			2.00	1.50	1.00	.50
No. 90.	Collections, not more than six varieties	5.00	4.00	3.00	2.00	1.00	

No. 91.   Fairfax   2.00 1.50 1.00   .50
No. 92.   Four baskets of strawberries,
          any variety   3.00 2.00 1.00

Currant, twenty-four bunches.—

No. 93.   For any variety, five dollars may be used for prizes.

Cherry, one quart.—

No. 94.   Black Tartarian   2.00 1.50 1.00   .50
No. 95.   Gov. Wood   2.00 1.50 1.00   .50
No. 96.   Best display, ten dollars may be used for prizes.
No. 97.   For varieties not scheduled, five dollars may be used
          for prizes.

Beet, open culture.—

No. 98.   Twelve specimens   2.00 1.50 1.00   .50

Carrot.—

No. 99.   Two bunches, six in each   2.00 1.50 1.00   .50

Pea, one-half peck.   0

No. 100. Gradus   2.00 1.00 1.00   .50
No. 101. Any other variety   2.00 1.50 1.0   .50

Cucumber, three specimens.—

No. 102. Any variety   1.50 1.00   .50

Thursday, July 7

*All articles for this exhibition must be
in the hall and ready for inspection by
the judges by 2 o'clock*

This exhibition will be open to the public from 3 to 9 p. m.

Cut Flowers.—

No. 103.   Display, 24 square
feet   4.00 3.00 2.50 2.00 1.50 1.00

No. 104.   Small display   2.50 2.00 1.50 1.00 .50

This number is intended for the growers who do not compete in call for large displays during the year.

Basket.—

No. 105.   3.00 2.50 2.00 1.50 1.00

Japanese Iris.—

No. 106.   Display, twenty dollars may be used for prizes.

No. 107.   Ten vases, one stem in a vase,
preferably named   2.00 1.50 1.00 .50

Delphinium.—

No. 108.   Display, fifteen dollars may be used for prizes.

Lilium Candidum.—

No. 109.   Vase   4.00 3.00 2.00 1.00

Wild Flowers, no duplicates.—

No. 110.   Fifteen vases, not more
than five stems in a vase 2.50 2.00 1.50 1.00 .50

Roses.—

No. 111.   Display of cut climbing roses. Fifteen dollars may be
used for prizes.

Strawberry, twenty-four berries.—

No. 112.   Downing's Bride   2.00 1.50 1.00 .50

No. 113.   Ten dollars may be used for
prizes.   Preference given to
worthy varieties of recent
introduction.

No. 114.   Display   5.00 4.00 3.00 2.00 1.00

Raspberry, Black Cap, one pint.—

No. 115.   Named variety   1.50 1.00 .50

Raspberry, one pint.—

No. 116.   Early varieties   2.00 1.50 1.00   .50
No. 117.   Varieties not scheduled, five dollars may be used for
           prizes.

Gooseberry, one quart.—

No. 118.   Any named variety   2.00 1.50 1.00   .50

Cherry, one quart.—

No. 119.   Coe's Transparent   1.50 1.00   .50
No. 120.   Montmorency   2.00 1.50 1.00   .50
No. 121.   Any other variety   2.00 1.50 1.00   .50

Currant, twenty-four bunches.—

No. 122.   For any variety, five dollars may be used for prizes.

Bean, Snap, one-half peck.—

No. 123.   Any named variety   2.00 1.50 1.00   .50

Pea, one-half peck.—

No. 124.   Sutton's Excelsior   2.00 1.50 1.00   .50
No. 125.   Alderman   2.00 1.50 1.00   .50
No. 126.   Display   3.00 2.50 2.00 1.00

Display of Vegetables.—

No. 127.   Not to exceed 24 square feet, $20.00 may be used
           for prizes. Notify the Secretary two days in advance.

Tomato, twelve specimens.—

No 128.   Any named variety   2.00 1.50 1.00   .50

Sweet Pea Exhibition
Thursday, July 14

*All articles for this exhibition must be
in the hall and ready for inspection by
the judges by 2 o'clock*

This exhibition will be open to the public from 3 to 9 p. m.

Sweet Peas, annual.—

No. 129.   Ten vases, not more than 25
flower stems in a vase   4.00 3.00 2.00

No. 130.   Table Decoration—Sweet Peas,
round table laid for four covers,
Gypsophila may be used. Flowers
grown by exhibitor. Notify the
Secretary two days in advance

4.00 3.00 2.50 2.00 1.00

Sweet Peas.—

No. 131.   Basket, any green may be used.

3.00 2.00 1.50 1.00

Obadiah Brown Hadwen Fund

D.   Collection of Sweet Peas, fifteen dollars may be used for prizes.

* * *

Japanese Iris.—

No. 132. Basket   3.00 2.00 1.00

Cut Flowers.—

No. 133. Display, not exceeding 30
square feet   4.00 3.00 2.50 2.00 1.50 1.00

Lilium Regale.—

No. 134.   Fifteen dollars may be used for prizes.

Centaurea.—

No. 135.   Display, Gypsophila may be
used   4.00 3.00 2.50 2.00

Petunia.—

No. 136.   Twenty vases, one flower in
each   3.00 2.50 2.00 1.00 .50

Raspberry, one pint.—

No. 137.	Latham	2.00 1.50 1.00	.50
No. 138.	Cuthbert	1.50 1.00	.50
No. 139.	Any other red variety	1.50 1.00	.50

Apple, twelve specimens.—

No. 140. Any variety, five dollars may be used for prizes.

Currant, twenty-four bunches.—

No. 141.	Red Cross	2.00 1.50 1.00	.50
No. 142.	Perfection	2.00 1.50 1.00	.50
No. 143.	White Grape	1.50 1.00	.50
No. 144.	Versaillaise	2.00 1.50 1.00	.50
No. 145.	Any other variety	2.00 1.50 1.00	.50

Pea, one-half peck—

No. 146. Telephone   2.00 1.50 1.00   .50

Bean, Snap, one-half peck.—

No. 147.	Wax	2.00 1. 0 1.00	.50
No. 148.	Green Pod	2.00 1.50 1.00	.50

Cucumber.—

No. 149. Three specimens   1.50 1.00   .50

Cabbage, three specimens.—

No. 150. Any variety   2.00 1.50 1.00   .50

Lettuce, Iceberg.—

No. 151. Twelve heads   2.00 1.50 1.00   .50

Squash, three specimens.—

No. 152. Summer   2.00 1.50 1.00   .50

Thursday, July 21

All articles for this exhibition must be in the hall and ready for inspection by the judges by 2 o'clock

This exhibition will be open to the public from 3 to 9 p. m.

Cut Flowers.—
No. 153. Display	4.00	3.00	2.50	2.00	1.50	1.00
No. 154. Standard	3.00	2.50	2.00	1.50	1.00	.50

No other standards to be shown.

Antirrhinum (Snap Dragon).—
No. 155. Display	3.00	2.00	1.00	.50

Table Decorations.—
No. 156. Oblong table, laid for four covers. Flowers to be grown by the exhibitor. Notify the Secretary two days in advance	4.00	3.50	3.00	2.50	2.00	1.50 1.00

Sweet Peas, annual.—
No. 157. Five vases, 25 flower stems in vase	3.00	2.50	2.00	1.50	1.00

Begonia, tuberous rooted.—
No. 158. Twelve vases	4.00	3.00	2.00	1.00

Apple, twelve specimens.—
No. 159. Yellow Transparent	2.00	1.50	1.00	.50

Raspberry.—
No. 160. Any red variety	2.00	1.50	1.00	.50

Blackberry, one quart.—

No. 161. Any variety, five dollars may be used for prizes.

Blueberry.—
No. 162. One quart	1.50	1.00	.50

Currants, twenty-four bunches.—
No. 163. Wilder	2.00	1.50	1.00	.50

Corn, twelve ears.—
No. 164. Sweet, any named variety	2.00	1.50	1.00	.50

Tomato, twelve specimens.—
No. 165. Any named variety	2.00	1.50	1.00	.50

Potato, twelve specimens.—
No. 166. Any variety	2.00	1.50	1.00	.50

Lettuce, twelve heads.—
No. 167. Any variety	2.00	1.50	1.00	.50

Thursday, July 28

All articles for this exhibition must be in the hall and ready for inspection by the judges by 2 o'clock

This exhibition will be open to the public from 3 to 9 p. m.

Cut Flowers.—

No. 168. Display, 24 square feet   4.00 3.00 2.50 2.00 1.50 1.00

No. 169. Small display   2.50 2.00 1.50 1.00 .50

This number is intended for the growers who do not compete in the call for large displays during the year.

Gladiolus.—

No. 170. Ten vases, named varieties, one spike in each   4.00 3.00 2.00 1.00

Phlox, perennial.—

No. 171. Large vase   3.00 2.00 1.00 .50

Annuals.—

No. 172. Display   3.00 2.50 2.00 1.50 1.00

Apple, twelve specimens.—

No. 173. Astrachan   2.00 1.50 1.00 .50

No. 174. Yellow Transparent   2.00 1.50 1.00 .50

Blackberry, one quart.—

No. 175. Any variety, five dollars may be used for prizes.

Blueberry, one quart.—

No. 176.   1.50 1.00 .50

Raspberry.—

No. 177. Any variety   1.50 1.00 .50

Plum, twelve specimens.—

No. 178. Red June   1.50 1.00 .50

Bean, Shell, one-half peck.—

No. 179. Any named variety   2.00 1.50 1.00 .50

Corn, twelve ears.—

No. 180.   Any named variety   2.00 1.50 1.00   .50

Squash, three specimens.—

No. 181.   Summer   2.00 1.50 1.00   .50

Potato, twelve specimens.—

No. 182.   Irish Cobbler   2.00 1.50 1.00   .50
No. 183.   Any other variety   2.00 1.50 1.00   .50

Vegetables.—

No. 184.   Display, Round Table, $20.00 may be used for prizes.   Notify the Secretary two days in advance.

Thursday, August 4

All articles for this exhibition must be
in the hall and ready for inspection by
the judges by 2 o'clock

This exhibition will be open to the public from 3 to 9 p. m.

Cut Flowers.—
No. 185. Basket   3.00 2.50 2.00 1.50 1.00

Flower Arrangement for Living Room.—
No. 186. Pottery container to be furnished
and flowers to be grown by exhibi-
tor   3.00 2.50 2.00 1.50 1.00   .50

Gladiolus.—
No. 187. Display   8.00 6.00 5.00 4.00 3.00

Larkspur, annual.—
No. 188. Display   3.00 2.50 2.00 1.00

Salpiglossis.—
No. 189. Display   4.00 3.00 2.00 1.00

Phlox, perennial.—
No. 190. Fifteen vases, one cluster
in each   3.00 2.00 1.50 1.00   .50

Zinnia.—
No. 191. Twenty vases, one flower in
each   3.00 2.50 2.00 1.50 1.00   .50

Wild Flowers.—
No. 192. Vase   2.00 1.50 1.00   .50

Special Prizes
Offered by Mr. Herbert R. Kinney

E. Table Decorations. Round table
laid for four covers   3.00 2.50 2.00 1.50 1.00

This call is intended for exhibitors who do not exhibit in other
table decorations during the year. Notify the Secretary two days
in advance.

Blueberry, one quart.—

No. 193. Cultivated		2.00	1.50	1.00

Apple, twelve specimens.—

No. 194. Oldenburg	2.00	1.50	1.00	.50
No. 195. Astrachan	2.00	1.50	1.00	.50

Peach, twelve specimens.—

No. 196. Any variety	2.00	1.50	1.00	.50

Bean, Shell, one-half peck.—

No. 197. Dwarf Horticultural	2.00	1.50	1.00	.50
No. 198. Any other variety	2.00	1.50	1.00	.50

Cabbage, three specimens.—

No. 199. Copenhagen	2.00	1.50	1.00	.50
No. 200. Any other named variety	2.00	1.50	1.00	.50

Corn, twelve ears.—

No. 201. Yellow, Sweet	2.50	2.00	1.50	1.00	.50

Potato, twelve specimens.—

No. 202. Rose	2.00	1.50	1.00	.50
No. 203. Varieties not scheduled	2.00	1.50	1.00	.50

Tomato, open culture, twelve specimens.—

No. 204. Any named variety	2.00	1.50	1.00	.50

Gladiolus Exhibition

Thursday, August 11

*All articles for this exhibition must be
in the hall and ready for inspection by
the judges by 2 o'clock*

This exhibition will be open to the public from 3 to 9 p. m.

Gladiolus.—

No. 205.   Display. Notify the Secretary two days in advance.
Forty dollars may be used for prizes.

No. 206.   Standard of gladiolus   3.00 2.50 2.00 1.00   .50
No other standards to be shown.

No. 207.   Twenty vases, one spike in
each   4.00 3.00 2.00 1.00   .50

Aster, large flowered, long stem.—

No. 208.   Vase of 20 blooms   3.00 2.50 2.00 1.00   .50

Salpiglossis.—

No. 209.   Bowl   2.50 2.00 1.00   .50

Phlox Drummondi.—

No. 210.   Display   2.00 1.50 1.00   .50

Annuals.—

No. 211.   Display, fifteen dollars may be used for prizes.

Flowers on a Mirror.—

No. 212.   Small vase to be shown on a mirror. Vase and mirror
to be furnished by the society. Flowers to be grown by
exhibitor.   Fifteen dollars may be used for prizes.
Highest award not to exceed $1.00.   One entry from
each exhibitor.

Apple, twelve specimens.—

No. 213.   Williams   2.00 1.50 1.00   .50
No. 214.   For varieties not scheduled, five dollars may be
used for prizes.

Apple, crab, twenty-four specimens.—

No. 215.   Varieties not scheduled   1.50 1.00   .50

Peach, twelve specimens.—
No. 216. Carman   1.50 1.00 .50
No. 217. Any other variety   1.50 1.00 .50

Plum, twelve specimens.—
No. 218. Japanese varieties, five dollars
          may be used for prizes.

Squash, three specimens.—
No. 219. Any named variety (excepting
          summer varieties)   2.00 1.50 1.00 .50

Bean, Shell, one-half peck.—
No. 220. Dwarf, any variety   2.00 1. 0 1.00 .50
No. 221. Pole, any variety   2.00 1.50 1.00 .50

Bean, String, one-half peck.—
No. 222. Kentucky Wonder   2.00 1.50 1.00 .50

Corn, Sweet, twelve ears.—
No. 223. Any named variety   2.00 1.50 1.00 .50

Tomato, twelve specimens.—
No. 224. Any named variety   2.50 2.00 1.50 1.00 .50

Mushroom, native.—
No. 225. Collection of edible varieties. Twenty dollars may
          be used for prizes.

Cucumber, for pickles.—
No. 226. One-half peck   2.00 1.50 1.00 .50

Thursday, August 18

*All articles for this exhibition must be
in the hall and ready for inspection by
the judges by 2 o'clock*

This exhibition will be open to the public from 3 to 9 p. m.

Gladiolus.—
No. 227.   Basket. Twenty dollars may be used for prizes.

Zinnia.—
No. 228.   Display, notify the Secretary
two days in advance   4.00 3.00 2.50 2.00 1.50 1.00

Dahlia.—
No. 229.   Display. Single, pompon,
and miniature   3.00 2.50 2.00 1.00

Obadiah Brown Hadwen Fund

Display of Garden Flowers.—
F.   Not to exceed 24 square feet.
Notify the Secretary two days
in advance   4.00 3.50 3.00 2.50 2.00 1.00

*   *   *

Flowers on Mirror.—
No. 230.   Small container to be shown on a mirror. Exhibitors
may use own containers. Fifteen dollars may be used
for prizes. Flowers to be grown by exhibitor. Highest
award not to exceed $1.00.   One entry from each
exhibitor.

Aster, single or anemone.—
No. 231.   Vase   2.00 1.50 1.00   .50

Apples, twelve specimens.—
No. 232.   Any variety   2.00 1.50 1.00   .50

Plums, twelve specimens.—
No. 233.   Washington   1.50 1.00   .50
No. 234.   Bradshaw   2.50 2.00 1.50 1.00   .50
No. 235.   Imperial Gage   2.00 1.50 1.00   .50
No. 236.   For varieties not scheduled, three
dollars may be used for prizes.

Peach, twelve specimens.—

No. 237.   Five dollars may be used for prizes.

Pear, twelve specimens.—

No. 238.   For varieties not scheduled, five dollars may be used for prizes.

Bean, Pole, one-half peck.—

No. 239.	Shell	2.00 1.50 1.00 .50
No. 240.	String, any variety	2.00 1.50 1.00 .50

Corn, twelve ears.—

No. 241.   Sweet, not less than twelve rows

2.00 1.50 1.00 .50

Vegetables.—

No. 242.   Display of vegetables from Home Gardens to cover 12 square feet   5.00 4.00 3.00 2.00 1.00

No. 243.   Market Basket of Vegetables. Baskets furnished by Society. Five dollars may be used for prizes.

Thursday, August 25

*All articles for this exhibition must be
in the hall and ready for inspection by
the judges by 2 o'clock*

This exhibition will be open to the public from 3 to 9 p. m.

Cut Flowers.—

No. 244.	Display. Class 1	5.00	4.00	3.50	3.00
	Class 2	4.00	3.50	3.00	2.50	2.00
No. 245.	Basket	3.00	2.50	2.00	1.50	1.00

Aster, large flowered.—

No. 246. Twenty vases, three
blooms in a vase   3.00 2.50 2.00 1.00 .50

Lilies.—

No. 247. Display   5.00 4.00 3.00 2.00
Notify the Secretary two days
in advance.

Dahlia.—

LARGE FLOWERED.—

No. 248. Twenty vases, one flower in
each   4.00 3.00 2.00 1.50 1.00

Zinnia, Lilliput variety.—

No. 249. Display   3.00 2.00 1.00 .50

Begonia, tuberous rooted.—

No. 250. Display   5.00 4.00 3.00 2.00 1.00

Verbena.—

No. 251. Basket or Bowl   2.50 2.00 1.50 1.00 .50

Five Miniature Containers.—

No. 252. Display. A group of five miniature containers,
6 inches over all in height. Containers to be owned
and flowers to be grown by exhibitors. Fifteen dollars
may be used for prizes. Highest award not to exceed
$1.00.

Apples, twelve specimens.—

No. 253. Porter   1.50 1.00 .50
No. 254. Red Gravenstein   2.50 2.00 1.50 1.00 .50
No. 255. For varieties not scheduled, five
              dollars may be used for prizes.

Plum.—

No. 256. Display, no restriction as to
              arrangements   4.00 3.00 2.00 1.00

Peach, twelve specimens.—

No. 257. Any variety   1.50 1.00 .50

Pear, twelve specimens.—

No. 258. Clapp's Favorite   3.00 2.50 2.00 1.50 1.00 .50

Squash, three specimens.—

No. 259. Any named variety   2.50 2.00 1.50 1.00

Pepper, twelve specimens.—

No. 260. Harris's Early   2.50 2.00 1.50 1.00
No. 261. Bell Type   2.50 2.00 1.50 1.00

Vegetables.—

No. 262. Display, not to exceed 24 square feet, $20.00 may
              be used for prizes. Notify the Secretary two days in
              advance.

Thursday, September 1

*All articles for this exhibition must be
in the hall and ready for inspection by
the judges by 2 o'clock*

This exhibition will be open to the public from 3 to 9 p. m.

Cut Flowers.—

No. 263.   Display. Class 1   5.00 4.00 3.50 3.00

                 Class 2   4.00 3.50 3.00 2.50 2.00

No. 264.   Pair mantel vases. Vases to be owned and flowers to
       be grown by exhibitor. Fifteen dollars may be used for
       prizes.

Dahlia.—

No. 265.   Standard—Dahlias

         predominating   2.50 2.00 1.50 1.00   .50

    No other standards to be shown.

Gladiolus.—

No. 266.   Basket   3.00 2.50 2.00 1.00   .50

Aster.—

No. 267.   Display, not exceeding

         25 square feet   5.00 4.00 3.00 2.00 1.00

Scabiosa.—

No. 268.   Vase   2.50 2.00 1.50 1.00   .50

Lilies.—

No. 269.   Vase   3.00 2.50 1.50 1.00

Apple, twelve specimens.—

No. 270.   Gravenstein   3.00 2.50 2.00 1.50 1.00   .50

No. 271.   Maiden's Blush   1.50 1.00   .50

No. 272.   Wealthy   2.50 2.00 1.50 1.00   .50

Apple, Crab, twenty-four specimens.—

No. 273.   Hyslop   2.50 2.00 1.50 1.00   .50

Peach, twelve specimens.—

No. 274.   Champion   1.50 1.00   .50

No. 275.   Golden Jubilee   2.00 1.50 1.00   .50

No. 276.   Seedlings   1.50 1.00   .50

No. 277.   Crawford (early)   2.00 1.50 1.00   .50

No. 278. Varieties not scheduled, five dollars may be used for prizes.

No. 279. New varieties. Five dollars may be used for prizes.

Plum, twelve specimens.—

No. 280.	Golden Varieties		1.50 1.00	.50
No. 281.	Lombard	2.00	1.50 1.00	.50
No. 282.	Burbank	2.00	1.50 1.00	.50
No. 283.	New varieties		1.50 1.00	.50

No. 284. For Japanese varieties not scheduled, five dollars may be used for prizes.

No. 285. Other varieties not scheduled, five dollars may be used for prizes.

Grape, three clusters.—

No. 286.	Green Mountain	2.00 1.50 1.00	.50
No. 287.	Moore's	1.50 1.00	.50
No. 288.	Ontario	1.50 1.00	.50
No. 289.	Varieties not scheduled	1.50 1.00	.50
No. 290.	New varieties	1.50 1.00	.50

Pepper, twelve specimens.—

No. 291.	Squash	2.00 1.50 1.00	.50
No. 292.	Any other variety	2.00 1.50 1.00	.50

Tomato, twelve specimens.—

No. 293.	Beauty	2.50 2.00 1.50 1.00	.50
No. 294.	Any other variety	2.50 2.00 1.50 1.00	.50

Bean, one-half peck.—

No. 295.	Dwarf Lima	2.00 1.50 1.00	.50
No. 296.	Pole Lima	2.00 1.50 1.00	.50

Cabbage, three specimens.—

No. 297.	Any named variety	2.00 1.50 1.00	.50

Celery, blanched (named) six specimens.—

No. 298.	Any variety	2.00 1.50 1.00	.50

Carrot, twelve specimens.—

No. 299.	Any variety	2.50 2.00 1.50 1.00	.50

Egg Plant.—

No. 300.	Three specimens	2.00 1.50 1.00	.50

Mushroom, native.—

No. 301. Collection of edible varieties. Twenty dollars may be used for prizes.

Thursday, September 8

*All articles for this exhibition must be
in the hall and ready for inspection by
the judges by 2 o'clock*

This exhibition will be open to the public from 3 to 9 p. m.

Cut Flowers.—

No. 302. Display. Class 1   5.00 4.00 3.50 3.00
               Class 2   4.00 3.50 3.00 2.50 2.00

No. 303. Metal container of cut flowers, container to be
furnished and flowers to be grown by exhibitor.
Fifteen dollars may be used for prizes.

Dahlia.—

No. 304. Twenty vases, one flower in
each vase   4.00 3.00 2.00 1.00

Cosmos.—

No. 305. Vase or basket   2.50 2.00 1.50 1.00 .50

Celosia.—

No. 306. Display   3.00 2.50 2.00 1.50 1.00
         Notify the Secretary two days in advance.

Apple, twelve specimens.—

No. 307. New varieties   2.00 1.50 1.00 .50
No. 308. Wealthy   2.00 1.50 1.00 .50

Pear, twelve specimens.—

No. 309. Louise Bonne de Jersey   1.50 1.00 .50
No. 310. Urbaniste   1.50 1.00 .50
No. 311. Varieties not scheduled, five dollars may be used
for prizes.

Peach, twelve specimens.—

No. 312. Crawford (late)   2.00 1.50 1.00 .50
No. 313. Elberta   2.00 1.50 1.00 .50
No. 314. Display, no restriction as to
arrangement   8.00 6.00 4.00 3.00

Plum, twelve specimens.—

No. 315. Any variety   2.00 1.50 1.00 .50

Grape, three clusters.—

No. 316.	Brighton			1.50	1.00	.50
No. 317.	Campbell			1.50	1.00	.50
No. 318.	Lindley			1.50	1.00	.50
No. 319.	Worden	2.50	2.00	1.50	1.00	.50
No. 320.	Concord	2.50	2.00	1.50	1.00	.50
No. 321.	Delaware		2.00	1.50	1.00	.50
No. 322.	Niagara	2.50	2.00	1.50	1.00	.50
No. 323.	Pocklington			1.50	1.00	.50
No 324.	Moore's Diamond			1.50	1.00	.50

No. 325. For other varieties, ten dollars may be used for prizes.
No. 326. New varieties, five dollars may be used for prizes.

Quince, twelve specimens.—

No. 327.	Any variety	2.00	1.50	1.00	.50

Melon, three specimens.—

No. 328.	Green Flesh	2.00	1.50	1.00	.50
No. 329.	Yellow Flesh	2.00	1.50	1.00	.50
No. 330.	Water	2.00	1.50	1.00	.50

Tomato.—

No. 331. Display. Fifteen dollars may be used for prizes.

Vegetables.—

No. 332. Display to cover 24 square
feet. Notify the Secretary
two days in advance   7.00 6.00 5.00 4.00 3.00

Dahlia Exhibition

Thursday, September 15

*All articles for this exhibition must be
in the hall and ready for inspection by
the judges by 2 o'clock*

This exhibition will be open to the public from 3 to 9 p. m.

Dahlia.—

No. 333. Fifty vases, one flower in each. Twenty-five dollars
may be used for prizes. Notify the Secretary two
days in advance.

No. 334. Twelve vases, one flower
in each   2.50 2.00 1.50 1.00   .50

This number is intended for the growers who do not compete
in other classes for Dahlias during the year.

No. 335. Single varieties, twenty vases 3.00 2.50 2.00 1.00

No. 336. Basket of large flowered   3.00 2.50 2.00 1.00

POMPON.

No. 337. Twenty vases, three sprays in
each   3.00 2.50 2.00 1.00

Display of Flower Arrangement.—

No. 338. No restrictions as to kind of tables used, not to cover
more than 24 square feet. Flowers to be grown by
exhibitor. Receptacles to be furnished by the exhibitors.
Notify the Secretary two days in advance. Twenty-five
dollars may be used for prizes. No baskets.

SCALE OF POINTS BY WHICH THE ABOVE CLASS IS TO BE JUDGED

Quality of flowers   40 points
Proportion and harmony of flowers with
receptacles   35
Arrangement of flowers   25

Begonia, tuberous rooted.—

No. 339. Cut flowers in vases. Ten dollars may be used for
prizes.

Edwin Draper Fund

Begonia, tuberous rooted.—
   G.   Display of Potted Plants.   Fifteen dollars may be used for
        prizes.
                         *   *   *

Apple, twelve specimens.—
   No. 340.   Varieties not scheduled, five dollars may be used for
        prizes.

Pear, twelve specimens.—
   No. 341.   Bartlett   3.00 2.50 2.00 1.50 1.00   .50
   No. 342.   Seckel   3.00 2.50 2.00 1.50 1.00   .50
   No. 343.   Any variety, not scheduled   1.50 1.00   .50

Peach.—
   No. 344.   Any variety   1.50 1.00   .50

Quince, twelve specimens.—
   No. 345.   Orange   2.00 1.50 1.00   .50

Grapes.—
   No. 346.   Display of Grapes. Ten dollars may be used for prizes.

Squash, three specimens.—
   No. 347.   Warren   2.00 1.50 1.00   .50
   No. 348.   Golden Hubbard   2.50 2.00 1.50 1.00   .50
   No. 349.   For varieties not scheduled, five dollars may be used
        for prizes.

Cabbage, three specimens.—
   No. 350.   Red   2.00 1.50 1.00   .50
   No. 351.   Savoy   1.50 1.00   .50
   No. 352.   Any other variety   2.50 2.00 1.50 1.00   .50

Cauliflower.—
   No. 353.   Three specimens   2.50 2.00 1.50 1.00   .50

Turnip.—
   No. 354.   Twelve specimens   1.50 1.00   .50

Broccoli.—
   No. 355.   Three specimens   2.00 1.50 1.00   .50

Thursday, September 22

*All articles for this exhibition must be
in the hall and ready for inspection by
the judges by 2 o'clock*

This exhibition will be open to the public from 3 to 9 p. m.

Dahlia.—

No. 356. Display. Fifty dollars may be used for prizes.
Notify the secretary two days in advance.
No. 357. Basket·   2.50 2.00 1.50 1.00   .50
This number is intended for growers who do not compete in
other classes for Dahlias during the year.

Cosmos.—

No. 358. Display. Notify the Secretary
two days in advance   2.50 2.00 1.50 1.00   .50

Marigold.—

No. 359. Display. Notify the Secre-
tary two days in advance 3.00 2.50 2.00 1.00   .50

Apple, one standard box, standard pack.—

No. 360. McIntosh   4.00 3.00 2.00 1.00   .50

Apple, twelve specimens.—

No. 361. Hubbardston   1.50 1.00   .50
No. 362. Tompkins King   2.00 1.50 1.00   .50
No. 363. McIntosh   3.50 3.00 2.50 2.00 1.50 1.00   .50
No. 364. For other varieties not scheduled, five dollars may be
used for prizes.

Pear, twelve specimens.—

No. 365. Sheldon   3.00 2.50 2.00 1.50 1.00   .50
No. 366. Display, no restrictions as to arrangement. Twenty
dollars to may used for prizes. Notify the Secretary two
days in advance.

Potato, six varieties (named).—

No. 367. Twelve specimens of each
5.00 4.00 3.00 2.00 1.50 1.00

Squash, three specimens.—

No. 368.   Green Delicious   2.00 1.50 1.00   .50
No. 369.   Any other variety, not scheduled 2.50 2.00 1.50 1.00

Cauliflower.—

No. 370.   Three specimens.   2.00 1.50 1.00   .50

Vegetables.—

No. 371.   Collection not to exceed 25
           varieties   10.00 8.00 7.00 6.00 5.00
           Notify the Secretary two days in advance.

Thursday, September 29

*All articles for this exhibition must be
in the hall and ready for inspection by
the judges by 2 o'clock*

This exhibition will be open to the public from 3 to 9 p. m.

Cut Flowers.—
No. 372. Display   4.00 3.50 3.00 2.50 2.00 1.50 1.00

Standard of Cut Flowers.—
No. 373. Twenty dollars may be used for prizes.

Dried Flowers, Statice, Strawflowers, Lunaria (Honesty).—
No. 374. Display.   4.00 3.50 2.00 1.00

Table Decorations of Flowers.—
No. 375. Oblong table laid for four
covers. Flowers grown by exhibitor. Notify the Secretary
two days in advance
5.00 4.50 4.00 3.00 2.00 1.50 1.00

Apple, one standard box, standard pack.—
No. 376. Any variety not scheduled
4.00 3.00 2.00 1.00   .50

Apple, twelve specimens.—
No. 377. Sutton Beauty   2.00 1.50 1.00   .50

Display of Fruit.—
No. 378. Not to exceed 20 square feet. Thirty dollars may be
used for prizes.

Pear, twelve specimens.—
No. 379. Bosc   3.00 2.50 2.00 1.50 1.00   .50

Grape, open culture.—
No. 380. Collection of not less than five varieties, three clusters
each.   3.00 2.50 2.00 1.50 1.00

Pumpkins, three specimens.—
No. 381. Sweet   2.00 1.50 1.00   .50

1938]

Cabt
No

Parsl
No

Pepp
No

Celei
No
No

Squa
No

I. I

Cabbage, three specimens.—
No. 382.   Any named variety   2.50 2.00 1.50 1.00   .50

Parsley.—
No. 383.   One-half peck   2.50 2.00 1.50 1.00   .50

Peppers.—
No. 384.   Display. Fifteen dollars to be used for prizes.

Celery, blanched, six specimens.—
No. 385.   Golden   2.50 2.00 1.50 1.00
No. 386.   Other varieties   2.50 2.00 1.50 1.00

Squash, three specimens.—
No. 387.   Blue Hubbard   3.00 2.50 2.00 1.50 1.00

Special Prizes
Offered by Mr. Herbert R. Kinney

I.   Display of vegetables from
         Home Gardens to
         cover 16 square feet   4.00 3.50 3.00 2.50 2.00 1.00

Fruit and Vegetable Exhibition
Thursday, October 6
*All articles for this exhibition must be
in the hall and ready for inspection by
the judges by 2 o'clock*

This exhibition will be open to the public from 3 to 9 p. m.

Cut Flowers.—

No. 388.   Display—$40.00 may be awarded for prizes.

Hardy Chrysanthemum, out-door culture.—

No. 389.   Cut flowers in vases. Ten dollars may be used for prizes.

Apple, one standard box, standard pack.—

No. 390   McIntosh   4.00 3.00 2.00 1.00 .50

Apple, twelve specimens.—

No. 391.	Baldwin	3.50	3.00	2.50	2.00	1.50	1.00	.50
No. 392.	Bellflower					1.50	1.00	.50
No. 393.	Winter Banana					1.50	1.00	.50
No. 394.	Peck's					1.50	1.00	.50
No. 395.	R. I. Greening			3.00	2.00	1.50	1.00	.50
No. 396.	Northern Spy			3.00	2.00	1.50	1.00	.50
No. 397.	Palmer					1.50	1.00	.50
No. 398.	Roxbury Russet			3.00	2.00	1.50	1.00	.50
No. 399.	Cortland				2.00	1.50	1.00	.50
No. 400.	Opalescent					1.50	1.00	.50
No. 401.	Delicious			2.50	2.00	1.50	1.00	.50

No. 402.   New varieties, five dollars may be used for prizes.

No. 403.   Sweet varieties, five dollars may be used for prizes.

No. 404.   For varieties other than sweet not scheduled, fifteen
dollars may be used for prizes.

No. 405.   For varieties that have been scheduled, fifteen dollars
may be used for prizes.

Pear, twelve specimens.—

No. 406.	Angouleme		1.50	1.00	.50
No. 407.	Clairgeau	2.00	1.50	1.00	.50

No. 408.   Anjou   3.00 2.50 2.00 1.50 1.00 .50
No. 409.   For varieties not scheduled, ten dollars may be used for prizes.
No. 410.   For varieties that have been scheduled, ten dollars may be used for prizes.

Grape, open culture.—
No. 411.   For any variety, six clusters, ten dollars may be used for prizes.

Peach, twelve specimens.—
No. 412.   Any variety, named, ten dollars may be used for prizes.

Quince, twelve specimens.—
No. 413.   Champion   2.00 1.50 1.00 .50

Cauliflower.—
No. 414.   Three specimens   2.50 2.00 1.50 1.00 .50

Celery, blanched, six specimens.—
No. 415.   Golden   2.50 2.00 1.50 1.00 .50
No. 416.   Any other varieties, not scheduled   2.00 1.50 1.00 .50

Endive.—
No. 417.   Six specimens   1.50 1.00 .50

Leeks.—
No. 418.   Twelve specimens   1.50 1.00 .50

Onion, twelve specimens.—
No. 419.   For varieties, five dollars may be used for prizes.

Salsify.—
No. 420.   Twelve specimens   1.50 1.00 .50

Turnip, twelve specimens.—
No. 421.   Purple Top Globe   2.00 1.50 1.00 .50
No. 422.   Any variety, not scheduled   2.00 1.50 1.00 .50

Thursday, October 13

*All articles for this exhibition must be
in the hall and ready for inspection by
the judges by 2 o'clock*

This exhibition will be open to the public from 3 to 9 p. m.

Ferns.—

No. 423. Display, potted ferns, named varieties. Fifteen
dollars may be used for prizes.

Specimen Fern.—

No. 424. One plant	3.00	2.00	1.00

Hardy Chrysanthemum, out-door culture.—

No. 425. Plants. Twenty dollars may be used for prizes.

Cut Flowers.—

No. 426. Basket. Ten dollars may be used for prizes.

Pear.—

No. 427. Lawrence	2.50	2.00	1.50	1.00	.50

Apple, one standard box, standard pack.—

No. 428. Baldwin	4.00	3.00	2.00	1.00	.50
No. 429. Any other variety except McIntosh	4.00	3.00	2.00	1.00	.50
No. 430. Collection, not to exceed 10 varieties	5.00	4.00	3.00	2.50	2.00	1.00
No. 431. Three flats, any variety	8.00	7.00	6.00	5.00	4.00	3.00

Apples, forty-nine specimens.—

No. 432. Any named variety	5.00	4.00	3.00	2.00	1.00

Table Decorations—Fruit.—

No. 433. Round table laid for four covers, no restrictions. Notify the Secretary two days in advance	5.00	4.00	3.00	2.00	1.00

Onion, twelve specimens.—

No. 434. Yellow Globe Danvers	2.50	2.00	1.50	1.00	.50

Parsnip, twelve specimens.—

No. 435. Any variety	2.00	1.50	1.00	.50

Squash.—

No. 436.   Collection   5.00 4.50 4.00 3.50 3.00

Turnip, twelve specimens.—

No. 437.   English varieties, not scheduled 2.00 1.50 1.00   .50

Celery, blanched, six specimens.—

No. 438.   Any variety   2.50 2.00 1.50 1.00   .50

Grains.—

No. 439.   Best exhibit, five dollars may be used for prizes.

Field Beans.—

No. 440   Best exhibit, ten dollars may be used for prizes.

Ornamental Gourds (Unvarnished)

No. 441.   Display. Twelve dollars may be used for prizes.

Chrysanthemum Exhibition

Thursday, Nov. 10, 3 to 9 p. m.
Friday, Nov. 11, 9 a. m. to 9 p. m.
Saturday, Nov. 12, 9 a. m. to 9 p. m.
Sunday, Nov. 13, 12 m. to 9 p. m.

*All articles for this exhibition must be
in the hall and ready for inspection by
the judges by 1 o'clock Thursday*

Chrysanthemums.—

No. 442.	Twelve blooms, not less than six varieties, to be named	12.00	10.00	8.00
No. 443.	Collection of twenty-five large blooms, long stems	20.00	15.00	10.00
No. 444.	Pompons, display in vases	5.00 4.00	3.00	2.00
No. 445.	Single varieties, display in vases	5.00 4.00	3.00	2.00
No. 446.	Korean varieties, display in vases	5.00 4.00	3.00	2.00
No. 447.	Anemones, display in vases	5.00 4.00	3.00	2.00
No. 448.	Six specimen plants	10.00	8.00	6.00
No. 449.	One specimen plant, one plant in pot	3.00	2.00	1.00

Standard Commercial Varieties.—

Use catalogue of Elmer D. Smith & Co. of Adrian, Michigan.

No. 450.	Chrysanthemums, vase of white	4.00	3.00	2.00
No. 451.	Chrysanthemums, vase of yellow	4.00	3.00	2.00
No. 452.	Chrysanthemums, vase of pink	4.00	3.00	2.00

Note. Six flowers in each, one variety in each vase. Stems not less than two feet.

Exhibition Varieties.—

No. 453.	Chrysanthemums, vase of white	4.00	3.00	2.00
No. 454.	Chrysanthemums, vase of yellow	4.00	3.00	2.00
No. 455.	Chrysanthemums, vase of pink	4.00	3.00	2.00

Note. Six flowers in each, one variety in each vase. Stems not less than two feet.

Chrysanthemums.—

No. 456.	Basket of Pompons	4.00	.00	.00	1.00
No. 457.	Basket of Single	4.00	.00	.00	1.00
No. 458.	Basket of Anemones	4.00	3.00	2.00	1.00

Garden Displays } A
Plant Displays } B   775.00

Persons competing for these premiums must notify the Secretary three weeks before date of Exhibition.

J. Special Exhibits.—
Seventy-five dollars may be used for prizes.

Frederick A. Blake Fund

K. **Chrysanthemums.—**Best bloom   4.00 3.00 2.00

Obadiah Brown Hadwen Fund

L. **Chrysanthemums.—**Large Flowers. Basket. Fifteen dollars may be awarded for prizes.

Special Prizes
Offered by Mrs. Mabel Knowles Gage

M. **Table Decorations.—**A Thanksgiving table. No restrictions. Laid for four covers. Notify the Secretary two days in advance. Fifty dollars to be used for prizes.

Fern Globes.—

No. 459.	3.00	2.00	1.50	1.00

Terrariums.—

No. 460. Large—Containers must be over 18 inches but must not exceed 36 inches in any dimension	4.00	3.00	2.00	1.00
No. 461. Small—Containers must not exceed 18 inches in any dimension	3.00	2.00	1.50	1.00

Wild Fruits and Berries.—
No. 462. Display   5.00 4.00 3.00 2.50 1.50 1.00

Physalis Franchettii (Chinese Lanterns).—
No. 463. Basket   4.00 3.00 2.00 1.00

Fruit Display.—
No. 464. No restriction as to arrangement. $40.00 may be used.
for prizes. Notify the Secretary two days in advance.

Apples, forty-nine specimens.—
No. 465. Baldwin   6.00 5.00 4.00 3.00 2.00 1.00
No. 466. McIntosh   6.00 5.00 4.00 3.00 2.00 1.00
No. 467. Delicious   5.00 4.00 3.00 2.00 1.00
No. 468. Any other named variety 5.00 4.00 3.00 2.00 1.00
No. 469. Fancy Basket of Apples 3.00 2.50 2.00 1.50 1.00
No. 470. Fancy Basket of Pears 3.00 2.50 2.00 1.50 1.00

Special Exhibition of Apples
William Eames Fund

A. **Baldwin, best twelve.—**
     Three premiums   1.50 1.00 .50
B. **Northern Spy.—**
     Three premiums   1.50 1.00 .50
C. **Delicious.—**
     Three premiums   1.50 1.00 .50
D. **Rhode Island Greening.—**
     Three premiums   1.50 1.00 .50
E. **Roxbury Russet.—**
     Three premiums   1.50 1.00 .50
F. **Sutton Beauty.—**
     Three premiums   1.50 1.00 .50
G. **McIntosh.—**
     Three premiums   1.50 1.00 .50
H. **Any other Variety.—**
     Three premiums   1.50 1.00 .50

*   *   *

Brussels Sprouts.—
No. 471. One-half peck   2.00 1.50 1.00 .50

Celery, blanched, six specimens.—

No. 472.	Giant Pascal		2.00	1.50	1.00	.50
No. 473.	Any other variety-	2.50	2.00	1.50	.00	.50

Onion, twelve specimens.—

No. 474.	White Globe		2.00	1.50	1.00	.50
No. 475.	Red Globe		2.00	1.50	1.00	.50
No. 476.	Cracker			1.50	1.00	.50
No. 477.	Any other variety	2.50	2.00	1.50	1.00	.50

Cabbage, three specimens.—

No. 478.	Any variety		2.00	1.50	1.00	.50

Parsnip, twelve specimens.—

No. 479.	Hollow Crown		2.00	1.50	1.00	.50

Squash, three specimens.—

No. 480.	Green Hubbard	2.50	2.00	1.50	1.00	.50

Turnip, twelve specimens.—

No. 481.	Purple Top Globe		2.00	1.50	1.00	.50

Turnip, six specimens.—

No. 482.	White Swede		2.00	1.50	1.00	.50
No. 483.	Yellow Swede		2.00	1.50	1.00	.50

Potato, twelve specimens.—

No. 484.	Green Mountain		2.50	2.00	1.50	1.00
No. 485.	Any other variety		2.50	2.00	1.50	1.00

Annual Meeting, Thursday, December 1, 1938.
Premiums will be paid on or after November 20, 1938.

THE LIBRARY OF THE
WORCESTER COUNTY HORTICULTURAL SOCIETY

The Library Committee wish to call your attention to the Library and Reading Room, where the librarian is always ready to extend every facility possible to those in search of horticultural information.

COMMITTEE ON
LIBRARY AND PUBLICATIONS

EDWARD W. BREED, Chairman   MRS. AMY W. SMITH
WILLIAM ANDERSON   HERBERT R. KINNEY
FLORENCE E. FIELD, Librarian

SOME OF THE RECENT ACCESSIONS TO THE LIBRARY

Pioneering with Fruits and Berries, by George D. Aikin—1936.

Roses of the World in Color, J. Horace McFarland—1936.

Succulent Plants, H. Jacobsen—1935.

The Identification of Trees and Shrubs, by F. K. Makins—1937.

Japanese Flower Arrangement for Modern Homes, by Margaret Preininger—1936.

Your City Garden, by Margaret McKenny and E. L. D. Seymour—1937.

The Royal Horticultural Society Lily Book—1936.

The American Rose Annual. Edited by J. Horace McFarland for The American Rose Society

American Delphinium Society Year Book—1936.

Design in Flower Arrangement, by John Taylor Arms and Dorothy Noyes Arms—1937.

The Book of Bulbs, by F. F. Rockwell—1932.

The Complete Book of Gardening. Edited by Leonard Barron—1936

The Book of Shrubs, by Alfred C. Hottes—1937

The Mushroom Handbook, by Louis C. C. Kreiger—1936.

How to Grow Roses (Revised and rewritten) by McFarland-Pyle—1937

Wild Gardens of New England, by Walter Prichard Eaton—1936

Cactus, by A. J. van Laren—1935

California Cactus, by E. M. Baxter—1935

The Gardener's How Book, by Chesla C. Sherlock—1935

Insect Enemies of Shade Trees, by Glenn W. Herrick—1935

1936 Gladiolus Year Book, New England Gladiolus Society

How to Know the Mosses, by Elizabeth Marie Dunham—1916

Ferns of the Vicinity of New York, by John Kunkel Small—1935

Bigger and Better Roses for Garden, House and Exhibition (English), by G. F. Mappin—1935

Lilies: Their Culture and Management, by H. Drysdale Woodcock and J. Coutts (London, 1935)

Rhododendrons and Azaleas, by Clement Gray Bowers—1935

A Year in the Rose Garden, by J. H. Nicolas—1936

The Garden Encyclopedia, Edited by E. L. D. Seymour—1936

Clematis (The Large and Small Flowered), by Ernest Markham (London, 1935)

Rock Gardens: How to Make and Maintain Them, by Lewis B. Meredith—1923

Plant Hunting on the Edge of the World, by F. Kingdon Ward (London, 1930)

The 1936 American Rose Annual, The American Rose Society

New Flower Arrangements, by Mrs. Walter R. Hine—1936

The Book of Perennials, by Alfred C. Hottes—1933

Gentians, by David Wilkie, (London, 1936)

Daylilies, by Dr. A. B. Stout—1934

The Flowering Plants, Grasses, Sedges and Ferns of Great Britain, by Ann Pratt, 6 vols.

Plant Propagation, by Alfred C. Hottes—1934

The Living Garden, by E. J. Salisbury (London, 1936)

First Gourd Book, by Helen M. Tillinghast—1935

Adventures with Hardy Bulbs, by Louise Beebe Wilder—1936

Vegetable Crops, by Dr. Homer C. Thompson—1931

Fertilizers and Crop Production, by Dr. L. L. Van Slyke—1932

Weeds, by W. C. Muenscher—1935

Mexican Plants for American Gardens, by Cecile Hulse Matschat

The Gladiolus Book, by Forman T. McLean

Our Native Cacti, by Edith Bailey Higgins

Succulents, by A. J. van Laren

House Plants, by Marjorie Norrell Sulzer

Herbs and the Earth, by Henry Beston

Old Roses, by Mrs. Frederick Love Keays

Flower and Table Arrangements, by Esther Longyear Murphy

Flower Arrangement, by F. F. Rockwell and Esther C. Grayson

Tuberous-Rooted Begonias and their Culture, by George Otten

American Ferns, by Edith A. Roberts and Julia R. Lawrence

Azaleas and Camellias, by H. Harold Hume

Gardening with Herbs, by Helen Morgenthau Fox

The Gladiolus and its Culture, by Alvin C. Beal, Ph.D.

American Orchid Culture, by Prof. E. A. White

Spring Flowering Bulbs, by Clark L. Thayer

Worcester County Horticultural Society

SCHEDULE OF PRIZES
Offered to
Children of Worcester County

Exhibitions to be held Saturday, August 20
and Saturday, September 10, 1938
Horticultural Building, 30 Elm Street

Worcester, Massachusetts

Saturday, August 20
All articles must be in the hall by 1 o'clock

> The exhibits must be the results of individ-
> ual effort of the child from the time of
> planting to the arranging of the exhibit.

Open to Children under 14 years of age

Display of Flowers.—

No. 1.   Not to exceed fifteen vases

                        2.00 1.50 1.25 1.00   .50   .25

No. 2.   Bouquet, mixed cut flowers   .75   .50   .25   .25

Zinnia.—

No. 3.   Not to exceed 10 vases   .75   .50   .25   .25

Asters.—

No. 4.   Not to exceed 10 vases   .75   .50   .25   .25

Petunia.—

No. 5.   Not to exceed 10 vases   .75   .50   .25   .25

Calendula.—

No. 6.   Not to exceed 10 vases   .75   .50   .25   .25

Wild Flowers.—

No. 7.   Not to exceed fifteen vases 1.50   1.25 1.00   .50   .25

No. 8.   Vase of Wild Flowers   1.00   .75   .50   .25   .25

Display of Vegetables.—

No. 9.   Not to exceed 12 varieties

                        2.00 1.75 1.50 1.25 1.00   .75   .50

Beets.—

No. 10.   Six specimens   .75   .50   .25   .25

Summer Squash.—

No. 11.   Two specimens   .75   .50   .25   .25

String Beans.—

No. 12.   Two quarts   .75   .50   .25   .25

Potato.—

No. 13.   Twelve specimens   1.00   .75   .50   .25

Sweet Corn.—

No. 14.   Six ears   1.00   .75   .50   .25

Tomato.—

No. 15.   Six specimens   .75   .50   .25   .25

Carrots.—

No. 16.   Six specimens   .75   .50   .25   .25

Cucumber.—

No. 17.   Two specimens   .75   .50   .25   .25

Open to Children between the ages of 14 and 21

Display of Flowers.—

No. 18.	Not to exceed 15 vases	2.50 2.00 1.75 1.00
No. 19.	Bouquet, mixed cut flowers	1.00 .75 .50 .25

Asters.—

No. 20.	Not to exceed 10 vases	1.00 .75 .50 .25

Petunia.—

No. 21.	Not to exceed 10 vases	1.00 .75 .50 .25

Gladiolus.—

No. 22.	Basket	1.00 .75 .50 .25

Zinnia.—

No. 23.	Not to exceed 10 vases	1.00 .75 .50 .25

Wild Flowers.—

No. 24.	Not to exceed 15 vases	1.50 1.25 1.00 .50 .25
No. 25.	Vase of Wild Flowers	1.00 .75 .50 .25 .25

Display of Vegetables.—

No. 26	Not over 15 varieties	
		2.50 2.00 1.75 1.50 1.25 1.00 .50

Potato.—

No. 27.	Twelve specimens	1.50 1.00 .75 .50 .25

Beets.—

No. 28.	Six specimens	1.00 .75 .50 .25

Carrots.—

No. 29.	Six specimens	1.00 .75 .50 .25

Shell Beans.—

No. 30.	Two quarts	1.00 .75 .50 .25

String Beans.—

No. 31.	Two quarts	1.00 .75 .50 .25

Sweet Corn.—

No. 32.	Six ears	1.00 .75 .50 .25

Tomato.—

No. 33.	Six specimens	1.25 1.00 .75 .50 .25

Cucumber.—

No. 34.	Two specimens	1.00 .75 .50 .25

Summer Squash.—

No. 35.	Two specimens	1.00 .75 .50 .25

Saturday, September 10

All articles must be in the hall by 1 o'clock

> The exhibits must be the results of individual effort of the child from the time of planting to the arranging of the exhibit.

Open to Children under 14 years of age

Display of Flowers.—

No. 36.	Not to exceed 15 vases	2.00	1.50	1.25	1.00	.50	.25
No. 37.	Bouquet, mixed cut flowers			.75	.50	.25	.25

Cosmos.—

No. 38.	Vase	.75	.50	.25	.25

Calendula.—

No. 39.	Not to exceed 10 vases	.75	.50	.25	.25

Petunia.—

No. 40.	Not to exceed 10 vases	.75	.50	.25	.25

Asters.—

No. 41.	Not to exceed 10 vases	.75	.50	.25	.25

Zinnia.—

No. 42.	Not to exceed 10 vases	.75	.50	.25	.25

Marigolds.—

No. 43.	Not to exceed 10 vases	.75	.50	.25	.25

Gladiolus.—

No. 44.	Basket	.75	.50	.25	.25

Wild Flowers.—

No. 45.	Not to exceed 15 vases	1.50	1.25	1.00	.50	.25
No. 46.	Vase of Wild Flowers	1.00	.75	.50	.25	.25

Display of Vegetables.—

No. 47.	Not to exceed 12 varieties	2.00	1.75	1.50	1.25	1.00	.75	.50

Shell Beans.—

No. 48.	Two quarts in pods	.75	.50	.25	.25

Beets.—

No. 49.	Six specimens	1.00	.75	.50	.25	.25

Carrots.—

No. 50.	Six specimens	1.00	.75	.50	.25	.25

Sweet Corn.—

No. 51.	Six ears	1.00	.75	.50	.25	.25

Green Peppers.—
　No. 52.　Six specimens　　　　　　　.75　.50　.25　.25

Tomato.—
　No. 53.　Six specimens　　　1.00　.75　.50　.25　.25

Winter Squash.—
　No. 54　Two specimens　　　　1.00　.75　.25　.25

Potato.—
　No. 55.　Twelve specimens　　1.00　.75　.50　.25　.25

Cucumber.—
　No. 56.　Two specimens　　　　　.75　.50　.25　.25

Open to Children between the ages of 14 and 21

Display of Flowers.—
　No. 57.　Not to exceed 15 vases　　2.50 2.00 1.75 1.50
　No. 58.　Bouquet, mixed cut flowers　1.00　.75　.50　.25

Petunia.—
　No. 59.　Not to exceed 10 vases　　1.00　.75　.50　.25

Dahlias.—
　No. 60.　Not to exceed 10 vases　　1.00　.75　.50　.25

Zinnia.—
　No. 61.　Not to exceed 10 vases　　1.00　.75　.50　.25

Marigold.—
　No. 62.　Not to exceed 10 vases　　1.00　.75　.50　.25

Cosmos.—
　No. 63.　One large vase　　　　1.00　.75　.50　.25

Gladiolus.—
　No. 64.　Basket　　　　　　　1.00　.75　.50　.25

Wild Flowers.—
　No. 65.　Not to exceed 15 vases　1.50 1.25 1.00　.50　.25
　No. 66.　Vase of Wild Flowers　1.00　.75　.50　.25　.25

Dahlia.—
　No. 67.　Vase　　　　　　　1.00　.75　.50　.25

Display of Vegetables.—
　No. 68.　Not to exceed 15 varieties
　　　　　　　　　2.50 2.00 1.75 1.50 1.25 1.00　.50

Potato.—
No. 69. Twelve specimens   1.50 1.00   .75   .50   .25

Carrots.—
No. 70. Six specimens   1.25 1.00   .75   .50   .25

Beets.—
No. 71. Six specimens   1.25 1.00   .75   .50   .25

Sweet Corn.—
No. 72. Six ears   1.25 1.00   .75   .50   .25

Peppers.—
No. 73. Six specimens   1.00   .75   .50   .25

Tomato.—
No. 74. Six specimens   1.25 1.00   .75   .50   .25

Cabbage.—
No. 75. Two specimens   .75   .50   .25

Winter Squash.—
No. 76. Two specimens   1.00   .75   .50   .25

Celery.—
No. 77. Three specimens   .75   .50   .25

Shell Beans.—
No. 78. Two quarts in the pod   1.00   .75   .50   .25

Onion.—
No. 79. Six specimens   1.00   .75   .50   .25

Cucumber.—
No. 80. Two specimens   1.00   .75   .50   .25

Prizes will be given for other meritorious exhibits.

Competition is open to all children of Worcester County under two classes. Those under 14 years and those between 14 and 21.

Only one child in a family can compete for the same prize.

The exhibits must be the results of individual effort of the child from the time of planting to the arranging of the exhibit.

All exhibits must be in the Hall ready for inspection by the Judges by 1 p. m. Exhibition will close at 4.30 p. m.

Prizes will be paid at the close of the exhibition.

Vases, plates and everything necessary for the exhibition of the flowers and vegetables will be furnished by the Horticultural Society.

Special Prizes Offered
by Secretary Herbert R. Kinney

To the ones receiving the two largest amounts under 14 years
f age. $3.00. $2.00.

To the ones receiving the two largest amounts over 14 years of
ge. $3.00. $2.00.

*   *   .*

For further information apply to

HERBERT R. KINNEY,
Secretary.

TRANSACTIONS

OF THE

WORCESTER COUNTY HORTICULTURAL SOCIETY

Reports of the Officers and Lectures

For the year ending December 2, 1938

HERBERT A. COOK
Vice-President 1920–1938

PRESIDENT'S ADDRESS

To the Members of the
Worcester County Horticultural Society:

The reports presented to you at this meeting are prepared for the purpose of accounting for the stewardship which you have entrusted to the various officers and committees. I am certain the reports which are to follow will demonstrate that the efforts put forth under the auspices of this Society have been blessed with worth while accomplishments.

The weather this summer was most unusual in that we had an overabundance of rain, a less than normal amount of sunshine, and the season ended with an unprecedented hurricane. The disaster thus inflicted on our exhibitors would have been reason enough to suspend part of the announced schedule; yet creditable exhibits were offered even at the regular Thursday show immediately following the hurricane of September twenty-first.

We have ample reason to be pleased with the results of the Lecture Course conducted during the early months of the year under direction of the Committee on Winter Meetings, and concluded with the Annual Reunion of the Society on the evening of Thursday, March third. The attendance at all of these occasions was numerous and appreciative.

It was a particular pleasure to have as the speaker at the Reunion Col. Samuel E. Winslow, a fifty-year member of the Society. Col. Winslow's early days were spent in this neighborhood. His accounts of the people of those days and of their doings, delivered in his own humorous style, enlightened and delighted the audience.

Reference already has been made to the excellence of the year's exhibits. Therefore, I will not further trespass on your time regarding them, excepting to commend especially the achievements of the special committee in charge of the Spring Show in March and of the Chrysanthemum Exhibit in November. With greenhouses damaged and some demolished by the September hurricane, it seemed incredible that energy and material would be available in November to provide the un-excelled exhibit presented at that time.

There are many special features in the flower kingdom such as the different varieties of Christmas Roses, Iris, Clematis, and others. Some of our members take a special interest in them. Those who do might gain advantage by forming a study group within this Society.

During the year we lost our friend and associate, Mr. Herbert A. Cook, whose long and useful life closed in May. He had been a prominent figure in these circles for many years. Mr. Davenport has prepared suitable resolutions with reference to his life work, which he will present to you during this session.

Dr. and Mrs. Homer Gage have ever evinced delightful interest in horticulture, and exhibits from Iristhorpe, their summer home in Shrewsbury, have been charming features of the Worcester Shows during these many years. Dr. Gage passed away peacefully on July third while in residence at Iristhorpe. We join with the friends of the family in extending sympathy to Mrs. Gage and in expressing the hope that she may be granted strength with which to carry on her many interests under these new and more difficult circumstances.

The year's work closes with its problems well in hand, and thus a feeling of satisfaction pervades throughout our organization.

Respectfully submitted,

MYRON F. CONVERSE, *President*

Worcester, Massachusetts
December 1, 1938

SECRETARY'S REPORT

Mr. President and Members of the
Worcester County Horticultural Society:

Our activities for the year have been carried on along lines followed by the Society for many years, having lectures during January and February, with a reunion and four-day Spring Exhibition in March, and exhibitions Thursday afternoons and evenings during June, July, August, and September.

We have one exhibition in April and one in May and one or two in October and the four-day Chrysanthemum Exhibition in November.

We have two Children's Exhibitions, one in August and one in September.

All of our lectures this year were illustrated.

January 13, "Garden Suggestions from Nature," by Dr. Frank A. Waugh, Amherst, Mass.

He showed many natural scenes of beauty and arrangements but did not advocate wild flowers for the garden.

January 20, "Vines," by Miss Dorothy Jenkins of Flushing, N. Y.

She said, "Vines are more the step-children of the garden, and seldom are considered as real personalities. We are apt to use them to cover or hide things. Vines are not a bit fussy. Many varieties planted in the open ground grow very rapidly." She showed and described many varieties, some beautiful ones.

January 27, "The Art of Gardening," by Henrietta M. Pope, Boston, Mass.

This was without doubt our most beautiful lecture during the course. There were many beautiful pictures of large and small gardens and they were described in an interesting manner.

February 3, "A Trip through Our National Parks," by Dr. Donald Wyman of Jamaica Plain, Mass.

These are noted for their many high mountains, beautiful water falls, mammoth trees, beautiful stones, and wild flowers.

February 10, "A Few Problems of the Average Gardener," by Professor Hugh Findlay, Columbia University, New York City. A good quotation from his lecture to remember is, "God breathed the breath of life into the soil and it smiled back at its Creator in the form of a flower."

"One way to solve some of our problems today is to sweat more in the garden and talk less."

February 17, "The Restoration of Williamsburg," by Mr. Sidney N. Shurcliff, of Boston, Mass.

I think this lecture drew the largest attendance we have had since we left Front Street. I think that the lecture would have been of rather more interest for a historical society than for a horticultural society.

The report of this lecture was written by Mr. Shurcliff and should be authentic.

February 24, "Bulbs for the Home Garden," by Mr. Allen W. Edminster, Boston, Mass.

"When one thinks of bulbs one thinks of Holland."

"In planting bulbs, it is important to consider color harmony."

March 3, Annual Reunion. The Library was decorated with palms and roses and lilies.

In the receiving line were President and Mrs. Myron F. Converse, Colonel and Mrs. Samuel E. Winslow, and Mrs. Homer Gage.

The ushers were Messrs. Malcolm C. Midgley, Harrison G. Taylor, George F. E. Story, Burt W. Greenwood, and Allen W. Hixon.

During the reception music was furnished by Felton's orchestra.

The receiving line led the march to the dining room, which was decorated with pink carnations.

Reverend Vincent E. Tomlinson invoked the Divine Blessing, followed by a beautiful rendition of the Lord's Prayer by the Ionic Male Quartet.

After the dinner, served by Mr. Lunt, the quartet sang "There Is a Tavern" and "Swing Low, Sweet Chariot."

President Myron F. Converse in his opening remarks called attention to the fact that Mr. Herbert A. Cook passed his ninetieth birthday recently.

He said that it was ten years since Horticultural Hall opened on Elm Street, but that ten years in the life of a Society that was ninety-five years old is a mere ten years past over lightly.

In introducing the speaker, Mr. Converse said that Col. Samuel E. Winslow had been a member of the Worcester County Horticultural Society for fifty years.

The Spring Exhibition was a very attractive one as a whole. The outstanding exhibit was by Iristhorpe, Mrs. Homer Gage's estate, which occupied the center of the Auditorium and the stage. Other exhibits of especial merit were those of Mr. Edward W. Breed, Charles Potter, and Sunnyside Greenhouses.

There were eleven entries in Class 1 and nine in Class 2.

There was only one rock garden.

Mr. Frank L. Abbott made an attractive exhibit of dwarf hemlocks.

Mr. Oren F. Whitney and Mr. S. Lothrop Davenport exhibited some nice carnations.

There was a large display of apples of good quality.

Vegetables were good.

The feature of the April Exhibition was the thirteen table decorations.

June 9, The Iris Exhibition was a good one with twenty-one exhibits of German iris, nine cut-flowers, eight peonies, and seven lupinus.

June 23, The Rose Exhibition was the best for several years. There were forty-nine entries of roses of good quality shown.

August 4, "Flower Arrangement for the Living Room." There were sixteen entries and they attracted much attention.

August 11, Gladiolus Exhibition. There were eight displays, eight, twenty vases and five standards. There were twenty-one "Small Vases on a Mirror."

August 18, "Flowers on Mirror" was again a very popular and attractive exhibit.

The display of garden flowers brought out eight entries.

September 1, "Pair Mantel Vases." There were eighteen entries and it made a very nice showing.

The two classes of cut flowers bring out some very nice arrangements.

September 8, "Metal Container of Cut Flowers" was both popular and attractive.   Twenty-four entries.

There was a light showing of fruit of poor quality.

September 15, Dahlia Exhibition.   While there were some nice flowers, it was not up to last year's standard in quality, but all classes were well filled.

There were twenty-three entries.

There has been no fine showings of tuberous-rooted begonias this season.

There were fifteen plates of Bartlett and eleven plates of Seckel pears.

September 22, The day after the very destructive windstorm, there were some nice exhibits, but only a small entry.

September 29, There were nine standards and twelve table decorations and eight good displays of fruit.

October 6,   Fruit and Vegetable Exhibition.   There were entries in all but one class, but the quality was not up to our standard with the exception of the table decorations of fruit. There were fifteen of them, some very fine.

November 10–13, Chrysanthemum Exhibition.   Mr. Breed had a very attractive exhibit in the center of the Auditorium and Iristhorpe had an excellent Japanese Garden in the West Room. Mr. Potter had the stage.

There were some very nice large chrysanthemums shown by Iristhorpe and a fine showing of pompons, singles and anemones.

Our Children's Exhibitions were again very satisfactory. There were 141 entries of flowers and 139 entries of vegetables in the classes called for and quite a number of extras, especially of flowers.

The children, both large and small have shown much interest in the arranging of their exhibits.

Respectfully submitted,

HERBERT R. KINNEY, Secretary

Worcester, Massachusetts
December 1, 1938

IRISTHORPE, MRS. HOMER GAGE, SPRING 1938

For the Year Ending November 30, 1938

Statement of Income and Expenditures

INCOME		
Rent:		
Hall............	$880.00	
Stores..........	39,999.96	$40,879.96
Permanent Funds:		
Membership Fund	$103.67	
Blake Fund......	31.00	
Dewey Fund.....	25.15	
Eames Fund.....	20.50	
Hadwen Fund....	61.00	
Morse Fund.....	11.00	252.32
Membership Fees...........		140.00
Interest Earned:		
Permanent Funds.	$132.87	
Investments......	231.03	363.90
Winter Meetings...........		196.00
Other Income:		
Mabel K. Gage...	$50.00	
H. R. Kinney....	29.50	79.50
Retirement of Class A Stock, Worcester County Trust Company................		130.00
Office Expense—Refund of telephone toll................		5.10
Furniture and Fixtures—Sale of chairs.................		228.00
Rebate of Insurance Premium.		2.98
		$42,277.76

EXPENDITURES		
Library....................		
Winter Meetings............		
Periodicals.................		
Publications................		
Premiums:		
Of 1938..........	$6,471.00	
Special..........	79.50	
Children's.......	261.70	
Blake Fund......	31.00	
Eames Fund.....	20.50	
Hadwen Fund....	61.00	
Morse Fund......	11.00	
Expense:		
Exhibitions......	$248.83	
Office...........	435.83	
Operating........	522.27	
Miscellaneous....	540.18	
Street Sprinkling............		
Maintenance:		
Furniture and Fixtures..........	$695.16	
Real Estate......	1,266.28	
Salaries.....................		
Interest Paid...............		
Interest Added to Permanent Funds....................		
Interest Added to Investments.		
Insurance...................		
Light, Heat, and Water......		
Janitor Service..............		
Mortgage Reduction (Front Street Property)...........		
Transfer to Membership Fund.		
Returned to Investments.....		
Contribution to McWilliam Fund....................		
Furniture and Fixtures.......		

Cash Balance, December 2, 1937	993.08
	$43,270.84

Cash Balance, Nov. 30, 1938...

Gains and Losses

LOSSES

Appropriations..............	$10,000.00
Depreciation................	1,325.05
Special and Permanent Fund Premiums................	203.00
Expense Accounts...........	1,742.01
Insurance..................	337.07
Interest...................	6,223.41
Janitor Service.............	2,688.75
Light, Heat, and Water......	1,210.60
Maintenance Accounts.......	1,961.44
Periodicals.................	94.82
Publications................	858.00
Street Sprinkling...........	5.70
Winter Meetings............	889.43
Contribution to McWilliam Fund....................	100.00
	$27,639.28
Net Gain to Surplus........	14,189.08
	$41,829.08

Statement of Resources and Liabilities

RESOURCES		
Permanent Funds (Investment):		
People's Sav. Bk.		
(Hadwen Fund) $1,166.61		
Wor. Five Cts. Sav. Bk.		
(Draper Fund)	420.16	
(Eames Fund)	588.89	
(Morse Fund)	523.58	
Wor. Mech. Sav. Bk.		
(Blake Fund).	1,408.34	
(Dewey Fund)	1,000.00	
(McWilliam		
Fund).....	203.97	$5,311.55
Investments:		
Wor. Co. Inst.		
for Sav......	$3,014.35	
Wor. Five Cts.		
Sav. Bk......	3,182.95	
Wor. Mech. Sav.		
Bk.........	3,376.04	
Wor. Co. Trust		
Co. Class A		
Stk. 65 shs. at		
$12 per share.	780.00	10,353.34
Membership Fund..........		4,270.00
Real Estate...............		480,000.00
Furniture and Fixtures......		20,866.08
Library..................		1,933.54
Cash....................		1,040.44
		$523,774.95

LIABILITIES

Blake Fund:
  Principal...............
  Income.................
Dewey Fund:
  Principal...............
  Income.................
Draper Fund:
  Principal...............
  Income.................
Eames Fund:
  Principal...............
  Income.................
Hadwen Fund:
  Principal...............
  Income.................
McWilliam Fund:
  Principal...............
  Income.................
Morse Fund:
  Principal...............
  Income.................
Mortgage Note, Front Street
  Property................ 1
Surplus:
  Balance, Dec. 2,
    1937........$350,273.60
  Net Gain, 1938. 14,189.80 3

$5

Respectfully submitted,
B. W. GREENWOOD, *Tr*

Auditor's Certificate

I have examined the books of the Treasurer of the Worcester County Horticultural Society, together with vouchers, securities and bank balances, for the year ending November 30, 1938, and find them to be correct
ADAH B. JOHNSON, *Auditor*

We have caused an audit of the books of the Treasurer to be made fo the year ending November 30, 1938, and the foregoing certificate is hereby approved.

Respectfully submitted,

H. WARD MOORE, HARRY C. MIDGLEY, ARTHUR H. BELLOWS,
Auditors

Worcester, Massachusetts

LIBRARIAN'S REPORT

Mr. President and Members of the
Worcester County Horticultural Society:

During the period since my last report the records show a marked increase in the use of the Library.

Four hundred books and many periodicals have been in circulation during the year and thirty-two books, twice as many as in 1937 have been added to our catalogue. All were on subjects frequently called for and greatly appreciated by our members.

Bulletins from the Arnold Arboretum and many informative bulletins from Agricultural Experiment Stations of Cornell University, the Purdue University and Connecticut State College at Storrs, Conn., have been received and our usual fine collection of horticultural magazines have been continued for reading in the Library.

In the interests of the maintenance of our permanent collections, it is important that the 1937 issues of *Horticulture* and *The Gardener's Chronicle of America* have been bound.

We have received and acknowledge with gratitude the gifts of books to the Library from the following donors in 1938:

Everybody's Garden, by Frank A. Waugh.
Vines, by Miss Dorothy H. Jenkins.
Garden Making and Keeping, by Hugh Findlay.

Other new titles added to the Library during the year 1938 were as follows:

The Garden in Color, by Louise Beebe Wilder, 1937.
Irises, by F. F. Rockwell, 1928.
Peonies, by F. F. Rockwell, 1933.
The Garden of Gourds, by L. H. Bailey, 1937.
Chrysanthemums (with supplement on forcing with the use of black cloth and training cascade chrysanthemums), by Alexander Laurie, 1930.
The Mushroom Handbook, by Louis C. C. Krieger, 1936.
How to Grow Roses, 1937 issue, by McFarland and Pyle.
The International edition of the 1938 Gladiolus Society Year-Book.

The 1937 Royal Horticultural Society Lily Year-Book.
Modern Dahlias, by J. Louis Roberts, 1938.
The Present-Day Rock Garden, by Sampson Clay (English), 1937.
The Delphinium Year-Book, 1937, by The American Delphinium Society.
Garden Bulbs in Color, by J. Horace McFarland, R. Marion Hatton, and Daniel J. Foley, 1938.
Flower Decoration, by Constance Spry (English), 1933.
Flowers in the House and Garden, by Constance Spry (English), 1937.
The 1938 American Rose Annual, Issued by The American Rose Society.
Herbaceous Borders and The Waterside, by Richard Sudell, 1938.
The Gardener's Omnibus, Edited by E. I. Farrington, 1938.
How to Know the Wild Flowers, by Frances Theodore Parsons, 1935.
Familiar Flowers of Field and Garden, by F. Schuyler Mathews.
Green Laurels, by Donald Culross Peattie, 1936.
Our Shade Trees, by Ephraim Porter Felt, 1938.
Creative Flower Arrangement, by Dorothy Biddle and Dorothea Blom, 1938.
Color in Everyday Life, by Louis Weinberg, 1937.
Soilless Growth of Plants, by Ellis and Swaney, 1938.
The Garden Dictionary, Edited by Norman Taylor, 1936.

Respectfully submitted,

FLORENCE E. FIELD, *Librarian*

Worcester, Massachusetts
December 1, 1938

EDWARD W. BREED, SPRING 1938

REPORT OF THE LIBRARY COMMITTEE

Mr. President and Members of the
  Worcester County Horticultural Society:

It is very interesting to note the increasing call for books from our Library, as well as the patronage afforded the magazine section.

We are always on the alert to acquire books that will be worth while and a valuable addition to our files. We are also glad to receive requests for such new volumes as may be helpful to our members.

Among the periodicals recently brought to our attention, we are pleased to mention one named *Real Gardening*, a new kind of magazine written and edited by experienced gardeners and nurserymen; for it is a magazine of the gardener, by the gardener and for the gardener. It is all solid meat, without advertising, and contains a fund of practical information. We think it is a real asset to our collection.

Then there is a magazine called *Gardening, Illustrated*, to which we have subscribed a number of years, but its publication has now been taken over by *English Country Life*, and has been somewhat enlarged. This also seems to be full of excellent reading matter.

May we suggest to our members that any knowledge worth while must be eagerly sought after and gained by personal study. Our Library offers these splendid opportunities.

EDWARD W. BREED, *Chairman*

Worcester, Massachusetts
December 1, 1938

REPORT OF THE JUDGE OF PLANTS AND FLOWERS

Mr. President and Members of the
Worcester County Horticultural Society:

In presenting to you my customary annual report, it is a pleasure to say that considering the changeable weather experienced during the season, the exhibits were generally of good quality and competition was very keen. This is especially true of class calling for twenty vases of cut flowers, nine competitors being the average number in this class.

The March Exhibition was notable for some fine garden and plant exhibits. Plants and cut flowers were shown in great variety and excellent quality.

Table decorations were the main feature of the April and May Exhibitions, and while there were a few tastefully arranged tables, the quality of the flowers used and the arrangement were generally poor. The same may be said of the table decorations throughout the season. They were not as good as in former years.

There was a fine display of Ixias from Iristhorpe and an exhibit of pansies remarkable in size and color from Dr. Cooper.

The June Exhibitions were notable for the fine displays of German and Siberian iris. Other cut flowers, especially roses and Aquilegias, were very good. Peonies were not as good as usual.

The feature of the July Exhibitions was the fine displays of Japanese iris and a remarkable exhibit of regal lilies from Mr. Kinney which occupied nearly all of the stage in the Main Hall and made a fine showing. The strength, length of stem, and size of flowers were unusually fine.

In August good gladioluses were shown both in baskets and vases. One vase of Lilium Philippenensis grown from seed was very fine. These came from Mr. Whitin of Uxbridge.

The Dahlia Exhibition was good. Some very fine blooms were shown in class for fifty blooms.

At the two October Exhibitions fine cut flowers were shown, including hardy Chrysanthemums.

At the Chrysanthemum Show in November the Main Hall was filled with well arranged garden and plant groups, although with two or three exceptions the quality of the flowers used was not up to the usual standard. The unusually warm weather for several weeks preceding the show made it difficult to hold flowers back. Classes calling for vases of specimen blooms were well filled with very fine flowers. The fern globes and terrariums were very good. A fine collection of wild fruits and berries was also shown.

During the season the Society also held two Children's Exhibitions, which were a credit to the exhibitors, particularly the exhibits of wild flowers.

Respectfully submitted,

WILLIAM ANDERSON, Judge of Plants and Flowers

Worcester, Massachusetts
December 1, 1938

REPORT OF JUDGE OF FRUIT

Mr. President and Members of the
Worcester County Horticultural Society:

As the year 1936 was noted for its extremes of weather conditions, so again during 1938 new records were established, the extreme rains during July with its flood conditions, the hurricane and flood of September 21, the two months of summer weather following the hurricane, and the beginning of winter conditions at Thanksgiving with its snow and extreme cold. These conditions during the year have inflicted severe losses on the fruit growers, not only in the loss of fruit, but in the loss of thousands of trees, and have presented them with many new problems of rehabilitation of their orchards. These conditions during 1938 have had a marked influence on the exhibits this season, and will continue to affect the exhibits of fruits for some years to come.

During the early part of the season our fruit exhibits showed a material increase over 1937. At the Spring Show we had a fine showing of fruit, with five displays, eleven classes of forty-nines, twenty-six plates, with boxes, baskets, etc.

On June 16 and 23, we had a fine showing of strawberries in plates and baskets, with Howard 17 still the leading variety.

Currants and gooseberries were well shown this season, with fourteen plates of currants on July 7.

The raspberry crop was almost a total failure, due to the extreme rains during July, but a few fine plates were shown.

Cherries, plums, and peaches were shown only lightly during the season and on some calls only a few pears were exhibited. However on August 25 eleven plates of fine Clapps Favorites were shown, and later we had some excellent Bartletts and Seckels, but due to the hurricane we only had a light showing of Bosc and Anjou.

The Grape Exhibits were not up to the usual standard, as many of the growers suffered heavy losses from the ravages of black rot. However, on September 8, Mr. Kinney exhibited some of the finest Concords and Wordens that have been shown for many years.

The older varieties of apples such as the Porter, Maiden Blush, Hubbardston, etc., are gradually disappearing and their places are being taken by the newer kinds.   McIntosh, Baldwins, Gravenstein, Wealthy, and Courtland are most in demand, and some fine fruit of these varieties were shown during the season. Crab apples were well shown this year with some fine plates of Hyslop, Martha, etc.

On October 13 the call for Table Decorations with Fruit was well filled with fourteen entries.   This is a fine class and brings out many attractive tables.

In spite of the hurricane of September 21 which caused the loss of 75 per cent or more of the winter fruits, apples, pears, etc., we had a most remarkable showing of fruit at the November Exhibition, with nine displays, fifteen classes of forty-nines, thirteen baskets and thirty plates of excellent quality which compares very favorably with other years.

Although the fruit growers this year have had many adverse conditions to contend with during the season, a remarkably good display of fruit has been shown.

Respectfully submitted,

S. Lothrop Davenport, Judge of Fruit

Worcester, Massachusetts
December 1, 1938

REPORT OF JUDGE OF VEGETABLES

Mr. President and Members of the
Worcester County Horticultural Society:

The vegetable growing season of 1938 was one of many vagaries, which were apparent in many different ways. First we had a spell of unusually warm weather in April which gave the early vegetables a quick start making them ready for exhibition earlier than they have been for the past few seasons. Following this were the cloudy weather and excessive rains of July and early August which delayed the ripening of some varieties and entirely destroyed others. Among the vegetables affected very adversely were potatoes and tomatoes, especially where these were grown on moist land.

For nearly three weeks during the blossoming time of the tomatoes there was not enough pleasant weather to permit the pollenization of the blossoms consequently very little fruit set during that time. Tomatoes which had set before the rains ripened poorly. Following this was a period of about three weeks during which almost no tomatoes ripened.

Other varieties were similarly affected so that the exhibits of vegetables have been fewer in number and poorer in quality since midsummer. To make matters worse along came the hurricane and ruined some of the vegetables that had survived the rains.

Among the varieties of which the number and the quality of the specimens shown was not up to the usual standard were sweet corn, squash, cabbage, celery, tomatoes, cauliflowers, melons, and potatoes. The collections and displays were not as good as usual, but that was to be expected.

However, not everything has been of poor quality this season. We had excellent showings of rhubarb, asparagus, beets, peas, and string beans in the early season and pole beans, some tomatoes, peppers, summer squash, carrots, and onions later.

The past season was particularly favorable for mushrooms. We had a large number of exhibits many of which were of exceptionally fine quality.

There were a large number of fine displays of both peppers and gourds.

The new call for "Market Baskets of Vegetables" was well filled. The half-bushel baskets of fine quality vegetables were very attractive.

The Children's Exhibitions were about the same as in past years.

Though we have passed through a rather unfavorable season, let us not be discouraged, but rather let us look forward to a better one in 1939, with more coöperation from the weather man.

Respectfully submitted,

H. WARD MOORE, *Judge of Vegetables*

Worcester, Massachusetts
December 1, 1938

R. J. ALLEN, SPRING 1938

REPORT OF FINANCE COMMITTEE

To the Members of the
  Worcester County Horticultural Society:

A satisfactory degree of progress was experienced during the year in the Society's financial affairs as reflected by the Treasurer's Report, although but little income was realized from Hall rentals.

The present Home Building is now ten years old, but because of its solid construction, requires but little attention except ordinary maintenance.

Your Finance Committee, after discussion with other officers, decided to replace the chairs in Horticultural Hall, and today's meeting affords an opportunity for the members to pass judgment on the transaction. The upholstery should lend a comfort which we hope will induce this audience to remain contentedly throughout the session.

Respectfully submitted,

MYRON F. CONVERSE,
LEONARD C. MIDGLEY,
HARRY HARRISON,
  Finance Committee

Worcester, Massachusetts
December 1, 1938

IN MEMORIAM

In the passing on May 23, 1938 of Mr. Herbert A. Cook of Shrewsbury, Vice-President of the Worcester County Horticultural Society since 1920, the Society lost a most loyal officer, and the members a dear friend.

Mr. Cook was a lifelong member of our society having joined in 1884 and he always maintained a keen interest in its affairs. He was always ready and willing to serve and for over thirty years he held one or more offices in the Society. In 1906 he was elected a Trustee and two years later in 1908 he became a member of the Committee of Arrangements. At the same time he was appointed the Judge of Fruit, which position he most conscientiously held for about twenty years. In 1920 he was chosen Vice-President which position he held until his death.

Mr. Cook devoted his life to agriculture, not only in the growing of quality vegetables, but fine fruit and beautiful flowers as well. For many years he was recognized as a leader in his chosen field, and through his love of nature and his persistent work he developed and improved various varieties of fruits and vegetables, which we today may enjoy. During his later years he still maintained his interest in the new varieties and had many growing in his own garden. He also led the way in developing various farm practices, and the Massachusetts Department of Agriculture, recognizing his achievements, presented him with a gold medal.

Not only did Mr. Cook excel in the production of fruits and vegetables, but developed one of the best ranges of greenhouses, specializing in carnations, in Worcester County. In growing such fine vegetables, fruit, and flowers, he always took a great interest in the exhibits and had the enjoyment of winning many prizes.

Mr. Cook was a busy man and yet he found time for civic duties and served his town on the School Committee and for seven years on the Board of Selectmen.

He was also active in many other agricultural organizations besides the Worcester County Horticultural Society, such as the Farm Bureau, the Market Gardener's Association, and the New England Carnation Growers Association.

Mr. Cook having passed his ninety-first birthday, enjoyed a long and well rounded out life and by his many accomplishments has set a high standard for us to maintain.

Therefore in appreciation of his fine work and his loving friendship, be it resolved that a copy of this memorial be spread upon our records.

Respectfully submitted,

S. LOTHROP DAVENPORT

Worcester, Massachusetts
December 1, 1938

ANNUAL MEETING OF THE SOCIETY

Thursday, December 2, 1937

President Myron F. Converse called the meeting to order at 10 o'clock a.m. Forty-five present.

Secretary read the call for the meeting.

The records of the last Annual Meeting were approved but not read.

President Myron F. Converse delivered his Annual Address.

The following reports were read:

Secretary, Herbert F. Kinney; Treasurer, Burt W. Greenwood; Librarian, Mrs. Florence E. Field; Judge of Flowers, William Anderson; Judge of Fruit, S. Lothrop Davenport; Judge of Vegetables, H. Ward Moore.

These reports were accepted and referred to the Committee on Library and Publications.

Mr. Allen J. Jenkins spoke for the Committee on Arrangements and Exhibitions.

Mr. Leonard C. Midgley read the report of the Finance Committee.

This report recommended an appropriation of ten thousand dollars for premiums and salaries for the coming year.

Mr. Harry Harrison made a motion that this report be accepted and adopted. So voted.

There being no member of the Nominating Committee present, President Converse appointed Messrs. H. Ward Moore and Ralph C. Breed a committee to distribute the list of candidates nominated.

President Converse asked if there were other candidates. There being none, he declared the candidates nominated, elected.

Adjourned.

HERBERT R. KINNEY, *Secretary*

ANNUAL MEETING OF THE TRUSTEES

Thursday, December 9, 1937

Meeting called to order by President Myron F. Converse at 10 o'clock a.m. Twenty-two present.

Secretary read the records of the last Annual Meeting of the Trustees.

President Converse declared them approved.

President Converse said that this meeting elected the Committees and Judges and apportioned the sum of $10,000 appropriated by the Finance Committee for premiums and salaries. He said, "You will find a list of the present Committees and allotments for the past year in the Premium List you have."

He read the list of the Committees and appropriations for the past year. He said that things had seemed to run quite satisfactorily. He awaited suggestions. There being none, Mr. Harry Harrison made a motion that the Committees, Judges and appropriations remain the same as last year. So voted.

Appropriation...................................... $10,000.00

PREMIUMS

Flowers...................	$1,800.00	
Fruits....................	1,000.00	
Vegetables	800.00	
Children's Exhibition.......	300.00	
Spring Exhibition..........	1,600.00	
Chrysanthemum Exhibition..	1,400.00	
Miscellaneous.............	225.00	$7,125.00

SALARIES

Treasurer................	$350.00	
Secretary.	1,000.00	
Librarian................	1,000.00	
Assistant to Secretary.......	125.00	
Judges...................	400.00	$2,875.00

$10,000.00

Adjourned.

HERBERT R. KINNEY, *Secretary*

ANNUAL MEETING OF THE COMMITTEE ON ARRANGEMENTS AND EXHIBITIONS

Thursday, December 9, 1937

Meeting called to order at 10:30 a.m. by President Myron F. Converse.

Present—Mrs. Field, Mrs. Denny, Mrs. Forbes, Mrs. Taft and Miss Bishop, Messrs. Jenkins, Breed, Potter, Allen Hixon, Mr. Davenport, Mr. Moore, Mr. Midgley, President Converse, and Secretary Kinney.

On Mrs. Forbes's motion, Mr. Jenkins was elected chairman.

After quite general discussion, it was voted that the rules should be brought to the attention of the exhibitors.

Rule 10 was considered at some length. As there was no general suggestion, Secretary Kinney made a motion that the Chairman appoint a committee of three to consider it and report after lunch. So voted.

Chairman Jenkins appointed Messrs. Davenport, Allen Hixon, and Mr. Moore.

Rule 21 was revised to read, "Hendricks' 'Fruits of New York' and S. A. Beach's 'The Apples of New York' will guide the Judge of Fruit in his decisions upon matters at issue."

It was voted to insert for the March Exhibition, "Notify the Secretary four weeks in advance for space."

The Chairman called the committee to order at 1:30 p.m. Committee on Rule 10 reported.

Rule 10. After the articles are arranged they will be under the exclusive charge of the Judges and Committee of Arrangements and not even the owners will have liberty to remove them until the exhibition is closed and no sale of fruit, flowers or vegetables shall be made in the building. This was adopted by a hand vote.

On the motion of Mr. Allen Hixon, it was voted that Rules 9, 10 and 14 in the Schedule be called to the special attention of the exhibitors.

The following changes were made:

April   28   Round Tables were cut out.
May   12   Round Tables were called.
June   30   Added, Vase of Peonies.
                   Strawberries, Fairfax.
                   Four baskets, any variety.
August   18   Market Basket of Vegetables.
September   22   Display of Pears from September 9.
October   13   Gourds from the Chrysanthemum Exhibition.

Adjourned.

HERBERT R. KINNEY, *Secretary*

EDWARD W. BREED AND CHARLES POTTER, FALL 1938

"GARDEN SUGGESTIONS FROM NATURE"

Illustrated Lecture

By Dr. Frank A. Waugh, Amherst, Massachusetts

Thursday, January 13, 1938

Nature is her own landscape architect. We may take hints or suggestions from her, but it is somewhat dangerous for us to make iron clad rules for gardens, since she does not build hers by rules. From one point of view, a garden is not at all the work of nature, but rather contains plants and flowers which grow outside of nature, and we have a perfect right to assert our supremacy over nature in the planning of our garden. From this point of view it is not desirable to grow wild flowers in the garden; they belong outside.

How often we would give almost anything to go out there close to nature, and so, once a year we sleep on the ground, cook our own meals, get our eyes full of smoke, and really enjoy life again. From her we can take a great many suggestions for any sort of garden. We ought to learn from nature that a great deal depends upon the soil and the subsoil.

In Central Kansas we find loose sand and here nature has made a garden with plants that develop in such surroundings. Even with water running over the brink or out of the side of a hill, or even in gravel, still nature develops plants which thrive under such circumstances.

If you would have a moraine garden, take the suggestion which nature gives us of beautiful crocuses growing at the foot of a glacier. And still another hint we see at the top of the Sierra Mountains in Oregon; a situation of soil and exposure, climate you might say, entirely different from that just given, yet flowers blossom there.

Spread along the roadside ledge, New England's most distinctive bluettes are perfectly at home. Nature grows some of her plants in groups of circular form and this may have some meaning for us. Another feature of nature's garden which ought to be of interest to us is the natural associations of plants. There are certain plants which associate freely together. Pine trees and the dwarf palmetto get along fine as do the juniper association. These are a beautiful grouping of plants in themselves.

Don't you think nature's planning looks pretty well? What landscape architect wouldn't like to plan his garden to look natural? Then why not take nature's suggestions and let her have her way in our gardens?

One of the most common of nature's combinations is the gray birch growing on moist, swampy land with fern. A grouping of pictorial value is the pitch pine, violets, and maianthemums. On a hill in Connecticut or Massachusetts we find hay-scented fern, a weed which grows excessively all over the country, associated with the gray birch. Don't you think they come together very nicely—like a cat with a kitten? To complete the association we add laurel, thus having fern, birch, and mountain laurel. This combination we cannot help but covet for our gardens.

Nature had been working on the arranging of plants along the roadside long before we started, and she has shown us some very beautiful examples.

Whether it be a bank in Oregon facing the south, very warm, dry, and the road new, or a barbed wire fence along the road in Kansas, nature has taken care of each such complex condition. Our own mountain laurel is the most beautiful along the roadside, if it has its own way. If we want to have laurel growing in our garden, we should take suggestions from nature as to where and how it should grow.

We have all heard the legend of the mushrooms: fairies coming out at night and dancing on the lawn in a circle, have the mushrooms to sit on, and thus they grow in a circle. This is a scientific fact, rather than a legend, and a fact which I firmly believe.

Nature seems to plan this garden in a circular form. If you notice in the spring, along the roadside you will find ferns growing in this pattern. Have we ever tried this? Here is another suggestion of nature. We plant them in rows, but God didn't plant them that way.

Iris forms groups not always clear, but in a circular form. We ought to know what nature is trying to do with native plants if we wish to cultivate a natural garden. Disc grouping is different from the circular, but essentially interesting.

Native plums in Shutesbury started in the center and spread

out in circular form. The old ones in the center grow higher and higher, and the new ones on the outside, just as the lilacs grow. By this we know the shorter trees or plants on either side of the center are new ones growing in. Wild roses grow just the same, following the rules of nature, and we should take these suggestions if we wish to have a natural garden.

No iron clad rules for nature; for we find the wild white asters make a complete group by themselves and these come up annually.

We interfere with nature in a great many different ways and then it is quite noticeable what the plants do.

We are getting away a little bit from our recent fad of rock gardens. I don't want to discourage you because it is really a nice form of gardening. We could very well match nature's rock gardens by better care, for she grows roses on top of bare rock, even better than those cultivated by us. You probably never heard of roses as a proper subject for rock gardens, yet here they are perfectly at home on bare rock. And too, she makes a garden of Hydrocotyle on wet rock where the water trickles down over it, and these rocks are as wet as anything that came out of Congress.

We don't really have any forest in our garden plots but we do sometimes have a forest margin and if trees grow around the side and inside the garden, we have a fringe of a forest. The most common fringe of forest is birches, then beeches, ferns, and laurel. Perfectly natural and once more—"This is just as pretty as any landscape architect could do." Nature gives us still another example of beauty with trees on a frosty morning in winter. Why don't we take a suggestion from nature and distribute trees along the margin of the water in marginal groups?

It is said that nature doesn't plant trees in a row, but we find a row of cottonwood trees in a straight line, and here they stand strong, against which the water comes when the snow goes off and the ice goes out.

Nature has her own system of distributing plants which makes them much happier and they make a much prettier picture. We can get a great many suggestions that may be of value to us in our garden; if we enjoy nature more we will get more pleasure out of our garden.

"VINES"

Illustrated Lecture

By Miss Dorothy H. Jenkins, Flushing, New York

Thursday, January 20, 1938

Vines are more or less the step-children of the garden, and seldom are they considered as real personalities. We are apt to make use of them to cover or hide things instead of realizing that they could be really attractive and would add a great deal of pleasure in tending our garden. Of course use them for screening, but what can't they do for porches or gardens, even if strings or pergolas have to be put up for them?

Birds will show great friendliness around the home and will visit often if berry vines are used.

A vine is a plant that develops a slender stem and cannot support itself. There are several classes of vines, divided according to their means of climbing. Roses will grow into a beautiful upright vine if they are given support.

Annual vines are not a bit fussy. Planted directly in the open ground they do become real personalities, because they mature so quickly and give such prompt results. For the most part they are not particular about soil or drainage. Bear in mind that perennial vines must be given time to establish themselves before they can really give the beautiful picture we have in mind.

A few examples will prove what annual vines can do: if an annual vine is wanted, that will grow very fast and cover a great deal of space, a package of Kudzu vine is the answer, since it will grow twenty-five or thirty feet during the first summer and probably fifty feet each year thereafter. The scarlet runner bean is another splendid one, giving some fifteen to twenty-five feet of growth, and, together with a great deal of nice, clean foliage, is a constant succession of bright red flowers all summer, not to mention the beans themselves, edible if picked when young and tender.

Japanese hop is a foliage vine which conceals admirably without calling attention to itself; and, although it doesn't refuse to grow in the sun, prefers to grow in the shade.

Another annual vine that would grow rapidly is the gourds, making one of the thickest screens known. The seeds are planted directly in the open ground and truly the very large white flowers are almost unbelievably fragile for the heavy gourd. Plant the seed for good vines, in the open ground; but watch out for pests.

It is a far cry from the common bindweed and morning glory to the Japanese imperial morning glory, streaked and striped in all sorts of colors. Even in this day and age, doubtless there is no vine that has caught people's interest and imagination more than this heavenly blue morning glory, which is so very graceful. Make a visit to Springfield, Mass., and see what a beautiful covering it makes for the arbors at the city dumping-ground. The morning glory is a large family, one of the most commonly known distant cousins being the sweet potato vine. Another relative is the white moonflower, with a flat broad flower. Very difficult to imagine, but nevertheless true, on the roof of one of the hotels in New York City is an old umbrella, once covered with canvas, but now covered with the heavenly blue moonflower, and during July, August, and September, the old umbrella is entirely hidden.

Another relation is the cardinal climber with a mass of fine-cut foliage, but with red flowers somewhat smaller than the morning glory. It loves sun and the more it gets, the more it is going to thrive.

My first choice of annual vines is the scarlet runner bean; the second, the cardinal climber because it is unusual, and the third, the hyacinth bean with flowers of a deep purple or a lovely lavender.

Cathedral bells, or cup and saucer vine (Cobea Scandens) should not be planted in the open ground. The most appropriate name is cathedral bells because it certainly denotes the dignity of the vine. Although this beautiful vine has a dull lavender or purplish flower, when early September comes, the stems and leaves take on quite a reddish tint. Seeds should be planted in the house in March and will have to be transplanted at least once or twice before planting out of doors in May, and remember that the flowers will not appear as early as the scarlet runner bean, for example.

Many people consider the wild cucumber a pest and will not grow it, yet it is nice for walls or fences, even fences of chicken wire or barbed wire. However, once you plant it, you may never get rid of it as it spreads.

Technically, sweet peas should not be included among the vines, since we grow them simply for their very lovely flowers. For these, rich soil and much water is needed and it is well to remember that they like cool nights and by having these, they do not mind so much the heat of the day.

The Japanese or Boston ivy, which should rightly be called "The vine that went to college" since there is hardly a college in New England whose walls are not covered or partially covered with it, is really our vine for buildings in this country.

One of the more popular vines fifteen or twenty years ago was the Dutchman's pipe, but it is still worthy of being popular if we will put up string or something on which it can climb. It got its name because of the flower that comes in the summer, and although it is hard to see underneath the heavy foliage, it is in the form of a pipe.

One vine whose leaves stay green all year round is the evergreen Euonymus. Many people are not satisfied with foliage alone and when there are so many vines with such beautiful flowers, one can hardly blame them.

Wisteria is one of the most beautiful vines. There is a superstition that it will not flower until it is seven years old, but this is just a superstition. We must, however, wait and give this lovely plant time to establish itself. We should choose a suitable place which provides rich soil. Do not be afraid to prune wisteria in order to make it grow the way you want it to and flower. The Japanese wisteria has extremely long clusters of flowers in many odd shades of lavender and blue, as well as pink.

Small flowered clematis is the easiest clematis to grow, as it obliges by flowering in sun or shade, but most people want to grow the large flowered clematis. There are many species and varieties of this latter kind, the pinkish one being quite different in shape, and is called the Duchess of Albany.

Coral honeysuckle is another beautiful vine, and, because of its fragrance, anyone who grows it is indeed fortunate, although you may have trouble with its growing too thickly.

The matrimony vine is one of those peculiar plants which will grow either as a shrub or vine, depending on where you plant it and how much pruning it is given.

Silver lace or fleece vine (Polygonum Auberti) is very hardy and exceptionally clean.

Even more beautiful than the wisteria is the flower of the passion vine, and while this is a semi-tropical vine, it is half hardy and will grow in this country, provided it is given a protected place where it will get plenty of sun. It needs a great deal of feeding. This beautiful blossom was used for the interpretation of Christianity to the South American Indians, each section of the flower having its own representation.

The vine in which we are most interested and would go anywhere to see, is the rose. The choice we make depends entirely on our own personal taste. Large and varied is the family. The pale pink Dr. Van Fleet was followed by the everblooming New Dawn. There is Mary Wallace, one of the lovelier climbing pink varieties which may be trained to grow upright or as a bush. Jacotte is a semi-double one which opens out rather wide, giving a coppery mixed tint. Dr. Huey is always a very rich dark red, and Bess Lovett, one of three Lovetts, is a crimson. Sunday Best is still a different red.

In the yellow family came Emily Gray, not very hardy and apt to be winter-killed. Then, Le Reve, once considered a nearly ideal yellow rose. Another is Mrs. Arthur Curtis James, which some say is hardy, but others complain of. The final answer in the search for the perfect yellow rose appears to be the new Doubloons.

One of the very large flowered roses is the Spanish Beauty which fairly takes one's breath away to come out the first morning in June and find it opening.

Still another good flowering climber is the climbing hydrangea. This will cling to a cement wall and pull itself up to the top.

Get out of the rut in planting. Choose a vine not necessarily for the hiding of objects, but a beautiful one you have not previously thought about. Then ask yourselves these most important questions:

Is the vine suitable for the place in which you are going to grow it?

Has it some distinction as to foliage, flower, or fruit?

Is it clean? Will pests and insects stay away from it? And lastly: if it is perennial, is it hardy in Worcester?

"THE ART OF GARDENING"

Illustrated Lecture

By Henrietta M. Pope, Boston, Massachusetts

Thursday Afternoon, January 27, 1938

What is this art of gardening?—for we have come to recognize gardening as one of the fine arts. One must first master the principles which govern proportion and line. Learn to recognize what causes harmony and discord.

While traveling in Mexico, it was very interesting to find colonial gardens, that is, gardens of the period when Mexico was a colony of Spain. These old gardens were carefully designed, each with the central area, round, square, or octagon, called the "Gloriette," with a Mirador placed high up. These gardens have been built over three hundred years and are still satisfying. However, right here in New England there are many gardens from which we can get inspiration and suggestions for use in our own gardens.

One very attractive little garden on Beacon Hill in Boston was made by building a basin against the wall and placing a plaque on the wall and then painting the wall a bright yellow. In building a city garden it is better to make the flower bed above the level of the garden. This makes it easier to keep the soil moist and easier to tend to the flowers. The potted plant is the salvation of the city garden. Another suggestion is Spirea Japonica and tulips.

As we travel, we may pick up unique pieces here and there to bring home for use in the garden. Use plants in pots a great deal, and too, tubs can be used for flowers, whether the tubs be large or small. Anyone can have a garden if they have a place where sun can penetrate.

With a dignified colonial house, a dignified garden should be planned. A very lovely garden was shown with beds of tulips and an edge of box, and the paving of the walk through the garden was made interesting by using red brick in the center.

A rock garden is perfectly permissible in the city. However, the rock garden is essentially a spring garden because the heat in our climate is very intense in the summer on the stones and dries up the moisture which the little roots need.

Another type of rock garden which we have in Massachusetts is obtained by utilizing the out-cropping rock ledges, and in this type of rock garden Alyssum Saxatile and Trollius Europaeus is very effective.

Many and varied are the types of gardens which can be made very attractive. A path at a lower level than the rock garden makes a very interesting way to take care of the rock garden. Another suggestion is a grotto where water trickles through, giving a delightful sound.

In building a rock garden, rocks should be carefully placed.

Still another style of garden is with stepping-stones for a path, with perennials on either side. This is a simple type for a garden, but one of the types of gardening which is most fascinating. The play of light and shade on this path is particularly beautiful. The question of light and shade is one that we study at all times in the "Art of Gardening."

A beautiful picture is made with rhododendron with holly trees on either side. Holly is hardy on Cape Cod, but we are inclined to think it is not in the area of Boston. However, we should grow it a great deal more, but it must be moved in the spring and not in the fall, and the foliage must be shielded from the February and March suns.

A trick which works extremely well and adds interest to the garden is the use of broken stone for a path, with a stone edge on either side to hold the edges of the flower beds. A lovely combination of flowers is daylilies, delphinium and Spirea Japonica.

If Canterbury bells are to be used in a garden, they are biennials and new plants must be brought into the garden each June. Another combination which makes a lovely picture under a heavy foliage of trees at the edge of a pool is azaleas with marsh marigold.

We might differ as to what we want, but here is still another picture of a pool which ends a walk through the woods. This pool is filled with pond lilies, and on the other side of the pool are plantings of iris. Marshy ground can be dug out to make a beautiful pool with pond lilies, and iris planted along the shore of it.

One of the questions in the "Art of Gardening" is how we are going to use our gardens; and the first requisite is to have a place to sit. Tea lawns in the garden are very effective, with furniture which stands the weather and yet a place to sit, with table and chairs. A maple tree gives much shade in which to make a tea lawn. Shade is essential in every garden, not for the growing of the plants, but as a place to sit.

Lobelias are very beautiful and lend themselves very well for use in pots at the edge of a terrace. As the types of gardens are many and varied, so are the types of terraces, some taking care of the difference in grade between the lower level and the garden level. An effective planting can be made with a section of lilies, beginning with regal and following clear through with Speciosum. Then there is the terrace introduced in the rose garden. The introduction of little terraces is of great help in adding to the beauty of the garden.

Do we succeed with our pergolas in getting the light and shade? The Japanese pergola is very simple in its design and yet how wonderful it is with wisteria drooping itself over it.

Another garden wall which is truly quite different is one covered with roses and at intervals all along the wall, standard roses are set. Wall fountains are very effective, with water introduced at the upper level and then it comes through the wall and drips into the basin below. Because this garden is at many levels and the basin below the level of the wall, is one of the interesting features of the garden.

Another entirely different type of pool is the large one where the sprays of water go way up as far as the sentinel Arbor Vitae. To have sprays of water as high as this, requires a pretty good pressure.

Garden steps are another way in which we can add interest to our gardens. All the things we have to have in gardens are not so much to be cared for as an opportunity to make something beautiful. You must always watch for the play of light and shade. Realize that we must endeavor in everything we do to get the play of light and shade.

There are many types of steps—ramp steps of grass—circular stone steps. Circular stone steps can be very attractively planned by placing one circle at one side of the wall and the other at the other side of the wall.

The gate is a great part of the garden. You can do almost anything with gates.

Much can be said about vistas and we should bear these in mind in connection with our gardens.

In the Japanese garden everything has a name and because we cannot understand just what they are, we do not get the full significance of the garden. All the stones and trees and everything in the garden has a name and a meaning.

The evergreen garden is another type of garden which is open to us and many people are interested in it. Dwarf Arbor Vitae with a little pool in the center makes another lovely picture. Box in New England never ought to winter-kill. Build a framework about six inches above the top and cover with burlap. In this way, no snow can get at it and yet air can get at it.

Our roses have been so improved by hybridzation that we have now a tremendous variety for the garden. From the polyantha stock we have been able to do many things. If we are going to have roses at all, they should be perfect roses. The use of grass in the rose garden tempers the heat of the very hot sun which we have.

Arches of the Dorothy Perkins rose are very lovely, because of the wealth of bloom of this particular rose.

We can all have a garden if we plan it well, as to light and shade, soil, location, and give it the care which the "Art of Gardening" requires.

"A TRIP THROUGH OUR WESTERN NATIONAL PARKS"

Illustrated Lecture

By Dr. Donald Wyman, Jamaica Plain, Massachusetts

Thursday Afternoon, February 3, 1938

Mountains are by no means rocks with no beauty of their own, but rather they contain more and varied beauty than can be imagined—rocks, streams, waterfalls, trees, and a wide variety of wild flowers.

Rocky Mountain National Park is noted chiefly for its large mountains which in many instances, are still snow-capped late in June. After driving hundreds of miles across flat prairie land, it is a relief to come upon pines, spruce, hemlocks and trembling aspen. In this National Park there is a most interesting automobile road at an altitude of twelve thousand feet from which can be seen the "Never Summer Ranges" literally covered with snow all year long. There is very little vegetation here though lower down gorgeous spots of Indian paint brush and other bright colored mountain flowers make numerous hikes well worth the effort.

Mesa Verde National Park was inhabited from the beginning of the Christian Era until about 1200 A.D. and you can still see the ruins of houses these cliff dwellers built in huge caves, safe from attack, high up in the rocks.

Few visitors know what to expect of the Grand Canyon, but in addition to the different colored rocks, which are all sorts of queer shapes and forms, are found many wild flowers, including the Gilia flower. The trail to the bottom, traveled by mule, is very treacherous. However, the cowboys assure you that they have never lost a mule and this is certainly encouraging to the timid traveler.

The Canyon, in reality is ten miles across in a straight line and a full mile deep. There are four climatic zones in the Canyon so the plant life there is most interesting.

In Bryce Canyon peculiar red and pink sandstone rocks have been seen worn to peculiar shapes by weather over thousands of years. Zion Canyon, close by, is also noted for its formations of sandstone. At one time there were cliff dwellers here, but little is said of them and the remains of their dwellings are not nearly as interesting as on Mesa Verde.

From here we went to Southern California where a greater proportion of annual flower seeds are grown. Acre upon acre of annuals in full flower, later harvested just as crops are harvested in the East, made very colorful displays.

In Sequoia National Park are the redwoods or "Big Trees" many of which are at least two thousand years old, yet the wood is still in perfect condition. These trees are not deep-rooted, but rather shallow-rooted and it is fortunate that they do not grow in windy situations, else many of them would be blown down. The largest and oldest of these trees is called "The General Sherman Tree," believed to be between three thousand and four thousand years old, and places on the bark where it has been burned by various fires is quite noticeable, yet the interior remains sturdy.

Then we went into Yosemite National Park. Here are the many beautiful waterfalls including Upper Yosemite, nine times higher than Niagara Falls, and Lower Yosemite, five times higher than Niagara. Usually in the late summer these streams dry out and very little water comes over the falls. Looking up the Yosemite Valley, one can get an idea of the height of the rocks on either side and extreme narrowness of the valley itself. Many travelers think the brown bears found in the parks are tame, but they are never to be trusted. Here also we see the beautiful Bridal Veil Falls, about six times higher than Niagara. Sometimes the water falls naturally and sometimes when the wind is just right, there is a beautiful misty spray, from which the falls takes its name. Late in the afternoon at the base of these lovely falls can be seen a perfect rainbow.

Going on up into Oregon we find Crater Lake National Park, which was at one time a huge volcano. This lake in the extinct crater is about twenty square miles in area and in some places, two thousand feet deep. There is much snow here and in the middle of July it is not surprising to find the roads just being opened for travel.

From here, we go on up into Washington and visit Mt. Rainier which is the third highest peak in the United States. This mountain is noted first for its glaciers and secondly, for its beautiful wild flowers, there being something like six hundred different kinds growing within the boundaries of the Park.

In Paradise Park or Paradise Meadow as it is sometimes called at Rainier, the wild flowers almost pop right out of the snow. Just as the snow disappears the avalanche lily comes through. We saw an unusual specimen of this flower with five blossoms on one stock. Here there are many anemones, and some western phlox which looks almost like snow itself. The trees are naturally tall, slender, and spirelike. If the branches were wide and broad they would be broken with the tremendous amount of ice and snow during the winters. There are many kinds of trees here also, including many spruces, firs and the western hemlock. Here also are such beautiful wild flowers as the columbine which is familiar in the East, the columbia lily and many anemones and buttercups.

From Mt. Rainier we went to Glacier National Park and on the way, saw lovely St. Mary's Lake with beautiful white caps whipped up by a very high wind. Then on down to Yellowstone which is the largest national park in this country, covering something like two thousand square miles noted for its three thousand geysers and hot springs. Not only has the natural beauty in this Park been preserved, but here are found whole herds of wild animals. One interesting feature is the feeding of the grizzly bears, which many people come to see.

There are many geysers here—The Devil's Paint Pot, literally boiling mud, and, of course, nearly everyone has heard, at least, of Old Faithful which spouts one hundred and thirty feet in the air every sixty-five minutes. The eruption itself lasts for about three minutes. Many of the geysers are not nearly as active as this for some may erupt constantly for a period and then be most inconsistent, but Old Faithful has been going on at the same rate for many, many years. Many of the pools are beautifully colored, one being called Morning Glory Pool, because it has the shape of a huge morning glory flower and is a beautiful blue. Another is called the Emerald Pool, because of its crystal clear green color. From Inspiration Point we viewed Yellowstone Falls, above which is splendid fishing as the lake above is continually being stocked by the United States Fisheries.

The Grand Teton National Park, just south of Yellowstone, is noted for the huge Grand Teton Mountain and several beautiful mountain lakes.

Some of the final views we had here exemplified the entire Rocky Mountain Region and we returned to the East from here with a much better impression of the beautiful West.

"PROBLEMS OF THE AVERAGE GARDENER"

Illustrated Lecture

By Dr. Hugh Findlay, New York City

Thursday Afternoon, February 10, 1938

The problem of the garden is very much like the problems of life. You start them when you begin to reason. How wonderful it would be to find at the end, an Eternity Garden. Why? Because somehow or other gardening is an insane business, and how beautiful it would be to find a perfect garden forever growing, with no problems.

The soil is the only thing on the earth at the present moment that has never told a lie. It doesn't wear a mask and always obeys the seasons. The soil is God's Ambassador of truth. We are in danger when we leave the soil and let our farms and gardens go to weeds. What we need today is a little more sweat and a little less talk.

The biggest problem of the garden is to know when to stop. There are two dangerous periods in gardening—one in January when the catalogs are out, and the second, when the spring of the year rolls around and something gets into our blood. We just must dig and plant. The big problem is just what to leave out. Another problem of gardening is—we send in big orders for seeds, keep them in dry places, and then expect to plant them all and get wonderful results.

Gardening is one way to keep people put. We are a migratory people in America, always on the move, and a little garden will help to keep us put.

When you go out into the garden and lift a little soil into your hand, it is a pretty sacred thing. There are over a thousand teachers at Columbia University, and mind you, they are smart men, scientists who know many things, and yet the whole of them put together cannot make as much as a single petal on a primrose. Just think for a moment about it, and you will realize just how sacred the soil is. You are handling the truth.

IRISTHORPE, MRS. HOMER GAGE, FALL 1938

The big problems come to us sometimes in trying to bring plants into a state where they simply will not grow. We are discovering that air pressure has a great deal to do with the growing of plants. Plants do most of the growing, particularly trees, from midnight until three in the morning. You can't fool the soil. It is going to have its way and the seasons cannot be changed so these are not problems, but we have a lot. The thing we must do is to have that feeling of love for the soil. Garden soil has no creed and any of us may have a little garden all our own.

One of the great problems in communities is to keep them from vandals. If vandals had gardens of their own, perhaps they wouldn't destroy other people's gardens.

By all means cut flowers and bring them into the home, but don't destroy the countryside, since it is the great garden country of America.

In the early spring, just as soon as the plants begin to push up out of the ground, it is well to use a little tobacco dust. It is a good food for plants.

Another problem that we have sometimes, is the matter of stones. Soil must be pulverized very fine in order for the roots to go straight through, rather than around lumps of soil or stones. This same principle holds with vegetables.

One of the greatest problems of the garden today is to get stable manure. Commercial fertilizers are good, but not as good as stable manure.

If you would have plants growing in the crevices of the rocks, do not put heavy clay soil in the crevices.

Cultivation of the soil is a real problem in the garden. If you live where there is sand which holds very little water and it is a warm soil, you must give it water, a little black muck or humus. Why is it when a soil is built up in your garden with lots of humus that plants hold their green so beautifully close to the earth? Because humus gives carbon dioxide.

The burning of leaves is a great waste, for leaves have a tendency to form acidity in the soil so we must put some fertilizer with them, but if we can't get stable manure, make it with leaves, using nitrate of soda and bone meal. Bone meal is a natural fertilizer and is a slow decomposing fertilizer. It is economical and will build your garden and last for a long time. The high-powered cocktails given to plants in the early spring make it amazing that the plants grow at all. Sometimes we give plants too much and they get "drunk" and they do not show up well when "drunk."

Stop feeding perennials about the last of August; then let the plant ripen and by ripening, it builds sugar into the tissues of the plant.

Sometimes we have masses of color in our garden—colors that are biting, sharp, irritating. The mixture of color is a real interesting problem. We do not use enough green. We should use more ornamental grasses and ferns.

Another problem in our garden is trees. How we do abuse our trees! The greatest problem with trees on our lawns is the matter of feeding. It is not the cavity in the tree which kills it. Many times it is the lack of proper feeding. As to the natural feeding of the tree and what the best food is for the tree, if you have a very choice tree on your lawn, cut holes three feet wide, three feet long, and about two feet deep around the roots of the tree; fill the holes with decayed leaves, a little bone meal, and a little fertilizer. Another thing which might be given a tree sometimes is dry blood. Just before a rain, scatter it around on the outside and let it sink in.

If we wish to keep a fruit tree dwarf, plant the dwarf tree up to the place where the bud is inserted. Apple trees growing over an arbor make a lovely picture.

White dogwood doesn't grow in Europe because it does not like limestone, but it is beautifully grown in America. "Nature spends all her time growing old gracefully." Do all you can to teach people not to destroy.

When you turn the soil in building a garden, don't turn it once—turn it four or five times. A beautiful garden may be built in sand by putting three or four inches of muck on the soil, with a little manure and bone meal.

It is difficult to cover all the problems of the garden. The lawn is one of the biggest problems in the American garden. Tree roots are another problem. Apply all commercial fertilizers the way you apply salt to your food and not any heavier. Sometimes the problem with our garden is space. Do not crowd too many plants in a small space. A homespun garden is like homespun cloth—it wears well and lasts a long time.

Another problem in the garden is to get wisteria to bloom. How not to get it to bloom is to feed it. Do not feed wisteria if you would have thick, heavy blooms. Prune the roots—about one-third of them a year—not all of them at one time. If you would increase the bloom of the lilac, put a quantity of lime around the bush, so the ground is white.

Heliotrope is the butterfly garden because butterflies like to get the sweet from the flower. Why don't we use more delphinium? Here it is five to six feet high, fed with nitrate, which is quite contrary to the book. Don't scoff at the petunia. They are minute men of the garden.

The annual garden requires sprinkling of plant food in the spring and always when the plant is up about four inches, give them a little tobacco dust. The shrub problem in the garden is a real one. Azaleas need an acid soil. Japanese quince or Cydonia Japonica do not root well from seed, but do well from cuttings. German iris thrive with a little well-rotted manure in the early spring, while Japanese iris hates lime. In fact, it frequently destroys the iris. Siberian iris may be put in sand and grow well. One of the great problems of gardening today is to visit somebody with a rock garden. We cannot imitate nature, but we can interpret nature. Place the rocks the way nature would place them. Sow seed frequently by rolling the seed into a little clay and then push it in the rocks. We can do it if we take time to.

Insects don't like Hemerocallis very much, and if it is thrown out of your car one year, you can go back the next year and find it growing. The Regal lily is thrifty and hardy.

Don't be too clean in the gardens. Let things ripen and let nature build herself restored strength.

Do not cover the primrose in winter. It will withstand the weather. Tulips should be planted six to eight inches below the ground, among the perennials. If the soil is light, plant them ten inches below.

Another problem is wind whipping the plants. Keep wind

away from the perennials. Another is "slugs." Put a board across the branches of the bush or tree, with a little bone meal, or dig out a potato and put in a little arsenic of lead.

Try some Prince of Wales violets in the garden. They bloom in the spring and again in the fall of the year. Get more green into the garden. Roses can be used in so many ways. Any colors can be mixed if you put in enough white and green.

We shouldn't build a garden that we have to apologize for. The trouble with some of our gardens today is that they have no spiritual quality. The beauty of the garden is something you cannot keep to yourself. You must share it with others.

"Bees go from flower to flower, gathering sweetness and Life is sweet, even with all the bitterness, and— Spring will come!"

"THE RESTORATION OF WILLIAMSBURG, COLONIAL CAPITAL OF VIRGINIA"

Illustrated Lecture

By SIDNEY N. SHURCLIFF, LANDSCAPE ARCHITECT,
11 BEACON STREET, BOSTON, MASSACHUSETTS

Thursday Afternoon, February 17, 1938

Williamsburg won renown as the second capital of the Virginia Colony. Jamestown, the first permanent settlement on our shores, was from 1607 to 1699 the original capital, heading a fast growing and increasingly prosperous colony.

The site of Jamestown, however, was regarded as unhealthy, and inconveniently far from the main line of land travel which had sprung up near the center of the peninsula formed by the James and York Rivers.

In 1698 plans were made for changing the location of the capital. As a fitting site for the head of so large and important a colony, part of the tract known as "Middle Plantation," seven miles north of Jamestown and directly on the main line of travel along the peninsula, was selected. It was entirely replanned, new buildings were built, and the name changed to Williamsburg in honor of the King.

In the years which followed, the new capital became the center of the political and social life of the colony. Its reputation for brilliance and gaiety in social activities and for sophistication in architecture and gardening was as well known in Europe as in the colonies. Williamsburg was at her height in 1751 when the ballroom wing was added to the fabulous Governor's Palace, and her reputation continued almost undimmed until the coming of the Revolution.

In 1779 the seat of government was removed to Richmond and with it went much of the prosperity and many of the influential people. This marked the beginning of a long decline which was hastened by the accidental burning of the Palace in

1781 and the destruction of the Capitol a few years later. The War between the States struck Williamsburg still another blow and the period of poverty which followed witnessed the destruction of many of the buildings and most of the gardens. Except for the College, Williamsburg became a forgotten town.

In 1903 Dr. W. A. R. Goodwin became Rector of the Bruton Parish Church, which, completed in 1715, has been called the Court Church of the Virginia colony. Becoming fascinated with Williamsburg's survivals of the past, Dr. Goodwin formulated plans for a restoration of its most important features. By 1905 he had raised sufficient funds from private sources to restore his church, and this was the beginning of Williamsburg's revival.

However, funds for additional work were difficult to procure and in an effort to raise interest in this subject in 1925, at a Phi Beta Kappa meeting in New York, Dr. Goodwin spoke. Mr. John D. Rockefeller Jr., who was present, was deeply impressed and within a few months made a visit to Williamsburg and conferred with Dr. Goodwin. At this time Mr. Rockefeller saw several of the old buildings still in a fair state of preservation. Others, however, had not fared so well. Some, including the Palace and the Capitol, had been burned. Many had been so mutilated by conversion into filling stations and stores as to be unrecognizable. Even the famed gardens in back of the Palace had been completely destroyed and on their site had been erected an unprepossessing electric light and power company.

In spite of these and other handicaps, Mr. Rockefeller was so impressed with the opportunity offered for creating an important historical monument that he decided to undertake the work at his own expense. As the project progressed, organizations were formed to direct the work of restoration, headed by Colonel Arthur Woods and Mr. Kenneth Chorley, and supplemented by Messrs. Perry, Shaw, and Hepburn, architects, and my father, Arthur A. Shurcliff, landscape architect.

It was realized only by degrees that the question of absolute authenticity in the restoration was of the utmost importance. At the very beginning of the work one extremely valuable piece of evidence was at hand: an unusually accurate paced plan of the

City made in 1782 by an unknown Frenchman. A glance at this map shows very clearly how the City was planned and built as a unified composition rather than permitting a haphazard growth as in most American cities. The important public buildings were placed so as to terminate carefully created vistas. Thus the Capitol was placed squarely across one end of the nearly mile-long Duke of Gloucester Street and the Wren Building of the College of William and Mary at the other. A special cross axis, two hundred feet wide, known as the Palace Green enhanced the approach to the Governor's Palace.

For the restoration of Williamsburg, it soon became clear that the Frenchman's map, plus the general professional knowledge of the architects did not total anywhere near enough understanding of the early appearance of Williamsburg to serve as a basis for its accurate re-creation. Therefore a research campaign was undertaken which has never before been equalled in this country. A search was made of the files of libraries and private collections of this hemisphere and Europe which might have a bearing on early Williamsburg.

Among the most important finds from a landscape viewpoint were a series of surveys made in 1769 of towns in North Carolina. Sauthier, the surveyor, had been so accurate in his work that he showed on his plans not only all the streets and houses but also the gardens complete with their paths and some of the planting. Knowledge of the garden patterns of the Sauthier maps was invaluable in determining the design of several Williamsburg gardens.

The most remarkable of the documentary finds was made by one of the research workers at the Bodleian Library at Oxford, England. Here was uncovered an ancient copperplate engraving which shows, accurately drawn in perspective on a single plate, the three most important buildings of the old City; front and back views of the Wren Building of the College of William and Mary; the Colonial Capitol of 1705 and the Governor's Palace complete with its two flanking offices and part of the garden.

While this documentary work was going on, the Restoration organizations were acquiring key properties and on these excavation was begun to determine what evidence remained in the ground.

New England Carnation Association, 1938

While the excavations were in progress, the architects made it
their task to visit and measure all the important old places still
standing within a radius of one hundred miles of Williamsburg.
Through these visits much was learned which otherwise might
have been missed. For instance, at Lower Brandon on the James,
upon measuring the garden, it becomes apparent that it was
originally geometrically laid out and, in fact, closely resembled
the gardens shown on the Sauthier maps.

So much of value was discovered during the early part of the
measuring work that it was considered worth while to map the
entire town of Port Royal, which once had the reputation of
containing the finest small box gardens of any Virginia town.
Luckily some of the oldest inhabitants were able to remember
where and how the box had been planted, thus making it possible
for us to record and preserve the charming designs which otherwise would have been lost forever.

During all our measuring work we took as much trouble with
the recording of details as with the plan and general layout of
the old places. Fences, well houses and pavements were studied
and a careful record of the size and type of each tree and shrub
on old places was kept. When the research was complete we had
a very clear idea of the authentic colonial plants. For instance,
at first we had no knowledge as to whether or not the colonists
used the wild American holly in their gardens. Although we did
know that the English holly will not thrive in Virginia, we did
not dare to use the American variety without good authority.
On one of the measuring expeditions I came upon a long line of
American holly trees growing near an old house. It was, in fact,
a colonial garden edging which, although unclipped all these
years, was still a living proof of the point we wanted to settle.

Before the research was considered complete, both my father
and I made a special trip to England to visit gardens of the
Williamsburg period. We were amazed at the similarities which
we discovered in these widely separated points. The garden
at Canons Ashby, in Northamptonshire, for example, has almost
exactly the same plan as that of Lower Brandon.

After the English trip, the research was considered virtually
complete and the actual reconstruction work at Williamsburg,
already under way, was speeded up.

Mr. Rockefeller has felt that the restoration should be carried out not merely as a monument to the past but also as a dwelling place for people of the present. Therefore, only two of the restored private dwellings are open to the public, the remainder being occupied by tenants. These tenants are in many cases the descendants of families who originally owned the houses and arrangements have been made to allow them life tenure.

The buildings which are daily open to the public consist in the main of the old governmental buildings, such as the Court House, Capitol, Governor's Palace, and the Public Gaol. There are also a few shops, homes, and inns kept open, including the Travis House, the Ludwell-Paradise House and the Market Square and Raleigh Taverns. In the garden in back of the Travis House are two very attractive little tea-houses, symmetrically located, in which visitors may be served during pleasant days in the summer.

Along the Duke of Gloucester Street are several of the small buildings which have been restored. At the Galt Cottage, across from the Bruton Parish Church, an experimental holly hedge was restored. Although the plants were at first shapeless sticks moved in from the adjoining woodlands, they bore clipping well and soon formed dense hedges so attractive in appearance that holly since has been used in many of the Williamsburg gardens.

At the John Custis Tenement place a box garden, adapted in plan from those on the Sauthier maps, has been built. Between the geometric figures of dwarf box run brick paths, and inside the hedges bloom a variety of colonial bulbs and flowers. A paper-mulberry tree shades this garden.

Among the larger houses purchased and restored by the Restoration is the Ludwell-Paradise House, colonial home of John Paradise, a member of the Essex Street Club in London, and a friend of Samuel Johnson. The Ludwell-Paradise House, a fine brick structure, was one of those which had survived the passage of years. Its restoration is authentic even to the omission of central heating. At the rear is a pleasant small garden planted with boxwood and crape myrtle trees. The crape myrtle is one of the distinctive Virginia small flowering trees and provides an abundance of pink bloom for about two weeks during the summer. Unfortunately, it is not hardy further north than Washington, D. C.

The various steps necessary to the restoration of a garden are typified by those taken at the Archibald Blair place. Here we knew there must have been a garden, because one was indicated on the Rochambeau map. We could find on the ground no vestige of the original garden, except one big box bush and a line of trees which, although young, might have been sprouts from old stumps. Subsequent excavations revealed the probable lines of the ancient paths. From these and our knowledge of Southern gardens, we were able to determine the layout. Next came the purchase of boxwood to complete the planting. Men were sent to North Carolina and Georgia to purchase such plants as could be obtained without injury to existing landscapes. After the purchase of the box, it had to be carefully dug and crated. Then most of it was shipped by rail, on flat cars, and removed from the railroad station at Williamsburg to the garden sites. After planting, it was necessary to shade the boxwood against the burning rays of the sun for a period of at least two years after the planting.

Another problem encountered in the transplanting of trees and boxwood occurred when it was discovered that the Williamsburg town water supply is too alkaline for watering large transplanted trees. This difficulty was solved by the purchase of tank wagons to haul good water from a pond outside the Town.

Among the larger buildings which comprise a part of the Restoration is the Court House which has been preserved complete with its large Green or "Market Square."

At the Coke-Garrett House is the largest of the gardens restored to any private dwelling. Here roses in great profusion grow inside the fragrant box edgings, and the original terraces have been planted again with crape myrtle trees.

In colonial days the permanent population of Williamsburg remained fairly constant between the figures of two thousand and two thousand and five hundred, but on holidays and during the "Public Times" the population of the Town increased tremendously, sometimes nearly doubling as visitors arrived to participate in political and social events. At such times life at

Williamsburg was at its gayest. There were horse races on a special track, parades, fireworks, and all kinds of religious, educational, political, and social functions. The first theater in America was run successfully in Williamsburg for several years. In order to accommodate the large temporary population, several large inns and taverns were operated. The most famous of these was the Raleigh Tavern where Washington frequently dined and Jefferson danced with "fair Belinda."

I have saved for the last a description of Williamsburg's two most important buildings—the Capitol and the Governor's Palace. The site of the Capitol had been preserved by the Society for the Preservation of Virginia Antiquities, who presented it to the Restoration. Excavations revealed the entire foundation of the old Capitol still intact. With the evidence of the foundations, the copperplate engraving, and records of the construction of the original building, the architects were able to reproduce almost exactly the colonial Capitol of the Virginia Colony. First constructed in 1705, this building was the seat of government for Virginia until the removal of the capital to Richmond in 1779. In it many events important in American history have occurred. Here Patrick Henry made one of his famous speeches; here were passed the resolutions calling for the adoption of the Declaration of Independence, and here was first adopted the Constitution of a free and independent State.

On the restoration of the Governor's Palace and grounds more time and thought were spent than on any other of the Williamsburg buildings. This was logical, since we know that Spotswood, who was lieutenant governor of Williamsburg between 1710 and 1722, expended much of his time and most of the available public funds on the construction of this building and its grounds. In fact he was so lavish in his use of the public money that an attempt was made to remove him from office, and the complaints against him, having been preserved, were extremely helpful in determining the features of the Palace as he built it.

The Palace and its grounds, at the time of their construction, were probably the most elaborate in America. Visitors from Europe and the other colonies commented on the splendor of the Governor's life, noted that he occasionally had over four hundred people for dinner and that his gardens were presided over by an English gardener. With these facts in mind, it is perhaps less surprising to look at the plan of the Palace gardens and grounds. The house is formal and symmetrical in the Virginian brick Georgian style. It is connected by curious reticulated brick walls to flanking guard houses. Between these is a courtyard entered through a very fine wrought iron gate, hung from brick gate posts which are surmounted by the carved stone figures of a lion and a unicorn. The façade of the Palace is set off to great advantage by its location at the end of the Palace Green.

On the garden front of the Palace beyond the Ballroom wing, added in 1751, is the very formal garden laid out in diamond-shaped figures, as shown on the copperplate engraving. Beyond this is the flower garden with its pleached arbors, and its curious brick wall, the posts of which are diamond shaped in plan and topped by round stone finials. To the east of the formal garden is the bowling green surrounded by the largest tree box used in the Restoration. On the east side is the Box Garden, the memorial to soldiers who were buried on this site during the Revolution, the maze and the mount over the ice house. Beyond these are a series of terraces sloping down to the canal adjoining the fish pond, which was Spotswood's special pride. Near the house on the west side was the service group consisting of the kitchen, a kitchen garden, scullery, smokehouse, salt-house, bathhouse and servants' quarters. On the other side of the main house, in a corresponding position, were the stables and more servants' quarters.

To think that such an elaborate and attractive layout could have been completed in this country only slightly over a century after the first permanent settlement, is astounding, yet if one examines the various perspectives made in 1709 by Kip, the English engraver, it becomes apparent that Spotswood was only re-creating in the new country the things with which he was familiar at home. Later, in the new country, even more elaborate places were built, among them Middleton Place at Charleston, South Carolina, but none of these grand estates were started as early as the Governor's Palace at Williamsburg.

The interior of the Palace, when it was first built, was a marvel to beholders and still is today. Spotswood and his successors spared no expense in obtaining the finest carvings, the most beautiful marble mantels, the most unusual wall paper, and the finest furniture which could be obtained in this country and abroad. This was all burned while the Palace was being used as a hospital during the Revolution.

As the years roll on, I think the citizens of America will come to realize that Mr. Rockefeller has done a very great service in restoring the Palace, as in restoring the rest of Williamsburg, thus permitting the visitor a breath-taking glance into a glorious but fast receding epoch. The motto adopted by Colonial Williamsburg, Inc., is "That the Future may learn from the Past." A visit to Williamsburg today is an unequalled opportunity for appreciation and understanding of colonial life in Virginia.

"BULBS FOR THE HOME GARDEN"

Illustrated Lecture

By Allen W. Edminster, Boston, Massachusetts

Thursday Afternoon, February 24, 1938

In a city there are so many opportunities for making lovely little bright spots here and there by adding a few of the first flowers of spring. One of the first to consider is the snowdrop or galanthus, which is one of the first to come through the ground; in fact, it sometimes comes through the snow. This is called one of the minor bulbs, not that it is minor in importance, but to differentiate from tulips, etc. Arriving in this country shortly after the first of September, they should be planted about that time.

When one thinks of bulbs, one naturally thinks of Holland, and, attending the International Flower Show there, a rare opportunity is given to see the vast fields of tulips which are grown simply for bulbs, and no blooms are ever cut or sold for the bloom itself. Here is found every conceivable way in which to use bulbs—beds, carpet work, along the edge of a canal, and in a wind swept area there is nothing better than the Early Single or Early Double Tulip.

Second to the galanthus is the crocus for appearing in the early spring. Coming up shortly after the galanthus, they are used to best advantage in the lawn, but can be used in bedding work also. In the lawn, they are particularly attractive. Do not, however, try to make a carpet design of them, for in doing this, the fine qualities of the crocus are lost. The crocus comes in several colors—yellow, white, lavender. The heavenly blue variety are particularly adaptable for rock garden use, although for the first two or three years, they do not grow especially well. After that, they will straighten out and come along in good shape. The main thing to remember when planting crocus in a lawn is that the lawn should not be mowed until the crocus leaves have turned brown and practically died away.

Another one of the minor bulbs is the scilla, which proves very delightful when worked around borders or trees in naturalistic form.

Before laying out a home garden or grounds, the color effect should be very carefully studied. It is very important to have harmonious colors in order to get the most enjoyment and the best way to do this is to plan the garden on paper before doing any work at all.

The Muscari is more or less of an oddity, but should be included in every home garden. This should be planted in early September in open, rich, gritty soil, and either bone meal or some type of manure is advisable to put on in the early spring before it begins to bloom. By doing this, much better results are obtained.

One of the major types of bulbs is the hyacinth, an old stand-by of the garden, and properly grown, it adds much beauty and charm to any garden. Use them for plants, scattered along the border, and they are particularly attractive along waterways. Hyacinths come in white, blue, pink, red, and also in yellow. The hyacinth is a heavy feeder and therefore, needs quite a bit of fertilization. They should be planted about the same time as the other bulbs, the middle of September or first of October, to a depth of at least four inches and even a little deeper will do no harm. One of the major points in growing hyacinths is that they should be lifted every year, around the first of June and should be stored in a tray. In place of the wooden bottom, it is better to cover them with a wire mesh, which allows for proper ventilation. They should be planted again about the middle of September.

The narcissus family is a large one, comprised of many different types, and they all have their place in the garden. These are usually planted about the middle of September, to a depth of four inches and sometimes a little deeper, with the same fertilization as the hyacinth. These, too, should be lifted after they flower, when the foliage has died down. This is not necessary, however, but to get the best out of them, they should be lifted and allowed to rest for four to six weeks.

In the narcissus family is the Incomparabilis, White Lady, and Thelma. The latter is most familiar to us, and is particularly fine for naturalistic work, while they are not so good for border work.

Like dressing a window in a shop along the street, the one with the least number of articles, but most quality, is the one which holds your attention the longest. So it is with the garden. It is far better to have only twelve bulbs planted correctly than to overcrowd the space available.

The tulip is practically the King bulb of the garden. It is in bloom from the latter part of April, through May, and into early June, starting with the Early Single and Early Double type, and then the Darwins. We, in this country, do not use enough of the early type tulips. An Early Double—Mr. Van Der Hoef, grows to a height of about twelve inches, and is especially fine for any bedding work, in areas that are apt to be wind swept. The tulip itself is a bulb which should be planted as late as possible in the fall. Most of them come up very early and should therefore be planted anywhere from the first of November on, depending upon the locality in which they are to be planted. For this particular section of New England, the first to the middle of November is not too late. They, too, should be given some protection the first winter at least, and should also be given quite a bit of food. If you are setting out a new tulip bed, it is wise to make certain that it is well prepared the fall before. Tulip bulbs should be taken up in the fall, like the hyacinth and the daffodil, but not until the foliage has turned brown and died down. They should be stored on trays.

The Orange Nassau, and Peach Blossom are particularly popular in this country. The United States is third in the use of Dutch bulbs, England using the most, and Germany is second. The Mendel type blooms two weeks before the Darwin, but is not especially good in garden work. The Triumph group is fast coming into popularity. It is a cross between one of the Early Single types and the Darwin, coming into bloom just a few days before the Darwin and a few days after the Early Single. There are a few Double Triumphs. Most of them, however, are single, but one of the better double types is known as Evening Sun, a very fine cutting variety, growing to a height of about eighteen inches and is a great addition to gardens in which double flowers are wanted.

The Breeder type of tulips is an interesting group and is quite

he one with
one which
garden. It
ity than to

n. It is in
into early
ble type,
te enough
Der Hoef,
ecially fine
nd swept.
as late as
and should
vember on,
nted. For
e middle of
given some
be given
bed, it is
re. Tulip
th and the
n and died

particularly
in the use
w is second.
ain, but is
oup is fast
the Early
a few days
le. There
are single,
ing Sun, a
t eighteen
ble flowers

nd is quite

surprising. The outer petals are brown and bronze and gold shades while the inside shows a sparkle of color.

The Parrot type are also coming into popularity. The stems are not as weak as they used to be, and these should be grown even more than they now are. One of the more popular types which is grown in a good deal of profusion is Fantasy. The petals are peculiarly shaped, not at all regular, and quite a bit of green is visible in the petals. The most beautiful is the Lily-Flowered. The Sirene is particularly good to use in border planting or even around the home surroundings, and will add a great deal of charm and beauty.

One of the most interesting types of tulips, that is the Botannical, has been much neglected. The colors are most attractive, and they grow to a height of only eight or nine inches, and are fine for use in rock garden formations. In a regular tulip border they would be quite out of place, except as an edging plant. These should be planted about the same time as any of the other tulip bulbs.

The Cottage type is next in importance to the Darwin in this country. These bloom in mid-May and one of the finest is the Walter T. Ware, a very large type which grows to a good height, is quite a robust grower, and is recommended to be grown in the home garden. Mongolia is a fine yellow; Rosabella is a very fine rose shade, Albina a white type, also Carrara, a pure white with a very lovely sheen on the outside, almost like silk, and Advance is one of the better types of red. One of the reasons we grow so many of the Cottage type is the color range and the height.

The Ideal Darwin has a larger color range than the True Darwin. Adoration is a particularly good variety for growing in the garden and there are a great many other fine varieties in this type.

The Darwin is the major tulip type. It blooms the latter part of May and the first of June. There is the Yellow Giant; Blue Amiable an attractive blue shade; Venus—very lovely; Princess Elizabeth—a pink variety; and City of Haarlem—a dark red. The Darwin will give you probably the best results of any of the tulips, since they are adaptable for many uses, not only for garden use, but also for cutting.

ANNUAL REUNION

March 3, 1938

Outside, the cold biting wind of a March night; inside, the Hall was decorated with smilax and colored balloons, and the stage was a veritable garden with daffodils, hyacinths, narcissi, tulips, snapdragons, and ferns, while the Library was decorated with palms, daffodils, snapdragons, roses and tulips.

In the receiving line were President and Mrs. Myron F. Converse, the guest-speaker, Col. Samuel E. Winslow, and Mrs. Winslow, and Mrs. Homer Gage.

The ushers were: Mr. Malcolm C. Midgley, Mr. Harrison G. Taylor, Mr. George F. E. Story, Mr. Burt W. Greenwood, and Allen W. Hixon. During the reception music was furnished by a few members of Harry Felton's orchestra.

Those in the receiving line led the march to the dining room where the tables looked very inviting with bouquets of the lovely carnation, "Virginia."

Rev. Vincent E. Tomlinson invoked the Divine Blessing, followed with a beautiful rendition of the "Lord's Prayer" by the Ionic Male Quartet, consisting of Ralph Adams, Dr. Malcolm Atkins, Dr. L. A. Bennett, John A. Jewell, with Leslie B. Goff, pianist.

After the dinner, served by Mr. Lunt, the Male Quartet sang "There Is a Tavern" and as an encore, "Swing Low, Sweet Chariot."

President Myron F. Converse made the opening remarks, after which the Quartet sang " 'Tis Morn."

Mr. Converse called attention to the fact that Mr. Cook, our senior vice-president, passed his 91st birthday recently, and was not able to come to the reunion. He asked that Mr. Kinney send a basket of fruit to Mr. Cook in memory of this occasion.

Mr. Converse recalled the swift passing of time—"Ten years since Horticultural Hall on Elm Street was opened. In the life of many societies, ten years is observed as an occasion, but in a society ninety-five years old, a mere ten years is passed over lightly."

He also called attention to the coming Spring Show opening March 10, and continuing through the following Sunday.

In introducing the speaker, Col. Samuel E. Winslow, or rather presenting him, Mr. Converse said that we were very fortunate in having with us an old friend of our society and also a friend of all of us, he having been a member of the Horticultural Society fifty years, joining in 1888.

Col. Winslow entertained us for an hour with a most interesting word picture of the different families occupying homes on the site of our present home and the adjacent neighborhood, he being especially qualified to do so, having lived and grown up in this neighborhood.

He closed his talk, saying, "If you have enjoyed this half as much as I have, I am well repaid for having come."

Whereupon we all assured him we had by our hearty applause.

Mr. Converse then thanked the Colonel for coming and giving us this delightful talk and also thanked Mrs. Winslow for coming with him.

We then adjourned to the Hall above, where the Male Quartet sang "The Sea Makes a Man, a Man" and as an encore "Ol' Gray Robe." Mr. David Horne gave two readings, and the Quartet then sang "Workin' on de Railroad" and "O! Suzannah."

After a grand march, dancing followed until midnight with music furnished by Harry Felton's orchestra.

INDEX